# SYMBOLS OF THE CAPITAL;

OR,

## CIVILIZATION IN NEW YORK.

BY

A. D. MAYO.

NEW YORK:
THATCHER & HUTCHINSON,
523 (ST. NICHOLAS HOTEL) BROADWAY.
1859.

W. H. Tinson, Stereotyper and Printer,
Rear of 43 & 45 Centre street, N. Y.

# PREFACE.

---

The subject of the following pages is American Civilization, as symbolized by the institutions of the chief State in the Republic. No State so completely represents the characteristic tendencies of society in our country as New York. Superior to all others in population, wealth and executive power; containing a representative of every style of character and ability at work in our new confederacy; closely linked with every interest in the Union; its condition is, perhaps, the best mirror in which we can behold the reflection of our present progress, and the obstacles that hinder our more rapid advancement.

The writer has selected the chief representative institutions of the capital city of New York, as suggestive of what life should be in every free commonwealth. The work is, therefore, concerned with local themes, only as they lead the mind to the consideration of the great privileges and obligations of American citizenship. It is a sincere endeavor to aid the young men and women of our land in their attempt to realize a character that shall justify our professions of republicanism, and to establish a civilization which, in becoming national, shall illustrate every principle of a pure Christianity.

# CONTENTS.

# SYMBOLS OF THE CAPITAL.

---

## I.

## THE HUDSON;

OR,

## LIFE IN THE COUNTRY.

There are many great rivers on the western continent; but nowhere within a valley of three hundred miles is there such an appeal to the love of nature and the higher love of man, as in the glorious region of the Hudson. Its springs hide themselves amid the secrets of that mysterious wilderness, whose "cloud-splitting" summit soars above a wide sweeping circle of primitive woods and hills, and glistening lakes and streams, with a faint gleam of civilization quivering in the far-off horizon. Within the broad bay, where its majestic tide lapses into the Atlantic, are reflected the masts of a commerce that searches the ends of the earth, and the spires of that city which represents in all its wondrous phases the new civilization of the western world. Midway between the Adirondack and the ocean, scaling the hills and nestling amid the ravines of its superb shores, rises the Capital City of the greatest Republican State. And every mile of its joyous current above, or its stately tide below, is crowded with nature's grandeur or loveliness. Whether it reflects the swelling hills and wooded islands that smile over its marriage with the beautiful Mohawk; or lingers reverently where the Catskills build their sapphire wall, terrace above terrace, along the western sky; or washes the lazy feet of old quiet villages, and foams around the wharves of busy towns; or glides by fertile fields that scale broad eastern uplands, shining like gardens of Paradise in the light of the sinking sun; or ripples at the end of shadowed paths, that lead to the embowered homes of culture and wealth and worth; or writhes through the girding Highlands; or diffuses itself in inland bays; or rolls by the solemn Palisades, to breast the ascending waves of the sea; its journey is everywhere a jubilee; the triumphal march of nature out of her primeval wilderness to her mystic union with the noblest works of man.

For glorious as may be this valley of the Hudson, yet around the least man that looks upon its waves, or treads its soil, lingers a charm as far above the magic of forest and sunset as the sky is lifted above the ground—the charm of an immortal spiritual existence. And nature's splendor along these three hundred wondrous miles is but a faint type of the grandeur of that human destiny wrought out amid her scenes. Two hundred and fifty years ago the little ship "Half Moon" first disturbed the waters of this unknown stream, bearing the heroic navigator whose name it has inherited. Seven years later a trading-post arose on one of its islands, and in 1623 were laid the foundations of Albany, the second town in those original colonies whose revolt from England created our Republic. Its junction with the sea witnessed the ceremonies that sealed its transmission to the English power in 1664; while on the region washed by its northern waters, the tide of French invasion was met and broken by the united bravery of New York and New England. Along its devoted banks ebbed and flowed the wave of the Revolutionary struggle; on the plains of Saratoga was struck the decisive blow that broke the spell of British success; under the shadows of the Highlands watched and thought and commanded our

Washington; here, at the end of the long and dreary war, was disbanded the army of the Thirteen Independent States; and in full view of its waters was the Father of his Country inaugurated first President of the Republic.

Just fifty years ago Robert Fulton opened its second great era of human interest, and stowed in the hull of his little steamer, that crawled up to Albany, were the mighty agencies of civilization that have changed this wilderness to the garden valley it has become. Thrice since that day has the mighty West reached out a long arm and seized its shores with a giant grasp; and now, along these avenues of wave and iron, surges the noise of nations going to their destiny beyond our sinking sun; while the genius of New England, from her long line of mountain ridges, looks down with hope and pride into its fruitful valleys. New York has arisen, like a city in a fairy tale, representative of the best and the worst of American life; and in the offices and halls of the buildings that crown the hills of Albany, has been elaborated the policy that has brought our State to its eminent position among the communities of men.

In all the elements of human interest no river can surpass our own; for while the plains of the Tiber and the Danube reflect the lingering glories of empires that have gone, or totter on the giddy summit of despotic misrule, and the Seine and the Thames mirror the best results of that civilization based on the contempt for the natural rights of man, our Hudson is stirred from her Atlantic wave to her mountain springs by the great conflict of freedom for the soul. Though the cannon of the old Revolution no longer awake the echoes of our hills, yet the American revolution now rages at its full noon-tide heat along these valleys; and when the armies of this revolution are disbanded on its shores, from the Capital City must go forth the joyous word that declares the people of the Empire State free from political oppression, and the more subtle tyranny of superstition, and the deadliest slavery of ignorance and social degeneracy. So does our Hudson flow towards the future, bearing on its swelling waves the hopes of a longing world for the final emancipation of man. And most fitting is it that the moral teacher who would point to the signs in the eastern heavens of this coming day of light and love should stand in the Capital City, of the most powerful commonwealth in the great republic, and make it, through its chief representative institutions, preach those Christian lessons that are the essence of the best culture of our time.

But as the cities that fill our lovely valley are

enfolded and shadowed on every hand by the country, so is their glory only representative, and they are only what they are made by those who till the plains, and toil upon the hillsides that stretch away from us to the limits of our State. Along the banks of the Hudson the cities and villages are but dots; while the country is the ever present object of view. Therefore let our estimate of the forces that cluster in the Capital City be prefaced by an estimate of the country life of our great State. With the Hudson for a text, let the teacher speak of the capabilities of that country life for the production of a civilization which shall be the American version of Christ's kingdom of heaven among men.

Every wise observer of the affairs of the Republic must confess that our hope of a Christian Democracy is in the country life of the nation. America cannot be ruled by her great cities except by the substitution of the interests of a class for the elevation of the whole. The influence of our great capitals is comparatively small in the array of public forces. In the southern half of the Union they are an insignificant element of power. The West has extemporized huge villages in the wilderness which, spite of their metropolitan pretensions, are only commercial depots erected by the immediate wants of a developing country. Even the older cities of the East, not excepting New York, are still gigantic caravansaries, so fluctuating in their population and tendencies that they cannot be estimated as a fixed power in the State. Their wealth, culture and moral enterprise are rivalled by thousands of smaller towns, bound together by rail-track and telegraph, which represent in turn a country population of landholders and independent laborers such as the world never before saw; and whose enlightened watchfulness will not permit the conceit of citizen aristocracy, or the brutality of citizen barbarism to dictate terms to our new civilization. While therefore the man of mature power may choose a city platform on which to work the machinery of his influence, yet his mission is not so much among the fickle crowds of the towns as out among the villages and farms. Whoever can make his mark deep and broad over the hills and fields of our Empire State can well afford to dispense with the homage paid by the metropolitan fashion of the hour to its favorite; for whatever idea of life rules the country must inevitably shape the destiny of the republic.

In speaking of country life we shall therefore avoid that greenness in which the hackneyed citizen so often clothes himself when pronouncing his oracles for the entertainment of his rural brethren. We shall avoid that sentimental Arcadian view which lures young ladies and gentlemen, deep in the mysteries of pastoral poetry and the latest *mode*, to invade the rural districts in midsummer, and display their innocent and verdant fancies for the entertainment of the farmers' sons and the village housewives; for though a pardonable hallucination in certain seasons of early adolescence, this pastoral view of country life can be dismissed by grown up men and women without serious damage to their mental integrity. We must also avoid the notion of a section of the mercantile world, whose views of the country have uniformly been through the telescope of speculation, and to whom the whole continent outside the pavement resolves itself into a universe of mill privileges, mercantile agencies, ups and downs of breadstuffs, and prospective corner-lots in cities yet hovering in the air. Equally useless for our purpose is that idea which painfully occupies the soul of the retired man of the town, who having recovered from the excitement of building his palace on the most inaccessible hill in the country, awakes to the direful apprehension that he has put himself into a fortress and must spend the remainder of his days in foraging for supplies of food and fuel and society. It is becoming quite unnecessary to dispel the fond dream of the city ecclesiastic or politician, that on the pulling of a certain wire above the chair of his sanctum whole districts of agricultural patriots and saints will dance most vigorously to his tune, since the cry of both these gentlemen is now to gods and men for relief against the oppression of these dwellers on farms who are bent on making their vocation a *sinecure*. We can do justice to the artistic view of country life and still understand that the chief end of the laborer or village maid is not to figure in a smock-frock or flower-decked flat in his charming landscape. In contemplating the country life of New York, such views must only be considered as glimpses of the real world, like those caught while swiftly crossing one of the hill streets of the Capital City. But we shall transport ourselves to the homes of the people, and consider the case of those, who, born into the whole circle of country toils, trials and advantages, will live and die outside of city walls. How does life appear to this vast majority of the American people; what opportunities aid and what hinderances discourage their efforts for Christian manhood; and how shall they solve the radical problem of our national destiny;—to combine individual freedom in every department of human existence with the duties of a citizen in our great general confederacy of independent States?

The advantages of country life will always bear repeating. First is health, which must deteriorate amid the poisonous vapors and artificial habits that now make our cities the graveyards of so much youth and beauty imported from the fields. Next is physical comfort, for a sober man will prefer the country where all things grow for his support and he can afford to be a hospitable neighbor to the city, where every addition of outward happiness must be bargained for and dearly bought. Better still is the opportunity for personal consideration in a community that soon understands the real worth of its every member and assigns him the position his character demands, while the city must to a great degree live in ignorance of character, and promote men and women according to their strength in achieving a special success. The alternation of labor and leisure in the life of the farmer or dweller in villages secures time for mental improvement, and if the masses in the country are not more enlightened in literature than the overdriven and excited crowds that throng the pavement, it is their own deep disgrace. Art is the advantage of the town, but in the present state of

American art and manners we shall not be thought singular if we maintain that the privilege of looking from one of the hills that overshadow the valley of the Hudson, or contemplating the pictures framed by the window-sash of the householder among the western lakes, is superior to the attraction of a reserved seat at the Academy of Music, a ticket to the Art Galleries, a promenade down Broadway, or a carriage once a fortnight, with the invitation to occupy six square inches of an uptown saloon, for two fearful hours contending for personal safety in a mob of dress coats and a wilderness of crinoline. And when the lover of Christianity is brought to know the unveracities and obscenities and inhumanities that deep below deep undermine our gilded metropolitan life, he will see that the hope of a purer religion in America is given to those whose independent country life makes social servility and moral depravity an unpardonable offence. The sum of this advantage is that in the country the individual man is a more prominent object in the landscape of life than in the city: and while corporations and institutions are the rulers of the town it is easier for the dweller with nature to possess himself and decide the great American problem between man and the state according to his best intelligence.

Yet in many sections of the country there are great drawbacks to these advantages. The monotony of lonely life often stupefies rather than deepens the character. The want of society representing varied interests and styles of thought may easily breed a conceit of superiority, which, alternating with the shyness of pride nourished in seclusion, shuts the door on improvement. The lack of that indefinable power we call manner or personal presence, which few can preserve away from intercourse with all varieties of people, is a great hinderance to the reserved countryman. The absence of these powerful excitements which awake the latent energies and introduce a man to himself is also injurious to many a sleepy soul that suns its life away on green banks and lets nature overpower and demoralize the will. The remoteness from the centres of concentrated influence often begets a mischievous dependence in thought and habit. There is danger that the rural mind will fall into the ruts, and live and die unconscious of its decided advantages of position; and many a one has doubtless been galvanized into a noble manhood by the shocks of city life, who would have glided down the slow current of a country career hardly disturbing the waters till the final plunge.

The upshot of this controversy between country and town is, that each has great advantages for a strong soul. It is time that our people were delivered from the cant that agriculture is an essentially ennobling pursuit, and that one has only to live in a farmhouse to be a worthy man. Selfishness as withering, meanness and craft as belittling, sensuality as brutalizing as any that dwells in city courts, often curses the farmer's home. Neither the land nor the pavement makes the man, but a high spirit makes both the theatre of life's grandest achievement. Every honest and useful profession is good for the best uses of the soul. Labor is not confined to the field or the shop, but is the severe angel that stands by the elbow of him who thinks, or traffics, or guides society, and whenever welcomed bestows her great rewards. Both countrymen and citizen need less false pride in their profession, more just pride to make that profession the means of human elevation. The best product of the farm and plantation is not wheat and cotton, but man; and our teeming prairies and rich uplands will only become a curse, unless the world values the planter above his bales, and the farmer beyond his grains. The especial need of the great agricultural classes in this land is more self-respect, founded not on their grounds, but on their nature as souls created in the image of God; and along with this a more rational estimate of their great opportunities to cultivate the best character in their position, with an unobtrusive independence in forming their habits of life on the basis of the country. A sham city in the rural districts is a painful sight which too often offends the eyes of the American. For, just now, commerce is flaunting her sudden successes and intolerable follies of luxury in the eyes of the country, inflaming young men with the aspiration to exchange the honors of health and independence at home for slavery and effeminacy in the town; and changing the good old race of country women into feeble imitators of the fashion plates, who sigh among the groves and gardens of the Hudson for the splendors of Broadway millinery and the exhausting pleasures of a city career. When our country youth come to their senses, and with no affectation of contempt for the town, devote themselves to the growth of their own manhood and womanhood in the ample spaces of their enviable lot, we shall be nearer the end of our American Revolution, and see more clearly how to organize upon our prairies, and river banks, and mountain sides, that Christian freedom of which they are the magnificent types and shadows.

This idea of a life of Christian independence, amid the circumstances of the country would, doubtless, introduce extensive reforms in every department of rural existence. Beginning in the unobtrusive freedom of good families, it would gradually make its way through neighborhoods and districts, till the whole aspect of country life would be elevated and refined.

First, it would remodel the physical arrangements of many of our country friends, and inaugurate a style of living which would secure a larger degree of health and comfort. It is melancholy that a people with such abundant means for health and comfort as the rural population of New York, should so often pervert the benevolent gifts of God into curses. Besides the intemperance in the use of alcoholic drinks, and that poisonous weed whose vile mark is seen over the whole face of America, there is a great neglect of the simplest laws of dress, diet, housing and labor by our country folks, which is laying the seeds of permanent physical degeneracy. Our capricious climate demands perpetual watchfulness, and the habit of reckless exposure, which in men is the result of carelessness, and in women of imitation of city fashions, lies at the foundation of our declining health. One would suppose that the daughters of the most intelligent nation of farmers in the world would perceive the folly of arraying themselves in apparel which can hardly be excused in the drawing-rooms of the cities, and braving the terrors of a New York winter and the caprice of its spring and summer with the gossamer contrivances denominated fashionable shoes and hats and drapery ; but the country women dress on the whole, more unsuitably for their exposure than those of the city. As a result, female health, the source of national health, is at a fearfully low ebb in our villages and rural districts. The wholesome preparation of good food, and the method of eating and drinking are yet an unknown science to millions of our countrymen. We know the depth and breadth of this stolid American prejudice against the religion of the kitchen. Many a family that worships God sincerely in morning and evening devotions is poisoning itself by a transgression of His laws around its daily table. The greed for more land often keeps the home of the farmer destitute of many essentials to the healthy education of the family. The habits of toil uncheered by amusements, or the higher culture of the soul, cut short the days of hosts of our earnest countrymen. We cannot suggest the details of this physical reformation. It will come when the more sensible inhabitants of every district begin to think of the best way to prolong life and increase comfort in their particular locality.

Every state and region has peculiarities of climate and circumstance to which the physical habits must be adjusted. We have outgrown the primitive pioneer life which hardened the bodies of our ancestors; we must live in a more elegant style than they; and the question for the country people in our State is, shall the town tailors, milliners, architects and cooks, dress your sons and daughters, build your houses, spread your tables, and dictate habits of labor and amusement, after some wretched imitations of old world folly; or will you exercise your own common sense in the premises, build your house to suit the country, dress according to the peculiar exposure, eat and drink what will keep you in the best state of health and spirits, and play as rational experience demands? The question is vital; for life out of town will never be the noble and cheering thing it can be while it drags after it this lengthening chain of American dietetic abuse, beginning in the farmhouse and ending in the hells of city debauchery and crime.

The next element of success in country life is the proper regulation of labor. Notwithstanding the boast of American Free Institutions, the American idea of work is still deplorably low. In half the nation the laborer is a slave. Much of our northern labor is still in the bonds of ignorance and degradation; better than slavery or serfdom chiefly because the laborer is a citizen and has an outlook for his posterity, who, by the blessings of a free education, can hope to rise above the life-long drudging of their fathers. In large districts of our State work is still the curse of Adam, and thousands of our toiling people on the land and in mechanical employments have not dreamed of what labor is to be under the transforming influence of a Christian civilization. Intelligent work is ennobling; but perpetual drudgery is a terrible calamity. The way out of this prison-house of unremitting toil for a mere bodily subsistence is not an overturn of society or any form of agrarian politics, but the old way of spiritual cultivation. The young farmer of New York is offered, in the common school and associate advantages, the means of rising above ignorance. Science and the mechanic arts are toiling to put into his hands machinery that will abolish drudgery in the field and home. A suitable practical education will fit any young man or woman to use these labor-saving agencies of modern agriculture. And when their use is acquired, let not the accursed spirit of gain come in and steal the leisure they afford for new accumulations. If our country people will educate themselves to use the scientific modes of labor which are the glory of our age, *and then remain content with a competency of goods, and devote their leisure to that cultivation of the soul which makes the true citizen and Christian*, the life of the farmer will become what God intended, and thousands who are now driven from its annihilating toils will gladly embrace it. If our working men and women do not choose to bend tamely under the tyranny of a growing aristocracy that already proclaims the odious doctrine that the laborer belongs to the landowner, let them give their children the cultivation to use the science of the 19th century to beat back the advancing tide of 14th century serfdom, and prove to the world that labor of the hands is one essential quality of the best Christian manhood in a republic.

The despotism of the old world divides society into a class of landed gentry and a mob of servile laborers. In trying to elevate and equalize manners in America, we too often imagine that true gentility is the imitation of a gentry which is quite foreign to our ideas of social life. We are fast rising above that rudeness and indelicacy which for centuries have been the inheritance of the tillers of the soil; but our people have not known that America must produce her own methods of social intercourse, and learn by long experiment to blend the freedom of a true individualism with the courtesy of a fine reverence for humanity. In our escape from the servile politeness and iron conventionalities of despotic nations, we must endure awhile that impudence which excites mingled laughter and indignation in our Young America school of precocious boys and girls; but this is not to be our national manner. Freedom implies respect for self, founded on reverence for man, and around no one should there hang a finer courtesy than the republican gentleman. Not the simplicity of ignorance, but of high intelligence; not the overthrow of conventions by unbridled sensuality and conceit, but their displacement by the broader and freer forms of a better moral culture; not the imitation of finical notions of refined intercourse, but the delicacy of pure and trusting lives is to be our contribution to the science of human behavior. Let the young men and women of our State first try to be worthy their great destiny, and then act out their best conceptions of social intercourse. This accomplished, we need not be ashamed before the more elaborate manners of the decaying civilization of the past.

Especially in the great problem of amusements

let our people be wise in time. Doubtless we have toiled too hard and become too stern and joyless getting our nation on its legs; and now the cry for a new organization of public and social recreation is rising quite too strong to be anathematized out of existence. But we are not pleading for the importation of that mixture of childish and sensual gaiety which charms our staid travellers out of their common sense on the continent. For these European popular amusements are the river of Lethe in which the masses plunge and forget the miseries of their actual lot. We want nothing in America to steep us in light-hearted indifference to our great problem of republican life; we are not far enough along to rejoice immoderately; we have no right to revel while the eyes of the world are looking on us for an example of self government. Thus, while we have no sympathy with asceticism, we would still urge simplicity and temperance; a heroic quality in our very sport, a something of thoughtful dignity even in our recreations. Our national amusements should be based on sincere admiration of American nature. We cannot see too much of the glorious scenery of our country; journeys, excursions, out-door pleasures will impart a tone to the mind, which will mould the pure and gentle delights of home, and out of our native taste create something more appropriate for public entertainment. Let our villagers and farmers not envy the metropolis its exhausting and artificial amusements. A majority of those who engage in them do not really enjoy or understand them. Let them not waste too much money running after city spectacles, but organize among themselves the best that the taste of the region will afford. Thus, by gradual experiment will our people learn the cheerfulness due to every citizen.

The education of the country must rest upon the public school as its corner stone. Would that the people of New York could know what a wound they give their State whenever they neglect this great republican institution. With a thorough organization of the free-school, and a judicious selection of the best public journals, a vigorous support of the lecture system untrammelled by sectarian or partisan bigotry, and a liberal provision of books through town and village libraries, there need be no want of mental enlightenment in the country. The farmers may have the most leisure of any class, and that leisure can be so used as to create a deep soil of thoughtful intelligence from which will spring genius in all its forms of commanding power. Never was there such a hope of mental illumination opened to a people as to the inhabitants of the northern states of America, and if the laboring masses of our great State choose to abide in the darkness of ignorance and prejudice they will deserve to be governed by the demagogues who now thrive on their defects and reckon on the 90,000 illiterate adults of New York, the benighted regions of Pennsylvania, and the shades of Egyptian Illinois, as so much capital in their infamous speculation upon the rights of humanity.

Our hope of a pure democracy in America must rest upon the country; not as it is, where whole districts are led by old prejudices or stolid traditions artfully used by politicians who wield the city press; but as it will be when the laboring masses know the history of America and fully comprehend the great conflict of ideas by which the nation is now shaken. Every good patriot must desire that the country should be the chief power in the State, not because a man who drives a plough is better than a man who drives a quill, rather because there is more hope that the dwellers outside of towns will administer government for man. There is but one controversy now dividing our politics:—*Is Government intended to protect classes or develop man?* For a feudal, a commercial, a manufacturing, a farming class to absorb the care of the state is equally dangerous and anti-

American. Only that republicanism will stand which proposes the recognition of human rights and their protection in a government that leaves to the individual the extreme of freedom compatible with the present safety of society, while its efforts are constantly directed to the wise enlargement of this area. And a truly educated rural population is better circumstanced to accept and administer this American idea than the dwellers in towns. In proportion as the millions of our laboring people make themselves capable of forming broad and independent judgments in public affairs will the occupation of the demagogues be gone, and the desperate diseases that now beset the state yield to a growing health in the body politic.

This condition of life in the country can exist only on the basis of a personal character founded upon that love which eighteen centuries ago was declared religion. Vain is the hope to build up a civilization in the fields of America which will resist the fearful pressure of our Republican temptations on other foundations than this. Pride of family, public spirit, reverence for our political ancestry, the fear of encountering a world-wide shame, a jealous and irritable spirit of nationality; how easily are such considerations washed down the tide of any fierce popular excitement! The citizen of our country is defended by its institutions against the forms of danger peculiar to established despotisms; but what shall defend him from the people, when inflamed by a great delusion, or debauched by a mighty temptation, it charges down on his manhood in a majority swelling like the maddened waves of a storm-tossed sea? Only character based on the everlasting rock of religious principle can offer to this onset a granite wall on which the popular surge shall be shivered to spray. Blessed will be the day when this fact shall be acknowledged all over our vast domain; when sects in and out of the church shall be stirred by a rivalry in righteousness more determined than their present warfare for precedence; when holiness shall be regarded the most imperative need of this very land wherein we live; when the widest freedom in the sacred affairs of the soul shall be reconciled with the most efficient union of all good men in behalf of that practical morality which exalteth a state; when the heathen sophism that religion should be separate from the daily life of the Republic, shall be left to those who need it to excuse their crimes against God and humanity; when the people shall exhibit their reverence for those who gained and preserved our heritage by scourging corruption, and blasphemy, and inhumanity from all high places in the name of that law which abides forever. Then will religious institutions, severed from all ecclesiastical connection with the government, dispense that sacred wisdom which shall become the life blood of character and consecrate our fair country to the holiest use of man.

With such a realization of country life, what a new splendor would pervade our glorious valley and brood over the mountains and plains of our Empire State. Then would the farms and villages of New York produce a race worthy to sustain the honor of the Republic. Reared amid the inspiring influences of nature and taught in the best school of youthful discipline, it would pour into our depraved and debilitated cities the life blood of a higher civilization. And when the hot, weary day of middle age toil was past, how gladly would the citizen return to the quiet country, and pass away from earth amid the blessings of his childhood's home. Where shall this idea be realized if not in this valley within whose borders lie all the appliances of modern life; where agriculture and commerce embrace; where the spires of the town are never out of sight; and from every city roof is a vision of swelling hills and gleaming waves? Who will not rejoice to dwell in a spot so favored by God and man; and who will not count it the greatest privilege of that lot to make the Hudson, now the symbol of all that is beautiful and sublime in nature, the higher type of those great and lovely elements of character and society which consecrate a Christian State.

## II.

# THE CAPITAL CITY;

OR

## SOCIETY IN TOWN.

The City of Albany may justly challenge comparison with the inland towns of America, for beauty of situation and peculiar historical interest. Midway in the lovely valley of the "Great River of the Mountains," it scales its triple-headed hill, crowned by the Capitol, from whose dome is seen a landscape of wondrous beauty. The shadowy Catskills contend with drifting mountains of clouds along her southern horizon, subsiding into the exquisite azure hues of the Helderberg. Down the valley, the Hudson slowly winds its placid way around projecting headlands to the distant sea; and smiling with cultivated slopes and wooded knolls, its western shores ascend to the hills whence the mountains of New England are seen to welcome the rising sun. All along these curving banks, up these woody ascents, and down this long, green vale is poured that indescribable atmosphere of magic quiet which lulls the whole region, from the Adirondack to the ocean, to a calm sleep, startled now and then into the hurried dream of a busy town. A hundred thousand people are working out the problem of life beneath the gazer's eye; their fret and toil and triumph enfolded in this drowsy enchantment of nature.

Seen from the western hills, the city crowns her blended heights with a surpassing grace; while, in her own streets the citizen is arrested in his hurried walk by a vision of glittering waves and wooded summits and fertile fields, at the end of a vista of bricks and pavements. With no pretensions to architectural grandeur, but with much of the reality of comfortable housing, healthful air, and solid prosperity, the dweller in our ancient town should long hesitate before he leaves her country-girdled streets for the prison of noisy ways and crushing toil, the great cities of our land have become.

And if, while standing in this post of observation, the history of our venerable Capital City could pass in panorama before our eyes, what remarkable changes would excite our admiration.

Through the dim mist of 250 years, we behold the "Half Moon," Hendrick Hudson, master, crawling along the shores, gazed at by savages surprised into the mood of gentle children. Six years pass, and above the low flats of yonder island rises a Dutch trading-house—26 by 36, stockaded fifty feet square, with its moat of eighteen feet, bristling with a few iron and stone guns, garrisoned by the ten men who have now become the 100,000 that people this area of ten miles. Anon the trading-house becomes a fort, first nestling where steamboats now do congregate, then bravely climbing the hill and laying its corner-stone as high as the roof of the present St. Peter's church. Another seven years finds the father of many Patroons the owner of his princely estate, stretching from the great Cohoes Falls, twenty-four miles on either side of the river; and lovelier manor never cheered the heart of feudal lord. In twelve years more the first minister of Christianity arrives and the germ of the most ancient church is planted. The little village of Beaverwyck, clustering beneath its fort, becomes the scene of fierce conflict, and violent hands from Manhattan tear down the flag of feudal proprietorship, and lay the foundations of the Corporation of Albany in the first court here instituted. Not long after the English power becomes supreme, in 1664, and in 1668 our town becomes the first chartered city in the United States of America; yet thirty years more will scarcely suffice to bring her a thousand citizens.

Now look ahead three-fourths of a century, and you behold our slow Capital City, in 1745, laced up in a stockade, lying on the hill-side like a pear, whose stem is the fort opposite St. Peter's, and whose base is washed by the river. Garrulous old Peter Kalm strays up here, gets hooted in the streets by the boys for his French fashions, goes off "in a huff," and tells sad stories about the little Dutch town on the borders of the interminable wilderness. Its quiet is often disturbed by the bustle of public affairs; a shudder runs through its drowsy streets as the news of French and Indian invasions come through the woods; here encamp and equip the armies that are to hurl back the successive waves that rolled from the St. Lawrence, only to spend themselves in the woods above; here congregate the colonial governors to deliberate on American taxation; and not a quarter of a century later the old town laughed outright as the famous procession, inaugurating the adoption of the Constitution of the United States, swept from the fields about Watervliet, to the big tent on the hill.

We look again at the beginning of the present

century, and behold a village of five thousand people, ten streets and lanes, one public hotel and six hundred houses, chiefly, according to the authority of the great Dr. Morse, "with their gable ends towards the streets." The pine groves close in this little provincial paradise; the brambles and wild roses clamber up the sides of the ravines, the three "kills" sing down their steep beds, the willows and tall elms line the river bank, half a hundred sloops stir the waters of the river; the patriarchs sit on their "stoops," along the sacred way of Pearl street, now and then pondering the meaning of a strange apparition of Yankeedom urging its sleds through the February snows to the "far west" of central New York—twelve hundred sleds in three days, five hundred in one day.

But the sentence of doom for the quiet old town has been pronounced; she is now the Capital City of the Republic of New York. Strong as were the first two centuries of her life, they are absorbed into the wider civilization of the State. As we look now we behold a modern city growing in wealth, honor, arts and industry, like a hundred cities of the republic in all save its representative capacity as the political capital of its chief state. Would that the genius of America that has changed this village of five thousand to a valley full of one hundred thousand and swept away the very landmarks of its old days, could have spared at least one street to remind us of the most peculiar civilization of our past. But they are gone, though the solid virtues that dwelt under these quaint gables are inwrought into the texture of our public and private life, an imperishable strand of that New York into which all the nationalities of earth are braided.

But it is not of the Albany of the past or present, in itself considered, that we speak; rather of Albany regarded first, as the type of city life in our land; and secondly, as containing those public institutions which represent the best civilization of our republic. To the first of these considerations, *Society in town as contrasted with life in the country*, attention is now invited.

While we regret the entire obliteration of our city of half a century ago, and contrast the present capital of New York with the cities of the old world, rich in monumental tokens and venerable associations of the long gone past, we must still congratulate ourselves on the cause. The reason of this obliteration of old landmarks is not that we are peculiarly vandalic in our rage for improvement, but that *an American city is essentially a different thing from an European capital.* The old cities abroad are the growth of another state of human affairs, and represent quite another phase in the history of human progress than our own. They were the centres of imperial influence; a court, a palace, a royal army, with the peculiar results of such institutions, made them the centres of permanent attraction. Here, too, were the famous seats of the ecclesiastical power that held the monarchy in check, and spite of its corruption, was for centuries the best thing in Europe. And most significant of all, the continental cities were the cradle of freedom, where the mercantile and industrial interest first rallied and beat back the insolent feudalism that ruled over the broad country in the shape of a barbarous nobility; and in the independence of the English and German towns laid the corner stone of the liberty we to-day enjoy. And here were the great foundations of learning and cultivation in the universities, scholars and artists, that are the real sovereigns of modern times. Thus an European city is a nation within a nation, a conglomeration of institutions rooted in the soil of centuries, firmly interlaced into a corporate structure that resists the convulsions of ages. What wonder that Rome, Paris and London, Berlin, Moscow and Vienna should rule the nations they represent as our cities never can control the destinies of America; and that they should exist in all their essential attributes, while dynasties, peoples, civilizations change; the gigantic monuments of the past, that no deluge of modern improvement can move from their foundations.

But an American city is only a convenient hotel, where a free country people come up to tarry and do business, with old recollections of nature haunting them amid its toil and confusion; where the foreigner halts at his landing, and, if able and enterprising, pushes on to the "Far West;" where the representative men of various kinds congregate during the few years of their culminating power to organize institutions and policies that represent the property and ideas of the millions that people the fields and villages without. Thus the American municipality can never have more than a representative character. Its money is the accumulation of the country's industry; its commerce is the exchange of the products of the prairie, plantation, lakes and rivers, and thousands of factory villages clustering about innumerable waterfalls among the hills; its scholarship is the growth of far away colleges; its literature culminates in the daily journals; its intelligence is rivalled by country towns; its society does not give the tone to, but is the growth of, the civilization of the district it represents; its politics finally yield to an outside pressure, and its institutions of philanthropy and religion are supported by contributions of men and means from the sects that spread over entire States. It is not the deep, firm root out of which rises the trunk and foliage of a great nationality; rather a boat tossed on the billows of American enterprise and emigration.

Let us rejoice that American cities must be representative, and cannot become our masters until the republic loses all but its name. Thank Heaven, liberty in New York is not compelled to burrow in forts and throw barricades across metropolitan streets, but ranges over her mountain tops, and along her plains, by the shores of her lakes, and down the valleys of her rivers. The open country is our fortress of freedom, and if the people know the worth of this precious boon, they will never permit the temporary classes of their cities to sacrifice it on the altar of municipal ambition. The cities of our State, even our proud "Metropolis," are but houses of industry, entertainment and public utility, built by our people; and while no individual right of the citizen is invaded, let them be so identified in the general body politic, that they cannot be seized by demagogues who would turn them into barbaric castles, fortified by ignorance and vice against the fresh and inspiring growth of new world civilization. The sophistry of "municipal independence" with which our people are so often befogged, is quite out of place to-day in the United States. It meant something in the middle ages, when a ferocious nobility occupied the country, and held the farmer as a serf, and the gates of the town were the only defence for the merchant and the artisan ; but in a State where the land is owned by the people, and an intelligent, virtuous, and prosperous country population build villages and cities for their commerce and convenience, the man who demands that these towns shall cut the vital cord that binds them to their creative and sustaining power, is advocating the cause of the Despotism that is passing away and not the welfare of the Humanity that is to come. Let the free winds of the country blow through every lane and whistle round every corner; let the people of New York always keep their towns in their own hands; then will the city in our republican life be what the garden is to the farm; the inclosure to which every forest and hill, and swamp, and brook and cultivated field has sent its tribute; that amid its bewildering walks and shaded arbors may be seen a representative from every nook and corner of the broad domain, controlled by the genius of a free society and a Christian State.

In view of these facts, the rage of the people of New York for city life is an evil that may well arrest the attention of the patriot and Christian. The Empire State contains 46,000 square miles of territory, of which only half, 13,000,000 acres, is cultivated at all, while 13,000,000 acres of unoccupied land, and untold mineral wealth invite to a century of industrial enterprise. Yet full one-third of our entire population of three and a half millions, is huddled into towns and exposed to the influences of American city life. Our young countrymen are born with a fever in their blood which drives them from the farm, or the factory, or the mine, where actual production is the result of their efforts, and economy of health, property, and soul is promoted, to the town where ninety per cent. of the merchants fail, and the mechanic toils with a pit of starvation ever yawning beneath his feet, and an ever increasing series of middle men enhances the cost of living, and pitiless competition of labor and perpetual temptation imperil integrity of mind and purity of life. Our country girls push for the city as by a natural instinct, seeming to relish better the intoxicating charm of being one colored wave of the torrent that rolls along a

Broadway than the centre of a neighborhood among the fields. We have the right to ask these heedless throngs what purpose drives them to the city; and compel them to contemplate its nicely balanced advantages and disadvantages before they step over the threshold of nature, and adventure in the labyrinth of artificial life.

Doubtless, a city is a large labor-saving machine, where the greatest amount of spiritual energy can be directed to a given point with the least waste of material resources. It is an undeniable advantage to an able man to occupy such a tower of observation, whence the forces of civilization can be seen in their accumulated vigor and mutual relation. Knowing what is the capacity of society in each department, and how much energy is enlisted for the development of each, he can adjust his own efforts, save himself useless expenditure of his powers, and direct his genius to the exact point of demand. Then it is a privilege to a strong man to enjoy companionship of his equals, to learn to make a straight path through the tangled feet of others as indefatigable as himself; to be drilled and criticised, and finally educated by his peers. This is the great charm of the city to the leaders of every realm of life. Here, too, the tendencies of classes, the need of crowds, and the secrets of public and wide-reaching influence over men, are best to be learned. And the town is a great workshop filled with the best tools in the shape of organized forces and institutions. Labor and business are systematized, society can be taken by the handle, literature is classified, and education and art in every branch assigned to its peculiar department. The caucus, the convention, the city church, the philanthropic institution, are the finest implements to do the kinds of work they represent. Doubtless, these are formidable tools for weak men to handle; and the incompetent man or woman who aspires to their use is like a child in an armory, reaching on tip-toe to lift the sword and bayonet from their rack above its imperilled head; but when a strong man of war appears, he can arm in the least time, with the best weapons. If one is up to the work, and can keep wide-awake without destruction to body and mind, there is a great opportunity in sitting at the end of the wire when the earliest message comes; in catching the last news of fluctuation in trade or society, before it falls into the hands of the reporters; in discerning the premonitory symptoms of all changes that modify the activity of man. The enterprising citizen thus always knows a little ahead of his rural brother, and so has a foot in advance in the race for success.

Able men will, therefore, always face towards the great centres of human activity, and since few young people count themselves fools, the American cities will be the battle-ground of annihilating competition in every department of republican society. From the newsboy whose voice best threads the labyrinth of street noises, to the preacher who knows the magic word that, spoken in the darkest chapel, will fill the street with a crowd of the best mind and heart of the town, every post of profit and influence will be contested inch by inch, and the victor stand at last surrounded by a score of fallen adventurers. The young who rush to the city thinking its brilliant positions are easily secured, do not understand that no man succeeds there otherwise than as a representative of a class ; that every citizen who permanently occupies an important position, holds it by virtue of some peculiar power in a certain direction persistently exercised. Many bad people rule in town, but no fool, no mediocre person long occupies a desirable eminence (unless in certain instances where the fools and platitudes need a representative, and choose the genius in stupidity to be their king or queen). That the vast majority of adventurers on the pavement do not succeed ; that they work harder, live closer, suffer tenfold the frets and sorrows of life, and peril the best prospects of character beyond comparison with the risks of a country career, is open to every one who will see; and only an insane man will assert that a majority of the one million two hundred thousand people who are waging this pitiless war of competition on the pavements of the Empire State, would not be vastly more useful to themselves and to society, if employed in developing the teeming resources of physical and spiritual wealth that prophecy the future of our noble State.

For out of this very representative character of citizen society spring the formidable disadvantages that to the mass of men quite overbalance the opportunities of the town. The quiet, affectionate youth comes from the genial atmosphere of the rural neighborhood, and finds himself struggling in a rushing crowd of adventurers, each bent on success. For here success is the only alternative of ruin. There is no long suffering, pitiful community behind the combatant to receive him, wounded and weary in defeat; he must leave the pavement for the country if he fails, and too often there is no home among the fields; and the deep vault of sin and sorrow which runs under every drawing-room and counting-room, claims him at the end. But even if this fate is escaped, through what prolonged and withering toils, amid what dangers of health and life, and sanity of soul, does the prosperous citizen approach his reward. The majority of successful dwellers in town are scarred in body and twisted in mind by their prolonged stimulation of all the powers of life, and in grasping the prize of ambition have lost their own best resources of enjoyment. *Happiness does not depend so much on what we have as on a certain freshness of nature that illuminates every corner of our life with a light from within;* and how few preserve that freshness amid the monotonous toils and discouraging collisions of the city.

But the greatest peril besets the soul. He who has impaired his reverence for man, duty, God, and the high religious self-respect which scorns any stooping to success, has made a failure of existence. And it is not easy to elbow the way through crowds of unknown faces—to lose almost the recognition of individual character in the contact with masses—to be forced to treat our best friends as rivals, and the multitude as instruments, without a disastrous decline in that love to man from which grows the reverence for duty and the supreme love of God. It is harder yet to own one's-self in a field where society in every direction claims you as one spoke in the wheel of some powerful organization, and to be "left out" is to live in a solitude more fearful than the primitive woods. When the outside of life is so large a point of immediate success, what a temptation to a soul-destroying career of fashion and luxury! and those who know best the seductions of sensuality that lurk beneath the gilding and propriety of the city, most distrust their own power of resistance.

All dangers of the town may be summed up in this: that here, withdrawn from the blessed influences of Nature, and set face to face against humanity, man loses his own nature and becomes a new and artificial creature—an unhuman cog in a social machinery that works like a fate, and cheats him of his true culture as a soul. The most unnatural fashions and habits, the strangest eccentricities of intellect, the wildest and most pernicious theories in social morals, and the most appalling and incurable barbarism, are the legitimate growth of city life. If one has strength of constitution, physical, mental and moral, to push through all these hinderances, and stand upon the summit of the town, doubtless his experience of man is more profound and curious, and his power to dexterously administer affairs greater than in a more secluded position; but who will risk the chances of a strife, where the mass are beaten and the one who outlives his companions succeeds, without deep reflection and for unanswerable reasons? Who but a lunatic will rush into this *mêlée*, trusting to luck, where luck is always on the side of the wise and strong?

Therefore, let our young people in the country take much counsel and be very well assured in their own sober judgment, before they cast their lot in the city. Remember that any point of New York is now in vital communication with the centres of civilization, and that every year is bringing all men nearer together. All the essential advantages of our republican life can be secured, by proper effort, in every village and cluster of farms in the Empire State; and the extraordinary successes of towns are but for the few. Let not these few be too eager to vault to their post of ultimate power; if the magnet is in them, the filings will concentrate anywhere; and only by long and patient experiment can any genuine man gain the magic platform whence electric wires course all over the land, and cause a thousand bosoms to thrill at every throb of his heart. For those adventurers who have concluded to sacrifice their manhood to a paltry success, we have nothing to advise; "where the carcass is, there will the eagles be gathered together." But we implore every honest youth in our land to ask this question of his innermost soul: "Am I sure I shall gain enough in happiness, worthy prosperity and manliness, to risk the perils and disadvantages of the town?" For this is the only test, a gain of manhood and womanhood. Oh, how far beneath any noble soul should be the weak hankering for such a success as comes to thousands of families in the city; a gain in money purchased by the sacrifice of honesty and reverence for man, a gain in comforts and luxuries which are a slow poison in the blood; of social position, which changes a sincere wife to a managing mother and a pure child to a reckless young man or a bedizened victim of female vanity; a success that is a dismal failure in all that is fit to be acquired. Better the most obscure lot in the bleakest northern wilderness with virtue, than a palace in town with such a wreck of souls within. Better far the opportunities and joys of our favored country life, for thousands who only leave it to tempt a certain damage to the highest interests of the individual and the demoralization of the republic.

It would be a great triumph of philanthropy if the large class of the poor could be removed from the cities of New York and planted all over her wide territory; and one dollar given to help a pauper family out of town is better charity than a year's support in the garret where they now fight with starvation. And with them should go thousands who are just living above the precipice of hopeless poverty, whom a few months' suspension of labor will hurl into the abyss of want and crime. And still more imperatively does public economy demand the exit of other thousands of middlemen, who are too able and respectable to fulfill their destiny by gaining a living from the mere handling the necessaries of existence, when they might be producing much that is useful elsewhere. Were our cities swept clean of these classes, there would be still enough to fulfill all the uses of the town; merchants whose talents and character are adequate to manage the machinery and resist the seductions of commerce; workmen of various kinds, whose superior skill and confirmed habits make them at home amid the intricacies of metropolitan industry; professional men, whose laudable ambition, fortified by ample experience, leads them to a municipal platform as their best position; and enough of the rich and cultivated in manners to reform the vices of social life and organize amusements on a generous and Christian scale. But we cannot build cities "to order;" they are and will be the huge receptacles for all varieties of humanity, and represent the worst as surely as the best in our American character. All the teacher of Christianity can do is to take men and women in towns as he finds them, and, spite of disheartening influences, keep on forever warning, instructing and inspiring to virtue.

One good man teaches better than all the sermons of the most eloquent doctors; let me therefore drop my vocation and introduce a worthy family, which will speak for itself on the interesting theme of city life. Coming down the steps of the capitol yesterday, whom should I meet but my old friend *Mr. John Manhattan*, who had stopped over Sunday in Albany, on a trip from New York to one of our pleasant western cities. He may even be reading these words; if so, I trust he will pardon my use of his example where my preaching would fail.

Mr. John Manhattan lived on his father's farm in a little town on the Hudson, where he saw light some fifty years ago, till he was eighteen years of age, when he took a turn of several years in the village "variety store;" and thence by a natural gravitation of his excellent business talents, was landed in Albany at twenty-five. It was not easy in any city twenty-five years ago for a rising young man to preserve his reputation and keep shy of the roistering habits, which were called "high life," by a large class of rich men's sons; and we have heard that Mr. Manhattan was at first snubbed by a good many young gentlemen who were afterwards very glad to intercede for his influence and cash to relieve them from the unpleasant consequences of their gentility. Friend John, after a few years' experience, came to the deliberate conclusion that nothing would be so good a protection against the attractions of his gay acquaintances as a good wife, and he reasonably concluded that a fashionable young lady who could not keep her brother from making a fool of himself at every party of the season, would not aid him in living a sober life. This idea was confirmed on a visit to a charming village in western New York (that treasury of sensible women), by the acquaintance of Miss Molly Mayflower, a young lady of Connecticut parentage, then keeping school in her native town. In due time (how it is unnecessary to explain), the schoolmistress became the wife of our friend, and, as Mrs. Molly Mayflower Manhattan, has demonstrated the best way of reconciling national peculiarities by creating a household in which the solidity and sagacity of New Netherlands and the enterprise and moral refinement of New England have combined to enrich the civilization of New York by a model home.

There was no danger of John falling asleep with a western schoolmistress of Yankee descent for a reminder; indeed his old friends thought his business capacity decidedly increased by this addition of a silent partner. But they very early concluded that to kill themselves with work, in order to make a fortune, would be ridiculous; so they pitched life on a moderate key—didn't try to sing in falsetto until they had mastered the lower regions of the scale. John buttoned up his coat after breakfast every morning and marched to his counting-room with the air of a man who knows just what he proposes to do, and intends to do it; and when he walked home to spend the evening with his beloved wife, the work was generally done. He congratulated his "fast" friends on their speculations, was glad when Flash, Frisk, & Co., set up their carriage, and moved up town, but respectfully declined to indorse their notes for corner lots in the New Jerusalem Metropolitan Company. By close observation he acquired the science of business as distinguished from commercial quackery, and he is one of the ten young men, among the one hundred who began with him, that have never been obliged to investigate the provisions of the bankrupt law, and his house is now a solid concern and has not figured in Mr. Bowen's list during the last panic. I never saw him angry but once, when he kicked a New York broker down stairs for proposing a partnership in the stock operations of a coal mine which he knew lay 500 feet under an inaccessible mountain; but many a sensible scheme for valuable public improvements has been the better for his advice or material aid.

Mrs. Molly needed no new-fangled doctor to inform her that if she poisoned her family three times a day by a luxurious table, or simple dishes villainously cooked, they would not live out half their days; it was always a pleasure to eat one of her dinners, for every course was seasoned with her common sense; the children did not need to have the military called out to disperse their riot among the victuals; but ate and drank and dressed as Mrs. Molly Mayflower Manhattan decided was best; much to the disgust of Mrs. Aurelia Bombazine across the way, whose first fifteen years of married life were passed chasing the milliners and French cooks, and her remaining days in chasing the doctors and studying into new systems of medicine. What rosy cheeks, what vigorous limbs, and straight backs these little Manhattans had; somewhat furious and noisy, and occasionally riotous, from fullness of life and that portion of the "old Adam," that falls to the best of families; but somehow they were managed, and I never heard in this house those peculiar domestic sounds which have greeted my ears when waiting in a fashionable parlor half an hour for the lady to array herself for a call of ten minutes, disciplining the nursery meanwhile.

Mr. Manhattan lived in a medium house, furnished by his own and his wife's good taste, not by upsetting a cart of miscellaneous upholstery into his drawing-rooms. He knew what he spent, lived well enough, never gave or went to "wine suppers," spent his summers in a way that in twenty years has filled the souls of parents and children with long galleries of pictures drawn by God's finger from the glorious mountain tops and valleys and lakes of our wondrous State. They live now in New York, very substantially and with that perfection of taste that everybody who enters their house seems to have found his own ideal of home.

Very early did John and Molly learn to keep out of the prison of an artificial fashionable caste. Instead of straining towards the West End, they put themselves on their human worth, and accepted such friends as God sent; and they have learned that "getting into society" is one of the chief American humbugs, that if *you are true, good and beautiful in life's relations, Providence will send from every region of society those who are to be your chosen friends.* Mr. Manhattan's house is the resort of the best society I ever knew; that is, the best people in every rank and class seem to have been drawn, as by a magnet, to his modest parlors, and society has been to his family a wide, rich and varied school of human experience, rather than the stifled inclosure of any conceited set of "first people." It was always his theory that there are good people in every place and every region of humanity, and a true man can find them without any creeping or masquerading, or going down on his knees before a plate glass window or a livery; and he has found his own and kept his manhood, and therewith he and his are content.

I don't think any of the little folks of this family ever were miseducated at a boarding-school, or forced into a precocious possession of useless knowledge. Of "yellow novels," they know only the name; and they have the shocking taste to prefer the sweet pages of Washington Irving to the rawhead-and-bloody-bones creations of Mr.

Sylvanus Cobb, jr. But they know English, read good books, study hard, are very intelligent, and, best of all, know how to think. Their amusements are so linked with duties and accomplishments that they seem to be the flower of all they do. Everything done indoors or out turns its sunny side; home is a varied landscape of ever blooming joys; society is a pleasing recreation. They go together to an occasional lecture when they suppose the man has anything to say; and once a month all hands are seen at the play, the concert, or some other place of entertainment; though the Rev. Dr. Doomsday one Sunday proved that the Devil is in all such carnal pleasures, in a sermon of intense dramatic power, in which he was himself star actor, supernumeraries, and orchestra, the scene changed every five minutes, and the fifth act went out in a gigantic tableau of all creation going to universal crash, and which old Tom Parquette, who ought to know, vowed was the best performance he had ever seen, on or off the boards.

Mr. Manhattan was never known to be absent from the caucus or the polls, and has used all his influence to make every city where he has lived a better community. He does not vote for a policy because it will benefit his trade, or to feather the nest of some political friend; but he tries to find out the best man to serve in city affairs; and in the politics of state and nation, he stands on the old platform laid down eighteen hundred years ago: "*Whatsoever you would that men should do to you, do ye even so to them,*" by which "glittering generality" he tests all public men and measures; and though he does not expect to be president in 1860, he believes that the country will be agitated more and more, as by whirlwinds and earthquakes, until all the good men unite on this platform of adamant, first to vote down and then to regenerate the demagogues and their troop of servile and ignorant followers. He is considered "visionary" by most of the party leaders; but any of them would give his ears to get his influence to back him at a contested election. He is a patriot Christian, and whether office goes or stays, he intends to stand by *man* who was made before governments and will outlast them all.

What a deal of ecclesiastical diplomacy has been used to get Mr. Manhattan into all the churches; meek suggestions of the value of his great influence; sad suggestions of heavy debts impending over the new church; hints that a vacant pew could be had next to Hon. So-and-so's seat; marvellous interest in the children and relish of

Mrs. Manhattan's teas by various worthy Doctors of Divinity. But for my life I don't know what church the good man attends; he is so good a man, that theological dissensions always seemed an impertinence in his presence, and the most severe-faced bigot relents under the experience of an evening by his fireside. An atmosphere of tender piety hallows his habitation; a full and silent tide of benevolence rolls from his doors, watering every interest of his brother man. The widow and orphan would bless him, but he is off, like a sunbeam, to escape their thanks, which fall on the hearts of Molly and the children like perpetual dew from summer skies. And though the Gospel trumpet is not blown before his steps in the street, a worldly policy has only to show its head in his presence to shrink out of sight before his noble manhood, rooted in the everlasting laws of the Almighty.

Such is my good old friend, and by such as he and his, will life in the American city become the fine and beautiful thing it may. Whoever can go and do likewise, let him seek the town, and there prove that after all it is not the sphere of action, but the soul that acts therein which ennobles our human existence. For a good soul is a breath of heaven among the fields and a sublimity among the hills; an angelic presence on the streets and a sanctity that makes every home in town a church of the living Father. Oh! that midway of this wondrous valley, on the sides of these sloping hills, among the streets and lanes, and in the chambers of this ancient town, might be realized that life of Christian manliness and womanly love which will make us indeed the Capital City of a State whose God is the Lord.

## III.

## THE FORCES OF FREE LABOR.

THE traveller who approaches our Capital City by any of its great routes of communication, is confronted by those Industrial Forces that represent the Free Labor of the Empire State. Warehouses and piers, crowded with produce and miles of lumber, suggest a mighty expanse of fertile western fields and the vast northern wilderness. The river banks, vocal with the hum of machinery and illuminated at night with the glow of furnaces, proclaim that here the myriad arms of manufacturing toil are moulding the crude elements of nature into forms of use and beauty. The flitting cloud of vessels and the stir of life along the docks declare the presence of a commerce whose roots touch the shores of far-off nations, and which shoots a fruit-bearing branch into every street and lane of our venerable town. And if he looks beyond this area of activity, and studies the habits and occupations of the 115,000 inhabitants who people this busy valley, he will not be surprised at the wealth, comforts and refinement that have rewarded the toil of the past two centuries; and he will surely not count that experiment of Free Labor a failure, which has already made an accumulation of property equal to $500, for every man, woman and child within the range of the strongest eye looking from the dome of the capitol, and reckons this gain of money the least of its many achievements in behalf of a true civilization.

Concentrated within this lovely valley are the six great agencies of our system of Free Industry. In the spring of the year 1807, the first of these wonder-working forces might be seen in the shape of a strange craft, 100 feet by 12, drawing seven feet of water, creeping up the river at the rate of five miles an hour, trailing a dense cloud of smoke and sparks, bearing twelve passengers, who for the sum of $7 apiece bought the renown of sailing from New York on the first steamboat, *The Clermont*, under the pilotage of Robert Fulton. A strange expedition was that accounted by the good people of the metropolis, not thirty of whom believed the vessel would move a mile from the wharf: one venerable man saying to Judge Wilson as he embarked, "*John, will thee risk thy life in such a concern? I tell thee, she is the most fearful wild fowl living, and* thy *father ought to restrain thee!*" Could her heroic commander, as he stood silent on deck as this craft *did move*, amid the cheers of thousands of astonished spectators, have been told that his little steamship was to inaugurate the first of the gigantic forces of our new American Industry, what a reward for long years of neglect and unrequited toil.

In the same year, 1803, that Fulton and Livingston obtained the exclusive right of navigating the waters of N. Y. with their new steamboat, Governeur Morris stirred up an active engineer to the gigantic idea of connecting the Hudson and the lakes by a great canal. Very slowly this second agency of our national civilization loitered towards its realization. Thirteen years passed before the final mandate went forth, in 1816, from yonder capitol, that the Hudson should be married to Lake Champlain and Lake Erie; and eight years were necessary to complete these magnificent works (in 1825), concerning which the wildest rhapsodies of Geddes, and Morris, and Clinton, now read like the most prosaic commonplace.

The year (1826) following the completion of the canals, was signalized by the passage of the first railroad charter in the Legislature of New York, and four years later (1830), the first train of cars rolling from the Mohawk to the Hudson, signalized the birth of the third of these servants of the Republic. And what a mighty power has that become. The Empire State is now veined by two thousand seven hundred and forty-nine miles of railroads, which furnish one-tenth of all our assessed valuation of real and personal estate, whose employees number one-fourteenth of our entire population and one-thirty-sixth of our voters; over which seven hundred and fifty thousand tons burden roll yearly, and forty thousand people ride every day. To each inhabitant of the State is due one hundred and thirty-five miles of travel a year, with only the remote risk of death to one passenger in one million two hundred and sixty-two thousand one hundred and sixty-five, or one for every forty-seven millions one hundred and sixty-four thousand four hundred and twenty-six miles of travel.

Contemporaneously with these has risen into power the wondrous energy of agricultural and manufacturing machinery, whereby the productive power of the Republic is enlarged tenfold, and one man, marshalling an army of wheels, and knives and spindles, can cut his way through nature's most obstinate defences, and stand victorious in wealth and power to reach the largest manhood of the age.

Crossing our streets and clustering under one watchful eye in an office on Broadway, we behold the fifth of these agencies in the Telegraph, that magic cord which weaves the people of a State into one family, and ere long will tie the family in New York to all the neighborhoods of the round globe, that Christ may come and make all one by the higher unity of Love.

And finally, the child of all these mighty forces, and the most spiritual agency of Free Labor, is the Press—crowded with the daily and weekly results of our toil, reaching forth with such hands as the steamship, canal, railroad, machinery and telegraph, and levying tribute over the whole world; scattering 3,334,940 copies of its various issues perpetually over the State; now a reflection of what is best and worst in our popular life, but destined hereafter to rise into the nobler form of an omnipresent leader and propagandist of the Republic that is to be.

These representative results and forces that cluster in the valley of the Capital City, are faint symbols of the mighty power of Labor that in 238 years has changed 46,000 square miles of wilderness into the world's chief Republican State. Of her 26,000,000 acres, 13,000,000 already have yielded to cultivation, and sustain a population of 3,470,059, divided into 663,124 families, who in all the elements of a Christian civilization, doubtless excel any equal number of people concentrated under one government. We have all read of the gigantic armies led forth by great commanders in ancient and modern times for the subjugation of empires. But could the army of Free Laborers in this Republic, through some long, bright day of our northern summer, on one of our broad western plains, defile in gigantic review before our eyes, how poor would seem the pomp and pageantry of destructive war.

Let us figure to ourselves this review of our Industrial host. First would appear a triumphal car, emblazoned with the records of the men and deeds, that make our history of 238 years, floated over by a banner inscribed with the proud device of our commonwealth—the rising sun and the inspiring "Excelsior."

Now appears the foremost rank of tillers of the earth—a host of 253,292 strong men, with their wives and children, bearing their implements of conquest, followed by a cloud of 7,000,000 domestic animals and innumerable flying fowl; trailing in great wagons, the varied productions of the land. Upon their standards would be read no chronicles of bloody fight, but such victories as these: Value of New York lands, $1,107,272,715; 3,256,948 tons of hay; 62,449,093 bushels of grain; 17,127,338 bushels esculent roots; 4,907,556 lbs. flax; 7,192,254 lbs. hops; 13,668,830 bushels apples; 9,231,959 lbs. wool; $2,400,000, value of poultry; $1,421,750 miscellaneous roots and fruits; 20,965,861 gallons milk; 90,293,077 lbs. butter; 33,944,249 lbs. cheese; 4,935,815 lbs. sugar; 2,557,876 lbs. honey; $1,138,082, value of gardens;—glorious, beneficent conquest of nature for the sustenance of man.

Now comes the second army of 214,899 free laborers in manufactures, not clad in ignorance and rags, but bearing the comforts of home, and treading the earth with the bold step of men who know their position and rights in the State. To what grander music could this host keep step than the iron harmonies of machinery that night and day, from the Ocean to Niagara, sing the song of man's coming deliverance from slavery and want, and subjection to material things. Look at their banners flashing in the sun, inscribed with their record: $106,349,977, capital of mechanical industry in New York; raw material employed, $178,394,329; manufactured articles, $317,636,685;

24,833 manufactories—or adorned with pictured representations of the myriad forms of grace, comfort and loveliness that issue from the workman's busy hand.

Next we behold the concentrated column of 20,758 merchants, who are the agents of the preceding host in transmitting the fruits of their labors to the ends of the earth. Here are the humble traders of the half-peopled wilderness, side by side with the merchant princes of the city, all bound into a brotherhood of interest, and flanked by the professions that depend upon their aid. What a gorgeous spectacle is this! Wares and merchandise, the products of all climes—the beauty, and manners, and civilization of every people—fleets of ships sailing and steaming on their ensigns—the long line of the freight car—the slow procession of boats moving through green fields—cities springing from the earth as by the summons of the enchanter, emblems of law, science, charity, religion, endowed and fostered by an all-embracing Commerce.

And not far off, coming nearer as the years roll on, would cluster the army of laborers on the highest soil of New York, the souls of her people. The teacher, who receives the child from its mother; the lawyer and legislator, who embalm the people's idea of justice in a statute; the editor, the lecturer and public speaker, who stand at the ear of the masses; the author and the scholar, who appeal from their obscurity of to-day to the future meed of fame; the artist, charming the crowd by the vision of beauty; the preacher, prophesying of righteousness and love eternal;—all these, now too often accounted the idlers in the field, shall one day be known as brother laborers, toiling on the summits of the Spiritual life, towards which the slopes of this material success ascend.

What a review were this—the most powerful Republic marshalling her armies of Industry—and bless God! all Free Men. Nowhere upon her broad and fair expanse does man toil in servitude to his brother man; and, so help us, the Father of all, while the Ocean washes the wharves of New York, and the Hudson flows to the sea, and the storms sing their anthems up in the Adirondack, and the sun sets, a golden glory beyond our western lakes—let no slave pollute our soil! And the day whose dawn shall behold this glorious army, as one soul, lifting up its voice before heaven, and registering an oath on high in behalf of man, shall not decline to its evening shades until it hears, borne on the south wind, the sigh of our Nation's barbarism, proclaiming that its sentence of death has been uttered, and its hour of abdication draws nigh.

Such is the spectacle presented by the Free Labor of New York in its material aggregates and secondary forces. But these lead us back to man, and while another class of teachers can best instruct the people on the details of political economy and the arts of industrial success, the most profound questions to the Christian philosopher will be: *To what spiritual end is all this? in what relation does a Free Industry stand to man's highest good? and are we now on the way to the style of Labor, which is the fit expression of that best Civilization founded on the everlasting law of Love?*

Labor is the point where the soul of man touches the physical world; and the quality of work is the test of man's superiority over nature and altitude in the spiritual existence. Free Labor, in its largest sense, is the gauge of National Advancement. Every nation, in ancient or modern times, has been truly great in proportion to the emancipation of its workers. The historian, Niebuhr, dates the real decline of Rome from the period when work ceased to be honorable, and the land once tilled in small farms by her statesmen and generals, was monopolized by rich men, and cultivated by hordes of slaves. Who cannot read the whole degeneracy of Spain in the proud laziness of her population, or the real grandeur of England in the variety and growing freedom of her mighty industry? Indeed, the best state must be that which offers the broadest field for the development of the active energies of its citizens; which is distinguished for the variety and vigor of its industrial professions; and where it is easiest for every man to obtain the post in which his peculiar genius may find scope in creative toil.

Free labor is the test of national superiority—not so much on account of what it produces, as for its results on the citizen. For only in such a condition of affairs can man receive the true education of all his powers, and use his circumstances for the building up of his manhood. Hence although the quantity and quality of production is one evidence of a prosperous people, yet a more striking proof is the effect of this work on the population itself. *Are the men and women of a state ennobled by their occupation, and is their daily business a school of Christian citizenship?* is the first question in this investigation. For the most astonishing works may doubtless be produced by the sacrifice of man; and such labor is only Satanic.

Compare the gigantic monuments of Eastern despotism with the achievement of our New York industry! We can show no pyramids, no labyrinths, no massive cities, tombs and temples, which will challenge the assaults of time. Bless God, we cannot point to mighty piles of stone and sculpture slowly raised by the hands of bondmen, cemented by the blood and tears of oppression; huge gravestones, marking the spot where the noblest aspirations of humanity were buried, and generations fell and wasted to please a despot's whim. But look at our monuments; an Erie Canal, whose projecting, construction and use, has been the primary school of the free industry of our State; a system of railroads, extemporized by the spontaneous enterprise of a whole people, groaning beneath the weight of free products or the armies of emigrants fleeing from oppression and poverty to comfort and liberty; cities not built for a century's endurance, but such as a new State, using every vital energy to the utmost, can throw together to shelter the families and transact the business of a Republican community.

So is the glory of our free Northern industry not found in its great material results of agriculture, manufactures, commerce; for doubtless our work is often crude, and partakes of the rawness of a continent coming out of the woods; but in what man has learned and become in producing it all, and the new powers and opportunities for the best society he is daily acquiring in this magnificent school. And the chief superiority of our system of labor over that of other lands and other districts of our own continent is, that through it we are coming to that point where all industrial operations shall play into the hands of that highest form of work, the development of the best men.

So the question of Free Labor is not to be argued so much from its economical results, though here the argument is triumphant, as from its spiritual aspects. Every true son of Adam will maintain that the happiest word that ever greeted his ears was his command to leave an Eden of childish innocence for a wilderness of manly toil. Free Industry is for the elevation and education of the race. All human experience has demonstrated that the only way to greatness of any kind is the straight and narrow way of labor. And when man toils, in the exercise of his great attribute of freedom, he is in the way to gain his chief distinction. Creation is the grandest attribute of man—the point in which he approaches nearest his Maker. To create new combinations from the material universe; by the discipline of free industry to discover the creative laws of Omnipotence, and by obedience to them to express his best conceptions of existence; to impress himself on the whole earth, and even fill the invisible elements with the finer energy of his victorious mind; especially to create in the realm of spirit; moulding human nature into higher forms of individual and social life, and by a far-reaching insight, peopling the realms of imagination with new and glorious beings, which bear the seal of reality and become the ideals of the generations; this is God-like; and only through Free Labor can man approach this throne of his power, and rise into the companionship of the creative love of the Father of all.

And herein is the overwhelming argument against the barbarous logic which is now filling the press of half our Union and the Legislative halls of the Republic with the assertion that labor belongs to capital, and the slave industry of the past is a greater success than the free labor of the present. No doubt statistics are against this theory, but when was a nation ever ciphered out of barbarism? Let its advocates pile up their bales of cotton, their tons of sugar, their rice and hemp and loathsome tobacco, to the heavens, and exultingly cry: This is ours! *But what has become of the Creative Power of Man meanwhile?* Where is your growth of that creative energy which lifts a people ever higher in the scale of humanity? Where are the inventions, the labor-saving machinery, the advanced modes of labor, the improvement of lands; all that bears witness to the growth of intelligence and power over nature? Your 4,000,000 of laborers are a smaller creative force in the world's industry than many a New England village. Not even able to use what the rest of the world has invented, they plod on, a great black mass of brutal toil, tagging behind the peasantry of Europe. Where has fled the creative force of your nobler race? What element is the white laboring class in slave regions, in the inventive power of the world? Insignificant beyond comparison. While England has built up an empire from a group of islands smaller than your oldest State, you have no resource but the barbarian's method of making one region a desert and striking your tents and moving to another. And where is your creative power in the higher regions of art, literature, theology, philosophy, politics, character? Let the best civilization of the age judge between you and itself. And this you call success—to sacrifice the creative energy of fifteen great States; to carry labor back to the age of the Pharaohs; to make yourself a cipher in the forces of an intelligent and Christianized industry; and boast of the cotton and sugar and tobacco you have received in exchange. And this Free Society you call a failure, which is increasing faster in creative power, in every realm of life, than any previous community on earth! Could you cover a continent with your products, and spin a shroud of your cotton wide enough to wrap humanity for her burial, one free man, educated in the school of a Christian industry, would be a sufficient refutation of your shallow philosophy.

And the same logic will scatter to the winds the affectation of superiority, which in a free State like ours, plumes itself on the distinction of laziness, and thinks gentility only the prerogative of the drone. Could the young man that saunters the streets to forget the lagging hours, and the maiden that scorns the severe toil of body and mind, but know what they are doing and becoming thereby, they would awaken from their dream of folly. For, pray tell me, is not true gentility also true nobility of character? Is there any genuine superiority other than spiritual power and worth? and when you despise labor of the hands and mind, do you not renounce that chief glory of man, his creative Life? If you make nothing in the realm of nature, or think nothing in the realm of ideas, or mould no character or shape no social result in the realm of Humanity—what are you but an underling, a worthless pensioner on society, taking the back track towards brutality and impotence? Is your laziness fraught with joys to compensate for the abdication of your throne of creative dominion? Are you satisfied to gravitate towards the irrational animals for the sake of their pleasant sensations and exemption from care? Do you shrink from that trouble, toil and anxiety which are the inevitable accompaniments of all human achievements? Learn that the utmost of these is only a penny toll paid at the gates which open into new regions of grandeur and loveliness; and that he who really understands himself, quite forgets these in the inspiration that burns higher, as he mounts the steep ways of Power. Aim to be the best, if you will, but show us your title in creative toil, superior to any other, before you expect of us a reception of your claim.

Since Free Labor is valuable, chiefly for its spiritual results on man, it will only be found in its genuine form where man applies the highest faculties of his nature to the occupations of his every-day existence. Where every citizen puts his whole soul into his work, and makes it the expression of his finest conception of manliness or womanhood; where a people writes out its grandest idea of truth, and justice and grace in the colossal dialect of an intense and varied industry, then shall we know what Free Labor can do. Thus we have only to look at the productions of any country to understand how far a liberal and elevated idea of work has advanced. Anybody could read the whole philosophy of Chinese art and life out of the manufactures of China. In the evidences of minute and patient drudgery, the gawky forms and richness of material displayed in their manufactures, we discover the mark of an unprogressive nation, where life is so cheap that a man's whole existence can easily be spared to the elaboration of one corner of a shawl, or the carving on the leg of a table, where with the richest material and the utmost patience to mould them, the same stereotype figures and shapes proclaim that generation after generation is inclosed in a wall of self-conceit and slavish routine. Compare with this spectacle the industry of the British islands, and behold in its ever-expanding variety, its constant improvement in all the appliances of machinery, its growing beauty, its thoroughness, the evidence that here man is gradually approaching a true idea of the mission of toil.

Tested by this rule, we shall find much to criticise in the industry of our State. We may suppose that Labor is free in our great commonwealth; and so it is redeemed from the infamy of personal slavery; but free from many hindrances to its highest development, it is not. We are yet in a transition state from the barbarism of servile labor to the Christian civilization of a truly enlightened and purified idea of work. Industry is yet embarrassed by the obstinate tyranny of corporations; by the tendency towards an aristocracy of wealth; by the lingering sense of degradation that hangs about toil; by the ignorance that oppresses so large a proportion of the toiling masses; and, above all, by the dishonesty and unveracity that permeate our system of manufactures and trade. Our whole idea of life, as a people, is far below any worthy conception of human existence. We are, as a State, great in our worldliness; pursuing material successes and temporary ambitions, to the woeful neglect of the higher achievements of life; more desirous of making splendid demonstrations in our own day, than of laying the deep foundations of an enduring Republic. This popular notion of life expresses itself in our Labor, which is enslaved in every way that a man or a State is enslaved by a narrow and sensual view of existence.

But let not our neighbors in the servile States exult over our panics and dangerous classes in commercial cities, and general short-comings; great as our difficulties are, they are such as these regions are not yet capable of feeling, nor will be for a century to come. Ours are the difficulties that ennoble a State by stimulating its best mind and heart into great effort, the struggles of millions of men, nominally free, to become spiritually emancipated; not the desperate, sullen heavings of a brutal race to rise to ownership of its own bodies and souls and the insolent and cruel effort of a superior caste to keep down this rising tide of human nature. Thus, while in half our country Free Labor can hardly be attained except by the very dissolution and reorganization of society, in New York we need no anarchy, no overturn in social and political constitutions; but only a better understanding by our people of the dignity and relations of labor, and a persistent effort to elevate the men and women who compose our armies of industry.

The first grand want of our present system of labor is intelligence. Ignorance is slavery by the inevitable laws of God; and whoever flatters ignorance anywhere does it for the purposes of despotism. Our labor is not truly free in New York, because it is not sufficiently cultivated. While thousands of farmers are prevented by their want of information and prejudice from adopting the myriad improvements of modern scientific agriculture, and other thousands of our mechanics and operatives know just enough to be tied to one kind of secondary work all their lives, and our young men enter into mercantile life so ill prepared that seventy per cent. fail, how can there be anything but a practical enslavement of whole regions of society? Men and women thus qualified are always at the mercy of the better instructed. Beyond a limited circle of plodding toil, they are lost, and must work as they are forced by the few clever people who organize the great machinery of labor and appoint them their place therein. They are exposed to distress in every great panic and are not able to avail themselves of times of prosperity.

It is vain for such laboring classes to protest against the injustice they suffer. Nobody disputes that they are practically shut up in a narrow place; but how came they there? Chiefly because they have preferred ignorance to intelligence. The State makes provision for the instruction of all, and the means of practical improvement are open to whomsoever desires them. But if two hundred thousand children are kept out of school by the wickedness of their parents, and other hundreds of thousands of young men and women prefer the luxury of ignorance, they are welcome to it; but they will learn that it is the most expensive luxury in which they can indulge. No man or woman is too old to learn, no girl or boy is too young to be taught, that love for improvement which is the great emancipator of the laboring man.

Especially let our youth of both sexes resolve to be generally cultivated, and whatever they undertake, learn to do in the best way. The young laborer in the household, in the shop or on the land, who is informed concerning his profession as a science, knows its central principles, its capacities for improvement, all its labor-saving machinery and its relations to other professions, is clothed with a power that will always defend him against the tyranny of his superior. Whoever resolves to have nothing to do with sham worth, to put the best he knows into all he does, and to learn the best there is to be learned, will gravitate to a higher position as he advances in skill and fidelity.

What a garden would scientific farming make of western New York and the valley of the Hudson; what a hive of industry could swarm in our mining districts; what wealth of manufacturing industry would a higher intelligence and wise legislation develop along our river banks; what a different thing were our commerce guided by a body of cultivated men; and what a new life would dawn in our homes if the art of housekeeping, the finest of all professions, were well known, and woman were thoroughly instructed in every avocation where she could maintain herself. Who can compute the additional comfort, wealth and opportunity for human advancement, such a reform would inaugurate?

And even a greater want than intelligence is truth in our present system of labor. It is impossible that industry in New York should be free until it is honest. Let any man study the different phases that this untruth assumes in all regions of our work, and he will no longer wonder at our thousand embarrassments. No class of laborers is exempt from it. The farmers are always too ready to slight their work, to cheat the land of its proper cultivation and defraud their crops and flocks and herds of their just attention, and therefore plunder society of what it has the right to expect from the soil; to say nothing of their questionable ways of dealing in their products. The root of all other industrial dishonesty is laid in the field, the pasture, the dairy and the kitchen. Thence the ill weed grows apace; the manufacturer, thus skinned by the producer, slights his work, makes clothes and tools and shoes and furniture to "sell" and not to use. The mechanic who buys diluted milk, and half fatted beef and mutton, and flour that won't "rise," has his revenge by building a house that will tumble down over the heads of a second generation, by charging exorbitant prices for poor service, and making his word as cheap as his work. The merchant, assailed by dishonesty on every side, strikes out to defend himself, and broken banks and exploding firms and gambling speculations make panic inevitable. The great corporations contain the flower of this iniquity, and a dozen respectable men as a "board of directors" will commit iniquities and oppressions of which either would be ashamed in his private affairs. Thus the rich, knowing that they have been obliged to fight to gain their money, have so little sense of public obligation in its use, and classes are set against each other, each fully aware of its own sins.

Of course this dishonesty vitiates all other professions; and the sons and daughters of people that cheat in labor will give us a sham instruction in school, a corrupt legislation in the senate, a literature that reads best while seen on the wall in passing, and a Gospel according to the fashion in the church. Let not the farmer, the mechanic and day-laborer accuse the men higher up of this dishonesty; they have created it by their own unfaithfulness. If the primitive employments of life are honestly performed, those that grow out of them will be of like character. Thousands of the servant girls and day-workers who this winter will shiver and starve have done all they could to bring on this panic by unfaithful and dishonest labor, by extortion and extravagant expenditure in prosperous times. There is untruth enough in our New York labor yet to produce a general financial explosion every quarter of a century. All professions are involved in it; and as a consequence Free Labor does not exist.

In proportion as industry is untrue to the eternal laws of rectitude, does it descend to the enslavement of the less clever by the more clever. When we can honor each other so much that we regard every attempt at sham or knavery as an unpardonable insult to human nature, we shall begin to realize that "glorious liberty" which only rectitude confers. Any man, whether a sweeper of streets or a president of a railroad; any woman, whether a cook or an artist, who slights work or wrongs a customer in any way, is to that extent laboring to enslave the human race; and whoever in the humblest walk of industry is faithful, is doing his utmost to emancipate society through the whole world.

A radical reform in such particulars could not fail to be accompanied with an advance in beauty. Our industry would take a more graceful shape; our life of toil would be less angular, coarse and uncongenial, and an increased appreciation of elegance appropriate to every production would every where make itself known. And through the State a more cheerful atmosphere and unostentatious loveliness would mark the growth of that industrial freedom which puts off at once the stolid, sullen gloom of the slave, and the gruff coarseness of the boor, and clothes itself in the natural and graceful deportment of the freeman.

And this system of intelligent, honest, graceful Free Labor, would place our people on a higher spiritual plane of existence; and it would then be understood, that the end of man is not "bread alone," but manhood in its greatest sense. Then the folly that toil is degrading would be silenced by the comprehension of the true purpose of effort. It would be understood that the end of all professions is to acquire power and opportunity to cultivate the highest qualities of our nature; that a day-laborer may obtain this privilege, and a legislator can do no more; and that men are not to be honored according to the work they do, but according to the use they make of the power which that work has obtained. All industry of hand or mind is mean if done only for itself, and hallowed by no aspiration for a loftier character; all effort is noble which is linked with the best improvement of our nature, and bears the fruits of an enlarging life. The labor of the Empire State will be truly free when its great powers and growing opportunities are used as persistently for the spiritual regeneration of man and the elevation of society, as they now are for private selfishness and public materialism. And let no sensual economist or political partisan promise the people larger freedom at any cheaper rate than a thorough reform in intelligence, truth and beauty, and a consecration of their wealth and all its opportunities to the service of man.

We shall, in the light of these principles, be at no loss to account for the great and deadly evils that still afflict our civilization. Does anybody wonder why New York, the most powerful Republican State in the world, is still, tried by the standard of Christianity, a half barbarous commonwealth; that her cities swarm with multitudes vibrating between beggary and crime; that ignorance still holds the balance of political power; and superstition is so deep and dense over whole districts of her dominion; and sensuality and intemperance eat out so much of her best vitality; why, in the great contest between the freedom of the whole and the tyranny of the few, she hardly seems yet to have a stable mind, and holds her great name as the watchword, now of a spasmodic liberty and now of an insolent despotism? The answer is too plain. She is not yet a free State because so much of the same dark blood runs through her own veins that clogs the heart of communities lower yet in the scale of civilization. She has yet too many proud, sensual, selfish men, who despise work, and would gladly lash a black or white slave to do their toil; too many frivolous and idle women, who care not whose body is bent or whose soul is cramped if they can live in ease and comfort; too many laborers who secretly despise their profession and only work to gain the means of degrading themselves by senseless material pleasures and low ambition; too few who have the courage to compliment the masses by telling them they are not what the citizens of such a State should be; that while they toil in their present spirit they must be content to see other States lead off in the sublime crusade for a freedom that here means Christian Democracy.

When the young men of New York resolve that they will regenerate industry from its present clogs of ignorance, untruth and vulgarity; when the young women of the Empire State decide to take the industrial field, and occupy and adorn every post of toil for which nature has given them the ability; when we cease to boast so much of our great canals, and cities, and crops, and wealth, and concentrate our highest ambition on the quality of our humanity; then may we hope to gain the renown of the freest commonwealth. But let no delusion possess our souls that liberty is extemporized in political campaigns, or will come any the sooner for our high-flown rhetorical adulation. Freedom comes only to a people that is resolved to work for it, protect it by all sacrifices, preserve it by individual consecration, and watch its enemies with an "eternal vigilance." So does our industry culminate in the sacred toil after that personal freedom which, inspiring every soul with the highest spiritual activity, shall mould a free commonwealth great and glorious beyond the empires of the earth.

# IV.

## MAN

### AND HIS MODERN INVENTIONS.

On a bright October day I looked from the heights of Hoboken over the Metropolitan City of the United States. Beautiful was it outspread, clasped in azure arms to the beating bosom of its ample bay, its spires and masts bristling like the pinnacles of a fairy temple in the rosy distance. The ferry-boats shot in and out, like living creatures; the Hudson steamer emerged from a golden vapor in the north, and every water craft was transformed by the magic atmosphere into a gilded barge navigating an enchanted sea. Viewed in the dreamy mood befitting the day, it was easy to transform the whole spectacle into a pictured symbol of the power of man. Out of a river, a bay and a savage island had this potent magician evoked the glorious creation, that hovered in this autumn haze. How easy to worship the Creator of all this, did not the reflection interpose, that even he is bound by a law that dates not from his own will, whose servant he is in his mightiest exercise of power. And then first dawned upon me the grand significance of these words, spoken in the old time, though fresher than the telegraphic dispatch of to-day: "*Seek ye first the kingdom of God and his righteousness, and all these things shall be added unto you.*"

What a declaration is here of the relation of man to these modern inventions, which so often excite him to a deification of humanity and a scornful defiance of God's everlasting laws of the soul. Translated into our form of thought, it means: Cultivate the highest style of manhood, and the forces of nature shall become your servants, and life shall be full of opportunities. The "kingdom of God" is not a place away off in space, but is a state of character as possible to-day in New York as in any future world, at any point in eternity. Anywhere in this state, or that world to come, he who makes the acquisition of a religious character founded on love to God and humanity his supreme object, will be able to use the opportunities offered by the state of existence in which he abides. Standing thus at the head of creation, man shall become its real sovereign by force of his moral energy, and "all things" needful to his eternal growth "shall be added unto him."

The peculiar state of American civilization today preaches a sermon from this text, which I shall only endeavor to report. Let me, with as little mixture of my own theories and fancies as may be, endeavor to interpret that civilization in its relations to man; show to what extent it is the creature of that spirit of invention which is the great obligation and privilege of our day; what we must be to live amid its opportunities with dignity and success; and what retributions will overwhelm us unless we become great and good enough to control it.

No man should understand the scope and significance of the modern spirit of invention so well as the citizen of our Republic, for no country is so much its creature. In the despotic governments of Europe we discover the awkward contrast between institutions a thousand years old and inventions of to-day; and the great effort of their ruling classes is to monopolize the use of these new agencies and thereby increase their own power ten fold. All the mechanics of the nineteenth century concentrate in the army of Louis Napoleon. Russia is pushing the railroad and telegraph towards Asia to pour down her armed millions with greater dispatch upon its enfeebled barbarism. The Prussian government has captured the common school, and made every teacher a policeman to aid in the manufacture of a Prussian citizen. Even in England the new powers of life are jealously retained by the few and only by faltering steps do the ignorant masses come into their inheritance. But in the United States of America these wonderful agencies are the possession of the people. Every man and woman of the ruling race has the nominal right to use them, and only ignorance or indifference is shut out from their enjoyment. Who, then, should understand the relation of man to his modern invention if not the citizen of that country which is itself the most surprising invention of these latter days?

Do we, indeed, realize how much in our circumstances is new? Truly, man is here, with his old nature; the same creature in all essential faculties and aspirations, as in the garden of Eden. But how novel are his surroundings! A thousand material forces aid him in his work. He cultivates the earth by machinery; shoots his own will and intelligence through an army of wheels and spindles, each of which is a better manufacturer than himself; and is driven about the world with a speed that makes the legs of man or beast ridiculous.

His house is fashioned by a stroke of every artisan's hammer since Tubal Cain; for the generations have treasured their best ideas of convenience under his roof. What a marvellous labor saving machine is our whole system of American business. A merchant in a counting-room on the banks of the Hudson, sits with his fingers on the pulse of the world's commerce.

We have all the old literature reprinted at our hands; yet the people are educated by the common school, the journal, the lecture, the caucus, the convention, and free discussion on every theme—a travelling college that keeps up with their haste, wherein, "he who runs may read." What a new thing is social life when the increase in home conveniences and means of communication expand a neighborhood to a nation, and we need not personal contact to know the condition of our beloved every hour. New ideas of amusement are rapidly coming in conflict with the old. Our system of government is a capital invention; for the ballot in America means all that king, court, army, nobility, revolution mean abroad. One ballot with brains behind it will do what Cæsar died to accomplish; and one election day in New York may change the reading of history. What an invention is the Protestant Church, founded on the voluntary system, divorced from the government. A world of ecclesiastical trash is superseded by the simple idea that every man shall worship God according to the dictates of his own manhood. And truly what is this Republic, with its fiery energies, tearing its way from the Atlantic to the Pacific, transforming the wilderness as it goes to fruitful States, but the latest invention of man to aid in that Christian civilization which is the kingdom of God on earth? Here, then, where the inventive spirit has done its utmost, is the problem between man and his modern inventions to be solved.

Now, there is astonishing confusion of thought among our people in regard to what may reasonably be expected from this gigantic array of American inventions. Millions of our population are to-day behaving as if our new circumstances were to create a millennium; and, of course, the land is full of demagogues, lay and clerical, who find it to their own advantage to persuade these confused millions that they are already in a Paradise of Freedom. But the thoughtful moral teacher must insist that *this magnificent array of contrivances can never do more than furnish new opportunities for true manhood.* Every new invention is a new opportunity, and every new opportunity imposes a new obligation.

The cultivated citizen of an American city, in comparison with the savage in Nebraska, has an incomparable advantage in his circumstances; but this advantage finds its compensation in his fearful increase of moral obligation. The Indian can use all his opportunities for nobility, and sleep half the day in his wigwam; the citizen can only use his privileges by a sleepless vigilance, and the exercise of energies unknown to the red man. New opportunities do not make new men, or create a new civilization; they only call man to arouse from his slumber, and put forth some faculty hitherto dormant, and fix his eye on a higher excellence, and climb up them as up a ladder scaling a new heaven.

And the awful fact about this matter is, *that there can be no labor-saving machine for the manufacture of character.* Man is called to-day to do and be what was never before conceived of excellence and power; a new world is around him—a world of slopes ascending to higher eminences, wandering off into a horizon of summits flushed with a glory as of angelic lands; but, alas! he can possess his new kingdom only in the old way. Just as Adam and Eve went out the gate of Eden and saw the earth before them, and began to mould that energy of moral manhood and womanhood which is the sovereign power of creation, must the Young American pass out the gates of his infant innocence, and earn a spiritual position by the sweat of the brow and the soul. There is only one way to be great and good, and that the old way. Spite of all modern inventions and opportunities, the essential conflict of life is the same. Perhaps we sneer at the old Theological Devil; but it is just as hard for us to resist evil as for those who believe in him. We scorn the monks, and hermits, and ascetics of the old days, yet under our broadcloth and satin and fine linen is the same death-grapple for manhood that bent Simeon Stylites on his pillar thirty years. Experience, character, cannot be inherited; opportunities can be inherited. You may come to your noble father's estate and position, but you cannot gain your father's nobility without working harder than he, for it is more to be noble to-day than in his day. America is the heir of all the ages; every battle of freedom that has shaken the earth, every gain in knowledge, comforts, policy, has drifted a treasure across the ocean to her; *but the experience of a nation in the use of its opportunities she cannot inherit;* that, she must learn for herself. Her character is her own to make or lose; and never was there such a task set for a people as to shape a true civilization out of our circumstances. Invention is both privilege and obligation; and only in accepting and using both is this great problem to be solved.

Whenever man fulfills this obligation and tries with all his might to become a noble being, as his opportunities increase, then is realized the law of success. "Seeking first the kingdom of God, and his righteousness, all these things are added unto him." All inventions, save drudgery, relieve man from the slavery to material things, and give him leisure to cultivate his higher nature. Thus, modern machinery will finally abolish slavery and ignorant labor. To manage a first-class kitchen is beyond the power of Kathleen or Minna, fresh from the other side; they must become educated women, or first class employment is closed against them. Sleepy old Jonathan or Knickerbocker, with his pipe in his mouth, cannot sit on a mowing machine; a man must be wide awake to keep out of the way of its sharp wheels, or to follow a horse-rake, a planter, or a thresher. Whoever hasn't brains must "stitch, stitch, stitch," and leave her brighter cousin to use the sewing machine. A fool can be a priest in Italy; but a minister in a Free Protestant Church must be much of a man to hold the people. So do all these inventions abolish drudgery, and demand culture for their use; and in our day, a successful farmer and his wife will use more science in their dairy or their fields, than most of our labor-despising, dilettante young people carry about at the end of the college or academical course. Drudgery and the class of drudges must gradually disappear, and what has been regarded menial work will become a fit employment for the most accomplished people.

Thus a good deal of time will be saved from the lower side of life, that may be used on the higher work of building a character in the image of God. And a true man will use his leisure for this purpose. He will recognize in his inventive faculty the key to let him out of the dungeon of material dependence; and when he is in the free air and light, he will put forth all the sublime and lovely attributes of his being. Think of the opportunity enjoyed by a young woman for the best culture to-day in town, compared with that of her grandmother out in the country fifty years ago. The grandmother had no time for cultivation; to cook, wash, bake and sew for self, husband and children was the life of a slave; travelling was slow, population scattered; nature had her under her feet. If she became cultivated and noble, it was her own great merit toiling against difficulties. The grand-daughter can have her work chiefly done by machinery; the water-pipe is in the wall, the light flashes at the touch of her finger, the furnace and the range warm her and cook her dinner, the sewing has ceased to be a nightmare; books, lectures, schools, cultivated society, and time enough to use all, are at her hand; she can do just what she has the patience to achieve, and be what she will. What a world of drudgery is saved to this generation; what centuries of time have been rescued from material uses, so that eternity is becoming our inheritance. And he who has this, and will employ it aright, may become such a man as will eclipse the heroism of the past; a sovereign with "all things under his feet," a man to whom we can say, in the glorious words of Paul: "All things are yours, whether the world, or life, or death, or things present, or things to come, all are yours." Yes; this world can even now be used so well that it may become the ante-court of Heaven, and amid our common opportunities we can realize the experience of that immortal life which is only the ascending growth of the soul through wider spheres of knowledge and power, and beauty and love.

But now suppose man, instead of doing this, does the contrary; *accepts the privilege and repudiates the obligation of this new condition of human cir-*

*cumstances.* He does not regard every invention as a new opportunity which demands new efforts after manliness, but clutches it as a fresh occasion for selfish indulgence. The wonderful improvements in modern labor and commerce he prizes chiefly as a more expeditious mode of making money. The increase in social conveniences is only an excuse for luxurious living. The facility of communication but enlarges his ambition for wide reputation. He abuses the freedom of religious worship by refusing to countenance the institutions of Christianity, or perverts the church of Christ to a movable platform of personal advancement. Our invaluable privilege of universal male suffrage he insults by the refusal to vote, or its prostitution to corrupt partisan ends. A free press means to him the liberty to flood the land with nonsense or scandal, and dilute his intellect by saturation in the thin gruel of popular literature. And Republicanism in America is to him but a conceit of selfish liberty to neglect the cause of his fellow man, and push his own whim to its utmost bound. Can there be any question what will be the consequences of such a criminal abandonment of the new obligations of an American citizen? Is any sober man so near a fool as to dream that he can use this splendid array of opportunities in the new world for selfish ends and come out safely? Are we so far gone in national conceit as to believe that God loves his children in these United States so much better than the rest of mankind, that he will permit us to ignore this eternal law, *that whosoever doth not improve his opportunities shall lose them or find them his curse?* Let the ministers of religion, spite of the rage of the demagogues who live on the degeneracy of the State, reiterate the lesson that if man does not grow in character in America as he gains in privileges, his new inventions, will not save him; nay, will become his special tormentors; and from the abuse of the very freedom of which he boasts, will come his more fearful destruction.

For see how these new inventions turn against him, when he makes himself morally incompetent to govern them. If a merchant has made up his mind to care for nothing but business, God help him in a modern counting-room; for, instead of the moderate and contracted life of the trader of former days which offered many an occasion for quiet and enjoyment, he is tied into a network of nerves that enfolds the globe, and his heart beats, and his imagination shudders at every change of business at home or abroad. The anxiety of millions of traders, the competition of nations, the hopes and fears of a world-wide speculation come like fiends to worry his poor brain; and he is as surely imprisoned from the nobler joys of existence as if he were buried in one of his own mines, or nailed up in his own warehouse. Behold the family that eagerly prostitutes its wealth to luxury and social ambition. No sensuality of ancient Rome or Ephesus or Corinth so quickly annihilated its victims, as the luxury of New York and Philadelphia, and Chicago; no social ambition is so demeaning as this American rage for an aristocracy of money. What avails a free Protestantism to a man who has not moral courage to declare his religious opinions, but must enact the farce of the hypocrite every Sunday before his Creator on the crimson seats of a fashionable temple? Gracious Heaven! Have martyrs died, and saints lived through persecutions, and Christians toiled and thought for eighteen centuries for this, that American Protestants should be the cowards that they have become—hiding within a new church, built on credit, at every little cloud of dust raised by the Devil in the streets? A free Protestantism indeed, when its liberty is interpreted as the license to transform the church of a crucified Saviour to a drawing-room, and the preacher of God's law to the gentleman usher in an ecclesiastical ceremony, and the awful prerogative of moral judgment to a separation of patrician sheep from plebeian goats.

If any one doubts that a good man is needed to wield a Free Press, let him open a morning paper and find his own name dragged before the community in connection with some criminal or foolish charge, or assailed for his own opinions with barbarian rancor, and comfort himself with the assurance that he will be the subject of execration or ridicule from the Bay of Fundy to San Francisco. Freedom of amusement is a great privilege, but when it turns out the freedom to get the delirium tremens and make one's self an appendage to a race-horse, an infamous woman, or a soul-destroying career of fashion, there is no question from what quarter that man's tormentors will come. The ballot is the last result of human government; the prize of all the revolutions that have shaken the nations; and now think of 20,000 men in the State of New York, and as many in Pennsylvania, the two most powerful States in the Union, wielding this fearful instrument, not one of them able to read the Constitution or write the name of America; then contemplate the increasing thousands in our more barbarous States, till you descend to the bloody arena of the territories, where the man who has the best rifle, and is least scrupulous as to its use, carries the election; and tell me if we may not vote ourselves into as terrible calamities this side of the water, as any into which the people of Europe have ever fought themselves?

If we are to have no greater elevation of manhood and womanhood in this age than the past, let us pray Heaven to destroy all our new inventions. For out of the opportunities of a people comes its reward, if it be worthy, or its retribution if it degenerates. We know the worst that old world privileges can inflict on a nation when man falls away from them. What he has suffered in Rome, in France, in Austria, history records; and that could be endured again. But what a fearful looking-for of judgment will there be for Americans, if they go down below their circumstances, and in the strife for selfish success forget their high obligation to God and man. Think of our commercial panics that scourge us for ignorance, haste and dishonesty in business; of railroads, and steamships and machinery everywhere built by unfaithful workmen, and managed by heedless and wicked superintendency; of the possibility of wreck to health and life implied in any street of modern residences inhabited by an effeminate population; of the chaos of atheism and fanaticism into which our popular Protestantism can any day be plunged by a people who have forgotten God and man; of the frantic gabbling of twenty-five millions of conceited tongues, educated on the trash that is daily hawked through the streets, and bound to settle every problem that the sages of the generations have left unsolved; of a nation like ours, driven into a war with a combined Europe, or a worse contest of sister States, by citizens too wicked to vote right, or too indifferent to vote intelligently! Is this hell that yawns beneath our new civilization a pleasant place to look into?

Ah! the old theological lake of fire is not the only hell with which the preacher in our land may threaten his hearers; nearer to them are the "infernal regions" that America could easily become with a population below its opportunities. Here might be seen a hell, where every other train ran off the track, and the dying shriek of the drowning passenger on the sea was caught by the sinking boat on the Hudson, and prolonged by the exploding craft upon the lakes, and swept down the Mississippi in a wail of death to the far off wreck-strewn shore of the Pacific—where dyspepsia and consumption, and "general debility" dwelt in every luxurious house, and the pale face of woman and the dimmed eye of man were the emblematic skeleton at every feast; where pecuniary disaster lurked in every bargain; and a reputation died at every stroke of the editor's pen; and the church pulled down Christ, and set up some foul abomination of our barbarism in His place; and the State was in a chronic revolution! What untold woes are hidden in this array of calamities, not fanciful, but such as even now, in part, we know—woes as new as the latest fashions, and as fearful as novel. Pray Heaven to avert such a fate, and second that prayer, by living up to your advantages. For should we get under the feet of our Inventions, no invasion of Goths and Vandals could be compared with the terrors of a State where man was the sport of his own contrivances, and every new agency with which his busy brain had peopled the earth, would be charged to an unhuman enemy for his persecution.

This is the inevitable law, eternally enacted for every soul, that if man "seeketh first the kingdom of God, and his righteousness, all these things shall be added unto him;" if, first, he seeketh his own selfishness, all things he has made shall turn against him. And thus the world he has created about himself, when viewed from the mount of Christian character, shall glow like the descending slopes of paradise beneath the sunshine of God's approving love; but viewed from the pit of unchristian degeneracy, shall glare like an impending firmament of storms lit by the lightnings of retributive doom. Do you need the application of this law to the public of to-day, and the land in which we live? Do you not understand that all our real prosperity as individuals and as a people, comes from the manly use which is made of our new life, and that all the varied troubles that harass our families and our States, and the more depressing fears that haunt those who can think and feel, are but the inevitable result of our neglect of American obligations? In the last seventy-five years, what have we not invented? Almost everything that makes us a "peculiar people," until we live in an outward world of our own. So far have we pushed out from the landmarks of the past that we are now drifting over an unexplored sea, of which there is no chart in any book of history, where only a force of character, such as was never before known, can save us. Have we that force of character adequate to guide the ship of our civilization to a safe port? I do not know what new energies may be developed, what great heads may be born, or what latent virtues may be dislodged by coming trials; but it looks now to a reflecting man as if character in America was creeping on at a snail's pace, and opportunity running on the wings of the wind.

Our commercial panic, which lately excited us into semi-insanity, was not an isolated affair, it was one phase of a chronic American disease. That disease is the semi-barbarism of the people, whereby *it happens that they have not moral wisdom enough to manage the involved machinery they have set up on this continent.* It is said that a celebrated engineer, having constructed an elaborate piece of machinery, on witnessing its first exhibition before a crowd, was so bewildered by the confusion of wheels, and mingled hum of axles, and shouts of applause, that he sprung into it and was torn in shreds by his own invention. Somewhat like this is the matter with the American people. They are confused with their own institutions. It needs an angelic clearness of mind and elevation of soul to guide aright this fearful mechanism of Republican government, church, literature, business, and society; but through a continent of whirling forces we rush as wildly, and disport ourselves with as little forethought and firmness as if we ran over an open prairie. What wonder that we receive our retribution on every hand. Now the disease breaks out in social life, and details of sensuality, luxury, crime and rottenness of domestic ties send a thrill of horror to every heart. Now it is a panic in the churches, Romanism and Atheism threatening the people and a Protestant ecclesiasticism too busy in fighting over shreds of doctrine, or building Sunday drawing-rooms for the elect, to stay the storm of error and sin. Now, our national ignorance looms above us like a black cloud, and our new agencies of intelligence are perverted to its advocates. Again, it is a sectional political controversy and a revolutionary campaign wherein it requires no superabundance of insight to discover barbarism and civilization fighting over their old conflict between man and man. And now the sympathies of the people are wrung even to insensibility by repeated disaster on land and sea. And now our commercial system explodes, and faith between man and man departs, and the nation, like Tantalus, sees its own abundance hanging as in mockery above its reach, while it wildly talks of starvation.

These varied agitations are but the symptoms of one disease which visits in turn every limb of the body politic. We are living below our opportunities, we are under the feet of our own inventions; and instead of rallying a new moral force of American manhood and womanhood for the crisis, we are dreaming that some new contrivance will get us out of the difficulty. How vain this hope!

*Not new inventions, but better men to manage those we have, is the need of the times.* We are debating whether we shall repudiate our manhood in America, and go in for a "free fight" for the selfish enjoyment of American privileges; already the shuddering throes in our national constitution proclaim the danger; and upon the decision of this question rests our success or disaster.

I speak not to those who scorn the word of warning; but I ask thoughtful men and women if they can say in conscience that their own elevation of character is what it should be to control these agencies of our time; are you honest enough, pure, intelligent enough; sufficiently economical and patriotic, and prudent? Do you live like wise men and women, determined to increase in rectitude as you increase in privileges, or are you catching the popular insanity? And if your conscience rebukes you for short coming, what shall we say of those who are below; the great whirling, frantic mass who drift hither and thither with no care for their own souls or the good of the State?

I have no professional opinions to offer on the late business complications, for I do not know just what screw is loose this time in our complex system of American trade. But I do know what some of you perhaps do not, that in such a time every dishonest, or careless, or ignorant transaction of the past years comes in to make "confusion worse confounded;" and commerce reaps the bitter fruit of a colossal selfishness and a corroding untruth. We have traded in an unchristian manner, and here is the retribution. We have worshipped our calf of gold, and now it is ground to dust, and we are drinking the fiery draught. Once in twenty years we explode in a general panic; if we loved our neighbor as ourself in our trade, would it be so with us?

Let these experiences teach us that never was it so imperative that man should rule his inventions as now. Never was Christian manhood so essential to safety; never degeneracy of any kind so fatal as just here to-day. Will we not arouse and be worthy to wield these forces of our own creation? Young men, young women, will not you become the kind of people America needs to guide her many-sided life and make it a blessing to the world? For present embarrassments and fears I have but this counsel: Do not lose the manliness you have in any confusion; come out of every "panic" better and wiser than you went in. In good time confidence will be restored, and your drooping fortunes will revive; but do not then forget the lesson of to-day. Let every man resolve that henceforth his character shall be his chief anxiety; let every woman keep her womanhood high above her estate in life. Thus will a slow reaction of health visit the feverish body of society. Thus will an example be afforded of that Christian consecration whose wider prevalence is the only power which in the fight between man and his modern inventions will lead him to victory and make his sovereignty in this world the type of the government of God.

## V.

## THE GOLD DOLLAR.

At the first Exhibition in the New York Crystal Palace, I observed a Gold Dollar covered with finely-engraved letters, which, on the application of a glass, were resolved into the Lord's Prayer. Amid that dazzling show of use and beauty, I remember nothing so distinctly as this new American Dollar, adorned with the oldest utterance of Christian devotion. By its intrinsic nature, the representative of the wondrous results of human industry around me; by the date of its coinage and its image and superscription, the type of the most characteristic age of our Republican civilization—suggesting our first great war of conquest, the golden visions of California, and the great development of heroic enterprise awakened by this period; the symbol of the great material achievements of our country, and almost the god of its idolatry; yet through that inscription seemingly consecrated to the Father whose law is the real constitution of freemen, and whose love can alone save us from our own folly and sin, what wonder that the objects around me appeared insignificant compared with this speaking emblem of a Christian society? I have forgotten almost everything I saw in this Exhibition; it floats in my memory like a gilded mist, in the centre of which hovers this Dollar most clearly defined. I know not the intention of the engraver in this singular fancy; but it was one of those things which, once done, become forever symbolic. It has preached to me so often on the great theme of our nation's peril and hope, that I will now declare to you some of its weighty lessons:

*The Gold Dollar: What does it represent? How shall we get it? And what shall we do with it?* Let this be the subject of the present discourse.

I need not inform a Christian reader that all material things are representative of spiritual realities. The faintest speck of dust that floats across a ray of light is the type of an eternal fact, as the noblest human form that ever walked the earth was the appropriate incarnation of the Redeeming Love. Every well-instructed child can tell what the Gold Dollar is—a bit of ore wrenched from the stern clutch of California rocks, refined, alloyed and finally, at one blow of the great hammer in the Mint, struck into coin. But into what wonderful relations that bit of shining metal is introduced by one decisive blow, not all the men and women in America can fully declare. For, as from a new birth, it rises from metal to money; and its natural worth as a piece of gold, is quite sunk in its spiritual value as the representative currency of the world's chief Republic.

From the earliest history of man, money has been as powerful as to-day. In the life of every people, ancient and modern, it has been a controlling force. Eighteen centuries ago, before this continent was discovered by civilized men, Jesus Christ in Judea told his disciples that the love of money is the root of all evil; and the panic of the last year is the commentary the American people are compelled to write on the margin of that awful scripture. It is all this, because it is the most permanent representative of that complex assemblage of possessions and powers which we call "This World." Money is the symbol of material things; not in their simply material aspect, but as they are related to man. Wherever man touches this world he must have a convenient emblem of what he can own in it, and what it can do for him; and that emblem is money. Whether a belt of wampum, a load of iron rings, a bank bill, or a gold dollar, money is always the same: the representative of the uses of this world to the human soul. Of no value in itself, its values are unestimated while used as the type of this perpetual human relation. So this little Gold Dollar runs ever to and fro over the charmed cord that unites the soul and the world; passing from hand to hand, it transmits earthly necessities, comforts, luxuries, hopes, energies, that terminate in worldly success, all individual power and position, all public grandeur and domination. I give this Dollar to my customer, and thereby endow him with a new power in American civilization; and as far as human success to-day is involved in the possessions and achievements which relate to this state of being and this state of action, this Dollar confers it.

So we may say that all the great visible America is compressed into this little Gold Dollar, for it represents the material aspects of the Republic. And were our eyes clear enough, we might behold delineated within its narrow rim the broad acres of American agriculture—fields of waving grass, hills of solemn forests, prairies of ripening grain, lonely plantations and reeking rice swamps, tilled by joy ous freemen, or scratched by lazy and sullen slave.

Beneath would appear the veins of coal underlying whole States; deep caverns grim with iron, or rocks of marble cropping out from the sides of New England hills; mountains of copper on Lake Superior, and rivers flowing over beds of gold into the Pacific. And girdling all with snowy sails, would Commerce weave her mystic dance about the coast, and every river beach and shore of inland sea be washed by the retreating wave of the steamship; and a snarl of iron cords would bind the land every year into a more inextricable knot of blended interests. Then what a picture of the varied industry of these millions; factories wherein is concentrated the invention of four thousand years; mechanics that arm man with the powers of a god. What a vision of comfort; towns and villages lying under the shade of country elms: great cities overlooking the rivers and the ocean. And with this, how much that goes to ennoble man; the Schoolhouse sown over the continent; the Press toiling day and night in the service of the soul; the Church warning the traveller a hundred times a day that there is a God; Art, that ever pleads for beauty; the Family, that mirrors heaven; Government, the imitation on earth of the justice that rules the universe. All this would pass as in a panoramic vision across this little yellow disc—a miniature of the America of to-day. Who wonders at the desire of men to gain this Gold Dollar, which is the talisman introducing the humblest son of the Republic to the enjoyment of all its opportunities?

But the Gold Dollar cannot be this without being a great deal more. For this great visible America is tied to the soul of every human being that dwells therein, and is, at any moment of her career, the type of the average state of the American mind. The meaning of this vast heterogeneous appearance is this alone; that here man, having reached a new and singular state of culture—in which the noblest theories, and the loftiest aspirations, are mingled with the most degrading inhumanities—has stamped himself on the new continent, and in American civilization drawn a picture of his own soul.

So this Gold Dollar, representing that visible civilization, has also a moral significance, and its inscription is the national idea of life, its objects of worship, its sense of duty, its consciousness of immortality. If those spiritual ideals of the country could be read on its face, as I read the dollar in the Crystal Palace, I fear the Lord's Prayer would not be found thereon inscribed; but quite another statement of religion, in which a Christian profession would be strangely mingled with a record of heathen practices. And could the real creed of

America be written thus on her gold dollar; could the secret, potent ideal of life that sways the forces of her nationality be compressed into a few words, and there read by every man who handles it, what an almost incredible distance would appear between the prayer of Jesus in Palestine and the petition of the great Republic to-day! We might then behold how slowly the world gravitates towards that divine love incarnate in the Saviour, and, by the slowness of its approach, measure at once the depth of its estrangement from God, and the mighty power of his redeeming grace.

But not alone is the Gold Dollar the emblem of the national ideal of spiritual affairs; it performs the same symbolic office for each of us. True, a dollar is the same to every man as long as he wishes to buy bread; but when taken as the representative of his character, what different inscriptions would it bear! In each man's hand it is a peculiar thing, bearing the image and superscription of his soul. For a dollar is really to each one of us the object proposed in gaining it, and the motive that dictates its use. Could every American, when he receives it, behold engraved on its face some picture explanatory of his motives in its acquisition, what a startling gospel would be read off every hour in the day, all over the land! To one man would appear the doleful picture of his brother in chains, his body stamped with the marks of property, his soul groping in his dark prison towards a ray of God's holy light of freedom. Another would behold a ruined home cursed by the demon of the bottle which he has sent in there to do its work of hell. To a third might appear a youth passing into the sad blight of honesty and honor, corrupted by it, and changed from a man to a sharper. To the murderer what a vision of his victim lying plundered and bleeding in some lonely spot, lighted by flickering flames that will burn deeper and deeper into his writhing soul! Let the corrupt ruler look at his Dollar, and see there a picture of his country insulted and disgraced before the world by his wicked bribe. Let the maiden in her bridal array consult this mirror, and perchance to her startled vision will appear sensual and covetous age, leading captive ambitious girlhood by the lure of gold. Might not the wearied merchant at his midnight toil for more wealth, would he look into this circle, behold his prodigal son, his imbecile daughter, his wife changed from the maid he loved to the scheming matron who now leads him chained to her car of social success? Could every form of suffering, degradation, meanness, crime that men encounter in gaining this dollar, appear on its face when they took it into their hand, what a sight were there! Yet it is all there as truly as if the magic picture were discerned; for every bad man's dollar is the type of his sin; every dollar gained by fraud and crime, by the unchristian devotion to gain, or the sacrifice of any element of manhood, is stained by the prostitution of the soul; and to such may we say in the words of the blunt and honest Apostle James: "*Your gold and silver is cankered; and the rust of them shall be a witness against you, and shall eat your flesh as it were fire.*"

But what a different thing is the Dollar when it represents the putting forth of industry for the noblest uses of life! The father who toils to sustain his home and make it the image of heaven, may behold thereon the beloved circle, the ruddy evening glow, the sweet faces lit by love and peace. The poor girl sewing in her garret to save her old decrepit mother from starvation, if she remain pure and thankful to God, may see an angel standing in the little golden mirror. The heroic mother saving and toiling for her darling boy may see a noble man in the Senate of his country, pouring forth a nation's rising indignation against a woeful wrong, till the pictured face of Washington almost smiles afresh from the walls, and the enemies of man gnash their teeth with infernal rage. What a Dollar was that which Fulton first received at New York for a fare on his new vessel; he says he felt half ashamed to take it—but if he kept it until he reached Albany, he could have seen all the rivers, lakes, and oceans of the world ebbing and flowing, and his vessels flying to and fro like the ministering spirits of the world's new day. The true artist's Dollar is but a frame, in which he beholds new forms of loveliness and majesty. The right-hearted citizen of our land, when he receives it as the reward of a day's toil, may behold it radiant with a patriot's hopes. The author, teacher, minister of religion may not fear to soil their hands with it for to them it is not base unless they have stained the whiteness of their genius by selling its power as a slave in the service of sin. The great statesman who has come out of office uncontaminated with bribes, can behold thereon the page of history whereon his name burns with a white light amid annals of infamy. And in private station, many is the good man who can read off the Lord's Prayer from his Dollar, and feel no sense of incongruity. So is this little coin the representative of our relation to our country; base or beautiful as we have been in gaining it. So is it the symbol of our relation to this world · and whatever use we propose to make of our earthly circumstances is there recorded. So is it the type of our position towards God; and the man who can honestly write the Saviour's Prayer on his Dollar has overcome the world by consecrating all its opportunities to the sublime office of fashioning a character in the image of "the perfect man, the measure of the stature of the fullness of Christ."

When, therefore, I proceed to answer the question, *How to get the Gold Dollar*, you will understand that I am speaking only of that which represents the best manhood in its relations to this world—the Dollar inscribed with the Lord's Prayer. For all kinds are to be obtained, and there are all kinds of teachers to instruct in the acquisition. One class of these instructors, whose certificate runs back to the money-changers whom Jesus scourged out of the Temple, protest against the interference of the clergy in financial matters; just as a class of statesmen, descended from Pilate and Herod, are grieved at the interference of the teachers of religion in public affairs. But let them not be cast down; as far as I know the clergy, they do not attempt to infringe on their vocation of teaching the art of "gaining the whole world and losing the soul." In all the tricks by which the base counterfeit Dollar, which symbolizes the loss of manhood, is gained, they are far too expert to dread any rivalry. But when it comes to telling the young how to gain the Dollar that gleams with the light of an elevated character, we have a word to say, since manhood is our province. I do not here attempt to describe the special operations in the varied forms of human effort by which this consecrated Dollar may be obtained—they are as numerous as the honorable professions and the righteous men in the world—but I maintain that the method in all is the same, and I only proclaim the everlasting law of Christian acquisition.

The Dollar is a new privilege in the life of this world, for which every man should pay his fair equivalent of work. Labor of some description; of the hands, or the mind, or subtler toil of noble living, is the God-ordained condition of the best earthly opportunities. For labor is not alone of the hands, and the worker on matter is not alone worthy of his hire. Whoever thinks a shorter way to do any necessary thing, or a better thing to do, or a finer grace of manliness to be obtained, deserves the Dollar, that he may occupy a wider field of effort, wherein he may bless mankind with his new discovery. And there are those who live so grandly that all the gold and jewels in the world are a poor tribute to their worth, and we are honored by giving them money, that their orbit of love and light may evermore expand. Service is manifold, and the worker in spiritual stuff is most deserving. Work alone deserves the Dollar; not that a bit of gold can *pay* any man for honest toil; but it is the key which unlocks the door to a new region of advantages, to which the laborer has gained the right to ascend. Therefore, let no man or woman, old or young, dream that laziness deserves anything but starvation and disgrace. Whoever will not work in some good way while he can —or when his strength is gone, live so nobly that his services increase as his body declines—shall not obtain the consecrated Dollar; if he obtain any it shall be a curse to his soul, for the lazy man's gold is a key that opens the ward of a lower hell, to which his sin has doomed him. Neither shall make-believe work deserve the true reward. Whoever gets his living by doing what hinders society, or is superfluous in its occupations, only disgraces himself; for there is a valuable thing for every soul to do that is born into this world, and whoever plays at work does the double mischief of leaving his task undone, and perpetrating a new sham. Oh! what a wreck does this savage old school-master, Panic, make with all this trumpery of unreal labor! How do whole professions disappear, and whole classes of men shrink to their native poverty, before his relentless gaze! Better live with him and munch your crust, than feast with a prosperity built on false pretences; for the world knows what it needs, and there will be confusion in the money market a good many centuries yet, until all men get into their own place and do their full measure of their own work.

Then do your best work on the highest plane of your manhood. Multitudes of men think business means going into the lower regions of their life to gain a base Dollar, and then coming up and putting on their clean clothes to enjoy it. But do you rather array yourselves in the purple robes of your largest manhood to go about your daily toil. Put your whole soul into your common life. Put in truth. Let every blow you strike come faithfully down on a real spot; and as you value yourself, do not sink to a dishonesty though buried deep as the bottom of the sea; for you cannot slight your work, or cheat your neighbor, or dodge your obligation, without taking it out of your own character, and erasing a letter of the Lord's Prayer from your Dollar. Put in patience and persistence—for there is no good thing, though hung up in the seventh heavens, that cannot be reached by sufficient toil; and no scandal, though rooted down in the seventh hell, that cannot be plucked up by him that "endureth to the end." Put in moderation—for a crazy man only gravitates to a strait-jacket in any region of life. Put in skill—for you are bound to do your work better in some way than it was ever done before. Put in reverence for man—for true work is always in his service—and your Saviour came to minister to us all; and to defraud in your toil is such an insult to him and disgrace to you as all the material prosperity upon earth cannot conceal. Put in self-reverence; love for family; respect for just law; patriotic devotion to your country's real good; philanthropic concern for all men—reverence for man implies all these. And no job is really done until all these appear in its doing. Do nothing in your work you are ashamed to publish to the world, to yourself, to your God.

Young woman, receive no Dollar that degrades your womanhood. If you are living as true daughter, wife, mother, friend, you are not in degrading dependence, but it is your right to receive as the privilege of man to give, the Dollar rightly earned. But oh! beware the curse of taking the base Dollar; of tempting man to earn it by the disgrace of his manlinesss: for could you see yourself walking in fine raiment bought by money wrung from your neighbor in the bitter competitions of dishonest trade; filched from the slow-witted; plundered from the foolish, the unfortunate, the desparing—as the angels behold you; could every dollar that goes to buy luxuries for your social state and position in the world, reveal the history of its acquisition, would you be able to face your present success? Pitch your wants on a key so low that they can all be satisfied by the consecrated Dollar, and scorn any advantage gained by other coin as you would shrink from pollution.

Say not this method of getting the Dollar is impracticable—a minister's fancy! For the only practical thing in business is to get money that represents the best manhood; and to sell your soul at retail to the devil, for a Dollar a fibre, is about the most unpractical sort of speculation in which a shrewd man can engage. I know it is not very easy to get rich in this way. It is very easy to get rich in America in many lower ways; but all the "fine gold" thus gained is "dimmed" in the getting, and we shall go down hill as we accumulate these riches. And of all men who thus obtain the Dollar, Jesus said: "It is easier for a camel to go through the eye of a needle than for them to enter the kingdom of God." It is as hard in America as it ever was in the world to earn the consecrated

Dollar; but the ambition to gain it is worthy our young men, and challenges their finest talent and their uttermost heroism. For to desire the consecrated Dollar is nothing less than to long for a larger field of usefulness; to wish for more of the world to fill with love; to pray for the power to be a providence among men. Such a love of money is the root of nobility, and whoever acquires wealth that represents the best he knows and can do in life, has treasure laid up in heaven.

This style of getting the Gold Dollar will insure the true method of its use. The fortune meanly gained will be meanly spent; for the plain reason that the same man who degraded himself to obtain his money, unless he becomes a better man, will continue to act from the same low level, and scourge the community worse in the use than in the getting of his wealth. The reason of so much criminal and foolish expenditure of money in America is found in the wicked modes of acquiring property. Is it strange that the scamp who has sprung a trap in speculution and caught a fortune, should go on speculating in higher things than railroad stocks, and prostitute his ill-gotten substance to pollute the ballot-box, or bribe the community into granting him a social position he does not deserve? Will not the young man who fills his pocket at the gaming-table, or by some shrewd legal way of swindling, conclude to buy the privilege of unlimited sensuality, or naturally aspire to the chance of spreading himself as an omnipresent coxcomb through the wide limbo of fashionable life? Is it surprising that a wife who shuts her eyes on the questionable tricks of her husband's trade, and tempts him to new meanness by her prodigality, will use her gold in spoiling the bodies and souls of her children, and putting out the light of heaven in her home? Whoever gains money like a knave will spend it like a snob, because the money-making sharper by success is naturally developed into the upstart of society. I want no better test of a man's way of using than a knowledge of his manner of getting; and when I see ostentation, or avarice, or hard, cold selfishness in the owner of large possessions, I can prophesy that if the whole story were told, his title of possession would be stained by many a damning sin before God, and outrage done to man. But when the Dollar has been so truly earned that it represents the best manhood of its possessor, I need no assurance that the same nobility will preside over its use, and bless the world as much in the spending as in the gaining.

Money is the talisman that opens the wards of

all regions of life, and he who has it can buy opportunities of many kinds. But since nobody is rich enough to buy all the opportunities of American society, or great enough to use them if they were possessed, there must be a choice in expenditure, and economy in use. Every man must save somewhere; it is honorable to stint ourselves in some directions, that we may obtain better things in others. Therefore, the wisest man is he who spends his Dollar to buy the opportunity most useful for his own growth in character and service to the world. Only a fool throws away his money on things that degrade himself or positions he can not occupy with honor to the people; but the greatest bargain is made when we buy those opportunities that we can fill full of our own power and make permanent positions of Christian influence among men. The bodily necessities of life are very few. Our Saviour while in the flesh was poorer than any of you whom I address; and almost every man can have something to purchase the position he can best use for himself and the world.

Have you then an especial talent for any honorable trade, or have you discovered a new and finer way of doing any necessary kind of work? Save everywhere else, and buy the opportunity to develop your genius in this direction—for this is the best gift you can bestow on society, and through such an elevation of labor, freedom and religion will gain a better chance among men. A true laborer, farmer, mechanic, merchant, who thus fills his profession brim full of his best mental and moral life, is a centre of power in any community, and his position is a seminary in the arts of a consecrated business. Do your abilities fit you best for social influence? then spend your money on a home, broad, elegant, hospitable; only remember to be so great that men shall forget your house while looking at you. Take your position in society, and then teach your neighbors Christian manners, Christian hospitality, Christian amusements. Let your family circle become a school of social wisdom and beauty; and win America from the worship of tapestry and gilding, and barbaric luxury and habits, to the love of true elegance and the grace of real gentility. Have you an unmistakable genius for letters or art, or are your children gifted with power to charm and bless the world? Then spend for the best culture of the mind. Let fine house, fine clothes, society, business, sink to subordinate matters, and buy the company of the best wisdom, the instruction of the most accomplished in the arts. And when gained, stand on your own manhood, and spend all your life to purchase greater opportunity to move the world in this excellent way. Are you gifted with that peculiar combination of faculties that fit you to heal the sick, to plead the law, to prophesy in the pulpit or outside the Church, on the people's platform? Let no expense be spared to get you into your place, and when there, do not spoil everything by using your position to make money, but use your money to enlarge your position, and trust to your service in that way for your vindication among men. You are born to rule, to live an executive life. You understand the movements of public affairs, and can keep cool and calm, and grow in manhood amid the fierce heats of political conflict. Use all the money you can get honestly to obtain a post of influence. Do not buy voters, or bribe editors, or insult any man by proposing any partnership in meanness; but buy honestly the opportunity to serve your country. Buy a newspaper, buy a stump, buy a standing-place, and begin to talk. Spend your money to sow the land from ocean to ocean with stirring appeals and invincible reasons for freedom; and every shoot you plant shall spring up in time a free and pure American voter. When you get power, do not try to seize a new place, before you know the duties of the old. If only a policeman, put your whole soul into your baton, and let it fall like a bolt of lightning upon the evil-doer, and flash like a ray of light before the oppressed within your "beat." And by saving everywhere else and using your money to enlarge your power to serve the people, you may become a statesman, such as lived in the old days, when great men dwelt under humble roofs, and went forth from narrow farms to guide the destinies of mighty states. And if you can be a wise philanthropist, and are sure that you know some good way to cure those social evils we all too plainly see, pray spend your Dollar to gain a place where you can be an angel of deliverance to the sorrowing, the sinful, the oppressed. *The crown of earthly privilege is to occupy your own place, and the only wise use of money is to buy that place.* And then all is in your hands—for the wisdom to fill it, and the virtue to make it a centre of power aud love, no money can buy; that must be gained by long, weary service, obedience to God, reverence for man, and devotion to those graces of the soul that mould the religious life.

The Gold Dollar is the type of American civilization. As it is a metallic plate on which we may write the Tempter's creed or the Saviour's prayer, so is our country such a material opportunity as was never seen, wherewith we can do what we will for man and God. But we have not yet learned how to gain the Dollar, nor do we really know how to use it. We run about calling to the nations—"Who will sell an empire? for our purse is full, we would buy—who can offer a new pleasure, a new luxury, a new way to pave the road of common life with gold? we have more than we can waste—who wants a new railroad? we will survey one to the moon—let us float a palace of gold and tapestry on every river and lake, and build up a fairy mart of commerce, wherein every man shall have a stall, and all be rich!" O foolish young nation! save your money, till you learn that the more you spend this way the leaner your soul will grow, till you learn in the fires of panic and the collapse of credit, and the wreck of your lofty hopes, to spend for man. For man is the summit of American civilization, and for him should we gain; for him use the golden talisman. Spend to organize a free and solid industry from sea to sea. Spend for the home; spend for the school; spend for a pure Gospel; spend for true art and generous manners; spend for justice, and order, and official integrity; oh! spend for freedom, the emancipation of man from the tyrannies of the past, that he may learn to obey the eternal laws of God. All virtue and skill in our outward life concentrates now in learning the value of this familiar Dollar: in stamping it with the image and superscription of liberty; in gaining it by the exercise of our uttermost nobility; in using it to buy success in our experiment of a Christian democracy. Always before our eyes shall hover this shining circle, illuminated with the words of Christ; and while following this gleam of the gold, a finer radiance shall mingle with its light, till along the horizon of our country's hopes its circle shall fade into the golden flush of a rising dawn, and over the hills shall leap the new day of love and joy, and the Christ shall again be born in a nation's life, and from the private heart and the public soul shall ascend the prayer: "Our Father who art in Heaven, hallowed be thy name. Thy kingdom come. Thy will be done in earth, as it is in Heaven."

# VI.

## THE NORMAL SCHOOL AND THE OBSERVATORY;

OR,

## EDUCATION IN NEW YORK.

On the 18th December, 1844, was inaugurated in the City of Albany the most characteristic of our institutions of learning—the State Normal School. Beginning with the humblest pretensions, a little group of twenty-nine pupils and their teachers, it has gradually increased to its present importance. A legislative appropriation in 1844 of $10,000 a year, for five years, was its first impulse. In 1848, $15,000, and subsequently $10,000 followed as an appropriation for the present building, which was occupied July 30th, 1849. During the thirteen years of its existence, 2,887 pupils have received educational discipline within its walls, at an expense of $45 a piece; and it would be difficult to name the public or private investment of $130,000, which has borne such fruits within our prosperous Republic.

The observatory which now crowns one of our most conspucious heights, and overlooks an enchanting landscape while it sweeps a vast horizon, is a later child of the same desire to promote the interests of sound learning. Founded in the spring of 1853, and enriched by the successive contributions of the citizens of Albany and our State, it was inaugurated at the meeting of the American Scientific Association in this city, Aug. 28th, 1856. The eloquent periods of the greatest living master of ceremonial oratory in our language still linger in our ears as we recall that day; and we may anticipate the time when his glowing prophecies will be realized in its valuable contributions to astronomical science.

But it is not to sound the praises of these admirable institutions, yet in their infancy, that I have placed their names at the head of my discourse. There are other and more celebrated observatories and Normal Schools than these, and the people of the greatest existing republic must enrich and enlarge all their educational establishments far beyond their present limits to supply their own wants. But situated as these institutions are, in the capital city of New York, and representing, as they do, the two great central ideas of mental culture, I may use them as symbolic of the complete intellectual development of our commonwealth.

The Normal School is the corner-stone of our system of free instruction; and from the 11,492 free school-houses of New York radiate those influences which create the newspaper, the magazine, our fugitive literature, the public library, the popular oratory in behalf of social and political interests, and the system of literary lectures which has done so much for the more advanced of our Northern States. These are the agencies of that mental culture of the people which is the glory of our civilization, and the foundation of popular intelligence: and of this side of the education of New York, the Normal School is the most characteristic type.

The Observatory, wherein are conducted the investigations of the most sublime of our natural sciences, is the best representative of that profound culture in abstract truth without which popular education and institutions inevitably degenerate to a superficial and transient existence. The reference to fundamental principles in every department of intellectual life will create a valuable body of scientific knowledge, a broad and reliable professional education, a permanent national literature; and from these springs among the highlands of thought will flow innumerable streams of fertilizing, practical energy. To show the relations of these two divisions of intellectual culture, and vindicate the imperative necessity of their perfect union in the mental development of our State, is the theme of the present discourse.

I certainly may be excused for declining to defend the necessity of a thorough Intellectual Culture for the whole population of New York. I do not question that there are many persons yet living in our State, who would demand proof of this commonplace. I could not convince the ignorant disciples of this gospel according to the dunces of their error; but fortunately a good Providence can be trusted sooner or later to bring every unlettered citizen of this republic into a position where he will at least stop boasting of his disgrace, and cease from any open attack upon his own best interests. And I have but one thing to say of any cultivated man or woman who openly or secretly resists the best culture of the people—that such a person is a public enemy and should be marked and watched as a traitor to Liberty and Humanity. Whether the opposition is from the conceit of a literary class, or the fanaticism of a mediæval religious sect, or the baser desire to play the demagogue at the head of a rabble; it is equally dangerous, and equally to be denounced by all who believe in American Freedom and the Christian Religion.

But there *is* an error, more deeply seated than we may imagine, which requires a more respectful notice; not because it is less dangerous, but is the result of honest misconception of the office of mental culture itself, and entertained by thousands of well meaning people.

There is doubtless a tendency in some regions of our most cultivated society to undervalue popular culture; to cut off from its support or the coöperation with its various agencies, and to sneer at the superficiality that does exist in the common school, the press, the fugitive literature, and the popular oratory, rather than to labor for their elevation. On the other hand, a tendency is developing among the masses of the people, fostered too often by their present instructors, to undervalue the study of abstract principles; to force all education to become what is falsely called "practical;" to break down the higher institutions of learning in favor of professional schools; to smother a permanent literature in a deluge of journalism; and to discourage the thinking head on the platform in favor of the most voluble tongue, and bring all subjects of intellectual culture into subjection to the suffrages of the people.

Both these delusions will vanish before the question, "*What is the use of mental education?*" It is evidently, first, to develop the individual man into the completeness of his humanity; and second, to unfold the mind of a State in its largest and noblest dimensions.

Intellectual culture has not done its work when it has made a scholar in any department of learning; for this scholar may be only half of a man, a mere child of impulse, void of commanding will or wisdom, intrusted with a casket of the jewels of knowledge. Until his acquisitions have become a part of his vital blood and bone and sinew, and science has borne its fruit of a wise and lofty character, he is yet a "freshman" in the great college of life. Neither has a man succeeded better who uses knowledge only so far as it serves him for some material end; and ignores the claims of a liberal culture as impractical. This man is as surely a pedant as the scholar he despises, and his pedantry is more degrading, shutting his soul in a prison of material and selfish occupations. Intellectual culture is first for the sake of manhood and womanhood; to unfold the divine faculty of reason, to impart the ability of reflection and accuracy of judgment in all regions of human experience, to clothe man with his complete power, which may be used in the service of truth and righteousness. It is not to prepare a man for one position, to do a special work, whether in a college or a workshop; these are but its incidental results; rather to develop souls into the likeness of Eternal wisdom.

The public function of education is not to raise up a literary or learned class in the State, or to teach the masses alone the best method of work. The experience of European society is not inspiring in its division into a learned fraternity and an ignorant populace. We are not so enamored of literature that we are willing to pay for it the price of political degradation. We want no servile cultivated class fawning about the feet of despotic power, holding the pen under the eye of a police, and flying off into regions of insane abstract speculation as a relief from the barbarous tyranny that forbids genius to speak on the rights of man; but that we must have unless we teach the whole people; we have it already in those portions of America most nearly resembling the old world. Better postpone the hopes of American scholarship a thousand years, than sacrifice the grander hopes of Republican life in our new world. But let us not swing off into the opposite danger of a purely material and superficial education; for thus we check the growth of the American mind in its infancy, and destroy the hope of an elevated civilization. If we are to have nothing better for all the trouble and peril of a democracy, than cheaper bread, better clothes and houses, more money in our pockets, and the ambitious shrewdness and unscrupulous energy that now dominates everywhere in our society, we have made a failure. And whoever discourages the most generous and profound culture, is helping to fix us in this disgraceful attitude before mankind. But we endure much that now offends us in the ardent hope that through our singular mixture of population and varied public and private experience, aided by the widest mental discipline, a new and grander order of mind is slowly growing up in our State and country; a mind in which ultimately the energy that now surveys railroads, and ploughs over territories, will mount to higher realms of spiritual activity and mightily advance the cause of man's eternal destiny. Thus the second use of intellectual culture, as a whole, is to serve this highest interest of our State in the training of an American character founded on the everlasting law of love as translated in our great national declaration of human rights.

Therefore let there be no jealousy between the scholars and the people. Each can live in New York only by the aid of the other. The most generous popular cultivation should lead men to perceive the infinite value of these central principals that lie at the foundations of the soul and life upon earth; the most profound scholarship should count the spiritual elevation of a Republic a work as far transcending any achievment in special science as man transcends the planet he inhabits. The Normal School and the Observatory are twin symbols of a culture that, laying its vast foundations in the education of every soul in the State, shall rise by gradual ascents to those sublime heights of abstract truth gilded by the eternal morning of an omnipresent love.

The Normal School is the corner-stone of the popular mental culture of our State. For the teacher is the soul of that free school where the vast majority of our people will learn the rudiments of knowledge. According to the quality of the 31,503 instructors who direct the 1,214,771 children of New York in the paths of learning, will be the future tastes of those children in intellectual pursuits. Whether they read the best or the worst of our public journals; whether they abide in the valleys of literature or strain up its invigorating heights; whether wisdom or folly in the popular assembly, and the high places of influence shall sway their opinions, is due chiefly to their first years of training in the school-room.

And without any special censure of these 31,000 teachers who now consent to lay the mental foundations of our Republic for the paltry compensation of less than $200 per year, we may boldly declare that while less than one-fifth of them receive any preliminary training in any preparatory institutions, inefficiency and failure must be the rule as often as the exception in this sacred sphere of effort. We venture to say that the people would complain if a shoal of preachers, doctors and lawyers were let loose on the State with no preparation for their important vocations. Yet none of these professional characters claim a tithe of the opportunity of permanent public influence possessed by the teacher in the free school; and, strange to declare, we commit the intellectual training of the whole coming generation to transient, poorly-paid and sustained agents, not one in five of whom pretends to have received any training for the most honorable office in the Commonwealth. While, therefore, we fully appreciate the fidelity of those who are laboring at the task of elevating the teachers in the one State Normal School, in the Teachers' Institutes, and in the academical departments, which out of our metropolis are the only establishments for such a work, we insist that the work of *creating a profession of competent and permanent common school teachers, whose services shall compel an adequate reward, is only begun.* This reform lies at the basis of all others in our complex and somewhat unwieldy school system. Let every friend of the people sound the cry from New York to Niagara: "*More Normal Schools; more training for the teachers!*" The cry of political parties is ever for economy. Let our public servants retrench in that enormous waste of money, and mind, and civilization which attends a body of unprepared teachers of the young; and inaugurate decided measures for enlarging and improving our establishments for the discipline of public instructors, and whatever politicians may say, the people will finally pronounce that they have seized the true principle of economy. Let the people demand and pay for the best opportunities of modern culture for these 31,000 sovereigns who now rule the millions of youth that are to rule the Commonwealth.

We have spoken of the Free School as that in which the vast majority of our people are to be educated. Already the number of children in it, compared with private schools, is as thirty to one, and the disproportion is yearly increasing. Indeed, it is doubtful whether the private schools of New York, except in occasional exceptions, are equal to our best public establishments, while the expense of education is fearfully greater. I am assured by competent authority that in a certain town in our State, containing 3,000 children, as much money is paid for the instruction of 240 youth in private schools as the entire expense for the remainder in good public institutions.

Out of this state of society I suppose the people expect a Democracy! But the extravagance in money is a small part of the evil. Of course, private special instruction will always be a necessity in a cultivated community; but to count upon any form of select schools to do the work of educating a State like New York is a folly that sensible men should outgrow. The experience of Prussia and New England are conclusive that the people can be best educated in public institutions, and the great results both in popular intelligence and elevated scholarship attained in these communities prove the efficacy of the system. It is almost impossible to find a Prussian citizen unable to read and write; and New England is fast approaching this condition; while the high culture and scholarship of these countries lead the literature of Germany and America. England, with no general system of free public instruction, is half untaught. Even New York, with her conflicting system, has 150,000 adult citizens unable to write. It may not appear to those whose social or sectarian prejudices make them look coldly on our noble system of public instruction, that they are unconsciously the allies of the worst barbarism in the State; that while they hesitate to pay their money and elevate their free schools to the front rank of merit, thousands of youth are joining the armies of the ignorant and swelling the vandal horde that already howls and thunders at the gates of our new civilization. If the children of a Webster or an Everett or of the great scholars of Germany can be taught as they have been in the public school, cannot we in New York make ours the suitable place for the culture of the whole people? I must believe that the most dangerous form of sectarianism is that which would break down this great interest, and commit whole regions of our society to the culture of a Catholic or Protestant priesthood. I count no social Aristocracy so odious as that which, out of contempt for the children of the people, withdraws money, influence and patronage from the great nursery of the State, and immures a select few in the walls of a narrow culture which must be a complete disqualification for any broad life.

The public school, organized by our best wisdom, supported by our wealth, and officered by a thoroughly trained corps of public servants, would be an influence as far above any form of select instruction, as the heart of a great people beats higher than the pulse of a clique or a corporation. Let our Capital City take her own youth in hand; call in the 2,000 vagrant children that roam her streets; cover her hills with school-houses after the pattern of the last ample structure; offer a seat therein to every child; from her abundant means secure the ablest teachers in the State; without delay establish a free school for girls and boys; and lend the due proportion of her vaunted political influence to the elevation of the whole people; or she may yet encounter the reproach of spending thousands for the select culture of the few, while she is training up an army of savages by the teachers of the street.

Next in importance to the common school in our popular culture, is the Press, as organized in the newspaper, magazine and fugitive literature. It would probably surprise any man to learn the extent to which the literary wants of our population are supplied from this source. The State census of 1855 reports 559 newspapers and 112 periodicals, whose circulation is: daily, 312,783; tri-weekly, 8,400; semi-weekly, 40,387; weekly, 1,294,340; semi-monthly, 264,600; monthly, 1,287,650; quarterly, 31,950; semi-annual, 11,000; annual, 96,950. Doubtless a considerable proportion of this matter circulates outside of the State, and is a part of the national influence of our popular culture; but enough remains in the State to excite the amazement of any uninformed observer. And when we add to this the vast number of books, written in essentially the same style, we must say that our wants for popular reading are most bountifully supplied.

It is one of the cheapest ways of affecting superior culture to sneer at this whole mass of popular literature; but it is a wiser thing to examine the phenomenon and report on its significance. This rage for transient reading proves, not that the taste of the cultivated has declined, but that *the people are learning to read.* Never were so *many persons reading anything before as now in a few of the States of the Union.* Whole classes now read that once were wholly ignorant. Of course, when a State begins its journey in the world of literature, it takes the easiest path; reads the news of the day; is interested chiefly in pithy and sketchy methods of conveying information; prefers monthly picture-books illustrated with reading to permanent works of genius; and if it enters the domain of books, craves those which have grown out of the newspaper and magazine, and demand only an ordinary comprehension for enjoyment. Thus we should rather rejoice that so many have began to read in New York, than turn with disgust from much they do read.

That this phenomenon of journalism in its present form is to be permanent, we have no belief. It is a sort of railroad to carry our people over from ignorance to a love for good literature, and is doing the work with as few accidents as could be expected. If a majority of the journals are partisan advocates, and feed the people with much that degrades their taste and embitters their spirit, it is also true that there is a minority which furnish writing of a respectable and often of a high degree of merit, conducted by editors of high attainments and elevated principles. The newspaper is the representative, not the leader, of the people. Every journal represents its public, and cannot long abide above its level. If there are papers that appear to be edited by Satan, it is because a class of the people is on good terms with that sulphurous functionary. If some of our best journals teem with the lowest details of crime and folly, it is because there are so many respectable people who like to sit in their arm-chair in the family, and look through this popular telescope down into the lowest hells of creation. If the political and theological "organs" are yet grossly partisan, and live on misrepresentation and suppression, it is because the majority of the people yet postpone the labor of thinking, for the more congenial occupation of training under leaders, and mustering upon platforms. But there is much that is good in all our journals. The best give us every day as good essays as were written by the wits of Queen Anne's time, for the delectation of the scholars: and altogether our popular writing is purer and more elevating than the whole body of English literature in some of its most illustrious periods. The duty of the cultivated and religious community is to urge selection, to hold this press to a stern literary and moral criticism, and demand the best the people can bear. A thousand editors will accept the chairs of those who now write when called to do higher work. Let good men rally about the best journals and periodicals, and unite to overwhelm the base and mean by a persistent letting alone of their foul wares.

Especially should we sustain the efforts making to develop a high-toned and free periodical worthy of the best state of American civilization. The word has already gone forth that no magazine shall live which does not go down into the dust before our national bigotry and despotism. There may be a popular censorship more destructive than an Austrian police of literature, and the efforts to crush out the best utterances of genius should be met by the stern rebuke of every man who desires to see literature a power in our Democracy, rather than the dancing attendant on a ruling class, or a dominant creed.

It is not clearly understood that this great outburst of popular writing in journals, magazines and fugitive books is the *birth of American literature.* Our national literature is not to be the reproduction of any foreign culture. It will not come from the brains of pedants or critical students of the past; but will spring out of the souls of men and women that are filled with the great American idea, inspired by her magnificent opportunities and solemnized by her wavering destiny. Already scattered through these fugitive leaves are not a few ominous words that sound the key note to the chorus of the future. Let us not complain too much of the mania for scribbling that infests all classes of our youth. Some of these boys and girls will catch a glimpse of our American realities and inscribe them in enduring lines. And with a thorough popular education and the unbounded facilities for reading, travel and social intercourse, added to the stimulant of our public life, many a scribbler will be trained in journalism for the loftier flights of authorship.

The help of public libraries is now greatly needed. Every town in New York needs a copious free library of good literature, where its youth can find a counter-influence to the fluctuating waves of journalism. With such aids to receive the child from the school-room, we may look for a soil of popular intelligence that shall bear fruits in literature and life worthy our best hopes.

These agencies of popular culture find their completion in our popular oratory. The stump to which our servants must all descend from their official chairs, and face their masters; the platform where the special reformer thunders out his indignation, sure of stirring some warm hearts to sympathy; and the desk where the "Lions" duly appear and shake their manes and roar to the delectation or disgust of the literary societies, are doubtless not inferior to any mental influence save the teachers. Books and journals will never extinguish man; Oratory is still the highest of human arts, and the most potent engine of human persuasion. Our people are greatly taught by this public speaking; and it only needs a more complete organization and a larger freedom to insure the grandest results. Of course, the same conditions accompany this as all forms of culture. In many localities a noisy humbug will talk to the people while a wise man cannot be heard; but the test of a true speaker is to wait and grow by the contact with the few until the people, tired of their quacks, come to him for relief. And then the same car that carries Prof. Windbags will convey the real orator to stir up a people in one hour so that henceforth they never can live as they have existed. The studious effort now making in many quarters to keep the best of our public orators from the platform, and compel the people to hear second rate talk, will return to plague its inventors, and only confirm the people in the resolution to hear all sides on the great questions of our civilization through their acknowledged representatives.

America is destined to be the home of such eloquence as never yet has shaken the nations. Great orators are made by great occasions and great listening; and the American orator, whose every thrilling period, and fervent thought, is flashed along the wires through the area of mighty States, whose themes range around the highest earthly interests of man amid the strange circumstances of a new existence, is exalted to an opportunity equal to the noblest human aspiration. Let the people listen rightly and their souls will not be unvisited by the prophecies and visions of truth which the men of former days desired in vain.

The best results of these combined agencies for popular cultivation, will be the production of a rich, deep soil of general intelligence; the best nursery of genius. Great minds are largely modified by the spirit of an age, birth-place, and social influence. A man of genius, born and trained amid a cultivated class, is quite another being from the offspring of a great and intelligent people. First class men oftenest have arisen outside the narrow circles of social caste or special scholarship; and so far from universal education dwarfing extraordinary talent, it will only form a deeper and stronger mould in which loftier trees may strike a firmer root. In proportion as the average of culture rises, will the variety and number of specially gifted souls increase. The true sy tem of Education in New York is one which, founded on the broadest basis of popular instruction, shall gradually rise through the Free High School to professional Seminaries, and the best University privileges of the time. Thus will the State be in a condition to arrest every man and woman of extraordinary promise, and proffer such encouragement as would develop all the genius of the commonwealth in the largest style. When we consider what a waste of talent is incurred by our present condition of affairs; how many young women of genius are hindered from their proper opportunities; and what a perversion of shining abilities there is into unsuitable employments, we must accuse our republic of a criminal prodigality in her best treasure. If we have done so much in spite of our lack of advantages, what could not be done by organization of all the appliances of the highest culture, and their union with the system of popular Education.

The Observatory is the type of that severe study of abstract principles, which is the final test of human culture; for we must never forget that facts and knowledge are only valuable to men as they are brought into relation to the everlasting ideas and laws on which life itself reposes. There is great danger that our youth will lose themselves in this drifting ocean of popular education, and fall into that most deplorable of mental states, the sport of every new theory and the victim of to-day's excitement. More than ever before, it is now important that we should have some deeply grounded ideas of existence—some immovable principle of character, and guide our conduct by an unchangeable law of public and private right; but such principals cannot be borrowed—cannot be shot into men from the stump, or crammed into the telegraphic column of the newspaper; they are the fruit of self-knowledge, toil, and thought; and unless the youthful mind is trained to the severe investigation of ideas in science and society, it is not probable that the task will be learned amid the cares and excitement of middle-age. Hence the very abundance of our popular privileges will be our worst enemy, unless we knit up into the system the most complete opportunities for the profoundest study, and the wisest range through the loftier fields of intellectual enterprise.

The University is the place where our chosen youth are to be instructed in the investigation of ideas and principles, and shown the extent and grandeur of the realms of human knowledge; while the Professional School receives those who require special training in each department of life; although all teaching in the Common School should aim at a discipline of the mind in reflection and the search for the central laws of thought.

That our present machinery for developing the higher intelligence of this State is adequate, we suppose no well instructed man will assert. While New York was passing through its transition from a wilderness to the world's first republic, it was necessary to plant an academy or college in every accessible place, and thus carry the best education that could be procured to the people. But New York, seamed with railroads, with her 3,500,000 souls virtually a family, will not long be content with this temporary arrangement. She has now 10 colleges, with 100 professors and 1,000 students; 210 academies, with 850 teachers and 23,000 scholars, conducted at an expense of more than $2,500,000; while her citizens proclaim that there is no university or school of commanding rank. Is it not time that Legislatures should cease from this dispersion of the means of high culture over such a wide area, and look for its concentration in some first class University worthy of this great State? The Free High School, properly developed, would do the work of a majority of our academies better and on a larger scale; while the best academical institutions might be elevated to preparatory schools for the University. Three colleges are better than ten; a concentration of Professional Schools would raise the character and usefulness of special culture; and the establishment of Seminaries for agricultural and mechanical training of various kinds, would complete the circle. Then what is to prevent a great University, enriched by the wealth and fostered by the protection of the State, where every young man and woman of extraordinary promise could be invited by the Commonwealth, and assisted in the enjoyment of the best advantages of modern culture? Contraction in the number of our higher Seminraies; larger opportunities in all, and the admission of woman to equal privileges with man; with a provision for free culture in the highest no less than the lowest departments of thought, is the direction in which we must move, or see our choicest youth drawn to other States to seek the generous training denied them in our own.

Who can contemplate the result of such reforms on the whole professional class? To say nothing of the advantage from elevating agricultural, domestic and mechanical pursuits, to the rank of professions, the whole body of men introduced to the pulpit, the bar, the legislative halls, medical science and editorship, would become more able and efficient. We shall be very blind if we do not perceive that such a population as our's needs every year more careful handling—demands wiser leaders in every region of public activity. Many evils that now afflict the American church, state and society, would vanish, were a new and higher class of men to appear and occupy the chief positions. Such youth we have, and only need our best training to prepare them for the inspiring duties of our future. And how would our native literature and art advance, could every youth of genius look confidently to the State for a helping hand at every step, from the alphabet to the highest opportunities of the age. What a field for the development of great genius is here; our superb and varied scenery; our growing vigor and influence; never were richer materials offered to the author and the artist. Let the Commonwealth welcome her gifted children to the whole circle of modern high culture, and her presses will groan with books that the nation will read and her galleries shine with the idealizations of her nature and her civilization.

From such a blending of interests the scholar would become the elder brother of the people, and from the heights of science would flow down perpetual blessings of practical power to the plains, even as the rivers that water the valleys, rise from silent far off mountain springs. Then would appear an ever-gaining intercourse between all classes of society; the vulgarity of ignorance would disappear, and the cultivated mind, no longer driven within a narrow circle, would range like a beneficent teacher through all the regions of our population. Then would the present monotony of our social affairs give place to a charming variety, since well educated men and women will always make life more varied and complex, and break down barriers founded on mere length of purse and pride of family or race. Then would the present jealousy between city and country disappear; for the barbarism of the city, and the vandalism of the country, which now lie at the foundation of such contentions, would vanish, and sensible people would soon perceive that between the field and the pavement there is no real opposition. And the present desolating contentions of partisan politics would depart with the extinction of the hordes of ignorant voters, who are now the body-guard of artful demagogues; and the State, no longer torn by internal feuds on secondary affairs, would move to her place as the leader of Freedom in National Affairs.

Doubtless the end of this scheme of culture would be the development of a peculiar civilization, founded on the genius of our people. The mind of New York is superior to that of any other American State, in breadth of view, the capacity for great public undertakings, executive ability, and powerful enthusiasm for the right. If New England is privileged to be the home of ideas, the nursery of the most accurate culture and the most fastidious refinement, it is equally the fact, that her ideas must be reorganized, adjusted and administered in New York, before they can operate on a scale as large as the whole of America. By our mixture of races, we can comprehend the wants of all. By our commanding position, we can receive the best the old world has to give, and mould it for the common wants of the new. Our cosmopolitan style of society and manners has repeated itself as far as the Pacific; our political and industrial energy concentrated in our great cities, is felt through the entire Union of States. Would to Heaven we could cease our proverbial boasting of opportunities we so shamefully abuse; would that, filled with a profound gratitude for our privileges and a solemn sense of our responsibility for our administration thereof, we could first lay deep and strong the foundation of permanent greatness and indestructible liberty in the education of every citizen. Then, instead of strewing the wilderness of the tropics with the bones of our young men, slain in the piratical conquest of savage lands, we might leave behind us institutions of learning and wisdom, which, in every generation, would send forth new armies of millions of intelligent freemen, who, in every part of the earth, would testify against the wrong, and mightily uphold the right.

## VII.

## PEDANTRY AND POWER.

In a former discourse we have unfolded the true idea of mental culture for the citizens of the Empire State. But we are aware that when this is attained we encounter an ancient and unreconciled quarrel between the man of letters and the man of action. The practical genius of our great commonwealth is always jealous of the interference of the scholastic mind in affairs. It would drive the scholar and professional man off into a narrow circle of mental operations and claim the whole field of actual life for itself. As a consequence, the scholar is forced to underrate practical efficiency and is confirmed in his own isolation from society. The great end of all human culture is yet imperfectly understood, even by those who claim to be cultivated. As a completion to our review of the education of the people of New York, let us state the true object of all developments of the mind; and as truth is often enforced by contrast, we may speak of that false culture whose result is seen in an all-prevailing pedantry, and set it over against that true education whose finest attainment is the acquisition of Power.

We shall be greatly mistaken if we suppose that what often goes by the name of "Culture" in Society develops spiritual Power. Indeed the well nigh universal result of culture in all departments of American life is pedantry. Pedantry and power are the antagonistic ends of two ideas of education. To the vast majority of men, culture means the imposition of knowledge and arbitrary rules from without,—an exercise chiefly taxing the memory, leaving the *man* unaffected. The cultivated man, according to this idea, is he whose memory is crowded with the results of other men's thoughts, whose life is spent in recollecting what he has learned, and squaring his opinions and conduct to such laws as may find their way to this storehouse of the mind. The deep places of his nature are undisturbed; his reason, affections, imagination, will have never been roused, fired, concentrated in any crisis of original thought, but are cold spectators of mental pictures thrown upon the walls of the soul by the camera obscura of memory. This kind of culture makes pedants, or men in whom life waits upon knowledge, not men in whom knowledge is fused into life.

We shall greatly mistake if we suppose the pedant is found only in the study. The literary pedant, the little man tottering under the crushing weight of his own memory, has been so often held up to ridicule, that it may be supposed his failing is the peculiar infirmity of the literary class. Not so! Society is crowded with pedants—the apt scholars of a system of education that would change men by dressing them in certain garments of conventional law and miscellaneous knowledge. Behold the merchant pedant, who has toiled himself into gray hairs and chronic restlessness, and never learned the alphabet of his trade; that a merchant is a man applying the eternal laws of nature and justice to practical affairs, not a man driven in a harness, whose reins are clutched in the unfeeling gripe of a false popular system of business. Behold the agricultural pedant, who spends fifty years trying to adjust the earth to the few notions of farming he has inherited from his ancestors or gathered from his neighbors. Have you not seen the female social pedant, whose idea of woman is a creature made to keep house and rear children like everybody else, be clothed upon as the Juno nods from the sacred mount of fashion whence descends the apparel of the "angels upon earth," to revolve in the monotonous treadmill which somebody calls good society, and pilot her soul within the breakers whereon she is assured all who venture outside the reigning conventionalism are fatally wrecked? I think I have seen the pedant of politics whose platform is "man for constitution," not "the constitution for man."

Practical people are fond of ascribing all pedantry to the men of letters—the preachers, the lawyers, the doctors, the scholars. We accept their most severe criticism, and only hope grace will be given us to see that man is the true centre of all professional life; but we cannot be ignorant that pedantry is the curse of common life and most destructive thereto. Whatever sinks the man into an appendage to the memory and crowds the mind with knowledge without arousing the soul, is false culture and ends in folly. How has the sacred office of instruction suffered at the hands of such men and women, schoolmasters and schoolmistresses who shout forevermore to their scholars from behind a barricade of words, disjointed facts, superficial theories, and conventional rules; whose souls never touch the soul they affect to teach; who know not what it is to stand by human nature and invoke its sublime energies to harmonious power.

There is another style of culture which arouses the nature, by the contact of life and the stimulant of science, and when the faculties are actually awakened and trained, leads the mind up to the avenues of knowledge, and points along these grand vistas the way to Spiritual Power. "Strait is the gate and narrow is the way" of this high culture, "and few there be that find it." Few indeed are they in any walk of life who have gained possession of their own powers, assimilated their knowledge and experience into the blood of life, who grow in human excellence as the years bear them on; who placed before a new subject of thought or thrown into a new complication of affairs, bring to the solution of their present problem a fresh original Spiritual Power. These souls are the rulers of life, the only "cultivated." It has been a tradition of the past, that these men must always remain a class; but we are bound to show that this is the natural training to which every soul has a right.

The constituents of Spiritual Power are Freedom, Earnestness and Purity.

It is a criminal mockery to demand Spiritual Power where Freedom is denied. Freedom is the unlimited privilege of searching for truth, and making its unrestricted application in life. Caprice is not freedom; willfulness is not freedom;

incontinence of body or soul is not freedom; these are the slavery of the higher to the lower faculties of man. Only through reverence for the true, and love for the good, does the soul rise into an ever-widening universe of thought and life, and under the lead of such an inspiration, no man can be safely hindered in his journey to Spiritual Power. For there is no faculty in man which may not rightly claim its legitimate exercise. Who shall forbid the ocean of human affection, whose waves conceal the awful boundary line between the soul and its Maker, to ebb and flow responsive to divine attraction in God and Man? What pretentious philosophy will dare to chain reason within the bounds of a foregone conclusion, and thus insult Omniscience through its only delegete on earth? Is any conventional notion of morality so valuable, that we can afford to sacrifice the imagination, whereby we behold and reproduce the eternal beauty on its altar? Is it not a shameful thing that man claims the absolute power over his fellow-man, and scorns the will, which is our most human possession? And if all our hopes of success in this state of being depend on the welfare of the temple in which our spirit dwells, is it not a crime to degrade the body and vilify nature, either by a narrow asceticism or a beastly sensuality?

And if all human faculties may rightfully claim Freedom, who will presume to fence off any portion of the field of human knowledge and life, and forbid the entrance of man therein? who knows what subjects are beyond the reach of human thought? who has surveyed the universe, that he should draw a chart of the coast along which man must inevitably sail? Away with this pedantry! Far more reverent is the most daring explorer of God's spiritual creation, than he who assumes to fix the limits of the soul at the point where he became tired and fell asleep. Limits to human knowledge there may or may not be, but no man yet knows where the adamantine hills cut off the horizon. Doubtless Freedom is perilous, but the peril is not of our creation; it is the peril of our nature, from which there is no escape, least of all through slavery. It is a very perilous thing to be a man, but we have been created men, and what shall we do with ourselves? We cannot become trees or clods, or irrational beings; we can spoil our manhood by throwing away the Freedom which is its glory and peril, or we can gird ourselves to the eternal work of vindicating ourselves. Weakness lies in the one path, the other path is the highway to spiritual power.

And who will dare to be at once a traitor to

human nature, and his native land, and withhold Freedom from the American youth? Do you point to the follies and crimes of Young America as the fruit of Freedom? This bad boy is the fruit of Despotism; his scandal is the reaction against the tyrannical social shams that have come over the water, and yet poison our Republican Society No American generation has yet been reared in. true independence; what wonder that those who have not been awakened to the glories of Spiritual Freedom should mistake license for liberty. The American young man and woman are compelled to go forth upon a new Continent, and organize a new State, Church, School, Household, Art, Business—for all these things spoil in a voyage over the ocean. There are many fine things of this sort abroad; grand results of the whole past of the Eastern Continent; and the admiring traveller longs to put them aboard the first steamer for home use; but somehow he cannot keep England, France, and Germany healthy, during a fortnight's voyage, and these majestic institutions issue from their state rooms in New York and Boston, the sickly shadow of what charms the conservative American abroad. No, we must make America out of the world's whole past, and the whole European present, *plus ourselves*, and if this latter quantity be false, where is America to come from? How can we know what is good in the world's past, what is valuable in Europe's present; how to adopt, how to combine, how to create, how to organize the life of a continent unless we are free? And free men and women are not extemporized on 4th July or election days, but are formed by a free *culture* —a culture that, beginning with trust in our nature, unfolds all human powers, throws open all fields of thought, leads the soul to the heights that overlook the vast areas of obligation, and sends it forth to become a citizen and a man in the might of Spiritual Power.

Another element in Spiritual Power is Earnestness. I use this term to indicate the whole group of qualities that form the habit of efficient labor. Thousands of well meaning people read books, associate with learned men, take degrees in literary institutions, or mingle in stirring scenes of life, without forming the idea of that habitual labor which is the working power of genius, and the assurance of success. To this Earnestness belongs a perpetual Industry which rejects every plea for laziness, however wreathed in pleasant fancies or disguised in the pretence of duty, that toils on unobserved, and rests only while energy may accumulate. And along with this goes Prudence, jealous of wasted efforts, with clear eyes watching for opportunities to accomplish difficult things in the most decisive way, guarding the thoughts, lips, and life, not to shirk responsibility, but to meet it in the most uncompromising style; a power whose absence brings confusion and defeat upon the most generous mind. And to this we must add Courage, without which Earnestness dwindles to a nervous irritability of the conscience on the side of truth; Courage, that fears not to encounter the eye of a foe, to differ from a friend, to face labor, to cut the meshes of skepticism, to take arms against whatever lurking selfishness would unman the spirit.

Its decisive moments are unknown to the world, for the things that *really* scare men are spectres seen by them alone. Beside these we must gain persistence, the power of doing things again and again, doing our best whether anybody is or is not looking on; for somebody knows of every noble word or deed; that enlists for life, uses failure for a school-master, despises any success that claims to be a finality, and has pressed on out of sight while men are shouting their approbation or displeasure. And what will all this come to without patience; the calm, forgiving, relentless waiting for the result, which keeps the true man firm when his companions fall into discouragement, that sees the end in vision and toils a whole life towards it. In these and similar virtues resides that quality of the soul which, under the name of earnestness, chains observers, wins men, overcomes obstacles and culminates in power.

We shall confess the necessity of this quality when we remember that spiritual power is not an instantaneous, natural endowment or an inheritance, but something into which a faithful man *grows.* No great soul could ever "tell its experience." The autobiographies of great lives surprise us by their meagre outlines; they relate how this admirable person got up in the morning and drank his tea, chatted with his neighbors, went to his study, his work, or his fighting, resting after dinner, saw company and went to sleep—in short, lived outwardly almost as every dunce has lived since Adam. Where is the history of the man's power? Ah, that is what he cannot write, what he knows less about than we suppose, what he sometimes doubts himself. All he or anybody knows is, that moved by the impulse, willing and faithful to conscience, he pushes on, his earnestness like a slow fire burning its way through whatever brushwood or rock obstructs his path. He does not think he has attained, but is dimly conscious of a growing vigor and consistency of being.

And now and then, lifted on the spring-tide of his own power, he is borne into new regions of hope, and feels along his nerves the sublime thrills of an incomprehensible energy, beholds new worlds to conquer, and resolves like an archangel. This is his hour of vision, when like the wanderer among interminable mountains, he comes out upon a new summit, and beholds far below the former peak of his ambition and throws his gaze with eager longing to the blue spectral heights that haunt the horizon line. Well it is for us that we cannot know the mysterious growth of spiritual power; better than such knowledge is the earnestness that drives us towards it with motion as steady and fatal as the march of the systems, or the swing of the sea.

Let me urge this complete earnestness upon the young who hear me. Do not mistake for it the mental neuralgia that afflicts so many American youth. An American is but a man, no law of life has been suspended for his sake, and any outrage of the virtues that make up true earnestness will bring him into the same trouble that besets all transgressors. Rashness, imprudence, caprice, foolhardy and heated action, thinking like chain lightning and doing like the thunderbolt, may be fine fun for a while, but such play turns out the dearest kind of work that must be done over again. "A fast man" is one thing, an earnest man quite another. Jehu the son of Jonathan drives furiously in the year 1858, as old Jehu drove in Bible days. He yokes the unwhipped horses of speculation and over-trading to his chariot of business and vanishes in a cloud of dust, and to-morrow is hauled out of the ditch from beneath the ruins of his equipage by some poor patient donkey that has been plodding on far behind. Jehu drives fast in domestic affairs; up goes the brown stone front, in and out the doors flash Mrs. Jehu and the little Jehus, resplendent in diamonds and taffeta; what a crowd mobs his saloon on reception nights! Alas! one silent gentleman rings the bell, calls Jehu aside, and, lo! the sheriff has dissolved the illusion, and old Slow jogs up to the auction and buys out the concern at a ruinous discount. How Jehu cracks his whip in the Senate. Onward and upward, new worlds to conquer; a fig for justice, hurra for success; man and God stand aside! Alas, the poor creature is only running himself blind and mad, and will soon lie breathless, his hot cheek pressed against the cold adamant of the higher law. Poor Jehu does no better at his books—he may study himself into any of the fifty new American diseases, shriek through high-pressure oratory, write new theories of the universe in extempore trance, rave in the newspapers, and swear upon the stump; old Germany can take the noisy boy on his knee and teach him his A B C's. Jehu is attractive, but his steeds always run away with him. It is a sorry ambition, this rage for being "fast;" better be an earnest man, an earnest woman, and grow as the years grow, and you will see all along your way the bleaching bones of these insane runners for the prize of life.

The crowning element in Spiritual Power is *Purity*. By Purity I mean more than that negative amiability, or general inoffensive habit, whose sphere is the drawing-room and whose resistance to evil culminates in a flood of tears, or a passive submission to violence. The virtue I enforce is the combination of all mental and moral powers in a character that responds to the Divine Perfections, and realizes the ideal of Humanity. In such a character, heroism, strength, firmness, invincible rectitude and uncompromising hostility to evil are the central substances, enveloped and harmonized by enduring love and unaffected grace; for men have yet to learn that power is really not power, till it is dissolved in affection and spiritualized into beauty.

Spiritual Power in its last analysis, is the consolidation of all gifts, acquirements, and opportunities into *Character*. A soul has not possession of its self, till it has banished every lower aim of life; for any partial object, however inspiring, becomes finally a chronic weakness. To cultivate all faculties, to seize every occasion, to acquire all possible learning, skill and experience, for the sake, first and last, always and everywhere of character; to toil in professional life as a help in this grand profession; to value social enjoyment and human affection, not for the pleasure they bring, but the manhood they enlarge; to become a good citizen, that one may be a noble man; to obey the decrees of nature, and wreathe life with joy, that the character may be refined; this is the end of life, this is Spiritual Power, the end of culture. For Character is good in itself, is not a coin to buy happiness, but is the sublime object of human existence in time and eternity.

How such a purpose, inaugurated in youth, aids the man at every step in the acquisition of Spiritual Power, can only be known by joyful experience. How many knotty problems of action does it solve for the young man winding through the mazes of common life. How many confusing dilemmas does it clear up for the young woman ensnared in the cobwebs of false society. A whole class of questionable occupations, perilous associations, and doubtful adventures, that beset every youth, are looked out of sight by the clear, forward-gazing eyes of Purity. Can it be a question to the young man or woman, resolved to make Character the end of life, whether dishonest business, selfish politics, sensual indulgence, calculating marriage without love, followed by an ambitious domestic career without peace, shall be accepted, or rejected? These are questions that bewilder half the world, and to which no refinement of logic will bring a solution, but which answer themselves the moment we step up to the heights of a worthy manhood. How does Purity clear the mind for all investigations; how it stirs the fire of industry; how it consoles and sustains us in failure; how wise it makes us in success; infinite are the modes in which it is our right hand of success in honorable enterprise. It brings the soul into union with the laws of nature, and led by the star of manhood, we go escorted by the servants of Omnipotence, and our best deeds are but the symbol of the grander works done through us.

And no less does Purity serve us in the use of our Power. The vital question with every human being, on which rests the whole claim to manhood is not "*what is the extent of his power; but, how does he use his power?*" Whether the power resides in great possessions, in vast acquirements, in splendid genius, is all the same; whether it has secured lofty position, or yet awaits its fitting place, is not the question; but what motive lies behind it, of what *quality* and *character* is the man who wields it? Divorced from Character, Power is as hateful for its evil as contemptible for its weakness.

There can be no compromise in the use of Power. In proportion to its quantity must it declare itself for good or evil. It is of little importance on which side the moral line a fool stands; he is impotent for good, harmless for evil; but as a man rises above that zero of human ability, the good claims him, the evil fights for him with deadly persistence. Anything short of entire consecration to the Truth is then treason to the Spiritual order of the universe. It is a sin to withhold countenance from the Truth; it is wicked to propose any agreement that admits the supposition that Error has right in the world; it is ruin to go over to the bad side, and be a respectable or a flagrant villain. All such experiments, often as they are tried, come out finally in Spiritual Suicide. A temporary success, however brilliant, is only part of a bad man's retribution, for it brings new responsibilities to be evaded and lays up a fearful account for the day of reckoning—a madness which finally compels sane men to rise and put him down. But Character is an ever growing wisdom, an ever culminating power, a quiet advocate for all men's suffrage: a success whose only question is of time. Happy the youth that has learned this fact out of his books, and teachers, and School years—that Purity is the synonym of Spiritual Power.

Every advance position of man makes Purity more indispensable and evil more destructive. Never was it so important that the power of a people should be wielded by character as to-day in America. What unnumbered curses beset us from a selfish culture! All over society, in every corner of our civilization, swarms this crowd of cultivated mercenaries. Practical men, strong with the gifts of modern science and large experience in affairs, ready to sell their influence for gold and monopoly; women, radiant with beauty, and more radiant with mental gifts and social tact woven into the most subtle power that guides the world, turning traitors to the eternal laws of love and honesty; refined Circassians, glorying in their price at the market-place, where fashion and Plutus bid for womanhood; shrewd men, versed in public affairs who know history, know the law, hold the mysteries of popular influence, and the Chinese puzzle of parliamentary tactics at their fingers' ends, calling out—"Who pays most for the cleverest defence of infamy, the subtlest cheat of the people, the most decisive betrayal of Freedom?" deeply read men of science; men that write books that everybody reads; editors that overlook the nation from their sanctum windows; poets and artists that the refined love and honor; men and women apt in conversation, whose presence is a magic centre in the community; divines who have studied the fathers and overlooked reverent crowds—all for sale—some bought with the pottage of personal comfort, some bribed with the devil's gold, some baited with popular approbation, some purchased with office; spiritual Hessians—each ready to fight for the Truth or against the Truth, according as either gives better pay and rations. This mob of cultivated mercenaries, not the mob of barbarians that make a night of civilization in the heart of the city and hold back the great day in the country, is making our republicanism a jest, and befogging a people in its search after manhood. The masses are driven hither and thither by contrary gusts of passion and interest, and clouds are scaling our zenith, frowning as they climb, because so many able men and women have their price—seem not to know that character in such as themselves is the nation's ballast—that where the culture of a generation is vitiated and debased by sovereign selfishness the crowds below are degraded to base instruments to work its wicked will. Every mercenary powerful mind in America is a gun charged with hot shot aimed at the inflammable citadel of our freedom. Will you, young men, young women of New York, go forth to join this pretorian band? or shall Purity lead you to the ranks of that little army, which hard beset and often driven from the field, bears in its heart the hope of the continent. We can go on with such mental culture as we have; there are clever people enough in the United States, if we can only have Purity to direct the actual energy we have. Oh, could all this skill, this money, this enterprise, this daring heroism, this learning, this popular intelligence, all that is strong in man and lovely in woman, become a weapon in the hand of a genuine national character, what a republic this would be!

We look to the youth of our commonwealth to bring in this reign of Spiritual Power, the antagonist of Pedantry, the result of Freedom and Earnestness culminating in Purity. In the great school of our best civilization, man and woman can be furnished together for the holy mission of civilizing the republic. Each may here be developed in characteristic power, both may here join hands in lofty purpose, together they may swear a great oath against the barbarism that yet shadows our sunniest uplands and broods over all the deep places of the land—one and all, they may resolve to give ignorance, ugliness, superstition and evil no quarters. Happy are you who are thus ready to meet your duties, for outside yonder door of maturity waits the proudest State of modern times, encircled by her children, to welcome you to a noble office. In every vocation, in every community, wherever you may be and whatever you may be called to do, in your fidelity reposes the hope of society. Go forth, young men, young women, and *mock this ideal* of power by the glorious reality of a cultivated and Christian State.

## VIII.

# THE CAPITOL

AND

# THE HIGHER LAW.

The sight-seer in search of gorgeous monuments of imperial dominion, would not linger on the hill crowned by the modest capitol of New York; but he who would behold in a public edifice the representative of a peculiar and protracted struggle for a Christian Democracy, need go no farther than the city of Albany. From the steps of our capitol he may overlook the scenes of the two most important political assemblies ever called in America—the meeting of colonial Governors in July, 1748, to deliberate on the scheme of taxing the people, and the convention of delegates in June, 1754, at which the plan of a Federal Union was presented by Franklin, who lived to see his early dream mocked by a more majestic reality. Out of the former of these conventions came the oppression of

Great Britain, out of the latter the American Union. Against that despotism no State rendered more signal services than New York, and New York is now the State whose final position will decide whether that Union shall degenerate to a new Empire, or advance to a Christian Republic. Our unpretending capitol sits upon its hill, the symbol of a political struggle in New York whose history, when truly written, will be a permanent accession to the annals of humanity.

Massachusetts was founded by the radical English mind of the 17th century; and starting from Plymouth Rock, the idea of *individual freedom* has scaled the Rocky Mountains and this year comes back from the Pacific shore the response to the Pilgrims in the new free Constitution of Oregon. Virginia was founded by the representatives of the English gentry of the 17th century; and the landed monopoly and chattel slavery of fifteen American States is but the lengthened shadow of that British aristocracy, ever creeping farther south to find in Central America the home now denied it in the North. To New York, seated midway between these radical States, was given the problem of moulding a population, the most diverse of any that has colonized this continent, into the most powerful Republic of modern times.

To briefly recall the elements of this great executive process and set forth the supreme law of a Christain citizenship for our Empire State, is the object of this discourse.

The genius of despotism stood by the cradle of New York civilization and has never ceased to threaten till the present day. The State was founded in 1614 by a trading company from a nation where popular liberty was then unknown: and from the possession of the Holland merchants it became, in 1668, the manor of the Duke of York. Feudalism was thus established on the Hudson River that for two centuries controlled her destinies in its two most odious forms of a great landed aristocracy and negro chattel slavery. Under the shadow of this oppression, popular intelligence languished and has slowly fought its way up to its present attainment. The diversity of nationality which always made our largest city a caravansary for the whole civilized world, and has planted obstinate prejudices of race all over our wide domain, long prevented that entire fusion of the people which is the soul of enterprise and the spirit of a compact Republicanism. The central and commanding position of New York in the original colonies has always exposed her civilization to formidable dangers. Her northern frontier long bore the brunt of French invasion, leagued with the most formidable of the Indian tribes. Her commercial metropolis was selected by English tyranny as the most suitable place for repeated experiment in despotism. On the banks of her great rivers the American revolution twice turned a short corner; and our Highlands were the watch-tower, and fortress of that long struggle for independence. Very early did her political importance as the opponent of Virginia involve her in the corrupting whirlpool of National affairs, and with the Administration of Washington commenced that conflict between federal and State patronage which still debauches every generation of her politicians. On the island of Manhattan has sprung up the commercial exchange of the old and new worlds, and the gold of two continents is every year cast into her scale, against the rights of man. Her landed aristocracy has perished before the more subtile invading power of the gigantic corporations that are fighting in the dark to replace the feudalism of the landowner by the oligarchy of the merchant: and the last twenty-five years has witnessed the conversion of her chief cities into little foreign nationalities, challenging the right and defying the power of the government to treat them as vital portions of the commonwealth.

But on the other side of the cradle of our Hercules, stood the genius of Freedom. Among the emigrants to New Netherlands came many smarting from the tyranny that had devastated their European homes and driven them exiles for liberty across the sea. Out of this element arose the struggle for representation which convulsed the Dutch colony, and was not staid by English power till it reached its goal, and in 1683, sixty-nine years after the settlement of Albany, gained that first assembly of seventeen representatives of the people of New York. For ninety-two years the history of that little Assembly marks the rugged road by which the colony fought its way up to independence. Brow-beaten and tempted and prorogued by a succession of insolent British governors, backed by a subservient council, it had a charmed existence, for it was the concentration of the free side of colonial life. It rallied again and again on the struggle for the revenue, protested in documents that might stir the blood of the most supple politician (if such individuals ever read the records of the Fathers); and when it succumbed to the rising storm of foreign wrath in 1775, out of its ashes sprung the Provincial Congress, which on the 9th of July, 1776, ratified the Declaration of Independence: in 1777 adopted the first constitution which for forty-four years was the organic law of the State: sat armed during the war wherever it could find a refuge, and with George Clinton for Governor, took its place in the Union in 1797.

Thanks to the tyranny that in 1663 placed the Judiciary of New York in complete dependence on the crown, a fire was kindled that has burned till every court in our great State is now created by the people. The very diversity of our population has always made ecclesiastical tyranny an impossibility. Every attempt by Catholic or Protestant church to control the State has brought down the people in an avalanche on its head; and every party formed on a sectarian platform has vanished as soon as it was born. And as a providential compensation for the temptations of our central position, our people have gained from it a certain largeness of view and facility of dealing with public affairs which has developed an executive power which, always eminent, has finally eclipsed every American State. Half a century ago, began that wondrous tide of emigration from the eastern hive, which has built up a new nation west of Albany, the ally of freedom on the Hudson, taking up the battle, where the old patriots left it, and carrying it on to victory. The day when De Witt Clinton discovered that to link his name with the Erie Canal was a more permanent honor than to become President of the Republic, inaugurated an era of popular enterprise, which in sending a railroad to every corner of the State, and creating the daily press of our great cities, and arousing the masses everywhere to activity, has become the missionary of freedom which, now, under the name of an "Emigrant Aid Society," has taken the field against piracy in Central America, and aspires to the colonization of a continent with free men. And, best of all, the free school is now fairly on its iron legs which will run to and fro, and never tire, till intelligence and freedom pervade our illustrious commonwealth.

This great conflict rapidly approaches its crisis, and no man doubts on whose banners victory will alight. A few more efforts to remodel the institutions of New York, on a scale demanded by her present growth and her greater future; the last relict of feudal vassalage and disability of race swept away; a few years more of unrelenting devotion to liberty; will forever consecrate the policy of our State to the rights of men. And when the Empire State finally assumes the leadership of the host of a Christian civilization, the revolution that began in 1615 in her Broadway will close by the assurance that through the countless ages of the future, the dominant and creative power on the western continent will be the civilization of the Saviour's golden rule: and over her avenues of travel, on her ships, and upon the wings of her press, the evangel of freedom will fly to all the nations of the world.

Citizens of New York, this is your past; your work is before you; your destiny beckons from the future. Standing in your Capital City, let me, as a citizen of your State, a citizen of the United States, and a teacher of Christianity, speak of your obligations, and direct your contemplation to the eternal law of God, which embosoms all earthly justice, and controls the affairs of men. In no spirit of sect or party, in no personal controversy with those who solicit the votes of to-day by blasphemy against Him who endureth forever, let me expound that *Higher Law* which holds every soul in the Republic by sanctions, as profound as the humanity of man, as everlasting as the divinity of the most High.

The conception of a government by the whole people is the inevitable result of the Christian idea of God and man. God is the Father of all men, and has made of one blood all nations upon the earth. The inhabitants of this world are all his children, inheritors of His nature and heirs of His immortality. Mankind is a family, related in its every member more closely than any earthly ties can bind together. The sole obligation of humanity as a whole, and in its every individual, is love to God and love to man. On this foundation of adamant rests our claim for human rights and democratic government.

For the government of God is not the ruling of an arbitrary despot over an empire of abject slaves, but the training of a world of immortal children into holiness of character through a moral discipline. Every citizen in God's vast republic is free, and, encompassed by influences human and divine, decides this crowning question of character alone. The inevitable law of a God of love is ever before, the wondrous agencies of an ineffable benignity invite and the certainty of retribution warn him, but no arbitrary fate drags him into heaven or thrusts him into perdition. No prisoner of despotic justice, man walks a free citizen of a divine government that respects his natural rights as a living immortal soul, and rules only to develop that soul into an ever expanding image of its Creator.

Then must every human government, in imitation of God's, rule men only to aid in the unfolding of a character founded on love, and the creation of a state which shall be the kingdom of heaven. In such a state no man or class can assume a power which God himself does not claim; to own and dispose of men by arbitrary selfishness. The natural rights of every citizen must be respected, and to every one must be guaranteed freedom to act out his human capacities and become what his Creator intended. The right of a man, a class, a race, to plunder the least soul of its freedom in such use of its faculties is no "divine right," for no divine being thus governs men; but a satanic travesty of God's supremacy. Human government thus becomes one of the agencies by which God educates His children into the citizenship of eternity; a humble imitation of His republic wherein love reigns supreme, and justice is but a divine method of its administration. All authority of human government is from its resemblance to this government of God; there is no other real authority among men, and in proportion as it departs from this law of love and reverence for human freedom does it forfeit its claim on our reverence and obedience. All just government is by divine right, and while acting according to God's law of love, claims our respect by divine authority; and to disobey it is to renounce the allegiance to the Father of all; to drop our high citizenship in the divine order and become the slave of disorder and its father, the devil.

But where resides the original authority to institute such government on earth, which shall be one of God's agents to mould this world into the kingdom of heaven? The source of all secondary authority in human affairs is the individual soul. Every intelligent being is first and last and forever, a citizen of God's great republic, and can never become an alien therefrom by any action of man. Whatever human arrangement he accepts, is with the full understanding that he shall be required to do nothing inconsistent with this primary obligation; *whatever constitution he swears to obey, the very oath is an affirmation that he will not disobey God's law of love;* for *what a blasphemous absurdity to swear in the name of God to disobey God.* And in every contested question between human government and the individual, the final appeal is to the higher and prior citizenship of the divine republic through conscience, its ever-present deputy in the soul. Such appeal is always heard on high, though scorned below, and in the long run every individual has his rights, to the confusion of a world in opposition. Conscience, the final deliberate voice of the soul, after all the evidence is in and the whole ground of duty has been surveyed, is the law of human duty; *not because the individual invariably will go right; but the obedience to conscience is the recognition of the supreme obligations to obey God's law of love forever.* This right to appeal to the higher law no man does or can lay down on his entrance into any association of men; could he, the renunciation would be the wreck of his manhood, and from a living soul he would fall to the degradation of a mechanical power.

With this reservation of appeal to God, man may enter the government which comes nearest the divine order, because in it the natural right to free development is best secured—a Republic. Here a majority rules to-day as the servant of the whole, subject in its act to the revision of every individual through free thought, speech, or influence, and liable at stated periods to be called to deliver up its trust, or change its policy. For the majority of the Republic is not the despot of the minority, but the servant of the whole; and when it comes down from its lofty elevation of acting for the best welfare of the whole state, and seeks to punish or oppress the minority, the act is not civil government, but barbarian piracy. And when a majority, by corrupt acts, bribery, the terrorism or seductions of power, or any way but an appeal to its services to the people, seeks to perpetuate its dominion, it is usurpation and ungodly tyranny. But where the majority serves the state, full in view of the conscience of every man, always subject to periodical dismissal or approval, there is the nearest approach to the divine order now possible on earth.

So is the government of the people, by the people through a representative majority, the best imitation of God's government now attainable, and claims the obedience and coöperation of every individual according as it realizes to him the divine order. Then is our republicanism founded on the authority of the Higher Law. Then is Democracy but another name for the Golden Rule. And the citizen at the ballot-box, the legislator in the Capitol, the Judge on the bench, the Executive in the chair of state, are all agents selected by the divine wisdom, to promote justice and holiness on earth. The least these agents can safely do the better for the man, since human government is not to supersede the divine, but chiefly to protect man from injustice, and place the weakest and strongest in the position to freely develop his nature into the stature of the perfect man in Christ.

And herein appears the folly of that Democracy which openly denounces God and proclaims a state free from every moral restraint. For if there be no God, as certain of the Red Republicans say, pray what becomes of the rights of man? If the soul be only the temporary result of material combination, with no claim to spirituality, where are its natural rights? Talk of the right of Freedom, to think, speak, act in a being that has no living soul, no radical moral obligation, no human allegiance to a creative mind, and an immortal humanity? Why, such a race as this is not a human race, but a great machine, whose cranks and wheels, and pulleys all spin around the laws of a remorseless fate, where freedom cannot exist and progress is a dream, and life itself, but the submission of the soul to the animal. We can understand that the suffering millions of Europe, maddened by the religious pretensions of their oppressors in church and state, should in their frenzy imagine that religion is itself their chief oppressor. But that a man should laboriously reason away his soul to prove his right to freedom is like the miser who killed himself to realize on his life insurance. The true remedy for Europe, is to unmask the hypocrites who steals the clothes of religion to serve the devil of their ambition, to explode the divine rights of kings by the assertion of the divine paternity of God, and the divine nature of man, his immortal child, and compel a satanic selfishness to abdicate in favor of a Christian civilization, founded on the love of the brother. May the day be far distant, when the pious heroism and devotional patriotism of our fathers shall give way either to the moon-struck meanderings of an atheistic republicanism, or the frantic appetite for tyranny by which men give melancholy evidence how deeply the iron of old oppression is rusted into their innermost souls.

Therefore, when we affirm that every citizen of New York should carry his religion into the sphere of his political conduct, we neither assert any union of church and state, nor claim any right of ecclesiastical dictation of legislation, nor justify the position outside of society assumed by a sincere but mistaken class of public reformers. No visionary and impracticable scheme of conduct, but the most practical and possible application of the everlasting laws of right to every act of public and private life is our demand. We reaffirm the simple truth announced by Jesus Christ: "Whatsoever ye would that men should do to you, do you even so to them." With every competent expounder of Christianity, since the day of Christ, we maintain that every member of human society is bound by an eternal obligation to gain a holy character founded on love to God and man, and to act from that character in every human relation. As the family, the market, the pulpit, the saloon claim our best manhood and womanhood, that home, trade, prophesy, and pleasure, may all be elevated by religion, so is the realm of citizenship no exception to this; but whoever goes in there shall carry his entire manhood and abate not one jot or tittle of his Christian integrity.

It has been affirmed that while the preacher should expound the abstract law of right, the statesman should ignore it in favor of expediency. *A true expediency is only a righteous man doing all the good that present circumstances permit as a stepping-stone to better achievements;* and any other expediency is as disgraceful in the senate as in the church. Strange morality this—that *while a man sits in his pew on Sunday where he can do nothing, he may acknowledge the obligations of God's law; but when he sits in the Capitol and holds the civilization of New York in the hollow of his hand, he is no longer bound by such obligation. Could Satan ask for a more complete license than this?* Life is the place where men prove their religious character; in the church they can only meditate and be instructed. What a caricature of Christianity to glow with sacred fires before the altar, and cast off the eternal law of love upon the temple steps. Let no sophistry of this kind delude the citizens of our State; for only on condition that every soul in New York labors for the highest Christian character and throws its whole force persistently on the side of righteousness in every corner of life, will our great domain lead the world as the first republic.

This religious obligation holds every inhabitant of New York in his relations to that form of social affairs into which he is born. For the evils of that system of government into which we are called by the fiat of Providence we are not responsible. They are the results of the wickedness of those who have gone before, and society as we find it at our appearance in life is our field of operations. Our whole duty concerning it is to reform as much evil and conserve as much good therein as we can by the healthy, constant exercise of our best powers through life. This done, our character is guiltless for that evil we cannot remove, and human affairs are left on a higher basis for our existence. Each inhabitant of the State should labor according to his opportunity in the best place he can honorably occupy and all endeavor to leave society a more heavenly thing than they found it.

What does this obligation demand of us as citizens, rulers and subjects of the law?

It demands that each individual of the Empire State shall gratefully accept all the faculties, rights, privileges and opportunities into which he is born, and out of these materials mould the best possible character and throw the whole force of manhood or womanhood in the scale of a Christian Democracy.

The *voter* is the most privileged person in our State; for, in addition to all the opportunities of moral influence, his yearly vote can shape the political policy of a great community and may be the turning point in the destiny of America. To say that he should use such a position, the highest in the world, to create a lofty religious character, apply the law of love in every sphere of life, and employ his political opportunities for the largest good of man, is a truism that is ignored not because it is unreasonable, but because it conflicts with the wickedness that scorns reason and right. The spectacle of a voter in New York using his whole weight of character and opportunity to hinder or crush out any portion of God's family is one over which evil spirits may well rejoice, and angels veil their faces in shame and grief. No man can prescribe the course of policy of any individual; that is an affair of his own conscience; but he may command every voting citizen, on the authority of

God's law, to use his glorious privilege to the utmost and follow the highest leading of his unseduced conscience in his relations to the State. And whatever inconvenience might occasionally result from a "crotchety conscience" in such case would be overcome a thousand fold by the advantages of righteousness in public affairs.

The religious obligation to the State holds that portion of our male citizens who are yet denied the right of suffrage, either from unjust prejudice against color, or a judicious preparatory naturalization. Some of the worst dangers to the community may arise from the notion that the members of this class are released from the duties of Christian patriotism. Under their present disabilities they are blessed beyond their brethren in other ages and nations. Will they use their influence to advance their own freedom and the general good, or to breed discord and disgrace by degeneracy of character and disobedience to law? Let these men remember, that if still denied the crowning privilege of citizenship, they are called by God to a determined advocacy of the rights of the oppressed. And on no man is there such a blessing as upon him who employs his own misfortune to gain the sympathy and espouse the cause of his brother in suffering. Every virtuous and patriotic alien in New York is strengthening the hands of those who are using their own privilege to fight his battles; every wicked and riotous man of this class is confirming the hostile purpose of those who yet deny his rights.

Next in outward privilege are the women of the Empire State: deprived of many social and political privileges by society, yet possessing, beyond their sisters of any state or age, the sacred opportunities of womanhood. Their political duties are not to be overlooked, because of certain disabilities. *To them, chiefly, is intrusted the moulding of character in youth—the greatest earthly opportunity; and the most intimate relation to, and subtlest influence over the heart of manhood—the second privilege of humanity.* The voice of God commands them to use this central and all-pervading influence for the highest good of the State. A race of mothers such as the women of New York can now become, might educate a race of men who would count it the highest privilege of their manhood to welcome them to every position they might claim. We cannot understand the feelings of any woman who permits herself to be crushed by her position, and neglects the practice of the most precious human obligations. Her political duties are no less important than those of man: let her perform them to the utmost, and if society refuse her what she then asks, it will be the first time American men have denied woman anything on which she has insisted.

To the youth of New York what an invitation is given to prepare themselves by the largest human culture for the republic of another generation, compared with whose grandeur of resource and inspiring obligations, our present State is but a family party. Do not fear, young men and women of New York, that you can know too much, or be too noble for the inheritance that awaits you. Heirs of the most splendid heritage of modern times, become the illustrious men and women whom it will gracefully adorn.

No inhabitant of New York can rightly separate himself from his obligations to society. The least privileged has a protection and opportunity deserving a boundless gratitude and claiming his best devotion to the State. It is a spurious assertion of individuality to affect to stand aside from this great family and criticise the doings of other men: for man was made for society, and his mission is to bear the law of love into human affairs, and share in the toils of the wise and good for a better day.

The law of God requires no impractical behavior in the rulers chosen to posts of influence in the Empire State. It does forbid that wretched traffic in offices by candidates, which makes the very name of free institutions a jest. *I know of no good a ruler can do to New York, which will compensate for the evil of bribing one voter, or corrupting the public mind by one falsehood.* Every structure of justice built over a defiled franchise, or a dishonest system of party machinery, is a house built on the crust of an abyss. Liberty suffers for every unveracity perpetrated in her name: and, *to buy a man in New York even to vote against despotism is to enslave a man to-day for the uncertain expectation of liberating humanity to-morrow.* The enemies of man will not heed our warnings: but on the escutcheon of the friends of man, let no stain of suspicion abide: for surely as they endeavor to gain power by any unworthy arts, will the defence of human rights be taken from them and given to those whose pure hands are fit to bear the banner of justice.

The legislator is not the attorney of his party; but first the servant of God and next the servant of the whole State. *His sole duty is to reënact as much of the law of God as the people can now sustain and enforce, and by his whole influence to educate society to a higher political morality.* To the judiciary is committed the office of interpreting the law and presiding over the administration of justice, and if there be a crime in America it is the prostitution of that exalted position to the uses of any party or interest lower than man.

When in the legislative, judical or executive sphere a controversy occurs, *let the ruling always be in favor of man—who was not made for laws and courts, but courts and laws and constitutions for him.* The organic law of the State is not an iron frame into which the public officer is to be driven to petrify into a machine, but the best realization of God's law that the State has so far obtained; *hence to interpret it downwards in favor of the barbarism of the past, is treason against humanity. A true statesmanship interprets organic laws upwards in favor of the civilization that is to come.* Read history and behold how every politician who has interpreted the organic laws of states downward towards barbarism has filed off into the limbo of human contempt and execration, and every statesman who has read constitutions upwards towards man has walked up to a throne where he now sits and receives the admiration of the world.

Were the law of God thus applied in the sphere of citizenship and official duty, the question of obedience to human laws would at once be simplified. For the case would hardly occur that a law could be enacted by a righteous people which a good man could not obey. But we are not yet in the millennium, and our rulers sometimes forget God and man and command us to do what a Christian manhood refuses to accept. A good man is not released from his obligations to the State by a bad law. He is still a citizen, though government turns against him, and his duty centres in sustaining a true order while he seeks to elevate the public conception of law. His duty increases in proportion to the degeneracy of legislation, and instead of quitting politics in disgust because of its corruption, the best men should especially go in then and turn the scale. A godly citizen will submit to much wrong for the sake of order: he will patiently use every legal means of redress, every force of moral influence, and count a life well spent in shaping a righteous policy that will gradually overcome the wrong. And if brought to a crisis, where the law commands him to commit a wicked act, he can testify his reverence to the State by suffering her penalties while he asserts his manhood by refusing to disobey God. This has been in every past age one of the most efficient means of reform; and no men have done more to advance a good government than those martyrs who have suffered or died because they would not commit sin against God and humanity.

I cannot recognize the right of armed revolution by the citizens of the State while the Republic preserves its reality. While men can speak and write and vote and hold office they may suffer for the right; but to grasp the sword is to dissolve the whole social fabric, to fall into anarchy and trust to luck for a reorganization of society. But under the forms of a republic a real despotism may creep in, and a minority be deprived of all just rights through the forms of law. Then revolution is the just appeal; because physical life is not the most sacred thing on earth, and when it and the natural rights of the soul are confronted, the soul must stand and the body must fall. But this right of revolution is to be exercised only in the last extremity and never should be perverted to the ends of party agitation, or used to excuse the toilsome duties of peaceful reform.

I am not ignorant of the possible abuse of these extreme rights of the subject of human law; but those who assert the contrary doctrine seem to be ignorant of the abuses of their own. If the one may drive a fanatical citizen to his destruction, or agitate a State with fears of anarchy, the other is the creed of despotism from the foundation of the world, and if adopted in a republic would leave every man and every minority at the unmitigated mercy of a wicked majority. The man who preaches unconditional submission to human law, preaches the political ideas of oriental tyranny, and if it be treason, as some say, to refuse to sin and suffer for that refusal, what shall we call the crime of sustaining an irresponsible despotism in the name of law? This right of resistance, so far from treasonable, is the real safeguard of the Republic. There are few classes of men, there are few parties in the State which would not commit enormities beyond endurance, did they not know that man never has, never will, and never ought to submit to the last extremity of wrong, but will now, as he ever has, overthrow the tyrant that drives him to the wall, or perish in the conflict for human rights. While religion would guard this right of disobedience, and the appeal to the God of battles from every abuse, it would still assert it as the last human safeguard in every state of society the world has yet attained.

These ideas of a religious patriotism are no figments of philosophical speculation, but the daily bread of life for the citizens of our Commonwealth. On their hearty acceptance and application, depends our success in the long struggle of two hundred and forty-four years for the freedom of man in this goodly domain of nature. New York has the materials for a magnificent nation, and her first duty is by all justice and righteousness to lift herself ever higher in the rank of noble States that stand for man; and her second duty is like unto it, to throw her entire influence on the side of a Christian Democracy in the Federal Union. When the Empire State shall have made up her mind for freedom, and spoken it in words that cannot be mistaken, and cannot be taken back, will the ungodly scramble for despotism in the national councils come to a swift end. From the midst of an age of conflict, from the summit of a crisis in the affairs of a Continent, rises the call as of an angel's voice to stand upright for Liberty, the cause of God and man. Shall the call be heard? When will New York spurn the rewards of tyranny, which endure but for a day, and accept the perils of that defence of freedom which ripens into the enduring glory of mankind?

# IX.

## THE STUDIOS;

### OR,

### ART IN NEW YORK.

THE most striking work of art, in the most attractive studio in the Capital City, is Palmer's model for his collossal group; "*The Landing of the Pilgrims.*" When elevated to its place in the pediment of a great public structure, this admirable work will afford a worthy symbol of the mission of Art in a Republican State. The barren landscape, haunted by the wolf and the savage, and brooded over by the wintry sky, incloses a group that represents the chief forces of a Christian civilization in their true relations. A strong man half reclines upon the cold ground, impatient of his overpowering fatigue. Between the shivered trunks of two gigantic trees, kneels another in meek resignation to a mysterious Providence. A venerable scholar bows his head in a prayer, that elevates his human knowledge to a divine wisdom. A boy clings to the arm of a maiden, and a little girl nestles by the knees of a youth; all in characteristic ways, oppressed or excited by the strange scene. A young man leans upon his axe. A soldier bows his head with arms folded in stern devotion. A young woman kneels in pious trust, and a mother folds her late born child to her bosom, in overflowing gratitude to the Heavenly love; while in the centre of the group, stands the majestic form of the Religious Teacher, with outstretched arms, and face upturned in a petition that binds all hearts in one, and prophecies a state, founded upon the Eternal Law. Every figure is representative of a vital force in American society. The bond of union is no tyrant's mandate, nor priestly dogma, but the voluntary unity of free souls, in the sublime idea of consecration to the Father of all. And glowing in every feature and attitude, and enfolding the whole group in an atmosphere of wondrous grace, is that austere beauty which descends from heaven to earth only when all the elements of humanity concentrate in due proportion to form the kingdom of God.

Let this achievement of a son of the Empire State, be our Symbol of an Art, which is no tasteful ornament of a factitious gentility, but the ideal-ization of our Commonwealth. No bird of foreign plumage flying over the sea, and perching on our metropolitan roofs, is the art which we celebrate, but that central Spirit of Beauty which apprehends and reproduces the splendors of our nature, penetrates to the sublimity of our idea of humanity, and through the carved marble, on the painted canvas, in the blended sounds of music, by the proportions of architecture, and the arrangements of a free industry, in the higher loveliness of home, and the graces and pleasures of a society as generous as refined, proclaims the Harmony of a Civilization, which, founded on the reverence for God and man in the soul of every inhabitant of New York, shall rise into the well-built fabric of a Republican State, great and glorious in its fidelity to the Eternal Rule of Love.

The State of New York has not withholden her tribute to the progress of Art in America. Among the earliest associations for the promotion of good taste in our country was the Academy of Fine Arts in our chief city, established in 1804, by the exertions of such men as Chancellor Livingston, De Witt Clinton and Robert Fulton. In 1826, was founded the National Academy of Design by the energy of the Artists of the same city, led by one whose name is forever connected with the Magnetic Telegraph, the crowning romance of Modern Life. At different times since, other associations have arisen in various portions of the State, which deserve the praise of awakening the inhabitants of a growing commonwealth to the claims of artistic cultivation. In the honorable array of names devoted to the arts none are more worthy than those who were born upon our soil or have been drawn hither by our opportunities for the practice of their high profession. And whatever may be the claims of other States in special refinement, the united voice of the country now declares our greatest city the centre of artistic influences for America. Within the memory of young men this door to European culture and refinement has been thrown wide open, and henceforth the old world will be laid under tribute for her best treasures to grace the life of the metropolis of the western continent. And by its commanding position our State must become the grand distributor of these influences through the vast area from the Atlantic to the Pacific shores. The social ideas and the conceptions of art which prevail in our commonwealth must, by the necessities of that position, become the most powerful instructors of millions of our countrymen. Elected by Providence to guide the youthful taste of a nation on whose fate the hopes of human freedom are now staked; with what purity of heart and energy of patriotic enthusiasm should we gird ourselves to the high task of making New York, now greatest in power, chief in the nobler eminence of a refinement that is the form of justice and love.

From our central and commanding position two decided tendencies in Artistic Life have already appeared. In many wealthy and cultivated circles of our cities no one can mistake a sincere prejudice in favor of those ideas of man and society which are the soul of old world despotism. This idea of man proceeds logically to the European idea of refinement as associated with a permanent nobility of wealth, rank, or cultivation and art as the finest luxury of an aristocracy rather than the idealization of a people's existence. This belief appears in that wholesale imitation of foreign society, amusements, and arts which turns in disgust from the vital developments of native civilization and aims at building a little Europe in the cities of New York, which shall give down the law of life to the benighted freemen of the Empire State.

In opposition to this effort to reproduce an old world conception of refinement, we everywhere discover the vigorous growth of that indescribable and original taste, which is known all over the civilized world as *New Yorkism.* In its best appearance it is the vigorous assertion of an enthusiastic and confident individuality. The true New Yorker firmly believes himself the most splendidly endowed and circumstanced creature of God's earth. He identifies himself with the greatness of his State, and from this mount of vision generously dispenses himself among the rest of mankind as their various needs may demand. When bounded by the limits of moral law, this character with its inspiring swing of executive force, the bewildering grandeur of its imagination and the contagious generosity of its sentiments, is one of the most irresistible ever let loose on this planet, and contains the elements of immense success or fearful wreck in American affairs. But while we are occasionally inspired with its highest manifestations, we are too often shocked and disgusted with the splendid selfishness and magnificent vulgarity that attend its lower demonstrations. Our new prosperity is playing such antics in every town and village as shock every mind of true refinement. In the audacity of a social aristocracy seated on its heap of gold; in the frightful sensuality of multitudes of first people from New York to Niagara; in the ostentatious style of building, upholstery, dress and equipage, and the steamboat manners and expensive pleasures by which hosts of our young people vainly attempt to become the gentlemen and ladies they never can be until they return to nature and common sense; and in that capacity of miscellaneous enthusiasm which leaves our metropolitan mind the victim to any powerful excitement from the horrors of a Burdell tragedy, or the fervors of a Great Awakening to the showy follies of a Broadway reception of a popular demagogue or the pompous funeral of a native bully; we are ever reminded that our native development of taste is still dashing through the low grounds of materialism and in danger of being swamped in the slough of a new barbarism.

Yet between these dangers of a servile worship of foreign ideas and a native barbarian luxury, we have no hesitation in choosing the tendency to *New Yorkism.* We know its present immorality and vulgarity, but this is not the whole, nor the most *vital* part of its life. *It is the people of New York* trying to *create a society and art expressive of their existence.* As such we hail its belief in individual man, its grandeur of purpose, its splendid generosity, its irresistible enthusiasm, and believe in these great elements is vigorous life to shake itself clear of the ridiculous and wicked habits that now deform its character. Every first effort of a whole people for refinement is necessarily rude and somewhat wrong-headed and low-hearted; but in the sincerity with which New York is rushing towards a splendid ideal, is a prophecy of success. And we can only praise that confident and enthusiastic sense of power, without which no great people can get out of the woods. A self-depreciating, finical, drawing-room refine ment, may be a pleasant guest at an evening entertainment in certain quarters, but it is a poor weapon to cut down the American forests of ignorance, vulgarity and sin, vanquish the thousand foes of freedom, and lay the corner-stone of a glorious State, deep and strong enough to bear up the majestic temple of a Christian society. We are not on the side of those who would detract from the refinement of the past and the old world. Thank God for all that has been and is there of beauty and cultivation. But New York has a better destiny than to go down on her knees before a class refinement, that dates from the contempt of man; even the destiny of inaugurating a refinement that includes the whole people of a great State. Let her take her stand boldly and hopefully on man and work for him, and as she advances in her sublime toil, generously appropriate every vital and congenial element of foreign or past culture that can be wrought into her web of beauty; and while withholding no admiration from the few souls whose genius and fame are of the world and for all time, still keep her footstep on her own soil and her eye lifted upward towards the rising sun and the "Excelsior" that inspired the faith of the fathers to make her what she is. *For our art must be the idealization of man in his native dignity, growing amid the circumstances of a new world into a nobler social state than the earth has yet beheld; an art to which all refinements of the old time and all culture of foreign lands shall finally become tributary: and which can afford to be young and crude for a century in hope of a glorious maturity, which shall be a new descent of Beauty from Heaven to man.*

We insist on the fidelity of New York to her best native taste as the chief condition of asserting her position as the dispenser of ideas of beauty in the Republic. The path to American art is the same that was opened by the immortal declaration of our national independence. The true culture of every nation is the idealization of its deepest conviction and highest admiration in art and character; and no people can permanently be attracted by what is not rooted in their most profound national life Every ordinary success in the realm of the beautiful has been achieved by obedience to this law.

The sculpture, and architecture, and poetry of Greece were only the majestic idealization of what all Greeks believed of man. If it still remains the grandest monument to physical beauty and intellectual power ever erected by human genius, it is because symbolic of one view of humanity which will never be repeated on so complete a scale. The painting, poesy and architecture of the great Catholic artists of the middle ages, were the highest representation of that sentiment of adoration for a Divine Polity which changed a barbarous Europe into the forms of modern civilization: and the permanence of this art is assured because the world can never again so entirely prostrate itself before this idea. Who does not know that the German music of the last century is the most subtle interpreter of the wondrous German character and civilization; and must forever remain a world apart, wherein humanity may read this phase of its varied history.

The most characteristic political genius of American civilization struck the key note of her art as the prophecy of her Republicanism in the sublime preamble to the Declaration of Independence.

Our nationality can become a commanding and enduring force in human affairs, only by fidelity to the belief in man, there announced. Man, the centre of the created universe, the crown of God's work and the brightest suggestion of His glory; under divine guidance capable of self-government in all things; instructed here in a school of moral and social freedom, for the larger realization of his destiny hereafter, is the corner-stone of American existence. On this rock of adamant must we build in our national art, or the foundations of our most showy imitations of foreign ideas will be undermined and the memory of our servility in the domain of beauty pass away from the earth.

Every success of the mind of New York in idealizing past ideas of man, however graceful and complete in appearance, will be only the small success of a clique, and recognized only as imitation of what can never be twice done for eternity. But the sincere endeavor to symbolize her best idea of man will abide, however rude may be its first endeavors. Many a page in the daily journal filled with the hot blood of our crude aspiration for freedom will endure beyond the most elegant reproduction of a literature that is passing away. And many an American artist of hopeful powers, is now laboriously paddling his craft back into the ideas of the middle ages only to be lost in it gilded haze, while others of feebler skill but sterner fidelity will be borne along the current of our life to the haven of an honorable fame. But that fame will be proportioned to the faith in the most profound ideas of the Republic.

There are many ways of believing in man, and the civilization of our Commonwealth is now befogged in the mists and bogs of a sensual "New Yorkism." It is easy for our young artists to drink of this highwine of our luxurious selfishness, till in their heady enthusiasm they sink to the representation of the material side of society and that part of nature where the brute and man unite in a common admiration. If they are satisfied with the money, and flatulent praise and hectic notoriety which comes from the idealization of a "rowdy" nature and a "fast" humanity, they may be safely left to their doom. But the young men and women who swear eternal fealty on the altar of man's spiritual dignity, and paint, carve, build, sing, live from that with a persistence that will resist every surge of popular sensuality and delusion, will be known and loved in the New York that is to be. Therefore, let every wise man free himself from all suspicions of a refinement that is less than the symbol of a paramount reverence for the soul as the brightest image of God; believing that no vulgarity is so fatal in the end as that which despises one human being, and no beauty will endure save that which mirrors the eternal love of God.

With this idea possessing his soul, let the citizen of New York wander over his own superb domain of nature and envy no man. For whether he meditates the fair picture of his Metropolitan City, blending with her surrounding waves in the golden dimness of an October afternoon; or from Catskill's summit beholds the valley of the Hudson smitten by the morning sun; or floats over the liquid mystery of Lake George and contemplates her silent mountains and enchanted shores; or from the towers of Utica, queen of inland towns, sees Oneida's fields sloping upwards to her encircling hills; or in the rail car exults in the grandeur that hurries past the traveller over Erie's path of splendor; or in the tossing skiff uncovers his face and gazes upward where the rejoicing sea bounds over Niagara's summit; or from out the storm of spray on the "Maid of the Mist" beholds through watery vistas the emerald gates of Paradise swinging amid the flitting glory of a thousand vanishing rainbows; or, tired of society, wanders off amid the awful summits of the Adirondack, and in the solitude of endless streams and boundless woods finds himself in his eternal union with the Author of creation; everywhere is her nature the wondrous type of his soul's destiny and the subtlest symbol of his earthly career.

Then let him rejoice to know that nowhere on this commonwealth does the land overlay the spirit, for 600,000 freemen own its 13,000,000 cultivated acres and its wildernesses invite the occupation of thousands more. So is the earth in its native features and its cultivated aspects, adjusted to its lord, and man beholds therein his garden of industry and his emblem of existence. If this citizen be gifted with the genius to adorn the canvas, let him follow the lead of our noblest painters, and in Durand's Catskill Cloves, and Hart's Esopus, and Boughton's fragrant hayfields of the Hudson, and Kensett's gorgeous autumnal view, and the Niagara of Church, recognize the true inspiration and follow the path to fame. But if it be not given him to idealize the nature of New York in any form of imitative art, let him remember that the perfect farm smiling out of a cultivated landscape, the railway springing over a Portage bridge, the factory clustering around the mountain torrent, the steamer gliding over Champlain, and the warehouse beautiful in its order, and, chief of all, the tasteful home, are children of the same imagination that carves an "Indian Girl," or sets a song of freedom to a people's voice. Let our youth be taught by parents and teachers the finest accomplishment of looking at the nature of the Empire State with eyes of refined and generous enthusiasm; of sketching her scenes of beauty; of living out of doors amid her ennobling and invigorating influences. So shall the people of this gracious domain learn to recognize the glory amid which they live; and through affectionate admiration for nature, ever grow into worthier masters of a matchless heritage.

When we come to the contemplation of the individual man as the subject of art, let us not fall into the heresy of representing him according to any fantasy of despotism. Let his servile relations be forgotten, let degrading associations be ignored, and be it the destiny of our artists to symbolize that native dignity and equality of right which is the deepest fact of his nature and the key to his history. We have no admiration to bestow on those skillful workmen who represent humanity according to an European or Asiatic pattern. We felt that an Art Union that was filling our country houses with pictures of society in which the colored American appeared only as a slave, was a sinner against good taste no less than humanity. We shall hail the day when our native music will strike a loftier string than its negro minstrelsy, which, spite of our laughter, is the mournful song of our national shame. When the drama is elevated enough to drop her flunkey adulation to kings and queens, and can see the tragedy and comedy in the life of Mr. and Mrs. John Smith, citizens of the United States of America, eminent divines will not quarrel over the barren question whether the theatre is the road to heaven or hell, for the people will go to the play and return nobler men and women, and leave the doctors to weave cobwebs at their leisure. The artists are now alive who dare challenge the people to admire the angelic childhood, generous womanhood and strong manhood of New York sculptured in living marble or breathing on the enchanted canvas. Let the youth of our State learn music in school, at home, everywhere in their daily life; and the harmony that sings of man's innate nobility will by and by entrance them beyond the mysteries of the foreign concert or opera, endured for dear fashion's sake. Wherever man in his individual dignity appears in our higher poetry, let us hail the advent of a new fact in literature, and let the severe test of admittance to our fraternity of artistic life be reverence for the soul, devotion to freedom, belief in the supreme beauty of men's eternal childhood to the father whose smile is the love of the universe.

This central reverence for man will be our guide through the region of those Ornamental Arts which beautify society while they stimulate the industry of the people. The architecture of New York should not, like that of Greece and Rome, work downward from palaces and temples, but upward from the American home. The temporary fashion of huddling in marble fronted caravansaries, in imitation of old-world habits, will finally disappear, and the home, built and furnished according to the means, convenience and finest taste of a Republican family, will become the germ of native architecture and ornamental arts. In New York the State and Church are but associations of free citizens, and our buildings for the accommodation of the servants of the people, and the ceremonies of Government and Religion, will finally represent a Christian Democracy, as certainly as the acres of palace and cathedral, and the royal parks and hunting grounds, symbolize the Despotism abroad. Whatever public structure in New York sacrifices the convenience of the people to any architectural effect, will eventually be condemned. The finest and most characteristic public rooms in America are the beautiful halls that are appearing in every city and village in our Northern States, where multitudes can assemble for every honorable purpose, from an evening's entertainment to a Sunday's worship. This Democratic assembly room will by and by expand to a People's Temple; as the new hotel has sprung up to minister to the wants of our migratory population.

Who will teach us to study the wants of a New York family, and build a home where economy, comfort, independence and the elegance of true refinement may concentrate? Our State offers such facilities for a charming domestic life as few spots on earth. Our long green valleys, threaded by the railroad, open their arms to the weary citizen; our thousand inland cities and villages can become as many centres of taste and virtue. When the young women of the Empire State learn to waive the excitements of a brick box on Madison Square, and the colored river of Broadway in favor of a spacious home, and a garden cultivated by their own hands, with cheerfulness, usefulness and long life in our lovely country; when the fashionable heresy of female idleness, shall be exploded in favor of the introduction of women to the practice of the many ornamental arts that transform a hard, barren existence to a genial and fruitful life; we may look for a new revelation of Beauty which will convert the exterior of the Commonwealth to a grander picture than artistic genius has conceived.

The polite society of our State must recognize the native worth of Man, and free itself from all narrow conceits, which hinder the development of that cosmopolitan fraternity of feeling which becomes a Republic composed of all civilized nations. While the descendants of each race, or the disciples of each "ism," or the retainers of each family, cuddle in little exclusive knots, we shall have no society worthy our great Civilization. Fortunately there is little danger that the aristocracy of money will ever become a permanent fact; our periodical panic can be trusted to dissolve any collection of expensive families to their original elements as often as may be desirable. The artificial manners of a clique will hardly corrupt our people while they only expose their unfortunate professors to that broad popular humor which is the best human instrument yet devised for "taking the starch out" of affected superiority.

We must understand here, that a true American society means, first: a Christian home, strong, bright, hospitable and simple as becomes the sovereigns of a free soil; and secondly, a wide, varied and natural style of social intercourse, excluding only vice and obstinate vulgarity. Doubtless in the organization of such a society, many a fastidious mind will find ample occasion for disgust at the rudeness and sensuality of the people. But since a Christian gentleman or lady should go abroad not to exhibit their own superiority, but to entertain, and elevate, and bless their fellow beings, we need waste no special pity on such finical griefs. Our social boisterousness and ambitious taste are but the effects of our popular vigor, and how much nobler to use the refinement we have to lift a neighborhood to the love of Beauty, than to draw off into the delicately tinted shell of our small conceit, and be a social snail in a world of living men.

Our natural amusements are not being developed in the metropolis where thousands are squandered for the delectation of the few; but in every neighborhood where the people are using the talent and resources they have to make life cheerful. Do not sit in your rocking-chair over the register or the stove, young woman of the New York village or farm, dreaming of the glare of gas or the blaze of diamonds and the glittering crowd, that you saw on your last visit to the town; but be up and astir among the people around you. The same human nature can here be developed into a refinement as genuine as that of the capital. Make your home a paradise; stir up your neighbors to pure and pleasant enjoyments, and identify your name with the growth of a community in Republican grace Do not wait till you have money and position there is money and pretension enough in the State now; our chief need is a pure, joyous, fearless spirit to organize our rich elements of life into the most inspiring society of the time. Reject the pitiful ambition to push yourself among any circle of "select," for before you get there a turn of the wheel may disperse the circle and leave you alone with your wasted time. But cherish the laudable desire to leave the people about you more closely united by that respect for each other's manhood and womanhood which will blossom into the only refinement that will abide.

Our habit of frequent public gathering in conventions and mass meetings will, by and by, put on another feature, and great public holidays relieve the monotomy of our life. The agricultural fair, the teachers' association, the political monster meetings where men, women, children and babies come by the acre and sit out the long, autumn day in council on the affairs of freedom are the natural holidays of New York; and few sights are more inspiring to a generous taste than such outpourings of popular enthusiasm and joy.

No man, no class is great enough to make society in New York ; but the wisest men and women can watch its native developments, and help the people realize their best ideas of social existence in the pure and refined union of an American brotherhood.

Thus are we led up the various degrees of ascent to the summit of Beauty, in a perfect state. For the culmination of art is not in painting, or statuary, or music, or architecture, or polite society, since all these do but hint the glory of a social order founded on the sentiment of human love. The sublimest achievement of man is a state wherein nature is wrought into the varied symbol of a free humanity ; and every great interest, class and profession is harmoniously adjusted ; and the commonwealth, poised on everlasting justice, is the lively image of the great republic on high. Grander work than this was never given to man ; to mould New York into the commanding force in a Christian confederacy of States. In this mighty enterprise every inhabitant of our large domain becomes a worker elected by God, bound to leave on his corner of the majestic fabric the best results of character. Then whether our lot be cast within the circle of professional Art, or range outside in the common area of life, each labors for the verdict of ages, beneath the eye of the Great Artist who created the world and pronounced it good. In such a calling let each fervent soul count it worthy of all devotion to become an image of the Divine Loveliness, and shape the commonwealth into a sublime figure of the kingdom of God.

# X.

## THE PENITENTIARY;

### OR,

## CRIME IN NEW YORK.

It is a lasting honor to the city of Albany that she has chosen one of the healthiest and most charming sites upon her lovely range of hills for her model Penitentiary. This noble institution has been in complete operation ten years, and may challenge comparison with any similar establishment in our country. Notwithstanding the great variety in national character among its convicts—nearly every civilized country being represented in the inmates—and the large number and frequent changes of its inhabitants, 1,000 persons yearly passing under its discipline, many of whom are committed for a brief period, the success of its management has been undoubted. A perfect discipline is enforced, habits of industry formed, and the receipts of the ten years amount to $10,000 beyond its expenditures. If more decided moral results are demanded we must not in justice expect them of the officers of the Penitentiary while the citizens of Albany permit 3,000 barbarous and untaught youth to roam her streets, pouring a constant stream of convicts in at its ever gaping doors and seething like a pit of perdition before every discharged criminal. To require the overworked officers of such an institution to reform in a month these persons, we have spent twenty years in debauching from the paths of virtue, is an insult to humanity and common sense.

The condition of criminal affairs in our own city, is a good type of this great state. We have the best penitentiary in America, and keep eight hundred grog-shops at work on 3,000 youthful vagrants, that it may not rot for want of tenants. Our State has a system of criminal jurisprudence and a prison organization, needing only the lopping away of here and there a barbaric feature, to make it the pride of a civilized community. But for want of wholesome prevention of crime and of Christian interest in the criminal, our laws are not executed, our courts too often made a mockery of justice, our State prisons left in the hands of partisan politicians, our jails and our poor-houses disgracefully neglected, our benevolent and reformatory institutions chocked with occupants, and altogether matters are in a bad state and rapidly becoming worse. To arouse the minds of the people to their duty on this great interest of the prevention and punishment of crime, and the Christian discipline of the criminal shall be the object of my present address.

The State of New York has not been remiss in her efforts to solve the question of the punishment of crime. The earliest movement for the melioration of her criminal code and the establishment of a system of prison discipline, was associated with the honored names of John Jay, Ambrose Spencer and General Schuyler. In 1776, sixteen offences were capitally punished by the laws of the State, and the Criminal Code was proportionally severe in other respects. Now, but three crimes are capitally punished, and the law in other respects is conformable to the growing humanity of the age. The first prison which resulted from this early movement—"Newgate," in the city of New York—was an imitation of the Pennsylvania system; but after repeated experiments in the social and solitary modes of discipline, it was reserved for Lyndes and Cray to inaugurate that system which is now adopted in nineteen States of the Union.

This method provides for associated, though

silent labor by day, and solitary confinement by night, and with sure penalties annexed to disobedience, and the aid of religious and literary privileges on Sundays and evenings of every day. In 1821, this system went into operation at Auburn, in 1825 the State Prison for male, and in 1835 for female convicts at Sing Sing, and in 1845, the Clinton prison, were built. New York has also the honor of being the first State to establish a House of Refuge for youthful offenders, and an Asylum for Idiots. We now have three State prisons, containing 2,000 convicts; two Houses of Refuge, and three county Penitentiaries, which, with our jails and work-houses, contain 4,000 more. In 1856 there were more than 11,000 convictions for crime in the State.

We are not prepared to criticise the criminal system of our State. From our point of observation, excepting its barbarous feature of capital punishment for three crimes (one of which was never committed, and the other two gaining impunity every year from the disinclination of the people to inflict their own inhuman penalty), the system appears well contrived and humane. Yet, it cannot be denied that, like every other great interest of humanity in New York, its working is a sad commentary on our Christianity. We are still weak enough to suppose that if a great public interest is well organized, it will take care of itself. Thus, having established a good system for educating the people, and regulating crime, we leave it and rush off into the mad pursuit of wealth, and are surprised when statistics point to 90,000 unlettered adult citizens , and the armies of savages in our great cities ; and the daily journals teem with astounding revelations of crime committed with impunity.

We appoint three Inspectors of State Prisons with almost despotic power for good or evil, and then permit the political parties to choose political aspirants to this great priesthood of humanity, who fill these schools of the State with a transient crowd of office seekers. We appoint chaplains and teachers and establish libraries in the prisons, but by our meagre salaries we bid for inefficiency in these sacred offices ; and while the preacher to a respectable congregation in New York has $5,000 a year, this great State hires a man to convert the congregation at Sing Sing for $500 ; while the teachers receive $150, and the libraries are meagre and insufficient. We are inexorable on the point that the State prisons shall "pay their way," not thinking that if these criminals can be reformed it will be a gain of manhood as well as money beyond computation. Our benevolent associations that are empowered to elevate the condition of the prisoner, languish for want of support, and the embarrassment cast in their way by refractory officials. We have sufficient legislation to secure a good condition of County Jails and Poor-houses, yet I am almost ashamed of human nature when I read the report of the Legislative committee of Jan. 9th, 1857, on the disgraceful state of many of these institutions. Our Lunatic Asylum is overflowing, and humanity demands additional facilities for the treatment of insanity and the classification of its victims. There is still great injustice committed in the imprisonment of witnessess. While the people choose the men they often do to administer justice, the best organized court and noblest code in Christendom will be powerless to protect the peace, property and life of the community. And let not our executive be made the scape-goat to bear the retribution for all this, while the people, as represented by their courts and juries, think that all these faults can be atoned for by demanding an indiscriminate pardon of convicts.

The cause of this state of anarchy into which our criminal affairs is drifting is found in the wicked indifference of the masses of our people to the whole subject of crime. Vainly will systems be devised, while their operation depends on a people who choose its officers and inspire its spirit with the strangest disregard to Christian reflection. A vast majority of those who choose judges, legislators, inspectors, and appoint virtually all the officials of justice, neither know what our criminal system is, nor concern themselves for its operation. Of course this culpable negligence reacts on themselves, and the fearful increase of crime hardens the hearts of the people against the criminal. There are always men enough ready to stimulate the barbarism of the community into a ferocious demand for more severe penalties, and a furious onslaught against humane ideas of justice. Of all sorts of demagogues, we count those among the most dangerous who use their position in press, pulpit, or official station to exasperate the people against the criminal; urging them to atone for their own negligence in the administration of a good system by a return to the savage practices of a bygone age. We do not need a more severe criminal code; indeed it is already in some points too stringent; we need no sudden reorganization of our courts and system of punishments. But we do need a revival of attention among the 600,000 voters of this State to the whole subject of crime—its causes, prevention and discipline—which shall result in filling all positions of this department of society with firm, able, humane men, who will work the machinery according to the intention of its founders, and take such measures to protect society from the commission of wrong as a Christianized people can devise. The most magnificently built and rigged ship cannot sail if the tide flows out from beneath her keel and leaves her in the muddy bottom of the harbor; the grandest system of criminal discipline in a Republic, can only float when public opinion runs deep, strong and full below it and wafts it to the haven of success.

We have, therefore, no right to impute the present working of our criminal affairs to the failure of that system of Humanity which proposes the protection of society through the reformation of the criminal as the great end. When the people have done their duty, it will be time to decide whether we shall cease dealing with the criminal as a man, and remand him to the conditions of a wild beast. We claim that the reformatory method of dealing with this fearful problem is the only one which will ultimately redeem society. And this method is not founded, as is so often asserted, on sympathy with, or even a light view of crime itself.

We do not base the demand for reformatory treatment of the criminal on a loose, but on a strict view of his moral condition. It would only be a caricature of philanthropy to assert that the offender is made so entirely by circumstances, and is a more unfortunate, not a worse man than his neighbors. To assert that any large class of men is compelled to do wrong by circumstances, is to declare that the devil, not God, rules on the earth. Every soul is provided with a defence against temptation; and the hardest extremity of human virtue always opens into the possibility of the glorious achievement of martyrdom. When we speak of circumstances we must be very uncertain who shall be excused on this ground, for it is by no means sure that the poor, ignorant and obscure are the most dangerously tempted. Nobody lives in such a fire of temptation in America, as the man chosen by thirty-two States to stand for four years as the Representative of the Republic. The richest man in every town, the ablest man in every State, is beset with such fiends as make his position not enviable even when compared with the poorest man that lives upon his bounty. Every soul has its forty days in the wilderness, and in some way Satan has a tug at the heart-strings of each one of us. And to every child of

God is given the power to resist the uttermost assaults of evil while reason and responsibility last. We propose no such fallacy as that of excusing any man for sin under the plea of his circumstances. We should doubtless endeavor to make the circumstances of all men more favorable to virtue; the higher as well as lower classes of society need deliverance from their unfavorable surroundings. God alone can measure the guilt of each spirit. We are to assume that every man who does wrong has violated his holy law, and act accordingly.

But here is our mistake: *that willful transgression demands vindictive punishment.* Nothing of the kind is authorized in our dealing with our fellow creatures. Every crime deserves at our hands, not revenge either for restitution or example, but discipline for the reformation of the offender. We deal with the criminal not as the final umpire on his fate—that is God's vocation—but to restore him to virtue. Thus only can we perform our duty to him or society. For society demands not the protection that comes from killing or caging a dangerous animal, but that which comes from the restoration of one of her members who has fallen out of his place. The criminal needs not punishment to embitter his lot; God will give him a pain of conscience amply sufficient for his powers of endurance; he needs the fatherly hand of society laid on him for wholesome restraint; needs to be sequestered from the scene of his old temptations and crimes and taught by deprivation of accustomed social privileges, by constant industry, by reflection, aided by the counsels of good men and good books, how far he has strayed from his obligation; if necessary, needs the whole moral force of society concentrated for his reformation.

The State cannot afford to lose a man; each soul is a vital individual in her brotherhood; and when one does fall away, it may well leave the ninety and nine and go out to seek for the lost one. If there be joy in heaven over one sinner that repenteth; if God is willing to adjust the whole moral universe to promote the restoration of the vilest offender; should not the State consider it the noblest exercise of its majesty to bring forth every agency for the conversion of its worst criminal, and never be wearied of efforts to bring him home to truth and rectitude? What a spectacle, should the world's chief Republic confess that it could not reform its own criminals; but must kill some, and ostracize all from the Christian sympathies of the people! Would not such a state of society be a failure when it could not convert one murderer, but would be obliged to put him out of the way? Shall we be content to lose 11,000 men, women and children a year from their posts of service in the State? Can we afford such a waste of manhood and womanhood? Oh, let us arouse from our wicked chase for a material success, and save our brethren for themselves, for society, for the cause of Liberty and civilization. Only the Reformatory system will do all these things; and to allege it will not, is a libel on Christianity.

I know all the respectable sophistry by which this method of dealing with crime is opposed. We are charged with nourishing a sympathy for the criminal at the expense of sympathy for the victim of his act, and society. Well, pray, with whom should we sympathize, if not with the criminal? Did God send Jesus Christ to call the righteous or sinners to repentance? Methinks a man needs our love in proportion as he is fallen from rectitude: needs it to arrest that despair which urges him to frantic excess of crime; to arouse hope; to evoke the latent vigor of his soul; to assure him first that man is still his brother, and will not let him go; then, that God is his Father and still pleads with him for repentance; to recall his self-respect and convince him that he can yet be a man. Is any one ashamed to bestow sympathy on a fallen man? Then he is ashamed of that which made Jesus the Saviour of mankind. Does any man fear he shall be accused of sympathy for crime if he indulges in love and service for the criminal? Jesus was called the "friend of publicans and sinners;" and there are Pharisees to-day, who love to taunt every philanthropic man with the same charge; but between Phariseeism and Christianity we should not be slow to choose. None should know better than those who utter this calumny, that we do not justify crime while we love and toil to save the criminal; and it is time such misrepresentation of Divine Charity should find its native home in the "Satanic Press" and not disturb the regions of respectable society in a Christian Republic.

Sympathy with the sufferer? Why, we suppose the best sympathy we can show to an injured man, is to help him reform his enemy. If he demands our help to revenge himself on a criminal, we as Christian believers must decline. Example? Why, what example are we bound to set before society: that of rendering vindictive punishment for crime, and thus compelling ourselves to become more barbarous for every offence of the man we punish, or the example of taking possession of every offender to make him a good man, and becoming ourselves more Christian for every sin he commits? Doubtless there may be a dangerous lenience, but it is usually the reaction from an overstrained severity. Let society insist on the punishment of death, and all good men will be tempted to let the murderer go; jury, judge, attorney, governor, populace, will be forced into a dangerous sympathy with the criminal, to vindicate our common humanity. Let society set herself to the glorious task of redeeming her outcasts, and all good men will conspire in every just method of restraint which will contribute to this end. Let us put away this unchristian hatred against the criminal, and apply ourselves to the Christian duty of recalling these estrays from society, to their renounced fellowship with man and thei repudiated obedience to God.

The first obligation, in this department of duty, is the Prevention of Crime; and the most important; since only by drying the fountain, can the poisonous stream be arrested. The most efficient agency in this work of prevention is the support of all those public and private means of improvement which make a Christian society. If you would prevent crime, teach your children to love industry and honesty in business. Idleness, and a habit of dishonesty in trade, are a fruitful source of offence. Every young man or woman sent into our Republican society too unskillful or too proud to obtain an honest living by hard labor of hands or mind, or too selfish to respect the rights of others in getting it, is at the mercy of the tempter. Education is a great safeguard against crime, especially if it be a true education, which develops all the powers of our humanity into a harmonious manhood, rather than sharpens the intellect at the expense of the soul. It costs $2 25 a week to support a convict in a jail in New York; and we can so administer our public schools that for $10 a year, every child in the State can be raised beyond the temptation of ignorance.

The family is the great school where children are fitted for honor or dishonor. Many a child in good society is systematically trained to be a villain by parents who weakly and wickedly indulge its whims, pamper its appetites and turn it loose, an organized willfulness, upon the world. The ambition and luxury of fashionable life tempt thousands to crimes of the deadliest nature; indeed much that is winked at in the ordinary course of fashionable society, is itself as culpable as offences that send their perpetrators to a prison. Art and amusements inwrought into the texture of society are a safeguard. A hundred youth are driven to wickedness by the *ennui* and monotony of our barren social American existence, where one falls through the temptations of such amusements as we now have ; and would Christian people cease their fruitless crusade against the recreations of society and attempt their reformation, we might hope for better things.

But especially will education in that radical love of God and man, which is Christianity, insure us against public immorality ; for, if anything is demonstrated, it is that respectability and superficial moral propriety are no reliable defence against the surges of evil desire. Every man does the most for the truth by living a holy life in his ordinary sphere of duty ; and every noble character is a constant protest and preventive against crime.

We have the right also to control those peculiar causes of offence which exist especially in densely populated communities. Blessed be the labors of those who gather together the orphans, the children of the street, the sorely tempted, the poor and the outcast into the fold of a Christian Charity. They are the true architects of society, restoring its fallen members to an honorable place in its harmonies. We may also lay our hand on such causes of public immorality as pander to the worst passions of men. I doubt that intemperance in intoxicating drinks is so large a source of crime as is alleged. Drunkenness itself, is commonly the result of a long deterioration of vitality in the will. The real cause of crime is a weakening of moral decision, which is the gradual result of a thousand influences. When this disease of moral enervation has reached a certain point, it leaves the victim open to the assaults of sensual passions and habits which doubtless react and hasten his descent to ruin. Still, Intemperance is a curse of such potent force, that the State may well overstrain, rather than fail to assert her powers in its suppression. Yet the only test of sumptuary laws is the probability of their enforcement. Not what corresponds to a preconceived theory of prohibition, but what can be thoroughly enforced, is the thing to be incorporated into a law. The failure of our legislation against intemperance, we believe, has been the result of its narrowness. We must include vagrant pauperism, sensuality and drunkenness in any system of legislation for the prevention of crime. Hitherto, we have separated these branches of the same tree, and our success has been doubtful. When a deeper philosophy comes into the consideration of that whole side of life given over to the debasement of man through his senses, we may be guided to a method which will save the sinner and protect the State. We suspect that Reformatory Asylums for the victims of the cup and the brothel are to figure largely in this system.

Every influence that unites the several interests and classes of society is a preventive of crime. The present tendency that threatens to ostracize the great North American, Asiatic and African races from all participation in the rights of American citizenship, will turn out a premium on disorder. Every class in this republic thrust outside the common privilege of freedom, will finally become a criminal class. Degraded as may be the emigrant that seeks our shores, or the servant that crouches beneath our power at home, our only safety is in educating them to the rights and rank of freemen.

Thus by fidelity to the culture of the community, by the wise management of the most obvious causes of offence, by patriotic union of all classes in the hopes and duties of a common civilization, may we greatly prevent the approaches of crime.

But while the human will remains free, our utmost effort at the prevention of crime will not insure its extirpation; and there seems little hope that our people will be suddenly awakened to their duties in this respect. We shall doubtless not lack for criminals, these many years, in New York. Let us consider our obligations to them.

The first and most imperative duty is to choose competent men to manage our existing system of criminal affairs. Let us apply our minds to ascertain just what our system can accomplish under a worthy administration. The greatest good that could happen would be the utter disconnection of our whole judicial and punitive system from partisan politics. While men are looking to seats in our halls of justice, and promotion to the responsible offices in our reformatory institutions, as a reward for caucus services, it is almost vain to hope that any system, however admirable, will be well administered. Woe to that State whose courts, police and prisons, are swayed to and fro by the fierce waves of political change. Yet the tendency seems a growing one, to regard all the officers in a republic as advocates of a victorious party. We believe the people will be driven by sheer necessity and common sense from the dangerous tendency into which they are now hurried by ambitious leaders. We anticipate a revival of wisdom, which shall insist, first of all, on competency, in every candidate for a position connected with our criminal affairs. Let us fill every judicial seat and every post down to the lowest official in jail and police, with a man of first rate integrity and undoubted capacity; pay well for services done, and be inexorable against neglect or abuse of the position. We may seem to many to be pleading in behalf of the millennium, when we demand such behavior from the sovereign people; but it is only by demanding it, and persuading or shaming the voters of New York into such a reasonable course, that there is any hope of the perpetuity of our society. Whoever tampers with the integrity of courts, or makes the administration of justice dependent on partisan favoritism, is knocking away the very foundations of social order, and doing his best to precipitate us all into the bottomless pit of anarchy. The people of New York have the alternative of choosing honest and competent managers of their criminal system, or of submitting to the organization of all decent men into a "Vigilance Committee," for the protection of life and property. Let them learn betimes, and insist that the method now on the ground shall have a fair administration.

When the court has performed its high obligation, and the criminal passes out of society within the walls of the prison, let him feel that he has not entered a chamber of torture where the Empire

State of the American Union wreaks its vengeance on his defenceless head; but rather a seminary, where the chief Republic of the world is not ashamed to become his father and mother and train him again in all the ways that lead to honorable manhood. Let the officials with whom he comes in contact, not appear so much the grim executioners of a despotic law, as the firm and humane representatives of a Christian Commonwealth that deplores the apostasy of her child, and will spare no pains to guide him into the ways of penitence and peace. Let him receive the comforts of life with none of its superfluities; for he who would reflect deeply on his duty should waste no time or thought on the indulgence of the senses. The first element of reformation is the establishment of a habit of industry, and the State does wisely that teaches every convict the preliminary lesson of labor in some necessary occupation. But to make a criminal's life all toil, is to degrade him to a machine and destroy the hope of his restoration to manhood. Therefore the industrial life of the convict should be only the basis on which should be reared a superstructure of Christian training. Let the wisest teachers divert his mind from the insane intensity of criminal meditation to the contemplation of truth. Let him be won to study and thought; and the mental training of the prison not be a mere recreation of the imagination, but a stimulus that shall arouse long slumbering energies and direct the intellect aright. And let religion appear, not in the shape of a frowning superstition, threatening the wretch with tortures and stripes in eternity, but as the father running to meet the prodigal while yet a great way off, and bathing his head with tears of holy joy. Let woman be greatly employed in all those offices that touch on spiritual discipline; for a pure and holy woman will often find a depth of repentant feeling in the soul of the outcast which would remain forever locked against the presence of man. And let the whole discipline of the Penitentiary resemble God's discipline of his creatures. As the offender rejects the proffered aid, let him behold society fading off from him, and his stone walls closing more firmly about his earthly life. As he accepts the offers of Christian discipline let a new light be cast on his path with every effort towards goodness. Thus may he be made by the State, as by God, in a measure the arbiter of his own destiny, and become an active partner in the exalted work of his own redemption.

And when, at last, his prison door opens and he stands again before the society he has offended, let him be met by those who will still be to him the representatives of a Christian brotherhood. No man should be permitted to fall a second time for lack of an arm to guide him away from scenes of old temptation. Here is a field that opens a wide sphere of usefulness to the benevolent heart. Oh, that thousands of the gifted and aspiring of our State might be made to feel that here they can serve their country more effectually than elsewhere. What are the joys of social applause, of literary reputation, of respectable position, compared with the heavenly consciousness of having met one man at the prison door and been his guardian angel back to the final trust and respect of his fellow men? Who will complain of "nothing to do" when 11,000 of our fellow beings yearly issue from the reformatory institutions of this State, each one a subject for Christian sympathy and influence? Thus, by a wise administration of a good system—the conversion of the prison into a convict's school, and of society into his instructor—we may solve this fearful problem according to the lights of Christianity.

But there is one class of criminals who are placed by our law outside this system of reformation. While the State sustains the attitude of a Christian missionary to the vast majority of her erring children, it still, in violation of her radical system, remains a pagan executioner towards those convicted of three capital crimes. Nothing so reminds us of the mingled barbarity and vacillating weakness of an Oriental tyranny, as the position of the State before the murderer. It claims the right to punish without mercy, but all the while is shaken with human doubts and relentings, the result of which is, that at some stage of the proceedings, between policeman and high sheriff, a majority of the worst criminals slip through the meshes of the law and go "unwhipped of justice." Those who protest so sternly against this state of affairs should remember that it is not so easy for a Governor of New York to change himself from a Christian gentleman to a pagan Brutus as they may imagine; and that to secure the invincible sternness they demand, they must go back at least five hundred years to an age of iron vindictiveness and bloodshed. This lenience of society is the universal protest against the law; and if the statute still threatens death, it will increase till conviction will be impossible, and the murderer become a licensed character. Why do we not learn wisdom of our past failures and repeal a law which now is a premium on the last extremity of crime?

It is to be hoped the time has passed when the

religious public will feel called upon to resist this greatly needed reform. We do not question the honesty of many religious people in obstructing this change, but we regard their view a superstition none the less dangerous for being the result of an honest conviction. It is time the Bible should be rescued from that interpretation which makes it the corner-stone of the gallows. The common sense of the whole scriptural argument is:—that the Hebrew Nation, like every other Asiatic people, claimed God Almighty as the author of their code of laws; and like every other Oriental nation, lived in the commission of slavery, polygamy, exterminating war and the punishment of death for crime. If the practice of the Jewish people is authority for capital punishment to-day, in New York, it is equally authority for slavery in South Carolina, for polygamy in Utah, for even more fierce wars of extermination than have yet been waged by our most savage backwoods soldiery against the pagan Indians. No man can logically defend the gallows from the Old Testament, while he rejects its testimony to these other ancient institutions. The way out of this difficulty, is to interpret the Old Testament according to reason and Christianity, and to regard the Hebrew people as a barbarous nation, living 3,000 years ago in Asia, whose customs, laws, ideas and practices have passed away into history, superseded by that better light of Christian love, under which only a Republic can exist. There is not a word, an act, an idea in the life of Jesus; there is not a principle of Christianity as he proclaimed it, that upholds the gallows. Christianity is the love of God and man; and by no possible arrangement of the law of Love can you deduce the halter and the executioner. If man has the right to deprive his fellow man of life at all, it can only be in the last extremity of self-defence, of himself or society; and to affirm that society in the Empire State is in imminent danger from the presence of a few murderers under Christian discipline in her prisons, is an assertion too puerile to need refutation. Even if the abolition of the death penalty for a time seemed to encourage crime, it would only prove that society was too indolent to do its duty by the convict, not that humanity was a failure. But the testimony is all on the side of mercy. Every melioration of the criminal code under favorable circumstances has increased the security of life, and the safest condition of society is not now that where the criminal code is most unrelenting, but that in which death is a punishment never or most rarely known to the law.

Every plea for the retention of the gallows resolves itself into a plea for moral inaction. Nobody doubts it is easier for the people of this State to hire a hangman to put a criminal out of the world than to concentrate the moral forces of the commonwealth for his reformation; but God will call us to a strict account for every man we thus destroy to save ourselves the trouble of his conversion. Are there not spiritual resources in this mighty Republic to reach the soul of any murderer in your domain? If not, let us hold a day of fasting and prayer, and implore God to revive our religion again and again, till it is strong enough to grapple with these outcast ones and melt them by the power of love into penitence and reconciliation to heaven and man.

Meanwhile, no service to our State is so valuable as labor directed to the reformation of the thousands of youth who are growing up in our cities and towns in an apprenticeship to misery, ignorance and vice. The report of the Albany Penitentiary for 1856, declares that no less than 2,000 such youth roam the streets of our ancient city, and we know the depths of youthful depravity that fester in every large community in our State. Oh, let us be ashamed to call ourselves a Christian State, while these heathen rise up to mock our pretence! Men and women of wealth and culture; young men and women whom I behold all about me, slowly perishing with *ennui* and social formality; ministers of Christ, professors of Christianity; people who only claim the reputation of common humanity; what are we doing for our heathen? Oh, fearful will be our retribution if we permit these youth to go on their gloomy way to crime and earthly ruin! Let us awake to our obligation to these, our perishing brothers and sisters! Let us all turn preachers in word and life, that society may be rescued from this moral scrofula in her blood; that every erring spirit may hear the tidings of salvation; be saved for himself, saved for the State, saved for citizenship in that Kingdom of Heaven, which will come when all men love God as the father, and the neighbor as themselves.

# XI.

## WOMAN IN AMERICA.

Our consideration of civilization would be incomplete without a chapter on *Woman in America*. What is the present condition, the true culture, the right position of woman in our Republican society?

America has no national type of female character and society. The American woman dwells in a nation that has not yet enjoyed a century of characteristic existence; indeed the present generation is the first that has lived in a self-conscious America. Ten millions of American women are let loose over an area of three millions of square miles to help ten millions of men and eight millions of children create a Republican society. From these women restraint is removed as in no former period of the world's history. Freedom, in its widest and best significance, is dawning upon woman in our land, and she cannot fail to be influenced in her whole existence by her novel position.

To say that the American woman fully appreciates this glorious opportunity, much less acts worthy of her position, would be to affirm her the angel she is only in the poetaster's and story-teller's columns of the monthly magazines. With the same human nature that played false with Mother Eve, she is here called to realize a grander fact than ever before existed—a Republican society. It is no slander to say she has not yet realized it, but is enslaved in sight of her boundless opportunity. The material advantages of freedom are always appropriated before men rise to its spiritual applications. If our young men too often differ from the young men of other countries, rather in their abuse, than appreciation of their social freedom, so, as far as our young women are American, do they to an equal extent exemplify the lower rather than the higher traits of the national character. Thus while everybody knows many fine women, nobody has found a fine republican neighborhood or a satisfactory state of social life.

American women are, just now, bewildered by their own position. The great mixture of people in cities and large towns, where customs and fashions originate, divides the mass into a thousand contradictory elements. Society is an uncertain fluctuating ocean, on whose shore every girl stands watching her opportunity to spring aboard the finest craft that is whirled within her reach.

During this formative period of social life, the material advantages of our condition have a fatal fascination to our young country women. There was never a race of men acquiring wealth and position so fast as the young men of America; so every farmer's, mechanic's or merchant's daughter; every girl at her needle, her studies, her school-teacher's desk, has a mighty temptation to keep the brightest corner of her best eye open for the coming man, who shall appear in his coach at her mother's door, carry her to a beautiful home, and bear her on from triumph to triumph in her social career. Honor to those who fix their eyes on the higher spiritual prizes of American freedom, and live out the resolve to found their success on something better than money and ease; but they are the chosen few. The crowd of American girls do what women would do everywhere; neglect the higher culture of the soul in the scheming or waiting for the sensual advantages of life, and spend the golden years of their first quarter of a century, rather in superficial occupations and inquiring after desirable husbands, than in toiling to become good wives and Republican mothers.

This fearful push for the material prizes of our

national life, explains the imperfect education of American young women. Mothers and daughters vie in the cultivation of those temporary graces and accomplishments which are supposed to bring young men to a crisis in the affections, while the solid qualities which can alone retain the love of a rational man, or fit a woman for genuine success, are postponed till life is upon them. It also accounts for the ridiculous imitation of foreign fashions, which makes Boston a sham London, and New York a sham Paris, and arrays the girls of every western town in obedience to the fashion plates of Godey and Harper. It is the chief cause of the restlessness of women, and the want of peace in family and social life; for young women who are crazed with this ambition, cannot be quiet enough to develop that sweetness and strength, which is the rock at the centre of earthly life, and next to God's love, the best support of man. And this is the secret cause of the fearful collapse of female health in America; for standing on tiptoe, watching the chance to leap aboard a fairy, floating palace that wavers over a stormy sea, is not a healthy, though an exciting occupation. It forces children through the grades of girlhood with steam power rapidity to young ladyhood, while they should be romping in pantalets, learning science or household duties under their teachers and mothers. This rush of energy to the surface of life, the excitements, hopes and fears of the young lady's career, leave the deep places of the heart dry, and create a morbid restlessness of the affections, that preys upon the very springs of physical existence; so the majority of American girls, when they have obtained their lover, are not physically fit to become his wife and the mother of his children, and the bright path of girlhood dips down into the valley of shadows, that married life is to woman in thousands of American homes.

This material ambition of the girls drives their companions of the other sex into overheated exertions in business and exhausts their health and freshness, by awakening at one-and-twenty the sense of obligation belonging to forty; while their ill-health and practical effeminacy prevent thousands of young men from marrying, and thus fearfully increase the sensuality of the community. It drives the young couple to live beyond their means and sacrifice constant comfort and true family life to occasional splendor and periodical excitement. American men wear out in business keeping up the household, and women wear out in straining after social position. Children are born with the mark of this career upon them, and brought up in a more exaggerated style. The mother at last "breaks down" under social cares, and distractions, and the father has no spot of rest on earth. The American woman has not yet created the American home. As a nation we are jaded, sad, nervous. Our men do not come out of their fine houses with the glory of the Lord shining in their faces, as Moses came down from the mount, but as tired and restless as they went in. The Republican home that shall cheer, console, and elevate the American people, and the Republican Society that is but its extension and idealization, are yet a vision.

Such is now the condition of woman in America, swayed to a dangerous extent by the temptations of the material side of Republicanism; and it becomes every wise man to drop that style of spread-eagle gallantry, with the Jonathonian order of rhetoric, which yet further inflames the sensualism of the people by false compliments, and speak severely of the faults of the American woman as he would invite her to a like criticism, in faith that she will respond to every true effort to raise her to the central power of the world's only Republican Society.

Already does this response begin to be heard. There is another tendency among American women, equally characteristic of their position and prophetic of the largest results. This tendency may be called "the woman's movement," including in the term the whole of that new interest in the elevation of the sex, which is now one of the most striking phenomena of the time.

Whoever travels among our people and listens to the talk of all classes, feels himself in the presence of a mighty inspiration of our national idea of Christian Freedom; an aspiration after a freer and wider life, and impatience with the present restraints and weaknesses of the sex—a blind impulse to do something more Republican than is now being done. This feeling, like all popular sentiments, reveals itself according to the character and circumstances of those it animates. In some isolated circles of pedantic culture, in many homes sunk in materialism, in the saloons of selfish and sensual fashion, it hardly lives at all; though even here a rousing blast from outside now and then slams an open door, or rattles the window shutters with portentous meaning. But in a thousand homes it prompts the serious inquiry into habits of living, economy, diet, dress, education, amusements, social ideas, and though such discussions are often but a tea-table vapor, their result is generally perceptible in the disuse of injurious customs, and the beginning of more rational family life. The fire gets into the maiden's soul, and she grows restive under the round of inanity that the fashionable courteously call "life." Now and then one succeeds in a new sphere and finds in a laborious independence, joys she never knew in a comfortable dependence. It sets people talking on marriage, and asking why, with such a liberty of choice, so many American women should be badly mated; and if such investigations now and then tip over a weak brother and sister into the gutter of free love, we cannot wonder that in a community where every other girl marries for something else than affection, there should arise an army who clamor for the free indulgence of the appetites. The school education of girls is being discussed with a vigor and breadth that promises the best results; the college is changing from a monastic cloister, where men study Latin and Greek, to a Republican University, where men and women vie in the beautiful emulation for the knowledge that maketh wise for life. Teaching in the school and church is fast becoming the special province of woman, and the press and art are free to all who come. The question of female labor is fairly before the people. Several professions are wholly or partly opened for the sex.

authorship is entirely free. Medicine is losing its masculine conceit. The lecture platform is open for any woman strong enough to face an audience and not be scared into a man; and the pulpit opens its reluctant door to a few eloquent female preachers. Woman is finding a wide and welcome sphere of activity in the various benevolent operations of the day, and the church would fall unless she held it up. Wherever a dozen young women are gathered together, we find some earnest soul asking what it shall do to be saved from the low contact of popular American life. If in many instances this longing begins with a chat and expires in a sigh, in many others it feeds a secret purpose that sooner or later ripens to a will and becomes a fact before the world.

Among the more radical class of minds this spirit has wrought more decisively, and driven thousands of intelligent men and women into public protest against the whole structure of society. These persons boldly affirm the equality of woman and man, in power, right and position. This demand they enforce with great vigor and ingenuity of reasoning, a fearful array of facts, and a scathing criticism of the present state of American society. We must not look to them for clearly defined ideas of woman's nature, or a philosophical estimate of her life; for most of them have been driven into their position by personal experience of, or a quick sympathy with, woman's wrongs; and pathetic and stirring as are their appeals, they are not self-consistent, much less do they agree with each other. But the conventions in which this development culminates, are distinguished for great ability, decorum, and power over popular sentiment; are least of a bore of any species of public conventions, because filled with live people. Every theory and vagary gets an airing on their platform, but after a liberal subtraction for nonsense and bad logic, a great mass of facts and argument remains that has never been answered, and on which only the next century of woman's career in America can be the commentary. The upshot of all this is, that we are bound to try the experiment of Democracy in America, and woman will have her part in the crusade; and those agitators who take the stump in favor of the millennium, are only doing in their way what every true man and woman in the land is doing in another. In contemplating this great movement we do not need so much a caricature of the foolish side of woman's conventions, or the exploding of rainbow social theories that will dissolve into their elemental suds at the first collision with real life, as a true and bold statement, by every man and woman who thinks at all, of what that mind has been able to believe on a great and complicated movement, which, after all, will turn out not according to our predictions but according to providential laws.

Every discussion of human rights presupposes a discussion of human capacities. Before we describe the path to true American womanhood let us give our best estimate of woman's nature; remembering that the nature of man and woman are so involved in each other, and both in God, that all attempts at description should be made with profound reverence, and held as a mere hint at a yet unfathomed mystery.

It must be that the human race, from the creation till this day, has not been deceived in ascribing superior energy of the affections to woman. In her, love is less mixed with passion, ambition or selfishness of any form than in man. The affection of few women is free from degrading weakness and instability, but even the perverted form in which it appears, testifies to the divine power lodged in every female soul. The development and the purification of the sentiments is the reward of all womanly culture. She is not paid for her hard toils and secret tears by outward advantages, but by gaining new capacity to love, and consequently to rule the world. In its noblest exercise, her affection penetrates to the possibilities of its object; beholds the germs of its life and the latent energies of its being, and declares not so much what it will be in this world, as what it can become in the vast revolutions of its eternal career. Woman's true love does not exaggerate its object; it is the only true estimate of its greatness of capacity. Like the divine love it annihilates time, space, and circumstances, and looking along the vast reach of the soul's achievements, loves and waits in patience the time of realization. Shakspeare, beyond all men, has shown this in the far-seeing celestial calmness of Desdemona. To this angelic woman the tempest of offended honor in her Othello's breast is but a hurricane, blowing them both through the waves of this stormy life into the peaceful deeps of the life beyond; and she dies by his angry hands, knowing his soul can have no rest till it finds her beyond the grave, and welcomes her with a love too great for new disturbance. The ideal affection of woman is the best representative of the divine love to man.

We are not prepared to assert that woman is inferior to man in imagination. Imagination is the power whereby the soul penetrates to the essential nature of existence and prophesies its perfect development. And this is woman's strong ground.

True, she has not written poems, painted and carved, created music and architecture like man; but she constantly does what is a more vital act of imagination: comprehends the secrets of the living soul, and moulds it into manhood and womanhood; creates the home, manners, amusements, social life, and through these, civilization. Her imagination is so vital, that it scorns imitation and drives at once to real existence, and there wins its lasting triumphs, of which art is but the record. There is more intense and constructive imagination shown by many a village mother in comprehending the natures of her children, and rearing them up without collision, into worthy men and women, than in writing poems or carving statues. Woman idealizes nature and spirit, and by her power thus to behold things as they were created to be, does she mould the world into constantly increasing forms of beauty and excellence.

Whether woman is equal to man in intellect, by which we mean the whole region of the higher reason, and the understanding, logical and practical, united in common sense, we cannot say. Certainly, in quickness of apprehension, in the perception of nice distinctions, in tact, in practical judgment, within a limited sphere, and generally in a common sense estimate of what is best to be done under any given complication of circumstances, she is the superior to man. But in that comprehensiveness of mental view, which overlooks vast interests in their entire relations, and in that sublime energy of pure reason, whereby nature and life are seen in their scientific correctness, and the laws discovered by which God rules his creation, she has not yet shown herself his equal. Here is the strong ground of man, and when truly himself, woman naturally looks upward to him as a superior intelligence.

Man is also the superior of woman in force of executive will. He possesses that restless energy, courage and consistency of purpose whereby he overruns the visible world, subdues nature, founds states, governments, institutions and civilizations. His physical being and the coarser texture of his mind qualify him for such a career. But when we go inward, and deal with more spiritual affairs, woman's will excels man as eminently as it falls below in the outward world. Before her incredible patience, her life-long endurance, her power of concentration and persistence of purpose, man hides his face and submits to be led by her irresistible force of will. That will despises outward triumphs, that it may the more effectually rally in its fullness of spiritual energy around those critical spots that determine human destiny.

Yet, whatever natural inferiorities woman suffers, are overbalanced by the superior fineness of her organization; all her powers are more ethereal than those of her companion. She, therefore, sits at the centre of life, and does through agents what man is compelled to run about the earth and accomplish by the sweat of his brow. She is the equal, perhaps the superior, of man in entire force of being; is perhaps a better manifestation of God in the flesh than he.

Now who will say that a being thus endowed can be developed within any narrow sphere of existence? Each of woman's known superiorities points to an infinite satisfaction. But her entire nature is more than a combination of rare qualities, even a soul fashioned in a peculiar image of the Creator, and spurns every boundary line drawn around it by human conceit and tyranny. We pity the man who has no better work on hand than fencing in a district of humanity, and writing over the gateway, "Woman's Sphere!" We doubly pity the woman who can be content to pace the restricted area of this feminine pound, and provided she is well fed, housed and filled with comforts and flatteries, gracefully fondle the hand that inscribes her sentence above her prison door. Man's sphere is what all the men in the world, working till the end of time, can naturally do. Woman's sphere is what all the women in the world, working till the end of time, can accomplish. Every individual man's or woman's sphere, is all that individual, working from birth till death, can naturally and gracefully perform. Therefore, we must not limit woman anywhere in the healthy and virtuous exercise of her energies; we must throw open the whole field of human enterprise, and call her like man to come up and occupy according to her ability.

Does the American woman, have this free field for the cultivation of her entire womanhood? Theoretically, she has it, especially in the northern States of the Republic, to an extent never before enjoyed, though not entirely. Practically, she has it not, but is yet living within various inclosures of custom, fashion, caste, which appear to her the granite walls of fate, but which are really walls of pasteboard, frescoed in imitation of the barriers of the universe. But, does the Creator place her in this hapless condition, as tyrants in the parlors, and hunkers in the pulpits solemnly proclaim? Surely not. Does man deprive her of the right she has inherited by nature, and doom her to a gilded slavery, as frantic bloomers shriek to sympathetic conventions? Just as surely not. God has treated her like all his creatures; given her a nature, and set his universe before her, saying: "Take what belongs to thee." Man is as much the slave of woman, as woman is the slave of man, and his tyranny is only the sign of her imbecility. She is chiefly responsible for her slavery in every department of life.

If her weak frame makes her a slave to nature, she has defaced that body, the perfection of nature's beauty, to a bundle of quivering nerves and diseased organs. If her want of practical efficiency makes her the slave of her servants, she has let her native activity and tact run to waste. If her capricious, sensual and restless affections make her the slave of her lover, husband, child, it is because she has vacated the throne of her womanly love, and crowned effeminate sentiment the queen of her heart. If her want of cultivation makes her the slave of social customs she despises while she obeys, it is because she has preferred ease in the present to the labor that swings open the gates of the future. If the want of religious experience leaves her under the feet of circumstances, it is because she has cared less for her soul than some temporary advantage, which, grasped, turns to ashes in her hands and leaves her in spiritual beggary. Her slavery is the retribution of her sins. Man does oppress her grievously, but in every battle she has the last word and the last blow, and never lies quietly in her chain, till she has fastened the other end on him.

There is no hindrance to the development of woman in America but woman. Freedom must be won everywhere. The gracious Creator offers woman America—an ocean of republican possibility—for her inheritance. She receives as much as she can dip in her cup. If she can only catch a tea-cup, or a thimbleful, or scoop in her trembling hand a little that runs through her fingers, it is her misfortune; but nobody's sin so much as hers. If she will go on with a brave heart, using what she has, she can be herself and occupy every position for which she is qualified, according to the same law by which man succeeds—unflinching toil in the acquisition and eternal vigilance in the preservation of Freedom.

But such an effort can only come from a deep inspiration of religious obligation. Not the superstition which makes woman the slave of a masculine priesthood, but the religion which is the new birth of the soul into love and freedom, can give her power, even to aspire to her destiny. The sentiment of freedom must be purified, widened and deepened by religion, to a controlling principle in the souls of our young countrywomen, before the victory will be won. For this woman's war of independence is no seven years' conflict that can be fought through with a great effort; but a series of petty skirmishes daily renewed, lengthening out through many generations. Her foes are not armies in the field, forts and navies on coast and sea, not even the restless throng of men; she cannot fight her father, brother, husband; but a thousand social gnats and mosquitoes, a swarm of domestic flies, little weaknesses that never take form, little selfishnesses that secretly spoil motives and conduct of elevation, little jealousies, sensualities, unveracities, mean hopes and cunning plans, and degrading half fears, that tie an invisible cord round every limb. She marches to her battle, not over ditches and up mounds where volleying cannon shake the ground, and hissing bombs flame through the smoking air; but along a field of spider's webs, through forests interlaced with flowery vines, and thickets where thorns lurk under blossoming roses. Through perpetual irritations does she gain her freedom. A half-drunken soldier can run like a screeching demon up the road to the parapet, swept by its storm of fire and iron, against a rampart of pointed steel; but only a religious woman can keep her nerves strong, and her spirit high, against the maddening vexations that, like mocking spirits, switch her with hairs, and prick her with needles, and throw flower dust in her eyes along the path of social freedom. But she who endures unto the end shall be saved; and as the fire burns deeper and calmer in her soul, shall a new vigor nerve her hands and feet, and a new grace hover about her form, and a lovelier halo of victorious womanhood encircle her brow, as she goes to her destiny like a queen to her coronation.

There are three stubborn difficulties in the way of the American woman's achievement of her destiny—want of health, lack of practical training, and deficiency in genuine cultivation of mind and manners. Until our women get more bodily vigor, all their aspirations will be at the mercy of a nervous fit; while they are so unpractical in common affairs, that their husbands must buy their dinners and keep their accounts, and their servants look down from the eminence of the cooking-stove and washing machine in insolent contempt of their mistress's shiftlessness, and a man with a cane and moustache must be the body-guard of their timorous steps abroad, and two untirable arms bear them unharmed through the perils of journey by railroad and steamship; why talk of more rights, when they have thrown away the primary human right of keeping out of fire and water and taking care of themselves? While they prefer a little embroidery and less French; a limb wrenched from the last opera, dissected again by the sharp edge of song; a little waltzing and a good deal of dressing and party-going, to the knowledge that is gained only by years of patient observation, reading and reflection, and the social tact that is but the largest and wisest expression of a good heart and a refined mind—how can they expect to make a society that shall allure the strongest and best within its charmed walls?

A great religious inspiration can alone keep woman fixed to the toils which shall overcome these obstacles. Inspired with this spirit of religious independence, and armed with the practical forces of health, skill and culture, the American woman will be prepared to commence the work of regenerating and reconstructing our social state. Here she must begin on her own familar ground—home. Woman must first have her rights under her own family roof, or all her attempts to gain them elsewhere will recoil upon herself. Therefore let the primary application of her newly inspired energy be made within those four sacred walls, where she is mistress, if anywhere on earth. We have no American home. We have, doubtless, thousands of families more or less harmoniously constructed; we have other thousands of houses where two hard-working people and their children toil, eat, dress and sleep, with exemplary diligence for a quarter of a century; we have gilded metropolitan hotels, more or less splendid, in all large towns, where husband, wife and little ones, are stowed away in narrow private apartments, that they may shine in the splendor of the saloon and the dining-hall; we have boarding of all sorts, from genteel to ungenteel, and one way and another, our people get more to eat, drink, wear and enjoy than any other people, but with a smaller result of real comfort and happiness. Our houses hardly rest on solid ground; they go on wheels and rock on waves. The life of the street, like a strong wind, rushes continually through them. We are restless in our own rocking-chair, by our own table, on our own bed; our family resources for happiness are meagre, and the morbid intensity of the household spoils health, and defeats the end of domestic life.

The cultivated American woman must recreate this sphere of life. She must lay the foundation of home in deep quiet love, in unflagging diligence, in sound health, in a solid culture, and unaffected refinement of manners. Let her begin by marrying for spiritual companionship, and a Christian home, not for a position. There can be no home to a pair falsely mated; there may be splendor and success of many kinds, but the paradise of according minds and hearts, which swims like a mirage before the eye of the youth, will never be theirs. Then let her whole influence be exerted to found the practical side of the household, in that noble economy and simplicity that scorns to use what it has not; and its spiritual side on a natural style of behavior and manners. Adopting foreign customs as far as they can be brought in vital connection with the life around her, and neglecting all nonsense, however popular, she may create a place where every power shall be refreshed, and every virtue developed. Let her keep her home, a home; and not pervert it to a means of social ambition; train her children to human worth, not to be spectacles in society; and as wealth and opportunities increase, build up on the side of true refinement and lasting comfort. Thus will there be at last a home, pervaded with the American spirit of a cultivated freedom, where all shall be free, yet, each be the minister of all; and life shall deepen into peace and expand into power and grace.

As soon as this home exists, woman will have all the rights over property and her own children, of which she is now unjustly deprived. Legislators will not dare to refuse the demand of the mass of cultivated wives and mothers, that they shall no longer be legally merged in man. The reason why the American people tolerate laws, derived from the society of the middle ages on these subjects, is that there are not women enough who care to enter or remain in domestic life, on dignified terms of equality with man to demand their alteration. It is easier for most women to trust to management and importunity for their pecuniary supplies, than to labor for the recognition of woman's just rights of property; and few mothers contemplate the event of being called to choose between a living death with their children in the house of a tyrant, or a selfish release to be shared alone; and thus the abuse continues. But a true family life will bring the community to the point where such inequalities can no longer exist; and when the American woman claims justice, as one pillar of the Republican home, it will not be denied.

Standing firmly at home, woman will be able to look beyond her household, and claim her rights in other spheres. First will come the demand for a better education. She may reasonably claim the highest opportunities for scholastic culture which are enjoyed by man. If she knew with what husks of knowledge she is put off, under the showy pretensions of fashionable girls' schools, ladies' magazines, popular lectures and female literature in general, she would scorn the flatteries by which her want of real culture is concealed. As a class, young women do not know the meaning of the word *study* as known to every educated man. Constantly fed on the flowers of science and literature, and accustomed to turn away from every granite wall of culture, along the vine-decked paths that skirt its base, they come up to womanhood, perhaps confirmed in the delusion that they are educated, while the intellectual life has never been awakened. Thus they are left at the beginning of their real life to the tender mercies of the polite literature of the day, and the popular lecture-room. The cure of this state of things is the union of the sexes in the whole career of scholastic culture. The boys and girls of America should be put in the same school, under equally skillful teachers, carried through an equally thorough course of instruction in high school, academy and college. Now, the girl is stopped at the college door by a polite usher, who conducts her to the fashionable female seminary, where she learns a more superficial science, and is narrowed by exclusive contact with her own sex. The boy is taught to study in the severe discipline of the University, but his nature hardens, and his manners, health and habits are in peril through his seven years' collegiate and professional career; and when the sexes meet again after this monastic separation, they are changed fatally for future companionship.

I solemnly believe that most of the foolish marriages and domestic unhappiness among educated men, are the results of this unnatural separation from women during the most sensitive portion of youth and early manhood. The only natural restraint on the rudeness and rampant passions of the growing boy, is the refining influence of a girl engaged in the same employment. Separate the two, and the boy becomes coarse and careless in manners, impure in thought, and half insane in imagination. Sitting on three chairs in a college room, in which disorder has become organized, deprived of his true society, he conjures up an ideal female, in whose construction his appetites and unpractical fancy fill the outline formed by the goddesses of Homer and Virgil, and the heroines of the English and French novelists; and when he comes out upon professional life, he issues into a new world, where every bright-eyed damsel suggests the ideal that wavered amid curling clouds of cigar smoke above his student head; and having married a goddess, he is very apt to awake to the saddening conviction that his happiness is wrecked on the rock of a false union. Were the sexes trained together they would know each other's strength and weakness, and not only stimulate each other to greater exertions, but also teach one another good breeding and knowledge of practical affairs. The tide of popular sentiment is now running strongly in favor of this educational right of woman in America. Already our revised system of common schools is placing the sexes on common ground; and several vigorous collegiate schools have demonstrated the advantage of union in the higher walks of culture. It only remains for our young women to spurn with womanly contempt this sham education that is proffered them in fashionable life, and at any sacrifice secure the best advantages, and never give over their importunity till their daughters shall be installed into the best privileges of American culture.

The result of this increase of intelligence will be a new desire to enlarge the sphere of female industry. Is there any reason that while the American boy is placed in a profession at one and twenty, the American girl is left dependent on her parents until this boy chooses to make her his wife? It is false and injurious. Dependence is as galling to a true woman as to a man; and whatever disguise of sentimental rhetoric you throw over it, every sensible girl in a large family knows it is absurd that she should be a young lady without employment, except such as she adopts to kill time, living on her father till she can find a husband. What restlessness, what disgust of life, what temptation to unmaidenly scheming in the sacred affairs of the heart, what untold domestic wretchedness this state of gilded slavery entails on the sex, only a wise woman can describe. The remedy for this is not kitchen work alone; there is not enough domestic work in families of several girls to arouse the industrial energies of all. Study is not enough; for true study without definite aim is only possible for highly cultivated minds, and only one girl in a thousand can regularly pursue a science or accomplishment for which she sees no practical bearing. The girls of America need a thorough training in some form of profitable and congenial labor, on which they can depend for steady occupation, which shall relieve them of pecuniary dependence, and keep their minds steadied by actual contact with the real work-day world. Then, study will have a new charm, health will not be spoiled by inactivity, and every young woman can wait till a suitable young man appears before she marries. Then, young men will look on marriage as a privilege, knowing a wife will be a "help meet for them," not a bundle of physical helplessness draped in expensive dry goods; and the practical skill of the woman will keep the man industrious and virtuous.

Whatever the last volume of poems you read may say to the contrary, young woman, nothing so claims the growing respect and holds the constant affection of men as the union of a womanly heart with womanly practical energy. Highly wrought raptures are very well in their time; smiles and tears and sentimental longings are surely a part of life; but the woman who can only sit in her rocking-chair, and drench her cambric handkerchief when hard labor, or narrow circumstances, or great sorrow darken the household; or can only dance when good fortune comes in at the door, cannot reckon on a permanent influence over any strong man. The most beautiful thing to our sex is an affection that is ever taking active forms of expression, that talks less than it does, that silently builds up a home while we are engrossed outside, that is competent to advise us in the conduct of affairs, and when we are at our wits' end has some happy plan in reserve by which we can go on. Such a woman takes her husband's arm and goes over every step in life, and when misfortune comes she does not become a dissolving view of inefficiency and vaporous sentiment, but only clasps the friendly arm a little closer, and new courage flows through every manly nerve, to overcome the worst that life can do.

We must throw open every species of labor to woman, and let her peculiar power choose what is best for herself. There is no danger that she will permanently occupy any place inconsistent with her womanly dignity, or drive men from any work they can do better than she. The community will know whose labor is most valuable in every department of activity, and ultimately sustain woman wherever she can sustain herself. I have no fear that our American girls will injure their womanhood behind the counter, in the manufactory, in the printing office, or wherever they choose to go. I know tastes differ; but I, in common with many sensible men, prefer the spectacle of a company of intelligent young women in active employment at any respectable occupation, to the melancholy procession of idle, bedizened femininity that daily sweeps the pavements with swelling satin and French kid; the funeral procession of American womanhood. And if young women knew their own souls and true destiny, they would not rest till their hands and minds found substantial employment that would at once do something for society, and sustain and ennoble themselves. Until this is done, there is no hope of woman's emancipation; for while man holds her in a pecuniary dependence from which she does not aspire to rise, her ideal of freedom will be only a school-girl's dream.

I am aware that this extension of the field of female industry will bring woman into the sphere of professional life to a greater extent than now, and I am not ignorant of the ridicule with which thousands of women are accustomed to visit the efforts of their sisters in this direction. But is not the radical question of woman in the professions already settled by the community? If ever the sex were to be shut out of this area of life, the time has passed, for women are already in several departments of professional activity. In authorship, school teaching, and the fine arts of painting, sculpture, music, and the drama, they are naturalized; and probably no persons would more vigorously oppose any attempt to eject them from these posts than those who are shocked at their attempt to win new positions. The fact is proven, that woman can act in public capacity and not lose one grace of her nature, while her service to the community is undoubted; and in two additional professions, medicine and popular lecturing, the people have already decided that she shall have her place.

Surely it would be hard to deny to her who in her capacity of housekeeper, parent and creator of social customs, is responsible for a large share of the disease in the world, an opportunity to aid in its cure. Surely the present success of the medical profession in preserving the health of the people is not so overwhelmingly evident that it can afford to spurn her proffered assistance. Nobody objects to a woman lecturer, if she lectures well, and I suppose nobody approves a man lecturer if he lectures ill. One sect of Christians has opened the office of religious instruction in the church to woman, and with no special evil results; indeed, the best preacher in the American sect of Friends is now a woman. I cannot but think the time is coming when some of the high Christian culture that now especially distinguishes the best women of the land, will find a tongue and waken new echoes in consecrated places. In the present subdivision of the legal profession, I can hardly under stand why women might not occupy many posts as successfully as men. This question of professional success is not to be decided *à priori*, but by experience. It is absurd to say a woman loses dignity in the pulpit and at the bar, and retains it in the concert, on the stage, and in the public ball-room. Whatever part of professional effort she can hold usefully to society and naturally to herself, is hers by the only right which man can assert—the right of conquest.

The more radical friends of the woman's movement affirm that the right of suffrage and elegibility to public office are essential to the freedom of the sex. With the logic that conducts to this conclusion I can discern no defect. If anybody can tell me why 20,000 men who cannot read and write should be permitted to vote in New York *because they are men*, and the 20,000 most cultivated women refused that privilege *because they are women*—why thousands of wealthy females should pay taxes which they never have a voice in imposing—why woman should be tried in courts of justice exclusively before masculine juries—why men alone should make laws that women must obey—I would be glad to hear a reasonable argument. I know the difficulties attending the whole complicated question of free suffrage; but it seems to me, we must either restrict the right of suffrage in America yet more than now, or throw it open, in time, to the other sex. We do not yet know the result of unlimited suffrage; the experiment is still being tried; experience alone will decide what is to come of it. Meanwhile women do already influence politics mightily. The women of our Southern States sustain the great evil of negro slavery that rules the Government of America. If they would rise to-morrow and proclaim human bondage wicked and vulgar, every chain would fall and the oppressed go free. The women of the Northern States move the men that make the laws according to their intelligence and interest in the history and life of the nation; and I cannot understand how a young American woman can be indifferent to the momentous ideas involved in our national experiment. I do not know whether the women of America will ever, as a body, demand the right of suffrage; certain I am, if they do, we shall be as eager to give it them as we are now to give them the wealth and luxury we wear out our lives to obtain. Whatever woman wants in this country she can have; and it rests with her whether she assumes the full privilege of American citizenship or acts for the state through man.

These are the several steps along which woman will advance to the Republican style of character, in America. At every step society will be richer and more characteristic of our great national idea. Only where acting freely and out of the fullness of her womanhood, can she construct that peculiar social state which is the outgrowth of our institutions. We do not know what that society will be; but surely it will be truthful, wise, strong and free as it is not now. Under the guidance of cultivated woman, the American man will be a different being from the man we know; for in gaining peace and happiness he will gain purity and refinement. The crowning grace of our life will then be a new beauty—the beauty of freedom—which shall adorn and elevate the home, the street, the halls of pleasure, the seats of learning, and mould the manners and refine the public life of the people. Then shall we know, that, much as woman has been and done in the world, it was reserved for the magic influence of national liberty to reveal her nature in its entire loveliness and power. Then, unhindered by outward restrictions and set free from the bondage of selfishness within, will she become the divine force of love she was made to be, and strew the land with flowers by her presence. No nation of men worship woman with an adoration so sincere and blind, as the Americans; will she be content to abuse this admiration, and while she is an idol, neglect the culture of that lofty womanhood which shall deserve it? This adoration we pay her is not folly; it is now extravagance, for she does not deserve it; but it is a prophecy of what woman can become under the inspiration of freedom. For when the true woman of America shall appear, she whose nature will mirror the glories and graces of a Republican State, as the waters of our lakes and rivers mirror the mountains with their crowning forests and the overarching skies, and who can rouse up men to adorn Liberty by their justice at home, and make it venerable to the nations abroad; then will there be one who deserves our utmost reverence, and, next to God, claims our manly devotion and adoring love.

That style of woman has not come; but, young women, you are born to hasten her coming. Shall I affront you by the suspicion that you will prefer the material side of freedom to this, her noblest spiritual results? Shall I not rather put into words the throbbing of your own hearts, now too wayward to revere demands, yet generous to the highest appeal, and say: Before God, this day shall witness a new consecration to the obligation of my time and country; for henceforth I live no more to self and sloth, but forgetting the mean prizes which slaves wring out of a newly-gained emancipation, move onward to the full consummation of that liberty which shall make me free in bonds of a love that binds self and home, society and country in a golden chain, and suspends the world below the throne of God.

## XII.

## THE CHURCHES;

OR,

## RELIGION IN NEW YORK.

It cannot be said the Capital City is destitute of Religious Institutions. The wants of its 60,000 people are ministered to by fifty churches, which, by their creeds and ceremonies, represent almost every form of faith, from the ancient Hebrew to the newest form of Protestant Christian. Fifty clergymen officiate in these houses of worship, and among the homes of the people. There is, probably, a seat in a church for two of every three in its population, though the brightest Sunday morning sees only one-third of the whole people under a consecrated roof. There are thirty-five Sunday-schools, containing 7,000 children; and several mission-schools and benevolent institutions complete the ecclesiastical machinery of the place.

This relative proportion holds good throughout

the State. New York contains 5,077 churches, affording seats for 2,141,159 of her 3,466,212 people, although the average attendance on public worship is estimated at only 1,124,211 ; and there are only 702,384 members of churches. These churches, with other property connected, are valued in the census table at $31,480,128 ; and the yearly salaries of clergymen at $2,411,683, giving an average of $400 a year to a body of men harder worked and poorer paid than any class in the Commonwealth. Of these 5,077 churches, the Catholics own the comparatively small number of 291 ; there are 19 Jewish Synagogues ; and the remainder are divided among the Protestant sects, in the following order: Methodist, 1,580; Baptist, 882 ; Presbyterian, 710 ; Episcopalian, 346 ; Evangelical Congregational, 301 ; Reformed Dutch, 260 ; Liberal Christians (including the Christians and Disciples), 250 ; Friends, 134 ; Lutheran and other German Evangelical, 132 ; Swedenborgian, 3 ; Second Advent, 8 ; Shakers, 3 ; while one solitary conventicle rejoices in the name of "Protestant Communion of Free Inspiration." But in estimating the religious institutions of our State, we must also reckon the large body of dissenters from all these forms of worship, whose wants are supplied by the numerous radical conventions and itinerant lecturers which have become a very characteristic mode of religious and philanthropic agitation in our northern States. It is not too much to say, that full one-fourth of our population obtain all their public instruction in religion from these new sources. When we consider, in addition, the immense circulation of the religious press, in its various forms of theological and reformatory newspapers, pamphlets and books; and remember, also, that the city of New York is fast becoming the centre from which all our organized religious institutions operate, and where the plans are matured for promoting the success of every sect and party, conservative and radical, we may well be astonished at the amount of energy, wealth, and ability, now engaged in representing the religious condition of our people; and the questions: How far does this vast machinery represent the religion of the State; and how well is it adapted to the application of a pure Christianity to our civilization? assume an importance transcending any others that can be asked of our great Commonwealth.

For to say that the success of a Republican civilization in New York depends on the success of a pure Christianity, is to report a fact demonstrated by the experience of mankind. In opposition to the strange assumptions of Mr. Buckle, that moral ideas have nothing to do with the progress of civilization, we believe the whole condition of every community on earth is an outgrowth from its religious faith. The depth and intelligence of a people's belief in such questions as the origin, duty, and destiny of man, measure their achievements in all respects; and those nations which have been farthest along in religion have ruled the earth by the power of their ideas, perpetuating themselves through generations. This State of New York is what she now is to-day by force, not of her superficial, but real belief or disbelief in these fundamental questions of being; and could we know the actual position of her people towards the ideas of love to God and man, which are the centre of Christianity, all the phenomena of her private and public life would be explained.

The whole significance of Jesus Christ and the history of Christianity is concentrated in this law of love. Whoever has attained a character shaped by the indwelling power of love to God and man is a Christian, and whatever people has achieved a civilization expressive of the same eternal love is a Christian state. The true Christian church in New York would therefore be the union of the Christian citizens of the State to resist every idea and practice opposed to the law of love, and to promote the elevation of public and private character towards this lofty ideal of human perfection; thus saving men from sin and making their present state of being a fit introduction to their immortal career. Whatever differences of ceremonial or organization might characterize its various divisions, these would never be permitted to obstruct the practical union of all good men and women for personal holiness and public virtue.

However numerous the theories concerning Christian theology, or the creeds in which the thought of the past is condensed, the freedom of opinion would not be invaded, and every man's thought would be judged by his life, instead of his character being measured by his creed. Thus while all needful independence of theological speculation, and variety of religious ceremonial would be secured, the church of New York would be the spiritual union of all Christians in love and charity, insuring a practical union for every emergency, when the powers of evil should challenge the friends of God and man to conflict for truth and righteousness. This is the idea of Christianity and the Christian Church, taught by the founder of our religion; and until both are realized in this State, no excess of wealth, or culture, or political power, or social refinement will do more than gild the barbarism in which man always remains until his life moves in glad obedience to the immutable law of the Divine Benevolence.

Tried by this standard of excellence, we cannot acknowledge that New York is a Christian State. For however pure and active a minority of her citizens may be, it cannot be affirmed that the majority have attained a character moulded by Christian love. Neither does her civilization prefigure the kingdom of heaven. Are her industry, her politics, her society, her literature founded on Christian benevolence? To ask the question is to answer it. Every good man knows that, however far in advance of former periods, or other communities, we are yet in the bonds of a materialistic idea of life; are not civilized enough to acknowledge that love is the corner-stone of true success.

Now what is the condition of the organized religion on which we are depending for the conversion of this half barbarism to a true social state? Is the church in New York, a true Christian Church, according to the ideas of Jesus? Can we hope that our present ecclesiastical institutions, in their present method of operation, will make the Empire State first in righteousness, as she is already first in power among the free communities of the earth?

That the church of New York is not doing this

work so well or so fast as good men could wish, is too obvious to be denied. In the first place, it can command the attendance of only one-third of the people on its ceremonies and instructions; and numbers only one-fifth as nominal members of the Christian fold. With a population in open agreement with Christianity, with the field entirely undisputed, with all the aids of wealth, the press, and the perpetual services of 6,000 ministers trusted and privileged like no other class, it is still obliged to confess to this want of success. Even this one-fifth which constitutes the visible body of communicants, cannot be called the leading force in the civilization of the State. The church has not uniformly led the people in the best social reforms of the past fifty years; it has oftener been forced abroad by an outside pressure. It does not lead the State, to-day, in the most vital life of an advancing society; a few divisions of it are abreast of the best life of the times, but other divisions are back in the middle ages; and as a whole, it is so divided by obstinate and bitter hostilities, so involved in its own machinery, that it has never, in one instance, united to do any one good work for the people. These 6,000 ministers are not the advance men of the day, not preëminently the moral leaders of the State. The people show them great outward respect; but four-fifths of them refuse to do what the clergy affirm is essential to eternal life, and they pay them $400 a year. As a necessary consequence, the majority of our people are unsettled in belief and practice to an alarming degree. A deep-rooted skepticism is spreading among the leading classes of every district, often concealed, but none the less destructive. Large masses of the people are adrift; now excited by a revival, now by a radical convention, unsatisfied with either. Who knows what his neighbor really believes on man's origin, duty, destiny? We do not affirm our organized religion a failure; its various merits need no defence, and it does immense good, at least in keeping things as well as they are. But we are still less prepared to call it a great success, while its real hold on the people is so uncertain, and it is forced to take the secondary position in every battle between barbarism and practical Christianity. We must assert that the church of New York is still far below the mark at which it may reasonably claim the superiority it now does; that its condition is becoming a painful problem for all wise religious men to contemplate.

While we acknowledge the whole truth in regard to the difficulty of elevating any community by the purest religion, we must still declare that the church is greatly at fault in the present state of affairs. We blame it not so much for its inability to convert the wicked and indifferent, as for the spurious character of much of the Christianity in its own fold. It is because the religion it really creates is so often futile, timid, useless; so much a thing of words and ceremonies, and so little a practical force for the right, that we feel compelled, as its best friend, to proclaim its shortcomings, and assert that the Protestantism of New York to-day needs a Reformation as certainly as the Catholicism of Europe in the days of Luther. We have no sympathy with the enemies of the church; we do not believe Christian institutions are to die out as man grows; but we believe the church must pass through many a period of regeneration before she will be the symbol of a pure Christianity. Reform or die is now the destiny of our popular ecclesiasticism. Not that the church of New York cannot exist as now, and become even more rich, splendid in its ceremonial, and popular in its dispensations than at present; but then it will cease to be a church of God, and become only an ecclesiastical, a social corporation in no way representative of Christianity. To apply the law of love to the life of New York demands the reforming of several popular vices, and the cultivation of several uncommon virtues. Let us indicate the direction which this revival of true religion in the church must take.

The great European Reformation of the 16th century, which resulted in Protestantism, was chiefly a revolt against ecclesiastical tyranny. A mighty thing was done when the church was burst asunder and the despotic unity of Roman Catholicism forever destroyed. But no great evil is cured at once, and ecclesiastical intolerance has been one of the greatest evils in Protestant lands. In the nations of Europe adopting the Reformed Religion, the most obstinate efforts of the people have not yet sufficed to shake off the oppression of great, consolidated establishments assuming the guardianship of God's truth. And in New York to-day, ecclesiasticism is a fearful power. Every Protestant sect is now a close corporation, working for power, often by very questionable means, coveting wealth and position, rewarding its friends and punishing its enemies. Its clergy and active laity are counted faithful in proportion as they toil for its aggrandizement. The enterprise and popular habits of our people are strongly implicated in this work; and to an outside observer, the manœuvering of these sects appears but little to excel those of the political parties in dignity or purity.

Like the parties, they have their platforms, their campaign issues, their fusions and schisms, their system of rewarding friends and shooting deserters, and he must be credulous indeed who permits the assumption of a party phraseology to blind him to the realities of the case. If there is found a certain security in the fact that these sects are so numerous and so evenly mated; on the other hand, this encourages that strife for popularity, which is the demon of the American Church. The results are the oppression of the people, who are wheeled about in masses by the church leaders, and cheated of their freedom by the force of social pressure and the theological fear of detraction; while each of the sects fears to commit itself to a pure morality, lest it should thereby be lowered in public estimation and outbid by a less scrupulous opponent.

We need a new application of the great Protestant idea that man is superior to sects. The church in New York must learn that Religion is above corporations and parties; that to create a great ecclesiasticism by flattering the vices of the people is not to do God's work but Satan's work; that to grow rich, strong, numerous, by the acts of a worldly policy, and use power thus gained to crush out opposition, is to kill Christian love, and bring in the reign of universal skepticism. Unless this tendency to sectarian partisanship is checked, it is not difficult to see that all true men will at last be disgusted, and driven from organizations that prefer their own enlargement and perpetuity to the glory of God and the good of man.

But the peculiar evil of Protestantism is not so much ecclesiasticism as dogmatism. The reign of the pope in the middle ages has been followed by the reign of the creed in modern days. And an imperative necessity in the church of New York is the abolition of the whole system of infallible dogmas. Each sect has now a creed which is practically made the test of religious character. Whoever accepts it and serves God *that way* has a hope of eternal life; whoever does not is in danger of perdition, or at least is reckoned unchristian. The Protestant Evangelical sects unite to call all the world unchristian who reject the so-called evangelical dogmas; the Roman-Catholic retorts with equal insolence and equal reason; the Liberalists too often catch the intolerance and make the creed the measure of the life. Now a creed is a good thing if properly used. Every creed is the condensed idea of some division of christendom on religion, and each probably contains some valuable truth. If men can be at liberty to investigate, compare, select, and hold them in the spirit of loyalty to truth, encouraged to enlarge their own belief as fast as they grow in knowledge, there is no harm in their use. But now, when they are used as fortresses in which to shut up and imprison their nominal beliefs, they have become a monstrous evil. What narrowness of mind, and uncharitableness of heart—what grinding tyranny over weak and timid minds—what wicked slander of opponents—what hypocrisy and self delusions, grow out of this wretched assumption of theological infallibility is becoming more apparent to every good man.

The Protestantism of the day must cease this mimicry of the worst sin of Papacy; withdraw its absurd pretensions of infallibility, which only expose it to the derision of reflecting minds; and while maintaining the truth given it with all its might, never deny the sacred right of free thought or expression on religion. We rejoice that a reform is already commencing in this direction. The best thing in the revival of last winter was the agreement of a few sects to ignore doctrinal distinctions for a time, in a work of Christian evangelization. The next great revival will demolish the remaining pretensions of a Protestant dogmatism to hold the keys of heaven and hell, and leave the people free to think, to the vast gain of pure religion.

Equally essential is a reform in humanity. The Protestant church of New York is, as a whole, unhuman. It is a factitious world of its own; a little realm of priests and churches and ceremonies and prayers outside the real world. It ignores New York in favor of some future heaven of which it talks much in proportion as it knows little. Consequently the church life of the State is quite too much aloof from the actual life of the people. The real evils of society, the real state of mind among the masses, the real course of events, are almost unknown to it. So it can gather the disciples into the charmed circle of the church and talk of future bliss, it gladly forgets the present. But whatever the church thinks, this State of New York is a great fact, that cannot be spirited away by the theories of a million doctors of divinity. And whatever the clergy may agree to consider orthodox, no religion is truly Christian which cannot go to the people as they are, and regenerate them where they are, and make them holy by the application of the law of love, and extirpate the evils of society by testing every region of life, and every form of character by the law of God. Every church that cannot do the work of applying Christianity to this three and a half millions of people, and making a heaven of this forty-six thousand square miles of territory, may as well vacate at once, for its days are numbered.

It would be gross injustice to deny that many portions of the church are awakening to this duty; it would be flattery to say that there does not yet remain so much to be done, and that speedily, that safety lies only in repentance. The best people of New York are fast coming to the conclusion that a church that loves itself more than man is not worth the expense of keeping alive; and the next quarter of a century will be shaken with an agitation, that will wake the sleepiest conventicle from its sacred repose to a perception of its duty to the struggling cause of righteousness in this Republic.

As the legitimate result of these vices of dogmatism, ecclesiasticism, and unhumanity, the church of New York is threatened with death from disintegration. Of course every man who cannot live under the yoke of the creed, or the corporation, goes out, and either becomes a radical, or forms a new church. Thus sects multiply, conventicles increase in number, and decrease in supporters. Every village and town in the country is struggling to sustain several Protestant churches. The money which would support one clergyman is divided among three or four; and this wretched system of compensation drives thousands of the best qualified youth away from a proper profession, and fills the pulpits with inferior men. This again reacts on the people, who lose interest in a Gospel so feebly proclaimed, and the church languishes towards a fall, and is only kept alive by frequent spasmodic excitements. A Christianity so divided and debilitated, can never unite to sustain the right in any great public emergency. Let any formidable enemy to society take the field, supported by the passions of multitudes and the prestige of wealth, and what a feeble opponent it finds in the sects. Every church is pressed to live at all; it cannot afford to offend even a few adherents, by actively exposing the truth. Every denomination is jealous of its neighbor, and will not unite with it, lest it should seem to indorse its deadly heresy. So the churches keep quiet, or talk in cloudy generalities, and the adversary walks over the course.

A great public evil is always a unit; it goes together and conquers, by dividing its opponents. When the church condescends to learn from the devil his great secret of *keeping his forces together*, it will conquer him; till that, he will ravage the country even under the shadows of the spires, and fear the sight of an ecclesiastical convention no more than an army would fear an undisciplined mob. The consequence of a reformation in the former respects will be a willingness to unite for all the uses of practical religion. Why, could this great church of New York heartily agree to make a holy crusade against any sin, it might render the most daring vice of our people execrable, and drive it out from the sight of decent society. Unless it can agree to do this, it will have a fearful account to settle with those who love God's truth, and will not long be silent over its eclipse. Better no church, than one that can never be found when most wanted. Let the present establishment continue to crumble, till it leaves some way of concentrating its forces for God and humanity.

How shall this good work of reform be accomplished? We answer, by the persistent efforts of the wisest and most religious people who still remain within the church; and by a new movement towards a liberal organization among those who have permanently left it.

There are two classes in the church, of whom little can be expected in this reformation. The first consists of the sincere bigots, who cannot understand how a soul can get to heaven except by crawling through the eye of their sectarian needle. We can do justice to the sincerity and moral worth of many of these persons, and yet feel that if the church falls they are chiefly responsible. Little is to be expected from an honest bigot, because bigotry implies narrowness of mind, and while the sufferer, under this malady can see only through his present eyes, reason and charity will be alike unavailing to move him onward. We can only leave him to the grace of God, and pray that his eyes may be opened in this world, or in some distant eternity.

For the second class of worldly people who seek the church for sake of social position, pecuniary or other emoluments, even less can be expected. Of all people who fill our churches these are the most hopeless. For they are using Religion for their own aggrandizement, and are quite indifferent to the meaning of Christianity. No sect is free from this class, although the most powerful are necessarily the most afflicted. Every attempt at reform will be frowned down by those who fear any loss of prosperity for their conventicle. They will shake hands with the most obstinate bigotry to keep affairs as they are, and it is chiefly by this unholy alliance of intolerance and worldliness that the church is kept so far behind the demands of the times.

Leaving these two classes as almost hopeless for any onward movement, we can with more confidence appeal to the large body of truly Christian men and women that still exist in every sect. These persons, the very flower of our church life, whose piety and philanthropy save it from stagnation, are now quite too often overborne by the obstinacy and craft of the two classes before named. Many of them are those quiet disciples who avoid contention and go on their own blameless way, not coveting the chief place in the organization; indeed often not knowing what the church as a public institution is about. Happy in their own private belief and the beautiful associations clustering about their spiritual home, they put off criticism of their ecclesiasticism, will not dwell on the unlovely and depressing signs of its unfaithfulness, and are drifted along by a current of which they know not the force or the direction. They do not see that although they are in the dear old ship, yet the hand of an intolerant or artful policy is at the helm; that the vessel is officered by those bold ambitious spirits who love to walk the slippery decks and climb the storm-tossed shrouds; and that while they are occupied in works of benevolence below, the old gospel craft is being steered on the breakers of intolerance, or the black flag of worldliness is run up, and she is turned to a pirate in the service of oppression. Neither do they know that their acquiescence, even their very graces of mildness and peacefulness, are used by these theological wire-pullers to shield themselves from the just odium of an indignant community, as a general piles up bales of the whitest cotton to ward off the shot from the batteries of the enemy.

Our only hope of Religious Institutions is in arousing this large body of true Christians to a knowledge of what is done in their name, and a determination to assume their due share of influence in the policy of the church. If they can be persuaded to look at the ecclesiastical intolerance, the dogmatic insolence, the inhumanity and the divisions of their organized Christianity through their own eyes; can be rallied to a persistent effort at their overthrow; we may hope much for religion in New York. We know how distasteful the warfare will be; how quiet men and amiable women loathe the agitation attendant on defacing corrupt leaders and upsetting a mediæval policy; how indolence can easily disguise itself in the garb of Christian peace; but we do not understand what claim the purest and gentlest have to live undisturbed in the service of a Christianity for whose establishment Jesus Christ and thousands of his followers have cheerfully gone to death, and others have borne the cross during their whole life. Does this loving, timid woman who fears the breath of slander or the sound of tumult near her home, reflect that her Saviour said, "I came not to send peace, but a sword?" Do these quiet men consider that just on them who know and feel the divine worth of a free religion God lays the martyr's mission in these later days? *They are the people who should not keep still;* who should rouse themselves and put forth all the might of holiness in them to regenerate these great sects, slowly dying with the infection of our materialism.

We do not ask them to renounce their belief as long as they can accept the creed; but we demand that they shall compel their church to renounce their absurd and wicked claim of infallibility. We ask them not to desert the ceremonial they have so long admired; but when the priest curses and shuns all outside that prayer-book as unconverted, let them teach *him* the Christian charity he has forgotten. We do not know where they could find a church as practical as it should be if they left their own; but we implore them to help wrench the iron foot of their own church from the wreck of a down-trodden humanity. If they will always stay in their present division of the fold, let them at least stretch their hands over the bridge and grasp the hands of Christians on the other side. These persons can yet save our Protestantism from the fate of Roman Catholicism if they awake in time. If they will not awake, their very graces of peacefulness and piety will become criminal, since they hold them back from their duty. It may be a privilege to belong to the church, but then it is an obligation likewise, and those who enjoy the privilege and ignore the difficult duty are not the true disciples of Him who walked up Mount Calvary that we might look upon his cross, and learn the grandeur of self-sacrifice for the cause of God and man.

We are disposed to be hopeful, and believe that this class will finally be aroused in our churches, and the sects be converted to the cause of religion. But there is a struggle impending in New York which will throw all previous agitation in the shade. The bigotry and the worldliness in these great, rich corporations, are not going to subside at the bidding of any power; and only when finally rooted out, will they give up the field. The preliminary skirmish can be witnessed in any week's reading of the church journals; but this is only the skirmish preparatory to a war which will purify, while it shakes, the churches. God speed all good men, who are toiling in this great reformation; they will have sorrow and labor enough for their portions in this life, but the favor of God and the deep gratitude of humanity will be their sure reward.

Meanwhile, there is a vast body of people who are out of the church on principle. They cannot, in conscience, be held responsible for its glaring evils, and they have no stomach for the warfare that must slowly achieve its purification. They think the way, both to regenerate the church and to advance religion, is to act outside the organized ecclesiasticism. They have the right to do so; and the wholesale slander with which this class, now far more numerous than the entire body of church members, and certainly not inferior in religious life, is visited by the regular clergy and the church organs, is a wicked outrage on Christian charity. But this body of dissenters have their duties to perform. It may be a great privilege to have parted company with the organized church, Evangelical and Roman Catholic; but that privilege is bought up with the obligation to teach and establish a purer religion. Thousands of these dissenters seem quite thoughtless of this obligation. So they can enjoy their own freedom of thought, expose the sins of the old establishments, and drop in once a month at a radical convention, or occasionally swell the crowd that throngs the steps of a great preacher, their work is done, while their families are often left utterly uninstructed in religious views and with no Christian associations.

It is hard to convince those persons, that by this course they are perpetuating the reign of bigotry and inhumanity in religion. The Evangelical and Catholic churches are armies well officered and manœuvered with consummate tact; and while the dissenting host is scattered over the field as now, both these armies will conquer by sheer weight of discipline. We have no hostility to mass conventions, and itinerant lecturers on religion and reform; in the present state of affairs they have their uses, however capable in bad hands of being abused. But what does Archbishop Hughes care for a mass convention? He knows it will be over in three days; that the public journals will emulate each other in calling it by any name their subscribers desire; that nobody there is responsible for anything said or done; that in any moral crisis the endeavor to summon it and make it work would be equivalent to marshalling an equal number of birds to face a whirlwind. What do the managers at the Tract House, and the Bible House, care for the system of lectures on reform and religion unsupported by organization? They have a rich, close corporation, a press, can buy shrewd and eloquent men to plead their cause, and well they know they cannot fall until liberalism concentrates its forces in something more potent than a curious crowd. Meanwhile a vast system of visitation is preparing to operate on every family in the State, and bring the children into the Evangelical Sunday-school. Once there, the revival machinery, like a great elevator, lifts them into the church, and so the work of a generation turns round upon itself.

The imperative duty of the dissenting force in New York now is organization. It is possible to gather the friends of free thought on religion into associations for the practice and study of religion. Let the best person attainable be selected as teacher, and a just freedom of thought be allowed in preacher and hearer; all agreeing to unite to do works of benevolence and aid each other towards the best wisdom. Out of such associations, would finally come a multitude of free churches in the State. The children would have religious associations, the minds of preacher and people be stimulated, and when the evil one blew his trumpet of defiance over the land, there would be an answering blast from these societies—for the time become one—to repel this invasion of public morality.

Already are there some 250 such organizations in New York, mostly small in number and resources, but all capable, by liberal and religious management, of being placed on firm foundations and made the centres of a new religious life. There are materials for as many more; and we urge upon the friends of religious liberty everywhere the duty of concentrating, and putting themselves in the way of permanent religious instruction. Even nothing more than a weekly assembly for the sincere discussion of truths affecting man's origin, duty, and destiny, would be a great advance on the disorganization of the present time. Thus alone can the great mass of truth imparted by conventions, lectures, and the press, be made available in the development of a growing life among the people.

Could we see at the end of twenty-five years, only a few hundred such liberal Christian churches in New York, united in the determination to have the law of love applied to the life of the State, it would be a great aid to the establishments now on the ground. Neither Catholicism nor Evangelicism could spring a plot against the freedom of the soul in the face of such a watchful organization. While they would both be pricked up to philanthropy and purity by its powerful criticisms and example. Meanwhile the friends of a Reformed

Christianity in these churches would succeed in beating down the evils that now cripple them. Feeble churches would unite on the ground of union in life and toleration in belief; the creeds would first lose their infallibility, and then become only the aids of men in learning of Christ. No ecclesiasticism would be able to shut up any large portion of the people away from the mass of believers; the practical work of reforming the State would take the place of useless ceremonial and indolent sentimentalism in the churches; and, year by year, the sects and the individual congregations would be learning to combine for great public influence on the side of the truth.

Would it be too much to hope that half a century in this country of rapid growth would quite modify the condition of the church of New York; and in place of a Babel of warring sects, give us a practical union of good men and women for the sanctification of society. To doubt that this is sometime to come is to condemn Christianity. For some religion must be had to regenerate this commonwealth by the power of united love and free thought; and if Christianity cannot do it, the people will have something that will. But Christianity can and will do it; this is Christianity as it came from Jesus Christ, when he said Love to God and man is the whole law, and this is the glorious ideal he beheld when he prayed: "*That they all may be one; as thou, Father, art in me, and I in thee, that they also may be one in us; that the world may believe that thou hast sent me.*"

Christians of the Empire State, is this blessed hope to be longer mocked and changed into despair through your intolerance and contentions and unhumanity? Behold the garden God has given you to till; the greatest free State upon earth, rich in all materials of a Republican society. In your hands is placed its destiny. You may say whether Christianity here shall exhaust herself through her sins and quarrels, till she becomes the prey to a new barbarism; or, freeing herself from present impurities, rise to the controlling power in the souls of the people. We seek no complicity of church with the State; no concentration of a great ecclesiasticism; no union with any outside interests. We only demand that those who love God and man shall agree to work together to make this magnificent commonwealth the garden of the Lord. What New York shall be religiously is, more and more, to determine the fate of Christianity in the Republic. From our great metropolis go forth plans and ideas that shape new States and mould new orders of society. All the forces of Religion and Irreligion are gathering here for a final struggle. Should we behold spiritual despotism and superstition laying the foundations of social and political tyranny, and not be up and doing, and save our State to a broad and pure Christianity? Save our country to the sacred cause of a righteous Liberty; save the Religion of Jesus from being driven from our own land to seek in distant shores the home denied in this? Never did a nobler field invite the toil; never will a richer harvest reward the fidelity of man.

# XIII.

## THE RURAL CEMETERY;

OR,

## LIFE AND DEATH.

Among the burial-places of our State, no one may better claim the admiration of the lover of beauty than the Albany Rural Cemetery. Situated three miles north of the city, upon the western bank of the Hudson, it includes, within the space of two hundred acres, a variety of surface remarkable even in this picturesque region. Its shaded avenues climb, by gradual acclivities, to lofty eminences, and hence the river is seen washing the wharves of two neighboring cities, and flowing between tranquil islands, down to the majestic curve, where it wheels off between a gateway of bold headlands. The cities and villages, the lovely wooded hills that soar to the opposite horizon, the distant spectral Catskills, the strange blending of human activity with the bewitched silence of the valley, detain the traveller long upon these enchanted summits. On descending, a new charm appears in a series of long ravines, extending down the entire slope, through which sequestered foot-paths lead among waterfalls and miniature lakes, and thread the flowery banks of perennial streams. Art has conspired with nature in the decoration of this beautiful city of the dead, which should be visited by every tourist to the ancient capital of our commonwealth.

This Rural Cemetery dates from a meeting of the citizens of Albany, on December 31, 1840. An eloquent discourse from a venerable clergyman, still living, had aroused the attention of the town to the necessity of better accommodations for the interment of the dead than the already crowded burial-places of the city afforded. In April, 1841, a legislative act of incorporation gave a new impulse to the scheme; and on the afternoon of October 7th, 1844, the grounds were solemnly dedicated, an immense concourse of citizens assembling to unite in the consecration. During the fourteen years of its existence, it has enlarged its boundaries, and is already one of the most attractive cemeteries in our country.

At the time of the dedication, the Rural Cemetery was almost an experiment in the United

States. As early as 1831 the first essay was made in Massachusetts, simultaneously with a like movement in England; for previous to 1832 this form of interment was almost unknown in Eastern Europe, though the Oriental nations have always inclined to this mode of burying the dead. Mount Auburn, near Boston, was the earliest result of this great movement of public feeling which has covered our States with countless cemeteries. When the Albany inclosure was dedicated, Laurel Hill, in Philadelphia, Mount Hope, in Rochester, Greenwood, in New York, with Mount Auburn, were its chief competitors for public admiration. The act of the legislature of New York, in 1847, was a great spur to the public enterprise in this respect. By this statute any company exceeding seven persons, may become a corporation, holding not more than two hundred acres of land, and $5,000, personal estate, for cemetery purposes. The proceeds from the sale of lots are to be appropriated to the purchase and improvement of the grounds. The corporation is governed by a board of trustees, elected by the owners of lots. The interment of one body in a plot of ground makes the spot unalienable. The lands are exempt from taxation and liability for individual debts; sacredly guarded from personal intrusion, and protected from the encroachments of a vandalic spirit of "improvement."

Under the impulse of this enactment, a great number of cemeteries have been established in our State during the past ten years. Few large towns are now destitute of such a spot, to which the stranger is invited with laudable pride; and every year witnesses the inauguration of new enterprises of this kind. The contagious enthusiasm of the American people is a great aid in the prosecution of any new and worthy undertaking; and although an occasional exhibition of fanatical excitement may provoke the disgust of the fastidious skeptic of Republican institutions, yet whoever beholds the susceptibility of our population to noble enthusiasm, will rejoice over it as a providential inspiration in the subjugation of a new world. Every new cemetery now stimulates a neighboring village to greater exertions in this direction, and another quarter of a century will doubtless see every community in New York supplied with a beautiful rural inclosure for the departed.

Already the cities of the dead that crown the hills adjoining our metropolis divide the interest of the contemplative traveller with the cities of the living. Within two hours' ride of New York are no less than twelve noble cemeteries, two of which include four hundred acres each, and most of which cover a space of one hundred acres and upwards. The situation of these cemeteries is unrivalled by any in the world. From the high grounds of the most extensive is spread out the wondrous view of the bay of New York, with intermingled cities, shipping, islands, rivers and ocean. Others overlook the valley of the Hudson. All are beautifully diversified with forest, lakes, cool glens and sunny slopes, and all are rapidly advancing in artistic merit. Oldest and most populous of these is Greenwood—incorporated in 1838, now containing 360 acres—a world of loveliness and grandeur, wherein one may wander for days with ever new objects of attraction challenging his attention.

Every friend of a Christian civilization in New York will rejoice over this growing evidence of respect for the departed. For it is not too much to say that the character of every people is tested by its mode of treating the bodies of the dead. The earliest glimpse of antiquity shows the belief in the sanctity of the body as a fixed sentiment in the race. It has been held by almost every people since the world began as a shameful outrage to deny to the temple of the soul a decent respect from the living. The Egyptians embalmed their dead with great care and built their grandest monumental piles for the resting-place of their bodies, that when the soul should revisit the world it might find its tabernacle awaiting it. The Greeks and the Romans held that the spirit of the unburied man was excluded from the Elysian Fields for a century; and enjoined upon the traveller, coming by chance upon a dead body, the pious duty of throwing dust three times on the inanimate form. How touching are those oft-repeated words in the elder Scriptures, describing the burial of their patriarchs: "He died and was gathered to his people." No funeral service ever exceeded in simple grandeur the words the ancient Hebrew was accustomed to utter at the grave of the deceased: "*Blessed be God who has formed thee, fed thee, maintained thee, and taken away thy life, oh, Dead. He knows your numbers and shall one day restore your life.*" It would seem that burial was the most ancient manner of disposing of the dead. The custom of burning was probably of later origin, and we think the early Christians did wisely in retaining the custom of the primeval ages. There is something akin to the later elaborate Paganisms in the violent and sudden annihilation of the body by flame; there is a beautiful harmony with Christianity in laying the deserted form in the ground amid the glory of the changing seasons, to slowly yield to the laws of nature and be resolved again into her lovely forms.

We could wish that the ancient custom of burying outside of towns and cities had never been invaded; and we approve the sentiment of the Christians of the first five centuries against burials in churches and churchyards. The original instincts of humanity often point to the most admirable customs; and after three thousand years of burning, and hiding in crypts and under pavements, and huddling in crowded churchyards, the better sense and finest taste of the American people are bringing us back to the beautiful practice of the old Hebrew times, of gathering our dead in cemeteries adorned with the tokens of our affections. For the service it has rendered in the education of the soul in this the primary school of its immortal existence, we will bear the body, no longer needed, to the most quiet and lovely place our united hands can prepare, and there leave it to mingle with the elements, and be wrought again into shapes of majesty and grace by those ever-acting laws of nature, which are but the direct presence of the all-creating God.

The improved ideas on the burial of the dead among us are a cheering sign of our advancement in a true Christian civilization. The stern necessities of a new country, and the divisions into rival classes and churches, incident to the transmission from a British province to a Republican Nation, still appear in the burial-places of many portions of our land. The old burying-grounds of the country towns in the original northern States, barren, bleak, poorly inclosed, and carelessly kept, bore witness to the hardships of a pioneer life, when a thousand pressing cares and hourly impending dangers almost compelled the people to neglect the resting-places of their dead. The custom of burying in private inclosures is a relict of the old divisions of European society, where the families of the rich and distinguished, even in death, were desirous of impressing the common people with a sense of their superiority. The practice of church-yard interment grew up from the similar desire to keep separate the rival churches of Christ even in death. We are no longer compelled to overlook our burial-places by poverty, or hardships, or the alarms of war; all family distinctions are fast merging in the only permanent distinction of character, which a Christian democracy can approve; and the contentious corporations that have too long waged unholy warfare in the name of Christ, are coming to see that the church of God in any community is all the Christian people of that place, working for the abolition of wickedness and the success of holiness in time and eternity. All things are tending, at least in the more advanced portions of our country, to a broad and pure Republicanism founded on the Christian law of love; and what emblem can be more significant of this happy tendency than the American cemetery, constructed by the money, taste, and sentiment of the whole people; containing the dust of the earliest generation, removed thither with pious care; receiving the body of every citizen when his earthly work is done, and he steps down from his little eminence of worldly distinction to mingle with the great democracy of death?

We would therefore cherish the American cemetery as a most significant type of the great democratic idea on which our society is founded; as a powerful aid in teaching the people the Christian view of life and death; as a perpetual preacher on the relations of those who live in this world and in the world of souls.

How impressive is the testimony of the cemetery to that true equality of man founded on respect for his nature; and that union of all men for the common welfare, which is the foundation stone of our national existence. However we may be forced by shallow theories or selfish projects to despise or run over any man or class, in the mad struggle of our week-day life, we have only to come up here to be converted from the sin of contempt for humanity. For in the cemetery all distinctions lie level with the dust. Friend and foe, rich and poor, wise and simple, good and bad, honored and obscure, are all here. Whatever they may have been, or may have done, above ground, our gentle mother earth opens her bosom to the least and greatest alike. However separated by the accidents of conventional society, Nature, the most illustrious hostess, keeps open house for all. From these green graves a voice shall speak to us saying: "Man is worthy of respect as man;" and this primal reverence transcends all secondary distinctions. Made in the image of a common Father; clothed in the dust of the common earth; bound to every spirit by a common nature; destined to a common immortality; the soul demands more reverence than any man can pay. Of all distinctions, but one endured beyond these walls; and this only for the common good of humanity.

Vainly will you seek to exalt the special rank of your dead by a show of monumental wealth and the elaborate recital of earthly superiorities. Cover the marble tomb of your most famous man all over with letters of gold; what is this to the majestic monument erected here by nature's God to the memory of the common humanity that sleeps beneath this turf? Will the flowers bloom more tenderly, or the grass wave more greenly, or the wind sing a sweeter song up in the vocal foliage; or the shower, the rain and the dew visit more generously, or the sounds from hill and valley wander hither with more harmonious murmur; or the blue heavens light up by day and glow by night with a glory more sublime, above the bed of the mightiest than over the corner where sleeps the weakest of you all? Come to the cemetery from the selfish competitions that divide man from man, and learn from the way our mother treats her every child, to reverence all men for their manhood derived from God; learn to live for each other, counting any superiority of native faculty, or culture, or character, as a trust to be used for the uplifting of the whole; to make society in this community, in our beloved country, one family bound together by respect for the nature and rights of all; a republic on earth, fit emblem of the kingdom of God in heaven.

It is a happy thought that places so many of our most beautiful cemeteries at easy distances from the centres of activity, and throws them open for the constant visitation of the people. Thereby is no loss of reverence for sacred things; but the popular views of life and death are insensibly elevated. The tendency of our insane activity is to shut the thought of death altogether from the mind; and this fanaticism for work reacts in a no less destructive fanaticism of meditation which overlooks this world, and lives in ecstatic dreams of a future heaven. A pure and wise Christianity unites time and eternity in one complete view of spiritual life. The time is past when this world's activity can be disparaged or despised in behalf of any other world. Look upon this planet to-day, virtually bound into one community; behold the vast sweep of its common interests; see how the ordinary occupations of our life are entangled with the highest spiritual relations. Science, so long despised, has woven her magic wire to demonstrate the fact so grandly proclaimed of old, that we are all members of one body of humanity. Commerce, so often scorned, turns out a pioneer of civilization and Christianity. Every blow of the spade or sweep of the mower on the uplands and in the valleys of New York, is felt in the spiritual experience of these who dwell in far-off lands. If our only hope of religion lies in teaching man to despise this world's affairs just as he is now becoming endowed with angelic powers, and prepared to live a magnificent life on earth, our hope is vain. But, thank Heaven, religion needs no such defence. Christianity teaches the glorious fact of one life for every soul; beginning with its emergence from God and running on forever; a life in which the change we call death is, perhaps, one of the least important events; a life which is exalted or base, not according to the place of occupation, but the quality of the motives and the holiness of the character. Religion commands the men and women of to-day, not to despise this glorious world, or underrate its opportunities, but to use it and all its manifold advantages for the production of that Christian manhood and womanhood, which survive all changes of mortality, and excel all achievements of human power.

Indeed, it is from this very worldly activity that stirs around, and burns within the veins of the American people, that the most cogent appeal arises for faith in the highest beliefs of religion. Were I challenged by the skeptics to show my strong reasons for the faith in God, and moral obligation and immortality, I do not think I should detain him in my study among the volumes of dead divines, but I would lead him to the very throbbing heart of this world's activity, to the decks of those steamers freighted with the science and burdened with the hopes of two continents. There I would stand, as these messengers ploughed their way through the waves, breasting an ocean of incredulity more chilling than the surges of the cold Atlantic, I would bid him mark the demeanor of those toil-worn men; their fidelity, their silent and sacred obedience to every command, the faith of their leader unsubdued by failure. I would ask him to follow that man as he walked up the shore of Newfoundland, and at night to awaken the sleeping electricians by the tidings that the continents were united—to behold that procession which bore the landed cable up to the station, and then bowed in prayer to God; and I would say, Is the instinct that bows great nations as one soul to a higher Power at such a time, a delusion? Is the idea of fidelity to a great obligation that nears the hearts of the swarming crews of two great vessels into one heart, vibrating to every rustle of a frail cord, nothing? Shall the thoughts of generations flash along these wires, while the souls of Morse, and Field, and Hudson go out forever like a wasted taper's flame? Believe who can, that he who thus pierces to the awful deeps of ocean, and shoots the lightnings through the sea and over the land, is the poor creature of chance; his soul a bundle of nerves, his duty the whim of the day, his life a spark struck off the electric wheel of being to go out in blackness everlasting; his holiest and highest beliefs on which he falls back, like a child upon its mother's breast, in the moment of his loftiest achievement, the dreams of a heated brain, that all things he has made shall outlive him; and he, the lord of earth, drop from his own throne into blank annihilation! Ah! because man is so powerful now, does he need to confess the God who made him, that, guided by the eternal laws of goodness, his activity may flow forth to Godlike uses, and bless while it astonishes the world.

How admirable, then, is the sentiment that often places the Rural Cemetery within sight of all the agencies of our new civilization. Walking among its silent graves, you can almost hear the hum of the machinery that crowds the adjacent stream; the meadows are sown and harvested beneath your eye; the spires and roofs of the city gleam in the distance, or the village streets are vocal below; the near river or blue ocean afar glitter with flitting sails; the thunder and the scream of the lightning train startle the echoes of innumerable ravines, and swift as thought, fly tidings of humanity over the glittering wire. All is life around; oh, yes, and there is no death here.

Could you explore the secrets of these green graves, you would behold the irresistible laws of nature changing the body of your friend to the grass blade, and the flower-cup, and the glancing foliage. This mute form you buried out of your sight as dead, is rising to another life. Why fancy, then, that death is a reality? Why not accept the lesson of the Rural Cemetery, that the soul is the centre of the life that throbs adown the hills, and along these river shores; that this soul is not here haunting its body; that body and soul have gone to their own place, the one to blossom in new material shapes, the other to inspire some grander sphere of toil in vaster worlds. Come not here to muse of death; for science has confirmed the glorious doctrine of religion that "death is abolished," and there is only perpetual change in life; but come to think deeply and truly of that spiritual existence which is the gift of God; what a glorious thing it is; how it expands into immortality; how it shall be employed, and how far along the road to perfection you shall be found, when the angel of shadowy countenance leads you through these flowery walks on to your future home.

Come, then, to the Rural Cemetery in every condition and mood of your earthly existence. Let not the child fear to play among these green mounds, for perchance some deep intuition of life shall be struck into his joyous spirit like a soft shadow suddenly darkening the corner of a dancing pool. Come here when love first blossoms in the unspeakable tenderness of man's and maiden's soul, and ask if that thou feelest so tumultuous within can look calmly on change and claim its own beyond the tomb: come here with your new-born darling, and think of the angels whose little forms lie so white and still below: come, man of business, and think over your plans among these trees, and test them by the thought of your eternal life: come, mother, weighed down with little cares and confused by haunting duties, and ask yourself how you shall train your children so that they shall water your headstone with tears from the deep wells of an undying gratitude: come when prosperity makes high noon in your life, and let these silent monitors whisper of rectitude and humility: come in adversity, and read the deep meaning of sunlight on graves and a blessed Providence behind every cloud of grief: come and think of your duties to your country, and ask, When I am here in my narrow house, will man be the better for my vote or my policy of to-day? come and deposit here the tabernacle of clay through which, as through an illuminated transparency, you knew the soul of your neighbor; and "mourn not as those without hope," but go away believing more of God, of man, of life everlasting. So shall this silent place be more eloquent than the haunts of earthly noise and toil; yea, only here shall you learn what this bustle on the earth means; for, viewed from this "green hill," this life and all its affairs shall appear as the foreground of a spiritual existence that fades off into deeper shadows and more dazzling lights, and vanishes into the mystery of the all-comprehending life of God.

Thus, by mingling your visits to this sacred place with all the occurrences of your daily life, you will be taught to live in contact with everlasting realities; your every action will be adjusted to eternal ideas of right; your whole existence become a series of variations on the deep and simple melody of love to God and man. And one thing more this cemetery will teach you: the way to think of your departed, and the highest mode of holding communion with the beloved in other states of being.

We may scorn as we will the perpetual desire to cling to those who are translated to other states of being; but still the deep heart of humanity yearns for the sweet companionship of the absent. It is easy to ridicule or reprove the myriad superstitions into which our fellow men are hurried by too much longing for those who are no longer in the flesh; but while we lop away any growth of rank fanaticism, let us be careful that our knife of criticism does not wound the most sacred instincts of human affection. We have only to see what a mighty power the desire to know the spirit world has always been in the individual and society, to learn that the only way to banish fanaticism on this awful theme, is to supply a true and healthy doctrine of our relations to those who have gone before us to the unexplored eternity.

I believe the establishment of a beautiful cemetery in every village would do much towards elevating the tone of popular feeling concerning the departed. The soothing influence of a visit to a place of flowers and fragrant quiet, would do much to allay those frantic moods in which we would almost break through the bars of our mortality to get at those who are away. Here the mourner may reflect on the beautiful process of nature by which the form of the beloved is changing into other shapes of loveliness, and will no longer shudder at the ghastly vision of decaying mortality. And here, lifted above the fret and fever of mere temporary excitements, the bereaved heart will find in the contemplation of the soul itself, the spiritual life, and those ideas and facts that endure forever, a strength which often is better than the mere joy of communing minds. It will then become more apparent why we are called to part company with those on whom we lean so fondly. For we shall see that it is often a needful discipline of our own spirits to be separated from those who were, perhaps, robbing us of our own strength, and hindering our best growth through the very excess of their attentions.

Nothing is so good for the soul as love; but love means a great deal more than the sweetest indulgence of the sentiments, and is often strongest and purest in the absence of its object. Many a one who has done for us what no other human soul could do by its presence, may, after a time, move us more potently, and stir a deeper place in our hearts, from its new home in the spirit world. You may scorch the surface of your fields by kindling a fire among the forests that shadow them, but when you would send a thrill of warmth into every vein of the frozen and clammy soil, you must wait till God moves the sun a few degrees higher above the horizon; and then, through incomprehensible distances, over the abysses of space, the level beams of light cleave their way to the centre of the earth, and the happy valley laughs out in a new spring. So, it is not by the loves of this state of being that our cold and selfish hearts are melted into a springtime of love and faith, so much as by those mighty, unseen influences that come like changes of seasons upon the soul; the tender compassion of the beloved in their heaven of holy service; the contemplations of the great and good, who move the world with every throb of their memory in the hearts of the generations; the Saviour, living and saving to-day more than when he dwelt in human form in Palestine; God, "whom no man hath seen at any time," but whom every child may know, at all times, through the life of obedience and consecration.

Thus contemplating the reasons of our separation, and the most elevating influences on our life, we shall gradually overcome the half insane desire to look perpetually in the faces of our friends. We know they live; if their love was real, we know it is immortal, since no reality can ever perish; we may trust God to keep us apart while it is best for us to live in solitude; and when our deepest wants crave a communion of souls, they will not be absent long.

So, let us not distract ourselves by vain and uneasy attempts to pursue the departing soul into the mysteries of its future home. If it be given to us to meet again, the path is not in this direction, but rather in the way of a pure life and patient faith in the providence of the Most High. Let no man flatter himself he will know his departed while buried in the dust of selfish toil, or plunged in the slough of guilty indulgence, or whirling down the maelstrom of a godless ambition. Let no woman think that her tears and repinings, and frantic wrenchings of will, can force the gates of Paradise. Let it not be dreamed that the lost are found in the company of half-sensual, half-lunatic enthusiasts, who trade in the sacred weakness of the afflicted. If we would know our best beloved again, and have our souls filled with the joy of their blissful presence as gardens are filled with the blown odor of fragrant roses, we must prepare for the visitation by long service and lofty meditations.

"How pure at heart and sound in head,
With what divine affections bold;
Should be the man whose thought would hold,
An hour's communion with the dead.

"In vain shalt thou, or any, call
The spirits from their golden day,
Except, like them, thou too canst say,
My spirit is at peace with all.

"They haunt the silence of the breast,
Imaginations calm and fair,

The memory like a cloudless air,
The conscience as a sea at rest;

"But when the heart is full of din,
And doubt beside the portal waits,
They can but listen at the gates,
And hear the household jar within!"

We best know our beloved in heaven, when in the sternest way of duty; when we have conquered our worst temptations; when we have loved our enemy and sacrificed ourself for our friend; when, in some great spasm of public folly and injustice, we have stood firm and just; when we have resolved to live the godly life, and feel that our prayer has been answered. We know the illustrious dead only when we are like them, and vainly do we insult their memory by words of praise, while our lives are traitors to their worth. Thus only by living nobly here do we know those who are living grandly elsewhere. Life gravitates to life, and while we are dead in any low state of existence, our communion will only be with "dead men's bones, and all uncleanness;" but, as we rise through the spaces of the life in God, at every step of our progress we are hailed by some glorious spirit, and claim the friendship of some exalted soul. The noonday idler on your hill-sides does not behold the finest aspect of nature, but the farmer who rests upon his plough to welcome the morning radiance streaking up the horizon; the busy traveller, borne through miles of autumnal glory, the mother who sits by her baby's cradle, while the sweet summer moonlight steals through the open doors. So do glimpses of Paradise and glances from angelic faces come oftenest to him who is most faithful in the nobler duties of life; and plodding along the dusty road of common service, his soul leaps up at a vision of far-off vistas in heavenly lands.

Thus shall we consecrate the Rural Cemetery to life and death. To the burial of the dead and the instruction of the living. Let every community esteem most holy, and guard with watchful care, this sacred inclosure. Consecrate it by making it every year more beautiful; by holy meditations, and lofty ideas of life, and cheerful views of death, and solemn resolutions and dedication of the soul to eternal things. What can be a greater adornment to any neighborhood than to have, within accessible distance, a spot of quiet beauty for the burial of the dead, which shall grow more beautiful as generations pass away; appealing to the holiest and calmest sentiments of our being through the spectacle of enchanting, natural scenery, and the associations of the beloved on earth, now beloved in the spirit land. Let the gentle and persuasive influences of this gathering-place of the departed steal through the neighborhood, like perfumes from the fields visiting the haunts of business and the sanctity of home. Let the life of the community be a perpetual consecration of this green inclosure by which, as through a flowery arch, the generations shall pass away to another clime. And may every town and village in our great State found a cemetery worthy its finest taste and adequate to its entire needs. Then, looking off from the hills that front the stormy Atlantic, nestling in the mystic ravines, and climbing the varied slopes of the Hudson; reposing upon the sun-lit shores of our lakes, blending the exhilaration of the traveller for pleasure with the solemn exaltation of the traveller to heaven; clustering all along the blooming valley of the Mohawk, from its springs among the western hills to where it plunges down its foaming precipice to lose itself amid an island labyrinth; the pride of every little village, the noblest sight to every visitor in the city; these fields of the dead will blossom with a harvest of ennobling influences for the living; proclaiming the equality and dignity of all men; reconciling the life that now is, with the life that is to be; lifting the souls that now tabernacle in clay to inspiring communion with spirits that have put on immortality; and mingling the waves of the life that now waters these earthly scenes with that river of being, whose billows roll on forevermore towards the boundless ocean of Almighty love.

THE END.

---

## PUBLISHERS' PREFACE.

The Anniversary of the "Young Men's Christian Union of New York," on the 13th and 14th days of May, 1858, may justly be considered as marking an era in the history of the progress of the Christian Church in America; inasmuch as it was the first instance in which so many of the leading minds in the various branches of the liberal and progressive portion of the Christian Church have met on one common platform, for the purpose of discussing the practical bearings of that higher type of Christianity which refuses to be limited by any dogma or fettered by any creed.

The occasion was one of peculiar interest. Such an array of talent as the speakers presented, would, under any circumstances, have given assurance of a rare literary feast; but when representatives of different branches of the Christian Church, hitherto somewhat antagonistic, found themselves side by side on a broad platform of Christian Charity and Brotherly Love, they could not but draw inspiration from the occasion as well as the soul-inspiring themes on which they dwelt.

Believing that the publication of these addresses, in a suitable form for preservation, as well as for general distribution, will be rendering a valuable service to the cause of practical Christianity, and one that practical Christians all over the land will appreciate and encourage, we have assumed the risk, confidently relying on the efforts of all who sympathize with the progressive Christian spirit of the age, to extend their circulation.

The "Religious Aspects of the Age," with a glance at the "Church of the Present and the Church of the Future," is a subject in which all are, or should be, interested, and this title has been adopted on account of its peculiar adaptation to the contents of the book.

To accommodate the means and tastes of all, we publish a cheap pamphlet edition, and another on superior paper, and neatly bound in cloth.

MARTIN THATCHER, }
ORREN HUTCHINSON, } PUBLISHERS.

## TABLE OF CONTENTS.



## OPINIONS OF THE PRESS.

"It is a work of great merit, and one which will furnish a rich literary feast to the reader."—*Canton Plain Dealer.*

"A work of great literary value and practical utility; the young will find attractions in it, and the old instruction and benefit."—*Black River Herald.*

"It is worth one hundred times its cost."—*Wisconsin Farmer.*

"We commend them (the Discourses) to our friends throughout the country." —*Christian Inquirer.*

"It is a valuable book."—*Literary Gazette.*

"This is a book which deserves to be widely circulated."—*New York Evening Post.*

"They treat of the most vital questions which can engage men's minds or hearts, and look carefully and seriously into the present religious aspects of the age. . . . The book ought to have, and will have, we believe, an extensive sale. . . . There are scores of men, and women too, we judge, now called Deists or Infidels, it may be, and who really reckon themselves as such, perhaps, who would rejoice with unspeakable gladness to become acquainted with the interpretation of Christianity, or Christian doctrine, and the Christian life, which is presented in this attractive volume, and without some new vision breaks upon them, they will wander into hopeless and confirmed unbelief. We hope the friends of liberal Christianity will circulate this and kindred books broadcast over the land."—*Star in the West.*

"Whoever procures and reads it will make a profitable investment of time and money."—*Universalist Quarterly.*

"The speakers are known to the public, and are known to be men of distinguished talents. Here are thirteen most valuable lectures—179 pages, paper covers, for the small sum of 25 cents. Order it, or instead of spending 25 cents you will lose more than 25 dollars."—*Christian Herald and Messenger.*

---

Law of Kindness, by Rev. G. W. Montgomery, . . . $0 50
Austin on the Attributes, . . 63
Voice to Youth, Voice to the Married, by Rev. M. Austin, each, 63
Beauty of Kindness, by Rev. D. K. Lee, . . . . . 50
Summerfield, by Rev. D. K. Lee. 75
Merrimack, Master Builder, by Rev. D. K. Lee, each, . . 1 00
Book of Promises. . . . 25
Pastor's Request, by Henry Bacon, . . . . . . 1 00
Sheaf from a Pastor's Field, by H. C. Leonard, . . . . 1 00
Beechdale, by Kate Carlton, . 50
Gospel Liturgy, . . . . 50
Gospel Sermons, . . . 1 00
Christian Helper, Vols. II. and III. each, . . . . . 1 00
Life, Present and Future, by Rev. J. H. Tuttle, . . . . 60
A Lady's Diary of the Siege of Lucknow, . . . . . 50
Commentary on Revelations, by Rev. T. Whittemore, . . 1 00
Pro and Con of Universalism, . 1 00
Smith on Divine Government. . 1 00
Pagan Origin of the Doctrine of Endless Punishment, . . 75
Lily of the Valley for 1859, . 1 50
Register and Almanac for 1859, . 12½
Religious Aspects of the Age, paper, . . . . . . 25
do. do. cloth, . . 63
Do. do. cloth, full gilt, 1 00
Writings of Rev. Theodore Clapp.
Paige's Selections, (new edition), 1 00
Sabbath School Books, . .
Hymn Books, and many others too numerous to mention.
Shahmah in Pursuit of Freedom, 1 25
Symbols of the Capital; or, Civilization in New York, by Rev. A. D. Mayo, . . . 1 00
Matrimonial Brokerage in the Metropolis, by a Reporter of the New York Press, . . 1 00
Selections from the Works of Wm. E. Channing, D.D., . . 60
Unitarian Principles Confirmed by Trinitarian Testimonies, 1 00
Channing's Memoirs, 3 vols., . 1 50
Norton's Statement of Reasons, $1 00
Theological Essays from various authors, . . . . 1 00
Sacerdotal and Spiritual Christianity, by Rev. James Martineau, . . . . . 1 00
Altar at Home, . . . . 50
Christian Doctrine of Prayer, by J. Freeman Clarke, . . 50
The Rod and the Staff, by Rev. T. T. Stone, . . . . 60
The Harp and the Cross, by Rev. S. G. Bulfinch, . . . 60
Athanasia; or, Foregleams of Immortality, by Rev. E. H. Sears, . . . . . 60
Stormy Sundays, . . . 60
Regeneration, by Rev. E. H. Sears, 36
The Christian Body and Form, by Rev. C. A. Bartol, . . 85
Early Piety; or, Recollections of Harriet B——, . . . 16
Sin and its Consequences, . . 15
The Memoir and Writings of James Handasyd Perkins, Edited by Wm. H. Canning, 2 vols., . . . . 1 50
Endeavors After the Christian Life, by James Martineau, . 60
Observations on the Bible, for the Use of Young Persons, . 30
Christian Aspects of Faith and Duty, by John J. Tayler, . 30
Doctrinal Lectures, by Rev. Wm. G. Elliot, . . . . 25
The Discipline of Sorrow, . . 30
The Gospel Narratives, by Rev. H. A. Miles, . . . 25
Grains of Gold—Selections from Bartol, . . . . . 20
History of the Cross, by Rev. William R. Alger, . . 15
Channing's Works, 3 vols., . 2 00
Genuineness of the Gospels, 3 vols., by Norton, . . 4 00
Bible News of the Father, Son, and Holy Spirit, by Noah Worcester, . . . . 36
Furness' Discourses, . . . 1 00
Thoughts on Jesus of Nazareth, by Furness, . . . . 1 00
Livermore's Commentaries, 4 vols., . . . . . . 3 00

They are also prepared to furnish Miscellaneous, School and Juvenile Books and Stationery, on the best terms. Books sent by mail, postage paid, on receipt of the retail price.

www.ingramcontent.com/pod-product-compliance
Lightning Source LLC
LaVergne TN
LVHW010136110826
845151LV00002B/367
*9781425539047*

THE

# AMERICAN TEXT BOOK

OF PRACTICAL AND SCIENTIFIC

# AGRICULTURE,

INTENDED FOR THE USE OF

COLLEGES, SCHOOLS, AND PRIVATE STUDENTS;

AS WELL AS FOR

# THE PRACTICAL FARMER.

INCLUDING

ANALYSES BY THE MOST EMINENT CHEMISTS.

BY CHARLES FOX,

SENIOR EDITOR OF THE "FARMER'S COMPANION, AND HORTICULTURAL GAZETTE;"
LECTURER ON AGRICULTURE IN THE UNIVERSITY OF MICHIGAN;
COR. MEM. OF THE N. Y. LYCEUM OF NAT. HIST.;
AND OF THE PHILADELPHIA AND CLEVELAND ACADEMIES OF SCIENCES;
MEMBER OF U. S. AGRICUL. SOCY., &C.

DETROIT:
PUBLISHED BY ELWOOD AND COMPANY.
1854.

DETROIT:
E. A. Wales, Printer, Advertiser Steam Presses.

TO

DR. SILAS H. DOUGLASS;

PROFESSOR OF CHEMISTRY, GEOLOGY, MINERALOGY, &C., IN THE

UNIVERSITY OF MICHIGAN;

TO WHOSE EXERTIONS AND ENERGY, THE

ESTABLISHMENT OF AGRICULTURAL LECTURES

IN THAT INSTITUTION,

IS,

TO A GREAT EXTENT, DUE.

AND WHO, FROM AN EARLY DAY, HAS EARNESTLY

AND PERSEVERINGLY LABORED IN THE CAUSE OF SCIENCE IN

THIS STATE:

**THIS VOLUME**

IS DEDICATED BY HIS MOST SINCERE AND

OBLIGED FRIEND

THE AUTHOR.

# PREFACE.

THE following work is strictly what it professes to be—A TEXT BOOK. It is not intended so much to teach the Science and Art of Agriculture, as to enable the Teacher to teach. In its character it is *suggestive*, and makes no pretensions to be a perfect Encyclopœdia of the subject. At the same time it is believed that there is no point—so far as the work professes to go—on which it is important that the Teacher should enlarge, or the student learn, to which they will not find their attention directed. Nor will the experienced Farmer, or the general reader fail to be interested. Practice and science are brought together, and compelled to assist each other; instead of being unnaturally divorced, as, unhappily, they have too long been in this department of knowledge.

This little work is the offspring of a sorely felt necessity. A year since, the Author was unexpectedly called upon to deliver a course of lectures on Agriculture, before the newly organized "Scientific Department" of the University of Michigan. He had for some years studied the subject, both practically and theoretically, and collected a valuable library in connection with it. But this he had done merely for his own gratification, without any direct object in view, and certainly with no intention of ever becoming a teacher of Agriculture. A sense of duty to the public would not allow him to refuse the invitation; and painfully conscious of his deficiencies, he assumed the office, determined to do the best he could. Upon the very threshold, however, he met with an unexpected difficulty. He could find no book, published either in America or Europe, adapted for a collegiate class, many of whom were practical and middle-aged farmers, and some to whom the very terms of Science were unknown. Professors Johnston, Norton, and Nash have each published elementary works, most excellent so far as they go; but they are confined almost entirely to the *chemical* portion of the subject, and "Practical Agriculture in its connection with Science" was the topic demanded. There are other books again, but deficient on the other side,—consisting merely of directions how to cultivate the land,—being chiefly compilations, and making no pretensions to a higher or scholastic character; so that the Author was obliged to prepare and write his entire course of lectures, and the students lost much from the want of some work which they might study in private, or refer to from time to time. This loss was chiefly felt in regard to analyses, figures and scientific words. It is quite impossible that a student can understand the one, or recollect the other by merely hearing them; and yet if these portions are lost, much of the value of the succeeding information is lost likewise.

Within the few last years, the study of Agriculture in the United States, has assumed a new form. It is beginning to be introduced, not only into Colleges, but also into Primary Schools; and in conversing with other gentlemen, the Author found that this want was as sensibly deplored by others, as it had been by himself. He therefore undertook to write out the substance of his lectures. Neither his more important engagements, nor his health permitted him to anticipate more. But having made a beginning, he found the subject constantly enlarging, and he has, to the best of his ability, collected and arranged a synopsis of all that is known,—so far as he could ascertain it—of the theoretical and practical truths and principles of Agriculture, up to the present moment. The analyses which are given, are, it is believed, the very latest that have been made, and, perhaps without exception, are worthy of all credit in the present position of the Science. The more strictly technical portion is either the result of the Author's own experience and experiments, or it is compiled from the most trustworthy sources adapted to the present position and necessities of the American Famer.

The only novelty, which can be claimed as such, is the arrangement, each subject being complete within itself. Much more might have been introduced, and one of the chief difficulties that have been experienced has been compressing the matter,—the omitting of all which did not appear to be absolutely necessary for the object in view, and the using as few words as possible.

It was essential that the book should be of moderate size, and cheap—this the Publisher insisted upon as a *sine qua non*,—and consequently much that might have been inserted has been left out. Thus, it is taken for granted that the Teacher or the Student is already familiar with Botany, and the elements of Agricultural Chemistry. Had these topics likewise been introduced further than they have been, they would have swelled the work far beyond the requisite size. For the boundaries of agricultural knowledge are like those of the horizon, ever enlarging as we travel on, till they embrace almost the entire circle of the sciences and Arts. So vast are the subjects, that a writer attempting to include the whole, would find that a library, not a volume, would be the result of his labors. Besides, with the excellent elementary works already mentioned, and Prof. Gray's Botanical Text-book, repetition could not have been avoided, and this too, has been most scrupulously abstained from, as regards works in general circulation among us. So again, the topics treated upon in the early chapters are presented merely in outline. Agricultural Meteorology—though essentially a most interesting and important application of Science,—is yet in its earliest infancy; and the materials do not exist for accurate or extended instruction; while the Natural History of Plants, the Air, Water, &c., belong rather to the department of the Chemist and the Vegetable Physiologist, than to the practical Agriculturist. Enough only is written on these subjects to serve as an introduction to what follows.

In many instances, and always in the Analyses, the authority quoted is mentioned, chiefly in order that the Teacher may be able to refer directly to the original, where he will usually meet with a more complete elucidation of the subject than could be admitted into these pages.

It will be observed that the work is printed in type of *three sizes.* Those portions which are considered as peculiarly important, or as being capable of comprehension by students of all ages, are printed in the largest type; that which is abstruse is in a second sized; and that which peculiarly interests the practical farmer is in the smallest type. The Chapters are likewise so arranged as to permit the teacher to select such subjects as he chooses.

No one can attempt to teach an irregular science, or a "scientific art" such as Agriculture is rapidly becoming, without discovering how much he must depend for explanation and illustration on his own resources. The strict sciences, such as mathematics, may be entirely taught by books; but in agriculture there is still so much that is uncertain, and so many sciences and arts are combined within it, that—without taking into consideration the discoveries that are almost daily made—a lifetime, laboriously devoted to the subject could scarcely render one individual master of the whole. It is hoped, therefore, that the Teacher who may use this book will enlarge upon the various subjects, and explain that which is difficult—in one word, that he will consider it as the mariner does his chart, as a director of his course, but a director from which he is at liberty to differ should his superior experience and knowledge induce him to do so.

The Author has no desire to assume to himself more credit than is due, nor to make excuses which are not strictly true. But constantly and seriously occupied in various other duties; for a length of time at a distance from the Press; and compelled to search for materials in a large number of books—considerably over one hundred volumes having been consulted and compared—he has not only found the labor of compiling these sheets a very arduous one, but is well aware, that had he been able to devote more time to the object he could have rendered them more truly worthy of the acceptance of the public. Should another Edition be called for, many emendations will probably be made.

The limits of this volume forbid the subject of Domestic

Animals, and some other topics being touched upon. For another work, a large amount of materials is on hand, and should life and health be spared, the writer may, perhaps, include them in another volume. That, however, must depend upon the success with which this meets.

*University, Ann Arbor, Mich.,*
*Feb.* 14, 1854.

# CHAPTER I.

## INTRODUCTORY.

1. The word AGRICULTURE is derived from two Latin words, AGER, *a Field*, and CULTURA, *Cultivating* or *Tilling*. It therefore means, strictly, *The working of the soil;* but is now used to describe every process connected with Farming.

2. Agriculture may be divided into *(a,)* growing of grains; of edible plants; of oil bearing plants; of vegetables used in dying, &c.; *(b,)* of grasses; *(c,)* breeding of stock; *(d,)* fattening of stock; *(e,)* producing wool; *(f,)* manufacture of cheese and butter; *(g,)* cultivation of fruit; *(h,)* of vegetables and flowers; *(i,)* viticulture, (or the culture of the grapevine,) and wine making; *(j,)* *Planting*, or the production of cotton, rice, sugar, tobacco, &c. And, in Europe, to the above are added, *(k,)* forest matters; *(l,)* manufacture of beet sugar; *(m,)* the production of silk; and of some other minor articles.

3. Any of these processes may be pursued by itself; though, in most instances, it is found profitable to include more than one of the above divisions on the same farm. In this respect, agriculture differs from manufactures; the latter becoming more profitable as the division of labor becomes more simple.

4. Agriculture is an ART, which, to be truly understood, requires the study of many SCIENCES.

ART is the application of knowledge to practical purposes. *Science* is a knowledge of the principles of Art. If the knowledge be merely accumulated experience, its application is *empirical art;* but if it be experience reasoned upon and brought under general principles, it assumes a higher character, and becomes a *scientific art.*

5. The following are usually considered the Sciences which are naturally included in the Art of Agriculture:—I. *Mathematical Science: (a,)* arithmetic; *(b,)* algebra; *(c,)* geometry; *(d,)* mechanics; *(e,)* surveying; *(f,)* levelling; *(g,)* stereometry, *(the measuring of solid bodies,) (h,)* linear drawing. II. *Physical and Natural Sciences: (a,)* physics; *(b,)* meteorology; *(c,)* mineral chemistry; *(d,)* mineralogy; *(e,)* geology; *(f,)* botany. III. *Technological Sciences: (a,)* organic chemistry; *(b,)* scientific agriculture; *(c,)* arboriculture; *(d,)* sylviculture; *(e,)* vegetable and animal physiology; *(f,)* veterinary art; *(g,)* zoology; *(h,)* equitation. IV. *Noological Sciences: (a,)* rural architecture; *(b,)* forest economy; *(c,)* book-keeping; *(d,)* rural economy; *(e,)* rural law. Each of these, again, is divisible into several sub-divisions; and the list may be still further added to with practical advantage.

6. While a knowledge of all these sciences is necessary to the thoroughly educated farmer, only a part of them is included in what is commonly termed *practical* agriculture. Of this latter portion, meteorology, chemistry, geology, mineralogy and botany, are usually taught by themselves; leaving field-work, arboriculture, animal physiology, zoology, and veterinary art in a class by themselves. To these last, the following pages will be devoted. It must, however, be observed, that so closely are the majority of these sciences interwoven in forming the agricultural art, that it is impossible entirely to disconnect the one from the other. This is especially the case with chemistry and botany: a knowledge of the principles of which must be considered as absolutely essential, and which, together with certain departments of geology, must be frequently referred to.

7. The farmer is a manufacturer. His art converts the soil and air into grain, meat, wool, oil, and other substances. He creates nothing:

he only causes a change of arrangement of materials already existing; which materials are governed by known and fixed laws. What the farmer, therefore, requires, is an intimate acquaintance with these materials, and with the natural laws to which they are subject. The earth and air are composed of a certain number of simple elements. But in this primitive shape, they are unfit for the support of animal life. Yet they will become either weeds or useful plants, according to the mode in which they are used. Again, if they become the latter, the quality produced on a given area will be large or small according to known and fixed rules; and if domestic animals are reared, these will be large or small, healthy or unhealthy, according to the same certain and unalterable laws. It depends, therefore, upon the knowledge which the practical farmer has of these laws, and the use he makes of this knowledge, whether he receives the largest possible return for his labor or not.

8. The object of the practical farmer is to raise from a given area of land the largest quantity of the most profitable produce at the least cost; and not only to avoid impoverishing the soil, but to render it gradually more productive. A knowledge of the above named sciences will enable him to do this; and thus he is repaid pecuniarily for the labor of his mind, as the workman is repaid for the labor of his body.

10. The earliest effort in Europe for the establishment of an Agricultural School, was made by M. L'Abbe Rosier in 1775; but, owing to the neglect of the government, it failed to go into operation. In 1799, Fellenberg, of Switzerland, established the Hofwyl School, which appears to have been the first institution of the kind. In 1818—1822, M. de Domsbasle commenced a Model Farm, of 375 acres, in connection with a place of education, at Roville, in France. In 1827, the Royal Agronomic Institution of Grignon, near Paris, was commenced, by the government. It owns a farm of 1,250 acres, and receives yearly a grant of about $12,000. In Germany, in 1806, the celebrated Dr. A. D. Thaer opened an Agricultural Academy at Moegelin, in Prussia, to educate superintendents for large estates. In 1845, the Royal Agricultural College of Cirencester, England, was chartered. Such institutions are now abundant in every part of Europe.

11. Dr. E. Hitchcock, in the "Report of Commissioners to the Commonwealth of Massachusetts concerning an Agricultural School, *January*, 1851," gives the following list of Agricultural Educational Establishments in Europe:

| SCHOOLS. | Superior Schools. | Intermediary Schools. | Inferior Schools. | Special Schools. | Connected with Colleges & Universities | Total. |
|---|---|---|---|---|---|---|
| In England, | 1 | | 4 | | | 5 |
| In Ireland, | 1 | 25 | 34 | | 3 | 63 |
| In Scotland, | | | | | 2 | 2 |
| In France, | 5 | | 70 | | | 75 |
| In Italy, | | | 1 | | 1 | 2 |
| In Belgium, | | 3 | 2 | 1 | 3 | 9 |
| In Prussia, | 3 | 2 | 12 | 13 | 2 | 32 |
| In Austria, | 4 | | 3 | 25 | 1 | 33 |
| In Wurtemberg, | 1 | 2 | 1 | 3 | | 7 |
| In Bavaria, | 1 | 1 | 32 | 1 | | 35 |
| In Saxony, | 1 | 3 | | 1 | | 5 |
| In Brunswick, | | 1 | 1 | | | 2 |
| In Mechlenburg Schwerin, | | 1 | | | | 1 |
| In Schleswig Holstein, | | 2 | 2 | | | 4 |
| In Anhault, | 1 | 1 | | | | 2 |
| In Duchy of Hesse, | | 2 | | | | 2 |
| In Duchy of Weimar, | | | | | 1 | 1 |
| In Duchy of Nassau, | 1 | | | | | 1 |
| In the Electorate of Hesse, | 1 | | | | | 1 |
| In Duchy of Baden, | | 1 | | | | 1 |
| In Duchy of Saxe Meiningen, | | | 1 | | | 1 |
| In Russia, | 2 | 10 | 51 | 4 | 1 | 68 |
| Total, | 22 | 54 | 214 | 48 | 14 | 352 |

12. Besides these, there are Colleges devoted to instruction in Veterinary Art, the most important of which are, the Imperial School at Alfort, in France, and the Royal College of Veterinary Surgeons, in London. In these institutions, a very complete education is afforded. Veterinary Colleges were first organized in France and Germany, in the beginning of the eighteenth century; and a great many valuable works from the pens of eminent practitioners have appeared on this subject. The first English College owes its origin, in 1792, to a Frenchman of the name of Saint Bel. In France, Veterinary Surgeons hold a high professional and social position, and many of them are members of the Order of the Legion of Honor. These schools, as well as the agricultural, receive annually liberal grants of money from government. One point of great importance is, that a Hospital for diseased animals is connected with each College, so that not only have the students an opportunity of studying living pathology; but, on the appearance of an endemic, there is great probability of the cause and cure being ascertained speedily.

13. Agricultural education is necessarily divided into the *theoretical* and the *practical*—or the Science of Agriculture and the Art of Agriculture. The former involving the reasons of action, is properly learnt first; and may be imparted without any connection with a farm; the second, including, as it does, manual dexterity, comparison, and experiment, must necessarily be taught in the field. Or the two may be taught simultaneously. There appear, however, in many cases, to be serious reasons against the latter course. A student of law or medicine first completes his *theoretical* education, and then proceeds to practice; and this seems to be the most rational course in agricultural education also. In the higher European Colleges, lectures are given in the field, *after* a large amount of information has been acquired; but, it is believed, that the students are not required to labor. There is certainly no efficient reason why a student of agriculture must necessarily spend a given portion of his time in physical toil; the more especially, as the manual operations of a farm are intrinsically simple, are easily learned, and require rather the exercise of the muscles than of the mind. A museum of rural objects, including models of implements, with likenesses of the best stock; and a hospital for diseased animals; connected with occasional visits to the best farms in the neighborhood, and to agricultural fairs, will supply everything that is requisite for the full education of a young man brought up on a farm; the practical skill being acquired when he returns home, to make agriculture the serious occupatian of his life.

# CHAPTER II.

## PLANTS.---THE AIR.---WATER.

14. Plants are formed by a re-arrangement of simple substances, (or elements,) already existing in *(a,)* the air, *(b,)* the water, and *(c,)* the soil. Animals are formed by a re-arrangement of these plants, of water, and of air. These changes are not simply mechanical, but chemical; and are under the direction of a power called Life, of which very little is yet known. Heat, light, electricity, the wind, the rain, and the sun, have also a powerful influence over vegetable and animal existence.

15. Wherever the proper elements and circumstances unite, there will vegetable life exist.

16. While all plants are composed of a certain quantity of different substances, the various orders of plants demand either a different proportion of the elements; or one requires an element which is not requisite to the existence of another plant. Thus, one species of plants grows in earth containing a large proportion of potash or soda, as wormwood *(artemisia)* and asparagus; while another requires little or no potash, as Indian corn. One grows in water, without any connection with the soil; while another grows in the air like the wind-plant of Florida; or the mistletoe of Europe, forcing its radicles into the sapwood of another tree.

17. While plants grow naturally where they find the elements, and other circumstances necessary for their formation;

they are also abundant or rare, according to the proportionate existence of these circumstances.

18. A plant not indigenous to a given locality, will grow and flourish, if transplanted, in exact proportion as it finds the materials and circumstances in its new locality the same as in its native one.

19. These facts are the ground-work of Agriculture as an intelligent art.

20. Comparatively few plants exist which are useful to man, and these, in their wild state, are naturally confined to narrow bounds. The business of the Farmer is, therefore, to cause such plants as he requires, to grow where he wishes them; and not only to grow, but by artificial adaptation of circumstances to compel them to yield so abundantly that their intrinsic value is greater than that of the labor bestowed upon them.

21. A striking example of this principle may be given in the growth of the Pine Apple in England. This is a plant requiring the heat of a long tropical summer in order that it may perfect its fruit. Until steamships plied between the West Indies and Great Britain, this fruit could not be carried to the latter country, without rotting. But so delicious is the flavor, that the English were not willing to be deprived of it. They consequently formed, by means of glass-houses and furnaces, a tropical atmosphere: they imitated the rich organic soil in which this plant is found to flourish; they supplied the moisture necessary at certain periods of growth; and not only brought the fruit to perfection, but greatly improved it in size and flavor.

22. The principles may therefore be laid down, *(a,)* "that out of nothing, nothing is made;" if it is desired to grow a given plant in abundance, all the elements that enter into that plant must be supplied in abundance, *(b,)* all other circumstances requisite to its perfection in its native state must also be furnished; *(c,)* that plants cannot be grown where these requisites are deficient; *(d,)* but that it is in the power of the Farmer, by

the acquisition of knowledge and by intelligent labor, so to modify existing circumstances as to cause a plant to grow profitably where naturally it could not do so.

23. On these simple principles, depends the utility of plowing, harrowing, manuring, irrigation, and the other mechanical processes of cultivation.

24. In other words, the art of Agriculture, when confined to growing plants, is simply adapting the soil, and surrounding circumstances to the natural demands of the plant; each plant varying somewhat from another, in its requirements.

25. In order to do this, it is necessary to understand, *(a,)* the materials which are or can be supplied by air, water, and soil; (for in this connection, manure is merely a modification of the soil,) *(b,)* the materials which enter into the composition of each plant; and *(c,)* the incidental changes, which meteorology and chemistry may produce.

26. THE AIR OR ATMOSPHERE.—According to M. Regnault, 100 cubic inches of atmospheric air, deprived of aqueous vapor and carbonic acid, weigh 30.82926 grains. At 62° Fahr. air is 810 times lighter than water, and 11,000 times lighter than mercury.

The chemical composition of air is, *(Dumas and Boussingault)*:—

| | | Air by Weight. | Air by Volume. |
|---|---|---|---|
| Oxygen, | Mechanically combined, | 23.10 | 20.90 |
| Nitrogen, | | 76.90 | 79.10 |
| | | 100.00 | 100.00 |

—Besides these constituents, the atmosphere always contains a variable quantity of watery vapor and carbonic acid gas, besides other gasses and vaporous bodies which are observed to enter into it. The younger Saussure has ascertained that the mean proportion of carbonic acid is 4.9 volumes in 10,000 volumes of air; or almost exactly 1 in 2,000 volumes; but it varies from 6.2 as a maximum to 3.7 as a minimum, in 10,000 volumes.

Its proportion near the surface of the earth, is greater in summer than in winter, and during night than during day. It is also more abundant on the summits of high mountains than in the plains.

27. COMPOSITION OF DRY AIR BY VOLUME.—

| | |
|---|---|
| Nitrogen, - - - - - - - | 7912 |
| Oxygen, - - - - - - - - | 2080 |
| Carbonic acid, - - - - - - | 4 |
| Carburetted hydrogen, - - - - | 4 |
| Ammonia, (3 vols. of hydrogen with one of nitrogen,) - - - - - - | varies |
| Ozone, - - - - - - - | " |
| Organic matter, and salts, - - - - | " |

28. Prof. Horsford, in experiments made in Boston, Mass., in 1849, *(Am. Assoc. of Science,)* found the quantity of ammonia in the air greatly to exceed that detected by Fresenius, at Wiesbaden. Liebig, at Giessen, found it in rain-water and snow; and estimates that one pound of rain-water contains a quarter of a grain of ammonia.*

" A field of 26,910 square feet must receive annually upwards of 88 lbs. of ammonia; or 71 lbs. of nitrogen; for by the observations of Schubler, about 770,000 lbs. of rain falls over this surface in four months, and consequently the annual fall must be 2,310,000 lbs."—*Liebig, Agricul. Chemistry.*

Liebig assumes, and justly, that such salts as are found in rain water must have been held in suspension in the air, and washed out by the shower.

29. M. Barrall, of Paris, has lately examined the composition

* The following table exhibits the results of several determinations by Prof. Horsford, at Boston, Mass., of the relative quantities of ammonia found in rain and snow-water.

AMMONIA IN RAIN AND MELTED SNOW IN ONE CUBIC METRE.

| | | | |
|---|---|---|---|
| 1849—Dec'r 22, in rain, | 1.56 grains. | 1850—March 18, in snow, | 1.49 grains |
| " 29, in snow, | 2.63 " | " 22-3, in snow, | 0.96 " |
| 1850—April 4, in rain, | 0.24 " | July 16, in rain, | 1.29 " |
| " 4, in snow, | 0.72 " | | |

*Annual of Scientific Discov.* 1851, *p.* 234.

of rain water; and from these examinations we find that if we take the annual depth of rain to be about 24 inches, this quantity conveys to every acre of land the following substances:—

| | | |
|---|---|---|
| Nitrogen, - - - - - - | 45½ lbs. | |
| Nitric acid, - - - - - - | 103 " | |
| Ammonia, - - - - - - | 19½ " | |
| Chlorine, - - - - - - | 12½ " | |
| Lime, - - - - - - - | 35 " | |
| Magnesia, - - - - - - | 11 " | |
| | —— | 227 lbs. |

30. Thence it appears that the quantity of ammonia held in the air varies according to the locality; and, probably, other circumstances.

31. Horsford, in continuing the experiments above referred to, found that at Boston, in the summer, when vegetable and animal decay is most rapid, the quantity of ammonia in the air is at a maximum, and afterwards decreases regularly until the winter season, when it is at a minimum. The following table shows the amount of thirteen different analyses:—

| Date. | Ammonia in 1,000,000 parts, by weight of air. |
|---|---|
| 1. July 3, - - - - - - - | 42.9995 |
| 2. July 9, - - - - - - - | 46.1246 |
| 3. July 9, - - - - - - - | 47.6308 |
| 4. September 1 to 20, - - - - | 29.7457 |
| 5. October 11, - - - - - - | 28.2396 |
| 6. October 14, - - - - - - | 25.7919 |
| 7. October 30, - - - - - - | 13.9315 |
| 8. November 6, - - - - - - | 8.0953 |
| 9. November 18, 12 and 13, - - | 8.0953 |
| 10. November 14, 15 and 16, - - - | 4.7066 |
| 11. November 17 to December 5, - - | 6.1328 |
| 12. December 20 and 21, - - - - | 6.9885 |
| 13. December 29, - - - - - | 1.2171 |

*Annual of Scient. Disc.* 1850, *p.* 221.

Liebig *(Agri. Chem.)* observes "that the ammonia contained in rain and snow water possesses an offensive smell of perspiration and animal excrements,—a fact which leaves no doubt respecting its origin." These experiments have been repeated in France, Germany, America, and England with the same results. It is probable that in the neighborhood of large cities, and in densely peopled countries, the air contains a much larger proportion of this valuable alkali, than in the wild and thinly settled districts. Some curious agricultural and pathological phenomena may be explained by these facts; but the subject still requires more extended and minute examination.

32. Henry and Chevallier have detected acetic acid and probably hippuric acid in the atmosphere. Horsford supposes, as the result of his experiments, that the organic effluvia in the air are of acid character.

33. Ozone, also, appears to vary in quantity.

*Ozone* is believed to be a form of oxygen, and is produced when electric sparks are taken through perfectly dry oxygen. It is formed in the air during thunder storms. Air impregnated with it acts very much as if a trace of chlorine gas were present, which ozone appears to resemble. Little is yet known of it, but it probably has some connection with health and epidemic illness; and is suspected to act on plants by effecting their growth.

34. Vaughan *(Am. Assoc. of Science,)* states that by means of feeble currents of electricity, the amount of carbonic acid which water and moist surfaces continually absorb from the air, is decomposed, and serves to supply the principal part of the humus of the soil.

35. Although, they have not been detected, there can be no doubt that the Sporules *(seeds)* of minute Cryptogamic plants, such as *Mould, Rust, &c.*, are generally floating in the air, ready to take root wherever they find proper conditions. The atmosphere is also full of Animalcules and infusorial forms.

36. Dr. Smith *(Proc. of British Assoc.)* in experiments on

the air of towns, detected sulphuric acid, chlorine, and a substance resembling impure albumen.* In a warm atmosphere the albuminous matter very soon putrifies, and emits disagreeable odors. By oxidation, this substance gives rise to carbonic acid, ammonia, sulphuretted hydrogen, and probably to other gasses.

37. Mulder found free muriatic acid in the rain water of Amsterdam, which he ascribes to the decomposition of the chloride

* This substance, which has been noticed in rain and snow water by several Chemists, has recently been carefully examined by Dr. A. A. Hayes, of Massachusetts. (*Proc. of Am. Assoc. of Science*, 1850, *B. pp.* 207–212.) It has been named *Pyrrhin*. Obtained from carefully filtered solutions, it appears as a brown yellow adhesive substance, having a strong oder of perspired matter, generally containing the remains of animalcula, spores of fungi, and atmospheric dust. After its solution has been freed from ammoniacal salts, the changes following in its fermentation produce ammonia. Dr. Hayes is inclined to attribute to this substance, a powerful influence over vegetation. When fertile soil is undergoing fermentation, the vapors, by condensation, afford a substance much like Pyrrhin ; but the state of admixture here renders it more compound than when it is obtained from the atmosphere through the aid of falling rain. To the falling of this substance from the air, Dr. H. attributes the remarkable growth of vegetation observed in New England and other places, when heavy rain succeeds a long continued period of dry weather in summer. "The more fertile a soil, either naturally or as resulting from judicious cultivation, the more the quantity of matter, having the character of a ferment, we always find in our analysis."

The following passage bearing on this subject appears in *Silliman's Am. Journal of Science and Arts, for September*, 1853, *page* 273:—"In continuation of his long researches on the composition of arable soils, M. Verdeil and M. Rissler have recognized in the aqueous extracts of these soils, the constant presence of a substance like sugar; and also a large proportion of mineral substances, little soluble or even insoluble in water. Thus in 100 parts of aqueous extract, they found 49 of organic matter and 54 of inorganic, consisting of sulphate, carbonate, and phosphate of lime, oxyde of iron, alumine, magnesia, all insoluble in water (or scarcely soluble) ; and as the presence of carbonic acid alone is not sufficient to explain the presence of these substances in the aqueous extract, MM. Verdeil and Rissler have sought for the cause of this solubility, and concluded that it is due to the saccharine ingredients, for only a very little water is required along with this sugar to dissolve large quantities of insoluble salts. They have recognized again the fact that nitrogen which enters into the composition of humus is found in the condition of an ammoniacal salt, and not in that of an organic substance ; for they have collected the whole under the form of ammonia in boiling the concentrated extract with milk of lime."

We refer to this not as yet proving anything certain, but as a subject well worthy of more investigation. There are many unexplained phenomena connected with vegetation which may receive elucidation if these facts prove to be correct. The rapid growth and change of color of plants after a thunder storm in summer has long been noticed by the writer, and probably by most persons living in the country.

of magnesium contained in the waters of the lake of Haarlem, by the action of the sun's rays.

38. The quantity of water in the atmosphere varies considerably, at different times and in different places. It is, besides, dependent on the temperature of the air and of the water evaporating from the earth's surface. The proportion of aqueous vapor has been determined by Verver, for the Netherlands. In 1000 volumes of air, he found the minimum 5.8; the maximum 10.18. The average of fifty observations during May, August, and September was 8.47. From an early hour in the morning to 10 o'clock, A. M. it was 7.97—from 10 to 2 o'clock, P. M., 8.58; and from 2 o'clock till the evening, 8.85 (*Mulder.*)

The atmosphere in New England is believed to be much drier than that of Germany. At a meeting of the Boston Natural History Society, 1852, this difference was discussed. In New England the dew point is several degrees lower. Various differences are noticed by foreign artizans in the processes of their different callings, attributable to this dryness of the air. The climate of New England is regarded as more nearly resembling that of the high Alps than that of any other part of Europe. Missouri, on the contrary, appears to have a still wetter atmosphere. At the winter season of the year the air of New England is so nearly anhydrous, (*free from moisture,*) that such articles as raw hides dry in a temperature just below freezing, without being frozen. (*Annual of Scient. Discov.*, 1853.)

39. All these constituents of the atmosphere have an important influence upon the character and luxuriance of vegetation. Of the whole, however, carbonic acid and water are the most important. Carbon, and the elements of water form the principle constituents of vegetables; the quantity of the substances which do not possess this compositon being in a very small proportion.

40. The leaves and other green parts of a plant exposed to

the light, absorb carbonic acid, decompose it, retain the carbon, and emit an equal volume of oxygen.

Plants thus improve the air by the removal of carbonic acid and by by the renewal of oxygen, which is immediately applied to the use of man and animals. The horizontal currents of the atmosphere bring with them as much as they carry away, and the interchange of air between the upper and lower strata, which their difference of temperature causes, is extremely trifling when compared with the hoiizontal movements of the winds. Thus vegetable culture heightens the healthy state of a country; and a previously healthy country would be rendered quite uninhabitable by the cessation of all cultivation.

47. But in the dark, or during the night, the reverse action takes place. Then green plants emit carbonic acid and absorb oxygen; while the whole volume of air undergoes diminution at the same time. From the latter fact it follows that the quantity of the oxygen gas absorbed is greater than the volume of carbonic acid seperated; for if this were not the case no diminution could occur.

42. Liebig has endeavored to prove that plants absorb directly from the atmosphere much of the nitrogen *(ammonia,)* which they require in their composition; but his views are now generally considered unsound; and the ablest physiologists teach that plants in a normal state imbibe carbonic acid and water only through the leaves, while all other constituents enter by the roots through the soil. Mulder lays down the following principle as sufficiently established:—*It is the function of the roots to convey to plants water, ammonia, organic salts, and a small quantity of inorganic salts; but that of the green parts, especially of the leaves, to increase the amount of the non-nitrogenous constituents of plants, by the absorption of carbonic acid, accompanied with an emission of oxygen.*

43. The other components of the atmosphere must, therefore, reach the plant through the soil; they being *generally* imparted to the soil by rain or snow. Their value and importance

will be better understood when we come to speak of the SOIL, of DRAINING, and of MANURES.

44. WATER consists of two *volumes* of hydrogen gas with one volume of oxygen, *chemically* combined: or by *weight*:—

| | | |
|---|---|---|
| Oxygen, - - - - - | 88.91 | 8 |
| Hydrogen, - - - - - | 11.09 | 1 |
| | 100.00 | 9 |

The oxygen and hydrogen are therefore combined exactly in the proportion 8 to 1, as appears by the proportion of the last column. (*Graham.*)

45. From the chemical combination of hydrogen and oxygen in water, a series of special consequences follows in the organic kingdom. It is a known fact that, when substances, chemically combined, are again decomposed, the action of other substances also, which are contained in the circle of action is reciprocally awakened. Wherever in the organic kingdom, water is decomposed—and this frequently happens—the decomposition re-acts on the substance from which the influence proceeded, and produces important chemical transformations of all the substances included in the circle of action. This chemical action proceeds, as regards water, from two elements, which are both chief constituents of organic bodies. (*Mulder.*)

46. (*a.*) The first effect of water on plants is that they are moistened by it. It acts chemically, forming hydrates with organic compounds; also, merely as a liquid, to moisten, dissolve, or keep solid substances in suspension.

47. (*b.*) Water is indispensable to keep the fleshy parts soft, to enable them to grow and be fed.

48. (*c.*) ——— also as a dissolving and suspending fluid. For it is only by the circulation of a fluid through the existing parts of an organic whole, that the support and nourishment of the whole organism can be effected; and many of its actions rest entirely upon this process.

49. (*d.*) The action of water differs in plants and animals as

to the way in which it disappears again from the organic substances.

50. Plants receive water from *(a,)* the dew, *(b,)* from rain, *(c,)* from the soil by evaporation; in case of irrigation, and in certain localities, directly *(d,)* from streams or ponds, and *(e,)* from vapor held in suspension in the atmosphere.

51. A cubic inch of water at 62 ° Fahr., Barometer 30 inches, weighs in air 252,458 grains. The imperial gallon has been defined to contain 10 pounds avoirdupois (70,000 grains) of distilled water at that temperature and pressure. Its capacity is, therefore, 277.19 cubic inches. The specific gravity of water at 60 ° Fahr. is 1, being the unit to which the densities of all other liquids and solids are conveniently referred; it is 815 times heavier than air at that temperature.

Water readily combines with or absorbs a great variety of solid or gasous bodies; and it is by means of water that most of the materials of the structure of plants are introduced. Consequently the composition of the water which cultivated plants may receive in any given locality is of great importance to the Farmer.

53. We have already seen (§28–37) that rain, washing the air, receives a variety of substances from the atmosphere which it conveys to the soil and plant; but the amount of these substances varies in different positions. Thus Dr. Madden has calculated that the quantity of rain which falls at Penicuick, in Scotland, in a year, brings down upon each acre of land in that neighborhood more than 600 ℔s. weight of common salt, *(Johnston.)* while in countries remote from the sea it is believed that no salt is held in suspension in the atmosphere. And thus, the rain may supply or withhold an important element of vegitation.

54. Rain water is purer than spring, river, or sea water. Dew is believed to be purer than ordinary rain water.

Dew is caused by the cooling of the earth, plants, &c., by *nocturnal radiation.* The appearance of dew always follows, never precedes the fall in temperature of the bodies on which it is deposited; thence the phenomenon cannot be attributed to anything more than a simple condensation of the watery vapor contained in the air, comparable in all respects to that which takes place upon the surface of a vessel containing a fluid that is colder than the air. The quantity of the moisture dissolved in the atmosphere is so much the greater as the temperature is higher. In very warm climates the dew is so copious as to assist vegetation essentially, supplying the place of rain during a great part of the year. When the sky is clear and calm during the night, vegetables cool down and very soon show a temperature *inferior* to that of the air which surrounds them. Thus plants are often destroyed by frost in spring, when the thermometer, a few feet above the ground, stands above the freezing point. But clouds, preventing the rapid radiation, also prevent plants cooling to the same point; and on cloudy nights, as also on those preceeding severe rain storms, there is no dew. The Farmers of Peru, South America, whose crops are often destroyed by this nocturnal radiation, have long been in the habit of making artificial clouds by setting fire to a heap of wet straw or dung, and by this means raising a cloud of smoke which destroys the transparency of the atmosphere, from which they have so much to apprehend. Unless the plants and surface of the earth cool *below* the temperature of the air there cannot be dew. (*Boussingault.*)

55. But it is from springs, and the water otherwise contained in the earth that plants cheifly receive their inorganic nourishment. As such water is always rising to the surface, it brings with it whatever substances are held in suspension by it, and deposits them either near the roots of the plants or on the surface, to be washed down again by rain. Thus the great marl beds, which form the bottom of most of the small lakes of the interior of Michigan, are deposits of lime dissolved in springs, and which becomes a carbonate of lime, and therefore insoluble, when exposed to the atmosphere. The great beds of nitrate of potash and soda, *(saltpetre,)* and other salts, found on the surface in various parts of the world, are believed to owe their existence to the same cause. Tables of the analyses of various waters will be here given, by which it will be seen how important an element it is in the production of vegetation:

56. SEA WATER, *(Schweitzer,)* from the English Channel.

| | |
|---|---|
| Water, - - - - - - - | 96,474 |
| Common Salt, - - - - - - | 2,706 |
| Chloride of Potassium, - - - | 76 |
| Chloride of Magnesium, - - - | 366 |
| Bromide of Magnesium, - - - | 3 |
| Sulphate of Magnesia, - - - - | 229 |
| Sulphate of Lime, - - - - - | 140 |
| Carbonate of Lime, - - - - | 3 |
| Iodine, - - - - - - - | traces. |
| Ammonia, - - - - - - - | traces. |
| | 100,000 |

57. SCUYLKILL WATER, *(B. Silliman, Jr.,)* taken from the Fairmount Reservoir, Philadelphia:

| | Grains in 1 gallon. |
|---|---|
| Chloride of Sodium, - - - - | 0.1470 |
| Chloride of Magnesium, - - - - | 0.0094 |
| Sulphate of Magnesia, - - - | 0.0570 |
| Carbonate of Lime, - - - - | 1.8720 |
| Carbonate of Magnesia, - - - | 0.3510 |
| Silica, - - - - - - - - | 0.0800 |
| Carbonate of Soda, - - - - | 1.6436 |
| Organic and other matter, volatile at red heat, | 1.2400 |
| | 5.5000 |

Carbonic acid given off by boiling from 1 gallon, 3.879 cubic inches.

THE SOLID, FIXED, AND INSOLUBLE RESIDUE OF THE SAME WATER.—

| | Grains in 1 gallon. |
|---|---|
| Solid residue at 212 ° fahr. - - - | 5.50 |
| Fixed at a red heat, - - - - - | 3.69 |
| Insoluble in water, - - - - - | 2.145 |

The Schuylkill water, when settled clear, is water of superior purity.

58. THE WATERS OF THE DEAD SEA, *(Poggendorff,)* procured near the North end, not far from the mouth of the Jordan:

| | |
|---|---|
| Chloride of Calcium, - - - - | 2.394 |
| Chloride of Magnesium, - - - - | 10.534 |
| Chloride of Potassium, - - - | 1.398 |
| Chloride of Sodium, - - - - | 6.578 |
| Chloride of Aluminum, - - - | 0.018 |
| Bromide of Magnesium, - - - - | 0.251 |
| Sulphate of Lime, - - - - | 0.088 |
| Silica, - - - - - - - | 0.003 |
| | 21.773 |

59. Water from the GREAT SALT LAKE, Utah Territory, *(Dr. L. D. Gale.)* The water was perfectly clear, and had the specific gravity of 1.170.

100 parts evaporated to dryness, and heated to 300° Fahr., gave solid contents 22.422, and consisted of

| | |
|---|---|
| Chloride of Sodium, - - - - | 20.196 |
| Sulphate of Soda, - - - - - | 1.834 |
| Chloride of Magnesium, - - - | 0.252 |
| Chloride of Calcium, - - - - - | 0. trace. |

60. WARM SPRING, OF SALT LAKE CITY, *(Dr. L. D. Gale,)* 100 parts of water gave:—

| | |
|---|---|
| Sulphuretted hydrogen, absorbed in the water, | 0.037454 |
| " " combined with basis, | 0.000728 |
| Carbonate of Lime, precipated by boiling | 0.075000 |
| Carbonate of Magnesia, " " | 0.022770 |
| Chloride of Calcium, - - - - | 0.005700 |
| Sulphate of Soda, - - - - - - | 0.064835 |
| Chloride of Sodium, - - - - | 0.816600 |
| | 1.023087 |

61. The Artesian Well, at Grenalle, near Paris, *(Payen,)* contains in 100,000 parts:—

| | |
|---|---|
| Carbonate of Lime, - - - - - | 6.80 |
| Carbonate of Magnesia, - - - - | 1.42 |
| Bicarbonate of Potash, - - - - | 2.96 |
| Sulphate of Potash, - - - - | 1.20 |
| Chloride of Potassium, - - - - | 1.09 |
| Silica, - - - - - - - - | 0.57 |
| Yellow matter, not defined, - - - | 0.02 |
| Organic nitrogenous matter, - - - | 0.24 |
| | 14.30 |

62. Several Springs at Hartford, Connecticut, *(Bull,)* give in 10,000 parts of water:—

| | I. | II. | III. | IV. | V. |
|---|---|---|---|---|---|
| Sulphate of Lime, - | 0.69 | 0.61 | 0.30 | 0.79 | 0.89 |
| Chloride of Magnesium, | 0.41 | 0.23 | 0.22 | 0.81 | 0.41 |
| Chloride of Calcium, - | 1.12 | 0.70 | 0.39 | | 1 79 |
| Chloride of Sodium, - | 1.91 | | | | 2.67 |
| Carbonate of Lime, - | 2.25 | 1.31 | 0.21 | 1.48 | |
| Carbonate of Magnesia, | 0.19 | | | | 1.51 |
| Crenate of Magnesia, - | | 0.13 | 0.76 | 0.44 | |
| Carbonate of Soda, - | 0.22 | 1.09 | 1.19 | 2.35 | 2.67 |
| Oxide of Iron, - - } Alumina, - - - - } | 0.04 | 0.38 | 0.14 | 0.04 | trace. |
| Lime, - - - - - | | | | 0.23 | |
| Silica, - - - - | 0.18 | 0.60 | 0.14 | 0.04 | 0.10 |
| Loss, - - - - - | 0.10 | 0.46 | | 0.18 | 1.78 |
| Total fixed ingredients, | 7.11 | 5.51 | 3.35 | 6.36 | 11.82 |

63. These examples are sufficient to show how water in the earth is charged with foreign matter, varying constantly, according to circumstances. The absolute quantity of saline matter contained in spring water, has been shown by Grange to be influenced in some cases, (as in the valley of the Isere,) by the relative height of the locality, and increases from the tops of the mountains towards the valleys. The relative quantities

of the different salts is variable; the soluble salts, particularly the chlorides, were found in this instance to diminish; while the insoluble, or difficultly soluble salts, gypsum and carbonate of lime increased as the site of the spring was at a lower level. The nature of the soil, likewise, alters the relative quantities of the different salts. The chlorides preponderate in magnesian soils, and vary from 25 to 32 per cent., while in anthracitic soil they do not amount to more than 10 or 16 per cent., and in calcareous soil to only between 4 and 8 per cent. of the saline matter. The sulphates are found in nearly the same proportions in calcareous and anthracitic soils; in the former, they vary from 24 to 31, and in the latter from 18 to 37 per cent. In the Nicomien, they do not amount to more than 5 or 12 per cent. of the dissolved saline matter. The carbonates vary from 36 to 47 per cent. in granitic soils; from 48 to 71 in anthracitic, and from 83 to 88 per cent. in chalk soils. Soda salts, (chlorides and sulphates,) preponderate in magnesian, and particularly in anthracitic soils; the total quantity of sulphates in the latter soils is much greater. Magnesian salts are remarkably constant in water from magnesian and anthracitic soils; their relative quantity averages between 19 and 23 per cent. in water from granitic salts and slates; and between 11 and 23 in anthracitic formations.—*(Knapp.)*

64. The quantity of saline and earthy matter in spring water, varies from about 20 grains to 1,800 grains in the gallon; when above 100 grains per gallon, it constitutes a mineral water. The average quantity in ordinary spring water is from 20 to 80 grains. The most common salts are sulphate and carbonate of lime, sulphate, muriate, and carbonate of potash and soda.

65. The presence of phosphoric acid in some waters has recently been discovered.

66. Three-fourths of the weight of the body of man and of the higher animals is composed of water; and the lower animals are constituted in like manner. Even the wood of trees

contains one-third and more of its weight of water. Dr. Salisbury gives the following tables exhibiting the per centage of water, dry matter, and ash in the horse chestnut, *(Æsculus hippocastanum,)* at Albany, N. Y., at two different periods:

MAY 4, 1849.

| | Imbricated scales of buds coated with wax. | Leaf Blades | Young twigs and petioles 2 to 3 inches long. | Bark from limbs 2 inches in diameter. | Wood from limbs 2 inches in diameter |
|---|---|---|---|---|---|
| Per cent. of water, - | 80.000 | 79.408 | 88.987 | 51.000 | 56.130 |
| Per cent. dry matter, - | 20.000 | 20.592 | 11.013 | 49.000 | 43.870 |
| Per cent. ash, - - | 1.852 | 1.838 | 1.271 | 5.000 | 0.510 |
| Per cent. ash, cal. on dry matter, - - | 9.359 | 8.927 | 12.479 | 10.204 | 1.162 |

MAY 18, 1849.

| | Peduncles. | Leaf blades. | Young twigs and petioles. | Bark from limbs 2 inches in diameter. | Wood from limbs 2 inches in diameter. |
|---|---|---|---|---|---|
| Per cent. of water, - | 87.047 | 78.485 | 84.730 | 50.500 | 48.000 |
| Per cent. dry matter, - | 12.953 | 20.515 | 15.270 | 46.500 | 51.970 |
| Per cent. ash, - - | 1.313 | 1.582 | 1.100 | 4.290 | 0.550 |
| Per cent. ash, cal. on dry matter, | 10.133 | 7.746 | 7.209 | 9.226 | 1.116 |

67. The air in water is a mixture of the same constituents as atmospheric air, but they are not present in the same proportions—the air contained in water being much richer in oxygen, and containing 32 per cent. of its volume of that element *(Knapp,)* and in water from freshly melted snow 34.8 per cent. The quantity of air retained by water at an altitude of 6 to 8000 feet is reduced to one-third of its usual proportion. Hence fishes cannot live in Alpine lakes.

63. Water contained in the soil may be so impregnated with salts or organic acids as to destroy vegetation. Some of the salts of iron are thus destructive. A cure may be effected by thorough draining. Water containing the salts of lime is called *Hard Water.* Its effect on horses is very remarkable. Hard

water drawn fresh from the well will make the coat of a horse unaccustomed to it *stare:* and it will not unfrequently gripe and otherwise injure him. *(Youatt.)* Milk, butter, and cheese are also sensibly affected by the quality of the water drunk by the cow. Dr. Wilson has found fluoride of calcium in milk, as well as in the blood and urine of animals, which must have been derived from this substance dissolved in the water usually drunk. *(Proc. British Assoc.)*

69. Goitre and Cretinism, diseases common in the vallies of the Alps, as well as in the other parts of the world, are believed to arise from the deleterious action of the water containing salts of magnesia, and the absence of a sufficient quantity of lime. In some places cattle are subject to a disease of the bones in consequence of a want of lime in the water. On the contrary, carbonic acid acts favorably on vegetable life. Dr. Daubeny found by experiments, that although very large quantities of carbonic acid were injurious to plants, yet that when present in water, from one to five per cent. more than is natural, it is beneficial.

70. M. Lassaigne has found arsenic present in the natural deposites of the mineral waters of Wattviller to the amount of 2.8 per cent.; but the poisonous property of the arsenic is destroyed by its combination with peroxide of iron. Free sulphuric acid has also been detected in springs in Virginia.

71. River water differs much in its constituents from spring water. It takes its character from the geological formations through which it flows. It is apt to hold in suspension much sand, earth, and organic matter. The quantity of sediment discharged by the Mississippi River annually is estimated at from 2,137,061,974 cubic feet *(Marr)* to 28,188,083,892 cubic feet *(Brown and Dickeson.)*

# CHAPTER III.

## THE SOIL.

72. To a common observer the soil is a heavy, cohesive, torpid substance; varying in color; and, more or less, mixed with stones. Examined scientifically, it is a compound substance; made up of many materials, each of them differing in its qualities; some of them lying in mere mechanical contact; others chemically combined. The soil is usually divided into two parts, *(a,)* the surface soil; *(b,)* the sub-soil. They usually differ *(c,)* in constitution; *(d,)* mechanical structure; and *(e,)* by the first *(a,)* containing more organic matter, and less salts than the other.

73. Strictly all accumulations of loose materials resting upon rock constitutes the soil. These loose materials vary in depth from a few inches to one or two hundred feet; and occasionally consist of different layers or beds placed one over the other.

74. The earthy matter of all soils has been produced by the gradual decay, degradation, or crumbling down of previously existing rocks.

75. Soils are formed *(a,)* immediately from the rock upon which they rest; or *(b,)* from deposites, drift, &c., brought by water and other geological causes from a distance. In the latter case, the soil may have no relation whatever, either in mineralogical characters or in chemical constitution, to the immediately subjacent rocks. To these constituents must be added the remains of plants and animals; and carbon.

76. The principal rocks whose decay has given rise to the formation of soil may be briefly enumerated as follows: (*Mulder.*)

(*a*,) Quartz Rocks; (*b*,) Feldspar Rocks; (*c*,) Mica Rocks; (*d*.) Hornblende Rocks; (*e*,) Serpentine Rocks; (*f*,) Augite Rocks; (*g*,) Alumina Rocks; (*h*,) Lime Rocks; (*i*,) Gypsum; (*j*,) Iron.

77. The value of Irrigation for the purpose of manure depends upon the geological formation through which the stream passes.

79. Soils differ much in the relative quality of the substances which compose them; but all *fertile* soils contain the same materials.

80. The great bulk of all such soils consists of three earths: (*a*,) Silica, (or sand,) (*b*,) Alumina, (or clay,) (*c*,) Lime. Generally, these lie in juxtaposition, inert, and producing no effect on each other. To these must be added (*d*,) Water, which is always present uniting them. Deprived of water, soil becomes dust; but the water varies in its relative quantity according to the proportionate mixture of these three materials.

81. The economical character and usefulness of the soil varies in proportion to the predominance of one or other of these substances.

82. On a general average, the earthy part of the soil constitutes about 96 per cent. of its whole weight when free from water. (*Johnston.*)

83. By *Silica*, is meant siliceous sand or siliceous gravel of various degrees of fineness from an impalpable powder to sand-stones. By *Clay* —a finely divided *chemical* compound consisting very nearly of 60 per cent. of Silica and 40 per cent. of Alumina, with a little oxide of iron, and from which no sandy matter can be separated mechanically or by decantation. By *Lime*—Carbonate of Lime, in the shape of chalk, limestones, marl, shell-sand, &c.

84. Soils may be classified as follows:—

(*a*,) Pure Clay, *pipe clay*, = 60 per cent. Silica, 40 per cent. Alumina, oxide of iron chemically combined. (*b*,) Strongest clay soil, *brick clay*, pure clay (*a*,) with 5 to 10 per cent. of sand which can be separated by boiling and decantation. (*c*,) Clay loam = 15 to 30 per cent. fine sand and pure clay.

*(d,)* Loamy clay = 30 to 60 per cent. sand and pure clay. *(e,)* Sandy loam = 60 to 90 per cent. sand and pure clay. *(f,)* Sandy soil contains no more than 10 per cent. of pure clay. *(g,)* Marley soils, in which the proportion of lime is more than 5, but does not exceed 20 per cent. of the whole weight of the dry soil. *(h,)* Calcareous soils, in which the lime exceeding 20 per cent. becomes the distinguishing constituent. *(i,)* Vegetable soils—of various kinds, from garden mould which contains from 5 to 10 per cent., to the peaty soil in which the organic matter may amount to 60 or 70 per cent. These soils are also clayey, loamy, or sandy, according to the predominant character of the earthy admixtures.

85. The only use of the great bulk of the soil appears to be *(a,)* the upholding of the plant, and giving it a firm basis from which to spring; *(b,)* the absorption of gasses, and the imbibing and retaining of other elements; *(c,)* the supplying of water.

86. The remaining constituents of the soil may be divided into *(a,) Organic matter; (b,)* and chemical substances and salts, or *Inorganic matter.*

87. All soils contain organic matter in a greater or less proportion. This organic matter consists, in part, of decayed animal, but chiefly of decayed vegetable substances; sometimes in brown or black fibrous portions; sometimes forming only a fine brown powder intimately intermixed with the mineral matters of the soil; sometimes scarcely perceptible in either of these forms; and existing only in a state of organic compounds more or less devoid of color; and at times entirely soluble in water. In soils which appear to consist only of pure sand or clay, organic matter in this latter form may often be detected in considerable quantities.'

88. Chemically the organic compounds of the soil are thus termed :—(*a*,) Crenic acid ; (*b*,) Apocrenic acid ; (*c*,) Geic acid ; (*d*,) Humic acid ; (*e*,) humin, (or humus) ; (*f*,) Ulmic acid ; (*g*,) Ulmin. Humin

and ulmin are insoluble in alkalies and in water; the others are readily soluble in alkalies, and more or less in water also.

89. All organic matter may be resolved into the four gasses, carbon, oxygen, hydrogen, and nitrogen; with or without a little *ash*, or inorganic matter.

90. The nature and quantity of organic matter in the soil have great influence upon its character and fertility.

91. The most useful portions of plants are chiefly organic; as the woody fibre, starch, gum, sugar, gluten, and albumen; and in animals, the flesh, milk, butter, cheese, &c. Barn-yard manures, are also chiefly composed of water and organic matter. Thus, in well-preserved manure is found *(Richardson,)* in 100 parts:—

| | |
|---|---|
| Water, - - - - - - | 65 parts. |
| Organic matter, - - - - - | 24½ " |
| Inorganic salts, - - - - - | 10 " |

92. The inorganic matter forms the smallest portion of the soil, but it is absolutely essential for the production of useful vegetation. Without it plants will not produce seed; and the deficiency of a single element may render the soil entirely barren.

93. The names of these inorganic elements are:—

| Name. | In combination with | Forming |
|---|---|---|
| Chlorine, *(Bleaching Gas,)* | Metals, | Chlorides. |
| Iodine, - - - | " | Iodides. |
| Sulphur, - - - | " | Sulphurets. |
| " - - - | Hydrogen, | Sulphuretted Hydrogen. |
| " - - - | Oxygen, | Sulphuric acid. |
| Phosphorus, - - - | " | Phosphoric acid. |
| Potassium, - - | " | Potash. |
| " - - - | Chlorine, | Chloride of Potassium. |
| Sodium, - - - | Oxygen, | Soda. |
| " - - - | Chlorine, | Common Salt. |
| Calcium, - - - | " | Chloride of Lime. |

| | | |
|---|---|---|
| Calcium, - - - | Oxygen, | Lime. |
| Magnesium, - - | " | Magnesia. |
| Aluminum, - - - | " | Alumina, *(Clay.)* |
| Silicon, - - - | " | Silica, *(Sand.)* |
| Iron and Manganese, - - | " | Oxides. |
| Iron and Manganese, - - | Sulphur, | Sulphurets. |

94. With the exception of Iodine, the above appear to be essential to the composition of all cultivated plants.

95. The organic and inorganic elements are chemically combined, and are always undergoing change. They perhaps never exist in plants in a simple form.

96. These inorganic materials may be so carried away from the soil by injudicious cropping that at last the land refuses to bear grain, until they are replaced, or, in other words, till the land is manured. Again, manure, by its chemical action, may set free these elements in the soil which were previously unfit for absorption by roots. To recapitulate

97. A fertile soil consists of three earths:—*(a,)* Sand; *(b,)* Clay, and *(c,)* Lime, mechanically combined; *(d,)* of four gasses, forming organic matter; and *(e,)* of eleven or twelve inorganic elements, in small quantities, chemically combined.

98. Practically, the difference between a rich and an impoverished soil is this:—A rich soil contains every thing a plant requires *in a soluble state*, ready to be at once absorbed by the roots of the plant. A worn-out soil contains the same constituents but *in an insoluble state*, not capable of being dissolved in water, and therefore unable to enter into the roots.

99. On whatever soil a plant is grown, if it shoots up in a healthy manner, and fairly ripens its seed, the quantity and quality of the ash is nearly the same.

100. No two plants of a different order contain the same quantity and quality of inorganic matter. The more widely two plants differ in their natural character, (*e. g.* turnips and wheat,) the wider will be the difference between their constituents.

101. On these principles, in practical farming, is based the utility of fallowing, and the rotation of crops.

102. The *mechanical texture* of the soil has a strong influence upon its practical fertility; very heavy clays, and very light sands, being both, for opposite reasons, apt to produce badly. The soil in which the particles are the finest, so that the air can enter, and the roots spread without difficulty, is, other things being equal, the best. In clay soils this division of the particles must be produced by the plow and other mechanical means; while in loose sands it is too great, and must be amended by an admixture of clay and other substances. The great fertility of the bottom lands of the Scioto River, Ohio, is attributed to the remarkable comminution of the particles of these soils.

103. The sub-soil also produces a sensible effect on the condition of the soil above it. If the soil is clay, it is impervious to water, and if the sub-soil is clay also, it also is impervious to water. The immediate effect of this arrangement is to render both soil and sub-soil habitually wet, and therefore cold, or perhaps barren, until evaporation dries first the one and then the other. A retentive sub-soil may render even a porous, sandy or gravelly soil above it habitually wet. A gravelly sub-soil, which is always porous, greatly assists in keeping a clay soil dry. When a porous soil rests on a sandy sub-soil, water can do no injury, while in dry weather, the evaporation from below may do great good. On the other hand, a clay sub-soil retains manure while a sandy one allows it to leach away, and in practice, renders the soil incapable of improvement. Rock may act either as a retentive or porous sub-soil, according to its structure. In many clay sub-soils, draining is absolutely necessary. In sandy and gravelly sub-soils, very rarely so.

103*. There is an important element which must always be taken into account in estimating the value of soils—*their depth or thickness.* In running a deepish furrow in a cultivated field, we generally distinguish, at a glance, the depth of the superficial layer, which is commonly called the *mould* or *vegetable earth;* this is a layer generally impregnated with humus, and is looser and more friable than the sub-soil upon which it rests. The thickness of this superficial layer is extremely variable; varying from two inches to two feet. Depth of mould or vegetable soil is always, practically, advantageous; it is one of the best conditions to successful agriculture. If we have depth of soil, and the roots of our plants do not penetrate sufficiently to derive benefit from the fertility that lies below, we can always, by working a little deeper, bring up the inferior layers to the surface, and so make them concur in fertilizing the soil. Farther, a deep soil suffers less from excess or deficiency of moisture; the rain that falls has more to moisten, and is therefore absorbed in greater quantity than by thin soils; and, once imbibed, it remains in store against drought.

104. Soils also vary much in color, as *(a,)* black; *(b,)* white; *(c,)* blue; *(d,)* red; *(e,)* brown. The colors of soil have a considerable influence in regulating the quantities of heat absorbed from the sun's rays; the darker colored absorb more heat than the lighter colored; and the dark colored reflect the least.

105. According to Shubler, while the thermometer was 77° in the shade in August, sand of a natural color indicated a temperature of 112½°; black sand, 123½°; and white sand, 110°, exhibiting a difference of 13° in favor of the black color.

106. Color also influences the power of soil in retaining the heat of the sun. Dark colored soils, in the absence of the sun's rays, radiate or part with the heat more quickly than light colored. Thus sand cools more slowly than clay, and clay than a soil containing much vegetable matter. This principle has a strong practical influence on the deposit of dew, and injury to vegetation by night frosts.

107. Soils also vary in their power of absorbing and retaining moisture. The absorption is greatest in clay soils, especially when they contain humus, (vegetable matter.)

Schubler gives the following table of the relative absorbing power of soils:

| KINDS OF EARTH. | 1,000 grains of earth on a surface of 50 square inches. absorbed in | | | |
|---|---|---|---|---|
| | 12 hours. | 24 hours. | 48 hours | 72 hours. |
| | Grains. | Grains. | Grains. | Grains. |
| Siliceous sand, - - | 0 water. | 0 water. | 0 water | 0 water |
| Sandy clay, - - | 21 " | 26 " | 28 " | 28 " |
| Loamy clay, - - | 25 " | 30 " | 34 " | 32 " |
| Brick clay, - - | 30 " | 36 " | 40 " | 41 " |
| Gray pure clay, - - | 37 " | 42 " | 48 " | 49 " |
| Garden mould, - - | 35 " | 45 " | 50 " | 52 " |
| Arable soil, - - | 16 " | 22 " | 23 " | 23 " |
| Humus, - - | 80 " | 97 " | 110 " | 120 " |

Thus, while sandy lands may suffer from long continuance of dry weather, a neighboring field abounding in humus may absorb sufficient moisture from the air to serve all the requirements of vegetation.

108. The power of saturation by water, and the retention of moisture, vary in the same manner, and nearly in the same degrees.

109. Another important physical property of soils, is their power to absorb oxygen from the air.

According to Schubler:—

| Grains. | Cubic inches. | |
|---|---|---|
| 1,000 Siliceous sand, in a wet state, absorbed oxygen, | 0.24 | From 15 cubic inches of atmospheric air, containing 21 per cent. of oxygen. |
| 1,000 Sandy clay, - - - - - | 1.39 | |
| 1,000 Loamy clay, - - - - - - | 1.65 | |
| 1,000 Brick clay, - - - - - | 2.04 | |
| 1,000 Gray pure clay, - - - - - - | 2.29 | |
| 1,000 Garden mould, - - - - - - | 2.60 | |
| 1,000 Arable soil, - - - - - - | 2.43 | |
| 1,000 Humus, - - - - - | 3.04 | |

Soils lose, in drying, the property of absorbing oxygen from the air, but regain it in the same proportion as before, on being moistened. The action of organic manures, and the production of carbonic acid, depend on the existence of oxygen in the soil; and, in practice, the difference is very great. Every farmer knows how little good is effected by his barn-yard manure on a crop in a very dry season, compared with a moderately wet one.

And, in the same manner, such manures act more rapidly in soils rich in humus than in those chiefly consisting of sand.

110. The different classes of soils are distinguished by growing different classes of weeds; and frequently by the existence of different noxious insects.

111. The capillary power of soils also differs.

*Capillary attraction or power,* means the power by which a liquid ascends in the interior of a capillary tube, or tube of small bore, above the surface of the liquid which surrounds it. The phenomenon occurs in solid bodies which are capable of being wetted. Thus, when water is poured into the basin of a flower-pot, the soil gradually sucks it in, and becomes moist even to the surface. The same takes place in the soil in the open fields. The water from beneath—that contained in the subsoil—is gradually sucked up to the surface. Where water is present in excess, this capillary action keeps the soil always moist and cold.

Evaporation takes place from the surface of the land, and as each atom of moisture is taken up into the atmosphere, its place is supplied by another atom, communicated by the contact of the particles of soil, the more superficial acting on the deeper particles like so many pumps, to elevate the water, and supply the loss. Thus a naturally porous soil may be kept injuriously wet by an impervious sub-soil several feet below.

Ordinary soils possess the power of separating, from solution in water, the different earthy and alkaline substances presented to them in manure. But these substances, necessary for the growth of the plant, are rapidly carried, by rain and other causes, down into the sub-soil, beyond the reach of roots. Were there no counteracting influences, these substances would soon be lost, and all soils become barren. But when warm weather comes, and the surface soil dries rapidly, then by capillary action the water rises from beneath, bringing with it the soluble substances that exist in the sub-soil, through which it ascends. And as this ascent and evaporation go on as long as the dry weather continues, the saline matter accumulates about the roots of the plants, so as put within their reach an ample supply of every soluble substance which is not really defective in the soil. Practically, this principle is of great importance in manuring and draining.

The relative capillary power of soils has not yet been thoroughly tested; but, generally, in sandy and light soils, of which the particles are very fine, this capillary action is of great importance, and is intimately connected with the power of producing remunerating crops.

112. The following analyses are given as examples of various classes of Soils:—

I. Clay:—Three specimens from the Zuider Zee, in the Netherlands. (*E. H. von Baumhauer.*)

| | First. | Second. | Third. |
|---|---|---|---|
| Insoluble quartzose sand, with alumina and silica, | 57.646 | 51.766 | 55.372 |
| Soluble silica, | 2.340 | 2.496 | 2.286 |
| Alumina, | 1.830 | 2.900 | 2.888 |
| Peroxide of iron, | 9.038 | 10.305 | 11.864 |
| Protoxide of iron, | 0.350 | 0.563 | 0.200 |
| Protoxide of manganese, | 0.288 | 0.354 | 0.284 |
| Lime, | 4.092 | 5.096 | 2.480 |
| Magnesia, | 0.130 | 0.140 | 0.128 |
| Potash, | 1.026 | 1.430 | 1.521 |
| Soda, | 1.972 | 2.069 | 1.937 |
| Ammonia, | 0.060 | 0.078 | 0.075 |
| Phosphoric acid, | 0.466 | 0.324 | 0.478 |
| Sulphuric acid, | 0.896 | 1.104 | 0.576 |
| Carbonic acid, | 6.085 | 6.940 | 4.775 |
| Chlorine, | 1.240 | 1.302 | 1.418 |
| Humic acid, | 2.798 | 3.991 | 3.428 |
| Crenic acid, | 0.771 | 0.731 | 0.037 |
| Apocrenic acid, | 0.107 | 0.160 | 0.152 |
| Humin, vegetable remains, and water chemically combined, | 8.324 | 7.700 | 9.340 |
| Wax and resin, | trace | trace | trace |
| Loss, | 0.542 | 0.611 | 0.753 |
| | 100.000 | 100.000 | 100.000 |

These are very rich soils, and derive their origin from the Rhine country, and are the product of decayed rocks.

113. II. Cotton Lands of Mississippi. (*J. P. Norton.*)

| | | A. | B. |
|---|---|---|---|
| | Organic matter, | 4.740 | 6.290 |
| SOLUBLE IN WATER. A, 2.470 pr ct. B. 0.147 " | Silica, | 1.299 | 0.072 |
| | Iron, alumina, and phosphates, | 0.230 | 0.019 |
| | Lime, | 0.389 | 0.020 |
| | Magnesia, | 0.090 | none |
| | Manganese, | 0.034 | none |
| | Potash, | 0.248 | 0.120 |
| | Chloride of sodium, (common salt,) | 0.107 | .... |
| | Soda, | .... | 0.015 |
| | Sulphuric acid, | 0.144 | 0.009 |
| SOLUBLE IN ACID. A 4.96 pr ct. B, 5.19 " | Silica, | 0.409 | 0.920 |
| | Alumina, | 1.644 | 1.820 |
| | Iron, | 1.448 | 0.670 |
| | Lime, | 0.535 | 1.340 |
| | Magnesia, | 0.576 | 0.080 |
| | Manganese, | 0.002 | none |
| | Potash, | 0.348 | 0.070 |
| | Soda, | .... | 0.180 |
| | Sulphuric acid, | 0.070 | 0.080 |
| | Phosphoric acid, | 0.042 | 0.003 |
| INSOLUBLE PORTION. A. 87.83 pr ct. B 88.373 " | Silica, | 78.845 | 84.930 |
| | Iron and alumina, | 5.946 | 2.370 |
| | Lime, | 1.098 | 0.260 |
| | Magnesia, | 1.142 | 0.680 |
| | Manganese, | 0.623 | none |
| | | 100.059 | 89.867 |

A. is from a strong cotton soil. B. was originally the same soil, but has been worn out by long cultivation. This analysis is peculiarly valuable as an illustration. The first table gives the organic elements soluble in water, and which alone are available for the growth of the plant. In the new soil this amounts to about 2½ per cent. of the whole. In the worn out soil, it is very trifling. A plant grown in the latter would be nearly starved; while it would be entirely deficient in two elements of nutrition. The second table gives the inorganic elements soluble in acid, but not in water. While, therefore, these are not available for a growing crop, yet by means of rest, by the action of carbonic acid, and of the atmosphere, or by *fallowing*, and by the application of *chemical* or dissolving manures, they may, to a certain extent, be rendered soluble in water, and the producing power of the soil be restored. Thus, shut up, there are materials enough to grow twice the amount of crops already taken from the land. The third table gives the inorganic constituents, which are not soluble by any available means; and therefore they must be considered only as the basis for the others.

Another fact to be observed is the very small proportion of such constituents available at any one time for the growth of plants; and the facility with which soils may be impoverished. In each 100 lbs. of the soil, free from moisture, only about 2 lbs. can be converted into vegetation.

This table will be again referred when we come to consider the subject of manures: but it is necessary to remark that, in actual growth, a plant *may* receive more than the above of necessary nutrition by means of water evaporating from below. (§111.)

114. III. Fertile pasture soil (A). Fertile arable soil (B). Barren or unfruitful soil (C). (*Johnston.*)

| | A. | B. | C. |
|---|---|---|---|
| Silica, Quartz, Sand, and Silicates, - | 71.849 | 87.143 | 61.576 |
| Alumina, - - - | 9.350 | 5.666 | 0.450 |
| Oxides of iron, - - - | 5.410 | 2.220 | 0.524 |
| Oxide of Manganese, - - | 0.925 | 0.360 | trace |
| Lime, - - - - | 0.987 | 0.564 | 0.320 |
| Magnesia, - - - | 0.245 | 0.312 | 0.130 |
| Potash and Soda, - - - | 0.007 | 0.145 | trace |
| Phosphoric acid, - - - | 0.131 | 0.060 | " |
| Sulphuric acid, - - - | 0.174 | 0.027 | " |
| Chlorine, - - - | 0.002 | 0.036 | " |
| Humic acid, - - - - | 1.270 | 1.304 | 11 470 |
| Insoluble humus, - - | 7.550 | 1.072 | 26.530 |
| Organic matter, containing nitrogen, | 2.000 | 1.011 | .... |
| Water, - - - - | 0.100 | .... | .... |
| Carbonic acid united to the lime, - | .... | 0.080 | trace |

The first is from a fertile alluvial district of Hanover, from the banks of the Weser; the second, from the banks of the Ohio River, is celebrated for yielding successive crops of corn for a long period without manure; and the third is from a moor in East Freisland.

115. IV. The following (A,) is from an analysis of an inferior wheat soil, at Three Rivers, Michigan, by *Dr. S. H. Douglass*, compared with a good and fertile soil (B,) analyzed by *Prof. Norton.*

| 1000 parts gave *soluble* in water | A. | B. |
|---|---|---|
| Humic acid and ammonia, | 0.264 | 4.740 |
| Silica, | 0.063 | 1.299 |
| Lime, | 0.256 | 0.389 |
| Potash and Soda, | 0.243 | 0.445 |
| Iron, alumina, and phosphates, | 0.120 | .... |
| 1000 parts gave *insoluble* in water | | |
| Silica, | 902. | 788.45 |
| Lime, | 1.7 | 10.98 |
| Iron, alumina, and phosphates, | 34. | 59.46 |
| Humic acid, | 4.7 | .... |
| Potash and Soda, | 2.04 | .... |
| Organic matter, | 54. | .... |
| Not ascertained, | .654 | .... |

116. V. Analysis of an impoverished soil in the town of Freehold, Monmouth County, New Jersey, (A,) with the constituents which it ought to contain to render it productive, (B.) (*Dr. Antisell.*)

| | A. | B. |
|---|---|---|
| Organic matters, | 4.50 | 9.70 |
| Silicates, | 87.60 | .... |
| Alumina, | 3.65 | 5.70 |
| Lime, | 0.45 | 5.90 |
| Magnesia, | trace | .... |
| Per-oxide of iron, | 1.39 | .... |
| Potash, | 0.01 | 0.20 |
| Soda, | 0.08 | 0.40 |
| Chlorine, | 0.06 | 0.20 |
| Sulphuric acid, | 0.12 | 0.20 |
| Phosphoric acid, with iron as phosphate, | 0.03 | 0.40 |
| Carbonic acid, | .... | 4.00 |
| Moisture, | 2.00 | .... |
| Loss, | 0.01 | .... |
| | 100.00 | |

117. VI. Marl from Bordentown, (A,) and from Squankum, (B,) New Jersey. (*Dr. Antisell.*)

| | A. | B. |
|---|---|---|
| Silicates, insoluble in hydrocholoric acid, | 68.66 | 76.00 |
| Alumina, | 7.00 | 5.00 |
| Lime, | 1.40 | 2.85 |
| Magnesia, | 0.38 | 0.18 |
| Peroxide of iron, | 9.00 | 3.20 |
| Potash, | 3.70 | 5.80 |
| Soda, | 0.30 | 1.10 |
| Chlorine, | 0.20 | 0.40 |
| Sulphuric acid. | 1.30 | 0.90 |
| Phosphoric acid, | 0.28 | 0.46 |
| Carbonic acid, | .... | 1.84 |
| Moisture, | 6.46 | 2.00 |
| Sulphur, combined with iron, | 1.32 | 0.27 |
| | 100.00 | 100.00 |

118. VII. Green Sand Marl, Shrewsbury, Monmouth county, New Jersey; two varieties. (*H. Wurtz.*)

| | A. | B. |
|---|---|---|
| Silica, | 48.24 | 47.83 |
| Alumina and oxide of iron, | 32.89 | 34.98 |
| Potash, | 6.38 | 4.94 |
| Magnesia, | 2.60 | .... |
| Hygroscopic water, | 4.81 | 11.50 |
| Combined water, | 5.69 | |
| | 100.61 | 99.25 |

119. VIII. Red Marl, Springfield, Mass. (*Dr. C. T. Jackson.*)

| | |
|---|---|
| Water, | 8.5 |
| Silex, | 51.3 |
| Alumina, | 16.0 |
| Peroxide of iron, with a trace of manganese, | 20.0 |
| Lime, | 2.8 |
| Magnesia, | 1.0 |
| | 99.6 |

120. IX. Analyses of Shell Marl, Forfarshire, (A,) and Clay Marl, Ayrshire, (B,) Scotland, (*Johnston.*)

| | A. | B. |
|---|---|---|
| Carbonate of lime, - - - - - | 81.7 | 8.4 |
| Oxide of iron and alumina, - - - - - | 0.6 | 2.2 |
| Organic matter, - - - - - - | 14.6 | 2.8 |
| Clay and silicious matter, - - - - - | 3.1 | 84.9 |
| Water, - - - - - - - | .... | 1.4 |
| | 100.0 | 99.7 |

# CHAPTER IV.

## METEOROLOGY.

121. A good soil, well worked, with good seed, is not the only element of success in farming; the CLIMATE has a powerful controlling influence on agricultural pursuits; an influence to which the farmer is compelled to submit. By knowledge, however, he may so adapt his business to the climate, as to render the changes to which it is subject, beneficial, instead of injurious to him.

122. The study of the laws which govern the climate is called *meteorology.*

The word "meteorology" means, literally, the science of meteors; but the term is applied, more extensively, to the investigation of all the physical causes which affect the condition of our globe; and particularly to the effects of light, heat, and winds on the earth, the ocean, and the atmosphere, and the results of these agents in the production of climate.

123. As meteorology is in itself an abstruse science, it will only be necessary, in this place, to give such principal laws and facts as bear upon agriculture.

124. The main elements of climate are, *(a,)* the temperature of the air; *(b,)* of the soil; *(c,)* the quantity of rain and dew that fall; *(d,)* the character of the prevailing winds; *(e,)* the length of the seasons of heat and cold; and *(f,)* the seasons at which, and the mode in which the rains prevail.

125. There is *(a,)* a general climate, and *(b,)* a local climate. The first is equal, over the whole globe, on the same *Iso-thermal*

lines; the second depends on local circumstances, such as mountains, table lands, large forests, lakes, &c., which affect the distribution of heat and rain; and which may render the local climate better or worse than the general one. In the United States, the local climate is found to change as the country is settled and cleared; and it often varies sufficiently, within a comparatively small area, to influence the sort of crops to be grown, and the stock to be kept.

*Iso-thermal lines* are lines of equal temperature; a term applied to imaginary lines drawn on a map connecting all those places on the surface of the globe which have the same mean temperature. Lines drawn through places having the same summer temperature, are termed *Iso-theral;* those drawn through places having the same winter temperature, are called *Iso cheimal;* while lines drawn through places having other common temperatures, receive other appropriate names. Fully to explain this to the student, it will be necessary for the teacher to exhibit a physical atlas of the globe, where the various lines are laid down.

126. The climate may be *practically* changed, to a certain extent, by the farmer, by means of cutting down forests, draining, deep plowing, high walls, and plantations of trees; and by the gardener, to any extent, by means of hot-beds, hot-walls, glass-houses, manures, &c.

127. The following changes take place, owing to the cultivation of a new country: *(a.)* Fogs disappear, and with them agues and other diseases; sometimes naturally; almost always, by a proper and sufficiently extensive system of drainage.* *(Brown & Dickeson, Prof. Johnston.)* *(b.)* Dews are less heavy; the quantity of running water is diminished; lakes and marshes dry up; hail-storms become more frequent; early and late frosts are more injurious to vegetation.—*(Boussingault.)*

128. On the contrary, by neglect, a previously healthy coun-

* A very striking instance of the improvement of health, and the ceasing of miasmatic diseases throughout a whole township, in consequence of draining, in Beverly, Mass., is given in the *Abstract from the Returns of Agricul. Soc. in Mass., for* 1846, *p.* 31.

try may become incapable of sustaining human life, as in the marshes surrounding Rome, Italy; and the waters may again encroach and cover land that was previously retrieved from them, as in the Aragua Valley, Venezuela, So. America.—(*Boussingault.*)

129. The cultivation of perennial plants is limited by the lowest temperature of winter; that of annual plants by the mean temperature of summer. Thus a country so cold as to be incapable of sustaining trees, may yet have a sufficiently long and hot summer to mature grains and vegetables; and annual plants may prosper in a latitude so far North that perennial ones, indigenous to the same climate, would perish from cold.

The heat of the atmosphere is measured by an instrument called a *thermometer*, consisting of quicksilver or alcohol, enclosed in a vacuum tube, with a hollow bulb at one end. This is placed upon a scale, graduated by actual experiment; and the quicksilver rises and falls in the tube, according to the amount of heat. Three different modes of graduation are employed in different countries; *Fahrenheit's* in America and Great Britain; *Centigrade* in France; and *Reaumur's* in France and other parts of Europe.

212 degrees, (°) of Fahrenheit equal 100° Centigrade, and 80° Reaumur.

32 degrees of Fahrenheit equal 0 Centigrade, and 0 Reaumur.

There are various forms of the Thermometer, but all on the same principle.

By the term *mean temperature*, is meant the temperature obtained by adding together the temperatures of the days or months required, and dividing by the number of days or months. *Mean annual temperature* is obtained by adding together the temperatures of all the months of the year, and dividing the sum by the number of the months; so that the *mean annual temperature* expresses the height at which the thermometer would stand at any place, if we could suppose it perfectly stationary throughout the year.

130. For the cultivation of annual plants, it is only necessary to know the mean temperature of the climate during the number of months requisite for growth and the maturation of the seed.

Boussingault gives the following list of temperatures favorable to the particular plants, in the success of which man is more especially interested. Some of them require a mean *annual* temperature, others only a mean *summer* temperature, as below:

| NAME. | Maximum. | Minimum. | NAME. | Maximum. | Minimum. |
|---|---|---|---|---|---|
| Chocolate Bean, | 82° F. | 73° | Rice, | 82° | 75° |
| Banana, | " | 64 | Pine Apple, | " | 68 |
| Indigo, | " | 71 | Melon, | " | 67 |
| Sugar Cane, | " | 71 | Coffee, | 79 | 74 |
| Cocoa Nut, | " | 78 | Wheat, | 74 | 44 |
| Palm, | " | 78 | Barley, | " | 59 |
| Tobacco, | " | 65 | Potatoes, | 75 | 52 |
| Maize, | " | 59 | Flax, | 74 | 54 |
| French Beans, | | | Apple, | 72 | 59 |
| (Haricots, | " | 59 | Oak, | 67 | 61 |

Thus we can grow melons, which only require a short period of summer for growth and maturation; but cannot grow pine-apples, which require at least two years before they bear fruit; although the former only needs one degree of mean temperature less than the latter.

131. The number of days that elapse between the commencement of vegetation and the period of ripeness is by so much the greater as the mean temperature is lower. Thus, wheat, with a mean temperature of 59° F., requires 137 days to mature; with a temperature of 56°, 160 days; with a temperature of 76°, 92 days. In other words, the lower the mean temperature of the climate, the longer the crop must be in the ground before harvesting. And thus Indian corn may ripen in a sheltered valley, but be annually cut off by frost on a mountain side a few miles distant.

Experiments, however, prove that many grains, brought from a climate with a markedly lower mean summer temperature, to one higher, only acquire the power of ripening early *by degrees of successive annual crops,* a fact which is practically important in the growth and quality of certain grains.

Upon every parallel of latitude, at all elevations above the level of the sea, the same plant receives in the course of its existence an equal quantity of heat.

132. The temperature of the soil, in summer, greatly exceeds that of the air. At Albany, N. Y., the temperature of the soil rises to 100° F. five feet below the surface, and to 140° half an inch below. *(Johnston.)* But this temperature varies according to the color and quality of the soil, the evaporation, the amount of water it contains, the nature of the subsoil, &c. This internal heat is of great importance in practical farming; a warm, dry soil allowing the seeds to sprout early in the spring; forcing forward the plant, as in a hot-bed; regulating the amount of dew deposited; controlling early and late night frosts; and probably influencing, favorably for the farmer, the growth of parasitic fungi, such as *rust, mildew, &c.* It also causes manures to act, and produces other beneficial effects, such as electrical currents. It can be regulated and increased by artificial means, but chiefly by proper drainage.

133. Seeds require a given temperature of air and soil for healthful germination; various plants differing in this respect; some requiring a much higher temperature than others. On this point, the following laws have been laid down: *(a.)* When the temperature at noon is given, (other things being equal,) the time necessary for the development of a seed may be ascertained. *(b,)* If the period of germination be given, the meridian temperature of the country during the period may be determined. *(c,)* When the seed fructifies in the same year in which it is planted, the proper time for putting it into the ground is when the meridian temperature is such as to produce vegetation in the shortest period. *(d,)* An increase of temperature beyond a certain point, does not expedite the vegetative process.

The following table has been drawn up from actual experiment,

*(J. T. Plummer;)* but it would have been more perfect if the temperature of the soil had also been recorded:

| When the average meridian temperature in the shade is | | | |
|---|---|---|---|
| | 62° F. | Lima Beans, *soaked*, require - - | 20 days. |
| | 76 | do s. - - - - - - - | 7 " |
| | 88 | do s. - - - - - - | 7 " |
| | 51 | Peas, s. - - - - - - - | 19 " |
| | 59 | do s. - - - - - - | 13 " |
| | 74 | do s. - - - - - - - | 11 " |
| | 80 | do - - - - - - - - | 14 " |
| | 60 | Bishop's early Peas, - - - - - | 10 " |
| | 62 | do do - - - - - - | 8 " |
| | 55 | Radishes, s. - - - - - - - | 12 " |
| | 60 | do s. - - - - - - | 7 " |
| | 70 | do s. - - - - - - - | 3 " |
| | 62 | Onion seed, s. - - - - - - | 15 " |
| | 77 | do s. - - - - - - - | 9 " |
| | 54 | Drum-head Cabbage, - - - - - | 12 " |
| | 60 | do s. - - - - - - - | 6 " |
| | 75 | do s. - - - - - - | 5 " |
| | 61 | Red Cabbage s. - - - - - - | 6 " |
| | 61 | Beet, s. - - - - - - | 11 " |
| | 63 | do - - - - - - - - - | 22 " |
| | 67 | do s. - - - - - - | 8 " |
| | 79 | do s. - - - - - - - | 5 " |
| | 58 | Cucumber, - - - - - - - | 30 " |
| | 81 | do - - - - - - - - | 7 " |

It is stated that at Albany, N. Y., of Indian corn planted when the temperature of the soil was but 45° in the spring, the seed all rotted; but when planted, when the temperature was about 60°, it vegetated.

This subject is one of great importance to the farmer; large quantities of seed and labor are annually lost in consequence of inattention to such particulars; and there is yet much to learn that is valuable in this regard. The proper time for seed-sowing may be accurately ascertained by means of experiment; and by the use of the thermometer and meteorological tables.

134. As is well known, a ray of the sun's light, consists of *seven* rays of different colors, which, uniting, form the ordinary white light. But, besides this, the sun's rays contain three different kinds of rays: *(a,)* a ray of light; *(b,)* of heat; *(c,)* of chemical agency. The effect of these on vegetation is essen-

tially different. Yellow light, *(a,)* impedes germination, and accelerates that decomposition of carbonic acid, which produces wood and woody tissues. Under its influence, leaves are small and wood short jointed. Red light, *(b,)* carries heat, and is favorable to germination if abundance of water is present, increases evaporation, supports the flowering quality, and improves fruit. Under its influence, color is diminished, and leaves are scorched. Blue light, *(c,)* (also called *chemical action*, or *actinism,)* accelerates germination, and causes rapid growth. Under its influence, plants become weak and long jointed. *(Hunt.)* These three agencies exist in different proportions in the sunbeam in the spring, summer, and autumn. The blue, *(c,)* is greater in spring; the yellow, *(a,)* in summer. The blue, (chemical ray,) is less in the fall; and then the heating ray, red, *(b,)* predominates. Thus the sun's rays differ in their properties at different seasons of year; and are adapted to the peculiar needs of the plant at the time. Still further, the proportion of these agencies vary in different latitudes and climates. Daguerreotypes, depending on these principles, are poor in England, better in France, superior in New York, but best in the Northwestern States. Probably the *chemical* rays are more abounding in the above proportion, but there is yet much to learn on this subject; and it is not unlikely that the many differences known to exist in animal and vegetable life in these countries will be found to be more or less controlled by these peculiarities of the sun's rays. Gardeners have attempted to make practical use of these facts by means of colored glasses, but, apparently, without much success.

135. Rain is necessary for the life of most plants. In those countries where rain never falls, vegetation is either wanting, or —depending on dews—very limited. In other countries, where it only falls at a certain season, leaving many months at a time without a shower, plants only grow during the rains, and are parched up and disappear during the rest of the year. The

amount of rain that falls in a year is governed by known laws. It varies in different parts of the same country, but is nearly the same, each year, in any given locality.

Rain is measured, for meteorological purposes, by *inches*. The instrument used is called a *Rain Guage*, and sometimes a *Pluviometer*. They are of various forms, but all acting upon the same principle—that of receiving the rain into a vessel of known size, with a graduated measurer, divided into inches and parts of inches. The one generally used in the United States is known as the "Conical Rain Guage of DeWitt"—equally simple and perfect. It consists of a copper cone, with a perforated cap to prevent evaporation. It is fixed on a post, in a situation sheltered from winds, about 8 feet from the ground. The measurement is made by putting down perpendicularly to the bottom of the guage, a measuring stick, graduated in inches and their decimals.

136. In Agriculture, rain is important as regards *(a,)* the season, and *(b,)* the mode in which it falls, whether in heavy storms, with long intervals between them, or frequently, in small quantities at a time; and *(c,)* the direction from which it comes. If rain chiefly fell late in the Fall, in Winter, or in early Spring, vegetation would receive but little benefit from it. If it fell continuously at seed and harvest time, it would preclude cultivation; if it fell in heavy storms, with long intervals between them, plants would be alternately forced forwards, and retarded. Where rain is very constant, as in the mountains of England and Scotland, grass-growing and cattle-raising are substituted for grain. Consequently, the *annual* amount of rain is of less importance than the frequency of it, and the seasons of the year over which it is spread.

The annual amount of rains, averages:—

| | |
|---|---|
| Under the tropics of the New World, - | 115 inches. |
| " " " " " Old World, - - | 76 " |
| Within the tropics generally, - - - | 95½ " |
| In the United States, - - - - | 45 " |
| Europe, - - - - - - - | 31¾ " |
| Generally over the world, - - - - | 34¾ " |

Much more rain falls annually in the United States than in Great Britain, if a few mountain districts in the latter be excepted; but the mode of falling is different in the two countries.

The following table will serve as an illustration of this subject, although being drawn from single years, it is not strictly accurate as regards each locality:—

| PLACE. | | Rainy Days | Inches. | Snowy Days. | Inches. |
|---|---|---|---|---|---|
| Truro, - - | England, | 152 | 50 | | |
| Exeter, - - | " | 150 | 33 | | |
| Bechington, - | " | 185 | 35 | | |
| Greenwich, - | " | 167 | 28 | | |
| Liverpool, - | " | 190 | 31 | | |
| Highfield, - - | " | 213 | 25 | | |
| Whitehaven, - | " | 200 | 45 | | |
| Durham, - - | " | 152 | 21 | | |
| Newcastle, - | " | 140 | 30 | | |
| Saco, Maine, - | U. States, | | 44 | | |
| Cambridge, Mass., | " | | 56 | | |
| Mendon, - " | " | *81½ | | 26 | |
| Worcester, " | " | 88 | 37 | 24 | 61 |
| New York, N. Y., | " | 57 | 39 | 8 | 31 |
| Savannah, Geo., | " | 72 | 59 | | |
| Natches, Miss., | " | 87 | 75 | | |
| Ann Arbor, Mich., | " | 79 | 23 | 33 | |

* Average of 15 years

In England, more rain falls on the West than on the East side of the Island; and the practical effect is that more green crops, which require more moisture than grain, are grown on the former; such crops making a larger return on the western side.

137. Every inch of rain falling annually is equal to a weight of rather more than 112 tons on each imperial acre; so that the mean annual weight of rain falling in the United States, exceeds the mean amount of rain on the eastern coast of England, by several hundreds of tons per acre.

138. Another important consideration is *(a,)* the season of the year in which rain chiefly falls; and *(b,)* the distance of

of time which usually intervenes between one day of rain and another.

Thus, in 1841, according to the *Army Meteorological Register*, there fell at Detroit, Mich., and New Orleans, La., the following inches of rain and snow in each quarter of the year, in so many days:

| DETROIT. | I. | II. | III. | IV. | N.ORLEANS | I. | II. | III. | IV. |
|---|---|---|---|---|---|---|---|---|---|
| Inches, | 5.36 | 7.87 | 7.84 | 5.99 | Inches, | 31.50 | 9.90 | 7.17 | 11.96 |
| Days, | 25 | 20 | 19 | 30 | Days, | 30 | 3 ? | 28 | 4 ? |

Thus we see, that in Detroit, during this year, of 27.06 inches of rain, 11.35 or less than half fell during the six winter months; leaving 15.71 inches for the use of vegetation; while in New Orleans, 43.46 inches, or nearly three quarters of the whole year's supply, fell during the winter months, leaving only 17.07 for the six summer months. So that, while there is much less rain in Michigan, it is more equally distributed.

139. The yield of grains, and root crops depends upon the mode in which the rain falls, whether in light showers, and dense fogs; or in heavy storms; and at the particular time of vegetating or flowering. These particulars again vary according to the soil, whether it is sand or clay, drained or undrained. Thus oats appear to demand a constantly damp atmosphere; buckwheat and peas light showers while flowering; while wheat is apt to be injured by rust, if much warm rain falls at the time it is ripening. The size and average weight of stock also seem to depend upon the mode in which rain falls. The health of sheep is certainly dependent on this peculiarity of the climate; and the naturalization of varieties *probably* depends upon it.

Dr. P. A. Brown, of Philadelphia, observes "that if a line be drawn diagonally through the United States from the South-east corner of New Hampshire to Texas, it will be found, that the woolly sheep, (*Merino variety*,) will breed and thrive everywhere North-west of it, and the hairy sheep, (long-woolled varieties,) everywhere South-east of this line;

but that neither will thrive on the other sides, respectively, of that line, nor will they if the species are crossed." The same peculiarities are found in other parts of the world. The *cause* is not yet satisfactorily ascertained, but is undoubtedly more or less dependent on climate.

140. Through a perfectly dry argillo-calcareous soil, in a state of fallow, rain descends in one day six times the depth of the quantity fallen. Thus a fall of 4-10ths of an inch will sink in a day through nearly 2½ inches. (*Gasparin.*)

141. The power of the soil to absorb and retain moisture, is practically, an important consideration, and greatly influences the effects of the annual quantity of rain falling. The amount of water which a cubic foot of various soils can contain before they allow any of it to run off was determined by M. Schubler:

A cubic foot of

| | | |
|---|---|---|
| Siliceous sand held of water | | 27.3 lbs. |
| Calcareous sand | " | 31.8 " |
| Sandy clay | " | 38.8 " |
| Loamy clay | " | 41.4 " |
| Stiff clay, or brick earth, | " | 45.4 " |
| Arable soil | " | 46.8 " |
| Garden mould | " | 48.4 " |

142. The relative degree of rapidity with which rain water is evaporated, was also ascertained. Of 200 parts of each earth exposed for four hours, on a thin surface in a closed room, at 65¾ Fahrenheit, there was an evaporation of absorbed water as follows:

| | | | | | | | |
|---|---|---|---|---|---|---|---|
| Siliceous sand lost | | 88.4 | parts in | 100 | parts of | absorbed | water. |
| Calcareous sand | " | 75.9 | " | " | " | " | " |
| Sand clay | " | 52.0 | " | " | " | " | " |
| Loamy clay | " | 45.7 | " | " | " | " | " |
| Stiff clay, | " | 35.9 | " | " | " | " | " |
| Arable soil | " | 32.0 | " | " | " | " | " |
| Garden mould | " | 24.3 | " | " | " | " | " |

It is readily perceived how different must be the effect of dry weather upon crops grown in these various soils.

143. Wheat, and probably other grains, vary in their quality and nutritive powers according to the warmth and relative dryness of the climate. Sir Humphrey Davy found in 1,000 parts of seed wheat in its natural state:

| | Mucilage or Starch | Gluten. | Total. |
|---|---|---|---|
| From Middlesex, England, - - | 765 | 190 | 955 |
| Thick-skinned Sicilian Wheat, - | 725 | 230 | 955 |
| Thin-skinned Sicilian Wheat, - - | 722 | 239 | 961 |
| Wheat from Poland, - - - | 750 | 200 | 950 |
| North American Wheat, - - - | 750 | 225 | 975 |

Thus the gluten of wheat, from the warm and dry climate of Sicily, far exceeded that of English wheat; while in wheat from the United States, the starch and mucilage, (the *heat-giving* constituents,) are nearly equal to those of England, and the gluten, (the *flesh-forming* constituent,) is far superior; or, in other words, the last is much more nutritious than the first.

"The real value of wheat and of the other cereals and bread stuffs depends mainly upon the proportion of gluten and albumen which they, contain, their starch, glucose, and dextrine, or gum, not being considered nutritive."—*(L. C. Beck.)*

According to Prof. Beck, American wheat flour shows the following comparative analysis:

| | | |
|---|---|---|
| Water, - - - - | 11.75 to 14.05 | per cent. |
| Gluten, - - - - - | 9.90 to 14.36 | " |
| Starch, - - - - - - | 66.00 to 70.20 | " |
| Glucose, Dextrine, &c., - - | 4.96 to 11.05 | " |

144. The quantity of water contained in wheat greatly effects its value, as regards, *(a,)* keeping; *(b,)* the quantity of bread it yields.

*(A.)* Large amounts of Western flour are annually damaged by a chemical change which takes place, owing to the water contained in it. This water amounts, on an average from 24 to 26 lbs. in every barrel of common flour. The total annual loss to the United States, from this cause alone, was estimated, in

1847, at from $3,000,000 to $5,000,000. It is not only the sourness which injures flour; but the gluten, and therefore the nutritive quality, is actually diminished. In Poland, and in some parts of the United States, wheat is dried before grinding, in which case, no change takes place. As much as 18 lbs. of water have been expelled from a barrel of Ohio flour.

*(B.)* Wheat grown in dry climates yields more bread than when grown in wet climates. A quarter of English wheat has yielded 13 lbs. more bread than the same quantity of Scotch wheat.

Wheat grown in New Jersey, lower Pennsylvania, the Southern part of Ohio, Maryland, Virginia, the Carolinas and Georgia, contains less water, and more nutritive matter than that from the more northern States Experiments have proved that manures produce an effect similar to climate in raising the nutritive value of wheat, in proportion as they contain nitrogen; and it is not improbable that the manure received from the air in dry climates has an especial effect in this respect.

145. "It is impossible, when we are examining these facts, not to feel how closely the meteorology of a neighborhood influences even the composition of the grain which it produces. The English miller is well aware of these things; he mixes with the wheat produced in the damper districts of that Island the dry wheat produced in lands where the mean temperature is much higher, the rain-fall considerably less, and, in consequence, more free from moisture. Such facts, too, are of practical use to the agriculturist, for he well knows how, by improved systems of cultivation, the obstacles presented by even climate are overcome." *(C. W. Johnson.)*

There is no reason for believing that the moon has any influence on the weather, or the crops, except as imparting light and heat. There are many old superstitions still popular on this subject. It has been closely investigated both in Germany for fifty years, and in England for twenty, and no connection between the moon and the weather could be detected. In every phase, the moon is the same to us, as a material agent, except as regards the power of reflected light; and no one supposes that moonlight produces wet or dry. Why, then, should that point in the moon's course, when it begins to emerge from the sun's rays, have any influence on our weather? Twice in each revolution, when in conjunction with the sun at new, and in opposition to it at the full, an atmospheric spring-tide may be supposed to exist, and to exert some sort of influence. But the existence of any such tide at all is denied, and the absence of fluctuations of the barometric pressure favors the negative of this proposition. Night-feeding birds and animals, however, and oysters, grow fat or thin, according to the state of the moon and tides. In Kentucky, horses are said to be subject to disease of the eye, amounting to blindness, during the period of full moon, which is not the case when the moon does not shine. Dark stables are the remedy; and the philosophy of the disease is easily understood.

In conclusion, every farmer is recommended to procure and use a good Barometer. It will, at all times warn him of the approach of rain and wind storms; and after a little experience, he will find no difficulty in deciding upon the weather for twelve or twenty-four hours in advance. When he goes to bed at night, he can make a shrewd guess whether it will rain or not in the morning; and during harvest he will be forewarned, and can prepare for rain, and thus often save his hay and grain from damage. At sea, a barometer is now of essential necessity. Mr. Redfield, of New York, has lately pointed out the great service it will render to those navigating our large lakes; and to the farmer, it is quite as useful. As agriculturists become more familiar with the barometer, they will cease to put faith in the weather-superstitions of the dark ages; and will find innumerable useful and interesting practical questions decided by it. There are two kinds in common use, the perpendicular or circular Barometer, depending for its action upon Mercury (Quicksilver); and the *Aneroid* Barometer—a French invention—depending on the action of gas in a thin metal case. The first is the most complete and expensive, but the latter is quite sufficient for ordinary purposes, is not easily damaged, and is much more compact. It requires, however, to be occasionally compared with a standard mercury barometer.

# CHAPTER V.

---

## FORMATION OF PLANTS.

146. It has been already stated that plants are formed of organic and inorganic elements, which they receive from the soil and air. (*See* § 81–93.) The living plant possesses the power of receiving into itself these bodies, of changing or digesting them, and of re-arranging them in a different way, so as to produce new substances. In the same manner a new born animal swallows milk, and changes the milk into blood, bones, muscles, brain, &c. The perfect tree is only air, water, and a portion of the soil in which it is growing; as the animal, a few months' old, is only milk in a different shape. If the soil does not contain all the materials requisite to form a plant, it either will not grow at all, or it will grow unhealthily.

147. A perfect plant consists of three parts, *(a,)* a root, which remains in the soil, *(b,)* a trunk or stem which branches into the air, and *(c,)* leaves. Each of these is differently formed, generally contains different proportions of the elements, and is endowed with a peculiar function.

148. The stems of plants differ in their construction, some being much more simple than others. The stem of a tree consists of three parts: *(a,)* the pith, in the centre; *(b,)* the wood surrounding the pith; and *(c,)* the barks which cover the whole. The pith consists of soft celular tissue *(or parenchyma,)* which is at first gorged with the nourishing juices of the plant, but

which in time become exhausted, leaving the older pith dry and light, or mere empty cells, which are of no further use to the plant. The wood consists of woody fibre, among which vessels are more or less copiously mingled, capable of carrying liquids up and down between the root and the leaves. The branches are only a continuation of the stem, and have a similar structure. The bark consists of three portions; *(a,)* the *liber* which lies next the wood; *(b,)* the outer bark, composed of two parts, 1, the green or cellular layer, 2 the corky layer, and *(c,)* the *epidermis* or skin which invests the whole.

149. The *root*, immediately on leaving the trunk or stem, has also a similar structure; but as the root tapers away, the pith gradually disappears, the bark also thins out, the wood softens, till the white tendrils, of which its extremities are composed, consist only of a colorless, spongy mass, full of pores, (or minute holes,) but in which no distinction of parts can be perceived. In this spongy mass, the vessels or tubes which descend through the stem and root, lose themselves, and by them these spongy extremities are connected with the leaves.

150. A leaf is an expansion of the stem. Like the stem therefore, the leaf is made up of two distinct parts, the *cellular* and the *woody*. The leaf is a highly organized structure, containing innumerable rounded globules, cells, and veins, regularly arranged. It is also full of pores through which air can enter.

151. In a growing plant, the sap enters by the extremities of the roots, *(spongioles,)* ascends through the vessels of the wood, and is passed over the inner surface of the leaf by the fibres which the wood contains. Thence, by the vessels in the green of the leaf, it is returned to the bark, and through the vessels of the inner bark it descends to the root.

# CHAPTER VI.

## WHEAT.—*(Triticum.)*

152. There are three kinds of grain on which mankind principally feed, *(a,)* Wheat, *(b,)* Rice, *(c,)* Indian Corn or Maize. Of these, Wheat is chiefly confined to the colder regions of the world; and, in the United States, is second in importance to Maize. It belongs to the botanical family of Grasses. It is not found in a wild state, and the country in which it originated is unknown.

Wheat has lately been produced by the continued cultivation of a plant wild on the shores of the Mediterranean, called *Ægilops.* This is no more extraordinary than the origin of most of our garden vegetables.

Wheat grows in a great variety of climates. In Europe, the polar limits are stated to be as follows:—

| | LATITUDE. | Mean Temperature. (Fahr.) of | | |
|---|---|---|---|---|
| | | YEAR. | WINTER. | SUMMER. |
| Scotland, (Ross-shire,) | 58° | 46° | 35° | 57° |
| Norway, (Drontheim,) | 64 | 40 | 25 | 59 |
| Sweden, | 62 | 40 | 25 | 59 |
| Russia, (St. Petersburgh,) | 60°15′ | 38 | 16 | 61 |

The iso-thermal curve of 57° 2′, which appears to be the minimum temperature requisite for the cultivation of wheat passes, in North America, through the uninhabited regions of the Hudson's Bay country. At Cumberland House, lat. 54° N., long. 102° 20′ West, this grain is successfully raised. The possible cultivation of wheat towards the Equator oscillates between lat. 20° and 25°. It is grown successfully in Chili, and Rio de la Plata. In southern Peru it grows at a height of 8,500 feet; and at the foot of the volcano of Arequipo, at a height of 10,600 feet.

The introduction of this grain into the United States was in 1602, when it was sown on the Elizabeth Islands in Massachusetts. In 1611 it was sown in Virginia; and in 1648 many hundred acres of it were cultivated in that colony; though it was afterwards neglected to give place to Tobacco. It was introduced into the Mississippi Valley in 1718, but owing to the character of the soil and climate, succeeded badly, running to straw instead of grain; yet in 1746 it became an article of export from the Wabash to New Orleans. The principal wheat-producing States are

| | BUSHELS. | | POPULATION. | |
|---|---|---|---|---|
| | 1840. | 1850. | 1840. | 1850. |
| New York, - - - | 12,286,418 | 13,121,498 | 2,428,921 | 3,097,394 |
| New Jersey, - - | 774,203 | 1,601,190 | 373,306 | 489,555 |
| Pennsylvania, - - | 13,213,077 | 15,367,691 | 1,724,033 | 2,311,786 |
| Delaware, - - - | 315,165 | 482,511 | 78,085 | 91,535 |
| Maryland, - - - | 3,345,783 | 4,494,680 | 470,019 | 583,035 |
| Virginia, - - - | 10,109,716 | 11,232,616 | 1,239,797 | 1,421,661 |
| Ohio, - - - - - | 16,571,661 | 14,487,351 | 1,519,467 | 1,980,408 |
| Kentucky, - - - | 4,803,152 | 2,140,822 | 779,828 | 982,405 |
| Michigan, - - - - | 2,157,108 | 4,925,889 | 212,267 | 397,654 |
| Indiana, - - - - | 4,049,375 | 6,214,458 | 685,866 | 988,416 |
| Illinois, - - - - | 3,335,393 | 9,414,575 | 476,183 | 851,470 |
| Missouri, - - - | 1,037,386 | 2,981,652 | 383,702 | 682,043 |
| Wisconsin, - - - | 212,116 | 4,286,131 | 30,945 | 305,191 |
| Iowa, - - - - | 154,693 | 1,530,581 | 43,112 | 192,214 |

During these ten years there was a gain on the whole crop of the United States of 15,645,378 bushels; while the crops of New England decreased from 2,014,000 to 1,090,000 bushels. In 1849, the wheat crop of the United States amounted to 100,503,899 bushels. It is estimated that one bushel of seed is used for every ten bushels produced; and that an average of three bushels is annually used by every individual of the population.

153. Botanists distinguish *eleven* species or sub-species, viz:—

| | | | |
|---|---|---|---|
| 1. | *Triticum* | *œstivum*, - - | Spring Wheat. |
| 2. | " | *hybernum*, - - | Winter Wheat. |
| 3. | " | *compositum*, - - | Egyptian Wheat. |
| 4. | " | *turgidum*, - - - | Turgid Wheat. |
| 5. | " | *Polonicum*, - - | Poland Wheat. |
| 6. | " | *Spelta*, - - - | Spelt Wheat. |
| 7. | " | *monocuccum*, - - | One-grained Wheat. |
| 8. | " | *compactum*, - - | Compact Wheat. |
| 9. | " | *atratum*, - - | Dark-spiked Wheat. |
| 10. | " | *hordeiforme*, - - | Barley-like Wheat. |
| 11. | " | *Zea*, - - - | Far Wheat. |

154. Of these, however, some may only be varieties. In the United States, two only, the Spring and Winter Wheat, are generally grown; though it is believed that Spelt may occasionally be met with as a spring wheat. The latter, which is the hardiest of the family, is cultivated in the south of Europe and Germany; and is known by its almost solid straw, and the chaff adhering to the grain so as to be separated with great difficulty. It may be grown on poor soils, but yields an inferior flour in small quantities. The others have no peculiar merit.

155. *Spring Wheat* was known in England as early as 1666, but has been cultivated only to a small extent there; and not to a much greater one in Scotland. In the United States, it does not appear to be as popular as formerly, except in districts, where Fall Wheat is apt to be killed during winter. As a general thing, the grain is not as large, contains more gluten, makes flour of a different quality and flavor, and brings a lower price in the market. Sir John Sinclair informs us that from 1767 to 1812 it was a practice with the best Scotch farmers to sow Fall Wheat

in Spring, from February to April, though March was generally the favorite month. The real Spring Wheat does not appear to have been generally known in that country till the begining of this century. Though sown in April or May it ripened as early as winter sown wheat. It was not, however so productive as winter wheat sown either in Winter or Spring, and the ears were shorter. There are many nominal varieties in the United States, the best probably being the Italian, the Siberian Bald, or Tea Wheat, and the Black Sea Wheat. Of this last there are again two varieties, the red and the white chaff ; both of which are bearded. It is not known that the practice of sowing Fall Wheat in Spring has ever prevailed in this country, though there is no apparent reason why it should not succeed as well as in Scotland, and be profitable in certain localities. In the Northern States, it is considered important that Spring Wheat should be sown as early as the season will permit. The soil may be lighter than for the Fall variety ; it ought to be in good condition ; and is generally better if it has been plowed, and laid up dry in the Fall. From one and a half to two bushels is the proper quantity of seed per acre ; more generally the latter. The after processes of harvesting and thrashing are similar to Fall Wheat.

156. The varieties of Fall Wheat are very numerous, differing not only in appearance, but also in constituents, in adaptation to soil and climate, in hardiness as regards disease and insects, and in productiveness. There appears to be one fact ascertained regarding them, which is, that they are constantly undergoing change in their relative productiveness. A new variety will be introduced into a given locality, and for a few years will succeed better than any other, after which it begins gradually to deteriorate in the qualities which at first recommended it. The ancient varieties appear to have been much inferior to some in the present day. There are four distinct divisions, *(a,)* White, *(b,)* Red, *(c,)* Bald, *(d,)* Bearded: the Red being *gen-*

*erally* hardier, but coarser than the White ; and the same may be said of the Bearded as compared with the Bald : but in other respects there is no material *practical* difference.

General Harmon, of Wheatland, Monroe County, N. Y., who has devoted a long life to the study of and experiments upon Wheat, in 1844 gave the following as the best varieties known in the United States:

1. *White Flint,* probably introduced from the Black Sea into New Jersey, in 1814. Its peculiarities are, (*a,*) strong straw ; (*b,*) solid grain with thin bran ; (*c,*) the chaff adheres to the grain so that it does not readily shell out ; (*d,*) it is little affected by frost ; (*e,*) it has withstood the Hessian Fly better than any other now cultivated. Its usual yield is from twenty to twenty-five bushels per acre, but it has produced fifty-four bushels to the acre. 2. *Improved White Flint.* It is superior to the last in the size of the berry, the thinness of the bran, and the weight per bushel. 3. *White Provence,* introduced from France, (*a,*) it grows rapidly, yielding much straw ; (*b,*) ripens four or five days earlier than the common varieties ; (*c,*) withstands cold, and is not injured by insects ; but the straw is soft and it is apt to fall down. It is *bald,* berry very large and white ; yielding flour well and of good quality. 3. *Old Red Chaff,* originated in Southern Pennsylvania. It is a bald wheat, with red chaff but a white grain ; and in other respects is similar to the last. On new oak lands it succeeds admirably, but on old lands it is subject to rust, mildew, insects, and winter-killing. 4. *Kentucky White Bearded,* (*Hutchinson, Bearded Flint, Canada Flint,*) a white chaff, bearded wheat. 5. *Indiana Wheat,* originated in Indiana, a white chaff, bald wheat ; peculiarly adapted to strong soils. 6. *Velvet Beard,* or *Crate Wheat* ; introduced from England twenty-five years ago : a red chaff, bearded, large berried wheat. It is very hardy, not apt to be thrown out by frost, nor injured by insects. 7. *Wheatland Red,* originated from the *Virginia May,* by Gen'l Harmon : it is red chaff, bald wheat, and not apt to rust. 8. *Golden Drop,* an English variety. 9. *Mediterranean,* introduced from the South of Europe fifteen years since. It is a light red chaff, bearded, berry red and long, bran thick, and flour inferior ; but it is not injured by insects, and ripens early. 10. *Blue Stem,* cultivated in Virginia about fifty years since, but now generally grown in the Northern States. Formerly it was a red wheat, but it is now changed to a beautiful white. It is very productive.

This list might be much extended, but it could not be of any practical utility.

157. The qualities desirable in Wheat may be thus shortly enumerated: Straw of medium length and size, not apt to fall down, to be attacked by insects or rust, nor killed by frost or wet; able to *stool out* or *tiller*, so that each grain gives several roots and stalks. The heads long, well filled; the chaff adhering to the grain so that it does not easily shell: the kernel white, flinty, solid and large, with thin bran, and yielding a white homogeneous flour in large quantity of first quality; the skin elastic, not breaking up into small particles in grinding, and filling the flour with specks of bran so small as to be incapable of seperation; not apt to sprout if necessarily exposed to wet after harvesting; germinating rapidly, and growing steadily after sowing. Any wheat that united all these qualities would be nearly perfect.

158. Wheat is expected to weigh sixty pounds to the American bushel. The crop varies from eight to sixty bushels to the acre; the average throughout the United States is between twelve and fifteen bushels per acre. Occasionally a bushel of wheat will weigh as high as sixty-six pounds.

The American Bushel contains, - - - 2,150.42 cubic inches.
The English (Imperial) Bushel contains - 2,218.192 "

The English *quarter* of Wheat is eight Imperial Bushels of 70 lbs. each, equal to 9⅓ American Bushels of 60 lbs. each. Wheat is sold in the States by the Bushel of 60 lbs. In England by the quarter of 560 lbs.

159. Ultimate ANALYSIS of Wheat grown at Bechelbronn, 1837.—*(Boussingault.)*

| | GRAIN. | STRAW. | |
|---|---|---|---|
| Carbon, | 46.10 | 48.48 | 48.38 |
| Hydrogen, | 5.80 | 5.41 | 5.21 |
| Oxygen, | 43.40 | 38.79 | 39.09 |
| Nitrogen, | 2.29 | 0.35 | 0.35 |
| Ash, | 2.41 | 6.97 | 6.97 |
| | 100.00 | 100.00 | 100.00 |

160. The composition of Wheat varies greatly according to

many circumstances, such as (*a*,) the soil; (*b*,) the manure used; (*c*,) the variety; (*d*,) the climate; (*e*,) the time it is harvested, &c. The following analysis by Sprengel may be taken as an average. 100,000 parts dry wheat contain 1177 parts of ash or inorganic matter; the same quantity of wheat straw contains 3518 parts of ash. They consist of the following substances:

| | GRAIN. | STRAW. |
|---|---|---|
| Potash, | 225 | 20 |
| Soda, | 240 | 29 |
| Lime, | 96 | 240 |
| Magnesia, | 690 | 32 |
| Alumina, | 26 | 90 |
| Silica, | 400 | 2370 |
| Sulphuric Acid, | 50 | 37 |
| Phosphoric Acid | 40 | 170 |
| Chlorine, | 10 | 30 |
| | 1777 | 3518 |

161. Analysis of the organic, or combustible portion. 100 parts of wheat in its natural state contain. (*Gregory.*)

| | |
|---|---|
| Albumen, | 3.0 |
| Gluten, | 9.9 |
| Starch, | 55.7 |
| Gum, Dextrine, Pectine and Sugar, | 4.6 |
| Fibre and Husk, | 11.9 |
| | 82.31 |

162. Or according to another analysis (*Gregory*,) the parts may be thus divided:

| | |
|---|---|
| Water, | 12.9 |
| Organic Matter, | 85.2 |
| Ash, | 1.90 |

163. The influence of variety of seed and mode of culture are shown by the following results of the examination by Boussingault of several varieties of wheat grown in the *Botanic Garden* at Paris:

| | Husk or Bran in the grain, per cent. | Water in the Flour, per cent. | Flour in the grain, per cent. | Gluten, &c. in the Flour, per cent. |
|---|---|---|---|---|
| Cape Wheat, - - | 19 | 81 | 7.0 | 20.6 |
| Russian Wheat, - | 18 | 82 | 6.4 | 24.8 |
| Dantzig Wheat, - - | 24 | 76 | 7.3 | 25.8 |
| Red Foix Wheat, - | 18.5 | 81.5 | 9.3 | 26.1 |
| Barrel Wheat, - - | 22 | 78 | 8.8 | 27.7 |
| Winter Wheat, - - | 38 | 62 | 14.1 | 33.0 |

164. The time of cutting affects the weight of produce, as well as the relative proportions of flour, bran, and gluten. Thus from three equal patches of the same field of wheat in Yorkshire, cut twenty days before the crop was ripe, ten days before ripeness, and when fully ripe, the produce was in *grain*. *(Johnston.)*

| 20 days before. | 10 days before. | Fully ripe. |
|---|---|---|
| 166 lbs. | 220 lbs. | 209 lbs. |

and the per centage of flour, sharps, and bran, yielded by each, and of water and gluten in the flour was as follows:

| When cut. | in the grain, per cent. | | | in the flour, per cent. | |
|---|---|---|---|---|---|
| | Flour. | Sharps. | Bran. | Water. | Gluten. |
| 20 days before it was ripe, | 74.7 | 7.2 | 17.5 | 15.7 | 9.3 |
| 10 days before, - - | 79.1 | 5.5 | 13.2 | 15.5 | 9.9 |
| Fully ripe, - - | 72.2 | 11.0 | 16.0 | 15.9 | 9.6 |

When cut a fortnight before it is ripe, therefore, the entire produce of the grain is greater, the yield of flour is larger, and of bran considerably less, while the proportion of gluten contained in the flour appears also to be in favor of that which was reaped before the wheat was fully ripe.

165. Bran, as is well known, constitutes, notwithstanding its dry appearance, a very excellent food, and is fattening for stock. Used in bread, it adds much to the nourishing qualities of it, especially in the case of children. The average composition of it is represented as follows: *(Johnston.)*

| | | |
|---|---|---|
| Water, - - - - - | 13.1 | per cent. |
| Albumen, (coagulated,) - - - - - | 19.3 | " |
| Oil, - - - - - - - | 4.7 | " |
| Husk and a little starch, - - - - | 55.6 | " |
| Saline matter, (ash,) - - - - | 7.3 | " |

The following is a more minute analysis of Bran from a Soft French Wheat, grown in 1848: (*Millon.*)

| | | |
|---|---|---|
| Starch, dextrine and sugar, | 53.00 | per cent. |
| Sugar of Liquorice, | 1.00 | " |
| Gluten, | 14.90 | " |
| Fatty matter, | 3.60 | " |
| Woody matter, | 9.70 | " |
| Salts, (inorganic,) | 0.50 | " |
| Water, | 13.90 | " |
| Incrusting matter and aromatic principles, | 3.40 | " |
| | 100.00* | |

A large portion of the inorganic matter in Bran is Phosphate of Magnesia, a very valuable salt both in food and for manure. Common bran, however, owing to the flour adhering to it, is generally much richer than the above analyses.

166. The following is another view of the constituents of wheat, being the extremes of fourteen analyses of as many different varieties, lately made by *Peligot*:

| | | |
|---|---|---|
| Water, | 13.2 to 15.2 | per cent. |
| Fatty matters, | 1.0 to 1.9 | " |
| Nitrogenous matters insoluble in water, | 8.1 to 19.8 | " |
| Soluble Nitrogenous matter, (albumen,) | 1.4 to 2.4 | " |
| Dextrine, | 5.4 to 10.5 | " |
| Starch, | 55.1 to 67.1 | " |
| Cellulose, (woody matter,) | 1.4 to 2.3 | " |
| Saline matter, | 1.4 to 1.9 | " |

*The reader is referred for further information on the nutritious value of Bran to an Essay by Prof. J. F. W. Johnston, published in Edinburgh, Scotland; and to the Report of Prof. L. C. Beck in the *Patent Office Report* for 1849, p. 55. Dr. Daubeny observes "that according to the experiments of Magendie, animals fed upon fine flour died in a few weeks, while they thrived upon the whole meal bread. Brown bread, therefore, should be adopted not merely on a principle of economy, but also as providing more of those ingredients which are perhaps deficient in the finer parts of the flour."

167. The composition of wheat may, therefore, be roughly stated, as:

| | | | | |
|---|---|---|---|---|
| Heat-producing constituents, | Starch, Sugar, Gum, | - | 50 to 60 | per cent |
| Flesh-forming " | Gluten and Albumen, | | 16 to 18 | " |
| Water, - " | | | 10 to 18 | " |
| Useless, " | woody fibre, | - | 22 to 26 | " |
| Inorganic, " | various salts, | - | 2 to 4 | " |

168. In damp climates, such as that of Great Britain, the grain of wheat is generally larger and plumper than in hot, dry climates; but analyses show that the small grain raised in the hotter and drier air greatly surpasses the former in its nutritive value.

169. Prof. Beck, in his numerous examinations, found that the wheat and wheat-flour of the United States are equal to, if not greater in nutritive value than those afforded by samples produced in any other part of the world.

170. The following is an analysis of Michigan *(A,)* and of Richmond Mill *(B,)* Flour: *(Beck.)*

| | A | B |
|---|---|---|
| Water, - - - - - - | 12.25 | 11.70 |
| Gluten and Albumen, - - - - | 10.00 | 13.00 |
| Starch, - - - - - - | 67.70 | 67.50 |
| Glucose, Dextrine, &c., - - - | 8.75 | 6.90 |
| Bran, - - - - - - | 0.75 | 0.50 |
| Ash, - - - - - - | 0.55 | 0.40 |
| | 100.00 | 100,00 |

171. The proportion of gluten in flour not only increases the nutritive value, but also the economical. It is to the peculiar mechanical property of this gluten that wheat flour owes its superior power of detaining the carbonic acid engendered by fermentation, and thus communicating to it the vesicular, spongy structure so characteristic of good bread. Where the proportion of gluten is large, the bread, absorbing more water, &c., weighs heavier. Thus, on an accurate and careful experiment, two pounds of Cincinnati flour, and two pounds of Alabama

flour were each, separately, mixed with a quarter of a pound of yeast, and were made into loaves and baked in the same oven.

The Cincinnati loaf weighed - - - - 3 lbs.
The Alabama loaf weighed - - - - - 3½ lbs.

The gain in the latter is 22 per cent. over the former; or five barrels of Southern flour are equal to six of Northern flour. (*Pat. Off. Rep.*, 1846, p. 150.)

172. When fermentation, or *rising*, in bread is affected by the addition of yeast or leaven to the paste or dough, the character of the mass is materially altered. A larger or smaller proportion of the flour is virtually lost; according to Dr. W. Gregory it amounts to a loss of one sixteenth part of the whole of the flour. To avoid this, it has been recommended to raise bread by means of carbonate of soda and muriatic acid, which produce the same effect as yeast, while the sugar and gluten are saved; these two former materials forming common salt; and giving off carbonic acid gas.

173. The best SOILS for Wheat are those which contain a good proportion of clay and lime. Light and sandy soils do not usually produce good wheat.

Boussingault gives the following classification of soils:

| Soils according to composition. | Usually Designated. | Clay. | Sand. | Lime or Chalk. | Humus. |
|---|---|---|---|---|---|
| Clay with humus, | Rich wheat land, | 74 | 10 | 4 | 11.5 |
| " " " | " " | 81 | 6 | 4 | 8.5 |
| " " " | " " | 79 | 10 | 4 | 6.5 |
| Marly Soil, | " " | 40 | 22 | 36 | 4 |
| Light soil, with humus, | Meadow land, | 14 | 47 | 10 | 27 |
| Sandy Soil, humus, | Rich Barley land, | 20 | 67 | 3 | 10 |
| Argillaceous land, | Good Wheat land, | 58 | 36 | 2 | 4 |
| Marly Soil, | Wheat land, | 56 | 30 | 12 | 2 |
| Argillaceous land, | " " | 60 | 38 | | 2 |
| Stiffer " " | " " | 48 | 50 | | 2 |
| Clay, | " " | 68 | 30 | | 2 |

| Soils according to composition. | Usually designated. | Clay. | Sand. | Lime or Chalk. | Humus. |
|---|---|---|---|---|---|
| Stiff argillaceous land, | Barley land, 1st class, | 38 | 60 | | 2 |
| " " " | " " 2d class, | 33 | 65 | | 2 |
| Sandy Clay, | " " " | 28 | 70 | | 2 |
| " " | Oat land, | 23.5 | 75 | | 1.5 |
| Clayey Sand, | " " | 18.5 | 80 | | 1.5 |
| " " | Rye land, | 14 | 85 | | 1 |
| Sandy Soil, | " " | 9 | 90 | | 1 |
| " " | " " | 4 | 95 | | 0.75 |
| " " | " " | 2 | 97.5 | | 0.5 |

Besides these constituents, a good wheat soil should contain a notable proportion of potash, soda, phosphoric acid, and nitrogen. In Great Britain, the introduction of turnips and clover culture and drainage has greatly extended the range of wheat producing soils; this grain being now cultivated in rotation, with profit, even on sandy soils; so true is it, that science can adapt the earth and climate to almost any crop which it is desirable to cultivate.

174. Wheat, is considered a *scourging* crop, rapidly impoverishing the soil, in consequence of its requiring for its composition large quantities of materials, chiefly inorganic, which are naturally rare in soils. In this respect, it is placed at the head, of *grains*. According to Boussingault, a medium crop of wheat takes from one acre of ground:

| | | | | ACIDS. | | | | | | | |
|---|---|---|---|---|---|---|---|---|---|---|---|
| | Dry Crop. | Ash, Per Cent. | Quantity of Ash Per Acre. | Phosphoric. | Sulphuric. | Chlorine. | Lime. | Magnesia. | Potash and Soda. | Silica. | Oxide of Iron, Alumina, &c. |
| | lbs | lbs | lbs | lbs | lbs | lbs | lbs | lbs | lbs | lbs | lbs |
| Wheat, - - - | 1052 | 2.4 | 25 | 12 | 0.3 | | 0.8 | 4 | 7 | 0.4 | |
| Wheat Straw, - - | 2558 | 7.0 | 179 | 5 | 1.5 | 1 | 15 | 9 | 17 | 121. | 1¾ |
| Total, - - - | 3610 | 9.4 | 204 | 17 | 1.8 | 1 | 15.8 | 13 | 24 | 121.4 | 1¾ |

An average crop takes of organic matter the following, in grain and straw:

| Carbon, | 2259 lbs. | Oxygen, | 1923 lbs. |
|---|---|---|---|
| Hydrogen, | 262 " | Nitrogen, | 52 " |

or, as Ammonia, 63 lbs.

In consequence, it is found, in practice, that it is impossible even upon the best wheat soils, to grow this grain for several years in succession, without injuring the land; and, in most cases, the crop becoming so small as to be unprofitable. What is taken away must be replaced either directly by manures, or by growing other crops which do not require the chief constituents of wheat.

175. There are many rich soils in the Western States, such as Prairies, and River Bottoms, in which wheat runs to straw, and produces very little grain. This is commonly said to be owing to the land being "*too rich;*" but, in reality, it must be in consequence of a deficiency of some constituents of the wheat; which judicious manuring would supply. We are not aware that a comparative analysis of such lands has been yet made, but they will probably be found deficient in the alkalies and lime.

176. The manures for wheat necessarily vary according to the nature of the soil, and the mode in which it has been cropped. It may, however, be stated as general proposition, that our wheat lands appear deficient in *ammonia*, and that they cannot fail to be benefitted by nitrogeneous manures, such as guano, flesh, blood, sheep-dung, *well-saved* barn-yard manure, and such like.

There are probably few fields in the country in which the crop may not be greatly increased by judicious manuring; and very many that require manures to continue them at or bring them up to their original fertility.

177. It has been already stated (§159,) that the composition of wheat varies greatly according to the manure employed.

Thus, manures which are rich in nitrogen *(ammonia,)* not only increase the crop, but also produce a grain richer in gluten, and therefore intrinsically more valuable. On ten patches, each one hundred square feet, of the same soil (a sandy loam,) manured with equal weights of different manures in the dry state, Hermbstadt sowed equal quantities ($\frac{1}{2}$ lb.) of the same wheat,—collected, weighed, and analyzed the produce. His results are represented in the following table:

| | Ox Blood. | Night Soil. | Sheep's dung | Goat's dung. | Human Urine. | Horse dung. | Pigeon dung | Cow dung. | Vegetable Manure. | Unmanured |
|---|---|---|---|---|---|---|---|---|---|---|
| RETURN | 14 fld | 14 fld | 12 fld | 12 fld | 12 fld | 10 fld | 9 fold | 7 fold | 5 fold | 3 fold |
| Water, - - - | 4.3 | 4.2 | 4.2 | 4.3 | 4.2 | 4.3 | 4.3 | 4.2 | 4.2 | 4.2 |
| Gluten, - - - | 34.2 | 33.9 | 32.9 | 32.9 | 35.1 | 13.7 | 12.2 | 12.0 | 9.6 | 9.2 |
| Albumen, - - | 1.0 | 1.3 | 1.3 | 1.3 | 1.4 | 1.1 | 0.9 | 1.0 | 0.8 | 0.7 |
| Starch, - - - - | 41.3 | 41.4 | 42.8 | 42.4 | 39.9 | 61.6 | 63.2 | 62.3 | 65.9 | 66.6 |
| Sugar, - - - | 1.9 | 1.6 | 1.5 | 1.5 | 1.4 | 1.6 | 1.9 | 1.9 | 1.9 | 1.9 |
| Gum, - - - - | 1.8 | 1.6 | 1.5 | 1.5 | 1.6 | 1.6 | 1:9 | 1.9 | 1.6 | 1.8 |
| Fatty oil, - - | 0.9 | 1.1 | 1.0 | 0.9 | 1.0 | 1.0 | 0.9 | 1.0 | 1.0 | 1.0 |
| Sol. phosphates, &c | 0.5 | 0.6 | 0.7 | 0.7 | 0.9 | 0.6 | 0.5 | 0.5 | 0.5 | 0.3 |
| Husk and Bran, | 13.9 | 14.0 | 13.8 | 14.2 | 14.2 | 14.0 | 14.0 | 14.9 | 14.0 | 14.0 |
| | 99.8 | 99.7 | 99.7 | 99.7 | 99.7 | 99.6 | 99.8 | 99.7 | 99.8 | 99.7 |

It must not, however, be forgotten, that these are *garden* experiments; and while the theory is probably quite true, in *field* culture the farmer may be unable to produce exactly the same results. Such experiments must be considered rather as illustrating a general principle, than as positively useful in practice, except to a limited extent.

178. The only mode in which a farmer can *judiciously* use manure, is by having an analysis of his land, showing what constituents are soluble, what may easily be rendered so, and what is wanting.

179. In many parts of the United States, wheat soils are manured by the complex action of clover, plaster (*sulphate of lime*) and sheep dung. The philosophy of this is as follows: The surface soil is naturally, or

has become by cultivation deficient in soluble lime and sulphuric acid, two constituents consumed in large quantities by clover; and which must be supplied before clover can grow. The clover is therefore sown with powdered plaster which contains these two elements, and it grows luxuriantly. But while the surface soil has been impoverished, the subsoil remains full of salts; and the clover sends down its deep tap roots into the subsoil, collects such inorganic matter as its finds there and brings it to the surface. The sheep eat the green part, and scatter the constituents of the clover over the ground, *together with* the ammonia formed in the urine. The clover is then plowed up, and all that it has received from the subsoil and the air, is again rendered more or less soluble by decay, and supplied to the surface soil where the wheat roots find it. This can scarcely be called *real* manuring. With the exception of a little lime and sulphuric acid, nothing is supplied to the field but what it or the air contained before. The clover has acted as a *collector*. It has brought together on the surface what was before scattered in the subsoil, but it affords *nothing new*. The effect, in time, of such practice must be, that not only the surface but the subsoil also becomes impoverished; and each crop of wheat carries off the constituents of a larger area, than it could possibly do without clover. Unless, manures from the barn-yard or other sources are also supplied, the soil must, finally, be very seriously injured.

180. There are various modes of preparing the land for Wheat; *(a,)* summer following, with three distinct plowings, *(b,)* plowing once; *(c,)* plowing once and rendering the surface mellow with a cultivator; all of which have their advocates, and all are probably good for peculiar soils, and under peculiar circumstances. (See PLOWING.)

181. There are also various modes of covering the grain, *(a,)* by a harrow or drag; *(b,)* by plowing it in with a shallow furrow with a plow or cultivator; *(c,)* by ribbing; *(d,)* with a Drill Machine. (See IMPLEMENTS.)

182. Wheat is sown *(a,)* either broadcast by hand or by a machine; *(b,)* by a drill; or in England *(c,)* by a dibble.

183. It is harvested *(a,)* by hand with a sickle or reaping-hook; *(b,)* with a cradle; *(c,)* by a machine worked by horses.

In all cases, it is usually bound with a band made of its own straw into *sheaves*, and set up in *shocks* to dry.

184. It is either *(a,) stacked* out of doors, or *(b,)* put into a barn; *(c,)* or thrashed in the field.

185. It is thrashed *(a,)* by a flail; *(b,)* by horses or cattle treading on it; *(c,)* by a machine moved by horse-power; *(d,)* or, among the French, by a machine called *Le Diable.*

186. The chaff is separated from the grain by *(a,)* a Fanning Mill, or *(b,)* by the wind.

186. It is then ready for *(a,)* storing in the granary, or *(b,)* sending to market, which is usually done in bags holding two measured bushels.

188. It has been already stated (§163) that the comparative ripeness affects the weight and quality of the grain. The best practical rule is to cut when a grain of wheat pressed between the finger and thumb is easily crushed, and yields a considerable quantity of juice; and when the straw is still more or less green, especially near the root. Some experience, however, is requisite in determining the exact time.

189. For *seed*, on the contrary, wheat should be allowed to stand until it is quite ripe; and then selected with care. The best wheat is raised from seed carefully selected from large heads. In former days, when wheat was winnowed by the wind, the largest and heaviest grains were preserved for seed. Great improvement, both in the variety and crop, may undoubtedly be affected by exercising care in this particular. Experiments seem to prove that wheat thrashed by a machine frequently has the germinating power destroyed; and though it may throw out leaves is deficient in roots, and therefore perishes.

The *Boston Cultivator*, 1845, gives an instance of a farmer in Vermont, who saved his seed wheat, who used, before thrashing, to select the best sheaves, and striking them over the side of an empty barrel as it lay on the floor, three or four times, he obtained a very superior seed wheat. Thus the largest and ripest kernels were seperated and collected. While the process was kept secret, so high a reputation had this wheat, that the neighbors willingly paid double the usual price for it.

190. The quantity of seed sown to the acre varies in the United States from one and a half to two bushels, *broadcast;* and about one bushel if drilled. In Great Britain, where much more seed of all the cereals is sown than with us, three to four bushels is the usual quantity, when broadcast.

191. The waste of seed in the soil is very great, especially when broadcast; chiefly in consequence of the irregular depth at which the grain is planted. The following calculation has been made, (*Stephens.*) "Wheat at 63 lbs. to the bushel, gives 87 of its seeds to the drachm; or 701,568 to the bushel (in apothecary's weight,) or 865,170, (in avoirdupois weight.) Now three bushels of seed are sown on the acre, or 2,595,510 grains of wheat. Suppose that each grain produces one stem; and every stem bears an ear containing the common number of 32 grains, the produce of the acre should be 96 bushels; but the heaviest crop in Scotland rarely exceeds 64 bushels to the acre, or 33 per cent. of the seed is lost in the best crops, and 58 per cent. in an ordinary one of 40 bushels." It is very important that such experiments as these should be made in the United States, so as to ascertain the exact quantity of seed to be sown in each soil and climate.

192. The depth at which seeds are sown, is also very important. In order to germinate, a seed must have acccess to moisture, air, and warmth, but be excluded from light. If covered too deep, it will not sprout; if too shallow it is apt to perish for want of moisture and from other causes. Seeds of different plants germinate at various depths. It is laid down as a rule that wheat sown before winter should be as deeply covered with earth as to be beyond the reach of injurious frost, say four or five inches; but when sown in spring it should be lightly covered, little exceeding one inch. In no case should wheat be deeper than six or seven inches. In light dry soils it should be

deeper than in wet adhesive clays; and where clods are numerous more seed is requisite than where the earth is in fine tilth. The following table is given on the authority of M. Moreau, of Paris. He formed thirteen beds in which he planted one hundred and fifty kernels of wheat at various depths:

| At Depth of | Came up. | No. of Heads. | No. of Grains. |
|---|---|---|---|
| 7 inches, | 5 | 53 | 682 |
| 6¼ " | 14 | 140 | 2,520 |
| 5¾ " | 20 | 174 | 3,818 |
| 4½ " | 40 | 400 | 8,000 |
| 4¼ " | 73 | 700 | 16,500 |
| 3¾ " | 93 | 992 | 18,534 |
| 2¾ " | 123 | 1417 | 35,434 |
| 2⅓ " | 130 | 1560 | 34,349 |
| 2 " | 140 | 1590 | 36,480 |
| 1¾ " | 142 | 1660 | 35,826 |
| 1 " | 137 | 1561 | 35,072 |
| 1½ " | 64 | 529 | 10,587 |
| On surface, | 20 | 107 | 1,600 |

From these experiments it would appear that the grain should not be sown at much greater depth than two inches, nor nearer the surface than one inch. The soil is not stated.

193. Wheat a year old is considered to be better for sowing in the Fall than new wheat. New wheat germinates quicker, but is more easily affected by bad weather and insects, and generally the stalks are neither as numerous nor as strong.

194. Wheat is frequently *steeped* or pickled *(a,)* to act as a manure; *(b,)* to destroy the sporules or seeds of smut. Various substances are used, as *(c,)* salt and water; *(d,)* green vitriol, *(sulphate of iron,)* *(e,)* stale urine; *(f,)* arsenic, &c. Arsenic, however, has been proved to be decidedly dangerous to the sower, and the use of it is forbidden by the French government. Various modes of steeping, according to convenience, are used; and the seed is dried with wood ashes, plaster, slacked lime, powdered clay, &c.

195. In *judging* of seed wheat, the dimpled end of the grain should be distinctly marked, and the point from which the little roots proceed must be somewhat prominent; the end from which the blade springs should also be slightly covered with hairiness or wooliness. The little protuberances at either of those ends must not have been rubbed off, as the grain is thereby deprived of vitality. Kiln-drying spoils grain for sowing. It may be known by unusual hardness, and a smoky odor. Wheat that has heated in the stack will taste bitter; if slightly sprouted, sweet; and if long kept in the granary it will smell musty, and look dull and dusty. If eaten by the weevil it may be detected by pressing the kernel with the fingers. If *rusted* it will be shrunk; if *smutty*, it will have a black appearance and a peculiar smell.

196. The weeds that principally injure wheat in the United States are *(a,)* Cockle, *(Lychnis Githago;)* *(b,)* Chess or Cheat, *(Bromus secalinus;)* *(c,)* Pigeon-weed, or Red-root, Steencrout, Stony-seed, Wheat-thief, *(Lithospermum arvense;)* *(d,)* (chiefly in spring wheat,) Field-mustard or Charlock, *(Sinapis arvensis;)* *(e,)* Vetch, or Black-pea, Tare, *(Vicia sativa?* and *Americana?)* *(f,)* Wild-radish, *also called* Charlock. *(Raphanus Raphanistrum.)* These are all annuals; for perennial weeds are confined to no particular crop.

*Cockle* (*a.*) is a strong growing upright plant, one to two and a half feet high, with a purple flower, and seed pod full of black seeds. It injures the wheat chiefly in grinding for flour, discoloring it, and giving an unpleasant bitter flavor.

*Chess*, (*b,*) a species of grass. There are two other species of the same genus indigenous to the United States, and two more introduced from England. The leaves and stalk, in their earlier stages, greatly resemble wheat, but the flowers, stamens, and seeds, are very different. It grows chiefly in soil plowed in the Fall, but is also met with in meadows, and among spring crops, where no wheat was ever sown. It is probably a native of most parts of the Northern States, and like other weeds, the germs are contained in the soil ready to vegitate as soon as the conditions of growth are favorable. The seeds are very numerous.

Seven thousand kernels have been counted growing from one root; enough to seed *three hundred* acres thickly the third year, were it cultivated. They are also very difficult to destroy, passing through animals and fowls without losing the germinative power. It was formerly as plentiful in England as it is with us, but by care in sowing clean seed, it is now all but exterminated. There is a notion among some farmers that "wheat turns into chess;" but this is wholly opposed to all facts and analogies; and the belief may be classed among the superstitions of the dark ages that still linger in our profession. (See *Patent Office Reports*, 1849, p. 455; 1851, p. 650.) By sowing wheat seed perfectly clean of chess, it soon disappears. It is chiefly troublesome by drawing the nourishment from the growing wheat, and overpowering it; and injuring the flour. When crushed, it is good food for horses and poultry, and if boiled, for hogs.

*Pigeon-weed*, (*c*,) has been introduced from Europe. It is an annual plant "slender, hoary with minute oppressed hairs, somewhat branched; leaves lanceolate, acutish, nearly veinless; racemes few-flowered, the lower flowers remote; corolla (yellowish white) not longer than the calyx." (*Gray.*)

This weed appears to be confined to certain soils, such as in New York are known by the name of Marcellus Shales, and in Michigan, as Oak Openings, and Burr Oak Plains. In this latter State, it is found in the Interior, while it yet seems to be unknown in the heavy clays, forming a belt around the Peninsula. Where it becomes plentiful it is exceedingly injurious to the wheat crop. It is not above thirty years since it was introduced into New York, and it has now spread wherever it finds a congenial soil. The peculiarities of the character and habit of this weed consist (*a*,) in the hard shell with which its seed or nut is covered; (*b*,) in the time at which it comes up and ripens its seed; (*c*,) in the superficial way in which its roots spread. The seed is so hard that it passes uninjured through cattle and birds, and lies for years in the ground without perishing. It grows very little in spring, but shoots up and ripens in the Fall, and its roots spread through the surface soil only, and exhaust the food by which the young wheat should be nourished. It is said to be so prolific as to increase more than two hundred fold annually. When it has once got into the land, two or three successive crops of wheat will give it entire possession of the soil. In Yates County, N. Y., the seeds are crushed with linseed, for the oil they contain, which is about 4 lbs. per bushel; and for the addition which the husk makes to the *oil cake*. The only mode of exterminating it is, when slight, to pick it out of the growing wheat by hand; and when abundant, to plow once or twice in the fall, after the seed has sprouted; and to cultivate spring hoed crops, avoiding wheat for some years. The seed must on no account be mixed with manure or given to stock, as it will thus be spread everywhere. As ordinary care and good farming will prevent its spreading further west, and as, in lands that suit, it is the most injurious wheat-weed in the United States, it is important that the whole community should attend to it. If allowed to grow on one farm, it will inevitably spread to others, being carried by birds, and other means.

Field Mustard (*d*,) and Wild Radish, (*f*,) are known by their bright yellow flowers. They are injurious by taking the place of the grain, and overpowering it. The seeds are small, numerous, and very persistent. The best mode of eradicating these plants, is to pull them by hand when in blossom.

Vetch, (*e*,) is a small creeping pea-like plant, adhering to the grain by its tendrils. In some soils it is very plentiful; and is chiefly injurious in grinding, discoloring the flour and giving it a bad flavor. The seeds are small, round, and black. It may be exterminated by one or two hoed spring crops, and laying the land to pasture for a year or two. A good fanning-mill would probably clean the grain completely, but the writer has seen wheat brought to mill in Western Canada, containing one third of the seeds of the Vetch. It appears to be confined to rich clay and loamy lands.

197. The parasitic fungi which are injurious to wheat are (*a*,) Smut or Bunt; (*b*,) Rust; (*c*,) Mildew.

A *Fungus* is a cellular flowerless plant, deriving its nutriment by means of spawn. It lives in air, and is propogated by *spores*, which are naked, or by *sporidia*, so called when enclosed in little vesicles. *Fungi* may be said to consist of a mass of little cells, or little threads, or of both combined in various ways. They have no seed or fruit except their *sporules*, *spores* or *sporidia*, of which the methods of attachment are singularly curious and beautiful. They derive their nourishment from the substance on which they grow, and not from the media in which they exist, Well known *Fungi* are Mushrooms, Toadstools, Puffballs, mould on cheese, &c., most of which are poisonous. Many of them grow on living plants, as Smut and Rust; but the small ones, to a great extent, on animal substances in a state of partial decay; or where they can find nitrogenous compounds, as in bread, &c. The spores are often of exceeding minuteness, and epidemic diseases have been attributed to their influence. Certain species are found in the living human body; and in the inferior animals. These are called *Entophyta*. A striking instance is the disease which kills so many silkworms, known as the *Muscardine*, where the Fungus is planted in the skin and grows externally. Dr. Leidy, (*Smithsonian Contrib. to Knowl.*) has described ten species of this order found in men.

198. There are two species of Smut, *(a,)*; the one *(b,) Uredo caries*, or *fœtidum*, a brownish black dust, greasy, and fetid, taking the place of the kernel of wheat. It does not appear externally, being confined within the husk. The other *(c,) Uredo segetum*, (Black ears, Brand, Dust Brand, Burnt Corn, &c.,) is met with in Barley and Oats as well as Wheat. It resembles a black dust, growing within the glumes of the plant. It destroys the seed, and its envelopes. The spores are so small that a square inch could contain 7,840,000 of them, and within these again are inumerable sporoles. Smut *(a,)* is undoubtedly propagated from the wheat seed to the living plant. M. Bauer *(Trans. of Linnean Soc'y., London, vol. xviii., p. 468,)* has shown that "Smut-balls" on grain can certainly be produced by inoculating the seed with the sporoles of the fungus. These bodies are carried into the interior of the plant by the sap, after being absorbed by the roots. Johnston says it can be seen where they have come up through the stalk. When examined, the tubes of the stalk were filled with black matter that had come through the vessels, affecting first the straw, then getting into the ear, whence it spreads itself all over. Thousands of the sporules may be attached to a single grain of wheat, and yet be invisible to the naked eye. This disease is most common on damp undrained soils, with impervious subsoils ; and may be eradicated by *(a,)* thorough draining of the land; *(b,)* and by washing the grain previous to sowing in some saline mixture (§193) and drying with slacked lime.

199. Of Rust *(b,)* there are also two species. One *(c,)* is found scattered over the inner surface of the outer chaff scales, the skin of which is raised into blisters. This is called by

Botanists *Uredo rubigo;* it is of an orange yellow color; and when severe, causes the grain to shrink, and prevents maturation. The other *(d,) Uredo linearis* is confined to the straw and leaf, and is the color of the rust of iron. It causes the epidermis to split, and it is supposed to permit the emission of the juices. The grain is affected by this in the same manner as by the former.

Wet soils are most subject to these fungi, but they especially appear during sultry, wet weather towards the flowering of the plant.

200. Mildew (i. e. *mel-dew*, from an old notion that it was produced by *honey-dew* falling from the air,) or Blight, *(c,)* is produced by *Puccinia graminis.* It forms blackish brown parallel, lives upon the straw, and seems to affect the entire plant, so that it deprives the sap of the power to form seed in a healthy state, and hence the grain is very much shrivelled, or no grain at all is formed. The spores of this fungus enter the straw by its breathing pores, which are closed in dry weather, but opened in a wet or damp atmosphere. This disease, like the last, attacks the plant in warm, moist weather, and often with remarkable suddeness and severity. Wet soils, and over-manured land are chiefly subject to it; and earth containing a large proportion of the salts of iron appears to add to the tendency. Draining is probably the only cure.

201. Wheat is also subject to attacks from various insects. The injury caused by these is sometimes so great and permanent as to prevent the culture of wheat at all, as has been the case in some parts of New England and New York. We shall shortly enumerate those most common in the United States, referring the student for scientific descriptions to *Dr. T. W. Harris' Treatise on some of the Insects of New England which are injurious to vegetation, 2d. Ed., Boston,* 1852, and for further information to the *Patent Office Reports* from 1844,

and to the older volumes of the Agricultural Periodicals of the United States.

202. *(A,)* Insects injurious to the seed, *when sown*, and to the young plant:

In Indiana, wheat has been injured both before and after germinating by a "red ant." It bores a small hole into the kernel, and consumes the germ; or cuts off the sprout, and eats into the grain. Drilled wheat appears to escape these ravages. (*Annual Report of Indiana State Board of Agriculture*, 1852. 2. The *Prairie Farmer*, in 1844, describes a small fly, a little more than an eighth of an inch in size, with four wings, and the odor of a bed-bug, which did much injury in Illinois. It first destroyed the heads of wheat previous to harvest; it then took to the corn-fields, killing that which was not too far ripened; and then attacked the young wheat, cutting it off just beneath the surface of the earth, "taking all clean as they go. They are of all stages of growth, and have been from the first, and the ground is perforated with the holes made by them." 3. In common with many other grains and vegetables, young wheat is sometimes injured by the "Cut-worms," (*Agrotididæ*,) "Wire-worms," (*Iuli*,) and "Grub-worms," (*Melolonthadæ*,) but these will be referred to more particularly hereafter.

*(B,)* Insects which injure the straw of wheat while growing:

1. The Chinch-bug (*Lygæus leucopterus*. SAY.) has done much severe injury in the South and West, including Wisconsin and Illinois. In its perfect state it is winged, and measures three-twentieths of an inch in length. The eggs are laid in the ground; and the young make their appearance on wheat about the middle of June, and still later attack all kinds of grain, corn, and herds-grass, during the whole summer. 2. The Joint-worm (Eurytoma——?) has proved eminently destructive in Virginia. It varies from one-tenth to nearly three-twentieths of an inch in length, is of a pale yellowish white color, with an internal dusky streak, and is destitute of hairs. It buries itself in the straw, generally at a joint, in or near the second or third joint from the ground. The substance of the straw for a distance exceeding half an inch is much swollen, and changed to a wood-like texture, while the surface exhibits long, pale spots, slightly elevated like a blister. The worm finally changes to a winged insect. Burning the stubble as soon as the grain is harvested is recommended as a cure. 3. The Hessian Fly (*Cecidomyia destructor*,) is supposed to have been introduced from

Germany into Long Island, R. I., by the Hessian troops, under Sir W. Howe, in 1776. Thence it gradually spread over the Southern parts of New York and Connecticut, at the rate of fifteen or twenty miles a year. It was found west of the Alleghany Mountains, in 1797. In many places, the culture of wheat was abandoned in consequence of its ravages. The body of the perfect insect measures about one-tenth of an inch in length, and the wings expand a quarter of an inch or more. Two broods are brought to maturity in the course of a year, and the flies appear in the spring and fall. In the latitude of New England, the female begins to lay its eggs on the blade of the young wheat at the end of September, or beginning of October. In four to fifteen days the egg hatches; the maggot, of a pale red color, crawls down the leaf, and works its way between it and the main stalk, passing down till it comes to a joint, just above which it remains, a little below the surface of the ground, with the head towards the root of the plant. Here it rests till its transformations are completed. It niether eats the stalk, nor penetrates within it, but lies lengthwise upon its surface, nourished wholly by the sap. As it increases in size, it becomes imbedded in the side of the stem, by pressure. If two or three are fixed in this manner they frequently cause the plant to fall down and die. In five or six weeks they grow to full size—three-twentieths of an inch in length. About the first of December, they harden and change to a bright chestnut color; in which form they are commonly likened to a flax seed. In this state, they gradually change to a fly, and appear again as such at the end of April or beginning of May. Very soon after, they are ready to lay their eggs on the leaves of the wheat sown in the previous fall, or the same spring. In three weeks they entirely disappear from the field. Undergoing the same changes, the maggets from these eggs take the flax-seed form in June and July. In this state they are found at the time of harvest, and when the grain is gathered they remain in the stubble in the fields. Some, however, are carried to the barn The principal migrations of the flies take place in the middle of August and September. 4. In 1843, Miss Morris discovered in Pennsylvania, another species of the Hessian Fly. (*Cecidomyia culmicola.*) It differs in its habits from the former, by depositing its eggs early in June *in the grain.* The egg remains unhatched till the grain is sown and germinates, and the maggot soon eats its way into and burries itself in the straw. Here it remains till it is ready to assume the flax-seed form, and then, emerging, fixes itself to the outside of the stalk. It has since disappeared from the locality, but may probably be met with elsewhere, being mistaken for the first species.

5. The larva or maggots of *Oscinis lineata, Chlorops pumilionis, and Chlorops glabra,* and other flies allied to them, live within the lower part of the stems of wheat, rye, and barley, thereby impoverishing the plants, and causing them to become stinted in their growth. They are rather larger insects than the *Frit-Fly.* It is highly probable that some of these species, or the *Oscinians* with similar habits may be found in the stems of wheat, and other grains, and perhaps also in the ears. "A careful examination of all the insects that inhabit our fields of grain is very much wanted." (*Harris.*)

6. The *Patent Office Report,* 1845, p. 144, mentions a worm which appeared among wheat in Buck's Co., Penn. "It is a green worm about an inch long; its head is brownish green, with two brown spots on it. It ascends the stalk of wheat, soon after it has headed, cuts off the head, and feeds upon the top of the standing part."

(*C,*) Insects which injure the grain of wheat in the field:

1. Wheat-fly, Grain-worm, Weevil, (*Cecidomayia Tritici.*) This is a small fly, one-tenth of an inch long, somewhat resembling a musquito in form, and was probably introduced from England. It is said to have been first seen in America in 1828, in North Vermont, and Lower Canada. It has since spread to Upper Canada, New York, New Hampshire, Massachusetts, Connecticut, and probably other States; and has, in some instances, caused the growth of wheat to be relinquished. The female appears from the begiuing of June to the end of August, in the wheat fields, in immense swarms, when they lay their eggs in the opening flowers of the grain. The eggs hatch in about eight days, and a little yellow magget is produced. It never exceeds an eight of an inch in length. From two to twenty have been found within the husk of a single grain. They prey on the wheat in its milky state, and stop when it becomes hard; in consequence, the kernels never fill out. Late in July and early in August, these maggets change their skins and enter the ground, where they remain through the winter; at the depth of an inch. Deep plowing in the fall, and the use of caustic lime as a manu·e are recommended for their destruction, as the best among many receipts.

2. Another small fly, very similar in its effects (*Thrips cerealium,*) has been met with in New Hampshire. 3. Brown Weevil, Grey Worm, Wheat-worm, (Caradrina cubicularis ?) This, which has proved very injurious in Western New York, Northern Pennsylvania, and other localities, has not yet been distinctly recognized as a species, nor is its

full history known. It is a catapillar or span-worm, from three to five-eighths of an inch long, of various shades of brown or yellow in color. It feeds not only on the kernel in the milky state, but also devours the germinating end of the ripened grain, without burying itself within the hull; and it is found in great numbers in the chaff when the grain is thrashed. They continue to eat the grain after harvest. Hot water should be poured on those met with in thrashing, and none should be allowed to escape.

## *(D,)* Insects which injure grain in the granary:

1. The Grain Weevil, (*Calandra* or *Curculio granarius.*) This belongs to the same family of insects as the Curculio which destroys plums. In its perfect state it is a slender beetle of a pitchy red color, about an eighth of an inch long. The female deposites her eggs upon the wheat after it is housed, and the young grubs hatched therefrom immediately burrow into the wheat, each individual occupying alone a single grain, the substance of which it devours so as to leave nothing but the hull, and the loss of weight is the only external evidence of the mischief that has been done. The adults also eat the grain. In Europe, it has proved peculiarly destructive to stored grain. Roasting or kiln-drying the wheat, effectually destroys the grub. 2. The Grain-moth (*Tinea granella.*) 3. The Angoumois moth (*Anacampsis cerealella,*) are small moths, resembling the well known carpet-morth of houses, the grubs of which prey on stored grain. They have spread very generally over the United States. The last species was probably introduced into Virginia from France.

There are probably many other insects than the above injurious to wheat at various stages of its growth; but unfortunately practical farmers pay little attention to entomology, and are apt to confound not only one known species with another, but also those which are described with those which are not. An intelligent farmer would confer a great benefit on the community were he to study carefully the habits of all insects injurious to vegetation in his own locality, and make the results known. Insects injurious to the farmer appear to be increasing in all parts of this country, and it is very essential that their habits should be accurately studied so that remedies may be devised. It is only by our becoming thoroughly acquainted with the character and peculiarities of our enemies, that we can hope to overcome them. Mere guesses, and random experiments, rarely if ever, prove of any benefit. The loss annually sustained by the country in consequence of the depredations of insects is exceeding great, and is calculated by millions of dollars.

203. The manufacture of flour is, in itself, a business independent of the farmer. It employs a large amount of capital, requiring expensive buildings and machinery; and consumes much timber in the making of barrels. It is not necessary to refer to it any further in this place, otherwise than to say that a good farmer will always endeavor to take his wheat to market in the best and cleanest condition. In 1850, 2,202,335 barrels of Flour were exported from the United States.

It is extremely important to the practical farmer to know the cost of producing wheat, so that he may be able to make his calculations, and avoid losses. The Commissioner of Patents has more than once endeavored to acquire a knowledge of the expense of bringing a bushel of wheat to market, in various parts of the United States; and though, owing to difficulties in the way, it has been found impossible to arrive at an accurate estimate, the actual cost of every bushel of wheat, to the farmer may be stated to be from 50 cents to $1⅛ according to the location, the value of the land, and the need of manure, &c. The following, which is a *bona fide* account by a very intelligent, practical farmer, may be considered as the actual cost in the older settled parts of Michigan. The field contained 12 and 2-100 acres of land.

| | |
|---|---|
| Plowing, 7 days, 3 pair oxen, 1 pair horses, 2 men and 1 boy, | $21,00 |
| Harrowing 2 days with team, | 2,00 |
| Cultivating 2 days, | 2,00 |
| 19½ bushels seed at $1,00, | 19,50 |
| Sowing 1 day, | 63 |
| Cultivating 3 days and harrowing 1 day, | 5,00 |
| Furrowing and cleaning furrows, 2 days, | 1,50 |
| Weeding ½ day, | 31 |
| Harvesting, &c., 37 days, | 32,38 |
| Team, | 1,50 |
| Thrashing and cleaning, | 28,82 |
| Manures, | 7,75 |
| Interest on value of land, ($6 per acre,) | 7,56 |
| | $128,95 |

The produce was 545 bushels of wheat or about 45 bushels per acre, making the cost about 23 cents a bushel. But if the crop had averaged 20 bushels only, which, on the average is a large crop, it would have cost nearly 54 cents a bushel. And had the crop been smaller still, say 15 bushels per acre, a fair average for the State, it would have cost over 71 cents a bushel, which is more than wheat was then selling for.

There is one apparent error in this account, and that is in the interest charged upon the land: land of such richness, drained, worked, and manured as it must be to produce such a crop, and with its share of the necessary buildings, was at the time worth from $40 to $50 an acre, ***intrinsically.*** Say the smallest sum, ($40,) and the interest charged, instead of being $7,56, ought to have been $48,00 for twelve months; but it is usual to charge eighteen months interest on land employed in growing wheat, or $72,00. This would still further raise the cost of the grain, on the farm, without allowing anything for profit, or remuneration for skill, or expences of marketing. The straw, however, is generally considered an equivalent for the latter. (*L. Cone. Trans. of State Agricul. Secy. of Mich.*, 1850, *p*, 487.)

# CHAPTER VII.

## RYE.—*(Secale cereale.)*

204. Next to Wheat, Rye is most consumed by mankind in those latitudes which are too cold for Indian Corn. It is believed to be a native of Western or Central Asia.

M. DeCandolle says that a M. Koch, who has traversed Anatolia, Armenia, the Caucasus, and Crimea, affirms that he has found Rye under circumstances where it appears to be really spontaneous and native. On the mountains of Pont, in the country of Hemschin, upon granite, at an elevation of five or six thousand feet, he found our common rye along side the road. It was thin in the ear, and about one to two and a half inches long. No one remembered that it had ever been cultivated in the neighborhood, and it was not even known as a cereal.

205. It is cultivated, to the North of Europe, in Scandinavia, on the western side of the parallel of latitude of 67° N.; and on the eastern side to latitude 65° or 66° N. In Russia, the polar limit of rye is indicated by the parallel of latitude 26° 30′. It is extensively cultivated in Europe, forming the chief part of the bread of Germany, Poland, Russia, Switzerland, and other countries. In Great Britain, and the southern countries of Europe it is little used. In America, it does no appear to be grown in Pembina, on Red River, in the Hudson Bay Territory, latitude 47° N., though wheat, barley, maize, tobacco, potatoes, &c., are cultivated with profit. It was introduced into the North American colonies soon after their settlement by the English,—into Nova Scotia, 1622; into

New England, 1648, and into South Virginia previous to that year.

206. The production of rye in the United States decreased in 1850, 4,457,000 bushels when compared with 1840; but in New York it had been *increased* in 1850 by about 40 per cent. In 1840 the total product of the country was 18,645,567 bushels; in 1850, 14,188,639 bushels.

The chief Rye producing States are—(1850:)

| | BUSHELS. | | BUSHELS. |
|---|---|---|---|
| Pennsylvania, - - | 4,805,160 | Connecticut, - - | 600,893 |
| New York, - - - | 4,148,182 | Ohio, - - - - | 425,718 |
| Massachusetts, - - | 481,021 | Kentucky, - - - | 415,073 |
| Virginia, - - - - | 458,930 | New Jersey, - - | 1,255,578 |
| Michigan, - - - | 105,871. | | |

It is grown, more or less, in all the States except California and New Mexico; but, with two exceptions, (Maryland and North Carolina,) none give over 200,000 bushels. It has been chiefly used for distilling and feeding stock, though bread is made of it in some localities. The export in 1850, was 44,152 bbls. of flour.

207. There is only one cultivated species, but several varieties: *(a,)* Common; *(b,)* Multicole; *(c,)* St. John's Day; *(d,)* Siberian; also, *(e,)* Spring, *(f,)* Winter, and *(g,)* Southern.

Of the Common *(a,)* nothing need be said. The Multicole *(many rooted,)* *(b,)* was introduced into this country by means of the Patent Office about 1844–5. It was found to produce heavy crops, and to stool out very perfectly,—ten to twenty stalks growing from every seed. It also appears to be well adapted for high northern latitudes. The St. John's Day *(c,)* is a native of the Italian Alps, and was introduced into England about ten years ago for soiling purposes. The seed is very small, dark, and hard, but the straw grows with great rapidity, to a great height, affording a remarkable quantity of green fodder. The Siberian *(d,)* is a German variety, noted for the gigantic product of grain and stalk. The grain is large with a thin skin, yielding an excellent flour. The other varieties have arisen from the period of sowing, or climate.

The yield is from ten to thirty, or more bushels per acre, weighing from 48 to 56 lbs. per bushel. In Michigan the *legal* weight of a bushel is 56 lbs.

208. Ultimate ANALYSIS of Rye and straw: *(Boussingault.)*

| | GRAIN. | STRAW. |
|---|---|---|
| Carbon, | 46.35 | 49.88 |
| Hydrogen, | 5.38 | 5.58 |
| Oxygen, | 44.21 | 40.56 |
| Nitrogen, | 1.69 | 0.30 |
| Ash, | 2.37 | 3,68 |
| | 100.00 | 100.00 |

209. Inorganic analysis of the grain of Rye. The grain of Rye leaves 2.425 per cent of ash, which is thus composed:

| | Will and Fresenius. | Bichon. | Mean. |
|---|---|---|---|
| Potash, | 32.76 | 11.43 | 22.08 |
| Soda, | 4.45 | 18.89 | 11.67 |
| Lime, | 2.92 | 7.05 | 4.93 |
| Magnesia, | 10 13 | 10.57 | 10.35 |
| Oxide of iron, | 0.82 | 1.90 | 1.36 |
| Phosphoric acid, | 47 29 | 51.81 | 49.55 |
| Sulphuric acid, | 1.46 | 0.51 | 0.98 |
| Silica, | 0.17 | 0.69 | 0.43 |

210. Organic analysis of Rye, dried at 212 ° F. *(Horsford & Krocker.)*

| | Rye flour from Vienna. | | Rye flour from Hohenheim. | |
|---|---|---|---|---|
| | No. 1. | No. 2. | Schilf. | Standen. |
| Gluten and albumen, | 11.92 | 18.69 | 17.73 | 15.76 |
| Starch, | 60.91 | 54.48 | 45.09 | 47.42 |
| Woody fibre, gum, sugar, | 24.74 | 24.49 | 35.77 | 35.25 |
| Ash. | 1.33 | 1.07 | 2.43 | 2.37 |
| | 98.90 | 98.73 | 101.02 | 100.80 |
| Moisture in fresh substance, | 13.78 | 14.68 | 13.94 | 13.82 |

211. It will be observed from the above, that Rye varies

much in its composition according to the soil in which it is grown. Hermbstadt experimenting with the grain as he did with wheat (§177,) found in 100 parts:

| Manured with - - | Ox blood. | Sheep's dung | Goat's dung. | Human urine. | Pigeons' dung. | Human excrement. | Horse dung. | Cows' dung | Vegetable mould. | Unmanured. |
|---|---|---|---|---|---|---|---|---|---|---|
| Gluten and albumen, - | 15.6 | 15.6 | 15.6 | 15.5 | 15.3 | 15.1 | 14.7 | 12.8 | 11.4 | 11.2 |
| Starch, gum, sugar, fat, - | 63.0 | 63.1 | 62.7 | 59.2 | 61.5 | 63.1 | 60.8 | 64.8 | 36.0 | 67.3 |
| Increase in grain, - - | 14 fold. | 13 f | 12½f | 13 f | 9 f | 13½ f | 11 f | 9 f | 3 f | 4 f |

212. Inorganic analysis of Rye straw. 100,000 parts of the straw, contain 2793 parts of inorganic matter. (*Sprengel.*)

| | | | |
|---|---|---|---|
| Potash, - - - | 32 | Oxide of manganese, - | — |
| Soda, - - - - | 11 | Silica, - - - | 2297 |
| Lime, - - - | 178 | Sulphuric acid, - - | 170 |
| Magnesia, - - - | 12 | Phosphoric acid, - - | 51 |
| Alumina, Oxide of iron, } - - | 25 | Chlorine, - - | 17 |
| | | | 2793 |

213. The flour of rye is not white like that of wheat, but has a pretty strong, grayish brown tint, and does not bind so firmly with water. It yields a short, much less tough dough, out of which it is impossible to seperate the gluten from the starch by washing with water. The cause of this is probably to be sought in some peculiarity of the gluten of rye. It contains very little fibrin, and on the contrary a nitrogenous substance, which Heldt has ascertained to be *vegetable gelatin.* The starch is of the same nature as that contained in other seeds.

214. Dombaste found that 100 parts of rye flour yielded, when baked, 145 lbs. of bread, or nearly the same quantity as is yielded by northern wheat. Johnston found rye bread, when leavened, to lose 44, when yeasted, 46 per cent. of water. 100 lbs. of flour containing naturally 16 per cent. of water, must then have yielded from 150 to 160 lbs. of bread.

215. The SOILS best adapted for rye are of a light, sandy

character. As wheat is the cereal of the clay, so rye is the cereal of the sandy soils. It will, however, grow well on all soils if rendered sufficiently friable, and not damp.

216. As will be observed by the analysis, (§208,) the principal inorganic constituents are Potash, Soda, Magnesia, and Phosphoric acid, but the per centage of ash is very small, rarely, if ever, above 2½ per cent. of the dry grain. Wood ashes, either unleached or leached are the most available manures.

217. Rye is sown as a winter and spring crop,—generally as the former. One plowing is given and the seed dragged in. If more care is taken in the preparation of the soil the crop will be larger. It is a custom in some localities to sow rye among standing corn, hoeing it in, and leaving the ground as level as possible. After the corn is removed, the rye is rolled. Harrowing and rolling in the spring, are recommended.

218. The time of sowing in the fall is, in the Northern States, from 20th August to 20th September. From 1¼ to two bushels of seed are sown, the richest lands demanding most. In spring it should be sown as early as the climate will permit.

219. In other respects, the culture, harvesting, &c., resemble those of wheat.

220. If cut before fully ripe, the grain makes better flour, and in larger quantity; but if intended for seed it should be fully ripened.

221. In some countries, rye and wheat are sown together. In England this mixture is called *Mesling*, *Mescelin*, or *Maslin*, (from an old French word *mester*, to mingle.)

222. Rye is frequently sown for fodder, being either pastured during the winter and spring, or cut green for soiling stock in stables. It affords a large amount of valuable food, and the crop of grain is improved by pasturing to a certain point.

223. It is also employed to plow in as a green manure. In the lighter class of wheat soils, it is recommended, after harvesting the wheat, to plow, and sow rye as early as possible; pasture with sheep and young stock through the winter, and then plow in for a spring crop. This system, alternated with two or more years of grass or clover, will rapidly restore unpoverished soils. For this purpose the Multicole, and *probably* St. John's Day variety are the best, but we are not aware that the latter has yet been tried in the United States.

224. There are no weeds peculiar to rye; but those which are troublesome to wheat will generally be found among this grain, according to the season in which it is sown.

225. The only parasitic fungus affecting rye is ERGOT *(Sclerotium clavis.)*

Ergot is a kind of spur which issues from the grain of rye. It is not a fungus itself, but a morbid growth caused by the existence of minute fungi in the grain. It is not confined to rye alone, but has been observed occasionally in wheat and barley, and some of the grasses. It is a poison when eaten in bread, producing a spontaneous gangrene, called *ergotism*. It is also a powerful medicine, for which purpose it was first used in the United States, in 1807. The composition of the ash of ergot is as follows: (*Engelmann.*)

| | | | |
|---|---|---|---|
| Potash, | 45.38 | Sulphuric acid, | 0.02 |
| Soda, | 16.79 | Chlorine, | 2.36 |
| Lime, | 1.68 | Silica, | 15.60 |
| Magnesia, | 5.34 | | |
| Oxide of iron, | 2.34 | | 104.95 |
| Phosphoric acid, | 15.44 | | |
| Per centage of Ash, | | | 0.36 |

It is chiefly found where rye grows in damp adhesive soils. Animals should not be allowed to eat it; as some will do when it is mixed with grain.

226. There are no insects peculiar to this cereal.

227. The straw, owing to its length and stiffness, is useful for many economical purposes, but not as good for feeding stock as some other sorts, unless cut and bruised.

227* Petri gives an experiment made to ascertain the proper depth for planting rye, as follows:

| Depth of seed, | Appeared above ground in | No. of plants that came up. |
|---|---|---|
| ½ inch. | 11 days. | ⅞ths. |
| 1 " | 12 " | all. |
| 2 inches. | 18 " | ⅞ths. |
| 3 " | 20 " | ¾ths. |
| 4 " | 21 " | ½ |
| 5 " | 22 " | ⅜ths. |
| 6 " | 23 " | ⅛th. |

The root stalk forms itself always next below the surface of the ground; and if we place the grain deep, it must first put out its sprouts to the surface, and form its side branches in a nearer connection with the air. We never find that the sucker-roots are arranged from below to above, but the contrary.

# CHAPTER VIII.

---

## BARLEY.—(*Hordeum.*)

228. The native country is unknown.

229. Barley is cultivated further north than any other of the grains. In Europe, its northern limits are as follows:

| | |
|---|---|
| Orkney and Shetland Islands, - | Lat. 61° N. |
| Faroe Islands, - - - - | " 61° to 61° 15′ N. |
| Western Lapland, - - - | " 70° N. |
| Russia (White Sea,) - - - | " 67° to 68° N. |
| Archangel, - - - | " 66° N. |
| Central Siberia, - - - - | " 58° to 59° N. |

It cannot be grown in Iceland, lat. 63° 30′ to 66° N.

In summer mean temperature, the northern limit varies between 46° 4′ and 49° F., in the latter being injured by rains. Its northern limit, in America, does not appear to have been ascertained.

230. It is cultivated in the four quarters of the globe: in Syria and Egypt for more than 3,000 years.

231. It was introduced into the United States by Gosnold in 1602, and by colonists into Virginia in 1611. By the year 1648, it was raised in abundance in that colony, but it afterwards diminished in quantity.

The annual amount of Barley grown in United States was, in 1840, 4,161,504 bushels; in 1850, 5,167,016 bushels. The principal States that produce it are, (1850:)

| | BUSHELS. | | BUSHELS. |
|---|---|---|---|
| New York, | 3,585,059 | Pennsylvania, | 165,584 |
| Ohio, | 354,358 | Maine, | 151,731 |
| Wisconsin, | 209,692 | Massachusetts, | 112,385 |
| Michigan, | 75,249 | | |

All the other States, except Florida, Louisiana, and Oregon, raise more or less, though four of them did not produce a thousand bushels each in 1850. There is little or none exported. It is chiefly consumed in the manufacture of malt and spiritous liquors, while some is fed to hogs and o.her stock.

232. Six species or varieties are cultivated:

1. *Hordeum distichum.*—Two-rowed Barley.
2. " *gymno-distichum.*—Two-rowed naked Barley.
3. " *disticho-zeocriton.*—Two-rowed Sprat, or Battledore Barley.
4. " *hexastichum.*—Six-rowed Barley.
5. " *gymno-hexasticum.*—Six-rowed naked Barley.
6. " *hexasticho-zeocriton.*—Six-rowed Sprat, or Battledore Barley.

Of these again, there are some thirty sub-varieties, such as the *Chevalier Barley;* the *Hudson's Bay*, &c.

The two-rowed variety is most commonly cultivated. The sub-varieties are distinguished by the quality of their grain, their period of ripening, and productiveness. In mild climates barley is sown, like wheat, in the fall, and is known as winter-barley. Occasionally the color of the corolla is black. In the *naked* barley, the corolla is not attached to the grain, and it thus resembles wheat. It was introduced into England in 1768, and is known in the United States, but in neither country does it appear to be much cultivated. The *Sprat* Barley has the spike short and conical, the awns long and spreading, and the seeds more compressed than in the first sort. The straw, also, is very short. It is little cultivated. In *six-rowed* Barley, three rows of flowers on each side of the spike are fertile, and consequently three rows of grains on each side are perfected. The chief sub-variety of this is known as *Bere* or *Bigg.* It is more hardy and productive then the two-rowed, and is used for fall sowing. In Europe it is much cultivated; in the United States but little. The yield of Barley is from twenty to sixty bushels per acre, weighing from 45 to 55 lbs. per bushel according to variety. In Michigan the legal weight of a bushel is 48 lbs.

233. Ultimate ANALYSIS of Barley, dry (A,) and with water, (B.) (*Thompson.*)

| | A | B |
|---|---|---|
| Carbon, | 46.11 | 41.64 |
| Hydrogen, | 6.65 | 0.02 |
| Nitrogen, | 1.91 | 1.81 |
| Oxygen, | 42.24 | 38.28 |
| Ash, | 3.09 | 2.79 |
| Water, | | 9.46 |
| | 100.00 | 100.00 |

233. Inorganic analysis of Barley. (*Thompson.*)

| | |
|---|---|
| Silica, | 29.67 |
| Phosphoric acid, | 36.80 |
| Sulphuric acid, | 0.16 |
| Chlorine, | 0.15 |
| Peroxide of iron, | 0.83 |
| Lime, | 3.23 |
| Magnesia, | 4.30 |
| Potash, | 16.00 |
| Soda, | 8.86 |

Mean of ten analyses of Barley grain, (*Way & Ogsden,*) from calcareous soils, Dorset, England:

| | |
|---|---|
| Ashes in 100 parts, in crop as taken from the ground, | 2.34 |
| Ashes in artificially dried plants, | 2.43 |
| Potash, | 19.77 |
| Soda, | 3.93 |
| Magnesia, | 8.55 |
| Lime, | 2.58 |
| Phosphoric acid, | 35.20 |

| | |
|---|---|
| Sulphuric acid, - - - - - - | 1.03 |
| Silica, - - - - - - - - | 26.49 |
| Peroxide of iron, - - - - - - - | 1.43 |
| Chloride of sodium, - - - - - | 0.47 |

In some specimens the chloride of sodium amounted to 1.01, and chloride of potassium to 5.65 per cent.

235. Organic analysis of Barley dried at 212 ° F. *(Krocker and Horsford, and Thompson.)*

| | Winter Barley Hohenheim. | Jerusalem Barley Hohenheim | Scotch Barley Scotland. |
|---|---|---|---|
| Gluten and albumen, - | 17.70 | 14.72 | 15.24 |
| Starch, - - - - | 38.31 | 42.34 | 39.86 |
| Husk, Gum, Sugar, - | 42.33 | 42.46 | 46 19 |
| Ash, - - - - | 5 52 | 2.84 | 3.26 |
| Moisture in the first grain, | 13.80 | 16.79 | 12.71 |

236. Barley has been less perfectly examined than any of the other cereals, except oats, and the nature of the gluten contained in them is totally unknown. All that can be said with certainty upon this point is confined to the observation that the gluten of these two grains is mechanically separated with much greater difficulty than that of either wheat or rye; that by the agency of some other substance in the flour, it is almost wholly dissolved in water, and is much less abundant than in either of the other two. It is also probable that it contains but little fibrin, and resembles in this respect the gluten of rye. *(Knapp.)*

237. Hermbstadt, in experimenting with Barley, found that the action of nitrogenous manures tends rather to increase the crop than to the production of gluten.

238. According to Proust, the greater part of the non-nitrogenous constituent in Barley is not starch, although a substance similar to it, but insoluble in boiling water, which he called *hordein.*

239. Analysis of Barley straw, (A,) *(Fresenius)* and awn, (B.) *(Way.)*

| | A | B |
|---|---|---|
| Sand and Silica, | 43.8 | 70.8 |
| Potash. | 21.0 | 7.7 |
| Soda, | 0.8 | 0.4 |
| Lime, | 7.2 | 10.4 |
| Magnesia, | 3 3 | 1.3 |
| Oxide of iron, | 0.2? | 1.4 |
| Chloride of Potassium, Chloride of Sodium, | 8.9 | 1.1 |
| Phosphoric acid, | 3.1 | 2.0 |
| Sulphuric acid, | 11 7 | 3.0 |
| Carbonic acid, | — | 2.0 |

240. The value of Barley depends much on the relative hardness of its husk, and this appears to be influenced by soil and manure in its culture. A soft thin skin adapts it better for malting, and a light chalk soil is best suited to produce it of this character. Fromberg has ascertained that the hard Barley contains less gluten and albumen than the softer kinds: thus be found:

| | Water. | Nitrogen equal to gluten, &c. |
|---|---|---|
| Soft or malting Barley to contain pr. ct., | 13.55 | 10.93 |
| Flinty or Pot Barley, | 13.4 | 8.03 |

The effect of soil upon the Barley crop is known to all practical farmers—so that, in Great Britain, the terms barley-land and wheat-land are the usual designations for light and heavy soils. On clay lands the produce of barley is greater, but it is of a coarser quality and does not malt so well,—on loams it is plump and full of meal, and on light chalk soils the crop is light, but the grain is thin in the skin and of a rich color, and well adapted for malting. (*Johnston.*)

241. *Malt* is Barley which has been made to germinate by moisture and warmth, and afterwards dried, by which the vitality of the seed is destroyed. By this process, a peculiar nitrogenous principle, called *diastase*, is produced. This, though it does not constitute more than 1-500th part of the malt, serves

to affect the conversion of the starch of the seed into dextrine and grape sugar. 100 lbs. of barley yield about 80 lbs. of malt, part of which difference is the loss of the water previously contained in the barley. Thompson gives the following comparative table of barley; and malt made from the same grain; showing the change which takes place in the organic constituents:

| | Barley. | Malt. |
|---|---|---|
| Carbon - - - - - - | 41.64 | 33.95 |
| Hydrogen - - - - - - - | 6.02 | 5.31 |
| Nitrogen - - - - - - - | 1.81 | 0.88 |
| Oxygen - - - - - - - | 37.66 | 34.46 |
| Ash - - - - - - - - | 3.41 | 1.34 |
| Water - - - - - - - - | 9.46 | 4.06 |
| | 100.00 | 80.00 |

Or the loss sustained by barley in malting may be stated as follows:

| | | |
|---|---|---|
| Water, - - - - - - - | 6.00 | per cent. |
| Saline matter, - - - - - - | 0.48 | " |
| Organic matter, - - - - - - | 12.52 | " |

242. Barley is rarely or never used in America and Great Britain as bread, but it is eaten in soups and given to the sick as *Pot* and *Pearl Barley*, in which condition it is considered very nourishing. This form is produced, by rubbing the grains in an appropriate machine, till they are deprived of the husk and outer coats, and become spherical. Such barley is generally imported into the United States from Scotland, but there is no reason why it should not be prepared here. A porridge made of barley meal is used in Scotland.

243. The quantities of mineral matter removed from the acre by a crop of 40 Imperial Bushels of Barley, and 2650 lbs. of straw are as follows:

| | By the Grain. | By the Straw. | TOTAL. |
|---|---|---|---|
| Potash - - - | 7.24 lbs. | 10.29 lbs. | 17.53 lbs. |
| Soda - - - - - | 4.32 " | 0.92 " | 5.24 " |
| Magnesia - - - | 3.97 " | 5.25 " | 9.22 " |
| Phosphoric acid - - | 20.74 " | 5.02 " | 25.76 " |
| Sulphuric acid - - | 0.05 " | 2.66 " | 2.71 " |
| Chlorine - - - | 0.02 " | 1.58 " | 1.60 " |
| | 36.34 lbs. | 25.72 lbs. | 62.06 lbs. |

244. As has been already observed, Barley succeeds best on lands more sandy and lighter than those adapted for wheat, yet containing a good proportion of calcareous matter. In the United States it is always sown in the spring; and in the Northern States, the earlier it is in the ground the better, so that it may have a long period of growth. Unless the soil is very light, it is well to plow in the fall, and again in the spring, and to render the earth mellow by the use of the cultivator and harrow before sowing. For a good crop the land should be rendered rich by previous manuring; but barn-yard manure applied directly to the crop is supposed to be injurious. From two to three bushels of seed are generally sown to the acre; and the land should be rolled immediately, or, which is perhaps preferable, as soon as the young plant is from one to two inches high. The productiveness of barley appears to depend much upon rolling. Judge Buel, of Albany, N. Y., recommends steeping the seed in a weak solution of Saltpetre *(Nitrate of Potash or Soda,)* for twenty-four hours; and some use the black water which collects in barn-yards around manure-heaps for the same purpose.

245. Barley is known to be ripe by the disappearance of the reddish hue on the ear; and by the ears beginning to droop against the stem. Unless intended for seed, it should be cut before it is fully ripe, both on account of the better quality and weight of the grain, and to prevent waste by shelling.

246. Harvesting of barley is the same as of other grains, except that it sometimes happens that the straw is too short for cradling, when it may be mowed and raked into bundles to dry.

247. The straw is used for fodder and litter, but for the former purpose is not so good as wheat and oat straw.

248. It is the best grain with which to sow grass and clover seed.

249. There are no weeds peculiar to this crop.

250. The only parasitic fungus which usually attacks barley is the smut *("Black Heads,") Uredo segetum*, (§197, *c*,) but in some parts of the United States this has proved very injurious, especially on the six-rowed varieties.

251. In New England, barley has, at times, suffered severely from the Joint-worm *(Eurytoma,)* (§201, *b*, 2.) Other insects may probably injure the crop, but they do not appear to have been described.

# CHAPTER IX.

## OATS.—*Avena.*

252. The Oat is supposed to be a native of Asia. A species is found wild in California.

253. The Northern limits of this grain in Europe appear to be in

| | |
|---|---|
| Scotland, - - - - | Lat. 58° 40′ N. |
| Norway, - - - - | Lat. 56° " |
| Sweden, - - - - | Lat. 63° 30′ " |
| Russia, - - - - | Lat. 62° 30′ " |

It is extensively cultivated in the Northern, but not in the Southern parts of Europe. It grows well in Bengal, India, lat. 25° N. In America it is cultivated as far as settlements extend Northwards. It was introduced into the United States at the same time as Rye. In this country it is confined principally to the middle, western, and northern States. Its profitable production would appear to depend much on the frequency of rain during its growth.

254. The total produce of the United States in 1840 was 123,071,341 bushels, in 1850, 146,678,879 bushels.

The chief oat-producing States are (1850:)

| | | | |
|---|---|---|---|
| New York, - | 26,552,814 bush. | Illinois, - - | 10,087,241 bush. |
| Pennsylvania, - | 21,538,156 " | Kentucky, - - | 8,201,311 " |
| Ohio, - - | 13,472,742 " | Tennessee, - | 7,703,086 " |
| Virginia, - - | 10,179,045 " | Missouri, - - | 5,278,079 " |
| Michigan, - | 2,866,056 bush. | | |

All the other States produce more or less,—fifteen of them from one to four millions of bushels. With the exception of

about 60,000 bushels used in making liquors, the whole is consumed in feeding stock. There is scarcely any exported.

255. Five species are cultivated:

1. *Avena strigosa.*—Bristle-pointed Oat.
2. *Avena brevis.*—Short Oat.
3. *Avena sativa.*—Common Oat.
4. *Avena orientalis.*—Tartarian Oat.
5. *Avena nuda.*—Naked Oat.

These again are divided into many varieties.

The first two are of inferior quality, but hardy, being cultivated in the mountainous parts, the one of Scotland, the other of France. The *common oat* is best known, and has been much improved by careful culture. The *Tartarian oat*, has its panicles shorter than the last, nearly of equal length, all on the same side of the rachis *(flower stalk)* and bearded. It is so hardy as to thrive in soils and climates where the other grains cannot be raised. It is much cultivated in England and not at all in Scotland. "It is a coarse grain more fit for horse feed than to make into meal." *(Stephens.)* The corolla is frequently black. The *naked oat*, like wheat and naked barley, has the corolla detached from the seed. It has long been cultivated in Europe, and it is said to be productive, and the meal to be fine. The popular varieties such as the Potato, Hopetown, Georgian, Siberian, Dyock oats, &c., belong to the *common oat.* (3)

256. In Scotland the oat yields very large crops, from 36 to 114 bushels per English acre. In the United States, the crop probably does not much exceed 30 bushels per acre, except in very favorable localities; but 90 bushels per acre have been raised, and prize crops of 60 to 75 bushels are not uncommon. The soil and climate of Michigan are not favorable to it. The weight, per bushel, varies from 30 to 48 lbs., according to variety and culture. In Michigan, the legal weight of a bushel is 32 lbs.

Stephens says that in Scotland:

The potato oat, weighing 47 lbs. per bushel, gives 806,144 grains per bushel.

The Siberian early oat, weighing 46 lbs. per bushel, gives 641,792 grains per bushel.

White Tartarian oat, weighing 42 lbs. per bushel, gives 731,136 grains per bushel.

257. Ultimate ANALYSIS of the grain (A,) and straw (B,) of oats (*Boussingault.*) One part of dried oats leaves 0.0398 of ash: one part of straw leaves 0.0509 of ash.

| | A | B |
|---|---|---|
| Carbon, | 51.09 | 50.25 |
| Hydrogen, | 6.44 | 5.48 |
| Oxygen, | 36.25 | 38.80 |
| Nitrogen, | 2.24 | 0.38 |
| Ash, | 3.98 | 5.09 |
| | 100.00 | 100.00 |

258. Inorganic analysis of oat grain. (*Way & Ogsden, and Norton.*)

| | Hopetown Oats. | Potato Oats. | Poland Oats. | Potato Oats without husk. | Hopetown Oats without husk. | Mean of 7 analyses of Oat Grain. | Mean of 2 analyses of Oats without husk. | Mean of 4 analyses of Oat Husks. |
|---|---|---|---|---|---|---|---|---|
| Ashes in 100 parts in crop as taken from ground | 2.27 | 2.45 | 2.65 | 2.22 | 2.14 | 2.90 | 2.18 | 6.79 |
| Ashes in artificially dried plants, | 2.50 | 2.73 | 2.97 | — | — | 3.02 | — | — |
| Potash | 17.80 | 19.70 | 24.30 | 21.22 | 31.15 | 16.76 | 26.18 | 8.13 |
| Soda | 3.84 | 1.35 | 5.51 | — | — | 2.49 | — | — |
| Magnesia | 7.33 | 8.25 | 8.26 | 11.26 | 8.64 | 7.70 | 9.95 | 1.[illegible]9 |
| Lime | 3.54 | 1.31 | 2.65 | 6.69 | 5.21 | 3.92 | 5.95 | 3.15 |
| Phosphoric acid | 26.46 | 18.87 | 14.49 | 38.48 | 49.19 | 18.19 | 43.34 | 1.54 |
| Sulphuric acid | 1.10 | 0.10 | 1.74 | 18.36 | 2.54 | 1.29 | 10.45 | 6.46 |
| Silica | 38.48 | 50.03 | 41.86 | 3.60 | 1.73 | 47.08 | 2.37 | 76.16 |
| Peroxide of iron | 0.49 | 0.27 | 0.69 | — | 0.80 | 0.64 | 0.40 | 1.33 |
| Chloride of sodium | 0.92 | 0.07 | 0.45 | — | — | 0.20 | — | — |
| Chloride of potassium | — | — | — | — | — | 0.14 | — | — |

259. Inorganic analysis of oat straw, (*Mean of Levi and Boussingault.*)

| | |
|---|---|
| Potash, | 19.14 |
| Soda, | 9.69 |
| Lime, | 8.07 |
| Magnesia, | 3.78 |
| Oxide of iron, | 1.83 |
| Phosphoric acid, | 2.56 |
| Sulphuric acid, | 3.26 |
| Chlorine, | 3.25 |
| Silica, | 48.42 |
| | 100.00 |

The nutritive matter afforded by an acre of oat straw weighing 2700 lbs. is, of husk or woody fibre 1210 lbs.; of starch, sugar, &c., 950 lbs.; of gluten, &c., 36 lbs.; of oil or fat, and of saline matter 175 lbs. *(Stephens.)*

260. Organic analysis of four varieties of Scotch oats, *(Norton and Fromberg,)* viz: Hopetown oats, *Northumberland*, (A,) Hopetown oats, *Ayshire*, (B,) Hopetown oats *Ayrshire* (C,) Potato oats, *Northumberland* (D.)

| | A. | B. | C. | D. |
|---|---|---|---|---|
| Starch | 65.24 | 64.80 | 64.79 | 65.60 |
| Sugar | 4.51 | 2.58 | 2.09 | 0.80 |
| Gum | 2.10 | 2.41 | 2.12 | 2.28 |
| Oil | 5.44 | 6.97 | 6.41 | 7.38 |
| Avenin, } nitrogenous compounds, | 15.76 | 16.26 | 17.72 | 16.29 |
| Albumen } nitrogenous compounds, | 0.46 | 1.29 | 1.76 | 2.17 |
| Gluten, } nitrogenous compounds, | 2.47 | 1.46 | 1.33 | 1.45 |
| Epidermis (or skin) | 1.18 | 2.39 | 2.84 | 2.28 |
| Alkaline salts and loss, | 2.84 | 1.84 | 0.94 | 1.75 |
| | 100.00 | 100.00 | 100.00 | 100.00 |

From these analysis it appears that the oat is very rich in oily matters and flesh-forming compounds.

*Avenin* is a substance resembling *casein* (or *cheese* when chemically pure) precipitated by acetic acid from the aqueous solution of oat meal. It appears to differ but slightly from *albumen* in its ultimate composition; and in its utility, as food, it is probably rather more nourishing.

261. The proportions of nitrogen and protein (*flesh-forming*) com-

pounds in nine specimens of oats have been determined as follows: (*Norton.*)

| | Hopetown oats | | | Potato oats | | Oats from Wigtonshire, Scotl'd | | | Oats from N. Y. |
|---|---|---|---|---|---|---|---|---|---|
| Nitrogen, - - - | 2.13 | 2.35 | 2.28 | 2.76 | 2.82 | 2.89 | 5.51 | 2.49 | 3 00 |
| Protein compounds, - | 14.0 | 14.78 | 14.04 | 17.36 | 17.77 | 18.24 | 22.01 | 15.66 | 18 86 |

The relative proportions of nitrogen and protein compounds in the husk, (A,) grain (B,) and whole oat (C,) are as follows:

| | A | B | C |
|---|---|---|---|
| Nitrogen, - - | 0.30 | 2.82 | 2.18 |
| Protein compounds, - - | 1.88 | 17.77 | 13.72 |

The mean of eight samples of Scotch oats gave Mr. Norton

| | |
|---|---|
| Grain, - - - - - | 76.28 |
| Husk, - - - - - - | 23.68 |

The maximum of husk being 28.2, and the minimum 22.C. Fresh oats contain from 16 to 21 per cent of water.

The organic composition of the Husk is:

| | Hopetown Oat. | Potato Oat. |
|---|---|---|
| Oil, - - - - | 1.50 | 0.92 |
| Sugar and gum, - - - | 0.47 | 0.75 |
| Gluten and coagulated albumen, - | 1.88 | 1.88 |
| Cellulose, - - - - | 89.68 | 89.46 |
| Saline matter, (ash,) - - | 6.47 | 6.99 |

262. Animal manures increase the crop and weight of the husk rather than the proportion of gluten.

263. In America, oats are used solely for feeding animals, and for this purpose they are equal to any other grain; combining the largest amount of useful qualities. For horses doing hard work, or where great speed is required nothing can replace them; and as the proportion of oil which they contain is but little inferior to that in Indian corn, while it is probably more readily digested and received into the system, they are used with great advantage for fattening hogs and other stock. For this purpose, however, owing to the hard husk, they ought to be crushed, and are preferable if boiled.

Where crushing or grinding cannot be effected, boiling serves nearly as good a purpose.

The peculiar form of the *casein* or *avenin* appears to give oats a nourishing power little inferior to that of animal food.

In Ireland, Scotland, and other countries, oat meal constitutes almost the entire food of the majority of the people; and those who live on it are not only physically perfect, but are able to undergo great exertion, and bear up against severe exposure and hardship. Owing to the small proportion of gluten, yeast-bread cannot be made with oat meal as with wheat flour, and it is usually eaten boiled, or made into thin cakes, dried in the air. Before grinding, it is necessary to kiln-dry oats; and they are ground in a mill constructed for the purpose, the mill-stones being different from those used in flouring mills.

264. Oats will grow upon almost any kind of soil, but the clays, and loams that are sufficiently retentive of moisture are the most favorable.

Owing to this facility of cultivation less pains are frequently bestowed upon this crop than upon others; though it will well repay proper culture.

There is a prevalent notion that oats particularly exhaust the soil on which they are grown, but we believe it to be a mistake. The form of the roots, however, predisposes the soil to collect in clods, and hard lumps, which are afterwards broken with difficulty, and unless these are carefully disintegrated, they may probably affect the succeeding crop injuriously. Barley, on the contrary, seperates the soil, rendering it mellow with its roots. As a mechanical agent, therefore, the roots of the oat plant may act unfavorably. The different varieties, containing such different proportions of organic constituents, are adapted to different soils and circumstances.

265. A crop of 50 bushels of oats, and 3800 lbs. of straw takes from the acre of soil the following quantities:

| | By the grain. | By the straw. | Total. |
|---|---|---|---|
| Potash and soda, - - | 10.88 lbs. | 64.78 lbs. | 75.66 lbs |
| Magnesia, - - | 3.52 " | 8.95 " | 12.47 " |
| Phosphoric acid, - | 14.48 " | 5.38 " | 19.86 " |
| Sulphuric acid, - - | 5 28 " | 9.95 " | 15 23 " |
| Chlorine, - - | 0.35 " | 8.51 " | 8 86 " |
| | 34.51 lbs. | 97.57 lbs. | 132.08 lbs. |

(*Stephens.*)

266. In the northern States, oats are always sown in spring, from the commencement of vegetation to the begining of June. They are a favorite crop to sow upon plowed sod. The quantity of seed varies from two to four bushels an acre; in Scotland six bushels are sown; under most circumstances, the larger quantity is preferable. The seed should be well harrowed in and rolled.

267. The best time for harvesting is before the grain is quite ripe, and while the straw is partially green. Oats may be cut with a sickle, cradle, scythe, or machine; but should be left for a few days in swath, before binding, when the grain will mature. Oats thus cut before they are quite ripe are larger, and heavier, while the straw, as fodder, is more nutritious. Oats, cut as above, do not appear to be inferior in any respect. (§312.)

268. Oat straw is more esteemed for fodder than that of wheat, barley, or rye. According to experiments made in Germany by Viet, 200 lbs. of oat straw with the chaff are equivalent to 100 lbs. of good hay, though, for the United States, this estimate is probably too low. If not too ripe when cut, and if saved in good condition, cattle in stables can be kept during winter in improving condition upon this straw alone. Late experiments in Scotland have proved oat-straw to be fully equal to hay for animals fattening on roots.

169. In this country, there is no insect peculiarly injurious to oats. In common with other grains, it occasionally suffers from the Wire worm.

270. Smut *(Black heads,)* *(Uredo Segetum,)* appears to be the only fungus to which it is generally subject, and this, rarely, to any great extent.

271. There are no weeds peculiar to this crop.

In soils where Wild Mustard *(Sinapis arvensis,)* and Wild Radish *(Raphanus raphanistrum,)* are abundant, oats are perhaps more seriously injured than any other grain. As many persons are ignorant how to root out these weeds, it may be well to copy the following rules by a late French writer in the *Annales de l'agriculture*, who had been entirely successful in clearing a farm overrun with them.

1. Plow *very* deep, so as to give all the seeds within reach of the plow facilities for germinating.

2. Harrow the ground till every clod is broken, for the seeds are often retained in clods, and only germinate when these are disintegrated by rain, &c., or by artificial means.

3. Cultivate two hoed crops before grain is sown, and do not allow a single plant of mustard to go to seed.

4. For the third crop, grow oats, *drilled* at a sufficient distance to permit hand hoeing between the rows.

By using these means, and not allowing a single plant to seed, the worst fields may be cleared in three or four years. It is important that the first plowing should be deeper than any succeeding one, as the soil frequently contains the seeds to a great depth, which will germinate as soon as exposed to the air.

Of course it is requisite that all grain sown should be *quite* free from the seeds of the mustard.

272. Common salt, from four to eight bushels per acre—spread three or four days before the seed is sown, and lightly harrowed in, has been found an useful manure for oats, especially at a distance from the sea. It supplies the soda, chlorine, and magnesia; it retains moisture in the soil; it acts as a solvent on the other constituents of the earth; and generally strengthens the straw. We warmly recommend a trial of it in those parts of Michigan where the oat crop is apt to fail. Wood ashes also (uncleached) are a valuable manure, especially in sandy soils, for oats.

# CHAPTER X.

---

## INDIAN CORN.—MAIZE.—*Zea Mays.*

273. The origin of the word "Maize" is from the Haytien *mahiz*. This grain is a native of the American continent, and was unknown to the rest of the world till the discoveries of Columbus. It is still found growing wild from the Rocky Mountains to Paraguay, but in this state, instead of having each grain naked, it is completely covered with glumes or husks. A variety of the wild corn has been cultivated of late years in the northern States, under the name of "Texas corn." This grain was found by the first European explorers of the continent to be everywhere cultivated by the natives.

Only one species has usually been recognized in this country, but the late M. Bonafous, director of the Royal Agricultural Garden of Turin, in his *Histoire naturelle agricole et economique de Mais*, describes four distinct species, viz :

1. Zea Mays—with leaves entire.
2. Zea caragua, with leaves denticulated.
3. Zea hirta, with hairy leaves.
4. Zea erythrolepis, with grains compressed, and red glumes—(husks.)

From these, but especially the first, all the varieties at present cultivated have sprung.

274. It has a wide range of temperature in America, flourishing from about 40° of Southern to beyond the 45° of Northern latitude. In Mexico its highest limits vary from 2000 to 8000 feet above the level of the sea; and the time necessary for it to ripen differs from six weeks to seven months, ac-

cording to the mean temperature. In Europe, it is grown from the shores of the Mediterranean as far north as the Netherlands. The region of cultivation appears to be gradually extending further north; probably by the origin of new and hardy varieties. It is also grown in Northern, Southern, and Western Africa, India, China, Japan, Australia, the Sandwich Islands, the Azores, the Madeiras, the Canaries, and numerous other ocean islands. With the exception of Rice, it is the food of a larger number of human beings than any other grain.

275. In the United States, it was first cultivated by the English on James River, Virginia, 1608; the Indian mode being closely followed. Since then it has been everywhere a favorite crop, and annually a larger quantity is produced. The increase from 1840 to 1850 was 214,000,000 bushels, equal to 56 per cent. over the former period. In New England it has increased nearly 50 per cent.; and no State has retrograded.

The following is the production of the most important States according to the census of 1840 and 1850:

| | | |
|---|---|---|
| New York, | 10,972,286 | 17,858,400 |
| Pennsylvania, | 14,240,022 | 19,835,214 |
| Maryland, | 8,233,086 | 11,104,631 |
| Virginia, | 34,577,591 | 35,254,319 |
| North Carolina, | 23,893,763 | 27,941,051 |
| Georgia, | 20,905,122 | 30,080,099 |
| Alabama, | 20,947,004 | 28,754,048 |
| Mississippi, | 13,161,237 | 22,446,552 |
| Tennessee, | 44,986,188 | 52,276,223 |
| Kentucky, | 39,847,120 | 58,675,591 |
| Ohio, | 33,668,144 | 59,078,695 |
| Indiana, | 28,155,887 | 52,964,363 |
| Illinois, | 22,634,211 | 57,646,984 |
| Missouri, | 17,332,524 | 36,214,537 |
| Michigan, | 2,277,039 | 5,641,420 |

Total production of the United States in 1850, 592,326,612, bushels, which at the low average of ten cents per bushel on the farm, gives an annual return of $59,232,661 in this one crop alone. The corn crop, however, represents not only the vegetable food of man, but also animal food in the shape of pork and beef; and also various manufactures, such as oil, stearine, bristles, Prussian Blue, &c.; and large quantities of valuable manure, in the shape of refuse and offal, In one or other of these forms, a large amount of corn is annually exported to foreign countries; and the industry of the United States greatly depends upon it. The same evils, however, which attached to the growth of the potato in Ireland, may, it is feared, hereafter follow the great production of corn in those States where it is most easily raised.

276. The varieties are very numerous, depending upon the character of the soil and climate, from the small shrubby corn of Northern Canada to the gigantic stalks of the Southern States; and the composition and nutritive qualities of the grain vary in like proportion. In practice this is a very important fact, as the nutritive value of corn is constantly varying according to circumstances.

(*A.*) The Phosphates differ in quantity according to variety. *Sweet Corn* appears to contain the most. Dr. Jackson analyzed two grains of corn (the Tuscarora and Sweet Corn) grown on the *same ear*, and he found nearly double the amount of phosphates in the latter, showing that even when mixed, so as to grow on the same plant, each variety retains its power of selecting its appropriate quantity of inorganic salts. A crop of Sweet Corn will take twice as much of the phosphates from the soil as the other variety, but at the same time will give more material to the animal for the formation of bone. On the same principle the stiffness of the joints and lameness of the feet common in horses fed too freely with corn may be explained, these affections arising from an unnatural growth of bone procured from the corn.

(*B.*) The proportion of Starch changes according to the variety and climate. Southern Corn contains more than Northern. Tuscarora contains the most of any variety examined. Rice Corn, and Pop Corn contain the least.

(*C.*) The relative proportions of oil and gluten also vary in the same manner. Rice Corn contains the most oil; Pop Corn, Canada Corn, and Brown Corn rank next. Burden Corn has a very fine white oil,

Tuscarora Corn does not contain either oil or gluten.* There is a difference also in the mode of distribution of the oily and glutinous parts of corn; the Southern and Dent varieties having the oil and gluten on the sides of the elongated seed, while the starch projects quite through the grain to its summit, and by its contraction in drying, produces the peculiar pit or depression in this variety of grain. Popping Corn contains the oil in little six-sided cells in the horny portions of the grain, in the form of minute drops. When heated, the oil is decomposed into carburetted hydrogen gas, and every cell is ruptured, the grain being completely voluted.

(*D.*) The meal of those varieties containing much oil is less liable to ferment and become sour.

(*E.*) The colors depend upon that of the hull and of the oil; the latter, when yellow showing its color through a transparent epidermis (or *skin.*) The color of the oil varies much in different varieties. Red and blue corn owe their hues to the colors of the epidermis.

(*F.*) The oil appears to reside chiefly immediately under the hull, so that when animals do not digest the outer coating of the grain, as is the case when corn is fed unground to hogs, much of the oil is lost.

(*G.*) The inorganic salts, and especially the phosphates appear to be confined to the chit and germ. (*Jackson.*)

(*H.*) The large eight-rowed yellow corn contains 13.9 per cent. of albumen, casein, and gluten, while the Sioux contains 16.5 per cent. of the same.

The eight-rowed Squaw Corn contains 60.6 per cent. of starch, sugar, oil, and gum, while the eight-rowed small white Flint contains 76.6 per cent of the same. If the Squaw Corn is worth fifty cents a bushel for fattening, the Flint would be equally cheap at fifty-eight cents a bushel. (*Gould.*)

---

*There are apparently two sorts of corn known as the "Tuscarora" the one mentioned above as devoid of oil, if the analysis is correct, and one analyzed by Dr. Salisbury (known also as "Turkey Wheat,") which contains 5.32 per cent. of oil, calculated without the water. What we ourselves have grown as "Tuscorora," was a peculiarly dry, starchy grain, with a thin skin, apparently deficient in oil. We would here refer the reader to the admirable Essay on Corn by Dr. Salisbury, containing the most complete and accurate examination of this grain perhaps ever made, in the *Transactions of the New York State Agricultural Society, vol. viii,* 1848. It occupies 199 closely printed octavo pages; and we would willingly have extracted more from it had our limits permitted. As these volumes, however, are not difficult to meet with, we prefer referring the reader to the Essay itself, as any quotations must prove deficient without the context.

From these facts it will be perceived how important it is that the farmer should study the adaptation of variety to the purpose intended in consumption. If he wishes to give young animals large bones, let him feed them on Sweet Corn; but at the same time manure the soil with dissolved bones, or other phosphate-bearing manures. He would endeavor in vain to fatten animals with the Tuscarora, as it contains no oil, while it makes the best bread, and is peculiarly adapted for the manufacture of corn starch. Again, the hard northern gluten-bearing corns are better for working animals than the southern-starch bearing varieties, though the latter, independent of the oil, will make most fat, the former most flesh. An accurate analysis of all varieties grown in the United States would be of great pecuniary value to the country.

277. The varieties of corn are generally distinguished by *(a,)* the number of rows of grain in the ear, as eight, twelve, fourteen, and sixteen-rowed; or by *(b,)* the color, as white yellow, brown, &c., but none of the common divisions are either accurate or scientific. It were useless to recite the names of the many varieties, the more especially as they are constantly changing by hybridizing. It may be noticed that northern corn will improve, if removed southwards, in size and productiveness, but southern corn taken to the north will either not ripen at all, or soon degenerate.

The origin of ***Sweet Corn*** is unknown, but it appears to have been used by the Indians of New England before the arrival of the Pilgrims. It appears like an unripe grain; and contains an unusually large proportion of the Phosphates. and a large quantity of sugar and gum with but little starch; while the stalks, being small, take up a less proportion of the saline matters of the soil.

278. The qualities desirable in a good variety differ according to the soil and climate. In the Central and Southern States the following may be laid down as peculiarities to be attained: *(a,)* good growth of stalk and leaf; *(b,)* several ears

on each stalk; *(c,)* cob small, but long, and grains long and numerous; *(d,)* husk thick and hard so as to shed water, and resist the attacks of birds; *(e,)* ripening sufficiently early to escape early frosts. In the Northeastern States, corn with a short light stalk, but with suckers, or supernumerary stalks bearing ears, as in the Dutton, is preferred.

279. The weight of a bushel of corn greatly varies. The legal weight in Michigan is 56 lbs. to the bushel. It is stated that corn on the cob loses 20 to 50 per cent. in *measure* by shrinkage in seven months, and 10 to 15 per cent. in weight. When sold on the cob by the bushel, 2 to 1½ bushels of ears are equivalent to one bushel of shelled corn according to variety. In the Southern States it is frequently measured by the barrel of five bushels.

280. The yield to the acre varies from 20 to 200 bushels of shelled corn.

The following premium crops of corn were grown in Kentucky in 1850. There were nine competitors, and the surface in cultivation ten acres by each competitor.

| | | | |
|---|---|---|---|
| J. Matson, | 189 | bushels, 1 quart | per acre. |
| P. Pean, | 189 | " | " |
| S. H. Chew, | 137½ | " | " |
| J. Hutchcraft, | 115 | " | " |
| A. Vanmeter, | 108⅓ | " | " |
| E. Hedges, | 107 | " | " |
| E. W. Hockaday, | 100 | " | " |
| Dr. B. W. Dudley, | 100 | " | " |
| H. Varnon, | 98 | " | " |

or, 11,440 bushels 10 quarts shelled corn oft 90 acres, perhaps the largest quantity ever raised from the same area. (*D. Lee.*) But it shows what corn can produce under good cultivation and favorable circumstances.

281. I. Inorganic ANALYSIS of white Flint corn, sown on a sandy loam and manured in part with coal ashes, (*Salisbury,*) New York:

| | Kernels. | Leaves. | Cob |
|---|---|---|---|
| Silica, | 9.50 | 53.550 | 13.600 |
| Alkaline Phosphates, | 35.500 | | |
| Earthy Phosphates, | | 19.250 | 23.920 |
| Lime, | 0.160 | 6.092 | 0.300 |
| Magnesia, | 2.410 | 1.250 | 0.900 |
| Potash, | 23 920 | 12.762 | 35.802 |
| Soda, | 22 590 | 8.512 | 5.914 |
| Chlorine, | 0.405 | 9.762 | 0.132 |
| Sulphuric acid, | 4 385 | 4.185 | 0.345 |
| Organic matter, | 0.367 | | 2.314 |
| Carbonic acid, | | | 6.134 |

II. Southern corn *(Shepherd,)* 100 parts gave 0.95 parts ash, composed:

| | |
|---|---|
| Silica, | 38.45 |
| Potash, with trace of Soda, | 19.51 |
| Phosphate of lime, | 17.17 |
| Phosphate of magnesia, | 18.83 |
| Phosphate of potash, | 2.24 |
| Carbonate of lime, | 2 50 |
| Carbonate of magnesia, | 2.16 |
| Sulphate of lime and magnesia, | 0.79 |
| Silica, (mechanically present,) | 1.70 |
| Alumina, | trace |
| Loss, | 1.65 |
| | 100.00 |

III. Corn, (United States.) *(Fromberg.)*

| | |
|---|---|
| Potash, | 26,63 |
| Soda, | 7.54 |
| Magnesia, | 15.44 |
| Lime, | 1.59 |
| Phosphoric acid, | 39.65 |
| Sulphuric acid, | 5.54 |
| Silica, | 2.09 |
| Peroxide of iron, | 0.60 |
| | 99.08 |

It will be perceived from these analyses that Indian corn varies very greatly in its inorganic constituents. But we are led to believe that it varies still more in Europe, if Liebig *(Agricul. Chem.,)* is correct in stating: "There are certain plants which contain either no potash or mere traces of it. Such is Indian Corn. *(Zea mays.)* For plants such as these the potash in the soil is of no use, and farmers are well aware that they can be cultivated without rotation on the same soil."

The water in dry corn varies from 10 to 15 per cent.; but as high as 37 per cent. when first ripened.

282. Organic analysis of various varieties of corn grown in New York. *(Salisbury.)* Golden Sioux corn, 12,—14-rowed, an improved variety of Buell's Dutton corn (A,) Ohio Dent corn (B,) small 8-rowed corn (C,) White Flint, grown on clay loam, and manured with coal ashes, horse dung, and unleached wood ashes (D,) large 8-rowed yellow corn (E.)

| | A. | B. | C. | D. | E. |
|---|---|---|---|---|---|
| Starch, - - | 36.06 | 41.85 | 30.290 | 40.34 | 49.22 |
| Gluten, - - - | 5.00 | 4.62 | 5.600 | 7.69 | 5.40 |
| Oil, - - - | 3.44 | 3.88 | 3.900 | 4.68 | 3.71 |
| Albumen, - - - | 4.42 | 2.64 | 6.000 | 3.40 | 3.32 |
| Casein, - - | 1.92 | 1.32 | 2.200 | 0.50 | 0.75 |
| Dextrine, - - - | 1.30 | 5.40 | 4.615 | 2.90 | 1.89 |
| Fibre, - - | 18.50 | 21.36 | 26.800 | 18.01 | 11.96 |
| Sugar and extractive matter, | 7.25 | 10.00 | 5.200 | 8.30 | 9.55 |
| Water, - - - | 15.02 | 10.00 | 13.400 | 14.00 | 14.00 |

When the dough of Indian corn is washed with water, a glutinous residue is left different from the gluten of wheat, and characterized by its solubility in alcohol, and therefore altered to vegetable gelatin.

The organic composition of corn in Europe differs from the above according to the following analyses. (*Knapp and Payen.*)

| | Indian Meal from Hohenheim. | Indian Meal from Polenta Vienna. | PAYEN. Grain of Corn. |
|---|---|---|---|
| Gluten, | 14.66 | 13.65 | 12.3 |
| Albumen, | | | |
| Starch, | 66.34 | 77.74 | 71.2 |
| Sugar, gum, | 18.18 | 7.16 | 0.4 |
| Fatty matter, | | | 9.0 |
| Husk, | | | 5.9 |
| Ash, | | | 1.2 |

The amount of inorganic matter taken from an acre of the soil by the small white Flint corn is: *(Gould.)*

| | |
|---|---|
| Silicic acid, | 210.14 lbs. |
| Phosphates of iron, lime, and magnesia, | 94 58 " |
| Potash, | 64 71 " |
| Soda, | 63.00 " |
| Lime, | 15.69 " |
| Magnesia, | 9.69 " |
| Chlorine, | 19.62 " |
| Sulphuric acid, | 30.34 " |
| | 881 85 lbs. |

Of organic matter there is taken from one acre:

| | |
|---|---|
| Sugar and extract, | 2,892 lbs. |
| Starch, (in kernel only,) | 5,139 " |
| Rosin, (in cob only,) | 15 " |
| Fibre, | 11,526 " |
| Albumen, | 817 " |
| Casein, | 396 " |
| Zein, (in kernel only,) | 113 " |
| Dextrine and gum, | 1027 " |
| Oil, (in kernel only,) | 312 " |
| Chlorophyl and wax, | 171¾ " |
| Glutinous matter, | 420 " |
| | 22,546 lbs. |

Of this, 8,008 lbs. are taken off by the kernels, leaving 14,538 lbs. for the rest of the plant. Of the inorganic matter 99 lbs. are contained in the kernels, leaving 782 lbs. for the stalks, leaves, &c.

Amount of the several proximate organic bodies in a ton of each of the following parts when ripe. *(Salisbury.)*

| | Leaves. | Sheaths. | Stalks. | Cob. | Kernels. |
|---|---|---|---|---|---|
| | lbs. | lbs. | lbs. | lbs. | lbs. |
| Sugar and extract, - | 336.000 | 180.000 | 186.660 | 94.000 | 266.40 |
| Starch, - - | | | | trace. | 1186.00 |
| Resin, - - - | | | | 12.500 | |
| Fibre, - - | 1086.000 | 1338.000 | 1402.660 | 883.760 | 17.80 |
| Matter by potash, - | 139.340 | 116.640 | 71.340 | 314.240 | 119.80 |
| Albumen, - - | 160.800 | 70.060 | 12.000 | 10.500 | 85.80 |
| Casein, - - - | 34.660 | 8.040 | 72.000 | 2.000 | 1.60 |
| Zein, - - - | | | | | 33.60 |
| Dextrine and gum, - | 116.00 | 57.600 | 165.340 | 16.000 | 65.20 |
| Oil, - - - | | | | | 72.00 |
| Resin, chlorophyl and wax, - | 82.660 | 12.040 | 84.000 | 51.240 | |
| Glutinous matter, - | | 57.400 | | | |
| Water, - - | 55.340 | 167 400 | 71.400 | 626.400 | 169.900 |

Percentage of dry matter in the following several parts of Small White Flint Corn, when ripe. *(Salisbury.)*

| | | | |
|---|---|---|---|
| Leaves, - - | 40.108 | Ear stalks, - - | 11.128 |
| Sheaths, - - - | 29.342 | Kernels, - - - | 62.540 |
| Stalk, - - | 13.635 | Cob, - - - - | 45.652 |
| Tassel, - - - | 58.722 | Silks, - - - | 18.825 |
| Sheaths of husks, - | 30.643 | | |

The following table shows about the amount of the several proximate organic bodies thrown away in rejecting the cob, calculated from the analysis of the Small White Flint variety. 1000 lbs. contain not far from 200 lbs. of cob, and 800 lbs. of grain. These contain the following proportions, expressed in pounds and decimals of a pound. *(Salisbury.)*

| | 200 lbs. Cobs. | 800 lbs. grain. | 1000 lbs. ears. |
|---|---|---|---|
| Sugar and extract, - | 13.582 | 115.320 | 128.902 |
| Starch, - - | 0.003 | 487.384 | 487.387 |
| Fibre, - - - | 127.687 | 7.712 | 135.399 |
| Oil, - - - | | 39.824 | 39.824 |
| Zein, - - - | | 31.856 | 21.856 |
| Matter seperated by potash from fibre, - | 45.404 | 51.856 | 97.360 |
| Albumen, - - | 1.518 | 37.136 | 38.654 |
| Casein, - - - | 0.288 | 00.688 | 0.976 |
| Dextrine or gum, - | 2.310 | 28.224 | 30.534 |
| Resin, - - - | 1.806 | | 1.806 |
| Glutinous matter, - | 7.402 | | 7.402 |

In the above table the inorganic matter is not seperately considered, it being distributed among the several organic bodies. By rejecting the cobs of 1000 lbs. of dry ears about 200 lbs. of organic matter is lost which consist of 13¼ lbs. of sugar and extract, 227½ lbs. of fibre 45½ lbs. of water soluble in potash, 1½ lbs. of albumen, ¼ lb. of casein, 2.31 lbs. of gum or dextrine, 1.8 lbs. of resin, and 7.4 lbs. of glutinous matter. Hence the cob, although not rich in nutritive matter, can by no means be said to be destitute of these proximate principles which go to support respiration and sustain animal heat, and those which are capable of being transformed into nerve, muscle, &c., and the phosphates which contribute so largely to the formation of bone.

Inorganic composition of the ash of the ripe cob. (*Salisbury.*)

| | |
|---|---|
| Carbonic acid, | 9.455 |
| Silicic acid, | 10.320 |
| Sulphuric acid, | 1.336 |
| Phosphoric acid, | 13 105 |
| Lime, | 8 833 |
| Magnesia, | 6.745 |
| Potash, | 34.400 |
| Soda, | 11 495 |
| Chloride of sodium, | 1 980 |
| Organic acids, | 6 430 |
| Phosphate of peroxide of iron, | .445 |
| | 99.544 |

Of all the twenty-seven varieties of corn examined by Dr. Salisbury, the Rhode Island Sweet is the richest in albumen, oil, and dextrine, and the most deficient in starch. As a general rule, those varieties with full corneous kernels are richer in the nitrogenized bodies and oil, and less rich in starch than the indented kinds; and of the corneous sorts with distended grains, the yellow seems to be richer than the white in oil, and those bodies which contain nitrogen, and less rich in starch.

According to Fresenius, the *oil* of corn consists of :

| | |
|---|---|
| Carbon, | 79.68 |
| Hydrogen, | 11.53 |
| Oxygen, | 8.79 |

283. Inorganic analysis of the leaves of corn at different stages. (*Salisbury.*)

| | July 19 | Aug. 2 | Aug. 23 | Aug. 30. | Oct. 18. |
|---|---|---|---|---|---|
| Carbonic acid, | 5.40 | 2.850 | 0.65 | 3.50 | 4.050 |
| Silica, | 13.50 | 19.850 | 34.90 | 36.27 | 58.650 |
| Sulphuric acid, | 2.16 | 1.995 | 4.92 | 5.84 | 4.881 |
| Phosphates, | 21.60 | 16.250 | 17.00 | 13.50 | 5.850 |
| Lime, | 0.69 | 4.035 | 2.00 | 3.38 | 4.510 |
| Magnesia, | 0.37 | 2.980 | 1.59 | 2.30 | 0.865 |
| Potash, | 9.98 | 11.675 | 10.85 | 9.15 | 7.333 |
| Soda, | 34.39 | 29.590 | 21.23 | 22.13 | 8.520 |
| Chlorine, | 4.55 | 6.020 | 3.06 | 1.63 | 2.664 |
| Organic acids, | 5.50 | 2.400 | 3.38 | 2.05 | 2.200 |
| | 98.14 | 97.750 | 99.58 | 99.75 | 99.523 |

Proximate organic analysis of the leaves at different stages of growth, calculated with the water. *(Salisbury.)*

| | Aug. 2. | Aug. 23. | Oct. 18. |
|---|---|---|---|
| Sugar and extract soluble in alcohol, | 1.110 | 3.300 | 16.800 |
| Do do insoluble in alcohol, | 1.890 | | |
| Fibre with a little chlorophyl, | 1.390 | 3.350 | 54.300 |
| Fibre, | 8.620 | 6.950 | |
| Matter seperated from fibre by a weak solution of caustic potash, | 0.290 | 2.380 | 6.967 |
| Albumen, | trace. | 0.020 | 8.040 |
| Casein, | 0.730 | 0.100 | 1.733 |
| Dextrine or gum, | 0.850 | 1.270 | 5.800 |
| Oil and resin, | 0.150 | 0.139 | 4.133 |
| Chlorophyl and wax, | | | |
| Water, | 86.762 | 82.482 | 2.767 |

284. Dr. Jackson found 100 grains of the *Chit* yield 6.4 grains of ashes (§279. ii) which consisted of:

| | |
|---|---|
| Phosphate of lime, | 2.4 |
| Phosphate of magnesia, | 0.8 |
| Phosphoric acid, a little potash, silica, and oxide of iron, | 3.2 |
| | 6.4 |

In composition, the Chit differs materially from the rest of the kernel in containing a very large per centage of oil and albumen, and a small per centage of starch. In the analyses of the Chit, the oil amounts to from 26 to 30 per cent., and the albumen from 17 to 20 per cent. of the dry matter, while the starch ranges from about 10 to 12½ per cent.

285. The feeding qualities of corn are universally known; and throughout the greater portion of the United States, it is used as bread for man, and depended on for fattening hogs and beef. There do not appear, however, to have been many accurate experiments made to ascertain how many pounds of corn are requisite to make a pound of meat. There are many difficulties in the way of arriving at accurate results in these respects. Different breeds, and even individuals of the same breed possess different fattening qualities; we have seen that the variety of the corn used must make much difference: cleanliness, and mode of feeding make more still; while corn ground and cooked is found to possess much more nutritive power, bushel for bushel, than when fed in its natural state. The following table, compiled from some experiments by Mr. H. L. Ellsworth, may be considered as an approximation towards the relative value of raw unground, and cooked ground corn,—though owing to peculiar circumstances the hogs fed on mush did not make as good progress as they ought to have done:

| No. | Weight when put up | Fed daily. | Weight at end of 15 days. | Gain. | Fed in all in 15 days. | Value of corn when pork is 3 cents per lb. |
|---|---|---|---|---|---|---|
| 1 | 131 lbs 4 oz | 5½ lbs. meal | 149 lbs 13oz | 18 lbs 9 oz. | 105lbs meal | 55 cts pr bush |
| 2 | 150 lbs 4 oz | cooked, each. | 165 lbs 13oz | 15 lbs 9 oz. | | |
| 3 | 157 lbs 4 oz | 7 lbs raw | 179 lbs 13oz | 22 lbs 9 oz. | 210lbs corn | |
| 4 | 120 lbs 4 oz | corn, each. | 146 lbs | 25 lbs 12 oz | | 38½ c pr bush |
| | | | End of 20 days. | | In 20 days. | |
| 1 | 149 lbs 13oz | 14 lbs raw | 179 lbs | 29 lbs 3 oz. | 280 lbs corn | |
| 2 | 165 lbs 13oz | corn, each. | 189 lbs | 23 lbs 3 oz. | | 31 cts pr bush |
| 3 | Sick. | 2½ lbs meal | | | | |
| 4 | 146 | cooked, each | 166 lbs | 20 lbs | 70lbs meal | 48 cts pr bush |

Thence it is deduced that raw food is to cooked food as 68 to 103, making the gain by cooking 55 per cent. over uncooked food; or 3 bushels of meal cooked is equal to 4½ bushels of dry hard corn. Or looking at this table in another light; the farmer selling his corn by turning it into pork, would receive 55 cents a bushel if it was fed cooked, while he would only receive 38½ cents per bushel if fed raw. It is generally estimated that if corn is cut up and fed to hogs in the field, 15 bushels will fatten each one; that is, add 100 lbs. weight of flesh. If hogs at gross weight are worth $3,00 per cwt., this makes corn worth 20 cents per bushel. If hogs are confined in pens, raw dry corn is worth 30 cents, and cooked meal 50 cents per bushel; so that the gain by grinding and cooking, over feeding in the field is 150 per cent. The manure, in the calculation of a skillfull farmer, should cover the incidental expenses of fire, feeding, &c. It is to be observed, however, from the above experiment, that hogs fed on mush did not increase in weight so *rapidly* as the others. Considering that many millions of bushels of corn are annually fed to animals in the United States, it is of great economical importance, worthy of the attention of the Federal and State Governments, that extensive and accurate experiments should be made as to the most economical mode of fattening stock. If we suppose—and we put the case in all respects lower than the truth is believed to be—200,000,000 of bushels of corn, bearing a market value of 25 cents per bushel, are annually fed to hogs, and by improved means of feeding a saving of 25 per cent could be made, it would leave 50,000,000 bushels, worth twelve millions five hundred thousand dollars to be applied to other purposes; and which now are annually thrown away, without being of any possible value, either direct, or indirect, to man.

Mr. Ellsworth, however, observes that "where land is cheap and easily tilled, and labor dear, as in the West, it may be best to make hogs their own harvesters. My present impression is, that [in Indiana] the most profitable way to feed corn, all things considered, is to cut the corn, as soon as it begins to turn hard; then hogs will eat corn, cob, and stalk; then too, the weather is mild, and swine will thrive much faster in September, October, and November, than in December, January, and February." This calculation is, of course, based on peculiar circumstances confined to certain localities.

286. Corn meal, owing to deficiency in gluten, &c., does not *rise* with yeast like wheat flour. The different varieties make different qualities of bread. The Southern and "Oregon" varieties are preferred for this purpose, as containing more starch. Yellow corn has more flavor, and absorbs more water than the white. In France it has been found that 150 lbs. of corn will make from 215 to 223 lbs. of good bread. Mr. Ellsworth found that 14 lbs. of good corn meal, thoroughly cooked, will make 90 lbs. of mush, so thick as not to run when taken out of the kettle; so that, in this form, the power of absorbing water is very great. The quality of bread likewise depends upon the mode in which the corn is ground. In the South, the mill stones are dressed so as to *cut* the meal into sharp particles, and not to *crush* it into powder as is done in wheat-flouring mills,—the corn being fed to the stones by handfuls at a time. Meal is often mixed with rye or wheat flour, and thus made into loaves.

Dr. Clos has lately given, in the *Journal d'Agriculture pratique*, the result of certain experiments made to ascertain the comparative economical value of Yellow and White corn, grown in the South of France. He found that Yellow corn meal when cooked absorbed water, and made mush as follows:

| Weight of Meal employed. | Weight of Mush. | Difference, or weight of water absorbed. |
|---|---|---|
| Kilogramme. | Kilogramme. | Kilogramme. |
| 3.794 | 11.932 | 8.138 |
| 3.488 | 11.136 | 7.648 |
| 3.549 | 12.054 | 8.505 |
| Total, 10.831 | 35.122 | 24.291 |
| White corn meal, cooked in the same manner gave: | | |
| 3.977 | 11.075 | 7.098 |
| 3.977 | 11.442 | 7.465 |
| 4.161 | 11.687 | 7.526 |
| Total, 12.115 | 34.204 | 22.089 |

The Yellow corn gives a larger quantity of mush in proportion to the meal used, and each kilogramme of meal absorbs over two kilogrammes of water, while the White corn meal absorbs less than two kilogrammes, or the mush of the Yellow is in proportion of 39.285 to 34.204 of the White from the same weights of meal. The Yellow meal, on sifting, gave les- bran and more useful meal than the White by one-twentieth. It was further shown (*a*,) that the Yellow corn is drier and harder ; (*b*,) resists moisture and is kept more easily ; and (*c*,) weighs more per bushel than the White. The same experiments repeated in America could not fail to be useful. (*A kilogramme*, is 2 1-5 lbs. avoirdupois.) Mr. Gould has stated that 10 lbs. 12 oz. of Long Island corn grew on a given space, while 15 lbs. 2 oz. of large 12-rowed red corn grew on the same space of a precisely similar soil. The large White Flint yields 2.4 tons of grain to the acre on the same soil where the large Yellow Sioux yields 3.5 tons per acre.

287. The stalks, leaves, and husks, have a great nutritive value for fodder. When well saved, being cut before they are fully ripe, they are probably very nearly equal in this respect to common hay. They contain much sugar; and are believed to be more valuable than hay when fed to milk cows; producing a larger quantity of milk; but no accurate experiments seem to have been made. In 1848, the Commissioner of Patents procured from seventeen States, estimates of the supposed value of corn fodder, and it varies from $1 to $5 per ton; exclusive of manure made from it. If stalks are given to cattle in their natural state, a large portion, and that the heaviest, is wasted; but if cut and mixed with a little meal, nearly the whole will be eaten. The relative value, therefore, will of course depend on the mode of feeding. Again, it must be taken into consideration whether the husks are left on the stalks or not; the practice varying in different localities. The size of stalks also makes a difference, the small northern corn containing more consumable fodder than the large southern; and some varieties are believed to be much richer in sugar, and probably albumen than others.

288. The cob, also, when divested of grain, contains a notable amount of nutriment. Most animals will eat it when soft, but refuse it when hard. Mr. Ellsworth had cobs crushed and ground, and kept his store hogs and other stock through the

winter upon the meal. The cob is often crushed and ground with the corn when intended for fattening animals, and produces a good effect mechanically as well as nutritiously. Oxen, however, are supposed to suffer from the fibres collecting in and obstructing the intestines.

289. Green corn stalks afford a saccharine juice which can be crystallized into sugar. Many experiments were made in this direction a few years ago, but the cost was found too great to compete with cane sugar. The time, however, may come when this manufacture will prove profitable, as that of Beet sugar is at present in France.

290. Corn is frequently sown broadcast to be cut green for *soiling*, when the grain becomes of secondary importance.

291. Corn may be made to grow, with manure and skilful cultivation, upon almost any kind of soil, but the land peculiarly adapted to it is that which contains a large per centage of vegetable matter, is fine, friable, warm, deep, and sufficiently supplied with moisture by evaporation. Prairies, and diluvial deposites along rivers, may be called the natural habitat of corn. It will grow where wheat prospers, but wheat will frequently not mature profitably in the best corn lands.

The following is an analysis of a rich corn-bearing soil in Ohio, occasionally overflowed by the Scioto River. It has been cultivated fifty-one years; and has borne forty-five crops of corn, and two or three of wheat, and been a few years in grass or clover. With the most ordinary culture it yields 80 bushels of corn to the acre. (*D. A. Wells.*)

I. Constituents soluble in pure water:

| | | |
|---|---|---|
| Total percentage 0.190 | Extract of earth, alkaline, chlorids, &c., | 0.032 |
| | Organic matter, crenic acid, | 0.010 |
| | Iron, lime and silica, | 0.012 |

II. Constituents soluble in dilute acid:

| | | |
|---|---|---|
| Total acid extract 5.011 | Iron, alumina, and manganese, | 2.760 |
| | Organic matter, combined with the above, | 0.860 |
| | Silica, | 0.560 |
| | Lime, | 0.390 |
| | Magnesia, | 0.280 |
| | Phosphoric acid, | traces. |
| | Potash and soda, | 0.161 |

| | |
|---|---|
| Organic matter rendered soluble by ammonia, - - | 3.140 |
| " " " " " - - - | 1.030 |
| " " remaining with insoluble residue, - - | 1.720 |
| Insoluble silicates, - - - - - - | 83.010 |

100 parts of the insoluble residue gave 59 parts silicious, and 41 parts clayey matter.

| | |
|---|---|
| Water, hygroscopic and combined, - - - | 3.500 |
| Resinous and waxy matter, - - - - - | .036 |

The most striking fact in connection with these soils is the exceeding fineness of their particles.

A deep rich mellow soil, in which the roots can freely extend a great distance in depth and laterally; and where, owing to the fineness of the soil, they will not be injured by drought, nor hidden from the heat of the sun, and from atmospheric influence, is what the corn grower should provide for this crop. A compact clay which excludes alike air, water, and rapid growth of roots, forbidding all chemical changes, is not the soil for corn. As it grows rapidly it requires a constant supply of food, and this can only be attained where there is water enough to act as a solvent to the solids. As will have been observed in the inorganic analyses, the per centage of ash in corn is comparatively small, organic matter and water forming the great mass of the tissue.

292. A great variety of manures are applied to this crop according to the requirements of the soil. Organic manures,—barn-yard dung and such like—are those which will most generally prove serviceable; and next to these, decayed vegetable matter. In consequence, corn is found to succeed well on grass or clover sod. Of the inorganic manures, dissolved bones, unleached wood ashes, salt, and plaster, promise to do good, *if* the soil is deficient in these elements.

293. When corn is planted on sod, *(a,)* spread manure on the grass; *(b,)* plow deep, laying the furrow flat; *(c,)* roll, and *(d,)* harrow with a long sharp toothed harrow, or a cultivator, till the surface is rendered friable two or three inches or more,

deep; both of these processes being lengthwise of the furrow; *(e,)* spread compost, or well decayed dung, and harrow it in again. If corn is to be planted on stubble, one plowing, and a thorough harrowing, with the same application of manure, is all that is requisite.

294. Corn is planted, *(a,)* by hand with a hoe, or *(b,)* by a drill, either *(c,)* in hills, or *(d,)* rows; and these latter either *(e,)* equal or *(f,)* alternate. If by hand, the lines are laid out by *(g,)* a light plow drawing a shallow furrow both ways across the field, so as to divide it into squares, at the proper distance, or *(h,)* by a *corn marker*, a coarse implement made somewhat similar to the form of a hay rake, with the teeth or pins at the distance apart proper for the corn; the whole being drawn by a horse; *(i,)* the drill will plant either in hills or rows. The usual distance apart for hills is three to five feet each way, according to the size of the corn; for rows three to four feet, and the plants nine to twelve inches apart in the row.

The amount per acre of the crop depends much on the mode of planting. In a favorable soil it rarely happens that each original stalk does not produce one ear; allowing these ears to produce in shelled corn one gill each, the amount produced per acre by different methods of planting will be as follows,—four stalks being allowed to each hill when planted in that form:

One acre in hills 4 feet apart, gives 2,722 hills or 10,885 stalks.
" " " 3 " " " 4,840 " 19,360 "
" " " 3 ft. by 2½ ft. " 5,808 " 82,232 "
" " in drills 3 ft. and 6 inches for plants, - 29,040 "
" " in double drills thus:

*      *      *      *      *      *

*      *      *      *      *      *      *

6 inches apart, the plants 9 inches in the rows, and 3 feet 9 inches from the centre of the drills would have 30,970 stalks. An acre planted 3 rows in a drill thus:

*      *      *      *      *      *      *

*      *      *      *      *      *

*      *      *      *      *      *      *

rows 6 inches apart, and the plants 9 inches in the rows, with a distance of 3 feet from the centre of the drills would have 43,560 stalks, or 170 bushels; while the hills, 4 feet by 4 feet, could only give 42 bushels. A crop of 170 bushels to the acre was actually raised, some years since, in Madison county, New York, on the three row system.

295. The proper depth at which to plant the corn is about 1 inch to 1½ inches.

The following experiment was made by Burger, in Germany:

Indian corn which was planted at the depth of

No. 1, 1 inch, came up in 8½ days.
No. 2, 1½ inches, came up in 9½ days.
No. 3, 2 inches, came up in 10 days.
No. 4, 2½ inches, came up in 11½ days.
No. 5, 3 inches, came up in 12 days.
No. 6, 3½ inches, came up in 13 days.
No. 7, 4 inches, came up in 13½ days.
No. 8, 4½ inches, came up in — days.
No. 9, 5 inches, came up in — days.
No. 10, 5½ inches, came up in 17½ days.
No. 11, 6 inches, came up in — days.

Nos. 8, 9, and 11, were dug up after 22 days, when it was found that No. 8, had an inch more to grow to reach the surface. Nos. 8, and 11, had just sprouted but were short, and 3 inches below the surface. No. 10, came up in 17½ days, but withered after 6 days growth. The more shallow the seed was covered by the earth, the more rapidly the sprout made its appearance, *and the stronger, afterwards, was the stalk.*

Corn will not germinate unless the temperature of the soil attains to 55° Fahr., and at a temperature higher than 110° it equally refuses to vegetate.

"Much of the damage which is supposed to arise from planting in the 'wrong time of the moon,' is really due to planting when the soil is at the wrong temperature, and if the time ever arrives when the average crop of the country is equal to what our premium crops now are, it must be when every farmer owns a thermometer and knows how to use it." (*J.S. Gould.*)

An experiment was made in Connecticut in 1844 to plant corn three inches deep. It came up and grew well until it was three or four inches high, and then stopped for a fortnight, while the same corn planted at a less depth grew rapidly. On examination it was found that a joint had been formed about an inch and half above the kernel, and that the roots had sprouted out from the joint *leaving all below to perish.* While the process of changing roots was going on the plant ceased to grow above ground, but in about a fortnight recovered its vigor; and it was about that length of time later in maturing the grain, than the seeds which were planted shallower.

296. The following table will show the quantity of seed, required, on an average, to plant an acre in hills.

| Distances of the hills apart. | Quantity required 4 grains to a hill. QUARTS. | Quantity required 5 grains to a hill. QUARTS. |
|---|---|---|
| 3 feet by 2 feet, | 14.52 | 18.15 |
| 3 " by 3 " | 9.68 | 12 10 |
| 3½ " by 3 " | 8.30 | 10 37 |
| 3½ " by 3½ " | 7.11 | 8.89 |
| 4 " by 3 " | 7.26 | 9 08 |
| 4 " by 3½ " | 6.22 | 7.78 |
| 4 " by 4 " | 5.44 | 6.80 |

297. The culture of the corn after it is above ground varies much. While some put a small quantity of ashes and plaster in the hill at planting, others wait until the corn is a few inches high. It will only be necessary shortly to state the various processes which are then pursued; *(a,)* hoe, plow both ways, throwing the earth into hills round the corn, hoe and plow again; *(b,)* hoe and plow, as above, but keep the earth level, and not raised, around the roots; *(c,)* hoe, but avoid plowing or hilling, cutting up the weeds, and rendering the surface friable with the cultivator. It is quite necessary that weeds should not be allowed to grow, and that the earth should be frequently stirred; but whether deep plowing, or the use of the hoe and cultivator alone are best is a disputed point; and probably depends on the nature and richness of the soil.

These directions only apply to the Northern and Atlantic States. In the rich Western Prairies and river bottoms, corn culture is a much more simple process.

298. It is a custom with some to plant corn five to eight feet apart in rows, and in the fall to plow between them, and sow wheat. As a system of rotation, this mode appears to possess peculiar advantages. For particulars, see *Mr. Bartlett's* letter in the *Farmer's Companion and Horticultural Gazette*, November, 1853. Pumpkins are generally planted in each alternate hill or row. In Virginia, peas are sown between the rows after the last hoeing, to be afterwards eaten off by hogs. In a similar manner clover is sown in New Jersey.

299. It is also customary to steep corn before planting to *(a,)* prevent birds and insects from injuring it; *(b,)* to act as a manure. For the first purpose soak the corn a few hours in warm water, and then mix it with tar thrown into water sufficiently hot to melt it. Each grain will be thinly coated with tar. Dry with plaster or ashes. For the second, use a weak solution of saltpetre, or salammoniac, *(Muriate of ammonia,)* 1 lb. to 4½ bushels, or 1 oz. to a quart of grain—mixed in warm water, and poured over, to remain upon the corn for 18 hours before planting. The corn sprouts with a rich green color, and grows rapidly, but whether it finally increases the crop is still disputed.

300. To grow corn broadcast for fodder, rich clean land is required. It is prepared with one plowing, is slightly harrowed, and the corn sown at the rate of 3 to 4 bushels to the acre. It is then harrowed in and rolled. It is sometimes planted in drills, and worked with the cultivator.

301. The best time for harvesting, or cutting the corn is when the grain is *glazed*, but not yet perfectly hard, and the stalks still partially green.

302. Previous to this process, and at the time when the ears

but not the grains were fully formed, it used to be the custom to *top the corn, i. e.*, cut off the stalks and leaves above the highest ears; but this is now generally abandoned. Truer views of the physiology of vegetation have taught that the leaves are necessary for the elaboration of the sap which forms the grain; and careful experiments proved that when the plant was thus deprived of part of its foliage, the grain was lighter and the ear not so well filled, although it might ripen a little earlier.

303. In the Southern States, it is customary to pluck the leaves of corn, dry them for fodder, and stack them, leaving the stalks standing in the field, to be afterwards eaten by stock, or plowed in. As this is generally done before the grain is formed, the same injurious results follow as in topping.

The following experiment was tried in South Carolina in 1846. Twelve rows of corn, as nearly equal in appearance as could be found, were selected. Nos. 1, 4, 7, 10, (A,) were left with the leaves on, until they were generally dry as high as the ear, and, on some stalks to the top. They were then cut up at the roots; shocked on the field until the other grain was gathered in; they were then hauled in and husked from the stalk. Nos. 2, 5, 8, 11, (B,) were left with the blades on until quite ripe. Nos. 3, 6, 9, 12, (C,) were stripped of their blades before ripening, but as late as usual. The results were as follows:

| | | | | | | | | |
|---|---|---|---|---|---|---|---|---|
| A, | when shelled, | measured | 4 pecks, | 1 gallon, | 2 quarts, | 1 pint, | weighed | 70½ lbs. |
| B, | " | " | 4 " | 1 " | 2 " | 1½ " | " | 71½ lbs |
| C, | " | " | 4 " | 0 " | 0 " | ½ " | " | 55 lbs |

The fodder, taken from the last, weighed 18 lbs., which added to the weight of the corn is 73 lbs.—1 1-2 lbs. more than the corn alone from which no leaves were taken. It thus appears that this process deprives the corn of nearly the weight of the fodder when cured, without reckoning the time also consumed in taking the leaves off.

304. Corn is harvested by cutting close to the ground, with a heavy knife manufactured for the purpose, or part of a scythe blade, fixed to a handled of some sort. Several hills are laid together, and bound with a corn stalk; with straw rope; or other cheap band. These bundles, to the number of 4 to 8, are then tied around the stalks of a hill left standing for the purpose.

There are various modifications of this process, but all on the same principle. The corn thus stands, until the leaves, stalks, and ears are dry; in the north, till after the first strong frost, the effect of which is to expel the remaining water.

Then the bundles are opened, and the ears of each stalk separated from the husk, thrown into baskets, and removed by wagon to the corn crib. The workman holds in his hand a short, sharp, piece of wood, generally attached by a string to the wrist, to facilitate the opening of the husk. The husks should remain attached to the stalk; and not be torn off as is too often done. The stalks are then again tied up, and left in the field till it is convenient to haul them to the barn, or stack them. When stacked out of doors great care must be taken that the rain does not get in, otherwise rot will rapidly ensue.

305. When sown broadcast, the stalks are usually cut while green, and fed to stock in stables. If retained till winter they may be cut, bound, and stacked as above. A little salt scattered among the stalks in stacking will be found useful to prevent moulding, and cause the animals to eat them more perfectly.

In 1845 over 31 tons of green corn stalks were raised to the acre in Massachusetts. The product of two acres 32 rods, fed 20 cows, 1 heifer, 2 bulls, and 5 spring calves for 7 weeks and 5 days; the *dried* produce off the same acre being estimated as equal to 15 tons of the best "Engligh" hay. This production, however, is much greater than what is generally obtained. Ten bushels of "white flat Maryland corn" were sown on the 2 32-160 acres. Corn is sometimes sown broadcast for the purpose of plowing it in as a manure for wheat.

306. Corn is seperated from the cob by (*a*,) thrashing with a flail; (*b*,) treading with horses; (*c*,) a machine called a *corn-sheller*, of which there are several sorts, some moved by hand, others by horse power. If required to be very clean the corn is then passed through a fanning mill.

The following is a rule for finding the quantity of corn, shelled or in ear, in a house of any dimensions. Having previously levelled the corn in the house, so that it will be of equal depth throughout, ascertain the length, breadth, and depth of the bulk; multiply these dimensions together; and their product by 4; then cut off one figure from the right hand of this last product. This gives the bushels, and decimal of a bushel of *shelled* corn. If corn *in the ear*, substitute 8 for 4, and cut off one figure as before.

EXAMPLE :—

| | |
|---:|---|
| 12 | feet long. |
| 11 | feet broad. |
| 132 | |
| 6 | feet deep. |
| 792 | |
| 4 | multiple for shelled corn. |
| 316.8 | bushels in house. |

When 8 is used as a multiple to find the quantity of corn in the ear, it is on the ground of 2 bushels of such making 1 of shelled grain.

There are other rules given for the same purpose which do not agree with this, and it appears that the accuracy of this mode of measuring requires further testing.

307. It is very important that the best ears should be saved for seed; as corn rapidly degenerates or improves according to the seed planted. Careful farmers select the best ears while husking; leave part of the husk attached to them; plait them together; and hang them up in a dry room. Corn not perfectly ripened or dried, *heats* when thrown together in large quantities, and the germinative power is lost. Two years ago, owing to early frosts, the corn in Michigan was imperfectly dried; and, in the spring, corn taken from the crib very generally failed to grow; while, preserved in the house, as above recommended, it is said no failures occurred. The loss of labor and time, and of the crop in consequence, was estimated at many thousand dollars in this one State alone. It is found advisable to change the seed every few years, procuring the new from a location further north, and from a different soil.

308. In the southern, and middle western States, it is customary to turn hogs and cattle into the field of standing corn, but this is a very

wasteful proceeding, unless labor is very costly. In south Ohio, the corn is cut and tied in bundles, and daily hauled to a small field, where stalks, grain, leaves, &c., are thrown on the ground for the fattening cattle to eat. The next day, these are removed to a second field, and their place is taken by a drove of hogs, which pick up what the cattle have wasted or refused. Thus, the two are fed alternately in different fields; and the swine fattened at comparatively little cost.

309. If the cobs are not ground for feed, they should be mixed with animal manures in a state of fermentation, when they will gradually decay. They contain many valuable elements of manure. They are occasionally used for smoking hams, and some other minor domestic purposes.

310. There are no weeds peculiar to this crop. Indeed a skilful farmer will not allow a solitary weed to grow among his corn; and thence it is an excellent crop for cleaning foul land.

311. Corn is subject to the growth of a very peculiar and destructive fungus or *Brand.*

Maize Brand (*Uredo maydis.* De Candolle,) attacks all the parenchymatous organs of the corn plant, and more or less completely destroys them. The stalk, however, the female, and the male blossoms, are the parts which it most especially affects. Its development is a peculiar one, as it forces out great masses of cellular tissue, formed from the tissue of the mother plant, and similar in formation to the latter. Some parts of the organs affected by the brand swell and become white. This species always impairs some blossoms, as soon as it is seated in the ear, while the other blossoms standing near bear good ripe kernels. The brand bladders can be very easily removed from the living plants by cutting them out, only this must be done as soon as possible, in order that in cutting them out the bladders may not scatter their powder, and thus a future crop of brand not be prevented. For seed only, kernels should be selected from plants which have remained wholly free from the brand. This fungus is, by the structure of its spores, different from all others, and only related to the wheat brand. Corn in rich, *damp* loam appears more subject to this disease than in any other situation, and draining would probably prove an effectual cure. (*See Trans. of N. Y. Agricul. Socy., vol.* viii., p. 842.)

In the *Patent Office Report* for 1847, a description of a disease which appeared in Maryland is given, and which we suspect to be another species of brand.

"The cap of the injured ear is discolored, and when opened a few grains near the apex of the ear, and one side of it, mark the commencement of the disease in their sickly and shrivelled appearance; this increases in space and intensity until the whole ear exhibits a deadly and gangreneous mass of black, rotten grains, while the whole plant on which it grows is erect, and of the most healthy and vigorous appearance." It did much injury to the crop.

312. The insects most injurious to the corn are:

(*A.*) *Cut-worms*. These are thick, greasy-looking caterpillars, from one to two inches in length, of a dark ashen grey color, with a brown head, a pale stripe along the back, and several minute black dots on each ring. They are the grub of a species of moth, belonging to a group called by Dr. Harris *Agrotidians*; and there are many species in the United States, each species *probably* confining itself to a particular family of plants, as one to the cabbage, another to grasses and grains, The moths fly by night, appearing in July and August. They lay their eggs either in the ground, or on the roots of plants in the autumn, and these are hatched in the spring, the Cut-worm being produced. These feed on plants, concealing themselves in holes in the ground during day, and appearing only at night. During the summer they become chrysalids; remain in that state about four weeks; and the moth again appears in the fall. The corn Cut-worm, is probably the *Agrostis messoria* of Harris. They feed only on the sprouts and young stalks and do not eat the seeds of plants.

(*B.*) *Wire-worm*, or *Iulus*, a hard, worm-like form, with the skin seperated into compartments or rings. It is not a true *Insect* as it undergoes no transformation; and belongs to the class *Myriapodia*, a name derived from the great number of feet with which most of the animals included in it are furnished. There are several species.

(*C.*) *Wire-worm*. In some localities, especially in new lands, and on plowing up old grass fields, another insect known by this name proves very injurious to young corn. They are long, slender, worm-like grubs nearly cylindrical, with a hard and smooth skin, of a buff or brownish yellow color, the head and tail only being a little darker; each of the first three rings are provided with a pair of short legs; underneath the last ring is a short retractile wart, or prop leg. These are the grub of a species of Beetle, the *Elaters* or Spring beetles, well known in this shape by the faculty they possess of throwing themselves upwards with a jerk, when laid on their backs. There are many species, some of which appear to be confined to rotten wood. It is believed that they remain in their feeding or larva state not less than five years, before changing into beetles. The grubs injure corn both by eating the grain when first sown, and also by cutting off the young plant just *below* the ground, as the Cut-worm eats *above* the surface.

(*D.*) *Spindle-worm.* This is the caterpillar of a moth (*Gortyna Zeæ,*) and is well known as destroying the *spindle* of corn. Its ravages, however, generally begin while the cornstalk is young, and before the spindle rises much above the tuft of leaves in which it is embosomed. The mischief is discovered by the withering of the leaves, and when these are taken hold of, they may often be drawn out with the included spindle. On examining the corn, a small hole may be seen in the side of the leafy stalk, near the ground, penetrating into the soft centre of the stalk, which when cut open will be found to be perforated, both upwards and downwards, by a slender worm-like caterpillar, whose excrementious castings surround the orifice of the hole. The grub grows to over an inch in length, and to the thickness of a goose quill. The chrysalis is lodged in the burrow formed by it; it is of a shining mahogany brown.

(*E.*) The grub of the *May-beetles,* (*Dor-bug, Cock-chafer, Anomala,*) injures corn by eating the roots. It is a white, thick, smooth skinned semipellucid-worm, with a brownish head, and when fully grown nearly half an inch in diameter. It is frequently thrown out of the ground in digging or plowing. When in a state of rest, it usually curls itself up in the shape of a crescent. It is supposed that it occupies from three to five years in the grub state, before changing.

(*F.*) *The Granary Weevil.* (*Fly Weevil—Grain moth—Angoumois moth,*) *Butalis cerealella,*) which is so destructive to stored wheat, is also injurious to corn in some localities, when it is kept unprotected more than six or eight months. (See §202.)

(*G.*) *The true Grain Weevil.* (*Curculio granarius,*) also attacks stored corn. (See § .)

(*H.*) The Grain moth (*Tinea granella,*) also feeds on corn under similar circumstances.

(*I.*) *Corn Weevil* (*Silvanus Surinamensis,*) is very commonly found among stored corn, as well as in other grains, and in sugar. It also infests mills. It is said that Sassafras Root, mixed with the grain, drives them away. *(For a very full description and a plate of this, and Calandra granaria, see N. Y. Trans. of Agricul. Society,* vol. viii., p. 656.)

313. A great variety of preventives have been tried, but only a few appear to be worthy of use. Salt, perhaps, is the most generally successful against such grubs as live in the ground: Two to four bushels per acre of fine salt being sown broadcast, and slightly harrowed in, a few days before planting. If the corn is to be planted on sod, fall plowing—late in the season—will affect some good; also steeping the grain in saline and ammonical liquors; and tarring. It has been recommended, and practised with success, to hang the seed corn in the smoke house, and smoke it with the hams: the pyroligneous acid appears to be offensive to insects and birds, while it does no injury to the grain. For insects injuring the ripe corn when stored, abundance of air, and thorough ventilation are the best preventives. A barrel, impregnated with tar, it is said will drive away the True Grain Weevil, (*C. granarius*,) (*g*,) if it is placed in the granary. It is thus employed in France. The farmer will find much profit in cherishing birds; even the red-winged Black Bird, (*Agelaius phœniceœus*,) and Crow Black Birds, (*Quiscalus versicolor* and *ferrugineus*,)—on his farm; for though they destroy some grain, it is but a choice of two evils; it being always found that where birds are driven away the loss by insects becomes extreme. A single pair of Crow Black birds will, in one season, destroy thousands of injurious grubs.

The whole subject of insects injurious to vegetation in America, still requires much study and persevering observation; and notwithstanding Dr. Harris' labors, there is yet much of practical importance to learn regarding it. We believe that the day will come when means will be discovered of preventing these ravages; but before this can take place, not only must the habits of the insects themselves, but also the peculiarities of the plants and soil be much better understood than at present. Many facts would lead us to believe, that an impoverishment of the soil is necessary before insects can become seriously injurious, as it is certainly connected with diseases of vegetation.

314. Many of the European physiologists, have for a length of time

been endeavoring to decide the question whether grains will germinate before they are fully ripe? The last writer on the subject, M. Duchartre, Professor of Botany in the Agronomic Institution of Versailles, has made many very complete experiments, with satisfactory results. We are only able to give here a summary of the truths he arrived at.

1. The grains of the cereals are able to germinate, if harvested at least twenty to twenty-five days before maturity, or complete ripeness, although the germ is yet very imperfect.

2. Such seeds require a longer time to sprout than those quite ripe, if sown immediately without drying.

3. The same proportionate number of seeds will grow in both cases, with the exception, perhaps, of barley.

4. Seeds imperfectly ripened germinate much more surely if they are well dried before sowing. In this case they sprout as soon as perfectly ripe seeds. It would appear that seeds harvested in an unripe state are able to mature themselves if kept for some time,—the embryo being nourished and developed at the expense of the moisture and albumen.

5. In practice, there need be no fear as regards sowing seeds of the cereals cut a long time before maturity, but the threshing should be deferred as long as possible.

6. Where the crop is large and laborers scarce, the harvest may be commenced much earlier than is usual, without any fear of injuring the grain.

7. The plants grown from seeds gathered twenty-five days before ripening, and allowed to dry for seven weeks, so far from being weak and inferior, were remarkable for their vigor, and on the whole no difference in this respect could be perceived in favor of well ripened grain. It would be well to make a series of similar experiments in America, as practically, it is a very important subject.

# CHAPTER XI.

## RICE.—BUCKWHEAT.—MILLET.—CANARY GRASS.

315. Rice has been known and cultivated from the earliest periods, and furnishes food to a large portion of the human family. Its native country is unknown.

316. There are two varieties, (*a*,) Common Rice; (*Oryza sativa*) and (*b*,) Cochin China, Dry, Upland, or Mountain Rice; with several subvarieties, as *Long Grain and Small Grain*, &c.

317. The first (*a*,) is cultivated in marshes; and, for a great part of its growth, is partially under water. It requires a warm climate. On the Eastern continent it matures as high as the 45th parallel of north lat. and as far south as the 38th. On the Atlantic side of the Western continent, as far north and south as 38° of lat. On the western coast as far north as 40° or more. It is cultivated in India, China, the Indian Archipelago, Eastern Africa, South of Europe, southern portion of the United States, and in parts of South America. It was introduced into Virginia in 1647, and into Louisiana in 1718. According to Boussingault it requires a minimum temperature of 75° F.

318. The second variety (*b*,) grows on mountains and dry soils; several degrees further north and south than the first. It is found high on the range of the Himalayan Mountains, and is cultivated in the northern provinces of China, in Hungary, Westphalia, Virginia, Maryland, Illinois, Missouri, &c. It was introduced into Charleston, S. C., from Canton, in 1772.

319. The States in which Rice is chiefly cultivated are

| | 1840. | 1850. |
|---|---|---|
| South Carolina, - | 60,590,861 lbs. | 159,930,613 lbs. |
| Georgia, - - | 12,384,732 " | 38,950,691 " |
| Louisiana, - | 3,604,534 " | 4,425,349 " |
| North Carolina, | 2,820,388 " | 5,465,868 " |
| Mississippi, - - | 777,195 " | 2,719,856 " |

Besides Virginia, Florida, Alabama, Texas, Arkansas, Tennessee, Kentucky, Missouri (700 lbs.) and Iowa (500 lbs.) The total crop of the United States was, 1840, 80,841,422 lbs; 1850, 215,312,710 lbs. The rice grown in South Carolina is considered the finest in the world, having much improved in quality in that State.

320. The *Wild Rice,* of the North Western Lakes, which is gathered and eaten by the Indians, belongs to a different botanical family, and is known as *Zizania aquatica.* It is not cultivated. The *Patent Office Report,* 1846,.p 289, mentions a grain by the name of *Hungry Rice,* cultivated at Sierra Leone, Africa, as worthy of introduction into this country ; but it is probably a species of *Millet,* and not a true Rice.

321. Unhusked rice consists of: (*Johnston.*)

| | |
|---|---|
| Husk, - - - - - - | 20.91 |
| Grain, - - - - - - - | 79.09 |

Carolina Rice, (A,) and Rice Flour (B,) gave:

| | A. | B. |
|---|---|---|
| Water, - - - - - - | 13.0 | 14.6 |
| Ash, - - - - - | 0.33 | 0.35 |

322. Considering a rice plant in its dry mature state to weigh 100 grains, the mineral matter in the different parts of the plant are as follows: (*Shepard.*)

| | |
|---|---|
| In the stubble and root, - - - - | 36.08 |
| Straw and leaves, - - - - - | 36.08 |
| Husk, - - - - - - | 14.20 |
| Cotyledon and Epidermis, - - - | 11.70 |
| Clean rice, - - - - - - | 1.94 |
| | 100.00 |

323. Dry rice contains: (*Payen.*)

| | |
|---|---|
| Starch, - - - - - - | 86.9 |
| Gluten, &c., - - - - - - | 7.5 |

| | |
|---|---|
| Fatty matter, | 0.8 |
| Sugar and Gum, | 0.5 |
| Epidermis, | 3.4 |
| Saline matter, (*ash*) | 0.9 |

Rice contains less fatty matter than any other grain, and the greater portion of the fat is contained in the outer coats. Johnston found in the siftings or cleanings of rice, from 5 to 5½ per cent. of fatty matter.

324. Inorganic analyses of Rice grain (A,) and husk (B.) (*Johnston.*)

| | A | B |
|---|---|---|
| Potash, | 18.48 | 1.60 |
| Soda, | 10.67 | 1.58 |
| Magnesia, | 11.69 | 1.96 |
| Lime, | 1.27 | 1.01 |
| Phosphoric acid, | 53.36 | 1.86 |
| Sulphuric acid, | —— | 0.92 |
| Silica, | 3.35 | 89.71 |
| Peroxide of iron, | 0.45 | 0.54 |

Varieties of rice from India give a much larger per centage of ash than those grown in the United States. This grain is probably less nutritious than any other ordinarily used by man; as it contains a comparatively small proportion of glutinous or nitrogenous matter.

325. The soil adapted for the common rice is of a marshy and wet character, containing much organic matter, which can be overflowed or drained when requisite; but it will grow (though less profitably) on light, moist uplands without irrigation, when cultivated with the hoe or plow. On wet lands, the embankments and ditches being prepared, the soil is well plowed, the seed sown at the rate of 1¾ io 2¼ bushels per acre, and harrowed in with a light harrow, thickly set with teeth. In South Carolina, from April to May, is the usual season. Immediately after, the water is let on, so as barely to overflow the ground. As soon as the grain begins to swell, the water is withdrawn. When the plant is three inches high, the water is

again let on, leaving the top leaves a little above it. A fortnight before harvest, the water is finally drawn off.

326. Rough rice, while the husk is still attached, is called *Paddy*; and large quantities are exported in this condition. A peculiar mill is required for cleaning the husk from the grain, and in this process large amounts of "Rice flour" are formed. The "flour," the chaff, and the straw are used as manure for this crop, and are deemed among the very best. The chaff is spread even over the surface, about three inches deep, and plowed in. The straw can be safely used when the field is fallowed. It is then put on the land thick, and bedded in. Prof. Shepard says "The planter who sells his crop in the condition of *Rough Rice*, robs his land of 27.84 per cent of the mineral ingredients of this species of produce, while on the other hand, he who sells it as clean rice, abstracts from them but 2 per cent. of these ingredients."

327. The Upland Rice is sown in April and is ripe in September. The usual method is to sow it in drills about 18 inches apart; but if the land is well prepared and clean, it may be sown broadcast.

328. The yield of an average crop of common rice in South Carolina is about 40 bushels per acre, while a good crop will give as high as 55 bushels. We find the product of 16 acres thus described when prepared for market:

Rough rice, 376 bushels, give of

| | |
|---|---|
| Clean rice, - - - - - | 10,754 lbs. |
| Small rice, - - - - - | 16¼ bushels. |
| Flour, - - - - - | 31 " |

The Upland Rice yields from 25 to 30 bushels an acre.

329. Rice is measured by the Barrel of 600 lbs, and by the Tierce.

330. This grain is eaten boiled in its clean state; it is ground into flour; and starch is made from it. Manufactured on a large scale, Patna rice yields 80 per cent of *marketable* starch;

8.2 per cent. of fibrous starch granules; and 11.8 per cent. of gluten, bran, and a small quantity of light starch. In India, a fermented intoxicating liquor called *arrack* is prepared from it. When damaged, it is occasionally used for feeding hogs and fowls, and though deficient in oil, the large amount of starch which it contains enables it to fatten. The refuse from rice-mills is probably more fattening than the clean grain.

331. Microscopic examination of the soil of rice fields shows it to be filled with minute animal forms and shells capable of supplying a large amount of phosphoric acid, the chief inorganic ingredient of this grain.

332. BUCKWHEAT (derived from the German *Buchweitzen* "Beech-wheat," from the resemblance of the seeds to the Beech mast) is not properly a *grain*, but belongs to the family of *knotweeds*, of which there are twenty species in the Northern United States. It is probably a native of China. There are three cultivated species; (*a*,) Common Buckwheat, *Polygonum Fagopyrum;* (*b*,) Tartarian Buckwheat, *P. tataricum*, and (*c*,) Notch-seeded Buckwheat, *P. emarginatum*. There do not appear to be any varieties.

In the *Trans. N. Y. State Agricultural Society*, 1848, p. 572, mention is made of a *Blue Buckwheat*, grown in Sullivan county. Its peculiarities are, 1. It is less injured by the sun. 2. Can be sown earlier. 3. Weighs heavier ; and 4. Makes from 3 to 5 lbs. per bushel more flour of a better quality, than common buckwheat. The flour sold for 25 cents per 100 lbs. more in the New York Market. In one instance it yielded 41 bushels per acre. Whether this is a variety, or one of the above mentioned, we are unable to decide.

The first is chiefly cultivated in America, the second in Italy, the last in China. In Europe it is grown for food from Russia to Italy, Great Britain excepted; and being a very short time in the ground, can be adapted to great differences of climate. In the United States it can be grown in every section, but is chiefly cultivated north of North Carolina and Tennessee. The total crop in 1840, was 7,291,743 bushels, and in 1850, 8,956,916; New York (3,183,955 bushels) and Pennsylvania

(2,193,692 bushels) being the largest producers. Michigan is the fifth largest, giving 472,917 bushels, being only inferior to Ohio and New Jersey. It has probably been grown in America about 150 years.

333. Organic analyses of Buckwheat flour from Vienna (A,) and Tartarian Buckwheat from Hohenheim (B.) (*Horsford and Krocker.*)

| | A | B |
|---|---|---|
| Gluten and Albumen, | 6.88 | 9.94 |
| Starch, | 65.05 | 44.12 |
| Woody fibre, Gum, Sugar, | 26 47 | 46.26 |
| Ash, | 1.09 | 2.30 |
| Moisture in fresh substance, | 15.12 | 14.19 |

334. Inorganic analyses of Buckwheat from Cleves (*Bichon*) (A,) and New York. (*Salisbury.*) (B,)

| | A | | B |
|---|---|---|---|
| Chlorine, | —— | | 0.20 |
| Potash, | 8.74 | | 23.33 |
| Soda, | 20.10 | | 2.04 |
| Lime, | 6.66 | | 0.14 |
| Magnesia, | 10.38 | | 2.66 |
| Oxide of iron, | 1.05 | | |
| Phosphoric acid, | 50.07 | Earthy phosphates, | 57.60 |
| Silica, | 0.69 | | 7.06 |
| Sulphuric acid, | 2.16 | | 7.30 |

There exists a striking identity in the composition of buckwheat and rye. In the seeds of the former there is 27 per cent. of husk. The 73 per cent. of flour, closely resembling that of rye in color and properties, contains 10½ of gluten, and 52 of ordinary starch. The greatest resemblance also exists in the constitution of the ash when both plants have been grown on the same soil. The dried grain of rye contained 2.4 per cent., that of buckwheat 2.1 per cent. of ash.

335. Boussingault gives the following as contained in the grain (A,) and straw (B,)

| | A | B |
|---|---|---|
| Water per cent, | 12.5 | 11.6 |
| Nitrogen per cent. of dried, | 2.40 | 0.54 |
| " " not dried, | 2.10 | 0.48 |
| Ammonia dried, calculated from the nitrogen, | 2.94 | 0.65 |

336. Inorganic analysis of Buckwheat straw (*Sprengel*) 100,000 parts of the dry straw contained 3203 parts cf ash:

| | |
|---|---|
| Potash, | 332 |
| Soda, | 62 |
| Lime, | 704 |
| Magnesia, | 1292 |
| Alumina, | 26 |
| Oxide of iron, | 15 |
| Oxide of manganese, | 32 |
| Silica, | 140 |
| Chlorine, | 95 |
| Sulphuric acid, | 217 |
| Phosphoric acid, | 288 |
| | 3,203 |

337. An acre of 28 bushels, weighing 56 lbs. per bushel, gives of the grain, an average of

| | |
|---|---|
| Organic matter, | 1326 lbs. |
| Ash, | 22 " |
| Nitrogen, | 32 " |
| Phosphoric acid, | 11 " |

338. Proximate organic analysis of Buckwheat: (*Salisbury.*)

| | |
|---|---|
| Starch, | 42.47 |
| Sugar and extractive matter, | 6.16 |
| Dextrine and gum, | 1.60 |
| Epidermis, | 14.42 |
| A light gray matter insoluble in water and boiling alcohol, | 10.10 |
| Albumen, | 6.70 |
| Casein, | 0.78 |
| Matter dissolved out of the bodies insoluble in water, by boiling alcohol; rising with a substance analogous to water, | 2.66 |
| Oil, | 0.47 |
| Water, | 12.88 |
| | 98.24 |

339. Buckwheat is used as food for man and animals, and is decidedly nutritious. Its fattening qualities are found in practice to be higher than could be supposed from analysis; and the meat formed by it is of peculiarly fine quality. The outer husk being hard, this grain should always be ground or cooked before feeding.

340. The uncrushed grain, and the fresh straw produce a remarkable and hitherto unexplained effect upon swine. If allowed to feed in a newly harvested buckwheat field, the head and ears are attacked by an eruption, with apparently intense itching, while the animal presents all the symptoms of intoxication. In severe cases death ensues. So, likewise, the fresh grain fed whole in large quantities, disorders the bowels; but if ground or cooked, these symptoms are not observed. In the latter case the husk is passed by the animal entirely undigested. Further investigation is necessary to explain these phenomena.

341. The straw is harsh, and not relished by horned cattle; but horses will eat all except the coarsest parts, and keep in good condition upon this alone. Buckwheat straw, unthrashed, and cut up is excellent fodder for working horses. It must be kept in a dry place, as it readily absorbs moisture, ferments, and spoils. If boiled, the straw will form a thick jelly.

342. Buckwheat is frequently sown for the purpose of plowing in as a green manure to precede the wheat crop. Though not equal to clover, it is yet beneficial to lands deficient in organic matter. It should be turned under when beginning to blossom.

343. The lighter class of soils is supposed to be the best for this grain, but it will prosper on any except the heaviest. Generally, the land receives but one plowing, and a light harrowing; from 2 to 3 pecks of seed to the acre are sown broadcast, and then well harrowed in. In the latitude of Michigan, about the 20th June, is the best time to sow; but we have known good crops to succeed barley, when the frosts were late.

344. In harvesting, the best mode is to cradle it; rake it

into small bundles, which are fastened by merely twisting the tops; and let it stand till dry. If cut with a scythe and left upon the ground, the seed is apt to shell out; the straw dries slowly; and much sand and dirt adhere to the grain. It should be thrashed at once as it is drawn into the barn, otherwise it will again absorb moisture, and heat. The best mode of thrashing is with horses, a machine being apt to break the grains. It must be cut before the whole is fully ripe.

345. The crop varies from 10 to 30 or 40 bushels; 20 to 25 being probably the average. It appears to depend much upon the state of the weather when in the fullest blossom.

346. The legal weight of a bushel of buckwheat in Michigan is 42 lbs.

347. MILLET. Under this name five plants of differing genera, which are cultivated for their seeds, are comprehended. They are all true grasses.

*(A.)* Common Millet, *Panicum miliaceum.*

*(B.)* Indian or Grand Millet, *Sorghum vulgare.*

*(C.)* Guinea Corn, *Sorghum cernuum.*

*(D.)* Bengal Grass, or Italian Millet, *Setaria italica.*

*(E.)* German Millet, *Setaria germanica.*

The first (*a*,) is most generally grown in the United States; the others being rarely met with. The second and third (*b*) and (*c*,) belong to the same family as Broom corn, (*Sorghum saccaratum.*) In other countries they are used as food for men and animals, and the straw or stalks as fodder.

The Indian Millet (*b*,) furnishes the bread of the Arabians and other people of the East, as well as of those of Africa. It is also eaten in Italy, Spain, South of Germany, and the West Indies. It matures perfectly in the neighborhood of Detroit. In its mode of growth it resembles Indian corn, but the seeds are different. In this country it is scarcely worth cultivating except as a curiosity, as it requires the same labor as corn, while its produce is smaller, and of an inferior quality.

348. As an article of food the Common Millet *(a,)* is very similar to rice. It does not appear to have been perfectly analysed; but the following are given as the inorganic constituents of the grain grown at Giessen, Germany. (*Rolich.*)

| | |
|---|---|
| Potash, | 9.58 |
| Soda, | 1.31 |
| Magnesia, | 7.66 |
| Lime, | 0.86 |
| Phosphoric acid, | 18.19 |
| Sulphuric acid, | 0.35 |
| Silica, | 59.63 |
| Peroxide of iron, | 0.63 |
| Chloride of sodium, | 1.43 |

349. The soil required for this crop is dry, rich, and well pulverized, sandy, rather than clay. It should be deeply plowed, and well harrowed. If sown broadcast, half a bushel of seed is the proper quantity, but on rich ground a peck may prove sufficient. If drilled, 8 quarts of seed are enough. If intended as a fodder crop, more seed should be used, it being regulated in proportion to the richness and condition of the soil. It will do well on land that is too light for grass. The time for sowing in Michigan is from the 1st of May to the 1st of July, or even later if intended for soiling; June is the usual month in New York. After sowing, the field should be rolled. When intended for a grain crop, it must not be allowed to become entirely ripe, or much will be lost by shelling. It may be cradled and bound, or cut with a scythe and raked into bundles. In New York, as much as 2¾ tons of fodder, and 32½ bushels of seeds have been raised to the acre. As high as 60 to 80 bushels of seed per acre are said to have been produced. *(Allen.)* The usual crops are from 1 to 2 tons of straw, and 20 to 30 bushels of seed.

350. In the United States, Millet seed is never used for human food; but when ground into meal it is excellent for fattening animals. The chief use of Millet is to take the place

of hay when that is likely to fail; or to serve for soiling; for both which purposes it is admirably adapted. According to Boussingault, dry Millet straw contains 0.96 per cent. of nitrogen, and 147 lbs. of it are equal in nourishment to 100 lbs. of ordinary natural meadow hay. If intended for hay alone, it should be cut as soon as the head is formed, and treated like any other grass.

351. CANARY GRASS, (*Phalaris canariensis*) is rarely cultivated in the United States, and what is used among us for feeding tame birds (its only value) is chiefly imported. It is, however, well adapted for most parts of this country; and might, it is believed, be rendered profitable, if grown on a small scale. It is a native of the Canary Islands, but is now grown in the south of England, and other countries. It requires a rich, fine, loamy soil. The seeds are drilled about a foot a part, as early in spring as frosts will permit, at the rate of 4 to 5 gallons per acre. Afterwards, the space between the rows must be kept well worked with a shovel plow, or some similar implement, and perfectly free from weeds. It may be harvested, cured, and thrashed like any other grain. From 30 to 35 bushels per acre is the ordinary yield, and from that to 50 bushels per acre. The straw is rough and coarse, but may serve for winter fodder and bedding.

These are all the Cereal plants grown in the Northern United States for their seeds.

# CHAPTER XII.

## LEGUMINOUS PLANTS.—BEANS; PEAS; LENTILS; VETCHES; AND LUPINES.

352. This class of plants derives its name from the seeds producing *legumin*, a substance identical in composition with the *casein* (or cheese) of milk; corresponding with the *gluten* (or nitrogenous compound) of the cereals. It is formed of Oxygen, Hydrogen, Carbon, and Nitrogen, with Phosphate of Lime and Sulphur incorporated; but the exact quantities do not appear to be accurately ascertained. (*Carpenter.*)

353. Under this head several botanical genera are included, most of them natives of temperate climates; and there are many varieties produced by cultivation. The following may be enumerated as those chiefly used by man:

| | |
|---|---|
| (*A*,) Common or English bean, including Field beans, Sow, Horse, Garden beans, &c. | *Faba vulgaris* |
| (*B*,) Kidney beans, | *Phaseolus vulgaris.* |
| (*C*,) Lima beans, with several other species and varieties. | *Phaseolus lunatus.* |
| (*D*,) Common lentil, | *Ervum lens.* |
| (*E*,) Bastard lentil, | *Ervum Ervilia.* |
| (*F*,) One flowered lentil, | *Ervum monanthos.* |
| (*G*,) Chick pea, | *Cicer arietinum.** |
| (*H*,) Common pea, with several species and varieties. | *Pisum sativum.* |

* This long cultivated pea was found by Capt. Stansbury's party, growing wild in the Interior of Oregon, and in the valleys of the Utah, in sandy bottom land. (*Exploration*, p. 385.) It is a native of the South of Europe, and is grown in India under the name of *Gram*. It has always been supposed to require a hot climate.

*(I,)* Lupines, *Lupinus albus.*
*(J,)* Tare or vetch. *Vicia sativa.*
with several other species.
*(K,)* Broad bean, windsor bean, *Vicia faba.*

354. In the United States the cultivation of leguminous plants is chiefly confined to Kidney Beans *(b,)* and Peas *(h,)* some varieties of which prosper in every section of the country. In the census they are united together; and no account appears to have been taken of them before 1850. In that year the total crop was 9,219,975 bushels, or nearly double the quantity of barley grown. North Carolina produced the largest amount, viz: 1,584,252 bushels, while South Carolina, Georgia, and Mississippi, alone besides, produced each, over a million of bushels. The crop of Michigan was 74,254 bushels. In the Northern States, these crops may be considered as of inferior value.

355. As regards the analyses, it will be most convenient to class them all together; and we shall be obliged to depend chiefly on the labors of foreign chemists.

The following by Horsford and Krocker of Germany, and Thompson of Scotland are believed to be correct.

| | Table Pea, Vienna. | Field Pea, Giessen. | Table Bean, Vienna. | Large White Bean, Giessen. | Lentils, Vienna. | Sow Bean, Scotland |
|---|---|---|---|---|---|---|
| Vegetable casein & albumen | 28 02 | 29 18 | 28 54 | 29 31 | 30 46 | 29.43 |
| Starch, - - - | 38 81 | } 66.23 | 37.50 | } 66.17 | 40.00 | } 63.61 |
| Gum, - - - | 28 50 | | 29 20 | | 25.06 | |
| Ash, - - - | 3.18 | 2 79 | 4 38 | 4.01 | 2.60 | 3.96 |
| Skin, - - - | 7 65 | 6 11 | 4.11 | 4.41 | ? | ? |
| Moisture in the fresh seed. | 13 43 | 19.50 | 13 41 | 15.80 | 13.01 | 10.60 |

From this table it appears that the nutritious qualities of each species is very nearly the same. The flesh-forming constituents are large, and there is sufficient starch for all the purposes of life, but little or nothing to form fat. Other analyses give from 1.5 to 2.1 per cent. of oil or fatty matter in beans, and from 1.9

to 2.7 per cent. in peas, probably in or immediately beneath the skin.

356. Ultimate analyses of White Peas, *(A,)* and Pea Straw *(B,)* *(Boussingault)* raised on manured land, yielding 16 bushels per acre, weighing 62 lbs. per bushel. One part of peas, after complete drying, weighed 0.914; one part of dried peas left of ash 0.0314. Of the straw, the acre produced 22 or 23 cwts. (of 112 lbs.) One part of the straw, after drying, weighed 0.802; one part of this left of ash 0.1132. And Scotch Beans, dried at 212° *(C.)* *(Thompson.)*

| | A | | B | C |
|---|---|---|---|---|
| | I | II | | |
| Carbon, | 46.06 | 46 94 | 45.80 | 45.59 |
| Hydrogen, | 6 09 | 6 24 | 5 00 | |
| Oxygen, | 40 53 | 39 50 | 35 57 | |
| Nitrogen, | 4.18 | 4.18 | 2.31 | 4.61 |
| Ash, | 3.14 | 3 14 | 11.32 | 3 96 |

10.60 per cent. of water was expelled from the Beans in the process of drying.

357. Inorganic analyses of leguminous plants:

| | Will and Fresenius. | Bichon. | Bichon | Levi. | | Thompson. |
|---|---|---|---|---|---|---|
| | Pea. | Pea. | Sow Bean. | Bean. | Lentil. | Scotch Bean Meal. |
| Potash | 39.51 | 34 19 | 20.82 | 38 89 | 34.31 | 23.15 |
| Soda | 3.98 | 12.76 | 19.06 | 11 78 | 13 30 | 9.42 |
| Lime | 5.91 | 2 46 | 7 26 | 5 90 | 6 21 | 5 18 |
| Magnesia | 6.43 | 8.60 | 8 81 | 9.[illegible]3 | 2 41 | 9.03 |
| Oxide of iron | 1.05 | 0.96 | 1 03 | 0.11 | 1 98 | 1 80 |
| Phosphoric acid | 34.50 | 34.57 | 37 94 | 31.34 | 35.82 | 35.26 |
| Chloride of sodium | 3.71 | | | | | |
| Chlorine | | 0.31 | 1.48 | 0 33 | 4.56 | 1.75 |
| Sulphuric acid | 4.91 | 3.56 | 1 34 | 2 47 | | 1.29 |
| Silica | | 0.25 | 2 46 | 0.44 | 1.31 | 13.12 |

358. Inorganic analyses of Field Pea (A,) and Straw (B.) *(Prof. Way.)*

| | A | B |
|---|---|---|
| Silica, | 1.24 | 5.36 |
| Phosphoric acid, | 34.81 | 4 50 |
| Sulphuric acid, | 5.68 | 5 66 |
| Carbonic acid, | 1 82 | 14.74 |
| Lime, | 6 32 | 37.99 |
| Magnesia, | 6.57 | 6.73 |
| Peroxide of iron, | 0.59 | 1.76 |
| Potash, | 40.19 | 17.17 |
| Soda, | 0.65 | 2 48 |
| Chloride of sodium, | 0.68 | 3.57 |
| Chloride of potassium, | 1.42 | |

These analyses prove that pea straw is a peculiarly valuable fodder. According to Boussingault, dried pea straw contains 1.95 per cent. of nitrogen; and 64 lbs. of it, are equivalent for nourishment to 100 lbs. of ordinary hay, while 27 lbs. of white peas, and 25 lbs. of beans *(b,)* are equivalent to 100 lbs. of hay.

359. Nutritive matter derived from an imperial acre of pease, producing 25 bushels or 1600 lbs. *(Stephens.)*

| | |
|---|---|
| Husk or woody fibre, | 130 lbs. |
| Starch, gum, &c., | 800 " |
| Gluten, | 380 " |
| Oil or fat, | 34 " |
| Saline matter, or ash, | 48 " |

360. Sugar appears to be contained in only a few of the leguminous plants as in the *Sugar-pea ;* gum, on the contrary, mucus, and pectic acid, a wax-like substance, and the same salts as in the cereals, are constant ingredients in all. In the skins, particularly of lentils, tannin is found. A large quantity of potash and soda, and a larger proportion than usual of sulphuric acid, characterize their ashes. The *legumin* of the pea and bean differs from the gluten of wheat in being soluble in water, and in very dilute acid or alkaline solutions.

361. THE PEA most commonly cultivated in the Northern States, in fields, is the *Grey* or *Canada Pea, (Pisum arvense;)* but varieties of the *White Pea (P. Sativum,)* are also grown on a large scale. In Virginia and the States southwards

*The Chickasaw Pea*, *The Cow Pea*, *The Black-eyed Pea*, and others, unknown at the north, are in common use, where they are depended upon for pasture, as clover is with us.

362. The soil best adapted to this crop is a loam, a little inclining to clay, abounding in the alkalies. Barn yard manures, freshly applied, are injurious as forming much straw at the expense of the seed; but ashes, plaster, and lime, and *probably* guano, may be used with much benefit. Land habitually wet should not be sown with peas.

363. Unless the soil is very highly cultivated and very friable, plow in the fall, laying the furrows up high; and again, crossways in the spring, so soon as the earth is sufficiently dried. Harrow thoroughly, and *deeply*. The common quantity sown in New York is 1 to 1½ bushels per acre, but the Scotch use 4½ bushels; and in the United States, from 3 to 4 bushels are preferable to the smaller quantity. The goodness of the crop greatly depends upon the roots being so deeply buried that they are beyond the risk of the earth around them drying up in summer. To ensure this, as it is very difficult if not impossible to cover the seed evenly with a harrow, they should be plowed in with a wheat cultivator, so as to leave them from 2 to 2½ inches or more below the surface, and then the field should be well rolled.

364. Harvesting is effected with the scythe, the straw being rather torn up and rolled into heaps than cut; or when fully ripe, the roots may be easily and quickly pulled with a horse rake. Pease are then left on the ground till dry, and are either put away in the barn; or, as is preferable, thrashed as they are hauled in. This may be done with the flail, or horses, the latter being the most expeditious and cheapest. The bottom of the wagon should be tight to prevent waste.

365. In Virginia, peas are frequently grown among corn, being planted between the corn hills, and made at the expence of

very little additional tillage, other than what the corn alone would receive. After securing enough for seed, the pease are usually fed off the land to hogs, and in that way, are a very important auxiliary to the crop of corn: while the dung, and straw plowed in, manure the land for the next season.

366. In other southern States, the *Cow*, *Indian*, or *Stock Pea*, is much relied on for pasture, and as a fertilizer. It is sown broadcast, or in drills, or it is hoed in among corn, when the culture of the latter is finished. Under any circumstances, the pea is valuable as a green manure; but the cost of seed is too great, and the quantity of straw too small to render it popular for this purpose.

367. The great enemy of this vegetable, and one which discourages its more extended cultivation is the Pea-weevil, or Pea-bug, (*Bruchus Pisi.*)

After the pea-vines have flowered, and when the peas are just beginning to swell in the pod, the weevils deposite their eggs singly, in the pod, just above the pea, chiefly at night, or during cloudy weather. The grubs, as soon as hatched, penetrate into the pease; and in time bore a round hole from the centre to the hull, leaving the latter, and generally the germ of the future sprout untouched. The grub is changed to a pupa within its hole in the pea, in the autumn; and from November to the spring casts its skin again, becomes a beetle, and gnaws a hole through the thin hull in order to escape, which frequently does not happen before the pease are planted for an early crop. Pease containing this insect may be detected by a minute hole, and dimple. It may be killed by immersion in very hot water; but as the mischief is already done, and as the weevil lives on other plants, this process can be of little use.

These attacks may be escaped, it is said, by sowing in the month of June, after the parent insect has ceased to deposite its eggs; but as the abundance of the crop appears to depend on a certain amount of rain or moisture while it is in blossom, and as great heat is injurious to it in its early growth, equal difficulties or risks exist in this attempt to find a remedy. Till lately, the district lying along the River Thames in Canada, was free from the weevil, and a large portion of the peas consumed in the Northern States were imported thence, but this immunity is said to have passed away. According to Dr. Harris, the weevil, as late as 1852, was rare in New Hampshire, and still unknown in Maine.

"The crow-blackbird (*Quiscalus versicolor,*) is said to devour great numbers of these beetles in the spring; and the Baltimore Oriole, (*Icterus Baltimore.*) splits open the green pods for the sake of the grub contained in the pease, thereby contributing greatly to prevent the increase of these noxious insects. The instinct that enables this beautiful bird to detect the lurking grub, concealed as the latter is, within the pod and the hull of the pea, is worthy our highest admiration" (*Harris.*)

368. The Statutes of Michigan provide no standard weight for the bushel of pease. The average crop is from 20 to 25 bushels, but as high as 50 bushels per acre is not very uncommon.

369. Pease are frequently fed to hogs. As has been already perceived they possess little capability to fatten, but no food can be given which will form *flesh* more rapidly; and in this respect they are essentially useful. They should be either ground and cooked, or soaked and partially soured before feeding. If fed whole, they are apt to swell greatly in the stomach, and injure or even kill the animal; but if this does not occur, much will be passed undigested, therefore wasted. At present, ground pease are made into bread in Scotland and some other countries. Soup or gruel made of ground pease is an excellent food for calves.

It is customary, in some localities, to sow pease and oats together, for the purpose, afterwards, of feeding to horses. The supposed benefit derived is the upholding of the pea, as it clings to the straw of the oat. We are inclined to think, however, that the oat will suffer as much or more from the overshadowing of the pea, as the pea gains from the protection of the oat; and prefer mixing the two afterwards as we require them.

In some soils, a heavy crop of pease proves beneficial in destroying weeds; and leaves the ground both clean and mellow. The roots of this plant render the soil very friable ; and in this respect are beneficial, mechanically, on adhesive clays.

370. BEANS. In the United States, the English Bean, *(a,)* (which in that country takes so important a place in the rotation in clay soils,) does not prosper. Our climate appears to be either too hot or too dry for it. With us three species or varieties, belonging to the genus *Phaseolus (b,)* are commonly grown as a field crop, the *large white bean, the small white bean*, and *the China bean*, the latter having a spot of deep red upon it. Some 30 other varieties may be found in gardens—known as *climbing beans* and *bush beans;* and in France and England as *Harricot Beans.*

371. The above *(b,)* will grow well on any soil, but sandy or gravelly lands are generally preferred, both on account of their being more easily kept clean, and because upon them the seed is less apt to be damaged in case of rain when ripening. Upon clay and other retentive soils, the pods which lie upon the ground are easily injured and rotted when nearly ready to harvest. Upon sandy lands, also, the seeds ripen earlier and more evenly.

372. Beans may be grown in hills, in rows, or broadcast. The following is considered the best mode of culture, succeeding a hoed crop manured the previous season. Plough twice, and harrow well, or plow once, and render the surface fine with the cultivator, and roll. About the 1st June, plant in rows 22 inches apart,—either using a drill, or having marked out the rows with a *corn marker*,—at the rate of six beans to the foot. Hoe about the 26th of June, and again about the 16th of July; perfectly destroying the weeds. It is believed by the most skilful growers of this crop, that it is better not to plow, or otherwise disturb the ground, if the weeds can be kept down by hoeing. When the pods have turned yellow they are ready for harvesting, which is done by pulling the plants, and striking the roots against a stick held in the left hand, till they are clean;

the plants are then lightly stacked on the ground, rails or blocks of wood having been laid for the purpose. The stacks should not be so large that the sun-shine and wind cannot enter. When entirely dry, they should be hauled, and immediately thrashed by flail, otherwise the pods will again absorb the moisture, and heat. The beans should be spread for a few days on the barn floor and occasionally turned until they are perfectly dry; as even, after thrashing, if thrown into too large a heap, they will be apt to mould.

373. The following is an account of the expense of raising a crop of one acre as above, in Jefferson county, N. Y., in 1851. The kind used was the "small early Vermont Bean."

| | |
|---|---|
| Plowing, harrowing and working, - - | $1.75 |
| Planting by hand, - - - | 75 |
| First hoeing, - - - | 1 13 |
| Second hoeing, - - - | 3.09 |
| Pulling and stacking, - - - | 2.40 |
| Drawing, thrashing, cleaning, and measuring, - | 1.75 |
| One bushel of beans for seed, - - | 1.00 |
| Board, - - - - | 2.50 |
| Interest on land, - - - | 3 50 |
| | $17.87 |
| VALUE OF CROP. | |
| 34 2-32 bushels beans at $1.00, - - | 34.06 |
| One ton of straw, &c., - - - | 5.00 |
| | $39 06 |
| Deduct expences, - - - | 17.87 |
| Net proceeds per acre, - - - | $21.19 |

374. The crop varies from 15 to 40 bushels. As high as 60 bushels is said to have been raised to the acre in New York. Of late years, the supply has rarely proved commensurate with the demand.

375. The straw is eaten by horned cattle and sheep. For the last it is, in common with pease and pea straw, particularly

excellent in consequence of the large amount of sulphur which it contains—this being an important element in wool.

376. LENTILS are rarely or never cultivated in the United States except as a garden plant. The seed has been distributed (1853) by the Patent Office; and in this manner this useful esculent may become better known. In the south of Europe and in Asia it enters largely into the food of the people. There are several varieties of it, distinguished by the color of their seeds, the greater or smaller growth of their stems, and the earliness of their period of ripening.

377. The Lentil requires a somewhat light soil and warmth. It is greatly less productive of straw than the pea and the bean, and the produce of seed is also comparatively small. There could be no benefit in introducing it into field-culture in this country. In gardens, it may be cultivated as peas are.

378. The TARE or VETCH is largely grown in Great Britain as a forage-plant, for which purpose it is much esteemed. In the United States it does not appear to be usually cultivated, though it will prosper in the northern States. There are several species and varieties; and in situations where grass is deficient, and regular rotations of crops are employed; or where grass fails early in the season, as on many of the Prairies, this crop would prove beneficial. All animals are fond of it, and all thrive on it in an eminent degree. Hogs may be fattened entirely on it. It causes milch cows to give more butter than any species of green food; and horses can be kept fat on it.

379. In Europe it is sown both in autumn and in spring, but in our Northern States, it would necessarily be a spring crop only. It requires land in good condition and free from weeds. In Scotland, manure is always given it, and the land is well worked. It possesses the advantage of growing on all classes of soils. It is *generally* sown broadcast, at the rate of 3 to 4 bushels per acre; but oats are frequently mixed with it, when

1½ to 2 bushels of Tares, and 1 bushel of oats are enough. Light or poor soils require more seed. The *Hopetown*, or *White-flowered Tare*, is considered the most valuable variety. When intended for fodder, Tares are usually cut and fed to stock in stables or yards. If intended for seed they may be treated as pease, being cut with a scythe. If fodder is wished for, sowing should take place in rotation: and the plant be used after the pods are formed, but long before the seeds become ripe.

380. LUPINES are grown with us as a garden flower, but in Italy are used both as food, and to plow under as a green manure, a practice derived from the ancient Romans. The flavor is said to be coarse and bitter. They flourish in light sandy lands, but can be of no value to us.

# CHAPTER XIII.

## GRASSES AND OTHER FODDER PLANTS.

381. As the production of domestic animals, and manure depends on grasses, we consider these as next in importance. The Belgians have a proverb which should be written in letters of gold on every barn-door: "Without dung, no crops; without cattle, no dung; without grass, no cattle."

382. The botanical family of Grasses *(Gramineæ,)* is extremely numerous; there are few parts of the world where some species are not found growing wild; while in moderate climates they form the great mass of vegetable production. In Agriculture, they are usually divided into *(a,)* wild grasses, and *(b,)* cultivated or tame grasses. These latter *(b,)* are grasses of peculiar value, which are regularly sown; while the former *(a,)* spring up naturally where they are found, without sowing. With very few exceptions, grasses do not change into varieties by cultivation, like other plants, but remain the same as when wild. In England, over thirty distinct species are employed for different soils and purposes. In the United States, not more than half a dozen, at the utmost, are usually sown, though we have a great variety of wild species. *Seventy-two* have already been detected in Michigan, without counting those that have been introduced. The culture of hay, at present, is principally confined to the Eastern, Middle, and Western States, from which the Southern markets are mainly supplied, in the form of pressed packages or bales.

**The reason for using so many species of grasses as the English do,**

(and in which respect it is very important that we should follow their example,) is that a greater weight can be produced on an acre; some are of temporary duration, some of permanent; the period of maturation differs, so that, when mixed, some are always in the best condition for pasture; the nutritive power differs; some are best adapted for pasture, others for meadow; and some prosper in one sort of soil, others in another sort. Mixed grasses are found to feed animals more profitably than one single kind; and it may be said, that the improvement of stock in Great Britain commenced, and has kept pace with the introduction of cultivated grasses, and other fodder plants. Great pains are taken in that country to find and cultivate the best species. In the United States we have been much too negligent in this respect.

In 1840, the hay crop of the United States was 10,248,-108¾ tons; in 1850, 13,838,579 tons; in which, however, clover is included.

383. The following species are the most valuable:

*(a,) Phleum pratense.* Timothy, Herd's grass. (Meadow Cats-tail.*)

*(b,) Agrostis vulgaris.* Red Top, Herd's grass.

*(c,) Agrostis alba.* White Bent Grass, White Red Top, Fiorin. (Marsh Bent Grass.)

*(d,) Muhlenbergia Mexicana.* Fowl Meadow Grass.

*(e,) Poa Pratensis.* Green Meadow Grass, June Grass. (Smooth-stalked Meadow Grass.)

*(f,) Poa compressa.* Blue Grass.

*(g,) Poa trivialis.* Rough-stalked Meadow Grass.

*(h,) Dactylis glomerata.* Orchard Grass. (Rough Cocks-foot Grass.)

*(i,) Lolium italicum.* Italian Rye Grass.

*(j,) Lolium perenne.* Perennial Rye Grass, or (Darnel.)

*(k,) Lolium annuum.* Annual do

There is a species of Rye or Darnel grass (*Lolium temulentum*,) greatly resembling the Perennia, which is poisonous to every thing but hogs. It is naturalized in Massachusetts. In some parts of Europe it is a weed among wheat, and when eaten in flour is frequently fatal. (*Abstract of Med. Scien., June* 1851, p. 299.)

*The last name within brackets in this list is that which is usually used by English writers. Those marked * belong to the South.

(*l*,) *Anthoxantham odoratum.* Sweet-scented Vernal Grass.
(*m*,) *Alopecurus pratensis.* Meadow Fox-Tail.
(*n*,) *Cynosurus cristatus.* Crested Dog's-Tail.
(*o*,) *Avena flavescens.* Yellow Oat Grass.
(*p*,) *Triticum dasystachyum.* Michigan Couch Grass.
(*q*,) *Phalaris Americana.* Ribbon Grass.
(*r*,) *Festuca elatior.* Tall Fescue Grass.
(*s*,) *Festuca pratensis.* Meadow do.
(*t*,) *Tripsacum dactyloides.* Gama Grass.*
(*u*,) *Sorghum halpense.* Guined or Egyptian Grass.*
(*v*,) *Cynodon dactylon.* Bermuda Grass.*
(*w*,) Grama.*

Besides these there are several species of *Poa* and *Festuca* that are valuable for pasture. When the subject is better investigated, undoubtedly many indigenous grasses will be added to the list, especially from California.

384. We will notice, in as small a space as possible, the peculiarities of these grasses: (*a*,) is a native of both Europe and the United States. It may be found growing wild in the counties of Ingham, Clinton, Shiawassee, &c., in Michigan, upon certain loamy clay soils, in great luxuriance, and it is known to spring up, without sowing, on clearing off the woods, and plowing. It is the most generally cultivated grass for dry soils in the United States, affording 1½ to 2½ tons of dry hay per acre; and in favorable situations remains permanently for very many years. It abounds in seed, which is easily saved, yielding from 10 to 34 bushels per acre. (*Wiggins.*) To save the seed, allow it nearly to ripen; mow; bind and shock like wheat, and thrash with horses. With a proper fanning mill, the seed can be perfectly cleaned, as readily as that of any of the cereals. According to Mr. Sinclair,* the nutritive value is double when ripe compared with the period

*A few years since a very extensive examination of the nutritive value of the English grasses was made by George Sinclair, under the direction of the Duke of Bedford at his estate of Woburn; and the results were published in an octavo volume, with colored copperplate engravings of most of the grasses, under the name of *Hortus Gramineus Woburnensis*. The work is now very difficult to obtain. The only copy we have seen in America is in the library of the Patent Office, Washington. Much interesting information was collected by Mr. S., but his labors are of less value than they ought to have been from his want of skill as an analyst, and his ignorance of the principles of nutrition. As, however, no one has gone over the same ground, his book is often quoted and referred to. The chief results will be found tabulated in *Allen's Amer. Farm Book*, p. 110.

of flowering, while the weight is the same. The ripe crop exceeds the flowering in value as 14 to 5. It is usually sown with wheat in the fall, or with oats or barley in spring—the latter being preferable—and red clover is generally mixed with it. If sown alone, half a bushel of seed, or if with clover 12 quarts of grass, and one pound of clover is the proper quantity. Many persons sow less than this, but there is no economy is stinting grass seed. There should be enough to form a thick sod the first season. In heavy clays even more seed may be requisite. Timothy may be cut in the morning, and hauled into sheds or barns the same afternoon, using a bucket full of salt to each ton; but if stacked, it must be drier. The faults of this grass are: 1, the coarse stem and head. 2. The deficiency of leaf. 3. The small quantity of the after crop; and 4, the dying out of the plant in winter in certain classes of soils. It is better adapted for horses and neat cattle than for sheep, and compares badly with the fine, leafy hay of the English meadows. It is well adapted for mixing with other grasses. (*b*) and (*c*) Both belong to wet or marshy lands, and will not prosper in entirely dry soils; they can, therefore, scarcely be called cultivated grasses, though they are often sown in such situations. They are natives of the United States. They have creeping roots or *stolons*, and are very difficult to eradicate. The two greatly resemble each other, but the latter has white instead of red heads or flowers. In England, they are not held in much estimation. With us they are placed as hay, by many persons, on a level with Timothy, and for sheep they probably surpass it, the stalks being fine, and the leaf abundant. They afford good pasture, and grow rapidly after being cut or grazed. The latter species (*c*,) is called *Fowl Meadow grass* in many parts of New York, a name which has led to much confusion. If sown in marshes, they readily exterminate the coarser grasses and weeds, and form a productive meadow. About one bushel of seed to the acre should be used, or two bushels if sown on clean plowed land. About 1½ tons to the acre of dry hay is the usual product, the grass diminishing greatly in weight after cutting. (*d*,) Till lately, this grass has only been sown in Massachusetts, where it is also called *Duck-grass*, and *Swamp-wire-grass*, but it is now getting into general favor. It is mentioned by the Rev. J. Eliot, of Connecticut, as early as 1751, from whom we learn that it was supposed to have been brought into a poor piece of meadow in Dedham, Mass., by ducks and other wild water-fowls, and therefore called by such an odd name. There can be little doubt, however, that it is indigenous to Michigan where it is frequently met with in swamps. It grows tall and thick, and makes a soft and pliable hay. One good quality is that it does not spoil by standing after it is ripe, but may be cut any time from July to October. It is represented as yielding heavy crops; grows about three feet high; and is essentially fine in the stalk with abundance of leaf, flower, and seed. Indeed, it appears to be the best American grass for damp soils yet known, and is worthy of very extensive culture. It is found to succeed best in *drained* marshes, which can be overflowed for two or three weeks in the spring and winter. When sown in such situations the land should be plowed, and between two and three bushels of seed harrowed in, with or without a grain crop. It may, however, be sown in lands too wet to plow, though yielding in such places an inferior crop; and it would be well to mix the two last species (*b*) and (*c*) with it. (*Dr. H. Wheatland in Farmer's Companion*, vol. ii, p. 5.) (*e*,) Is or has been abundant in all the Northern States, coming up immediately after the forests have been cut down, though it is now said to fail in the older Eastern States. It belongs to dry soils, and forms a thick, though shallow sod, and excellent pasture, especially for sheep. In heavy timbered clay soils it is generally mixed with the indigenous white clover. (*Trifolium repens.*) The stalks or culms are short and naked, the leaves reclining partially on the ground, and it is only when peculiarly luxuriant that it is worth cutting for hay. It is found, however, in all old meadows where the soil is adapted to it. It is rarely, if ever, sown, though the seed may be collected without difficulty. It dries up after flowering in June, but in the damp climate of England, it appears to grow more luxuriantly. "At the time of flowering, the produce on an acre is 10,209 lbs., when ripe 8,507 lbs., and the lattermath (*aftergrass*) is 4,083 lbs., and bears nearly an equal value with the ripe crop."

(*f*,) Is the well known *Kentucky Blue Grass*, so famous as pasture. It much resembles the last, but is of a deep color, with a bluish hue, and is better adapted for making hay. The late Hon. Henry Clay informed the writer that when he first went to Lexington, Ky., that country was covered with cane-brakes, the trees standing at distant intervals; and as soon as the cane was destroyed the blue-grass appeared. It is said to be confined to a peculiar geological formation, one of the lower lime-rocks of the great western coal field; and that the underlying rocks can be distinctly traced both in Kentucky and Ohio by the existence of this grass. If this proves to be everywhere the case, as present circumstances incline us to believe, this grass must be considered as strictly local in its habitat. The seed may be purchased at the Cincinnati seed stores.

(*g*,) According to Prof. Gray, this grass is not a native of America, though naturalized in some parts of the Eastern States. It resembles the June grass (*e.*) Donaldson in his *Treatise on Grasses* does not speak favorably of its productiveness in England, although it is sown among others for pastures. It requires a sheltered situation on damp clays and strong loamy soils, and is easily hurt by frosts.

(*h,*) This grass is also a native of England, but has become entirely naturalized in the Atlantic States. It belongs to dry soils, though it does well in moderately damp situations, and, in its native state, grows in clays and heavy loams. It prospers well in the neighborhood of Detroit, proving quite hardy, and is about a fortnight earlier in the spring than either *Timothy* or *June grass.* It is a large, strong, tall grass, with somewhat coarse culms, and abundance of leaf; but, unless annually pastured, it has a tendency to grow in clumps instead of covering the ground. This is corrected by grazing the meadow in spring and fall. It succeeds well under trees, (hence its American name,) and the leaf, when cut or eaten, continues to grow; unlike *Timothy,* which must throw up a new leaf. "The produce, when flowering, is 27,905 lbs., per acre; when ripe, 26,544 lbs., and the lattermath, 11,910 lbs." Under most circumstances, it is essentially a most valuable grass, and is much relished by all kind of stock. It is the favorite grass of the rich pastures around Dublin, Ireland. The aftergrass is very abundant, and does not seem to suffer from heat as much as our grasses. It should always be sown with other species, but it ripens about a fortnight before *Timothy.* The Balled Drop-seed grass, (*Muhlenbergia glomerata, Trin,*) somewhat resembles it, and might, we are inclined to think, be profitably sown with other species in wet places. The latter is a native of Michigan.

(*i,*) Undoubtedly stands at the head of all cultivated grasses for productiveness, for feeding qualities, and for hay, but like all the Rye grasses, it has a tendency, if allowed to seed, to impoverish the soil. It is probably a distinct species and not a mere variety. Compared with the common Rye grass, it arrives sooner at maturity; has a greater abundance of foliage, which is broader and of a lighter color; grows taller; spreads less on the ground; its spikes are longer; the seed is lighter, smaller, and less in quantity. It is preferred by cattle to any other grass. It grows through winter; is earlier in spring; does not suffer from heat; and continues growing luxuriantly till checked by frost. The *true* species is perennial, and prospers well in the neighborhood of Detroit. The great difficulty we have found with it, is that cattle, horses, and sheep are so fond of it, that when mixed with many other varieties they leave all the rest, and eat this grass deep into the soil, thus destroying it. When not allowed to be pastured, it is very luxuriant, and makes excellent hay, generally seeding twice a year in this latitude. We are inclined to believe that the common and the annual species, have often been sold for the *Italian* in the United States, and indeed, it is said that it can only be procured pure from a few great seed-dealers in England. In that country, it is usually sown with red clover, at the rate of 1 to 3 bushels of grass seed, and 3 to 16 lbs., of clover seed to the acre. (*See Patent Office Reports*, 1845, pp. 373, 376; 1846, p. 258.)

(*j*,) Is more used in Great Britain for meadows on all kinds of soil, and mixed with other grasses in pastures, than any other species; (*k*,) resembles it in all respects with the exception that it is an annual, and therefore used in rotations, where one year's grass only is required. Experience has given them a very high reputation, and late analyses, it is said, have proved them to be the most nutritive of grasses. They are generally sown with the clovers at the same rate as the previous one (*i*). They would be found highly profitable in the wheat soils of Michigan to sow with clover; the clover not being diminished in quantity, while this excellent grass is added to it. They are gradually finding their way into favor in the Atlantic States, though their *appearance*, compared with *Timothy* is unfavorable to them. There are several improved varieties, as *Pacey's*, *Stickney's*, *Russel's*, &c. A late writer in the *Journal of the Highland Agricul. Society*, (October, 1853, p. 111,) mentions the following objections to the Perennial Rye grass, (*j*) "Its growth is much stunted by being cropped or cut over; it is impatient of drought; it throws out few roots or radicle leaves; it covers the land during summer with dry innutritious herbage." These objections, which are probably exaggerated, do not apply to the Italian species.

(*l*,) Is chiefly valuable as pasture, the leaf being short, and the rich perfume being lost when the grass is ripe or dried. It is to this that the English meadows owe their well known odor; and the butter made in Delaware County, Pennsylvania, (where this grass has long been naturalized,) its excellent flavor. It prospers well in the neighborhood of Detroit, though it is a native of Great Britain. It is there considered the earliest of all the grasses, and succeeds best in moist localities, such as rich deep loams, but not in *wet* soils. Its owes its peculiar scent to an aromatic essential oil of which *benzoic acid* is the base. The same flavor may be imparted to butter, by giving the cows 20 to 30 grains of *Benzoin* twice a day, previously dissolved in hot water, and mixed with meal. This should constitute a part of all mixtures of grass seeds, intended for permament pastures. The seed is difficult to procure, and therefore expensive, but it is found that in Pennsylvania, when once it is rooted, it is only exterminated by the plow. (*See Patent Office Report*, 1849, p. 373.) With the writer, in a very rich damp loam, the culm grows fully three feet high.

(*m*,) Is held to be the best permament meadow grass in England, for rich lands. It so greatly resembles *Timothy* that it is difficult to distinguish it when not in blossom, but it affords much more leaf, the culm is finer, and the aftergrowth heavier. We have found the winters too cold for it in Michigan, and would not recommend it in this latitude.

(*n*,) Is also an English grass, of second rate value, and has proved too tender for this climate. Where it prospers it is chiefly valuable for pasture.

(*o*.) The same remarks will apply to this. (*p*,) Our experience with this has been accidental, it having appeared in the corner of a permament meadow, and spread over a large space, exterminating all the other grasses. It is an early, rich growing species, with great abundance of leaf, stalk and seed, makes excellent hay, and cattle of all kinds prefer it to *Timothy*. We mention it here that more experiments may be made with it. Should it not prove difficult to exterminate, like the English Couch grass, we know no native species that has more to recommend it on clay soils. (*q*.) This, known as the *Ribbon-grass* of the Gardens, prospers luxuriantly in wet marshes, soon covering them over, and forming a dry elastic surface. After a few years, the leaf assumes one color. Horned cattle eat it, but horses do not appear to like it. It may be planted, by throwing roots into the water, at a foot or two distance from each other. The seed appears to be barren, and it is subject to a species of *Ergot*. Mr. Allen failed to make it prosper on a clay marsh in New York. (*r*) and (*s*.) Prof. Gray, supposes these grasses to be naturalized from Great Britain, and that the latter is probably a mere variety of the former, but a more valuable grass. They prosper best in moist or boggy alluvial soils, but are of little general interest in this country. Of the Southern grasses we know nothing personally. The best accounts of them will be found in various volumes of the *Patent Office Reports*.*

*Since writing the above, a communication has been received from J. M. McAllister, Esqr., Summerville, Cass Co., Michigan, who has experimented upon a great variety of native and foreign grasses. He finds *Orchard grass* peculiarly valuable; but the most important that he has met with, is *Randal Grass*, the seed of which was received from Virginia. He has succeeded in introducing this extensively into Cass and the neighboring counties. (*See Farmer's Companion*, vol. iii, p. 30.) The seed resembles that of the Rye Grass; the living plant we have not seen, and do not know the botanical name.

The *Tussac Grass*, from the Falkland Islands; and the *Pampas Grass*, from the Prairies of South America, have been introduced, the first into Ireland, and the latter into Scotland, with great promise of success. There is little doubt but that they would be found valuable in our Southern and Middle States. They are both remarkable for their feeding qualities. It is believed that the *Tussac Grass* requires the neighborhood of the Sea; or at least, of salt springs.

385. As regards the ANALYSIS of grasses, little seems yet to have been done with accuracy. *Perennial and Italian Rye Grass* have been carefully examined by *Thompson* and *Way;* but with this exception we have no means of ascertaining what species are included under the terms "Hay" and "Grass," analyzed by the various chemists; while the probability is that each grass differs in its constituents, in its amount of nitrogen, and in the peculiar salts which it requires; and, likewise, according to the soil and climate in which it is grown. The English meadow hay is usually formed of 20 or 30 species, besides clovers; of the German we have no particulars. Mr. Norton gives the following "average of organic substances in Meadow Hay, from Boussingault and Johnston," but thinks the amount of nutritive matter too high.

| | | | |
|---|---|---|---|
| Water, | 16 | Nitrogenous substances, | 7 |
| Starch, | 4 | Oil, | 3 |
| Gum and sugar, | 12 | Woody fibre, | 50 |
| Ash, | 8 | | |

386. Thompson gives the following analysis "of almost entirely Rye grass, (*Lolium perenne.*")

| | |
|---|---|
| Water, | 75 |
| Soluble Salts, Silica and Insoluble Salts, | 1.34 |
| Organic matter, | 23.66 |

Or reducing the same to its ultimate constituents, when fresh (A,) and dried at 212° F. (B,) together with hay made at Giessen, (*Dr. Will;*) species of grass not mentioned (C;) and hay grown in the neighborhood of Strasburg, France, (*Boussingault;*) species not mentioned (D):—

| | A. | B. | C. | D. |
|---|---|---|---|---|
| Carbon, | 11.35 | 45.41 | 45.87 | 45.80 |
| Hydrogen, | 1.48 | 5.93 | 5.76 | 5.00 |
| Nitrogen, | 0.46 | 1.84 | } 41.55 | 1.50 |
| Oxygen, | 10.39 | 41.54 | | 38.70 |
| Ash, | 1.32 | 5.28 | 6.82 | 9.00 |
| Water, | 75.00 | | | |

Thompson found the amount of solid matter in this grass to vary from 18 to upwards of 30 per cent, according to the early or late period of growth. When grass first springs above the surface of the earth the principal constituent of its early blades is water, the amount of solid matter being comparatively trifling; as it grows, the deposition of a more indurated form of carbon gradually becomes more considerable; the sugar and soluble matter at first increasing, then gradually diminishing, to give way to the deposition of woody substance.

Table of Rye grass before and after ripening.

| | 18th June. | 23d June. | 13th July. |
|---|---|---|---|
| Water, | 76.19 | 81.23 | 69.00 |
| Solid matter, | 23.81 | 18.77 | 31.00 |

These are important facts; for if the sugar be an important element of the food of animals, then the farmer should cut grass for the purpose of hay-making at that period when the largest amount of matter soluble in water is contained in it. This is at an earlier period of its growth than when it has shot into seed, for it is then that woody matter predominates—a substance totally insoluble in water, and therefore less calculated to serve as food to animals than substances capable of assuming a soluble condition. This is the first point for consideration in making hay, since it ought to be the object of the farmer to preserve the hay for winter use in the condition most resembling the grass in its highest state of perfection.

100 parts of the stem and seeds of Rye grass when dried as hay, gave:

| | Stem. | Stem. | Seed. |
|---|---|---|---|
| Water, | 15.50 | 19.30 | 11.376 |
| Organic matter, | 79.52 | 75.72 | 82.548 |
| Ash, | 4.98 | 4.98 | 6.070 |

387. Inorganic constituents of Rye Grass *(Lolium Perenne,)* Stem, (A,) and seed (B,) *(Thompson,)* and Italian Rye Grass *(L. italicum,)* in flower, (C,) and in seed (D.) *(Way.)*

| | A. | B. | C. | D. |
|---|---|---|---|---|
| Silica, | 64.57 | 43.28 | 59.18 | 60.6 |
| Phosphoric acid, | 12.51 | 16.89 | 6.34 | 6.3 |
| Sulphuric acid, | | 3.12 | 2.82 | 1.3 |
| Chlorine, | | trace. | 2.27* | 5.6* |
| Carbonic acid, | | 3.61 | | |
| Magnesia, | 4.01 | 5.31 | 2.23 | 2.6 |
| Lime, | 6.50 | 18.55 | 9.95 | 12.3 |
| Peroxide of iron, &c., | 0.36 | 2.10 | 0.78 | 0.3 |
| Potash, | 8.03 | 5.80 | 12.45 | 10.8 |
| Soda, | 2.17 | 1.38 | 3.98 | 0.1 |

Thompson observes "There is no doubt that these numbers undergo very considerable modifications on different soils." The seed tends to remove a larger portion of phosphoric acid from the soil than the stem; the quantity of acid found in the seed exceeding that in the stem by one-fourth. The same remark applies to the lime. The quantity of alkalies is twice as great in the stem as in the seed, while the total ash of the seed is a sixth part superior in amount to that of the stem.

388. According to Boussingault, 10,000 parts good meadow hay (species not mentioned) contain 547 parts of inorganic matter, consisting of:

| | |
|---|---|
| Potash, | 130 |
| Soda, | 10 |
| Lime, | 107 |
| Magnesia, | 43 |
| Oxide of iron, | 5 |

*Chloride of Sodium. The amount of this is remarkable, and may be the reason why cattle are so fond of this grass.

| | |
|---|---|
| Silica, | 189 |
| Sulphuric acid, | 16 |
| Phosphoric acid, | 32 |
| Chlorine, | 15 |
| | 547 |

The Nitrogen amounts to 1.65 equal to 2 per cent of Ammonia ; the fat, wax, or oil to 3.8 ; and the starch, gum, dextrine, and pectine to 50 per cent, the rest being woody fibre and waste.

389. Liebig gives the following summary analysis of "Hay:"

100 parts of hay dried in the air contain 86 of dry matter.
14 of water.
100

100 parts of hay dried at 212° F.=116.2 dried in air contain:

| | |
|---|---|
| Carbon, | 45.8 |
| Hydrogen. | 5.0 |
| Oxygen, | 38.7 |
| Nitrogen, | 1.5 |
| Ashes, | 9.0 |
| | 100.0 |

100 lbs. of hay dried at the ordinary temperature contain 1.29 nitrogen.

240 oz. of such hay=15 lbs. contain 3.095 oz. of nitrogen.
72 oz. of oats, =4½ lbs. contain 1.34 oz. of nitrogen.
4.435

390. Prof. Way has given the water (A,) and flesh forming constituents (B,) of the following grasses, in 100 parts.

| | A. | B. |
|---|---|---|
| Sweet-scented Vernal grass, | 80.35 | 2.05 |
| Orchard grass, | 70 | 4.06 |
| Meadow barley, | 58.85 | 4.59 |
| Timothy, | 57.21 | 4.86 |

391. The following principles may be laid down. *(a,)* The proportion of soluble matter yielded by any species of grass, when made into hay, varies not only with the age of the grasses, when cut, but with the soil, the climate, the season, the rapidity of growth, the variety of seed sown, and with many other circumstances which are susceptable of constant variation. *(b,)*

Animals have the power of digesting a greater or less proportion of that part of their food which is insoluble in water. Even the woody fibre of the hay is not entirely useless as an article of nourishment. *(c,)* The most valuable constituents of the grass, such as the albumen, casein, starch, sugar, &c., may undergo great and ruinous change by fermentation and washing before and after the hay is put in stack or barn; so that ill-made hay, exposed to rain, may be inferior in nutritive quality to the coarsest straw. *(d,)* The riper the straw or grass, the less soluble matter does it contain; and soil, season, and manure will equally affect the quality of hay. One field will grow a hard wiry grass, while another will produce a soft and flexible plant, and highly nutritious hay. In England, a much higher price is given for hay cut off old grass fields, than for the first crop grown; and race and hunting horses are fed on hay over a year old, new hay injuring their *wind* and condition. *(e,)* Thompson found that the soluble matter of hay capable of being taken up by cold water, was as much as 5 per cent, or nearly a third of the whole soluble matter in hay. Thence we may form some notion of the injury liable to be produced by every shower of rain which drenches the fields during hay harvest. But hot water will extract over 16 per cent. of soluble matter; and if we consider the warmth of the soil and hay, and also of the rain in summer, the loss in this country is probably much greater than 5 per cent. *(f,)* The *bleaching* of hay is owing to the loss of wax, as much as 2 per cent of which may readily disappear. But this wax is important for fattening; and *bleached* hay is decidedly deteriorated in feeding qualities. In Scotland 100 parts of hay were found to be equivalent to 387½ parts of grass; or it requires nearly eight tons of grass to yield two tons of hay to the acre. By late analyses at the Royal Agricultural College, Cirencester, England, *Italian Rye Grass* was found to contain:

Water (in natural or green state,) - - - 80.770

| | | |
|---|---|---|
| Nitrogenized, or flesh-forming matters, | natural state, | 2.861 |
| | dried at 212° F. | 14.87 |
| Non-nitrogenous, or heat and fat-forming matters, | natural state, | 14.389 |
| | dried at 212° F. | 75.09 |
| Inorganic matter or ash, | natural state, | 1.980 |
| | dried at 212° F. | 10.04 |

In making hay for our own use, but more especially in purchasing hay, all these points must be taken into consideration. A load of hay, before seeding, carefully dried, not exposed to rain or heavy dews, put by in sheds with salt so that fermentation is impossible, bears a much higher *intrinsic* and therefore *money* value than hay carlessly made, on which rain has fallen, and which has been stacked damp. A *spirituous* smell is not uncommon in stacks, which shows that the sugar is lost, and with it, probably, most of, or all the nitrogenous constituents. Such hay as we have mentioned last, is probably inferior in value to well saved oat straw. To be a good judge of hay, requires both much experience, and the consideration of many particulars; while the difference in nutritive qualities between good and bad samples—frequently resembling each other to the eye—is very great. Old hay, that is, hay which is over a year old, other things being equal, is always the most valuable. Some chemical change takes place by which it is supposed to be rendered more nutritive; and as has been already stated, horses prosper better upon it. The same peculiarity is found in grasses when used for pasture. It has been noticed, in the valley of the Kennet, England, that sheep might safely be fed upon, or soiled with the grass of the *first* crop of the water-meadows, but it was dangerous to do either with the *second* crop of the same grass, (*C. W. Johnson.*) Prof. Way analysed the grass of such meadows taken April 30th (A,) and 26th June (B,) and found that in 100 parts in a green state there were contained:

| | A. | B. |
|---|---|---|
| Water, | 87.58 | 74.53 |
| Nitrogenous matter, | 3.22 | 2.78 |
| Fatty matter, | 0.81 | 0.52 |
| Starch, gum, sugar, &c., | 3.98 | 11.17 |
| Woody Fibre, | 3.13 | 8.76 |
| Ash, | 1.28 | 2.24 |

This not only shows that the very season at which grass is cut or fed is a matter of importance, but elucidates a beautiful provision of nature. In spring, growth is provided for, and heat or fat is not requisite, but in order to provide for the cold of winter, the later grass abounds in fat forming constituents, so that a provision may be laid up for the inclement season.

392. Grasses prosper, on the great majority of soils,—not on all—but those containing a fair proportion of clay and loam, with moisture, are the most profitable both for meadow and grazing.

393. A field laid down to grass for a length of time improves the soil for grain crops,—much if pastured, partially if mowed.

394. The manures requisite for grasses, necessarily vary with the needs of the soil, which can only be ascertained by analysis; but these plants peculiarly require the alkalies in the form of soluble silicates, the phosphates of magnesia, and lime, with nitrogen. Unleached wood-ashes contain the silicate of potash in the same proportion as straw, besides several other important salts, and consequently are an excellent manure for this crop. Barn-yard manures may also be applied with profit, but they are generally preferred in the shape of *composts*. Guano, plaster, &c., are found profitable in some localities. Salt is highly beneficial in some soils,—2 to 3 bushels per acre sown in spring. In England, nitrate of soda *(Saltpetre,)* at the cost of $6.00 per acre, has been used with profit. If barn-yard manure is used, it should be hauled and evenly spread on all lands containing clay, soon after the hay is taken off; on sandy lands, in spring. In both instances, harrow in spring, as soon the ground will bear the team without poaching, and mix the manure into the soil, till the whole looks black. There can be no injury done by tearing up the surface grass. If the sod is thin, sow on a little more seed and roll. By such a dressing of well-saved barn-yard manure every three years, a meadow may be kept in high condition. Such fields should not be pastured in spring, nor at any time when wet.

395. *Timothy* seed, in the United States, is usually sown with a grain crop; if with wheat in the fall or spring; with oats, or barley in spring. Barley is decidedly the best crop for the purpose. The first year's grass on the same field, one-half sown with oats, and half with barley, will show a very decided profit

in favor of the latter. In laying down a permanent meadow, the field should be well manured, plowed deeper than usual, and put in good condition in every way. In clay soils, finish putting in the grain crop, and harrow fine and evenly. Then sow the grass seed, and roll in, till the surface is smooth, and the clods entirely broken up. In such lands *Timothy* seed does not require to be deeply buried, and the same applies to clover when sown with it. In sand, give the grain one harrowing, sow the grass seed, harrow cross ways, and finish by rolling. In Great Britain, harrows made much lighter than the usual ones, with long, narrow teeth, placed rather near together, are used expressly for putting in grasses. In some cases a "brush harrow" is used for the same purpose. In very heavy soils, it is recommended to roll as soon as the grain-sowing is finished, sow the grass on the smooth surface, and finish with light harrowing.

To sow evenly requires some experience. The seed is caught between two fingers and the thumb, instead of the whole hand, and the casts are more frequent than in grain-sowing. There are machines, fastened by a strap to the sower's neck, for the purpose of sowing grass and clover seeds, which do the work well, and cost only a small sum. Weeds are often conveyed in grass seeds, and none but the perfectly clean should be purchased. Such will cost more at first but will be cheapest in the end. The *Journal of Agriculture* gives a table from actual experiment of the proper depth at which to sow these seeds. Fourteen species of grasses and clover were tried, and in all cases those on the surface, and not more than a quarter of an inch in depth sprouted the best; at 3 inches none at all appeared. In certain sandy and gravelly soils, however, grasses and clovers are apt to dry up in summer, if the roots are superficial. *(See Patent Office Reports*, 1846, p. 694.)

396. Under some circumstances, it is beneficial to steep such seeds previous to sowing, to strengthen and insure the germinating powers. The best mode of doing this, is to spread the

seeds on the barn floor, and shower over them gradually, with frequent turnings, as much water, at a time, as they can absorb without any running off. Do this for a whole day, at separate intervals, until they are thoroughly saturated. At night, make them up into a heap and cover with cloths so as to raise the temperature. Before sowing, spread out on a cloth to dry in the sun for a short time, so that they can be easily separated. Old or damaged seeds, incapable of germinating, are sometimes sold. This may be discovered by placing a piece of flannel at the bottom of a common saucer, saturating it with water, and sowing a few seeds on it. Keep in a warm place, renewing the water as it evaporates, and in three or four days all the seeds capable of germinating, will sprout. The same test may be applied to any kind of seed.

In Maine, the grain intended to be sown, is wet or soaked, the grass seed is mixed with the grain in this wet state, to which it readily adheres, and in this manner it is sown. We only mention this mode to condemn it; as either the grain must be buried too shallow, or the grass too deeply; in growing, the two will be apt to interfere; and the plants will be uneven.

397. These rules, with slight modifications which must be learnt from experience, will apply to all species of grasses. The small and light seeds are usually sold by the pound weight. The statutes of Michigan do not determine the weight of a bushel of Timothy seed, but 60 lbs. is the usual standard.

398. A great diversity of practice occurs as to the time when grass should be cut for hay. So far as can be ascertained by theory, the period at which grasses contain the largest proportion of nutritive matter is just previous to flowering, and while in blossom; but in practice, some species appear to be as good if not better when the seed is ripe. The question can only be determined by many carefully conducted experiments; and we trust that a matter of such great importance will not be allowed to remain in its present uncertain condition. Timothy cut

while in blossom, makes *dusty* hay, owing to the pollen; which is unpleasant, if not injurious to stabled animals.

Late experiments, very carefully made in Scotland, show that Italian and Perennial Rye grass, mixed hay, and clover, cut before flowering (*a*,) when in flower (*b*,) and when ripe (*c*,) fatten in unlike proportion, so as to be valued at (*a*,) 6d. per stone of 28 lbs., (*b*,) at 5½d., and (*c*,) at 5d. At the same time it was found that good oat straw was just as valuable as hay for fattening beef animals, when roots, oil-cake, &c., were given as the main food.

399. The more simple the operation of hay-making the better. The following plan has been followed for many years with complete success, the grass being pure Timothy, and Timothy, Red Clover, and June Grass mixed. If the meadows are extensive, begin mowing when first the heads appear. Do not cut till the dew is nearly or quite risen, leave till afternoon in swathe, rake into windrows with horse rake, and form into light cocks, each containing about one hundred pounds of *dry* hay; next morning, as soon as the dew is risen, throw these cocks open; and leave them so for a couple of hours, and then haul into sheds. Let a man stand with a bucket of salt, and scatter about half a handful on each large fork-full as it is packed away; using about an ordinary bucket-full of salt to a ton of hay. This is all that is necessary. The hay will come out in the winter nearly as soft and green as when put by; and will be eaten with avidity by the stock. If it is intended to be stacked, it had better stand the second day in cock, and be treated in the same manner as above on the third. If the grass has flowered, even this labor is not necessary. It may be cut in the morning, raked into windrows in the afternoon, and immediately hauled into sheds. By this rapid process, nothing is lost; the wax, the nitrogen, and the salts are saved; much labor is saved; and risk from rain and dew is not incurred; while the common salt prevents fermentation, souring, and the growth of the fungus so common on badly made hay, usually known as *mould* or *mustiness*, and which is so injurious to horses*

*The following passage contains much valuable practical matter, based on true

"Bad hay will change a horse's appearance in two days, even with an unlimited quantity of oats. The kidneys are excited by it to extraordinary activity. The urine, which in this disease is always perfectly transparent, is discharged very frequently and in copious profusion. The horse soon becomes hide-bound, emaciated, and feeble. His thirst is excessive. He never refuses water, and he drinks as if he would never give over. The disease does not produce death, but it renders the horse useless, and ruins the constitution. *Musty* hay is said "to be bad for the wind," and it is certainly so for every part of the body." (*Stephens.*)

400. Grass is cut with *(a,)* a scythe, or *(b,)* a mowing machine. It is raked with *(c,)* a hand-rake, or *(d,)* a horse rake, of which there are several kinds. It is pitched with a hay-fork, for which purpose the two-tined is generally preferred. The mowing-machine and the best horse-rake will cut and rake about 12 to 15 acres a day, under favorable circumstances, with four horses and two men. The same work to be done by hand would require about 18 men.

401. It is laid down as a principle, which appears to be strictly true, that hay can scarcely be injured by *its own juices alone*, but if wet with rain or heavy dews it requires very careful drying before being put away.

402. In hauling, three and sometimes four men are required.

---

principles. "Damp hay, or even grass, may be stacked with layers of straw, or of old hay, sprinkled with salt to prevent heating, and to draw out the juice from the damp grass, which is then absorbed by the straw." [Rev. A. Huxtable, an eminent English Agriculturist, has long practiced this mode of putting hay by; and he finds that by so doing, not only does the grass require but little drying, but it so imparts its juices to the straw, as to render the latter still more valuable. The two are placed in layers, and in use are cut through, and mixed.] "Mouldy hay, put together with salt, from 8 lbs. to 25 lbs. per ton, was better relished by cattle, and did them more good than sound hay stacked without salt; of which many instances are recorded. (*Johnson on salt*, p. 165.) In Germany they even cure fresh cut grass by pitting with salt, 1 lb. to the 112 lbs.; it comes out quite a paste, and is said to go further as food than the same quantity of grass made into hay. When hay is packed with straw, the latter may vary from one-eighth to one-quarter, and the salt from 1 lb. to 3 lbs. per cwt., according to the dampness of the new hay. If old dry hay is used instead of straw, it must be in larger proportion because less absorbent. And where neither can be had, chaff might do, or even bran if salted enough to prevent fermentation." *Farmer's Magazine*, vol. iv, (1853) p. 280.

One stands on the wagon, one or two pitch to him, and one rakes the ground. It is not often, however, that the man on the wagon is able to stow it away as rapidly as two can pitch to him. Where hands are scarce, the raker is sometimes dispensed with, the hay-rake being run over the field when all is hauled. In changeable weather, no more should be cut in a day than can be well taken care of before night.

403. If sheds are used, the stowing away is very simple; one man standing on the load pitching, one inside catching and spreading the hay, and one salting and treading down. If stacked, the man on the stack requires experience, which can scarcely be taught by writing, so as to carry it up straight, of proper size and weight all round. An ill-made stack is very apt to fall over, or to let the wet into crevices and cracks. However, stacking is very deficient in economy. More or less hay is inevitably spoilt; and in winter it has either to be carried to to the barn to be consumed, exposing the remainder to wet, or the cattle, while feeding, are exposed to all vicissitudes of weather, waste much, and manure the ground, immediately around the stack, inordinately. It is calculated that a good shed, adapted for hay above, and for stock beneath, with proper racks, pays its own cost in three seasons, in saving alone.

404. There is a mode of increasing the yield of grass called *Gurneyism*, from its discoverer, the Hon. G. Gurney, of Cornwall, England. It consists of covering the field with 1¼ tons to the acre of straw, letting this lie for some time, and then raking it off. The grass is then cut or grazed, and the straw again returned. The principle on which this acts is unknown, but every one must have observed that grass covered with straw, or a bush grows more rapidly than when not covered. This mode does not appear to have been much used in England, and probably not at all in America. *(See Patent Office Reports,* 1846, p. 254,*)*

405. *Irrigation* of meadows is of high antiquity; and

greatly increases the yield. It requires the land to lie peculiarly in connection with running water, and a complex and artistic series of ditches and draining is necessary. It is too extensive a subject to enter upon in this work, though there are many positions in the United States where it may be favorably employed.

406. Good old hay is long and large, hard and tough; color inclining to green rather than to white, has a sweet taste and fragrant smell, and when infused in hot water produces a rich, dark-colored tea. In damp weather good hay absorbs moisture, and becomes heavier. "A truss" of good old hay weighs 56 lbs. (*Stephens.*) The following rule is given to find the weight of hay in bulk, but we have not tested it. It necessarily varies with circumstances, *old* hay weighing heavier per square foot than new; and ripe hay heavier than if cut before blossoming.

"Multiply the length, breadth, and height into each other, and if the hay is somewhat settled, ten solid yards will make a ton. Clover will require 11 to 12 such yards."

A peculiar mode of renovating worn out meadows has been employed of late years in Massachusetts. At the end of August or begining of September, the grass land is carefully and neatly plowed and rolled down. Fifteen to twenty loads of compost are next spread to the acre, and harrowed both ways. The grass seed is then sown and covered with a brush harrow, and is ready to cut the next summer, though perhaps a little later. The seed must be applied liberally, say three to four pecks per acre. (*Trans. of Agricul. Societies of Mass.*, 1852, p. 769.)

There are various other modes of renovating worn out meadows when it is not convenient to plow them, for which see *The Farmer's Companion and Horticultural Gazette*, vol. ii, (1853,) p. 20.

"In forming mixtures of grass seeds, every soil should be supplied with its appropriate mixture, both as regards succession and qualities; and as the permament ones require time to come to maturity, some of the more short lived should be introduced that there may be a crop from the begining, and also that there should be as great a variety as possible. The grasses thrive permamently only when mixed, some forming herbage in the spring and autumn, and a few throughout the warmer months; if they did not closely succeed each other, weeds would soon appear."

The following table, arranged by one of the large English Seed

Dealers, may prove practically valuable. This assortment of grasses, &c., is recommended as forming peculiarly excellent pasture. It were well if our American grains and grasses were tabulated in the same way. The number of seeds in an ounce are found by counting the number in a grain weight. The prices are given in English sterling, 5 shillings being rather more than one dollar—one penny to two cents.

| Scientific names. | Price of seed in London. per bus. | per lb. | Average weight. per bush | Average number of seeds in one ounce. |
|---|---|---|---|---|
| | s. d. | s. d. | lbs. | |
| Lolium italicum, | 6.0 | 0.6 | 15 | 27,000 |
| Dactylis glomerata, | 4.0 | | 11½ | 40,000 |
| Trifolium pretense, | | 0.6 | 64 | 16,000 |
| Trifolium pratense perenne, | | 0.7 | 64 | 16,000 |
| Alopecurus pratensis, | 5.0 | 0.8 | 5½ | 76,000 |
| Festuca pratensis, | 6.0 | 0.6 | 13 | 26,000 |
| ——— duriuscula, | 6.0 | 0.6 | 9½ | 39,000 |
| Poa nemoralis sempervirens, | | 1.6 | 15½ | 133,000 |
| Lotus corniculatus, | | 6.0 | 62 | 28,000 |
| Achillea Millefolium, | | 2.0 | 29¼ | 200,000 |
| Lolium perenne, | 5.6 | 0.3 | 24 | 14,850 |
| Trifolium repens, | | 0.6 | 65 | 32,000 |

# CHAPTER XIV.

---

## CLOVER (*Trifolium,*) AND OTHER FORAGE PLANTS.

407. Next to the Grasses, the Clovers are the most valuable as fodder plants. They belong to an entirely different botanical family, that of the *Leguminosœ, or Pulse Family*, and are known by the generic name *Trifolium* from *tree*, and *folium*, a leaf. Thence they are frequently called in English *Trefoils;* the leaves mostly presenting three lobes. Eight distinct species are found in the North United States; others again in the Southern States and California; and others in Europe. More than 160 species in all are enumerated by botanists. Nine species are cultivated in Great Britain; usually, only two in the Northern States of America. The following are the the most important:

| | | |
|---|---|---|
| (*a*,) | *Trifolium pratense*, | Annual or Biennial Red Clover.* |
| (*b*,) | " *pratense perenne*, | Perennial Red Clover, Cow grass.* |
| (*c*,) | " *repens.* | Dutch or English White Clover. |
| (*d*,) | " *repens*, | American White Clover.* |
| (*e*,) | " *hybridum*, | Hybrid or Alsyke Clover. |
| (*f*,) | " *minus.* | Lesser Yellow Trefoil, |
| (*g*,) | " *procumbens*, | Low Hop Trefoil. |
| (*h*,) | " *medium*, | Cow or Marl Grass, Southern |

---

*Those marked * are either natives of America, or extensively naturalized.

| | | | Clover, (?)* |
|---|---|---|---|
| *(i,)* | " | *incarnatum,* | Crimson Clover. |
| *(j,)* | " | *alexandrinum,* | Egyptian Clover. |
| *(k,)* | " | *arvense,* | Rabbit-foot Clover.* |
| *(l,)* | " | *reflexum,* | Buffalo Clover.* |
| *(m,)* | " | *agrarium,* | Hop Clover.* |

Of the above, 4 are "Red" Clovers; 3 are "White;" 3 are "Yellow;" and the rest varying. (*b,*) (*h,*) and (*l,*) are in common use with us, the latter chiefly in the Western States where it is indigenous. We have distinguished between the "Dutch" and "American" White Clovers, which Botanists do not usually do, but having grown them side by side, we find them essentially different in habit; the first (*c,*) is a tall, strong growing plant, well adapted for meadows, standing frequently, when supported, 18 inches high; while the latter (*d,*) is short, adhering to the ground, and wholly unfit for meadows. If one is only a variety of the other, which appears probable, they are, economically, very distinct. The Dutch or English White Clover would be a valuable addition to our plants of this family. Attempts have been lately made to introduce into America the Alsyke Clover, (*e,*) and the seed has been distributed by the Patent Office. It is a native of the South of Europe, but has long been cultivated in Sweden and Germany, where it is very highly esteemed, and latterly in Great Britain. It is described as peculiarly luxuriant. The root is fibrous, and the heads globular. The stems are recumbent, but they do not root in the soil; "in short it may be described as a *giant* white clover, with flesh colored flowers." It yields two mowings annually. It will grow luxuriantly on poor, bare, obdurate clays as well as on light sands. It ripens its seed much earlier, and continues in vigor much longer than the Red Clovers. When once rooted it will remain for a great many years in full vigor, and produce annually a great quantity of herbage of excellent quality. A heavier crop of wheat is invariably produced after this than after other clover. The quantity of seed requisite is from 10 to 15 pounds per acre, while it will yield over two cwt. on the same area. It does not suffer from the severest frosts; it will flourish on barren land where few grasses will grow at all; and with it the soil never becomes "clover sick." (*Dr. Lindley.*) Such is its European reputation, and it is certainly worth trying extensively in this country. The seed in London is worth two shillings sterling—50 cents—per pound; and at that price might become with us an article of export.

The Crimson Clover (*i*,) is a native of the Southern and Central parts of Europe. It is an annual, and must be sown in autumn that it may flower and arrive at maturity in the following season. It has latterly attracted much attention in England. The Egyptian clover (*j*,) is also an annual. The other species are small, and unfit to be sown alone, but are commonly mixed by the English with grasses, for which purposes they are well adapted as varying the food, and filling up blank spaces. They would be profitable with us in permanent pastures.*

408. Red Clover prefers clayey soils; it generally thrives in good wheat lands; in light and sandy ground it gets bare and frosted. During its early growth it always requires the shelter of some other plant. It is apt to be lifted out of the ground and destroyed by frost in winter, if eaten bare, and not covered by snow. White Clover grows spontaneously in most clay soils, such as are known as "heavy timbered lands;" appearing as soon as the forest is removed. For sheep-pasture nothing can surpass it; but it is usually rather short for larger stock. It has a peculiar effect on horses in producing severe salivation when in blossom, but without apparently injuring the health or strength:—why, does not appear to be ascertained. This, we believe, has not been observed in the European variety.

409. The Red species are extensively grown throughout the Northern United States, chiefly, however, in the moderate climates. In wheat-culture, they are greatly depended upon as a sort of manure.

---

*The difference between the annual Red Clover (*a*,) and Cow Grass (*h*,) is thus given by a late English writer. (*Farmer's Magazine*, vol. iii., 1853, p. 424.) "The first has a somewhat spindle shaped root, with but few fibres, grows more upright, has fewer hairs on the stem and leaves, thrives luxuriantly, stem generally hollow or pipey, broad leaves, and reddish-purple flowers; the latter has a somewhat creeping root, the stem grows zigzag and less globular than the other, and is solid or pithy, with a narrow leaf which, with the flowers, has a paler hue; it comes into flower from twelve to fourteen days later than the first." We do not remember ever meeting with the first in our Western States, where we are inclined to believe that our "large" species is the *Buffalo Clover*. It is, however, very difficult to distinguish the various species of this family. The California Clovers are spoken of as far surpassing any we at present cultivate in the Eastern portion of the continent.

410. Ultimate ANALYSIS of Red Clover (*a*?) (*Boussingault*,) one part of clover hay after complete desiccation weighed 0.790: one part of dried hay left, 0.078 of ash.

| | I. | II. |
|---|---|---|
| Carbon, - - | 47.53 | 47.19 |
| Hydrogen, - - - | 4.69 | 5.33 |
| Oxygen, - - | 57.96 | 37.66 |
| Nitrogen, - - - | 2.06 | 2.06 |
| Ash, - - | 7.76 | 7.76 |
| | 100.00 | 100.00 |

A surface of 120 square yards gave 44 lbs. roots, weighed after being thoroughly dried in the sun; when pulverized after drying in the stove the weight was reduced to 37 lbs. When perfectly dry one acre would furnish 1428 lbs. of residue. Composed as follows:

| | | |
|---|---|---|
| Carbon, - - - | 43.4 | per cent. |
| Hydrogen, - - | 5.3 | " |
| Oxygen, - - - | 36.9 | " |
| Nitrogen, - - | 1.8 | " |
| Salts and earth, - - | 12.6 | " |
| | 100.00 | |

The same writer shows the amount of clover hay obtained from, and clover roots left in the soil of one acre with the elementary matter of the latter, which forms manure when plowed under, as follows:

| | |
|---|---|
| Produce of hay per acre in 1839, - - | 2292 lbs. |
| do dried at 212° F., - - | 1810 lbs. |
| Roots dried in the sun, per acre, - - | 1833 lbs. |
| do do at 110° F., - - | 1418 lbs. |
| These roots consisted of, per acre, | |
| Carbon, - - - | 615 lbs. |
| Hydrogen, - - - | 75 lbs. |
| Oxygen, - - - | 523 lbs. |
| Nitrogen, - - - | 26 lbs. |
| Salts and earth, - - - | 178 lbs. |
| | 1417 lbs. |

Thus returning, for the use of the next crop, only 204 lbs. of nitrogen and salts, per acre.

411. Prof. Way finds 100 parts of the following clovers in their fresh state, to contain of water (A,) and flesh forming principles (B.)

| | A. | B. |
|---|---|---|
| Crimson clover, (*i*,) - - | 82.14 | 2.96 |
| Red clover, (*a*,) - - | 81.06 | 4.27 |
| Cow grass, (*h*,) - - | 74.10 | 6.30 |
| Sainfoin, - - - | 76.64 | 4.32 |

And Dr. Anderson, (*Trans. Highland Agricul. Society*, 1853, p. 509,) gives the amount of albuminous or flesh forming matters in the second crop of clover *hay* at 13.52 per cent.

Schwertz reckons that 2 cwt. (=224 lbs.) of green clover yield 48 lbs of hay. The relation of green to dry fodder varies with the age of the plant, and the meteorogical circumstances under which it has grown. At Bechelbronn 1 ton of clover in flower (second year,) afforded in hay 7 cwt.; 1 ton of clover in flower (first year,) afforded in hay 4 cwt. 2 qurs. 24 lbs. The average produce of this fodder reduced to hay was 41 cwt. (=112 lbs. per cwt.) 3 qurs. per acre. (*Boussingault.*)

412. Approximate composition of the green stems of Red Clover (A,) and White Clover (B.) (*Johnston.*)

| | A. | B. |
|---|---|---|
| Water, - - - | 76.0 | 80.0 |
| Starch, - - - | 1.4 | 1.0 |
| Woody Fibre, - - | 13.9 | 11.5 |
| Sugar, - - - | 2.1 | 1.5 |
| Albumen, - - - | 2.0 | 1.5 |
| Extractive matter and gum, - - | 3.5 | 3.4 |
| Phosphate of Lime, - - | 1.0 | 0.8 |
| Wax and Resin, - - - | 0.1 | 0.2 |

413. Inorganic analysis of Red Clover; Broad Clover (A,) White Clover (B,) and Cow Grass, (*T. Medium*) (C.)

| | Red Clover. | | | A. | B. | C. |
|---|---|---|---|---|---|---|
| | Boussingault. | Way. | Liebig. | | Way. | |
| Carbonic acid, - - | 25.0 | 16.9 | | 23.47 | 18.0 | 25.51 |
| Sulphuric acid, - | 2.5 | 4.2 | 1.1 | 1.85 | 7.2 | 1.08 |
| Phosphoric acid, - - | 6.3 | 6.3 | 4.1 | 6.71 | 11.5 | 5.41 |
| Chlorine, & chloride of sodi'm | 2.6 | 2.4 | 4.7 | | 5.0 | |
| Lime, - - | 24.6 | 35.4 | 21.9 | 22.62 | 26.4 | 24.56 |
| Magnesia, - - | 6.3 | 11.2 | 8.3 | 4.08 | 8.2 | 4.52 |
| Potash, - - | 26.6 | 14.9 | 16.1 | 36.45 | 14.3 | 34.72 |
| Soda, - - - | 0.5 | 1.4 | 40.7 | | 3.7 | |
| Silica, - - | 5.3 | 3.3 | 2.6 | 0.59 | 3.7 | 0.63 |
| Oxide of iron, &c., - | 0.3 | 1.0 | 0.5 | | 2.0 | |
| Chloride of potassium, - | | 3.0 | | | | |
| Dried ash, - - | | | | 9.56 | | 7.97 |

According to Sprengel, 100,000 parts of White clover in a fresh state contain 1735 parts of inorganic matter.

414. The following is a late comparative analysis of White clover (A,) Trefoil (B,) Red clover *(a,)* (C,) and Tares (D,) all grown on the same land in a natural condition, on the farm of the Royal Agricultural College, Cirencester, England. *(Dr. Voelcker.)*

| | A. | B. | C. | D. |
|---|---|---|---|---|
| Water, - - | 83.65 | 77.570 | 80.640 | 82.16 |
| Nitrogenized matter capable of producing flesh, - - | 4.52 | 4.481 | 3.606 | 3.56 |
| Substances free from nitrogen capable of sustaining respiration. | 10.26 | 15.949 | 13.784 | 12.74 |
| Inorganic substances, - - | 1.57 | 2.000 | 1.970 | 1.54 |

By "*Trefoil*" the context leads us to suppose that Hop clover (*T. procumbeus,*) (*g*) is meant, but as the writer neglects to give the botanical name we cannot be sure.

415. The following tables, show the difference of the water and inorganic constituents of Red and White Clover hay, on different soils. *(Way.)*

| | Red Clover. | | White Clover. | |
|---|---|---|---|---|
| | Silicious Sand. | Clay. | Silicious Sand. | Clay. |
| Water, - - | 13.97 | 12.20 | 12.60 | 12.00 |
| Ash, - - | 6.77 | 7.12 | 7.70 | 7.61 |
| Ash calculated on the dry, - | 7.87 | 8.11 | 8.81 | 8.65 |

Composition of 100 parts of ash of Red and White Clover hay. (*Way.*)

| | Red Clover. | | White Clover. | |
|---|---|---|---|---|
| | Silicious Sand. | Clay. | Silicious Sand. | Clay. |
| Silica, - - | 4.03 | 2.66 | 4.63 | 2.74 |
| Phosphoric acid, - - | 5.82 | 6.88 | 10.93 | 12.12 |
| Sulphuric acid, - | 3.91 | 4.46 | 7.05 | 7.38 |
| Carbonic acid, - - | 12.92 | 20.94 | 18.64 | 17.41 |
| Lime, - - | 35.02 | 35.76 | 26.32 | 26.51 |
| Magnesia, - - | 11.91 | 10.53 | 7.46 | 8.83 |
| Peroxide of iron, - | 0.98 | 0.95 | 1.17 | 2.76 |
| Potash, - - | 18.44 | 11.30 | 15.17 | 13.50 |
| Soda, - - | 2.79 | | 3.03 | 4.41 |
| Chloride of sodium, - | 4.13 | 0.58 | 5.56 | 4.32 |
| Chloride of potassium, - - | | 5.92 | | |

416. Mineral matters contained in a ton of Red (A,) and White Clover (B,) hay. (In pounds and tenths.) (*Way.*)

| | A. | B. |
|---|---|---|
| | lbs. | lbs. |
| Silica, - - - | 5.2 | 6.3 |
| Phosphoric acid, - - - | 10.0 | 19.9 |
| Sulphuric acid, - - | 6.6 | 12.4 |
| Lime, - - - - | 55.6 | 45.5 |
| Magnesia, - - - | 17.7 | 14.0 |
| Peroxide of iron, - - - | 1.5 | 3.4 |
| Potash, - - - | 23.2 | 24.7 |
| Soda, - - - - | 2.2 | 6.4 |
| Chloride of sodium, - - | 3.7 | 8.5 |
| Chloride of potassium, - - | 4.7 | |
| | 128.4 | 141.1 |

417. As will be seen by these various analyses, the clovers are all peculiarly nutritious, containing everything that can be wanted for the growth and sustenance of an animal. The flesh and fat-forming constituents are large, and phosphate of lime, for the formation of bone predominates. The long tap-roots force them away deeply into the subsoil, the fibrous roots collect nutriment from the surface, and the large fleshy leaves, as

in all leguminous plants, are capable of absorbing such constituents as the air can afford. At the same time, if cut as hay, and carried off the ground, the clovers remove a comparatively large amount of valuable materials from the soil, and it is only owing to the fact that much of the material is collected in the subsoil, below the usual depth of the plow, and the roots of the cereals, that it does not become a *scourging* crop. As it is, it returns to the surface of the soil that which it has gathered from the subsoil, and which, under the ordinary system of cultivation would not have become available. Under a system of *thorough-draining*, which allows the roots of *all* plants to go to a great depth, many of the supposed advantages of clover as a manure would be lost.

418. From these analyses, also, we learn what manures are likely to be peculiarly advantageous; viz, such as contain nitrogen,—guano, barn-yard dung, urine, &c.; and such as contain the inorganic constituents—lime; phosphoric acid, in the shape of ground bones; sulphuric acid, in the shape of Plaster; Potash, as wood ashes; and soda, as common salt. Unless land contains a notable proportion of all these, Clover cannot prosper upon it.

419. Clover is always sown with some grain crops, and usually in the spring, as hard frosts are apt to injure the young plants. If with fall wheat, the seed is frequently sown upon the last snow in the spring, the covering which it receives from absorption being sufficient, or it may be harrowed and rolled. If sown with spring grain it should be treated as is recommended for grasses. The quantity of seed requisite, when unmixed, is from 10 to 18 lbs., according to the character, condition, and richness of the soil. Some persons steep the seed for twenty-four hours and roll it in plaster.

420. If intended for hay, it should be cut immediately after blossoming, and before the seed begins to form. The same

rule applies to the second crop. Seed is saved only from the second crop; and may be cut in the usual manner and thrashed, or the heads are pulled off by an implement for the purpose, and the hay left as pasture. Before thrashing, the seed should be allowed to become perfectly dry. The produce varies from 2½ to 6 bushels per acre, when cleaned. Cleaning the seed for market, requires a machine for the purpose worked by horse-power. In consequence, many farmers sow it mixed with the chaff, in which case they must judge as well as they can of the quantity.

Clover seed should be large, full, glossy, and of bright orange yellow and bold purple mixed; when handled it has an oily feel. Damaged seed is said to be frequently dried and polished in England for sale, but this can generally be detected by the rougher feel, and the duller appearance; and still better by sprouting it as directed for the grasses. The Statute weight in Michigan is 60 lbs. to the bushel, but the best seed will weigh as much as 64 lbs. or over. At 64 lbs. to the Imperial Bushel, 2000 grains weigh one drachm. (*Stephens.*) The seed of White Clover is very small, of a rich golden yellow color, weighing 65 lbs. to the bushel, and affording 4000 grains to a drachm weight. (*Stephens.*) New seeds are the best, the germinating power failing the second year. Large quantities of the seed of Red Clover are annually exported to Europe.

421. In making clover hay, great care must be taken that the leaf is not so scorched and dried up as to break into powder; which too often happens, to the great injury of the hay. This may be avoided by the following process. While mowing, have men to follow, and put every swathe into small cocks, at about a rod distance. On the second day, or if the weather is damp, not till the third, turn over one of those small cocks, and place two more upon it, laying the greenest part nicely on the top so as to shed rain; then let it remain several days. It becomes a little heated, and the moisture all evaporates through the cock. Before hauling in, open the cocks, and air them for an hour previous. By loading and unloading it receives air enough to be thoroughly cured, if sufficiently sweated in the cock.

It remains green, with all the leaves upon the hay, just as it came from the scythe. *(A. Y. Moore.)* The same may be accomplished more rapidly, though perhaps not quite as perfectly, by allowing the clover to lie in swathe just long enough to wilt, and be warmed through. Then put in small cocks, and leave two days, if the weather is dry and hot, longer if cloudy or damp; air before hauling, and salt as directed for grass-hay. We have followed this plan for many years with great success. The clover is not quite dry when put in the shed, but the salt prevents any injury. We prefer it to be damp enough to melt the salt, and partially heat.

422. In the United States clover appears to be free from any peculiar enemies or diseases. In Europe it suffers from several.

In some of the Eastern States, a caterpillar has been found in large numbers spinning its webs over the clover, but it does not appear to be very injurious, nor is the species accurately determined. *(Harris' Treatise,* 2nd ed. p. 354.*)*

But in both continents, the land sometimes fails to produce clover when sown, a condition known by the name of *Clover Sickness.* While Agricultural Chemistry was unstudied, this peculiarity was the cause of much wonder and many disputes. It is now well known to be owing to the deficiency of the soil in one or more of the inorganic constituents requisite for clover; and can be cured by special manures; by sowing it at longer intervals; or by using a different rotation of crops. To this cause may also be attributed the dying out of clover after having partially attained its growth, which sometimes occurs in over-cropped wheat lands. Seed still retaining its chaff, or outward covering, is supposed to be less subject to failure than when clean, which is probably true. Where Red Clover is apt to be destroyed in winter, by the frost raising the roots out of the ground, it may be partially or wholly prevented either by leaving the aftergrowth uneaten, or by spreading straw heavily over the sod to be left all winter, and then raked off.

423. Besides the true Clovers or Trefoils, several other plants closely resembling them are more or less used, in Great Britain, to mix with grass seeds. Two of them are natives of the United States—(*a.*) Sweet Clover, or Yellow Melilot (*Melilotus officinalis,*) and (*b,*) White Melilot (*M. leaucantha,*) but the most important of this genus is (*c,*) the Bokhara Clover, (*M. leucantha major,*) a biennial. It stands the winters in Scotland, and probably would in our middle States. Two species of the Bird's-foot Trefoil are also used in England. (*Lotus corniculatus,* and *L. major.*) Besides these, the following might be profitably introduced among us. (*d,*) Burnet, (*Poterium Sanguisorba.*) This is frequently grown in gardens as an herb ; and we find it quite hardy in damp loam on the Detroit River, though it naturally belongs to dry and calcareous soils. It is one of the first plants to become green in spring. It enters largely into old English meadows and pastures, and from its peculiar bitter and aromatic flavor, would probably be beneficial for sheep in miasmatic climates. (For picture and description, see *Patent Office Report,* 1847.) (*e,*) Yarrow or Milfoil, (*Achillea Millefolium*)—a native of the United States. It is closely eaten by pasturing animals, and has long been cultivated in Great Britain along with other herbage plants. (*f,*) Ribwort, or Plantain. (*Plantago lanceolata.*) According to Prof. Gray, this is extensively naturalized in the Eastern States. Cattle greedily eat our common Plantain, (*P. Major,*) a well-known weed around houses.

424. LUCERN (*Medicago sativa,*) together with the next mentioned, are extensively cultivated as fodder plants in some parts of Europe, but are of little practical interest, at present, in the United States. This is a perennial, grows a foot and a half to two feet high, and flowers in June and July. It requires a deep light soil, with an open subsoil. It is sown either broadcast, or in rows, and cultivated with the hoe and cultivator, which process must be continued for at least three years; till which period it does not arrive at its full growth. When sown broadcast, it has also to be kept clean with the hoe, like turnips. There are two species, both of which have become naturalized in the Eastern States.

425. SAINFOIN (*Onobrychis sativa,*)—(from the French *sain, healthy—foin hay*)—is, likewise, a perennial, but belongs almost exclusively to the chalk and lime formations and light sands. It is on dry rocky soils that the chief advantages of its cultivation are observed.

It may be cultivated like clover, or grown in rows like the last. It is used either as hay, for soiling, or pasture. It contains 76.64 per cent of water, and 4.32 flesh-forming principles, being slightly more nutritious than Red Clover. (*Way.*)

Boussingault (See *Rural Economy,* chap. vi., p. 321, New York ed.,) found this crop to vary, per acre:

| | |
|---|---|
| Dry herb, | 2068 lbs. to 5462 lbs. |
| Seed, | 66 lbs. to 582 lbs. |
| Weight of total crop, | 2134 lbs. to 6044 lbs. |

Plaster has as remarkable an effect upon it as on clover.

426. Analyses of Lucern (*Sprengel*) (A,) and Sainfoin (*Way*) (B):

| | A. | B. |
|---|---|---|
| Organic matter, | 89.6 | 93.7 |
| Ash, | 10.3 | 6.36 |

Inorganic analyses of the above, (*Liebig and Way.*)

| | A. | B. |
|---|---|---|
| Sand and Silica, | 2.3 | 3.2 |
| Potash, | 17.3 | 31.9 |
| Soda, | 4.9 | |
| Lime, | 28.5 | 24.3 |
| Magnesia, | 6.7 | 5.0 |
| Oxide of iron, | 0.4 | 0.6 |
| Chloride of sodium, | 2.3 | 0.8 |
| Phosphoric acid, | 6.6 | 9.4 |
| Sulphuric acid, | 1.0 | 3.3 |
| Carbonic acid, | 29.0 | 15.2 |
| Chloride of potassium, | | 6.2 |

427. CHICORY (*Cichorium Intybus,*) also called "Succory," is a native of England, but it has become naturalized in the Atlantic States. It is recommended as a fodder plant, and the root is extensively used in Europe to mix with, or as a substitute for, coffee. The rich aromatic bitter of the French coffee is chiefly owing to this. In Italy it is made into hay; in

France it is cultivated extensively for forage, and enters into the regular rotations of the fields. It is attracting much attention at present in England. It will withstand the severest cold, and bear drought well, its large leaves covering the ground, and the root striking deep into it. It comes very early in the spring, and may be cut for soiling several times in the year. It is a perennial with very ornamental blue blossoms.

428. Comparative analysis of the dry root (A,) and fresh root (B,) of Chiccory. (*Dr. Anderson.*)

| | A. | B. |
|---|---|---|
| Water, | 18.01 | 80.58 |
| Ash, on dry, | 3.64 | 6.77 |
| Nitrogen, on dry, | 1.60 | 1.48 |
| Ash on moist substance, | | 1.31 |

429. Inorganic analysis. (*Ibid.*)

| | I. | II. |
|---|---|---|
| Silica, | 3.790 | 0.99 |
| Peroxide of iron, | 0.657 | 0.81 |
| Lime, | 8.644 | 6.09 |
| Magnesia, | 5.777 | 3.15 |
| Sulphuric acid, | 13.048 | 4.80 |
| Phosphoric acid, | 13.882 | 10.02 |
| Potash, | 29.687 | 42.60 |
| Chloride of potassium, | | 1.78 |
| Soda, | 7.641 | |
| Chloride of sodium, | 2.555 | 6.83 |
| Sand, | 3.271 | 1.12 |
| Charcoal, | 2.567 | 9.90 |
| Carbonic acid, | 7.927 | 11.40 |

It seems from the above that the plant has great powers of appropriation or replacement of constituents. It probably is able to replace the potash with soda.

430. Where this plant is grown for the sake of the root the following is the English mode of cultivation. The autumn previous to sowing, the land must be manured and deeply plowed, and if it be dry and porous,—the best for this crop—harrowed before winter. About the second week in May, the soil is ridged up so as to deepen it, and facilitate subsequent

hoeing, and the seed sown at the rate of 3¼ to 4 lbs. per acre in drills, 12 to 14 inches apart. The plants will not appear for a month or six weeks, and during this period care must be taken to keep down the weeds with the cultivator. The plants, if too thick, should be thinned to 5 or 6 inches. The subsequent cultivation consists in careful hand-hoeing. Late in October the roots are dug with a three-pronged fork. The leaves may be previously removed and fed to sheep. When taken up the roots are topped and tailed, then washed, and cut into slices like turnips, only in lengths as equal as possible. They must be dried, either by exposure to the sun, or in kilns, when they are ready for market. The usual yield is from 12 to 15 tons of the wet roots per acre, the latter diminishing when dried to about 1½ tons. The price in England varies from $50 to $150 per ton. When used, the slices are roasted and ground like coffee. The principal objection to this crop is the great difficulty with which it is afterwards eradicated, the smallest fibre left in the ground forming a plant. Still this may be accomplished, or nearly so, by hoeing. Sheep, in common with all stock, are very fond of the leaves, and prosper well upon them; and a few acres devoted to this esculent would prove valuable for early and late sheep-feed, and for horses and cattle in summer. If sown broadcast 12 to 14 lbs. of seed to the acre are required.

431. White Mustard, *(Sinapis alba,)* has of late years been cultivated in England as a forage plant, but from experiments we have made with it, it does not appear to be suitable to this climate. The heat dwarfs it, and it is seriously injured by a minute black beetle, which attacks it early in spring. In light soils, however, it might succeed better.

These constitute all the forage plants that can be of interest in the Northern States; except Rape which will be described in the next chapter.

# CHAPTER XV.

## PLANTS CULTIVATED FOR THEIR ROOTS, AND LEAVES. TURNIPS. *(Brassica.)* KOHL RABI. CABBAGE. RAPE.

432. In Great Britain and Germany roots are grown to a very great extent to feed stock, and to act, indirectly, as a renovator of the soil, in rotations. It is not yet a century, since the present *system* of root culture was introduced, but it has entirely revolutionized Agriculture, and the Art could not now be profitably exercised without it. This class of plants is not numerous, and they owe their beneficial effect on the soil chiefly to the fact that they are not allowed to seed. If they bear seed, they cease to be "fallow crops," and in their effects become similar to the cereals. They may be comprised in the genera, *(a,)* Turnips, (including Cabbages;) *(b,)* Potatoes; *(c,)* Carrots; *(d,)* Parsneps; *(e,)* Beets; *(f,)* Jerusalem Artichokes; *(g,)* Onions; *(h,)* Sweet Potatoes. Still more are cultivated as garden plants. The climate of a great portion of the United States is but illy adapted for the winter-preservation of several of these roots; and this fact, together with our less scientific and more careless mode of farming, has tended to discourarge their cultivation. In the older States, however, more attention is now being paid to this subject, and there are none of the above which may not be successfully and profitably cultivated in Michigan. The profit of a root crop is two fold—direct and indirect:—*direct*, when we sell or so consume the produce in feeding animals as to realize more money than the production has cost us; *indirect*, when our only profit is in

the manure and the improvement of the soil for succeeding crops. English farmers are content to grow large fields of turnips, &c., and fatten many head of stock, merely for the benefit which the succeeding grain crops will receive.

433. Turnips belong to the botanical family of CABBAGE, *(Brassica,)* of which the following species are cultivated in the United States.

| | | |
|---|---|---|
| *(a,)* | *Brassica Rapa,* | Common Turnip. |
| *(b,)* | " *Napus,* | Rape, or Cole. |
| *(c,)* | " *Oleracea,* | Cabbage, |

The true Turnips again are thus divided:

| | | |
|---|---|---|
| *(a,)* | *Brassica Rapa,* | Common Turnip. |
| *(b,)* | " *Campestris Napo-brassica,* | Swedish Turnip. |
| *(c,)* | " *Napus esculenta,* | Turnip-rooted Cole. |
| *(d,)* | " *Oleracea Caulo-rapa,* | Turnip-stemmed Cabbage or Kohl-rabi. |

Of the turnips, there are very many sub-varieties originated by cultivation, such as round, depressed, fusiform, white, green, and red, each of which is supposed to possess some peculiar good qualities. We shall, probably, originate in the United States varieties better adapted to our climate than those of Europe. The three great divisions at present are, *(a,)* The Common Turnip; *(b,)* The Hybrid Turnip; and *(c,)* the Swede, (or *Ruta-Baga,* a name, but rarely used by English writers.)

434. The Common Turnip is too well known to need description. The Hybrid *(b,)* has the leaves of the Common Turnip, and the character of Rape and of the Swede, and is supposed to be formed by a cross of these three. It is hardy, nutritious, and less apt to be injured by frost. The Swede *(c,)* is hard, yellow, containing less moisture, and keeps longer into spring, so that it is the last consumed.

435. The soil best adapted to this crop contains a small amount of clayey matters, and is characterized by its light, loamy texture. Barley and Turnips usually prosper well on the same soil. The following are analyses made in Scotland, of two different specimens of good "Turnip soils," on which such crops had just been grown. *(Dr. Anderson.)*

| | | |
|---|---|---|
| Insoluble silicates, | 87 89 | 90.695 |
| Soluble silica, | 0.07 | 0.073 |
| Peroxide of iron, | 2.94 | 1.233 |
| Alumina, | 1.59 | 0.893 |
| Lime, | 0.38 | 0.319 |
| Magnesia, | 0.13 | 0.279 |
| Potash, | 0.14 | 0.056 |
| Chloride of sodium, | 0.10 | Soda 0.043 |
| Sulphuric acid, | 0.05 | 0.039 |
| Phosphoric acid, | 0.04 | 0.018 |
| Organic matter, | 4.66 | 4.996 |
| Water, | 1.75 | 1.444 |
| Chlorine, | | trace. |
| Nitrogen, | | 0.164 |

These analyses, are valuable not only in this peculiar aspect, but as a standard whereby to compare our own soils. They had long been cultivated and highly manured.

436. The meteorological conditions of the country seriously influence the yield of turnips. Thus Scotland and the West of England, with their greater amount and frequency of rain, produce larger crops than the Eastern shores of the same country, *(C. W. Johnson;)* while in most parts of the United States, we are obliged to sow late to escape the heat, and the roots are very much smaller.

437. Ultimate ANALYSIS of the Turnip. *(Boussingault.)* A slice weighing 2 oz. 17 dwts. dried in the stove was reduced to 4 dwts. After thorough desiccation, one part of turnip weighed 0.075, consequently the root contains 92.5 per cent of water. One part of dried turnip left 0.0758 of ash :

| | I. | II. |
|---|---|---|
| Carbon, | 42.80 | 49.93 |
| Hydrogen, | 5.54 | 5.61 |
| Oxygen, | 42.40 | 42.20 |
| Nitrogen, | 1.68 | 1.68 |
| Ash, | 7.58 | 7.58 |

438. Water (A;) solid matter (B) and ash(C;)—100 parts in moist state—in turnips, grown in four different localities in Scotland. (*Dr. Anderson.*)

| | A. | B. | C. |
|---|---|---|---|
| White Globe Turnips (*a*,) | 93.18 | 6.82 | 0.67 |
| do do (*b*,) | 92.85 | 7.15 | 0.78 |
| do do (*c*,) | 94.03 | 5.97 | 0.69 |
| Swedes, do (*d*,) | 90.07 | 9.91 | 0.57 |

439. Inorganic analysis of the same turnips. (*Dr. Anderson.*)

| | A. | B. | C. | D. |
|---|---|---|---|---|
| Silica, | | 0.60 | 0.18 | 0.28 |
| Potash, | 47.460 | 44.11 | 42.83 | 48.02 |
| Soda, | 2.655 | 5.48 | 13.66 | 3.93 |
| Chloride of sodium, | 13.990 | 21.99 | 5.45 | 7.04 |
| Lime, | 8.689 | 7.91 | 9.23 | 10.67 |
| Magnesia, | 4.555 | 3.88 | 4.97 | 4.45 |
| Sulphuric acid, | 12.603 | 9.03 | 12.23 | 12.16 |
| Phosphoric acid, | 8.613 | 6.81 | 11.14 | 13.07 |
| Peroxide of iron, | 1.435 | 0.19 | 0.31 | 0.38 |

The proportion of nitrogen in healthy turnips varies within extremely wide limits, and that without any assignable cause. In two of the above specimens the nitrogen was respectively 3.81 and 2.54. By comparing the analyses of other chemists the nitrogen may be averaged from 1.65 to 4.31, equivalent to 2.00 and 5.22 of Ammonia. From these facts we learn that this plant varies not only in its agricultural requirements but also greatly in its nutritive powers; and that one ton of turnips may be capable of forming as much flesh, as two and a half tons grown on a different soil. Dr. Anderson places the average of the flesh-forming matter in turnips as low as 1.27 in 100 parts of the fresh substance. The phosphates vary in a like manner. In 12 analyses of turnips of two varieties, grown on different soils, and with different manures, these varied from

6.8 on clay to 17.6 on "black land;" while the nitrogen in the fibre, and the nitrogen in the juice, equally uncertain, appear to bear no relative proportion to each other.

440. Organic analysis of Swedes. *(Johnston.)*

| | |
|---|---|
| Albumen, | 3.5 |
| Fat and oil, | 2.0 |
| Gum, Dextrine and pectine, | 14.9 |
| Sugar, | 58.9 |
| Fibre and husk, | 20.3 |

"The potato is characterised by containing a large proportion of starch in connection with a small quantity of albumen —the turnip and carrot by containing in place of the starch a variable proportion of sugar, and of a gelatinous gummy-like substance, to which the name of *pectin* has been given. In the Swedish Turnip and in the carrot the pectin is usually present in the larger quantity." *(Johnston.)* The same writer gives the following comparative table; remarking, however, that "these analyses are very defective, and apply with any degree of correctness only to the specimens actually operated on." They will answer, at the same time, to give a general view of these plants.

| | Variety of Turnips. | | | | | |
|---|---|---|---|---|---|---|
| | White. | Swedes. | Cabbage. | Common carrot. | Sugar beet. | Parsnip. |
| Water, | 79.0 | 80.0 | 78.0 | 80.0 | 85.0 | 79.4 |
| Starch and fibre, | 7.2 | 5.3 | 6.0 | 9.0 | 3.0 | 6.9 |
| Gum (pectin,) | 2.5 | 3.0 | 3.5 | 1.75 | 2.0 | 6.1 |
| Sugar, | 8.0 | 9.0 | 9.0 | 7.8 | 10.0 | 5.5 |
| Albumen, | 2.5 | 2.0 | 2.5 | 1.1 | ? | 2.1 |
| Salt, | 0.5 | 0.5 | 0.5 | — | ? | ? |
| Loss, | 0.5 | 0.2 | 0.5 | oil 0.35 | — | ? |

441. Average of water (A.) and ash (B.) in turnips grown in England, *(Way and Ogsden.)*

| | Water. | | | Ash. | | | Ash Dry. | | |
|---|---|---|---|---|---|---|---|---|---|
| | Highest. | Lowest. | Mean. | Highest. | Lowest. | Mean. | Highest. | Lowest. | Mean. |
| Bulb, | 92.7 | 86.0 | 90.0 | 1.13 | 0.48 | 0.73 | 10.90 | 4.00 | 7.30 |
| Top, | 90.0 | 79.0 | 85.5 | 2.64 | 1.19 | 1.84 | 18.00 | 8.00 | 12.98 |

The nitrogen in the tops appears to average much higher than in the bulb.

442. A crop of 20 tons of bulbs or roots, and 4 tons of leaves of turnips, mangel wurtzel, and carrots will respectively withdraw from the soil of an acre as follows:—(*Way.*)

| | Turnips. | M. Wurtzel. | Carrots. |
|---|---|---|---|
| Phosphoric acid, | 45 lbs. | 21 lbs. | 39 lbs. |
| Sulphuric acid, | 50 " | 22 " | 57 " |
| Lime, | 90 " | 21 " | 197 " |
| Magnesia, | 14 " | 22 " | 29 " |
| Potash, | 140 " | 133 " | 134 " |
| Soda, | 33 " | 70 " | 103 " |
| Chloride of sodium, | 57 " | 160 " | 85 " |
| | 429 " | 449 " | 664 " |

443. *Pectin*, or Pectic acid ($C_{12}H_8O_{10}$) (*Solly*) is a substance analogous to gum, which exists in many plants, and especially in fruit. It is a tasteless solid, which swells up, and gelatinizes with water. It possesses feeble acid powers, combining with bases to form *pectates*. Containing no nitrogen, it belongs to the heat or fat forming constituents of food—and in this respect appears to act as an equivalent, in food, to starch. Pectic acid has been found in every plant for which it has been sought for; but in some it usurps the chief place, as in turnips, carrots, beets, Jerusalem artichokes, onions, and in all kinds of fruits. It is also found in the stalks and leaves of herbaceous plants, in the wood and bark of all the trees examined, &c. *See Boussingault Rural Econ. p.* 129. *Pereira on Food and Diet*. Ch. ii. § 6.

444. The characteristics desirable in the turnip are hardiness against insects and disease; rapid growth; moderate size of bulb; and capability of keeping sound and fresh. Not only are very large bulbs apt to be hollow, or cellular, but late examinations have shown that they contain, proportionably, less nutritive matter than smaller ones: in some instances the difference was as high as 50 per cent. In England some varieties are found much more liable to disease than others; and some retain their flavor and solidity longer than others. In all these respects, the Swedes appear to stand preeminent.

445. In Great Britain, the average *good* crop varies from 15 to 40 tons of bulbs "topped, tailed, and well cleaned" per acre, according to soil, and meteorological locality; while the *tops* of Swedes reach as high as 17 tons on the same area.

"If planted 28 inches from row to row, and 10 inches from turnip to turnip, each turnip taking up 280 square inches, there would be 22,402 turnips, which at 3 lbs. each is 30 tons, 6 lbs. per acre; at 4 lbs. each turnip, 40 tons, 8 lbs. per acre."

In New York and Pennsylvania 600 bushels per acre of the common turnip are generally considered a good crop. The *Farmers' Cabinet*, iii. 17, mentions an instance where 850 bushels were raised to the acre. The Swedes yield one-third more than the common variety; of these 1200 to 1600 bushels have been raised to the acre. (*Wiggins.*) In Rensselaer Co., N. Y. a premium was given in 1848, for a crop of the last of 1,238½ bushels per acre.

446. The cost of cultivating the last named crop was as follows, the quantity of land being 1 2-10 acres.

| | |
|---|---|
| Plowing the fall previous, | $2.25 |
| do and harrowing in spring, | 6.50 |
| Light harrowing, previous to sowing, | 50 |
| Seed, | 75 |
| Drilling in seed at $1 per day, | 31 |
| Thinning, weeding and after culture, 11 days, | 8.25 |
| Man and horse with cultivator 3 times, | 2.50 |
| 14 days harvesting and securing, | 10.50 |
| 20 loads of manure, | 13.00 |
| Interest on land at $150 per acre, | 12.60 |
| | $57.16 |
| 1,486 bushels at 12½ cents per bushel, | $185.75 |
| Net proceeds, | $128.59 |

(*Trans. of N. Y. State Agricultural Society*, Vol. viii: p. 328.)

447. The culture of this crop in Great Britain is very complex, and has, perhaps, been more thoroughly studied than any

other. We must refer our readers to works especially upon the subject, merely laying down the following principles.

*(a,)* The soil for this crop should be light, rich, thoroughly plowed, and pulverized. Fair crops may be raised on some clay soils, but they require more labor to put them in a proper condition. No crop demands more thorough tillage previous to the sowing.

*(b,)* Drilling the seed, at 20 to 24 inches, the distance of the rows, instead of broadcasting, saves much after labor.

*(c,)* The land must be kept perfectly clean, and often stirred with the hoe.

*(d,)* The manures requisite are those which will supply nitrogen, and the peculiar inorganic constituents. Supposing the soil to be in a fair average condition, the following may be applied: 1. Super phosphate of lime; 2. Ground bones, in various states of preparation; 3. Guano; 4. Barnyard manure, or compost; 5. Common salt; 6. Wood ashes; 7. Lime; 8. Plaster. In rich English soils, guano, bones, and ashes, are usually considered sufficient.

*(e,)* It is exceedingly important that the young plant should be rapidly forced into the "rough leaf." Previous to this, it is subject to the attacks of several insects; and its future prosperity appears to depend on the early rapidity of growth.

448. In the United States, turnips are usually grown as a *second* crop in the fall, being sown in New York and Michigan from the end of July to the 12th of August. The Swedes require the longest period of growth. If sown broadcast, a quart of seed, if by drill, a pint is sufficient. The harvesting must be performed before hard frosts set in. The roots are pulled by hand, laid on the ground, the tops of the two rows facing each other. A man follows with a bill hook, and separates the tops from the roots. Three men will harvest 300 bushels a day. The tops are taken to the barn yard for the cattle. The best mode of storing is in root-cellars, with straw; but hills or pits—

such as are used for potatoes—may be made in the field. On feeding, the bulbs should be cut up. This may be done with a common shovel, but there are various machines for the purpose, which save much labor.

449. Fattening cattle, averaging 900 lbs. live weight, will eat 150 lbs. of common turnips daily, with 7 lbs. of oat straw.

450. In Europe, many diseases, such as *Fingers and toes, Black cracks,* &c. seriously injure this crop. In the United States it appears to be free from any general malady.

451. There are several insects which are more or less injurious in this country. The worst is the Black Flea-beetle (*Haltica pubescens.* Ill ?) if we do not have the *true* Turnip fly of Europe (*H. nemorum*); but little is yet known of this family. On a small scale, it may be driven off by scattering over the plants finely powdered plaster, or *boiled* plaster mixed with spirits of turpentine, and dried ; but the best preventative is rapidly forcing the plant into the rough leaf. This insect is peculiarly fond of *White Mustard,* which may be sown in the neighborhood. In Massachusetts, the caterpillar of a white butterfly (*Pontia oleracea*) devours turnip leaves. The Iulus also bores into the roots, and even the common Earth-worm appears, in some way, to penetrate them.

452. If seed is required, the best roots should be selected in spring, set out about 2 feet apart, in good land, and hoed while growing. If any particular variety is required it must be kept far apart from any other.

453. The seeds of turnips contain much oil. The following production of seed and oil is given by Boussingault.

| | Swedish Turnip. | Rape. | Kohl Rabi. |
|---|---|---|---|
| Seed produc'd per acre, | 15cwt. 1qr. 25lbs. | 16cwt. 2qrs. 18lbs. | 13cwt. 3qrs. 19lbs. |
| Whole qnt'ty oil pr acre, | 595.8 lbs. | 641.6 lbs. | 565.4 lbs. |
| Oil obtained per cent. | 33 | 33 | 33 |
| Cake pr. cent. | 62 | 62 | 61 |

454. Kohl Rabi, *Turnip stemmed Cabbage,* is chiefly cultivated in Germany, where it is eaten both by man and animals. It is perfectly hardy on the Detroit river, is subject to few casualities, and is little affected by frost. It may be grown in the

seed-bed and then transplanted, like a cabbage, or drilled, and thinned out, and cultivated as turnips are. It should be sown as early in spring as the temperature will permit. It is much harder than any of the turnips, and in rich lands, apt to become stringy. We consider it worthy of more extended cultivation. There are two varieties,—the *green* and *purple*. *Horsford* gives the nitrogen as 2.17 per cent.

455. CABBAGE *(Brassica oleracea.)* Of this there is a great number of varieties, most of them adapted to garden cultivation. In some parts of Great Britain, the larger varieties are cultivated in fields for the purpose of feeding cows and other stock; but in the United States, the price of labor, and the climate will probably long preclude cabbages from being a field crop. They require very rich clayey soils, as well as high cultivation. The leaves average 92 per cent. and the stalks 84 per cent. of water. The nitrogen is believed to be proportionably greater than in any other plant consumed by man except perhaps mushrooms. The flower of one species (cauliflower) in the dry state has been found to contain as much as 64 per cent. of the flesh-forming constituents *(Johnston.)* The inorganic constituents resemble those required by the rest of the family, viz: the alkalies, sulphuric, and phosphoric acids, and chlorine.

456. RAPE. Two species of this are usually cultivated, Rape or Cole *(Brassica Napus)* and Colza *(B. campestris.)* The use is twofold—*(a)* as a forage plant; *(b)* to afford oil from the seed, the *cake* of which is largely consumed as a manure and as top dressing for wheat and other cereals. Rape is a native of England; is a hardy plant; and has a wider range of soils than the turnip. It requires also, less culture and manure; and can be produced under circumstances in which the turnip cannot be profitably cultivated. The root is of no value. As a pasture plant it is admirably adapted for sheep. Where the climate will permit, it may be sown in spring, for fall feed. It is usually drilled 24 inches apart, in the rows, and kept clean by

a cultivator, but, if the land is free from weeds, large crops may be raised by broad-casting. If drilled, 2 lbs. of seed to the acre will suffice. It weighs about 53 lbs. to the imperial bushel. The *cake* in London, sells for about $25 a ton, being one half the value of *Linseed cake*. In 1846, the Patent Office distributed the seed, and recommended its culture as an oil plant; but we are not aware that it has yet been generally introduced. As sheep-feed, in our large prairie country, south of Michigan, it is deserving of much attention, to take the place of grass in the fall. *(See Patent Office Report*, 1846, *pp*. 314, 400.*)*

In the same work for 1850, p. 190, J. E. Dodge, of Erie, Penn., thus writes :—" I have cultivated Rape for several years, and find it very profitable. The soil for growing Rape on should be rich and clean. A thorough old-fashioned summer fallow is probably the best for the Rape crop. It should be sown the last of August,—3 pints of seed to the acre. It will be ready to cut in the last of June or first of July. We cut it with large reaping hooks, and lay it in small bunches to dry, for eight or ten days. Then, with a large cloth spread over the hay-ladder, we proceed to haul in, and thrash with a flail immediately. The greater portion of the chaff is to be raked off, and the remainder left, with the seed, one or two weeks on the barn-floor to dry. It will produce from 30 to 50 bushels per acre. It is worth $1.00 per bushel in Erie."

It is understood, however, that the crop is occasionally injured by frosts, if uncovered by snow, in this latitude. As a green manure, to be eaten by sheep, and the roots plowed under, it is considered essentially valuable, and may profitably take the place of an occasional clover crop in wheat culture.

457. We have been unable to meet with trustworthy analyses of this plant; but in its general character it resembles the rest of its family.

458. Inorganic analysis of Rape *(Rammelsburg)* 100 parts of seed gave of ash 4.54,—of straw, 5.21.

| | Seed. | Straw. |
|---|---|---|
| Potash, | 25.18 | 8.13 |
| Soda, | —— | 19.82 |
| Lime, | 12.91 | 20.05 |

| | | |
|---|---|---|
| Magnesia, | 11.39 } | 2.56 |
| Peroxide of Iron, | 0.62 } | |
| Phosphoric acid, | 45.95 | 4.76 |
| Sulphuric acid, | 0.53 | 7.60 |
| Carbonic acid, | 2.20 | 16.31 |
| Muriatic acid, | 0.11 | 19.93 |
| Silicic acid, | 1.11 | 0.89 |

Dr Madden gives the constituents of the cake as—

| | |
|---|---|
| Water, | 10.5 |
| Organic matter, | 85.5 |
| Earthy phosphates, | 3.0 |
| Siliciate of potash, | 1 |

Frequently as much as 9 per cent. of soil remains in the cake, which affords nearly double the fattening matter of Indian corn, if it should prove equally available in digestion. Cattle are said to dislike the flavor of Rape cake, so that it is rarely used for feeding.

It may be stated in this connection, that Boussingault and Dumas consider that the oil of seeds is intended for the production of heat by undergoing combustion at the period of germination. Generally, oily seeds retain their germinative powers for a long period, but this does not appear to be the case with the cabbage family. Such seeds should always be fresh ; and certainly not more than two years old.

Mr. Low concludes his essay on this family in the following words, which are worthy of the serious consideration of American farmers :— "The extended culture of the turnip has enabled us to carry the practice of breeding and feeding our domestic animals to a state of perfection, in which no other country has yet been able to rival Great Britain. The cultivation of the plant in rows, instead of the former method of broadcast, may well be regarded as an improvement of the highest importance. It has enabled the farmer to secure abundant returns, which the former methods of cultivation did not admit of, and so to increase the number of useful animals that may be maintained upon the farm, and to subject the lighter soils to a species of culture more beneficial than any other that had been before devised for them."

To this it may be added, that while, in the northern United States, turnip culture may never be as profitable as in Europe, yet it may be very greatly increased, and by the production of new and hardy varieties adapted to our climate, and by improved processes of culture it may be rendered as beneficial to the soil here as elsewhere. Not only will the improvement of our stock depend on the introduction of green or root-feeding during winter, but also the retaining the good qualities of the animals we import, must necessarily do so. They have been rendered what they are by such feeding, and without it they must inevitably deteriorate.

In §444, it is stated that large bulbs "contain less nutritive matter than small ones." This subject has just been examined with great care and accuracy by Messrs. Sullivan and Gages, *Chemists to the Museum of Irish Industry;* and as some very important practical facts are now for the first time brought to light, we add them here: "On the continent where beet-roots are grown for the purpose of manufacturing sugar, it was long since remarked, that large sized roots yielded less sugar than moderate sized ones, between one and three pounds in weight. With a few exceptions it is now found, that as a general rule, small roots contain a larger per-centage of solid matter than larger roots. Thus 100 tons of the small roots of sugar beet would be equal to 167.43 tons of the large; 100 tons of small Mangel-wurzels contain as much solid matter as 142.18 tons of large; 100 tons of small Swedish turnips would be equal to 118.37 tons of the large, *in specimens of all these roots actually examined.*

The following table contains a summary of the mean results of the examinations of 450 roots.

| Size of Roots. | White Selisian or Sugar Beet. | Long Red Mangel-wurzel. | Orange Globe Mangel. | Red Globe Mangel. | Swede Turnips. | Red Carrots. | White Belgian Carrots. |
|---|---|---|---|---|---|---|---|
| Average of roots above 7 lbs. - | 10.204 | 10.017 | 10.785 | 8.704 | 10.755 | | |
| " " " 5 lbs. - | 11.653 | 11.476 | 11.028 | 10.115 | 11.257 | | |
| From 3 to 5 lbs. - - - | 15.708 | 14.934 | 13.974 | 12.059 | 12.810 | | |
| Average of all roots, - - - | 14.532 | 13.635 | 12.645 | 11.188 | 12.031 | 13.370 | 12.99[illegible] |

This table shows some unexpected results. Thus the sugar-beet contains the largest amount of solid matter of any of the root crops now cultivated; and red and white carrots, though usually sold at a much higher price per ton, are very little superior to ordinary Swedes, and much inferior to the varieties of beet. Of course, it is not pretended that the value of roots can be determined by the per-centage of solid matter alone, as its composition must be taken into account. But in the same variety of plant, it will give an approximation to the truth—indeed practically speaking a very close one; in different species, or different families of plants, it is absolutely necessary to take the composition as well as the quantity of solid matter into consideration. In the case of carrots, however, an examination of the solid matter does not show that they are superior to that of the beet. As a general rule we have found that those roots of a particular variety of the beet which had white flesh were superior to those exhibiting a colored flesh. Another cause of exception was that the roots which grew out of the soil, and whose upper segment was colored more or less green, contained less solid matter than those which had fully grown *under* the soil; hence if a large part of the root grows out of the soil, the portion thus exposed will partake of the character of the segment immediately below the crown. This would seem to recommend a change in the usual practice of culture."

# CHAPTER XVI.

---

## POTATO (*Solanum tuberosum.*) JERUSALEM ATICHOKE (*Helianthus tuberosus.*)

458*. POTATO. This well known, and till lately, most useful esculent, belongs to the botanical family of *Sclaneæ*, or the Night-shade Tribe, of which many of the species are poisonous. The potato itself, in an uncooked state, is, to a certain extent, injurious to human beings; and if kept till spring, in a dark place, a new chemical alkaline principle called *Solanine* is formed in the shoots, which is a powerful poison. (*For analysis, see Liebig's Animal Chemistry, note* 38.)

459. As the potato has much diminished in value as a field crop, and there is no prospect at present of the *Rot* being remedied, we shall say but little about it, considering it rather as interesting to the gardener than the farmer.

460. It is a native of South America, and is still found wild in Chili.

In 1545, a Slave merchant, John Hawkins, introduced the potato from New Grenada into Ireland. From Ireland the plant passed to Belgium in 1590. It was neglected in England till introduced by Sir Walter Raleigh in the beginning of the 17th century; and was not in general cultivation in Scotland till near the end of the eighteenth century. When the potato came from Virginia into England, for the second time, it was already disseminated over Spain and Italy. It has been ascertained that this root has been cultivated on the great scale in Lancashire, England, since 1684; in Saxony, since 1717; in Prussia in 1738. In 1710, it began to spread in Germany, but the famines of 1771 and 1772 seemed necessary to lead the Germans to cultivate it upon the great scale. In less than two centuries it has literally overspread the earth;

and at the present day is found growing from the Cape of Good Hope to Iceland and Lapland. (*Boussingault and Sir J. Sinclair.*)

The Egg Plant (*Solanum Melongena*;) the Tomato (*Lycopersicum esculentum,*) and the Red Pepper (*Capsicum annuum,*) as esculents; and Deadly Night-shade, (*Atropa Belladonna,*) a well known medicine, belong to the same family. The Bittersweet of our own woods and fences (*S. Dulcamara,*) may be mentioned as the Type in the Northern United States.

461. The plant may be propagated by *seed*, in which case a vast number of new varieties is originated; or by the *tubers*, which contain buds or germs from each of which a stem will arise; and the variety continue constant. The germ will grow equally well if severed from the tuber, retaining merely a small fragment of the skin and substance; and it submits to desiccation by a hot stove without losing vitality.

It has long been a disputed point whether it were better to plant the entire tuber, or to cut it up into fragments, but no accurate decision seems to have been arrived at. In consequence, we may conclude that the practical difference is very small. General custom leans towards the latter plan. "It has been observed that "eyes" or germs taken from tuber that have not been fully ripened are more vigorous than those that have been taken from such as have been very fully ripened. This leads to a rule in practice, that the tuber to be planted shall be those which were taken up before the stems had begun to decay in autumn." (*Low.*)

The number of varieties is very great, and always increasing. The chief distinction is that of early and late kinds.

462. The peculiar characteristic of this root is the quantity of starch that it contains in combination with much water, and potash in its ash. The quantity of dry solid matter depends much upon the state of ripeness to which it has attained. The ripest leave 30 to 32 per cent of dry matter, the least ripe only 24 per cent. The quantity of starch varies according to variety from 10¾ to 32 per cent; and, accordicg to Liebig, in the *wild* state, this root is almost destitute of nourishing constituents. Since the *rot* has prevailed, potatoes appear to have lost much of the starch they previously possessed. The crop, also, other

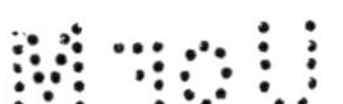

things being equal, varies in the weight per acre, according to variety, more than perhaps any other cultivated plant. The quantity of starch is at its maximum in the winter. In the spring, vegetation becomes active, and the buds begin to grow at the expense of the starch contained in the tuber. Hence, at this season, potatoes are less mealy, and, in consequence, less esteemed for eating. The tissue of the potato consists of a mass of cells, and in these the starch is stored up in the form of grains, of the ordinary shape, and these congregate principally in a zone near the skin, and are less abundant toward the center; the remaining space, in and between the cells, is occupied by a thin albuminous liquor, constituting three-fourths of the total weight of the tubers. All the nitrogenous matter is dissolved in the juice, and consists almost entirely of albumen, with a very small quantity of *asparagin* and free acids. The substance of which the cells consist is essentially different from that found in other plants. It possesses the property of swelling in water into a translucent jelly, and of being transformed into sugar and gum by the action of acids, and consequently occupies a position intermediate between starch and woody fibre. Potatoes are readily frozen at a few degrees below freezing point, and when again thawed are soft and sodden, and allow the greater part of the juice to flow out—in fact, the cells are burst by the ice formed within them, the organic structure is destroyed and vitality lost; while decay speedily succeeds. A chemical change, when the freezing has been gradual, is often perceptible; the tubers become remarkably sweet, and contain an appreciable quantity of uncrystallizable sugar.

463. Ultimate ANALYSIS of the Potato:—(*Boussingault.*)

| | | | |
|---|---|---|---|
| Carbon, | 44.0 | Water, | 75.9 |
| Hydrogen, | 5.8 | Solid matter dried at 230° | |
| Oxygen, | 44.7 | *Var. in vacuo,* | 24.1 |
| Nitrogen, | 1.5 | | |
| Ashes, | 4.0 | | 100.0 |

From this we see that the proportion of Nitrogen is very small; but it is still smaller in potatoes that have been kept for some time.

| 100 parts of - - - - - | Moisture. | Nitrogen in dried substance. | Nitrogen in undried substance. |
|---|---|---|---|
| Potato, fresh, - - - | 79.4 | 1.80 | 0.37 |
| Potato, kept ten months, - - | 76.8 | 1.18 | 0.28 |

464. Proximate analysis of the Potato:

| MICHAELIS. | | JOHNSTON. | | |
|---|---|---|---|---|
| Red Potato. | | | Natural state. | Dry. |
| Water, - - | 66.875 | Water, - - | 75 52 | |
| Starch and amylaceous fibre, | 30.469 | Starch, - | 15.72 | 64.20 |
| Albumen, - - | 0.503 | Dextrine, - | 0 55 | 2.25 |
| Gluten, - - - - | 0.055 | Sugar, - - | 3.30 | 13.47 |
| Fat, - - - - | 0.056 | Albumen, casein } Gluten, - } | 1 41 | 5.77 |
| Gum, - - - - | 0.020 | | | |
| Asparagin, - - | 0.063 | Fat, - - | 0.24 | 1 00 |
| Extractive, - - - | 9.921 | Fibre, - | 3.26 | 13.31 |
| Chloride of potassium, - | 0 176 | | | |
| Silicate, alumina, and salts, - | 0 815 | | | |
| Free citric acid, (?) - - | 0.047 | | | |

According to Illisch, what was formerly believed to be *citric acid* is phosphoric, muriatic, and malic acids.

465. Inorganic analysis of the Potato. *(Boussingault; Fromberg; and Daubeny.)*

| | Ash in 100 parts | Ash in artificially dried plant. | Potash. | Soda. | Magnesia. | Lime. | Phosphoric acid | Sulphuric acid. | Silica. | Peroxide of iron | Chlo. of sodium | Carbonic acid. |
|---|---|---|---|---|---|---|---|---|---|---|---|---|
| Potato tubers, | | 4.0 | 59 96 | | 6.28 | 2.09 | 13.16 | 8 27 | 6.52 | 0.59 | 5 20 | } Deduct. |
| d | | 4 01 | 57 58 | 3 66 | 4.53 | 0.81 | 9 98 | 14.63 | 3.68 | 0.42 | [illegible].6 | |
| do | | 3.75 | 49.73 | 1.93 | 5.03 | 3.31 | 14 58 | 18.04 | 2.49 | 0.56 | 7 5 | |
| do | 1.27 | | 46.60 | | 8 70 | 4.54 | 13.30 | 4.66 | 1.95 | 3.30 | 3.43 | 13.30 |
| do | 1.08 | | 50.00 | 0.84 | 6 85 | 2.70 | 16.20 | 2.37 | 7.15 | 5.15 | 1.95 | 11.90 |
| do | 0.76 | | 43 80 | | 12.65 | 3.10 | 11.15 | 6.0 | 6.67 | 6.85 | 2.39 | 6.70 |
| Mean of six analyses, } Carb. acid deducted. } | | 3.92 | 55 75 | 1.86 | 5 28 | 2.07 | 12.57 | 13 64 | 4 23 | 0.52 | 7.01 | |

466. According to Boussingault and Liebig, the nutritive power of the potato is very low. "A horse may be kept alive" says the latter "by feeding it with potatoes, but life thus supported is gradual starvation; the animal increases neither in size or strength, and sinks under every exertion." The true value of this tuber, as food, is evidently to supply carbon, in the shape

of starch, for the purpose of sustaining breath and heat, not for building up the body. Pereira estimates that 1 lb. of butcher's meat is equal to 10½ lbs. of potatoes. In consequence, those who live solely upon them are obliged to consume inordinate quantities; and the stomach, habitually distended with the great bulk, becomes unnaturally enlarged, and incapable of digesting concentrated food. This was shown during the Irish famine, when more than an equivalent of corn meal, or other nitrogenous food, being much smaller in quantity, entirely failed to suspend that craving which the stomach feels when empty.

At the same time, in consequence of the great yield per acre, much more nourishment can be produced from a given area of soil by this crop, than by any other except perhaps corn. The following example will prove this *(Knapp)*:—

From one hectare of land (= 2.471 acres) there were produced under similar circumstances,

| | | | |
|---|---|---|---|
| 3,400 lbs. wheat, | 2,800 lbs. rye, | 2,200 lbs. peas, | 38,000 lbs. potatoes, or |
| 3,036 do | 2,538 do | 2,980 do | 9,500 do |

after deducting the amount of moisture. In this quantity of dry produce there is contained:

| | In wheat. | In rye. | In peas. | In potatoes. |
|---|---|---|---|---|
| Nitrogenous matters, | 570 lbs. | 440 lbs. | 560 lbs. | 950 lbs. |
| Starch, | 1,590 " | 1,196 " | 780 " | 6,840 " |
| Mineral ingredients, | 90 " | 62 " | 60 " | 323 " |

And in consequence, when the Irish learnt to depend on this food alone, cultivating chiefly with the spade, population very rapidly increased; the land was subdivided into portions too small to be profitably applied to grain—for where one acre of potatoes would sustain a family, it would require many acres of grain to do the same, together with the necessary cattle—and when this crop failed, there was nothing to fall back upon, starvation ensuing in consequence. In India, the same results follow the dependence on rice, in many respects a very similar food. It may be laid down as a general principle, that the more highly civilized, intelligent, and prosperous nations are, the greater amount of nitrogenous vegetable and animal aliment do they consume; and in wearing out the soil of a single farm, or of a State, the decline is gradually from muscle-forming to heat-producing products, and finally to grass, for cattle raising, for the use of distant communities. But as the grass-product becomes general the population gradually decreases in numbers.

467. We shall not attempt to explain the cause of the Rot, nor yet repeat the various theories which have been originated. The ablest scientific men—while each has his own private opinion—acknowledge their inability, satisfactorily to account for it, any further than for the cholera and similar human epidemics. It is probably owing to some undetected atmospheric influence, and *may* be connected with electrical phenomena. One fact, however, appears to be generally acknowledged, viz, that rich, ammoniacal fermenting manures, tend to increase the disease, and that new soils, of a porous character, or old soils supplied with inorganic manures, are apt to produce the healthiest tubers. It is a peculiarity in this case, that remedies which are successful in one instance or locality, entirely fail in others; and thus, all specific curative means are now looked upon with suspicion. In Russia, drying the potato soon after digging, by artificial heat, has been found successful, yet failed in England; while, in Michigan, Mr. Mott and others have remedied the evil by leaving the tubers intended for seed in the ground where they grew until required for planting, taking the precaution to plant deep and cover with straw to prevent freezing. It is certain that in some soils this is a perfect preventive, and some unexplained change goes on in the potato; for, in the second season, the old potato which has acted as seed will be found perfectly sound, but altered in flavor. The same gentleman recommends leaving the tubers, intended for eating in the spring, in the ground all winter, when they will be found as fresh and unaltered as they were in the preceding autumn. *(See Farmer's Companion and Horticultural Gazette, Vol.* i, p. 77. ii, p. 14.*)* The following receipt has been lately published by an English farmer, not only as a manure, for which purpose it is undoubtedly excellent, but also as a preventive:—*(Agricultural Gazette.)*

| | |
|---|---|
| 30 lbs. wood ashes, | 20 lbs. common salt, |
| 15 lbs. burnt bones, in fine powder, | 30 lbs. air-slacked lime, |
| 10 lbs. plaster, (*sulphate of lime,*) | 7 lbs. nitrate of soda, (*saltpetre*) |

The whole to be intimately mixed. When planting, put into every hole an ounce of the above, cover it with some earth, and plant the tuber, or cutting above it. Habitually damp, undrained, adhesive clays should be avoided for this crop, while sands, gravels, and loams, lying on a porous subsoil, may often be successfully tried, even now.

468. In Great Britain, the potato was considered as a *fallow-crop*, and improved the land still more in consequence of being liberally supplied with fresh animal manures; and the surface, between the plants, being frequently plowed and hoed. Great pains were taken in preparing the field, and it was left in fine condition for wheat or other grains, which will not bear the direct application of dung. In our rotations, corn may take this tuber's place, especially if planted at distant intervals. In that country it was and is usually grown in rows, the earth being heaped up around the potato plant as it grew. In the United States much less pains have generally been taken, and the *hill* system is commonly followed; 4 potatoes, or *sets*, being planted close together in each hill. These hills are from three to four feet apart, and the interval is worked and kept clean with the plow and hoe. Undoubtedly the largest crops per acre can be raised on the English plan. When healthy, the time for digging, is when the stalks and leaves have partially withered; or when the skin of a tuber, recently unearthed, cannot be readily rubbed off with the hand. In Michigan, there is usually a period in October of *the* two or three weeks, when the weather is steadily fine, dry, and warm; but is succeeded by rains and frosts. This time, then, should be seized for the harvesting of this crop. The Irish dig with a spade or shovel; the New Englanders with a fork; or potato-hoe. The first, our experience teaches us to be the most rapid, and cleanest; but the shovel,

when lifted, requires a peculiar twist of the wrist, by which the earth and tubers are separated, and deposited in different places, which *twist* requires practice to accomplish successfully. In harvesting, it is important that the potatoes be not left exposed to the air and sun longer than can possibly be avoided. When first dug they are peculiarly sensitive to light, and if kept covered in the wagon with a thick cloth, or straw, till laid by in a dark place, they will retain their *mealy* qualities much longer than otherwise. A potato, exposed partially to the air in growing, turns green, moist, and unpleasantly waxy. This mistake is often made; the tubers being left on the ground in small heaps, for at least a whole day, or even several days. While this was an important crop with us, we always threw them into a corn-basket; and this, as soon as it was full, was emptied into a covered wagon; the consequence was, that the potatoes were remarkable for their fine flavor, and good qualities.

469. Besides being used in the ordinary shape, many preparations of starch were prepared from the potato. The larger quantity of the starch used by the laundress, and articles sold under the name of *Arrowroot Farina*, &c., were derived from this plant. *British gum*, (Dextrine,) extensively used in stiffening calicos, and applied to the back of postage stamps, is formed from *wheat* starch by roasting, or by nitric or sulphuric acid, *potato* starch failing to produce it. The water, in which potatoes have been boiled, is destructive to lice upon hogs, cattle, &c. The potato possesses a peculiar curative power over the Scurvy which attacks sailors confined to salt meat. In France, an extensive manufacture of Sugar from Potato Fecula or Starch is carried on. "Thus by the aid of Chemistry we obtain sugar from potato-starch, sulphuric acid, chalk, and water. The sugar is used for giving "body" to Burgundy wine, and for confectionary." (*Annual of Scien. Disc. Vol.* 1, *p.* 173.)

470. JERUSALEM ARTICHOKE (derived from the Italian word for Sunflower, *girasole;* i. e. *girare*, to turn, and *sole* sun,—bearing no reference to the *City of Jerusalem*,) belongs to the family of Sunflowers, and is a native of America. It was introduced into Europe probably from Mexico in 1497; and was much esteemed before potatoes were generally used; and in case

of the total loss of the latter esculent, may be so again. In France and Germany it is extensively grown as food for stock; we remember seeing, a few years since, large fields of it near Massilon in Ohio, and it has been successfully tried in New York, Alabama, &c. In the United States, however, it is not usually cultivated, except in gardens. Both the tubers and stalks are valuable. The first are occasionally eaten, either boiled or roasted, by men, but are not in the present day much esteemed as a vegetable, being apt to produce flatulency. The tubers grow in clusters attached to the true root, somewhat in the manner of potatoes, and the stems are from 5 to 10 feet in height, with a considerable quantity of large leaves. In Michigan it flowers, but does not bear seed. The crop is large, giving from 10 tons, to 1,200 bushels of tubers, and 11½ cwts. of *dried* stems per acre. *(Boussingault, and N. Y. Cultivator.)* The tubers, when once planted, are very apt to spread, and are difficult to eradicate; but in Europe this inconvenience appears to be obviated by turning swine into the field. "Taking into account the hardy qualities of this plant, its productiveness, and easy culture, it may be doubted whether it merits the neglect into which it has fallen. Granting its inferiority as an article of food for cattle to turnips, &c, it must be of some importance, especially since the potato has failed, to have a plant that can be so easily raised, and on soils so low in the scale of fertility." *(Lou.)*

471. Ultimate Analysis of the Tuber (A) and dried Stem (B) of the Jerusalem Artichoke. *(Boussingault.)*

A tuber fresh from the ground weighed 1 oz. 15 6-10 dwts: after drying in the stove 7-10ths dwts: after complete desiccation, one part was reduced to 0.208.

| | A | | B |
|---|---|---|---|
| | I. | II. | |
| Carbon, | 43.02 | 43.62 | 45.66 |
| Hydrogen, | 5.91 | 5.80 | 5.43 |
| Oxygen, | 43.56 | 43.07 | 45.72 |
| Nitrogen, | 1.57 | 1.57 | 0.43 |
| Ash | 5.94 | 5.94 | 2.76 |

In this analysis of the stalks, the carbon and nitrogen are probably rated too low. It will be observed that these tubers are almost identical in composition with the potato, the only essential difference being a little more ash in the first. According to the same writer, 30.8 lbs. of Jerusalem Artichokes are equal to 11 lbs. hay, as food for horses. "These roots are excellent food for the horse; they are eaten greedily, and he thrives upon them."

472. Proximate analysis of the tubers of the Jerusalem Artichoke. *(Braconnot.)*

| | |
|---|---|
| Uncrystallizable Sugar, | 14.80 |
| Inuline, | 3.00 |
| Gum, | 1.22 |
| Albumen, | 1.00 |
| Fatty Matter, | 0.09 |
| Citrates of patash and lime, | 1.15 |
| Phosphates of potash and lime, | 0.20 |
| Sulphate of potash, | 0 12 |
| Chloride of potassium, | 0.08 |
| Malates and tartrates of potash and lime, | 0.05 |
| Woody fibre, | 1.22 |
| Silica, | 0.03 |
| Water, | 77.05 |

M. Payen found a larger proportion of Sugar in this tuber than that stated above, and he ascertained that the fatty matter consists of stearine and elaine.

Boussingault found :—

Of dry matter, 20.8 | Water, 79.2.

473. Inorganic analysis of the tuber of the Jerusalem Artichoke. *(Boussingault.)* Per centage of ash in dry state 6.00.

| | |
|---|---|
| Potash, | 54.67 |
| Soda, | traces |
| Lime, | 2.82 |
| Magnesia, | 2.21 |
| Oxide of iron, alumina, &c., | 6.39 |
| Phosphoric acid, | 13.27 |
| Sulphuric acid, | 2.70 |
| Chlorine, | 1.97 |
| Silica, | 15.97 |

It will be observed how rich in phosphoric acid this plant is, and consequently how beneficial for growing animals; but in order to derive all the benefit possible from this fact, either water rich in lime, or some food containing an abundance of calcium should be supplied at the same time.

*Inuline* ($C_{24}$, $H_{21}$, $O_{21}$.) is a variety of starch found in the dahlia, and many other plants; specific gravity, 1.356, fuses at 212°; rendered yellow by iodine. Its aqueous solution does not gelatinize in cooling. (*Solly.*)

The following is the result of the analyses of two varieties of Jerusalem Artichoke—the white and red—made by Dr. Salisbury of Albany, N. Y., in 1850:—

| | White Tubers, | Red Tubers, | Tops of red variety. |
|---|---|---|---|
| Water, | 83.608 | 68.35 | 40.08 |
| Dry matter, | 16.392 | 31.65 | 59.92 |
| Ash, | 0.774 | 1.352 | 3.85 |
| Ash Calc. or dry matter, | 4.728 | 4.27 | 6.425 |

Inorganic analyses of the tubers of White [A,] and Red [B,] Jerusalem Artichokes, and the tops of the Red variety, [C,] grown near Albany, N. Y.:—

| | A | B | C |
|---|---|---|---|
| Carbonic acid, | 21.75 | 23.10 | trace |
| Silicic acid, | 1.60 | 1.40 | 26.55 |
| Phosphoric acid, | 9.75 | 12.05 | 11.10 |
| Phosphate of iron, | 1.20 | 1.25 | 3.25 |
| Lime, | 1.95 | 3.35 | 18.30 |
| Magnesia, | 0.55 | 0.30 | 8.85 |
| Potash, | 42.20 | 43.65 | 11.40 |
| Soda, | 15.25 | 6.60 | 15.85 |
| Chlorine, | 2.55 | 2.65 | 0.85 |
| Sulphuric acid, | 1.95 | 4.45 | 4.05 |
| | 98.75 | 98.80 | 99.60 |

Proximate analysis of the fresh tubers of the White [A,] and Red [B,] Jerusalem Artichoke; and of the fresh tubers of the Potato, [C.]

| | A | B | C |
|---|---|---|---|
| Water, | 83.608 | 68.330 | 74.712 |
| Fibre, | 2.232 | 3.676 | 6.839 |
| Sugar and extract, | 3.952 | 7.688 | 2.367 |
| Dextrine, | 2.652 | 5.436 | 0.923 |
| Casein, | 2.052 | 4.400 | 2.054 |

| | A | B | C |
|---|---|---|---|
| Albumen, - - - | 2.080 | 4.086 | 0.185 |
| Starch, - - - | 2.850 | 5.884 | 12.399 |
| Resin, - - - | 0.168 | 0.184 | trace. |
| Glutinous matter, - - | 0.096 | 0.122 | 0.009 |
| Fat, - - - - | 0.024 | 0.018 | 0.008 |

Ultimate organic analysis of the dry tubers of the White [A.] and Red [B,] Jerusalem Artichokes:—

| | A | B |
|---|---|---|
| Carbon, - - - | 45.817 | 45.918 |
| Oxygen, - - - - | 40.926 | 40.566 |
| Hydrogen, - - - | 5 768 | 4.829 |
| Nitrogen, - - - | 3.378 | 3.597 |
| Ash, - - - | 4 728 | 4.270 |

474. The tubers are an excellent food for milch cows, horses, and sheep, but should be used in connection with dry food and salt. Hogs likewise prosper upon them; and when the ground is not frozen, they can help themselves and save the cost of harvesting. The nourishing quality of the root is very little, if any lower than that of the potato, while its inorganic constituents are more useful. The stalks are nearly as valuable as the tubers; and in this respect it has an advantage over the potato. Although cutting the stalk in the beginning of September may diminish the growth of the tubers—which is questionable—the fodder that is obtained at that season will fully compensate for the loss.

According to Schwertz, 100 kilogrammes (=220.548 lbs. avoirdupois) of *green* stalks, equal as regards nutritious qualities 31.250 kilogrammes of hay; but the value is increased if they are mixed with other vegetable matters. If for winter fodder, the stalks should be left as late as possible, cut, and dried as hay; and in this condition all domeetic animals eat them. In some parts of Europe, the stalks are also used as fuel; and Boussingault found them profitable as absorbers of liquid manure,—owing to the amount of pith—when thrown into hog-pens.

475. The soil and climate appear to matter little. The tu-

bers, either above or below ground, bear a degree of cold that no other cultivated root will do. They are thus of essential utility in northern climates, and may be left in the ground all winter, if wanted for early spring use. This plant can bear the effects of great heat equally well. With the exception of marshes, all places and all soils suit; and even the shade of trees, in moderation, is not injurious. The following results have been arrived at by experiments in France:—

| | | |
|---|---|---|
| Alluvial land gave, | 20.868 | Kilog. of tubers. |
| Turfy land, *very dry*, | 26.768 | " " |
| Sandy clay, | 22.563 | " " |
| Calcareous earth, | 18.908 | " " |

From which it would appear that dry and light soils agree best with this plant.

476. In Europe, where Artichokes enter regularly into rotations, the ground is prepared and manured as if for potatoes, in the spring: and planting should be accomplished, as early as possible. They may, however, be planted, equally well, late in the fall, in dry soils. Whole tubers are used, and placed in rows, at about 1 inch below the surface, leaving sufficient space between the rows to use the cultivator, and the plants about nine inches apart. When they appear above ground, the soil is kept clean with the plow or cultivator, and hand hoe. If not harvested the first year, they will cover the whole surface of the ground the second season.

477. The stalks, if intended for dry fodder, must be left as late as the climate will allow of their being entirely dried. They may be cut with a strong sickle, or a corn-knife, from 2 to 3 feet above the ground, if tall; or in proportion, if short. They are lightly bound in bundles, and seven of these bundles are placed in shocks. After a week, and when the outside leaves are well dried, the shocks are separated, and replaced, so that 14 stand together, and 7 are placed on the top, like a roof, with the cut ends upward, and strongly fastened toward that end. In this way they stand till perfectly dry.

478. The tubers may be dug when convenient, in the same manner that potatoes are; but, if another crop is intended to succeed, great care must be taken to gather up every portion. As they grow in clumps, a little experience will render this easy. If it is intended to continue artichokes on the same ground enough small tubers may be left to serve for seed next season.

479. If they are to be used during the winter, they may be piled in heaps in a dry place, and covered with straw and earth. Wet injures them more than frost. (*Girardin and Debreul; See also Patent Office Report* 1844, p. 145; 1845, p. 321; 1846, p. 186; 1848, p. 159, 578.)

480. In the above references, much interesting information will be found. We would hardly, in our present state of agriculture, recommend this crop to be introduced into our rotations or upon rich soils, but we are confident that every farmer would find it profitable to set apart a field for this plant, and use the stalks in place of hay, and the tubers for his horses, sheep, milch cows, and hogs in winter and spring. There are certainly few plants which can be raised so readily, nor one which will yield more food at less cost. After a few years the artichoke will die out, in many localities; having exhausted the soil of the peculiar food it requires.

# CHAPTER XVII.

**PARSNIP** *(Pastinaca sativa.)* **CARROT** *(Daucus Carota.)* **BEET** *(Beta Vulgaris.)*

481. The Parsnip is a native of England, of the Continent of Europe, and of Asia, but in its wild state is useless, if not poisonous. It has become naturalized as a wild plant in the United States, *(Gray;)* and when once established as a weed, is very difficult to exterminate, while the root diminishes in size. Formerly, it was in more general use than at present, and it is now more cultivated in Catholic countries than in Protestant. Shakespear refers to it in the old proverb that "smooth words butter no parsnips." It is cultivated both as a field and garden crop; and in the Channel Islands, (Jersey, Guernsey, and Alderney,) and in parts of France, it is greatly depended on for fattening hogs and cattle, and as food for milch cows, for all which purposes it is perhaps superior to any other root.

482. There is probably only one species, but several varieties, of which, in Great Britain and America, the *Large Jersey* is considered the best for field culture. Of this there are two sub-varieties, *(a,)* the *fusiform*, which strikes deeply into the earth, and *(b,)* the *napiform*, which becomes thick, and grows near the surface. French writers mention three varieties as worthy of attention; *(c,)* the *Coquaine*, with a long root, and tall leaves; *(d,)* the *Lisbonnaise*, with a shorter and thicker root; and *(e,)* the *Siam*, small, and of a yellowish tinge, tender, and richer in flavor than the others. Any of these, however, will degenerate in poor soil, or by careless culture.

483. Late examinations have proved this root to be more nutritive than the Carrot, while it greatly excels the latter in hardiness; freedom from disease and insects; in its adaptation to soils; in its yield; and facility of culture. We believe that it is far too much neglected, and were the *fashion* to change in our Northern States it would be greatly for the benefit of farmers.

All animals are fond of the Parsnip. To milch cows it is eminently favorable, giving a flavor and richness to their milk which no other winter vegetable but the Carrot can give. The cows of Jersey and Guernsey fed with Parsnips and hay, yield butter during the winter of as fine a tinge, and nearly as good flavor, as if they were fed in pastures. To horses it is equally suited as the Carrot. Hogs are extremely fond of it, and, when boiled, poultry may be fed upon it. (*Low.*) To this may be added, that next to the Artichoke, it bears frost the best of any of our cultivated roots, and it may be left in the ground through winter, not only without injury, but even with an apparent increase of saccharine matter.

484. No ultimate analysis of this root appears to have been made. (*E. T. Hemming*, 1852.)

485. Proximate analysis of the Parsnip root (*Voelcker*, 1852;) grown on stony, shallow soil, on the farm of the Royal Agricultural College, Cirencester, England.

| | I. | II. | Average. |
|---|---|---|---|
| Water, | 81.780 | 82.320 | 82.050 |
| Inorganic matter, (ash,) | 0.941 | 0.924 | 0.932 |
| Nitrogenized organic substances, | 1.310 | 1 250 | 1.280 |
| Carbonaceous matters, | 15.969 | 15.506 | 15.738 |
| | 100.00 | 100.00 | 100.00 |

or the same dried at 212° F.—

| | I. | II. | Average, |
|---|---|---|---|
| Nitrogenized substances, | 7.43 | 7.12 | 7.27 |
| Carbonaceous matter, | 87.41 | 87.65 | 87.54 |
| Inorganic matters, (ash,) | 5.16 | 5 23 | 5.19 |
| | 100.00 | 100.00 | 100.00 |

Parsnips contain 6 to 8 per cent less water than turnips, and 5 to 6 per cent less than mangolds. The quantity of flesh-forming substances in fresh Parsnips is about the same as that contained in turnips. In a dried state, however, turnips are richer in protein compounds than parsnips.

486. Detailed proximate composition of Parsnips. (*Voelcker.*)

| | In natural state. | Calculated dry. |
|---|---|---|
| Water, - - - | 82.050 | |
| Cellular fibre, - - | 8.022 | 44.691 |
| Ash united with the fibre, - - | 0.208 | 1.159 |
| Insoluble protein compounds, - | 0.550 | 3.064 |
| Soluble casein, - - - | 0.665 | 3.704 |
| Gum and Pectin, - - | 0.748 | 4.166 |
| Salts insoluble in alcohol, - - | 0.455 | 2.535 |
| Sugar, - - - | 2.882 | 16.055 |
| Salts soluble in alcohol, - - | 0.339 | 1.888 |
| Ammonia in the state of ammonical salts, | 0.033 | 0.184 |
| Starch, - - - | 3.507 | 19.537 |
| Oil, - - - | 0.546 | 3.041 |

487. Inorganic analysis of the Parsnip. (*Richardson.*)

| | |
|---|---|
| Potash, - - - - - | 36.12 |
| Soda, - - - - | 3.11 |
| Magnesia, - - - - - | 9.94 |
| Lime, - - - - - | 11.43 |
| Phosphoric acid, - - - - | 18.66 |
| Sulphuric acid, - - - - | 6.50 |
| Silica, - - - - - | 4.10 |
| Phosphate of iron, - - - - | 3.71 |
| Chloride of sodium, - - - - | 5.54 |

By this it will be perceived that it belongs to the class of *potash plants*, but that it is also rich in the phosphates. The starch is all deposited in the external layers of the roots; the second layers contain much more protein compounds than either the heart or the outer layers. It will thus be noticed that the albuminous or protein compounds are not uniformly distributed throughout the whole mass of the root.

| | In outer layers. | Heart. | Layers between the heart and the outer layers. |
|---|---|---|---|
| Per centage of nitrogen, | 1.039 | 1.069 | 1.500 |
| Equal to | | | |
| Protein compounds, | 6.493 | 6.668 | 9.375 |

15

488. Parsnips succeed best in a deep, well pulverized, loamy soil, but will prosper in much heavier clays than carrots, especially if the soil is formed of granitic rocks. They require depth, and consequently the ground should be plowed deeply, or subsoiled, which is better still; but they will force their roots in spite of obstructions. Fresh barn-yard manure is not injurious to them.

489. The land being manured, (if requisite,) and plowed, is harrowed and rolled, and the seed sown broad-cast, by hand in rows, or by drill.* If by either of the first modes, it must be lightly harrowed, care being taken not to bury it above 1 or 1½ inches deep. It is important that the seed be fresh: if two years old it will not vegetate. In Jersey 3 or 4 lbs. *(Le Couteur)* in Scotland 10 lbs. *(Stephens)* per acre of seed are required. It generally vegetates slowly. Some soak it and mix it with damp sand to hasten germination, but in this case it should not be sown in dry land. If in drills, they should be just wide enough to admit a one horse plow or cultivator,—about 20 inches—and by degrees the plants must be thinned to 6 or 9 inches apart, according to the size of the variety, and the richness of the soil; but it is better to sow rather heavily to prevent misses. When the plants are one inch high they are to be weeded with a hoe, and the land must be kept clean in this manner till they are large enough to admit a cultivator. After this they grow very rapidly, and soon cover the ground with their leaves, and prevent the further growth of weeds.

The following plan is recommended, where a good drill cannot be procured. When the land is well harrowed and leveled, sow the seed broad-cast, harrow, and roll it; then when the plants appear, hoe into drills, either with a hoe-plow or hand-hoe.

The chief labor requisite, is keeping down the weeds till the parsnips gain sufficient size to do it themselves.

---

*The Drills manufactured by Emery & Co., of Albany, N. Y., sow this seed regularly and at a proper depth.

490. Harvesting is most readily performed with a plow, with a blunt or worn out share, drawn by a pair of horses, along or across the rows. The pressure of the plow and earth forces the roots out of the ground, when they are gathered into baskets by hand. They may be left in the ground, if intended for winter use, as long as the frost will permit; and, if for spring use, through the whole winter. They may be kept in cellars, or as is recommended for artichokes.

491. In Jersey, the crop averages from 9 to 11 tons per acre, but has been known to be as great as 27 tons 8 cwt.

492. When the leaves begin to fade, they should be cut off and given to cows; but if they are moist from rain or dew they are apt to inflame the udder. A good armful a day to each cow will impart nearly as much richness to the milk as the parsnip itself.

493. Domestic animals will eat the roots raw, but hogs are believed to prosper better upon them if they are cooked. Pork made of turnips is said to be quite equal to that made of corn. (*See Trans. of N. Y. State Agricultural Society*, Vol. xi, p. 360.)

494. Wine has been made of this root, and a pure spirit may be obtained from it by distillation.

495. For seed, the plants should be allowed to stand till the second season, or the best roots may be set out two feet apart each way, the crowns being under the surface of the ground. In the latter mode from 1½ to 4 lbs. of seed may be expected from a square rod of 16½ feet. (*Stephens.*) The seeds ripen irregularly, and should be gathered by hand when ready, being spread under cover till quite dry.

The seeds are apt to produce blisters and watery vesicles on the hands and arms of those gathering them, which may be prevented by rubbing well with grease previous to commencing.

496. Neither insects nor disease of any kind appear to injure this plant in the United States.

497. The best manures, are rich dung, guano, bones in some form, wood ashes, plaster, and common salt. The inorganic compound should be drilled in with the seed.

498. THE CARROT—like the parsnip—belongs to the botanical order of *Umbelliferæ*, the Hemlock or Parsley family, some of the species of which are mutritive, and many of them poisonous. The wild carrot is a common weed in Europe, and is wholly useless, having a hard, slender, fusiform root. Mr. Low is inclined to think that our edible variety has been derived from warmer countries, and not from the wild plant of northern Europe, which no modern cultivation has been able to change. It was known to the Romans, and is described by Pliny. It was introduced into England, as a field crop, by Flemish refugees, towards the end of the 16th century. The varieties are very numerous, being divided into *(a,)* field, *(b,)* garden, *(c,)* red, *(d,)* white, &c., while the root varies in shape from fusiform to napiform. The most esteemed for field culture are the *(e,)* White Belgian, *(f,)* Altringham, *(g,)* orange, and *(h,)* long red carrot.

499. The culture of this root for the feeding of stock has rapidly increased both in America and Europe, during late years: still, with us, it is rare, and grown in small quantities. It requires a peculiar soil, and careful cultivation, and in its early stages is difficult to attend to. At the same time, it is nutritive, and when every thing is suited to it, very heavy crops may be grown.

Analysis appears to indicate that 350 to 400 parts of carrots are required to replace 100 parts of good meadow hay in feeding horses ; and this root is much inferior to the equivalent of potatoes, in practice. *(Boussingault.)* Thaer says that a working horse may be kept in condition on 70 or 80 lbs. of carrots, and 8 lbs. of hay daily.

500. No ultimate analysis appears to have been made. The organic matter, ash, and nitrogen have been found to vary as follows, calculated dry.

| | Boussingault and Horsford. | Voelcker. | Way. | | Fromberg. | |
|---|---|---|---|---|---|---|
| | | Root. | Root. | Top. | Root. | Top. |
| Organic matter, | | 93.710 | 93 5 | 81.3 | 90.5 | 84.6 |
| Ash, | | 6.290 | 6.50 | 18.7 | 9.49 | 15.4 |
| Nitrogen, | 1.34 to 3.61 | | | | | |
| Water, | | 88.260 | | | | |

501. Proximate analysis of fresh white Belgian carrot (A,) compared with the fresh parsnip, (B,) grown on same soils:—*(Voelcker,* 1852.)

| | A. | B. |
|---|---|---|
| Water, - - - | 88.260 | 82.050 |
| Organic matter, containing nitrogen, - | 0.596 | 1.280 |
| Organic matter, fitted for the support of respiration and formation of fat, | 10.399 | 15.738 |
| Inorganic substances, - - | 0.745 | 0.932 |

In round numbers, carrots may be assumed to contain about 88 per cent. of water, and 12 per cent. of solid matter.

502. Proximate analyses of the fresh (A) and dried (B) white Belgian carrots, *(Voelcker,)* at 112° F.

| | A. | B. |
|---|---|---|
| Water, - - - - - | 87.338 | ——— |
| Cellular fibre, - - - | 3.471 | 27.412 |
| Inorganic matters attached to fibre, - - | 0.145 | 1.145 |
| Sugar, - - - - | 6.544 | 51.682 |
| Salts soluble in alcohol, - - - | 0.409 | 3.230 |
| Gum and pectin, - - - | 0.885 | 6.989 |
| Inorganic salts insoluble in alcohol, - - | 0.293 | 2.314 |
| Soluble casein, - - - | 0.498 | 3.934 |
| Insoluble protein compounds, - - | 0.169 | 1 334 |
| Oil, - - - - | 0.203 | 1.604 |
| Nitrogen, in state of ammoniacal salts, - | 0.008 | 0.063 |

503. Inorganic analysis of the white Belgian carrot (A,) *(Way,)* and of the parsnip, (B,) *(Richardson.)*

| | A. | B. |
|---|---|---|
| Silica, - - - - - - | 1.19 | 4.10 |
| Phosphoric acid - - - - | 8.55 | 18.66 |
| Sulphuric acid, - - - | 6.55 | 6.50 |
| Carbonic acid, - - - | 17.30 | |
| Lime, - - - - - - | 8.83 | 11.43 |
| Magnesia, - - - | 3.96 | 9.94 |
| Peroxide of iron, - - - | 1.10 | |
| Potash, - - - - - | 32.44 | 36.12 |
| Soda, - - - - - | 13.52 | 3.11 |
| Chloride of sodium, - - - - | 6.50 | 5.54 |
| Phosphate of iron, - - - - - | | 3.71 |

504. Dr. Voelcker (*Jour. Royal Agricultural Society of England, Vol.* xiii, p. 395,) thus compares the white carrots and parsnips together :— 1. There is a general resemblance in the composition of both roots. 2. Parsnips contain less sugar than carrots, the deficiency of which is replaced by starch, not occurring in carrots. 3. Carrots contain an average of 12 per cent. of solid substances, parsnips 18 per cent. Thus parsnips will be found much more nutritious than carrots. 4. The flesh-forming constituent of parsnips is greater than that of carrots. Parsnips are about as rich in albuminous compounds as mangolds. Thus *fresh* parsnips contain 1.30 per cent. and *dry*, 7.25 per cent of flesh forming constituents ; the above carrots, fresh, 0.612 per cent, and dry, 5.46 per cent. of the same. Parsnips also contain more nitrogen in the form of ammoniacal salts. 5. Parsnips contain a double proportion of fatty matters. 6. The difference in the relative proportions of cellular fibre in both roots is very great. The cellular fibre, occurring in carrots, parsnips, turnips, mangolds, &c., must not be regarded as useless in the animal economy ; for there can be little doubt that the soft and young fibres of these roots are readily converted in the stomach of animals into gum and sugar, and applied in the system to feed the respiration, or for the formation of fat. 7. Parsnips possess greater value than white Belgian carrots as a feeding or fattening material. Parsnips are, indeed very valuable as an article of food ; they are liked by cattle, and highly esteemed by Continental farmers for fattening stock. Moreover they stand the frost better than any other root-crop cultivated in England.

505. Carrots require greater care in cultivation, than any other plant of the sort. The soil must be light, sandy, rich, and fertile to the depth of at least a foot, to produce good crops. Freedom from weeds is also very essential, as the young plant

is delicate, and at first grows slowly. The ground should be plowed and prepared, as far as possible, in the fall, and the seed sown in spring, as early as the climate will permit:—Thaer says, "even before the winter is over, and while the snow remains on the ground," in Prussia. Manure adds much to the yield, but if dung be used, it ought to be well rotted or composted; or raw manure may be plowed in, in the fall, and compost *dragged* in, in the spring previous to sowing. In Scotland, it is applied at the rate of 25 tons to the acre, and placed in the drills immediately below the seed, (*Stephens.*)

506. The seed should be fresh, for if two years old it frequently fails. From 3½ to 6 lbs. to the acre are required. As it germinates slowly, at the ordinary spring temperature, the following process is recommended. Enclose the quantity wanted in a bag, and soak in water for 48 hours—and this 8 or 9 days before sowing. After soaking, spread the seed about a foot in thickness on the barn floor, and germination will take place in 6 or 7 days. When the seed is observed to be "chipped," it should be sown, being previously mixed with fine dry sand, to about 4 pecks to the acre, seed and sand together. By drill is the best mode of sowing, the ground being previously rolled, and rendered very smooth; but it may be sown by hand, rows being previously marked out, and the seed covered with a hoe. Broad-casting would require so much expense in weeding, as to be entirely inapplicable. Seed dealers now prepare carrot seed by rubbing off the hairs or points; but where this is not done the seed may be separated by mixing intimately with sand or ashes; or rubbing forcibly between the hands. The seed should be slightly covered. In wet weather, it will penetrate the ground spontaneously. The rows or drills should be about 20 inches, and the plants 6 to 8 inches apart, according to the size of the variety. In such roots, nothing is gained by crowding, as much being lost in size, as is gained in number.

507. When the carrots show themselves, they should be raked,

hoed, and thinned; the hoeing must be repeated at least twice. When sufficiently large, so as not to be injured, the cultivator may be run between them, and the weeds kept down till the leaves cover the ground.

508. The leaves are of little value for feeding stock, cattle not liking them. Carrots may be dug with an iron fork, or by a blunt plow, as is recommended for parsnips, the tops being cut off. They are not injured by moderate frost, but when severely frozen they are apt to rot as they thaw. On the other hand, when put in large heaps, and kept very warm, they soon ferment and rot. The safest mode is to place them in layers alternately with straw, in cellars or heaps, ventillation being allowed till the approach of severe cold, when the heaps must be covered with straw or earth.

509. The following is the cost of raising a crop of one acre of carrots, at Fredonia, Chautauque county, New York, in 1848, on green sward turned under, rolled down, and harrowed with a fine harrow, and sowed on top of the sod, May 4th. (*Trans. of N. Y. Agricul. Soc'y.* vol. viii. p. 327.)

| | |
|---|---|
| Plowing and harrowing 1½ days, team $1.25 | $1.88 |
| Raking and sowing 10 days @62½ cents, | 6.25 |
| Hoeing and weeding 16 " " " | 10. 0 |
| do second time 10 " " " | 6.25 |
| Harvesting 33 " " " | 20.63 |
| 4 ℔s Seed 40 " | 1.60 |
| Interest on land, | 3.50 |
| | $50.11 |
| 996 bushels carrots at 12½ cents, | 120.75 |
| Profit, | $70.64 |

70½ days of man's labor, and 1½ days of horse labor upon one acre of land. Twelve and a half cents per bushel is apparently a very high price, when the true nutritive value, and the quantity of water contained are compared with the price of oats, buckwheat, or some other roots.*

*If Oats are worth 37½ cents per bushel, Carrots are evidently too dear at 12½ cents, if the following mode of estimating the value of food is correct. We take equal weights of the two vegetables to be compared and find the equivalent proportions of nutriment in each. Thus:—

| | Oats | Carrots |
|---|---|---|
| | 100 ℔ | 100 ℔ |
| Deduct water, | 16 " | 88 " |
| Solids left | 84 " | 22 " |

510. The Carrot contains in place of starch, as also the turnip, a variable proportion of a gelatinous gummy like substance, to which the name of *Pectin* has been given. It is a tasteless solid, which swells up and gelatinizes with water. It possesses feeble acid powers, combining with bases to form *pectates*. It is represented by the symbol $C_{12}$; $H_8$ ; $O_{10}$. (*Solly.*)

511. The average crop in the the United States, with good cultivation, is from six to eight hundred bushels per acre. (*Wiggins.*)

The following crops of Carrots have been raised by L. Risley, of Fredonia, Chautauque Co., New York, allowing 56 lbs of the fresh roots to the bushel. (*Pat Office Reports* 1850, *p.* 385.) Mr. R. took the Premium of the State Agricultural Society, annually, for 10 years; so these may be considered *above* the average:

| | | | | | | | | | |
|---|---|---|---|---|---|---|---|---|---|
| 1 | acre gave | 1590¼ | bushels, | at a cost of | $104.75, or | 119½ | days | labor at | 62½ cents. |
| ½ | " | 498 | " | " | 25.76, | | | | " |
| ⅞ | " | 826½ | " | " | 42.69, | | | | " |
| 1 | " | 966 | " | " | 60.11 or | 70½ | " | " | " |
| 1⅜ | " | 2318½ | " | " | 54.37 | | | | " |
| 1 | " | 951½ | " | " | 46.63 | | | | " |

With the exception of the first and fourth, the particulars are not given. The Carrots were sown in drills from 12 to 14 inches apart, and hoed as soon as the young plant could be seen. The plants were left from 2 to 4 inches in the row. In the cost of the first crop, $15.00 is charged for manure, and $10,50 for "Improvement of land"; the rest is the actual outlay for labor, and seed without interest. The charge for wages is unusually low.

---

Of this

| | | | | | | |
|---|---|---|---|---|---|---|
| Nitrogeneous matter | forms 16 per cent, | - | 13.44 lb | 5 per cent | - | 1.10 lb |
| Carbonaceous matter | " 77 " | - | 64.68 " | 88 " | - | 19.36 " |
| Ash | " 3 " | - | 2.52 " | 6 " (Ash and Husk) | - | 1.32 " |
| Husk | " 3 " | - | 2.52 " | | | |

Now, allowing that a bushel of Carrots weighs twice as much as a bushel of Oats, though 56 lbs per bushel is the usual estimate, 37½ cents worth of Oats contain over 6 times as much nitrogenous matter as 12½ cents worth of Carrots.
1¾ " " carbonaceous " " "
2 " " ash and residue " " "
but as the nitrogenous matter is by far the most valuable for common food, the Oats greatly overbalance the Carrots in value in this respect. In another point of view, i. e. the fattening qualities of the two, the dry Oat contains from 5 to 7½ per cent of oil, while the dry Carrot contains only about 1½ per cent.; so that in every aspect, except the supplying *fresh* food, in winter, to the animal, the Carrots appear to be very much overcharged at that price. As has been already mentioned, Boussingault, experimenting on a horse, places the value of Carrots compared with hay as 400 to 100; and hay being worth to the farmer for feeding or wool growing (*not for sale into cities*, in which case other elements of cost enter,) not more than $5 a ton, 100 lbs. of Carrots would be worth about 6 cents or 3¼ cents per bushel. Still, in proportion to Oats, this is too high. We offer this view of the subject for further consideration.

512. THE BEET belongs to the botanical order of *Chenopodiaceæ*, the Goose-foot family.

Spinach, (*Spinacia oleracea,*) and Lamb's-quarters, (*Chenopodium album,*) belong to the same family.

The original type of the garden and field-beet, is the *Beta maritima*, or sea-beet, a plant indigenous to the sea shore of many parts of Great Britain, especially where an argillaceous formation borders the sea-line; the root is somewhat fleshy, and the leaves are gathered and eaten. The cultivated varieties are the *Beta hortensis* or *cycla*, the Chard Beet, which is cultivated for its leaves alone; and the *Beta vulgaris*, which comprises all the red, white, and variegated beets, the root of which is of chief value, whether used for garden or field culture. Of both these, there are very many varieties in size, color, shape of the root, and mode of growth. The field-beet is generally known by the name *Mangel-Wurzel*, (German for "*Root of Scarcity;*") or *Mangold-Wurzel*, (which literally means, the "*Root of the White Beet;*") or it is simply, and more usually termed *Mangold.* Field-beets may be again subdivided into those which are cultivated for the feeding of cattle, and those from which sugar is made, which latter contain more saccharine matter, and are generally white.

Such sugar is now manufactured on the Continent of Europe, including Russia, to a very great extent; and the quantity is annually increasing, as Chemistry simplifies and renders cheaper the process. This manufacturing is said to have been lately introduced into Utah. The best varieties of sugar-beets are (*a,*) the *Disette*, with a white root, skin and leaves, each root weighing from 25 to 34 lbs.; (*b,*) the *Silesian* beet, the sweetest, but smaller; (*c,*) the *Yellow* beet, (*d,*) the Siberian beet. (For a very minute and accurate account of the Beet-sugar manufactories of Europe, see *Knapp's Chemical Technology*: London Ed., 1851, vol. iii., pp. 339—416.)

In 1841, the production of Beet-sugar in Europe was estimated at 55,000 tons; in 1847 at 100,000 tons; in 1850 at 190,000 tons. In 1842 France produced 40 millions of kilogrammes, (=45,000 tons;) in 1853, 80 millions kilogrammes, (=90,000 tons.) This progress has been owing to improvements, chiefly chemical, each year in the manufacture. (*Ann. of Scien. Disc.*, vol. iv., p. 95.; *Silliman's Journal*, vol. xvi., N. S., p. 275.)

513. The Mangold can be grown successfully for sugar-extraction at all places between 45 ° and 56 ° N. Lat. in Europe. At Tobolsk, in Siberia, this crop is cultivated for food, but the root is supposed to contain a smaller proportion of sugar than than that raised farther south; judging from the effect of a warm climate on wheat, the nitrogenous matter should likewise be smaller. The Sugar or Silesian Beet is more particular as to climate, and consequently does not succeed so well in general cultivation. *(Prof. Wilson.)*

514. The *root* of this plant is not strictly a *true* root, but a thick fleshy protuberance of the stem, to which the actual roots are attached. The bulbous portion of some kinds of beet is formed below the surface of the earth; in others, it is above, exposed to the air; and again, in some it is placed midway between earth and air. Most varieties are spindle shaped; some, long and narrow, like the radish; others thicker, and more round; some nearly square, with deep indentations; and seldom flattened. The varieties are also distinguished by the leaves, curled or smooth; light or dark green; fringed with red; or entirely red.

515. If a root is cut across, it will be seen to be composed of concentric zones or layers of fibrous vessels and cellular tissue differing in color more or less according to variety. It will be remarked, that the leaf-stalks take their origin pretty deeply in the body of the bulb, and there form an extensive region called *the heart*, characterized by its greenish color and abundance of fibrous vessels; and, chemically, more analogous to the leafstalk than to the rest of the bulb. The actual bulbous matter is distributed in a zone about this heart, extending below it to the point. The exterior, or skin, is composed of a peculiar compact cellular substance, containing mineral and nitrogenous matter;

immediately beneath which lies the herbaceous tissue, containing the coloring matter, an essential oil, and several other peculiar organic compounds; then succeed the concentric zones of vascular and cellular tissue. In the cellular tissue is deposited the saccharine matter, the proportion seeming to be greatest in those cells immediately in contact with the vascular tissue. The *germ* (where the leaves enter the bulb) contains a large proportion of the saline matters, but no sugar. The cells contain neither starch, nor crystalline salts, but only a liquid, consisting chiefly of dissolved sugar. The fibrous vessels, on the other hand, contain no sugar, at least those do not which are situated in the heart, but they contain salts in a crystalline form. Some 25 or 30 distinct substances are found in this root.

516. In Great Britain the root is held in high estimation as a fallow-crop, and as food for fattening stock; and the culture is understood to be increasing. No statistics regarding it in the United States appear to exist. We are inclined to believe that this crop is annually becoming more common in the Atlantic States.

517. Ultimate analysis of the root, (A;) and leaves, (B;) of the Mangold. *(Boussingault.)*

| | A. | | B. |
|---|---|---|---|
| | I | II. | |
| Carbon, | 42.75 | 42.93 | 38.1 |
| Hydrogen, | 5.77 | 5.94 | 5.1 |
| Oxygen, | 43.58 | 43.23 | 30.8 |
| Nitrogen, | 1.66 | 1.66 | 4.5 |
| Ash, | 6.24 | 6.24 | 21.5 |

The leaves appear to possess a far higher value, both as a *feeding*, and as a manuring substance, than is usually assigned to them. The proportions of water were about the same in each; and the analysis shows that, in a chemical point of view, the leaves were *three* times as valuable as the same weight of roots would be. *(Prof. Wilson.)*

518. Proximate average of several analyses of Mangold. *(Knapp.)*

| | |
|---|---|
| Sugar, - - - - | 10 |
| Soluble salts, pectin, certain azotized compounds, &c., - | 3 |
| Water, - - - - | 83 |
| Woody fibre, insoluble salts, albumen, and other azotized compounds, - - - - | 4 |
| | 100 |

519. Proximate analysis of Mangold—"Sugar Beet."—(*Horsford and Krocker.*) Root grown at Giessen:

| | Fresh. | Dry. |
|---|---|---|
| Albuminous matter, - - | 2.04 | 11.5 |
| Sugar, - - - | 12.26 | 68.8 |
| Cellulose and other nitrogenous substances, | 2.56 | 14.6 |
| Mineral substances, - - | 0.89 | 5.0 |
| Water, - - | 82.25 | |

520. Inorganic analysis of Mangold. (*Way.*)

| | Tops. | Roots. |
|---|---|---|
| Silica, - - - | 1.99 | 2.57 |
| Phosphoric acid, - - - | 5.15 | 3.08 |
| Sulphuric acid, - - - | 5.3 | 3.37 |
| Carbonic acid, - - - | 6.49 | 18.32 |
| Lime, - - - | 8.65 | 1.95 |
| Magnesia, - - - | 8.63 | 2.11 |
| Peroxide of iron, - - | 0.95 | 0.6 |
| Potash, - - - - | 21.25 | 24.79 |
| Soda, - - - | 7.01 | 13.75 |
| Chloride of sodium, - - - | 33.96 | 29.41 |
| Per centage of ash, - - - | 1.7 | 0.886 |

Payen found 1.11 per cent of nitrogen in dry beet, of which one-third was due to the albumen. Horsford, obtained from beet-root, which lost in drying 82¼ per cent of water, 1.8 per cent of nitrogen. Under the very probable supposition that all these nitrogenous substances are of an albuminous nature, these numbers would correspond with 11.54 per cent of albuminous matters, or 6.16 per cent of the amount of sugar. (*Knapp.*)

As will be noticed above, Chloride of Sodium (common salt) enters largely into the composition of the Mangold. Prof. Way gives the following comparative table of the quantity of salt yielded by *one ton* of each of these plants:

| | Roots. | Tops. |
|---|---|---|
| Mangold Wurtzels, - - | 5.29 - - | 12.82 per cent. |
| Carrots, - - | 1.42 - | 11.25 " |
| Turnips, - - | 1.49 - - | 6.15 " |

521. The average quantity of nutritious matter afforded by a crop of Mangolds of 20 tons, or 45,000 lbs. per acre, consists of 900 lbs. of husk or woody fibre; 4,950 lbs. of starch, sugar, &c; 900 lbs. of gluten, &c; and 450 lbs. of saline matter, or ash. No oil or fatty matter has yet been detected in an appreciable quantity. *(Johnston.)*

522. This crop prospers on much heavier soils than either turnips or carrots; but a light clay soil, containing a fair proportion of humus, and rendered rich by manures, is the best. Moisture, especially in the beginning of the season, is very necessary, in order to develop its full size and good qualities. An excess of moisture is very rapidly absorbed by beet roots.

523. In France, it is a common practice to sow the seed in a seed-bed, and afterwards transplant. In England, the soil is plowed twice in the fall, laid up dry in the winter, manured and plowed again in the spring. With us one plowing is generally considered all that is required. Depth and friability are necessary in order to procure large crops, and the sub-soil plow may be used to great advantage. The land must be thoroughly harrowed, and the seed drilled at the rate of 3 or 4 lbs. per acre, not more than *one inch* in depth, and from 12--14 to 24 inches apart. Sowing may take place as early as frosts will permit. The seed should be steeped from 12 to 24 hours in water, to cause rapid germination; though if the soil and season are very dry, this may prove injurious. The subsequent cultivation consists of hoeing, and using the cultivator, keeping the earth fresh and perfectly clean. When well up, the plants must be thinned. Many leave the plants too close to each other, which interferes with growth, hoeing, and cleaning. If planted 2 feet apart, there will be a produce on the acre of 10,890

plants; that is both two feet apart, lengthways and breadthways.

According to Boussingault, the culture of a hectare (=2.471 acres,) of sugar-beet, requires, in France, the labor of a man for 113 days, and of a horse for 35 days; but much of this labor might probably be saved by a better system of management and improved implements.

524. The peculiar organization of this root requires great care to be exercised in harvesting the crop, as the slightest injury to it is sure to be followed by a tendency to decay when it is stored. At the same time, it keeps well to a late period of summer if carefully stored without injury by frost, or rain, or mechanical causes. The beets which grow above the ground are best gathered with the hand; kinds that grow underground require to be loosened by running a plow along the drill. The tops are then carefully cut off, without injuring the *heart.* In Alsace, it is the custom to take away the leaves, and trim the roots upon the ground, the refuse, which is a valuable manure, being plowed in immediately. Or the leaves may be fed to cattle, though they are said not to be very fond of them. Fine weather should be selected for the operation, and especial care must be taken to preserve the roots from wet and frost. It is desirable that they should be exposed on the ground, for three or four days before they are stored away, in order that they may lose as much of their moisture as possible.

525. Various modes of preserving them are used, such as *(a)* storing in pits dug in the ground, 4 to 5 feet deep, and covering with straw, and a thick layer of earth. To insure ventillation, narrow ditches or gutters are made in the soil under the heap, and chimnies are formed by inserting stakes to be afterwards withdrawn. Or *(b)* the roots are piled between two rows of hurdles, set up at 6 or 8 feet apart, and then built up from the top of the hurdles in a long pyramidal form. A second row of hurdles is then set all round, at a distance of 9 inches from the other, and the space between the two filled with loose straw well

pressed down. A good thatch is laid over the centre. In our Northern States, the most economical plan, when this crop is to be regularly cultivated, would probably be the preparation of root houses, or cellars under barns on hill sides.

526. The crop varies very much according to soil, manure, and cultivation. In France, the average maximum is about 278 cwts. per acre; the minimum 67 cwts. per acre. Boussingault gives, for the same country:—

| | Tons. | Cwts. | Qrs. | lbs. |
|---|---|---|---|---|
| Pas de Calais, - - | 12 | 9 | 1 | 19 |
| Department of the North, - - | 12 | 10 | 2 | 25 |
| Department of Cher, - - | 15 | 1 | 39 | |

or an average for the whole country of 10 tons, 9 cwt. 1 qur. 13 lbs. per acre. In England as high as 39 tons, 13 cwts. per acre have been procured, by not applying manure *directly* to the crop; but 20 tons are considered a good average on soils yielding 5 quarters (=46 American bushels,) of wheat to the acre. Wiggins gives the yield, in Delaware, of the Silician Sugar Beet at 800 bushels per acre, but a premium crop was grown in Monroe County, New York, of 1,489 bushels per acre, of 50 lbs. per bushel (=37½ American or 33 English Tons,) at a total cost, including manure, of about $22,00. (*Trans. of N. Y. Agricul. Soc'y. vol viii. p.* 328.

527. Cattle are readily fattened on this root. Late experiments in Scotland have proved Mangolds to be as profitable for this purpose as any other food that can be given. Steers weighing 935 lbs. live weight, consumed 120 lbs. of Mangolds per day, divided into three feeds, and 7 lbs. of straw besides. In 100 days each animal gained 161 lbs. (*Trans. of High. and Agricul. Soc'y. of Scotland* 1853.)

528. Manures act very variably upon this root. Ammoniacal manures increase the size and yield, but injure the sugar, while organic manures add to the sugar, but the crop is smaller. Guano is beneficial if the roots are intended for feed. Common salt is specifically beneficial, and should be applied in moderate

quantities under nearly all circumstances. It appears to be best to apply barn-yard manures to the previous crop.

An instance is given where an application of 3 cwt. of salt to the acre increased the crop from 26 to 40 tons.

The Beet at all stages of its growth, including the period of its flowering, exhibits the same relative proportions of water and solid ingredients; consequently half grown and full grown bulbs, flowering and not flowering plants, leave very nearly the same amount of dry residue. With the period of bearing seed, this residue rapidly diminishes in quantity. But the separate constituents vary in proportion. Thus, the Sugar gradually increases with the growth, attains a maximum at a certain period before ripening, when it again diminishes, and disappears with the formation of seed.

529. In England this root is frequently sold at £1 (=$4.88) per ton, but the *real* value to the farmer for feeding, is estimated at about one half, or $2.00. In this country, where meat brings a lower price, the value is of course less. The improvement of the land, when properly cultivated, ought, however, to be estimated as a profit.

530. No peculiar diseases or insects appear to injure this crop in the United States. In Europe, there are several of both, and of late in France it has suffered from a *Rot* similar to that of the Potato.

531. A sort of beer is sometimes made of it, at a low cost.

A good vinegar may also be procured by grating the root, expressing the juice into a barrel, and allowing it to undergo fermentation in a warm place. Six gallons have been made from a bushel of the root of the Sugar-beet. A cider-mill might be used for the purpose.

As this root is the raw material of an extensive manufacture, which demands great scientific skill, its culture and peculiarities have been thorougly studied; and more, probably, has been written upon it than almost any other vegetable product whatever except wheat. In these pages, we have only been able to give a compressed abstract, and therefore refer the reader to the following works among many others. Thaer's Principles of Agriculture; Johnston's Agricul. Chemist.; Journ. of Royal Agricul. Socy. of England, vol. xiii.; Pat. Off. Reports 1849; British Farmers' Magazine vols. xxii, xxiii.; Knapp's Technology vol. iii.; Journal d' Agriculture pratique, Tome vii. Low's practical Agriculture, Stephen's Farmer's Guide; Wiggin's American Farmer, &c., &c.

16

# CHAPTER XVIII.

## SWEET POTATOES, *(Convolvulus Batatas.)* MUSTARD, *(Sinapis nigra and alba.)* HOPS, *(Humulus Lupulus.)*

532. The Sweet Potato, belongs to the order *Convolvulaceæ*, the *Convolvulus* or *Bindweed* family, of which the common Morning Glory of the gardens *(C. purpureus,)* may be mentioned as a type. The *Yams* of South America, and the medicine *Jalap* are also of the same genus. The Sweet Potato is biennial, growing with a large, long shaped bulb at the root.

533. As an agricultural plant, it may be considered as properly belonging to warm climates, but can be cultivated profitably, on suitable soils, as far north as Michigan. In New Jersey, large quantities are annually grown; but in all the northern States, the plant rapidly degenerates, and must be replaced by fresh bulbs from the South. In the southern States, this plant takes the place of the common potato, and is used not only for man's food, but for cattle, hogs, &c. It is there raised with great ease, and returns from 200 or 300 to 1500 bushels per acre, according to soil and climate. *(Patent Office Reports,* 1845, pp. 452, 453.*)* In this present article we shall confine ourselves to its culture in the North.

534. The only analysis of this root with which we are acquainted is one made in the West Indies, *(O. Henry.)*

| | |
|---|---|
| Starch, - - - - - - - | 133 |
| Albumen, - - - - - - | 9 |
| Sugar, - - - - - - - | 33 |
| Cellular matter, - - - - - - | 68 |

| | |
|---|---|
| Fixed oil, - - - - - - - | 11 |
| Malic acid and salts, - - - - - | 14 |
| Water, - - - - - - - | 732 |
| | 1,000 |

535. This plant requires a sandy, rather light, deep, and well stirred soil, which must be located on a dry subsoil; and the whole either naturally rich in organic matter, or rendered so by manuring. Stiff clay does not suit it. Slips or sprouts, from the previous year's tubers, are used for planting, and these are prepared in either of the following manners, (*a.*) In a bed of earth, make a box with planks set edgewise, and fill in about a foot in depth of good warm horse-stable manure, over which spread two inches of fine rich earth; on this lay the potatoes so near as to almost touch each other, and cover them from 2 to 2½ inches deep with the same earth. If the nights are cold, this bed must be carefully covered with straw, or some other warm covering, which is to be removed during the day. There is a danger in making the bed too warm, and so spoiling the roots. They must be kept tolerably wet after the sprouts appear: when these are 3 inches long, they are fit to set out. (*b.*) Dig a hole a foot deep, the size of the space required, and fill in with manure from the horse-stable, sufficient to make a good hot-bed. It should be raised 10 or 12 inches above the surface of the ground, and the top of the bed should be sand and loam. Place the potatoes in rows, about 6 inches apart, and cover them to the depth of 2½ or 3 inches. Afterwards proceed as above.

536. The ground should be plowed very deep, and thrown up in ridges or hills; if the latter, such as common potato hills, after they have been hoed. This should be done immediately before planting, so that the soil may be moist and fresh. Set two plants in a hill, 2 or 3 inches apart, and make the top of the hill sufficiently hollow to hold a pint of water. If there is

no rain, watering in the evening is requisite for a few days. If in ridges plant the slips 8 or 10 inches apart. When the weeds begin to appear dig or plow between the rows, clean round the plants with a hoe, and draw a little dirt round them. When plowed the last time — about the last of July — hill them up. If the vines have grown across the furrows, turn them carefully back, and afterwards replace them. No earth should be allowed to fall upon the vines; and if they root, they should be pulled up, otherwise small and worthless potatoes will be produced at each root, and the main ones will be inferior in size. They should be dug as soon as the frosts kill the vines.

537. There is great difficulty in the north, in preserving these tubers from decay during winter. The best mode appears to be placing them in moderately sized boxes, and keeping them, in a room sufficiently heated to prevent frost, at an equal temperature; allowing them, however, to "sweat" before packing them away. *(See Patent Office Report,* 1846, pp. 450-457. *Trans. of N. Y. Agricultural Society,* Vol. viii, p. 426.)

538. Mustard. *(Sinapis nigra, and alba.)* This plant is very rarely cultivated in the United States, except on a small scale; most of the mustard consumed in this country being imported from England, where the manufacture is confined to a very few localities. There are or were mustard manufactories in Philadelphia and New York, but the seed was chiefly imported from Holland and Germany. The *Black* mustard is preferred for this purpose, but becomes a very troublesome weed when cultivated. Of late years, the *White* mustard has been sown in rich soils in England for sheep feed during summer, for which purpose it is found to be profitable, but in the United States both the climate and the Turnip Flea are injurious to it. This species cannot become a weed, as it is killed by a very slight frost. It is occasionally used medicinally; and in Europe oil

is extracted from it at the rate of 36 lbs. of the white, and 18 lbs. of the black species from 100 lbs. of seed. (*For a very complete account of this plant see Patent Office Report*, 1845, pp. 312, 397, 959-966 ; *compared with Ib.* 1848, p. 160.)

539. THE HOP is a native of the United States (*Gray.*); but the cultivated varieties, of which there are many, are believed to have been introduced from England, in which country it is likewise indigenous.

540. The only uses to which it is usually put are in medicine and the imparting a bitter principle to malt liquors; and in the United States the chief field of cultivation has been New York. It was introduced into England from Flanders in the reign of Henry VIII, A. D. 1509–1547; and in that country it is grown chiefly in the counties of Kent and Sussex. The quantity produced in New York in 1840, was less than half a million pounds; in 1850, 2,500,000 lbs, which exceeds five-sevenths of the whole crop of the United States.

New York also stands foremost in the production of ale, beer, and porter. The breweries of the State produced in 1850, 645,000 barrels of ale, &c., being more than a third of the quantity returned for the whole Union. (*Census Report Dec.* 1, 1852, p. 75.)

541. The hop is a perennial, the stems dying each winter, and being reproduced. The male and female flowers are on different plants, the latter only being of use; but a few male plants are generally grown among the others. The flower is the part used; the active principle,—a waxy yellow powder, called *Lupulin*,—being produced under the scales of the strobiles.

542 The following analysis of the Lupulinic grains, and of the scales, are copied from *Pereira's Elements of Materia Medica.*

| Lupulinic grains. | | | | Scales. |
|---|---|---|---|---|
| PAYEN, CHEVALLIER, and PELLETAN. | | IVES. | | PAYEN, &c. |
| Volatile oil, | 2.00 | Tannin, | 4.16 | Astringent matter. |
| Bitter principle, (Lupulite,) | 10.30 | Extractive, | 8.33 | Inert coloring do |
| Resin, | 50 to 55.00 | Bitter principle | 9.16 | Chlorophylle. |
| Lignin, | 32.00 | Wax, | 10.00 | Gum. |
| Fatty, astringent, gummy matters, ozmazome, malic and carbonic acid, malate of lime, acetate of ammonia, chloride of potash, sulphate of potash, &c., | traces. | Resin, | 30.00 | Lignin. |
| | | Lignin, | 38.33 | Potash, lime, and ammonia with acetic, hydrochloric, sulphuric, nitric, &c. Acids. |
| | | | | Lupulinic matter. |
| | 99.30 | | 100.00 | |

543. Inorganic analysis of the Hop (A;) and Leaves (B;) and Bind or Stem (C;) of the Hop Plant. (*Nesbit.*)

The 2 lbs. of Hops, dried at a steam heat, lost 3 oz. of moisture, leaving 1 lb. 13 oz. of dry hops. These furnished 1282 grains of ashes, or nine-tenth per cent.—9⅜ oz. of leaves, dried, lost 1⅛ of moisture, leaving 8¼ oz. of leaves. These left 572 grains of ashes, or 16⅓ per cent.—1 lb. 2½ oz. of the Bind, dried, lost 1⅞ oz. of moisture, and left 1 lb. 0⅝ oz. of dry Bind. These gave 353 grains of ashes, nearly 5 per cent.

| | A | B | C |
|---|---|---|---|
| Silica, | 21 50 | 12.14 | 6.07 |
| Cloride of Sodium, | 7.24 | 9.49 | 6.47 |
| Chloride of Potassium, | 1.67 | —— | 9.64 |
| Soda, | —— | 0.39 | —— |
| Potash, | 25 18 | 14.95 | 24 35 |
| Lime, | 15 98 | 49 67 | 38.73 |
| Magnesia, | 5.77 | 2.39 | 4.10 |
| Sulphuric acid, | 5.41 | 5.04 | 3.44 |
| Phosphoric acid, | 9.80 | 2 42 | 6.80 |
| Phosphate of iron, | 7.45 | 3.51 | 0.40 |
| Per centage of ash, (dried) | 9.87 | 13.06 | 3.74 |

544. Amount of inorganic matter removed from the soil by an acre of Farnham Hops. (*Nesbit.*)

The number of hills to an acre varies in different localities. In some places 1000, in others 1260, in other 1440 hills to the acre. The following is estimated from actual analysis of 4 hills, at the rate of 1000 per acre. (*Nesbit*)

| | 500 lbs. Hops ℔ | oz. | 146½ lbs. Leaves ℔ | oz. | 239 lbs. Bind ℔ | oz. | Total Plant ℔ | oz. |
|---|---|---|---|---|---|---|---|---|
| Silica, - - | 9 | 9 | 2 | 2 | 0 | 9½ | 12 | 4½ |
| Chloride of Sodicum, | 3 | 3½ | 1 | 10 | 0 | 10 | 5 | 7½ |
| Chloride of Potassium, | 0 | 12 | —— | | 0 | 15 | 1 | 11 |
| Soda, - - | —— | | 0 | 01 | —— | | 0 | 1 |
| Potash, - - | 11 | 3½ | 2 | 10 | 2 | 6 | 16 | 3½ |
| Lime, - - | 7 | 1¼ | 8 | 10 | 3 | 13 | 19 | 8¼ |
| Magnesia, - - | 2 | 9 | 0 | 6 | 0 | 6½ | 3 | 5½ |
| Sulphuric acid, - | 2 | 6¾ | 0 | 14 | 0 | 5¼ | 3 | 10 |
| Phosphoric acid, - | 4 | 6 | 0 | 7 | 0 | 9½ | 5 | 6½ |
| Phosphate of iron, | 3 | 5 | 0 | 10 | 0 | 0¾ | 3 | 15¾ |
| Total, | 44 | 8 | 17 | 6 | 9 | 11½ | 71 | 9½ |

545. There are several varieties, of which the *Farnham*, the *Golding*, the *Yellow Grape*, are considered the best.

These are found to differ much in the *proportion* of their inorganic constituents, and consequently the above analyses must only be considered as an approximation as regards the species, while it is accurate as regards one variety. (*See Stephen's Farmer's Guide. vol. ii, p.* 45, 320.)

546. The soil peculiarly adapted to this plant is a rich, deep, rather adhesive clay, with abundance of organic matter, or vegetable mould; and a porous rocky subsoil. A dry subsoil is considered essential. The variety grown, and the quality of the produce depend entirely upon the character of the soil; and the peculiarities from these causes are almost as numerous as they are in wine-culture. In England, large quantities of valuable manure are expended on hops; such as bones, woollen rags, &c. The following, for the inorganic portion, may be given as a sample :—(*Journal of Royal Agricul. Society*, 1846, *part* I.)

| | I. | II. | |
|---|---|---|---|
| Guano, - - | 3 cwt. | 1 cwt. | per acre. |
| Common Salt, - - | 1 " | 1 " | |
| Saltpetre, (or - - | 1½ " | — | |
| Silicate of Potash,) - | 1½ " | — | |
| Plaster, (gypsum,) - | 1½ " | 1½ | |
| Superphosphate of lime, - | — | 1½ " | |
| Pearlash, - - | — | 1 " | |

It may be laid down as a principle, that the more richly hops are manured, the better will be the quality and yield.

547. The culture of this plant, the picking, drying, packing, &c., demand a great outlay of labor, much skill, and more experience; and it would be useless to attempt to teach the practical manipulations in our limited space. We must therefore refer the reader anxious to know more of the subject to other works, and recommend those who wish to to cultivate the hop to visit a plantation, and thus acquire on the spot the necessary knowledge.

548. Hops are planted in hills; and long poles are driven in for the bind to climb on. They do not come to full bearing till the third season after planting, and will yield profitably from 12 to 20 years. In the United States in a good season, each hill will average 2 lbs. of hops ready for market; but more frequently the produce is below that. Appropriate buildings and kilns are necessary for drying, as well as peculiar baskets, cloths, bags, &c. The price is subject to very great and sudden variations; and the grower must have a large number of workmen at his command, as the crop, when ready for picking will not permit delay without serious injury. *(For a very complete account of hop culture in the United States, see Wiggins' American Farmer, and Trans. of N. Y. Agricultural Society, Vol.* iv, p. 447, &c.)

549. Cost of cultivating 2 acres of hops at Morrisville, N. Y. (*Trans. of N. Y. Agricultural Society*, 1845, p. 497.) The soil was a mixture of dark loam and gravel, well adapted for grass. It was well plowed and manured with 40 loads of barn yard manure per acre, and planted with hops and corn. The next season the account stood as follows :—

| | |
|---|---|
| 41 loads of manure put in hills, | $30.00 |
| Rise of poles, | 45.00 |
| Labor of cultivating, | 40.00 |
| Interest on land, | 14.00 |
| Harvesting and bagging, | 87,50 |
| | $216.50 |
| Produce of 2 acres, 2500 lbs. at 12½ cents, | 312.50 |
| Net profits, | $96.00 |

# CHAPTER XIX.

## ONIONS, PUMPKINS, TOBACCO, CASTOR-OIL BEAN, LIQUORICE, UNCOMMON PLANTS.

550. The Onion *(Allium Cepa,)* though usually ranked among roots (bulbous roots) is in reality a bud, formed at or underneath the ground, and whose scales are thick and fleshy. It is a biennial.

There are several species known in garden culture as Garlic, (*Allium Sativum*); Rocambole, (*A. Scorodoprasum*); Chive, (*A. Schœnoprasum*);* Leek, (*A. Porrum*); Shallot, (*A. Ascalonium*); and several varieties of the first (*A. Cepa*), as the Top onion (*A. Viviparum,*) bearing perfect bulbs or buds in place of seed; the Potato onion, producing by the formation of young bulbs on the parent root, an ample crop below the ground; red, white, yellow onions, &c., &c. There are five species indigenous to the northern United States, (*Gray,*) which sometimes become very troublesome weeds in pastures, in consequence of being eaten by cows, and flavoring the milk. The medical plant *Squills* belongs to the same family.

551. The native country of this esculent is unknown, but it has been cultivated from a very remote antiquity; as we find it—in its different species—the common food of the Egyptians in the time of the Pharaohs, before the Exodus of the Israelites. It is now cultivated in all parts of the world. In Hindoostan it is considered sacred, and not eaten. In Europe, the Portugal onions are the finest. In the United States, the *field culture* of the onion is chiefly confined to limited districts of Connecticut, Massachusetts, New Hampshire, and New York, certain towns

*Found growing wild on Lake Superior, by Prof. Agassiz. Also a native of the Alps, to the height of 7000 feet. (*Agassiz L. Superior*, p. 166.)

being celebrated for the quantity of good onions which they produce and export. What are not required for home consumption are sent chiefly to the West Indies and South America. The census takes no notice of this plant. From 1835 to 1845, 30,000 to 40,000 bushels and from 1850 to 1853 from 125,000 to 150,000 bushels a year were raised in the town of Danvers, Massachusetts, alone; and though, to the *farmer* it is rather an insignificant product, yet it employs many men and women in its culture, and adds largely to the comfort of the small cultivators of New England. Its moral effect is beneficial, as it teaches the value of manure, of clean, neat cultivation, and steady industry; and it is said that onion-growing districts are always remarkable for their prosperity, economy, and intelligence.

552. Onions do not appear to have been accurately analysed. They owe their peculiar odor and flavor, as well as their pungent and stimulating qualities, to an acrid volatile oil which contains sulphur. When eaten, the oil becomes absorbed, quickens the circulation and occasions thirst. According to *Fourcroy*, *Vauquelin* and *Le Grange*, the following is the composition:—

| | |
|---|---|
| Acid volatile oil, | Starch, |
| Uncrystallizable sugar, | Woody fibre, |
| Gum, | Acetic and phosphoric acids, |
| Vegetable albumen, | Phosphate and carbonate of lime, |
| Sulphur, | Water. |

The nourishing quality probably depends on some unknown property of the oil, or an alkaline base, resembling *creatine* in meat; and may be classed with such sustaining substances as chocolate, opium, &c., of the principle of which we are yet totally ignorant. The ashes contain alkaline and earthy salts. This plant is used medicinally as a local irritant both internally and externally; as an expectorant, diuretic, and anthelmintic. Garlic is the most active of the family in its properties.

553. The soil should be mellow, dry and rich: it need not,

necessarily be deep. A rich sand, sandy loam, or gravelly loam, when well manured will answer. Onions do not appear to exhaust the soil, and may be grown for many years in succession without deteriorating. The following is the mode of culture pursued in Danvers, Mass, (*D. Buxton, Jun., in Farmer's Companion and Horticultural Gazette*, Vol. ii, p. 86; iii, No. 3.)

Such land is selected as would give a good crop of corn; wet land will answer if the seed can be got in by the first of May. It must have been plowed from the sod at least three years, unless a crop of carrots was raised the second year. Land may be rich and well manured, and yet not bear onions the first year of planting; afterwards the crops will be good as long as the land is kept well manured. Six or seven cords of good barnyard manure per acre are sufficient. Salt mud and "mussel-bed" are valuable for a change. Ashes, particularly on new land, are beneficial. The land is plowed shallow, rendered fine, and rolled as early in spring as the climate will permit, and the seed is sown in drills 10 or 12 inches apart by a machine made for the purpose. With it, a man can sow two acres a day, and drop the seed thick or thin. New land requires 3 lbs., old land 2½ lbs. of seed per acre; the young plants being more likely to live on old than on new land. Weeding is performed with a wheel-hoe (which costs about $1,) two or three times before the plants are large. A man can weed 1½ acres per day. The rest of the weeding is chiefly done by boys, and the expence depends on the management of the land the first year or two; it being of the utmost importance not to allow any weed to go to seed. The crop must be kept perfectly clean. When the stalks shrivel, and fall spontaneously, the bulbs have ceased to grow, and should then be pulled up and laid on the ground for some days to dry. If the weather is moist they must be turned. After this they must be spread in the barn till thoroughly dried, and then wove into ropes, or the stalks cut off before putting in barn, and the onions, when dry, packed in barrels.

554. In selecting onions for seed, take the largest and those which ripen the earliest, as by so doing the crops will ripen in warm weather. If no care is taken, onions will soon run out, ripening late, and growing with large stiff necks in October. In Massachusetts they should be harvested and dried by the first of August.

555. The average crop at Danvers is about 450 bushels per acre, though 600 or 700 are not uncommon, and occasionally 1000; the wholesale price from 40 to 50 cents per bushel. An instance is given in the *Albany Cultivator*, where 1209½ bushels of carrots, and 630 bushels of onions were raised off the same acre.

556. In Russia, the Potato Onion is cut into 4 parts, leaving the quarters hanging together at the root, the onions having first been hung up and dried in the smoke. Smoking, however, is not necessary. The quarters thus united are planted, and produce 4 fine onions. This course has been successfully pursued for thirty years, resulting in abundant crops. (*Pat. Office Report*, 1847, p. 188.)

557. In Vermont, New Hampshire, and north Massachusetts, a maggot has, of late years, proved very destructive to this plant. It is the young of the Onion Fly, (*Anthomyia Ceparum,*) which lives in the roots and causes them to perish. It appears to be the same insect that destroys the onion in Europe, and has probably been imported. It lays its eggs on the leaves of the onion, close to the earth, so that the maggots, when hatched, readily make their way to the heart of the onion. They come to their growth in about two weeks, turn to pupæ within the onions, and come out as flies a fortnight afterwards. It is said that the onion crop may be preserved from the attacks of this fly by sowing the seed on ground upon which a quantity of straw has been previously burned. (*Harris' Treatise on Insects*, p. 494.) In Scotland, the evil is remedied by dusting

the soil with dry coal soot once a fortnight. (*London Gardener's Chronicle, May* 26, 1853.)

558. Besides this, onions appear to be free from the attacks of insects and disease. It sometimes happens that many of the plants grow with thick stems and small bulbs. These may be left in the ground during the winter. Many of them will stand the frost, and in the spring they may be taken up and set in a bed where they will grow to be good onions.

559. THE PUMPKIN, (*Cucurbita Pepo,*) is the only plant of this family usually cultivated as a *field crop;* though in many parts of the United States, the other genera might be grown in the same manner with facility.

The Cucumber, (*Cucumis sativus*); the Musk Melon, (*C. Melo*); the Water Melon, (*C. Citrullus*); the Round Squash, (*Cucurbita Melopepo*); the Long Squash, (*C. verrucosa*); the Orange Gourd, (*C. aurantia*); and the Vegetable Marrow, (*C. ovifera*); the Bottle Gourd, (*Lagenaria vulgaris*); the Balsam Apple, (*Momordica Balsamina*), belong to the same family. There are two species indigenous to the northern United States,—The One-seeded Star Cucumber, (*Sicyos angulatus*); and the Wild Balsam Apple, (*Echinocystis lobata,*) (*Gray.*) The *varieties* of this family are exceedingly numerous, and they hybridize with great facility, even among different genera, as the cucumber and pumpkin, &c. The Pumpkins and Squashes are natives of America, and were unknown in Europe previous to the time of Columbus. The early voyagers found them in common use among the Indians through the whole extent of country from Florida to Canada, and probably far to the west. Melons and Gourds are derived from Southern Asia. Persia has long been famous for the former. (*Dr. Harris in the Trans. of the Amer. Asso. of Science.*) In medicine, Colocynth, (*Cucumis Colocynthis*), and Squirting Cucumber, (*Momordica elaterium,*) belong to this family.

560. Although this plant is so so generally cultivated, and enters so largely into the winter food of animals and men throughout the Western States, and notwithstanding that it has acquired a national importance in New England, very little information has been collected regarding it, and we are unable to meet with an analysis of it. Cucumbers and melons have been more fortunate, and we shall quote these as presenting a family

resemblance. The pumpkin probably owes its chief value to the sugar and starch which the flesh contains, and the oil in which the seeds are rich. For fattening, the latter appear to be chiefly of value. This plant probably contains a less per centage of water, than any of the rest of the family; but that per centage must still be large. There is a *sweet* variety, cultivated in gardens, which promises to be more profitable as food than the common sorts, though it does not usually grow to as great a size, and we recommend its adoption in the field.

561. The per centage of water, dry matter and ash, in the Musk Melon, (A,) and Water Melon, (B,) *(Salisbury.)*

| | A. | B. |
|---|---|---|
| Per centage of water, | 90.987 | 94 898 |
| do dry matter, | 9 013 | 5.102 |
| do ash, | 0.271 | 0.248 |
| do ash in dry matter, | 3.007 | 4.861 |

36,900 lbs of Musk Melons, and 40,322 lbs. of Water Melons contain each 100 lbs of inorganic matter or ash, as follows:—

| | 100 lbs. ash of Musk Melon. | 100 lbs. ash of Water Melon. |
|---|---|---|
| Carbonic acid, | 11 55 | 11.42 |
| Silicic acid, | 2 20 | 1.21 |
| Phosphoric acid, | 25.40 | 14 93 |
| Sulphuric acid, | 3.90 | 1.63 |
| Phosphate of iron, | 2.30 | 4.52 |
| Lime, | 5.85 | 7 32 |
| Magnesia, | 0.60 | 1.31 |
| Potash, | 8 35 | 23.95 |
| Soda, | 34.35 | 30.63 |
| Chlorine, | 5.20 | 1.81 |

(*See Trans. of Amer. Assoc.* 1851, pp. 195, 221.)

562. Composition of the Green Cucumber, *(John.)* The peeled fruit (A,) the fresh peel, (B.)

| | A. | | B. |
|---|---|---|---|
| Sugar and extractive, | 1 66 | Solid matter, similar to that of the pealed fruit but containing much Lignin, | 15 |
| Chlorophylle, | 0 04 | | |
| Lignin with phosphate of lime, | 0.53 | | |
| Mucas, with phosphoric acid ammonical salt, malate, phosphate, sulphate, and muriate of potash, phosphate of lime and iron, | 0.50 | Water, | 85 |
| Water, | 97.14 | | |

563. The pumpkin is generally grown in connection with corn, occasionally with potatoes; and rarely or never alone. Two or three seeds are planted with the corn in the hill or row, and thinned out to one afterwards, the plants being left from 6 to 8 feet apart. No further care is requisite except to gather and store before frosts occur.

564. The usual yield is probably from 3 to 4 tons per acre; but there are instances on record of 7 tons per acre among corn, and 15 tons per acre among potatoes. (*Patent Office Reports*, 1844, p. 144; 1847, p. 188.)

565. There is great difficulty in preserving this fruit during winter; as, in consequence of the quantity of water it contains, frost readily destroys it; and even without frost, rot will occur wherever the skin is bruised. The best mode is to pack upon a tier of rails laid on the ground, under a warm shed, with straw between each tier of pumpkins; and before severe frost occurs, cover thoroughly in all directions with a heavy covering of straw. This latter must be deferred as long as possible, in order to allow the superfluous moisture to escape.

566. It has been recommended to grow the Vegetable Marrow in the same manner, to feed hogs and other animals. This is a very hardy and productive species, but whether it has any advantages above the pumpkin, in an agricultural point of view, has not been tested. An instance is mentioned where 20 tons had been produced on an acre.

567. For fattening hogs, these fruits are supposed to be more nutritive if boiled. For ruminant animals, living on dry food, they are probably preferable in their natural state. Pumpkins increase the yield and richness, and improve the color of milk.

568. The young plants are apt to be destroyed by the Cutworms, and Cucumber Beetle, (*Galeruca vittata;*) and therefore more seed should be planted than is required. Many remedies have been proposed for the injury caused by this Beetle.

The cheapest and most effective is the dusting the leaves with common plaster; or with boiled plaster (such as is used by masons) mixed with spirits of turpentine, and dried. This application must be repeated after rain until the rough leaf is well grown. Occasionally, this insect, and another much larger species injure the fruit when ripe by burrowing into it to a considerable depth. The only remedy is harvesting as rapidly as possible. In some localities the Cucumber Flea Beetle *(Haltica pubescens.)* is also injurious to the young plants.

569. TOBACCO, *(Nicotiana Tabacum)* belongs to the *Solanaceæ*, or Nightshade family, and is nearly connected with the Jamestown Weed *(Datura Stramonium)* and Henbane *(Hyoscyamus niger,)* well known weeds and medical poisons. One species, Wild Tobacco, *(N. rustica)* is found indigenous to the Northern States. There are several other species, *(N. repanda, Persica, Glutinosa, Macrophilla, &c.)* the first of which forms the best Havanna cigars; and the second, "the delicate and fragrant tobacco of Shiraz;" besides many varieties. It is a native of America; and was found by Columbus to be in common use among the Indians in 1492. It was introduced into France in 1559, and into England in 1586. It is now cultivated in most parts of the world, except Great Britain where its culture is prohibited by law; but the tobacco of Cuba, Virginia, Maryland, Kentucky, and Connecticut is the most celebrated. No plant, perhaps, more readily adapts itself to greater differences in climate, or none, except the grape, changes more in its composition and economical value. At the same time it is remarkable for the injurious and impoverishing effect that it produces upon the soil. The tobacco of Michigan is said, so far, to have proved inferior in flavor and strength; while a valuable article is brought to market from Western Canada.

In three or four years, the tobacco grown in Germany from American seed, acquires an aroma perfectly distinct from that of fine tobacco, and this it retains pertinaciously. Too rapid and luxuriant growth spoils the flavor of the leaf, which on the contrary is heightened by pruning.

570. The Virginians began to cultivate this plant very early, following the Indian mode. In 1611, it was first grown by the use of the spade, and shortly increased to so great an extent as almost to preclude the sowing of grain. Before the Revolution merchantable tobacco was a legal tender in which taxes and ministers' salaries were paid, and it almost became the currency of the colony. At present the culture in the United States appears to be on the decline. In 1840, the total produce of this country was 219,163,319 lbs; in 1850, 199,752,646 lbs, showing a decrease of 19,410,673 lbs.

The chief tobacco producing States in 1850 were:—

| | | | |
|---|---|---|---|
| Virginia, | 56,803,218 lbs. | North Carolina, | 11,984,786 lbs. |
| Kentucky, | 55,501,196 " | Ohio, | 10,454,449 " |
| Maryland, | 21,407,497 " | Connecticut, | 1,267,624 " |
| Tennessee, | 20,148,932 " | Indiana. | 1,044,620 " |
| Missouri, | 17,113,784 " | | |

No other State gives one million of pounds; Michigan returns only 1,245 lbs.; while Maine, Vermont, Rhode Island, Delaware, and Minnesota produce none.* The principal varieties cultivated in the United States, are the Virginian; Large-leaved; Dwarf; Cuba; Common Green; Summerville; Light Burley, &c.

571. Proximate analysis of the fresh leaves of Tobacco. (*Posselt and Reinmann.* 1827.)

| | | | |
|---|---|---|---|
| Nicotina, | 0.06 | Malic acid, | 0.51 |
| Nicotianin, | 0.01 | Lignin and a trace of starch | 4.969 |
| Bitter extractive, | 2.87 | Salts, | 0.734 |
| Gum with malate of lime, | 1.74 | Silica, | 0.088 |
| Chlorophylle, | 0.267 | Water, | 88 280 |
| Albumen and gluten, | 1.308 | | |

*From 1800 to 1839 the whole quantity of tobacco exported from the United States, annually, was about 82,000 hogsheads. The Western States, during this period, never exported, on an average, over 35,000 hogsheads. In 1840, the West exported 40,000; in 1841, 54,600; in 1842, 68,000; in 1843, 89,800; and in 1844, 81,200 hogsheads. This last was nearly as much as the consumption of Europe then demanded From 18 000 to 20,000 hogsheads of Virginia tobacco were consumed at home. Above 75,000 hogsheads were supposed to be raised in other conntries than the United States.

572. Inorganic analyses of eight specimens of Hungarian tobacco-leaf. (*Will and Fresenius.*)

| | Mean of 4 analyses. | Mean of 4 analyses. |
|---|---|---|
| Potash, | 26.46 | 12.14 |
| Soda, | 0.56 | 0.07 |
| Lime, | 27.87 | 45.90 |
| Magnesia, | 9.72 | 13.09 |
| Chloride of sodium, | 6.91 | 3.49 |
| Chloride of potassium, | 2.21 | 3.98 |
| Phosphate of iron, | 7.00 | 5.48 |
| Phosphate of lime, | —— | 1.49 |
| Sulphate of lime, | 7.14 | 6.35 |
| Silica, | 12.13 | 8.01 |
| Per centage of ash, | 21.28 | 23.68 |

(*See, for particulars, Knapp's Chemical Technology,* Vol. iii, p. 149, *and Johnston's Agricultural Chem. last Ed.*)

Among the constituents of the tobacco leaf, *Nicotine* is the most characteristic. This is a volatile vegetable alkaloid ($C_{10}\ H_{16}\ N_2$) belonging to a class of nitrogenous organic substances which are, for the most part, gifted with a very energetic and remarkable action on the animal system. Pure nicotine is a colorless oily liquid with a slight smell of tobacco, which, when the liquid is heated, or mixed with ammonia, becomes very intense and biting; it has also a sharp irritating taste, a few drops acting as a poison on small animals. This substance, which gives value to tobacco, does not exist in a state of nature, but is a product of fermentation. The *fresh* leaves possess very little or no smell. When they are distilled with water, a weak ammoniacal liquid is obtained, upon which a fatty crystallizable substance swims, which does not contain nitrogen and is quite destitute of smell. But when the same plant, after being dried, is moistened with water, tied together in small bundles, and placed in heaps, a peculiar process of decomposition takes place. Fermentation commences, and is accompanied by the absorption of oxygen, the leaves become warm, and emit the characteristic smell of prepared tobacco. When the fermentation is carefully promoted, this smell increases; and after the fermentation is completed an oily azotised volatile matter, called *nicotine,* is found in the leaves. This substance was not present before the fermentation. The different kinds of tobacco are distinguished by having very different odoriferous substances, which are generated along with nicotine. (*Liebig Ag. Chem.*) This fermentation begins during the harvesting, or even before, but is stopped by the process of drying. The quantity of nicotine in the *fresh* leaves has been estimated at $\frac{6}{10000}$; in *commercial* leaves at [illegible]/10000 to $\frac{100}{10000}$. It varies according to the locality in which the plant is grown, rendering it stronger or weaker, as follows:—(*Schlosing.*)

| | Per centage in the dry leaves. | | Per centage in the dry leaves. |
|---|---|---|---|
| Department Lot, (France,) | 7.96 | Department Elsas, (France,) | 3.12 |
| " Lot-Garonne, " | 7.34 | Virginia, | 6.87 |
| " Nord. " | 6.58 | Kentucky, | 6.09 |
| " Ille Vilaine, " | 6.29 | Maryland, | 2.29 |
| " Channel of Calais, " | 4.91 | Havanna, less than | 2. |

Besides Nicotine, tobacco contains albumen, and a gluten-like substance, gum, resin, malic, and citric acid.

It has been discovered by the "Tobacco Administration" in Paris, that the value of tobacco stands in a certain relation to the quantity of potash contained in the ashes. Another striking fact was also disclosed. Certain celebrated kinds of American tobacco were found gradually to yield a smaller quantity of ashes, and their value diminished in the same proportion. (*Liebig Agricul. Chem.*) The large quantity of ammonia, of lime, and the alkalies required by this plant is the cause of its so rapidly impoverishing the soil, while it supplies no material for the production of manure. The mode of cultivation, also, exposing the soil to the evaporating effect of the hot sun undoubtedly adds to the evil. In rich loams, where the solution of the minerals of the soil is rapid, and where 10 to 20 per cent of vegetable matter is incorporated in the earth, tobacco may be obtained for many years, but it is always an exhausting crop. It has been stated, that a crop of tobacco removes, in less than three months, 170 lbs. of mineral matter from one acre of land, without estimating the silica. The important mineral substances presented in Havanna tobacco, were in 100 parts ashes:—(*Hertwig, in Liebig's Annalen, April* 1843.)

| | | | |
|---|---|---|---|
| Salts of Potash, - | 34.15 | Salts of Lime, - - | 51.38 |
| Magnesia, - - | 4.09 | Phosphates, - | 9.04 |

"The total quantity of tobacco retained for English consumption in 1848, was nearly 17,000,000 lbs. North America alone produces upwards of 200,000,000. The combustion of this mass of vegetable matter would yield about 340 000,000 lbs. of carbonic acid gas; so that the yearly increase of carbonic acid gas from tobacco smoke alone cannot be less than 1,000,000 lbs; a large contribution to the annual demand for this gas made upon the atmosphere for the vegetation of the world." (*Ellis.*)

573. The manure for this crop should be such as can rapidly and readily supply ammonia; for instance, guano, night-soil,

hog's dung, well rotted sheep and cow stable manure, &c. In Europe, malt-dust, and rape-cake, either powdered or dissolved in urine are highly prized. The manure and urine of horses are objectionable as giving a bad taste to the tobacco. (*Colman's Europ. Agricul. ii.* 548.)

All the ingredients necessary to replace the ash of 100 lbs. of tobacco leaves, are present in the following mixture:—(*Johnston.*)

| | | | |
|---|---|---|---|
| Bone dust, - | 15 lbs. | Carbonate of Soda, (dry) | 5 lbs. |
| Sulphuric acid, - | 8 " | Carbonate of Magnesia, | 25 " |
| Carbonate of Potash, (dry) | 31 " | Carbonate of lime, (chalk) | 60 " |

The leaf appears to have the power of replacing a deficiency of potash in the soil with lime; while, as was before shown, the soil and climate produce a great difference in the proportion of the inorganic constituents.

574. The best soil for this plant is a light sandy loam; or a light soil rich in organic matter, having a portion of sand mixed with it. Clay soils are not adapted for it. New or fresh land is better than old; and pretty steep hill-sides, if light and rich, are better for the production of fine tobacco, than level land.

575. The following is the mode of culture pursued in Connecticut and New York; and in the West, north of the Ohio river. (*a,*) A "seed-bed" is prepared as early in April as possible, for which the richest and best land, moist but not wet, is chosen. It is manured, dug deeply, pulverized, and rendered fine and smooth; and the seed sown broad-cast, at the rate of one table-spoonful to the square rod, before the earth becomes dry. After this it is raked, but the seed is not buried; it is rolled, or a man treads it in, rendering the surface of the bed as hard as possible. Weeds must be carefully extirpated. When the plants have leaves two or three inches long they are fit for transplanting—about the beginning of June. (*b,*) The field intended to be planted should be well manured, and plowed at least twice; harrowed, and rolled, and left as smooth as possible.

The rows are marked out, 3 feet, or 3 feet 4 inches, according to the variety grown; and on these rows small hills are formed for the reception of the plant, at 2 feet, or 2½ feet apart. To make *fine* tobacco it is important to plant early, so that the leaves may be cured when the weather is warm and dry. If it rains at the time of setting out, advantage is taken to plant as many as possible. If not, about half a pint of water is poured into each hill, and the plants immediately set.* After this, the field is examined several times, and where plants are dead, or injured by the worm, others are set in. *(c,)* As soon as they stand well, they are either carefully hoed and the vacant places filled with new plants, or the cultivator is merely passed between the rows. After this the plants are kept clean with cultivator and hoe, being hoed three or four times without hilling. The plants are frequently and thoroughly examined for the tobacco worms; and they must be destroyed, or the crop will be greatly injured. *(d,)* When in blossom, and before the formation of the seed, the plants are *topped* about 32 inches from the ground, leaving from 16 to 20 leaves on each stalk. If there are late plants, in consequence of re-setting, break them low, and they will grow faster and ripen sooner. All suckers must be broken off. *(e,)* When ripe, the time of cutting—the leaf is spotted, thick, and will crack when pressed between thumb and finger. It may be cut any time in the day after the dew is off; left in the row till wilted; then turned; and if there is a hot sun, it is turned often to prevent burning. After being wilted, it is put into small heaps of 6 or 8 plants, and carted to the sheds for hanging. Here it is hung with cotton twine on poles 12 feet long, and about 20 plants on each side. It must hang until the stem of

*It may be useful to mention that all young plants, either in garden or field, may be transplanted with great certainty of success by forming a deep hole with a round stick an inch in diameter; insert the root in the centre of this hole, holding the plant with the left hand; pour in water till it overflows; and immediately fill it up with fine earth dribbled in with the right hand. Even cucumbers and melons may be safely transplanted by this method.

the leaf is thoroughly cured to the stalk—from 6 to 10 weeks. It is then taken down, in a damp day (to prevent the leaves from crumbling,) and placed in large piles by letting the tops of the plants lap each other, leaving the butts of the plants out. It remains in these heaps from 3 to 10 days, before it is stripped, depending on the state of the weather, but must not be allowed to heat. When stripped, it is made into, or tied in 3 small "hands," the small and broken leaves being kept by themselves. When fit for market, it is collected in large quantities,andslightly pressed in boxes containing about 400 lbs. each.

576. In some places in the South, it is the custom to dry the leaf by fires, a process which requires much care and experience; and a peculiar class of buildings or sheds. The seed-bed is also, at times, burned or charred before the seed is sown; a process which, in certain soils only, enriches the soil by setting free the inorganic nourishment; adds ashes, from the fuel consumed; and destroys the seeds of weeds, but also much of the organic matter of the soil.

577. In Kentucky and Indiana, and some other districts, hogsheads are used for packing. The hogshead should be 4½ feet long, and 3½ broad in the head, with a bulge only sufficient to hold the hoops. Such a cask should hold, without too hard pressing, which is injurious, 1300 or 1400 lbs. of net tobacco. The cask should weigh 150 or 160 lbs. Ash timber is the best for the purpose.

578. The crop varies from 1000 to 2000 lbs. of dry leaf to the acre, according to the variety, closeness of planting, and soil. An average crop of 2700 lbs. has been grown on several acres. In France the crop is stated to be 4000 lbs. *(Colman.)*

579. The following was the cost of cultivating one acre in Massachusetts in 1845:

| | | |
|---|---|---|
| Interest on land, | | $15.00 |
| 10 carts of manure, @ $2.50 | 25.00 } one half, | 15.00 |
| Carting and spreading, | 5.00 } | |
| Plowing twice, | | 3.00 |
| Harrowing and marking, | | 1.00 |
| Seven thousand tobacco plants, | | 3.50 |
| Holding and setting, | | 3.00 |

| | |
|---|---|
| Hoeing 4 times, | 5.00 |
| Securing and killing worms, | 2.00 |
| Topping and securing, | 4.00 |
| Cutting and hanging to dry, | 4.00 |
| Shipping and packing, | 5.00 |
| Rent of drying shed, | 4.00 |
| Freight, | 3.00 |
| | $67.50 |
| Produce 2000 lbs. @ 8 cents, | 160.00 |
| Net profit, | $92.50 |

580. The chief disease which affects the tobacco leaf is the "spot" or "firing," believed to be owing to rot. It appears when there is too much rain; and is more liable to occur on sandy soils, than on those that are "stiff, red and thirsty." We suspect that it is owing to too rapid an absorption of some material from the soil, during wet weather; and that it resembles the "curl" of the Peach-tree leaf under similar circumstances. The practical cure is said to be deep plowing between the rows as soon as it appears. A careful analysis of the leaf would probably show a change in the proportion of some inorganic constituents.

581. The only insects usually liable to injure this plant, are a Cut-worm, and the Tobacco-worm; the latter follows this crop wherever it is cultivated. Dr. Harris does appear to mention it. The worms attack the plant twice in a season, first when the latter are one third or one half grown, and again when the tobacco is ready for cutting. The most effectual remedy is gathering them by hand and killing them; but Turkeys are found of great assistance in destroying these insects: they eat, and kill thousands which they do not eat. The first brood may be readily destroyed by Turkeis, but when the second one appears the tobacco is generally so large that Turkies do but little good. *(See Farmer's Library for* 1848, *for a full account of this Insect.)*

582. To save the seed, allow a few of the strongest plants to produce their flowers. Each plant will ripen, in September, as

much seed as may be necessary for stocking half a dozen acres.

(For further information on this extensive subject the reader is referred to the various works on practical agriculture; *the Patent Office Reports*, especially the vols. for 1846, pp. 740–754, and 1849, pp. 318–326, containing a *Prize Essay, by W. W. W. Bowie of Maryland*, and for the manufacture, to *Knapp's Technology*, vol. iii.)

583. THE CASTOR OIL PLANT, PALMA CHRISTI, (*Ricinus communis,*) belongs to the *Euphorbiaceæ*, or Spurge family;—a family which contains the Croton Bean, and many other medical plants.

It is a native of India, but has been known from the earliest antiquity, seeds of it having been found in some Egyptian Sarcophagi, and it was used by the Greeks. It is naturally a perennial, attaining the height of 15 or 20 feet, with a thick stem; but in cold climates it becomes an annual, not more than 3 to 6 feet high. There are many instances of perennial plants becoming annuals by change of climate, as is the case with the common English daisey when transplanted to, or grown from seed in India. There are 5 distinct varieties or species, differing chiefly in the color and pruinous condition of the stem, and the quantity of oil yielded by the seed.

584. This plant is cultivated to some extent in Indiana, Illinois, Georgia, and other States enjoying a like temperature. The only useful part is the seed, or "bean," from which an oil is expressed, to be used in medicine; for the manufacture of hair-oil by barbers; for machinery; and for burning. In its common state, the odor and taste are exceedingly disagreeable, but these can be eradicated by refining. The American oil is of very fine quality. and has a less unpleasant flavor than the East Indian; but it is often objected to by Druggists in consequence of its depositing a solid fat in cold weather. (*Pereira.*)

585. No analysis of any value to the Farmer has been published.

586. A good crop will yield 35 bushels of beans per acre, and the oil will be from 25 to 60 per cent according to the goodness of the seed and manufacture. The cultivation is similar to that

of corn. The beans from which the oil has been expressed are said to form a valuable manure. They appear to contain a large amount of nitrogenous matter; and the stems, roots. &c. can be plowed in again.

587. LIQUORICE, (*Glycyrrhiza glabra.*) This, also, is a medical plant, with a local agricultural importance, and it might be still further profitably introduced into the United States as one of the minor products of the soil. It is a native of, and cultivated in the South of Europe, but prospers in England. Our annual import of it is said to exceed $250,000, and the demand is constantly increasing. The root, (the only useful part,) has recently been employed in France for the manufacture of paper. It was introduced into Georgia and the Carolinas at an early day, but the great attention now paid to Cotton has caused it to be neglected. It is a perennial, with long tap-roots extending very deep into the ground, and creeping to a considerable distance.

588. The soil should be a moist, loose, sandy loam; or diluvial of river-bottoms. If not rich, it must be manured with *well rotted* dung, ashes &c. It should be subsoiled or trenched 3 or 4 feet deep; and if sufficiently rich, thrown into three and a half foot beds, including the alleys, in the centres of which the sets are planted early in March, 18 inches apart. If the ground is not sufficiently rich, trenches must be dug throughout the field, 3½ feet apart, from centre to centre, and 3 or 4 feet deep. When one trench is dug, it must be filled with earth from the next, well incorporated with compost, and alleys made 7 or 8 inches wide, mid-way between the trenches, the earth being spread over them, so as to form raised beds throughout the plantation.

589. The "sets" being procured, and cut into five or six inch pieces, dibble holes along the centres of the beds, 18 inches apart, and 8 inches deep, into which thrust a piece of root, and cover

it up. The after culture, for that season, consists in keeping the beds perfectly free from weeds, by the hoe. In the fall, when the stems are decaying, they are cut down, and a light dressing of rotten manure is spread on the surface. Early the following Spring, dig lightly between the rows, taking care not to injure the roots. During the second and third summers, the only labor is hoeing to kill the weeds.

590. At the end of three years the roots are fit for harvesting; which is done when the stalks are fully decayed. Begin by digging at one end of the rows, and so take up all the roots. When they are collected, the small side shoots are trimmed off, and preserved in dry sand in a cellar for fresh "sets"; and the large roots are prepared for sale. They are offered in three shapes—the entire root—the same dried and ground to powder—and the inspissated juice. The sooner liquorice is sold the heavier it weighs; and the greener it is the more virtue it contains. An acre has sometimes produced 4000 to 5000 lbs. of roots, valued at $400 to $500. *(Jour. of the U. S. Agricul. Socy. July* 1853, *p.* 53.*)*

591. There are various other plants which have been recommended for cultivation in the United States, which have not yet been introduced to any extent, such as (*a*,) *Madia Sativa*, grown in Germany for its oil; (*b*.) *Myagrum Sativa*, Gold of Pleasure, also cultivated in Europe for oil; and in England for Sheep-feed and oil, as it may be pastured early and yield a good crop of seed afterwards. It is perfectly hardy in the neighborhood of Detroit, bearing the coldest weather, and being among the first flowers in Spring to blossom. In the South of Europe it gives two crops in a season. (*See Patent Office Report* 1846, *page* 314; *Thaer's Princ. of Agricul. ii.* 528. (*c*,) The Bene Plant, (*Sesamum Orientale*,) cultivated in South Carolina and Georgia for its oil, which is as good as that of the Olive for table use; andthe leaf is employed as a cure for summer diarrhœa in children. (*d*,) Madder, (*Rubia Tinctorum*,) and (*e*,) Indigo, used in dyeing, the former remaining 2 or 3 years in the ground before harvesting: both of these require a warm climate. (*f*,) Dyer's Weld (*Reseda Luteola*,) grown in Germany as a dye; the cultivation is represented as both easy and profitable. (*g*,) Dyer's Woad, (*Isatis tinc-*

*toria,*) the seed of which, with that of Weld, has lately been dristributed by the Patent Office. The leaves are the part used. There are others of a similar character; but in general they require too much time and labor to perfect, or the demand is too limited to attract general attention.

(For a full account of the culture of *Madder*, *Woad* and *Weld*, in Flanders, see Colman's *European Agriculture, vol. ii. pp.* 550–552.)

# CHAPTER XX.

---

## TEASEL. FLAX. HEMP. BROOM CORN. OZIER WILLOW.

592. Teasel *(Dipsacus Fullonum,)* is a native of Europe, and is used by the manufacturers of woollen cloth to raise a nap on the surface, by means of the fine and elastic hooks with which the seed pod is armed. There is a native American species *(D. sylvestris,)* devoid of these hooks, and therefore useless.

593. It was not till about 1820 that this plant was introduced into field culture in the United States. It is now grown in parts of New York and New England, in sufficient quantities to supply the demand. The first raised in this country sold for $10 per thousand ; as late as 1835, they were imported at a cost of $4 or $5 per thousand; from 1845 to 1850, they were afforded as low as 75 cents to $1 per thousand. The demand for them necessarily increases with the number of woollen manufacturies, and as these are met with in most of our Western States, this plant could probably be grown with sufficient facility and profit, on a limited scale, to make it worth the attention of Western farmers, for home use.

594. Having a tap-root, the teasel requires a deep rich soil. A strong, gravelly loam produces the best and most serviceable heads; and sward-land plowed deep, and well turned under in April is preferred. After plowing, the soil is pulverized and made smooth and even. The land is marked out in rows 3 or 3½ feet apart, or a drill is used, and the seed sown at the rate of 6 quarts to the acre, and lightly covered. This should be done early in May. In about a month, the field is thoroughly weeded with the hoe and fingers, and the plants thinned out to a distance of from 4 to 6 inches. After this, a cultivator is used

between the rows, and the earth drawn lightly around the plants with a hoe, thinning them to a distance of 6 to 8 inches. During the rest of the season, the weeds must be kept down, and the earth preserved mellow by the cultivator and hoe. Early the next spring the cultivator is again used, and earth drawn around the roots with the hoe. In July, the blossoms will appear; and about the first of August the earliest are sufficiently ripe for cutting. This is done as soon as the blossom is entirely off the "bur," and before the seed is fully matured. It is necessary to go through the field two or three times to collect them all at the proper age, to prevent any being injured by remaining on the stem while others are being matured. Cutting is performed with a large knife, held by the workman in one hand, while he seizes the teasel with the other, leaving from 3 to 6 inches of stalk, and throwing it into a basket. An experienced workman will cut from 20,000 to 25,000 in a day, if the crop is a good one. When taken from the field, they are carefully spread, 6 inches deep, on *open* floors, in an airy place, under cover. If the weather is damp, they must be frequently turned. When sufficiently dry, which is known by the seed seperating freely in moving, they are stored away, or packed in boxes for market. The yield is from 50,000 to 200,000 per acre, worth from 75 cents to $2 per thousand. In Europe, they are sorted according to quality, each quality being known by a peculiar name, and they are bound up in a curious manner.

595. The only insect injurious to this plant is "the common white grub" which feeds on the young roots; in some instances to such an extent as to destroy a whole crop. The winter, also, occasionally makes great destruction; the plants being partially or entirely killed [in Oneida county, N. Y.,] by an open winter, accompanied by severe frost. Late frosts in Spring are likewise injurious. A sort of "rust" is also destructive, caused by a long continuance of warm, wet weather, after the flower bud is fully formed. (*Patent Office Report*, 1850, p. 315.)

596. The use of teasels has been, to a considerable extent, superseded in the United States, within a few years, by the introduction of machinery to produce the same effect. *(Allen.)*

597. To procure seed, it is only necessary to leave a few of the strongest plants, till they are quite ripe, dry them well, and thrash with a flail.

598. FLAX *(Linum usitatissimum)* is a native of Europe but has long been cultivated in this country. There are two indigenous species in the Northern United States, *(L. Virginianum,* and *rigidum,)* of no economical value. Two species or varieties are cultivated, the common, and one with a yellowish seed, lately introduced into Ohio, which is said to yield a larger crop, and to be in many respects superior. We have seen the seed, but not the plant.

599. The census returns of flax are stated to be incorrect, and not to be depended on; but there is reason to believe that its cultivation is rather decreasing than otherwise, in consequence of the difficulty of preparing the fibre for market; and the seed alone not proving sufficiently renumerative.

600. Inorganic analysis of the entire plant of the flax grown in Ireland. *(Sir R. Kane.)*

| | |
|---|---|
| Potash, | 11.78 |
| Soda, | 11.82 |
| Lime, | 14.85 |
| Magnesia, | 9.38 |
| Alumina and oxide of iron, | 7.32 |
| Phosphoric acid, | 13.05 |
| Sulphuric acid, | 3.19 |
| Chlorine, | 2.90 |
| Silica, | 25.71 |
| Per centage of ash, dry, | 5.00 |

601. Inorganic analysis of Linseed. *(Johnston.)*

| | | Riga. | Dutch. |
|---|---|---|---|
| Potash, | 25.85 | 17.59 | 30.01 |
| Soda, | 0.71 | 6.92 | 1.88 |
| Lime, | 25.27 | 8.46 | 8.12 |

| | | Riga. | Dutch. |
|---|---|---|---|
| Magnesia, - - | 0.22 | 14.83 | 14.52 |
| Oxide of iron, - - | 3.67 | 1 25 | 0 68 |
| Phosphoric acid, - | 40.11 | 36.42 | 37.64 |
| Sulphuric acid, - - | | 2.47 | 2 16 |
| Sulphate of lime, - | 1.70 | | |
| Chlorine, - - | | 0.17 | 0.29 |
| Chloride of sodium, - | 1.55 | | |
| Silica, - - | 0.92 | 10.58 | 5 60 |
| Percentage of ash, - | 4.63 | | |

602. Inorganic analysis of English (A;) and American (B,) Linseed cake. *(Johnston.)*

| | A. | B. |
|---|---|---|
| Alkaline salts, - - | 32.72 | 38.28 |
| Phosphates of lime and magnesia, - | 49.44 | 56.40 |
| Lime, - - - | 5.06 | 1.25 |
| Magnesia, - - | 1.57 | trace. |
| Silica and sand, - - | 11.21 | 4.07 |
| Percentage of ash, - - | 7.3 | 6.04 |

The alkaline phosphates are included among the alkaline salts.

603. When the Flax plant is steeped in the ordinary way of preparing it for the flax-mill, much of the saline matter it contains is extracted by the water. This water, when evaporated (in Ireland) left a dry solid extract, which being burned gave 42 per cent of ash, of which the composition was: *(Sir R. Kane.)*

| | |
|---|---|
| Chloride of Potassiam, - - | 9.05 |
| Sulphate of potash, - - - | 10.48 |
| Carbonate of potash, - - | 9.05 |
| Carbonate of soda, - - - | 31 43 |
| Phosphate of iron and alumina, - - | 7.62 |
| Phosphate of lime, - - - | 5.00 |
| Carbonate of magnesia, - - | 4.76 |
| Carbonate of lime, - - - | 9.52 |
| Silica, - - - | 13.09 |

The saline matter is not by any means all removed by steeping. Both the outside portion taken off at the flax-mill, and the pure fibre leave when burned a considerable proportion of ash.

604. Ultimate analysis of Linseed. *(Thompson.)*

| | Fresh. | Dried at 212° F. |
|---|---|---|
| Carbon, | 42.51 | 49.55 |
| Hydrogen, | 6.22 | 7 26 |
| Nitrogen, | 3.78 | 4.41 |
| Oxygen, | 26.35 | 30.68 |
| Ash, | 6.94 | 8.10 |
| Water, | 11.20 | |

605. We are unable to meet with a perfect organic analysis of either the plant or seed, but the following results of 44 analyses by Way, Nesbit, and Lawes, of English, American and Dutch Linseed, will give an idea of the composition:

| | | | | |
|---|---|---|---|---|
| Water, | 7.6 | to | 12.4 | per cent. |
| Organic matter, | 81.0 | to | 84.1 | " |
| Ash, | 5.44 | to | 11.40 | " |
| Nitrogen, | 4.57 | to | 5.28 | " |
| Albumen, gluten, and casein, | 22.2 | | | " |
| Fat or oil, | 9.1 | to | 13.5 | " |
| Gum, dextrine, &c., | 36.3 | to | 39.1 | " |
| Fibre and Husk, | 9.5 | to | 12.7 | " |

606. The following recipes are given as special manures to return to the soil what is carried of by the seed (A;) and stem (B,) of Flax. *(Johnston.)*

| | A. | B. |
|---|---|---|
| Bone dust, | 144 lbs. | 50 lbs. |
| Sulphuric acid, | 72 " | 25 " |
| Carbonate of potash (dry,) | 36 " | 17 " |
| Carbonate of soda, (dry,) | 6 " | 20 " |
| Carbonate of magnesia, | 22 " | 21 " |
| | 280 lbs. | 133 lbs. |

Linseed leaves (on an average) 6 1-2 per cent of ash, so that for every 100 lbs. of linseed harvested, 13 lbs. of the above mixture require to be added to the land. The dry stem leaves 5 per cent of ash; every ton therefore carries off the land 112 lbs. of inorganic matter, to replace which 150 lbs., of the above mixture must be added. If this be carefully done, and if the fermented scutchings be returned to the land, the culture of flax will cease to be exhausting. The flax-fibre is almost pure *Liguin*.

Flax is cultivated in the United States for two purposes, for the fibre for weaving, and for the oil. The States which chiefly grow it are Kentucky, New York, Ohio, Pennsylvania, Virginia, Indiana, Missouri, &c. Nearly every State returns, in the census, more or less. Were an easy and cheap mode of preparing the fibre introduced, as there is every probability of there being, this crop would become both profitable and popular; as the supply, both here and in Europe, is inferior to the demand. The oil, the cake, and the seed are exported to Great Britain to some extent. The fibre is believed to be principally consumed at home. This is one of the farm products which demand the assistance of the manufacturer along side of the farmer to render it truly valuable; or the farmer has to relinquish his legitimate business, as a producer of raw material, and prepare the article for market, in its first stages of utility. Machines have lately been invented in Europe which entirely relieve the grower of the plant of the unpleasant labor of steeping, scutching, &c.; and by one of these new processes, the liquor, in which the flax is prepared, is employed, with success, for fattening hogs and cattle.* *(Journal of Highl. and Agricul. Soc'y of Scotland,* No. 42, 1853.

In this place, we shall omit any mention of the European mode of cultivating this crop, as being much too laborious and expensive for the United States, and merely give an outline of the usual way of growing it here; nor shall we describe the steeping, &c., as these after-processes demand a practical skill and experince which cannot be taught by writing.

607. *(a,)* The character of the soil depends upon the purpose for which the flax is required: if for seed it can scarcely be too rich; if for fibre, it must not be such as will cause rank growth. The general principles are, to employ *clean* land, free

*In the Weekly N. Y. Tribune of January 14, 1854, appears an advertisement of "Flax and Hemp Machinery" for pulling flax, and breaking and dressing flax and hemp. It is said to require but few hands and little power to operate it, leaving the Flax and Hemp line in better condition than has been attained by machinery heretofore in any country.

from weeds, as the flax-plant is delicate and easily smothered; land containing much organic matter, as rich prairie; and either naturally, or artificially abounding in lime. Lime, ashes, and well rotten manure may always be used to advantage. *(b,)* Plow *deep*, as soon as the crop is off the field in the fall. Where frosts are severe, it is advantageous to throw the land up in ridges, so as to allow entire disintegration. In the spring, plow again, four or five inches deep; or if the soil is tenacious and weedy, plow twice in the spring. The object is to render the land really friable, and exterminate the weeds as thoroughly as possible; and this may be done in any manner that the farmer finds the most expedient. Harrow lightly. *(c,)* Sow broadcast, 2½ to 3 bushels per acre of seed, and harrow thoroughly both ways. With *thick* sowing the fibre is of greater length and fineness than in thin sowing; in the first case, the stem grows tall and straight producing little seed; in the latter the plant grows coarse, producing much seed, and a very inferior quality of fibre. As *thin* and *thick* sowing are merely comparative terms, experiments should be tried by each farmer in order to ascertain the best quantity on his own land. The seed should be deposited about an inch deep. Finish by rolling, which is considered essential. *(d,)* The field is kept clean of weeds by the close thick growth of the plant, or by hand-weeding. *(e,)* If intended for the fibre, much experience is required in harvesting; as the marketable value of the straw depends altogether on the manner in which it is saved. The degree of ripeness is of peculiar importance. In Ireland, the best time is decided to be when the seeds are begining to change from a green to a pale brown, the stalks for two-thirds of their height being yellow. In Europe, it is pulled by hand. In America the crop is often cradled, the scythe being from 18 to 22 inches long. In this case it is recommended to cut as soon as the blossoms begin to fall. If intended only for seed, leave till the *bolls* are generally turned yellow; and treat like wheat. The after-process, when fibre is wanted, must be learnt by experience.

608. The crop of fibre in the United States is said to average 200 lbs. per acre, if the plant is allowed to seed; but 400 lbs. if it is harvested when in blossom. The quantity of seed is from 8 to 15 bushels per acre; and about 2 gallons of oil are expressed from one bushel. But we find premium crops in New York of 28½, and 20 bushels of clean seed, and 567 lbs. of dressed flax per acre.

609. Cost of cultivating 1.54—100 acres of Flax in Rensselaer county, N. Y., in 1851. The soil was a heavy loam, on upland, the crop next preceding was oats; and the crop preceding that was corn; on land many years in pasture. No manure was used.

| | | | |
|---|---|---|---|
| 1½ days plowing, | | | $3.00 |
| ½ " harrowing and sowing, | | | 1.00 |
| 6 " pulling Flax at one dollar per day, | | | 600 |
| 2 " thrashing and cleaning seed at one dollar per day, | | | 2.00 |
| 1 day spreading and taking up, | | | 1.00 |
| 1 " drawing in, and drawing to mill, | | | 2.00 |
| 1½ bushels seed at $1.50, | | | 2.25 |
| Paid for dressing and marking flax, | | | 15.96 |
| Interest on land, | | | 10.50 |
| | | | 43.71 |
| CROP. | | | |
| By 23 bushels clean seed at $1.50, | $35.50 | | |
| By 798 lbs. dressed flax at 10 cents, | 79 80 | 115.30 | |
| Net profit, | | 71.59 | |

(See, also, another account in New York Transactions of Agricultural Society, vol. v, p. 338.)

610. An interesting account is given, in 1846, of the growing of Barley and Flax together, in the town of Earlville, N. Y. An acre of land was prepared for barley; after sowing two bushels of this, one bushel of flax-seed was also sown, and the whole harvested together. They were harvested in the usual manner, threshed with a machine, and cleaned;—it is supposed that the seeds were separated by the different sized screens in the fanning mill.—The sale of the crop was:—

| | |
|---|---|
| 30 bushels of barley at 50 cents, | $15 00 |
| 15 " flax-seed at $1, | 15 00 |
| | $30 00 |

It was believed that the barley crop was as good as if no flax had been sown; neighboring fields of barley alone giving the same yield of 30 bushels. *(Patent Office Reports* 1846, *p.* 728.*)*

611. Linseed oil, being essential for painting, is in constantly increasing demand. The *Cake* is greatly depended on in Great Britain for fattening stock, and adding to the richness of manure heaps. It is quoted at wholesale prices in New York at $28 to $35, and in London at $45 to 50 per ton. The best quality of the fibre in Ireland is worth from $250 to $300 per ton.

Thompson, in his experiments on cows, found that Linseed-meal produced less milk and butter than Bean-meal. In feeding, too large quantities of linseed must not be given. About 2 lbs. of meal, boiled for 3 hours in 3½ gallons of water, is a sufficient daily allowance, with other food, for an animal weighing 800 lbs. The refuse of the pods is valuable as feed.

612. In large sections of the West, it were of much importance to Agriculturists to influence the establishment of Mills for the preparation of fibre, and for oil-making. The two should always go together.

Two patents for the preparation of the fibre are now used in Europe, and are represented as working economically, and requiring only a small capital. They are Schenk's and Watt's Patents, an account of which will be found in the *Journal and Trans. of the Highland and Agricul. Socy. of Scotland No.* 42, *p.* 116. The *Royal Flax Society* have published much of importance on this subject. Not only is the farmer interested in the direct profit of the crop, but also in the fattening and manure-forming refuse; and as the business of preparing cattle in the West, for the Eastern market increases, flax will become essentially more important to us. But above all, it brings the manufacturer in direct contact with the farmer; and forms a market for his produce at his very door. It is not usually very advisable for the farmer to connect himself with manufacturing processes, but this is an exception; and there are thousands of acres devoted to corn and pork-making, in consequence of the difficulty of reaching a market for coarse grains, where flax culture, with appropriate mills controlled by a company of farmers, would be found exceedingly profitable.

Imports of Linseed into the United States for the past five years:—

| | | | |
|---|---|---|---|
| 1849 | bags 85,970 | 1852 | bags 191.979 |
| 1850 | " 108,401 | 1853 | " 228,737 |
| 1852 | " 192,090 | | |

Imports and exports of Linseed oil:—

| Imports. | | Exports. | |
|---|---|---|---|
| 1852 | bbls. 11,364 | 1852 | bbls. 12,427 |
| 1853 | " 17,056 | 1853 | " 20,536 |

(*N. Y. Weekly Tribune, Jan.* 14, 1854.)

Oil meal is quoted in New York at $1.44 to $1.50 per 100 lbs.

613. Hemp, (*Cannabis Sativa,*) is a well known plant cultivated, like the last, for the sake of its fibre, employed in the making of ropes, and coarse fabrics. It is probably a native of India, but it is now extensively cultivated in Russia, as well as in the United States, in Germany, and in other parts of Europe, in Arabia, Africa, &c. It is of the same family as the *Hop* and *Nettle*, the fibres of both of which genera have been used for the same purpose. According to Prof. Gray, Hemp has become naturalized as a wild plant in this country.

The Indian Hemp (*C. Indica,*) (which is the same species (*Pereira,*) as the above,) is well known as affording a resinous exudation, which is used in various forms, to produce a species of intoxication, among a large portion of the human race. In hot climates, the fibre degenerates in quality, while the narcotic ingredients increase in quantity and in apparent strength. "This is another of the many interesting facts now known, which show the influence of climate in modifying the chemical changes that take place in the interior of plants, and the nature and proportions of the several substances which are produced by these changes." (*Johnston in Blackwood's Magazine, Vol. xxxvii. No.* 5, *p.* 617.) This plant is employed to produce a narcotic effect by probably not less than two or three hundred millions of the human race in Asia, Africa, and South America.

614. In the United States, the growing of Hemp is chiefly confined to Kentucky and Missouri; ten other States producing trifling quantities only. In 1850 this plant was not cultivated in Michigan. It is supposed to be decreasing in the annual product.

615. Proximate analysis of Hempseed. *(Bucholz.)*

| | | | |
|---|---|---|---|
| Oil | 19.1 | Mucilage | 9.0 |
| Husk &c. | 38.3 | Soluble albumen (casein?) | 24.7 |
| Woody fibre and Starch, | 5.0 | Fatty matter, | 1.6 |
| Sugar &c | 1.6 | Loss | 0.7 |

616. Inorganic analysis of Hemp-seed (A,) *(Johnston.)* and the Straw (B,) *(Kane.)*

| | A | B |
|---|---|---|
| Potash, | 21.67 | 10.99 |
| Soda, | 0.66 | 1.06 |
| Lime, | 26.63 | 61.75 |
| Magnesia, | 1.00 | 7.16 |
| Oxide of iron, | 0.77 | 0.54 |
| Phosphoric acid, | 34 96 | 4.73 |
| Sulphate of lime, | 0.18 | —— |
| Sulphuric acid, | —— | 1.61 |
| Chlorine, | —— | 5.54 |
| Chloride of sodium, | 0.09 | —— |
| Silica, | 14.04 | 9.92 |
| Percentage of ash, | 2.50 | 4.54 |

617. Analysis of the Scutchings of American Hemp. *(Johnston.)*

| | |
|---|---|
| Alkaline salts, chiefly common salt and sulphate of soda, | 3.32 |
| Phosphates of lime and magnesia, and a little phosphate of lime, | 19.15 |
| Sulphate of lime, (plaster,) | 3.26 |
| Carbonate of lime, | 26.45 |
| Carbonate of magnesia, | 2.80 |
| Insoluble siliceous matter, | 45.02 |
| Per centage of ash in dry fibre, | 14.43 |

618. In Commerce, Russian Hemp bears the highest value, being quoted in the New York Price currents at $265 to $300 per ton, while the best American only brings $180 to $220 per ton. The difference appears to be in the mode of preparation, Russian Hemp not being carried to the fermenting point in rotting; while in the American, incipient decay has already set in. In the latter country, two processes are employed,—"water-rotting," and "dew-rotting." In the American federal and mercantile navies Russian hemp is cheifly employed for cordage. "Russian hemp, when kept moist and warm, will lose its strength in about three weeks;—the American water-rotted in two weeks; and the dew-rotted in from five to ten days." *(Crook & Co.,*

*Maysville, Ky.* 1848.) The value of American hemp, however, is said to be rapidly increasing, owing to greater care and experience in preparing it for market. In 1845, the Navy Department decided that "American water-rotted hemp when made into cordage *without* the application of tar proved to be greater in strenth than Russian; and the application of tar proved to depreciate its strength to that of Russian." Large quantities of Western hemp are annually manufactured into cotton-bagging and bale rope. In 1845 the quantity so consumed was estimated at 40,000,000 lbs., sufficient to cover, 2,600,000 bales of cotton.

619. The best land for hemp is that which has been timbered with black walnut, buckeye, hackberry, and white oak; or rich bottom lands. If sward land, plow in the fall, and again in the spring; if fallow, one deep plowing, well harrowed, in the spring is sufficient. In Missouri, 1½ bushels of seed are sown broadcast per acre, from the 1st of April to the 10th of May. When the blossoms begin to fall, (from the middle of July to the 1st of August,) the hemp is cut. If left later, the quality is injured. An impliment similar to the point of an ordinary scythe, is used for harvesting. The plant is cut as close to the ground as possible, and the tops are lopped off as far as the seed ends, and the stalks are either thrown into the shade, or kiln-dried. While cutting, the stalks are assorted according to size; and bound up into bundles, 6 or 8 inches in diameter at the the butts, with two bands. A stick an inch in thickness, is placed in the center of each bundle, to facilitate handling. The bundles are then placed in properly prepared pools. or cisterns for rotting. Hemp, less than five feet in length, is reserved for dew-rotting. After a proper period, the bundles are withdrawn from the water, dried and stacked. After this, the mechanical operations of breaking, &c, succeed. (For a full account of this subject, in all its aspects, see *Pat. Off. Rep.* 1845 and 1846, and the other volumes.)

620. A species of wild hemp, resembling the Manilla, is said to be found in St. Louis county, Missouri; but it does not appear to be described by the Botanists. (*Pat. Off. Rep.* 1846, *p.* 261.) A "Centen-

nial Hemp" cultivated in China is recommended as adapted to this country.

621. Cost of cultivating 1 acre of Hemp, in Missouri, 1849. (*Patent Office Report*, 1849, *p*. 328.)

| | |
|---|---|
| Rent of land, | $2.00 |
| 1½ bushel of Seed, | 0.94 |
| Seeding, | 3.00 |
| Cutting, | 3.00 |
| Shocking, | 0.50 |
| Spreading, | 0.50 |
| Taking up after rotting, | 0.50 |
| Breaking 800 lbs. | 8.00 |
| Hauling to river, | 2.00 |
| | $20.44 |
| 800 lbs. @ $5 per cwt. | 40 |
| Net profit, | $19.56 |

After this profit to the farmer, it falls into the hands of the merchant or buyer, who, after paying expenses to the St. Louis market realizes as follows:

| | |
|---|---|
| Cost of 1 ton on bank of river, | $100.00 |
| Baling for shipment' | 3.00 |
| Storage, | 2.00 |
| Freight to St. Louis, | 8.00 |
| Insurance, | 1.80 |
| Commission for selling, | 3.00 |
| Weighing, | 0.40 |
| Drayage and storage 1 month, | 1.00 |
| | $119.20 |
| Market value, | 125.00 |
| Net profit to merchant, | $5.80 |

622. BROOM CORN (*Sorghum saccharatum,*) is cultivated solely for the purpose that its name indicates. It is said to be a native of India; and that its introduction into the United States was owing to Franklin, who, finding a seed upon an imported whisk, planted it, and thus disseminated the plant.

623. It is grown on a large scale on rich bottom lands in New York and Ohio, and to a more limited extent in nearly all the States. It prospers best on soil abounding in organic matter, damp but not wet. Heavy clays are improper for it. The ground is plowed in the fall, and again in the spring; well-har-

rowed; and the seed sown by a drill, in rows 3½ feet apart, as early as the climate will permit. As soon as it is above ground it is hoed, and soon after thinned, leaving the stalks 2 or 3 inches apart. It is only hoed in the rows to remove the weeds near the plants; the harrow and cultivator are then run through to keep down the weeds, and a small double mould-board plow is likewise used between the rows. It is not left to ripen but cut green. Some persons lop the tops early, and let them hang down to straighten: others leave it till nearly ready to cut. In this case, one set of hands goes forward, and lops or bends the tops on one side, and another follows and cuts them off when bent; a third gathers them into carts or wagons. At the Factory, they are sorted over. and put in bunches, each bunch of brush of equal length. The seed is then taken off by appropriate machinery, worked either by hand or horse-power. The brush is then spread thin to dry on racks, in buildings. In about a week it can be packed away. The brooms are made in winter, at about the rate of 75 dozen per acre. The stalks are left on the ground to be plowed in for manure. The seed is used for feeding stock. *(Albany Cultivator.)* The average yield in New York is 600 lbs. per acre, at a cost of cultivating and securing the crop of $10 or $12. *(N. Y. Trans.* 1849, *p.* 54.*)*

624. Cost of a raising a crop of Broom-corn in Oswego County N. Y., 1846. (*Trans. N. Y. Agricul Socy. Vol. v, p.* 340.) The soil was a rich black loam; the previous crop Indian Corn. The field low and wet with blind ditches. The area is not mentioned.

| | |
|---|---|
| 25 loads of manure, | $3.13 |
| Hauling and spreading same, | 3.13 |
| Plowing 1 day, (with horses) | 1.00 |
| Dragging ½ day, | 0.50 |
| Marking out ground for planting, 3 X 1½ feet, | 0.50 |
| 8 quarts of seed | 0.13 |
| Planting 5 days, at 50 cents, | 2.50 |
| Dragging between rows ½ day, | 0.50 |
| Hoeing and thinning, 8 to 10 stalks in a hill, 6 days, | 3.00 |
| Dragging, | 0.25 |
| Hoeing 4 days, | 2.00 |
| Tabling the corn, 5½ days, | 2.75 |

| | | |
|---|---|---|
| Binding and hauling in, - - - | | $0.75 |
| Scraping of the seed by machinery, - - | | 3.00 |
| Cleaning up seed, - - - | | 0.50 |
| Interest on land, - - - | | 3.50 |
| | | $29.86 |
| Crop :—1155 lbs. brush a$4.50, - - - - | $51.97 | |
| 81 " Seed at 18 cents - - - | 15.19 | |
| Manure for next crop, - - - | 3.14 | |
| | | $70.29 |
| Net profit, - - - - - - - | | $40.40 |

It will be observed that the wages and cost of horse labor are charged much lower than the present rates.

625. When cultivated on a large scale, with appropriate buildings and machinery for the manufacture of the brooms, the profit is said to be much greater, than when the operations are performed on a small scale. At present, much of the expense incurred in the above account would be saved by the use of improved implements, and with better management. The goodness and elasticity of the brush appear to depend partly on harvesting at the right moment, and partly on the soil and climate. It is said that some soils invariably produce brush of a brittle character. The seeds, for feeding purposes, are estimated as equal to oats, but we are unable to find an organic analysis of them. (*See Pat. Office Report* 1849, *p.* 462.)

626. Inorganic analysis of the ripe Broom-corn brush with the seeds (A,); and the quantity of such matter removed from the soil in a ton of Brush and Seeds, (B). (*Salisbury.*)

| | A | B |
|---|---|---|
| Silex - - - | 32.50 | 11.960 lbs. |
| Earthy phosphates, - - - | 36.15 | 13.303 " |
| Lime, - - - | 0.40 | 0.147 " |
| Magnesia, - - - | 0.10 | 0.036 " |
| Potash, - - - | 27.32 | 10.053 " |
| Soda, - - - | 2 37 | 0.870 " |
| Chlorine, - - - | 2.50 | 0.846 " |
| Sulphuric acid, - - | undetermined | |

Composition of the ash of Broom-corn seed. (*Salisbury.*)

| | |
|---|---|
| Carbonic acid, - - | not determined. |
| Silicic acid, - - - | 41.975 |
| Sulphuric acid, - - | not determined. |
| Phosphoric acid, - - - | 28.760 |
| Phosphate of peroxide of iron, - - | 0.525 |

| | |
|---|---|
| Lime, | 0.845 |
| Magnesia, | 3.010 |
| Potash, | 3.920 |
| Soda, | 7.247 |
| Chlorine, | 0.245 |
| Organic acids, | 4.200 |

—(*See Pat. Off. Rep.* 1849, *p.* 473.)

627. Ozier Willow (*Salix.*) This plant is used for the manufacture of baskets, and other willow-ware. The cultivation of it is only commencing among us. Hitherto, some of the wild species, of which there are 22 in the Northern States, have been used for coarse work; and the imports from Europe are stated at $5,000,000 annnally; each ton costing from $100 to $250. If attention were turned to this crop, there is no reason in either the mode of cultivation, in the climate, or appropriate soils, why willows might not become a very profitable product among us. At present, they are grown for market by a few individuals only, in New York, Mississippi, &c. John Reed, of Staten Island, N. Y. is said to have been the first person in America who systematically cultivated the ozier.

628. The species and varieties, useful for this purpose, are very numerous. Dr. C. W. Grant, of Newburgh, N. Y., has in his possession (1854) nearly 100 varieties, more than 70 of which are from England. Several, which are esteemed in that country, have failed with us, probably from their leaves being too delicate to withstand the scorching of the summer sun.

The following species are thus characterized by Dr. Grant. (*a*) Black ozier, (*Salix nigricans,*) brittle, worthless, and not a vigorous grower. (*b*) Round leaved Willow, (*S. Caprea,*) Color dark, quality indifferent, tolerates more water than any tolerably good ozier. (*c*) *S. Viminalis*, in England, the most vigorous growing and generally cultivated; (*d*) and a sub-variety called *Long-skin*, both utterly unsuited to the climate of New York. (*e*) Yellow Willow, (*S. vitellina,*) and (*f*) Huntingdon or White Willow (*S. alba,*) both moderately good; the first as oziers, the second for hoops; and greatly admired as ornamental trees. The following have been found the most valuable, as oziers, in New York. (*g*)

Long-leaved Triandrous Willow, (*S. Triandra,*) very vigorous and productive, excellent for basket work, and especially for "split work." (*h*) *S. Forbyana,* emphatically excellent in all respects. (*i*) Purple Willow (*S. purpurea,*) "If there were but one ozier in existence, this would supply more of the wants of willow-workers than any other *one.*" It is so intensely bitter that neither animals nor insects will touch it. In the West, a decoction of the bark would be valuable in place of Quinine. It is also well adapted for bands and withes for nurserymen. (*j*) A new species from the county of Suffolk, England; it grows with astonishing vigor and is in every respect valuable. (For particulars, see *Farmer's Companion and Horticultural Gazette,* Vol. iii, p. 13.)

629. Willows will grow in a great variety of soils, especially if moist, but not profitably in any greatly unsuited to their habits. Drained swamps, when brought into tillage, afford fine sites for willow plantations, or "halts." Deep, rich intervale, if with a little inclination the better, having a retentive subsoil, with a warm exposure, and some protection from wind, would leave nothing to be desired. A deep rich bottom of sandy loam, that is occasionally overflowed, such as would yield excellent potatoes, but subject to June freshets,—not so much elevated above the summer level of the stream, that by penetrating to the depth of 3 feet, the roots would find moisture,—would have no superior. Any amount of overflowing, not in the growing season, would do no damage, but increase the fertility. Richness of soil is important, great depth indispensable, and easy culture desirable and profitable.

630. Having sufficiently drained, plow deeply, or dig and trench thoroughly, and prepare the field as if for corn. Then insert the cuttings, (which should be two feet long,) perpendicularly and firmly in the soil, leaving only 2 inches above the surface. Plant in rows 3 or 4 feet apart, and one foot between the plants. Keep clean from weeds, at least for the two first years, with the hoe or cultivator. At the end of the second year, the oziers will be ready to harvest. There is a difference of opinion as to the proper season, some recommending the fall, or winter after the stopping of the circulation of the sap;

others, the spring, when the sap starts freely and the buds begin to swell. If cut in winter, the oziers are tied in bundles, and stood up in cold water till spring. Every shoot must be cleared from the stool; leaving, however, about two inches in length for the young shoots to spring from. The oziers are then pealed by a very simple implement. *(See figure.)* It is merely a round stick of hard wood, about an inch thick and a foot long, quartered about half the length of the stick, and the two opposite quarters cut off, so that it will leave a sharp edge on both the remaining two. This tool is taken in the right hand, and the willow inserted in the slit with the left one, and pulled through, the bark coming off. Sometimes, a piece of split iron with half rounded edges on the inside, set in a bench, is used for the purpose. With this a man and three or four children ought to peel 400 lbs. a day. As fast as a little bundle is stripped they are cured by laying them in the sun till they are perfectly dried; and then tied in bundles three feet round the butt; being stowed away in a dry place free from dust. They are sold by weight.

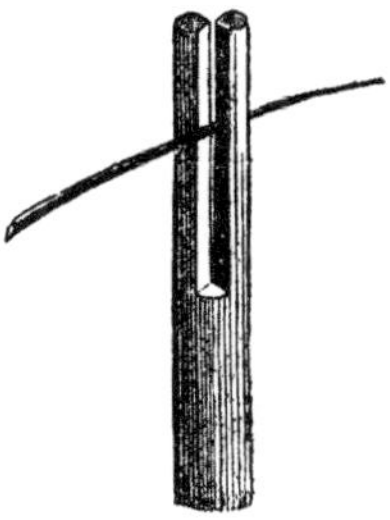

631. In Mississippi the "Italian ozier" is cultivated; it grows on the uplands when well manured, to the height of 8 or 10 feet in a season, clear shoots. Peeled shoots sell in Natchez and New Orleans, for 8 and 10 cents per pound; and cut green, with the leaves stripped, only, in September, for 2 cents per pound. The demand in New Orleans is greater than the supply. *(T. Affleck in N. Y. Agricultor*, Jan., 1853.)

632. We have no data from which we can ascertain the yield per acre, or the profits, but the latter are said to be very large when once the "halt" is fully established. It is to be hoped that our swamp lands in the west will soon be turned to this use; as not only will the country become more healthy, but

thousands of acres can be rendered profitable to the community while at present they are valueless. It is rather a reflection upon us that we are obliged to import such an article as willow sticks; and so rapidly does the demand increase that it must be long before the market can be overstocked.

In John Reed's case we are told that he received more profit from a few acres of willow than from the whole upland portion of his farm. Medicinally, *Salicin*, used, and perhaps, frequently sold as *Quinine*, is prepared from willow bark. This, also, affords much *Tannin*, the cause of its astringency.

# CHAPTER XXI.

## FRUIT TREES AND VEGETABLES.

633. To enter fully into a detail of orchard and garden plants would too greatly enlarge this volume; but the following notes and analyses are given, the latter not being easily met with, and as being both of interest and practical value to the cultivator. The teacher will experience no difficulty in procuring such practical works in this department as will suffice for his purpose; and more persons appear to be familiar with fruits and esculent vegetables than with agricultural.

634. THE APPLE (*Pyrus Malus,*) (*a,*) a native of Europe, greatly changed by cultivation (*b,*) varieties very numerous, as sour, sweet, summer, autumn, winter, (*c,*) propogated by seeds—grafts—budding—(cuttings) (*d,*) American varieties superior: quality, and value depend on soil and climate (*e,*) cultivation, pruning, gathering, packing, and preserving during winter (*f,*) dried, a considerable article of commerce; machines for the purpose, various, (*g,*) profitable as food for stock, especially the sweet varieties; for hogs better cooked; sour apples said to dry up milch cows, (*h,*) cider making; peculiar varieties for the purpose; process and implements; fermentation, spiritous, acetic; mustard seed delays the latter; when bottled, contains free carbonic acid gas; the use of a raisin in each bottle in assisting to form this gas, (*i,*) manures, bones,—sulphuric acid—ashes—plaster—salt—lime—ammonia—wheat bran. (*j,*) Insects and diseases, (*k,*) the ash of fruit small, in quantity.

635. Analysis of the Pulp (A;) and Skin (B,) of the Swaar apple. (*Salisbury.*)

| | A. | B. |
|---|---|---|
| Percentage of water, | 84.75 | 61.20 |
| " " dry matter, | 15.25 | 38.80 |
| " " ash. | 0.26 | 0.72 |
| Ash, calculated on dry matter, | 1.705 | 1.856 |

636. Percentage of water and dry matter in the Tolman Sweeting (B;) Roxbury Russet (C;) Kilham Hill (D;) English Russet (E;) Rhode Island Greening (F.)

| | B. | C. | D. | E. | F. |
|---|---|---|---|---|---|
| Percentage of water, - | - 81.52 | 81.35 | 86.31 | 79.21 | 82.85 |
| " of dry matter, | 18.48 | 18.65 | 13.69 | 20.79 | 17.15 |
| Mean of the six analyses, per centage of water, - - | | | | | 82.664 |

637. Inorganic analysis of the above, excepting the Tolman's Sweeting; and including the Swaar (A;) without carbonic acid:

| | A. | C. | D. | E. | F. |
|---|---|---|---|---|---|
| Silica, - - | 1.750 | 2.278 | 1.693 | 1.051 | 1.412 |
| Phosphate of iron, - | 2.227 | 1.564 | 1.838 | 1.062 | 1.277 |
| Phosphoric acid, - | 14.083 | 15.057 | 13.922 | 11.110 | 11.664 |
| Lime, - - | 4.956 | 4.857 | 2.999 | 3.263 | 4.421 |
| Magnesia, - | 1.786 | 1.903 | 1.379 | 1.068 | 2.211 |
| Potash, - - | 42.016 | 34.958 | 35.821 | 38.323 | 38.440 |
| Soda, - | 19 296 | 25.173 | 25.826 | 30.408 | 22.781 |
| Chlorine, - - | 2.092 | 2.300 | 2 334 | 1.848 | 2.272 |
| Sulphuric acid, - | 6.656 | 6.889 | 7.898 | 6.684 | 8.019 |
| Organic matter, - | 5.139 | 5.021 | 6.290 | 5.187 | 7.503 |

1000 lbs. of fresh apples contain about 827 lbs. water; 170.4 lbs. organic matter; and 2.6 lbs. of ash. 1000 lbs. of *dry* apples contain 17 to 18 lbs. of ash.

638. Proximate organic analysis of 1000 parts of fresh Tolman's Sweeting; (B) Rhode Island Greening; (F,) and Mean of the analyses of the six foregoing varieties (G.)

| | B. | F. | G. |
|---|---|---|---|
| Cellular fibre, - - | 33.90 | 33.58 | 32.03 |
| Glutenous matter with a little wax and fat, | 3.52 | 1.32 | 1.94 |
| Dextrine, - - - | 28.96 | 32.07 | 31.44 |
| Sugar and extract, - - | 99.05 | 76.37 | 83.25 |
| Malic acid, - - - | 2.50 | 3.04 | 3.17 |
| Albumen, - - - | 8.97 | 16.37 | 13.79 |
| Casein, - - | 0.89 | 1.89 | 1.64 |
| Dry matter, - - - | 177.79 | 164.64 | 167.26 |
| Water, - - | 815.20 | 828.46 | 826.64 |
| Loss, - - - | 7.01 | 6.90 | 6.10 |

Besides the above, apples contain a little tannic and gallic acids, especially the Russets. The Tolman Sweeting showed a trace of starch. A small quantity of white wax, and a respectable percentage of gluten also exist. These analyses were made in the month of March.

639. Comparison of the apple (A) with the ripe peach (B,) pear (C,) cherry (D,) and potato (E.)

| | A. | B. | C. | D. | E. |
|---|---|---|---|---|---|
| Chlorophyl, &c., - | | 1.10 | 0.08 | | |
| Sugar, - | 8.3 | 16.48 | 6.45 | 18.12 | 0.25 |
| Dextrine, - - | 3.1 | 5.12 | 3.17 | 3.23 | |
| Fibre, - | 3.2 | 1.86 | 3.80 | 1.12 | 5.8 |
| Albumen, - - | 1.4 | 0.17 | 0.08 | 0.57 | |
| Malic acid, - | 0.3 | 1.80 | 0.11 | 2.01 | |
| Citric acid, - - | | | | | trace. |
| Lime, - | 4.19 | trace | 0.03 | 0.01 | |
| Water, - - | 82.66 | 74.87 | 86.28 | 74.85 | 79.7 |
| Gluten, fat, &c., - | 0.2 | | | | 0.3 |
| Casein, - - | 0.16 | | | | |
| Starch, - | | | | | 9.7 |

The apple, if of good quality, may be regarded equally, if not more rich in fat-producing products than the potato. The apple is also richer in nitrogenous, or flesh-forming, products; and its inorganic constituents are peculiarly valuable. (*Salisbury*, in Trans. of N. Y. Soc'y, vol. ix. pp. 737—743.)

640. Inorganic analysis of a Sweet Apple Tree; 19 years old. (*Emmons.*)

| | Bark. | Outside wood. | Heart wood. | Bark of root. | Wood of root. |
|---|---|---|---|---|---|
| Potash, - - | 0.44 | 3.288 | 2.75 | 0.66 | 15.07 |
| Soda, - | 1.53 | 3.33 | 1.62 | 11.38 | 21.99 |
| Chloride of sodium, - | 0.30 | 0.33 | 0.51 | 0.10 | 0.11 |
| Sulphuric acid, - | 38.39 | 12.21 | 22.17 | 30.83 | 1.84 |
| Carbonic acid, - | 49.56 | 15.79 | 38.98 | | |
| Lime, - - | 1.86 | 15.56 | 2.66 | 1.00 | 11.64 |
| Magnesia, - - | 2.56 | 3.52 | 2.93 | 8.72 | 0.16 |
| Phosphate of iron, | | | | 0.72 | 0.91 |
| Phosphate of lime, - | 3.60 | 37.50 | 24.40 | 6.39 | 13.96 |
| Phosphate of magnesia, | | | | ...... | 31.35 |
| Organic matter, - | 3.35 | 3.20 | 3.60 | 1.80 | 1.20 |
| Insoluble silica, - | 1.26 | 0.45 | 0.20 | 2.86 | 1.46 |
| Coal, - - | 1.26 | 0.35 | 0.01 | 0.72 | |

641. Inorganic analysis of the leaves of the Early Harvest Apple, collected September 30: bearing fruit. *(Emmons.)*

| | | |
|---|---|---|
| Silica, | | 5.775 |
| Phosphate of iron, | 4.875 | |
| Phosphate of lime, | 1.416 | |
| Phosphate of magnesia, | trace | |
| Silica, | 5.125 | |
| Phosphoric acid, | 5.359 | 16 775 |
| Lime, | | 36.398 |
| Magnesia, | | 0.075 |
| Potash, | | 13.179 |
| Soda, | | 11.616 |
| Chloride of sodium, | | 0.060 |
| Sulphuric acid, | | 0.137 |
| Carbonic acid, | | 15.200 |
| Organic matter, | | 2.850 |
| PROPORTIONS. | | |
| Water, | | 54.341 |
| Dry, | | 45.659 |
| Ash, | | 4.194 |
| Ash, calculated dry, | | 9.163 |

642. THE PEAR *(Pyrus communis,)* *(a,)* a native of Europe, cultivated from remote antiquity; *(b,)* at present, Belgium is celebrated for this fruit; *(c,)* several fine American varieties; *(d,)* propagated by seeds, (for stocks,) by grafting—budding—dwarf pears on Quince roots; *(e,)* requires a soil rich in the *phosphates*, much more difficult to cultivate than the last; *(f,)* subject to several diseases, from the seed to maturity, as *Insect-blight*, *Frozen-sap-blight*, &c; *(g,)* ripened artificially in the house, to acquire perfection of flavor; *(h,)* brings high prices in market; *(i,)* Perry—manufacture *(i,)* manures, unleached ashes, bones, lime, plaster, salt.

643. Comparative analysis of the Sap-wood (A,) Heart-wood (B,) Bark of Trunk (C,) of the Pear Tree, and the Wood (D,) and Bark (E.) of the Root of the same. *(Emmons.)*

| | A | B | C | D | E |
|---|---|---|---|---|---|
| Water, - - | 48.80 | 22.05 | 63.70 | 22.33 | 58.80 |
| Dry matter, - | 37.20 | 77.95 | 30.30 | 79.67 | 46.20 |
| Ash - - | 0.20 | 0 10 | 1.99 | 0.40 | 3.26 |

644. Analysis of the leaves of the Bergamot Pear tree, (collected September 30, bearing fruit;) (A,) and of a Pear tree, (picked May 23, flowers just fallen,) (B.) *(Emmons.)*

| A | | B | |
|---|---|---|---|
| Silica, - | 4.250 | Silicic acid, - | 1.750 |
| Phosphates, (with 5 bases,) | 16.550 | - | 25.050 |
| Lime - - | 39.853 | - - | .4.715 |
| Magnesia, - | 5.920 | - - | 4.500 |
| Potash, - - | 8.793 | - - | 18.950 |
| Soda, - | —— | - - | 15.190 |
| Chloride of Sodium, | 0.554 | - - | not determined |
| Sulphuric acid, - | - 4.464 | | do |
| Carbonic acid, - | 17.125 | - - | 11.560 |
| Organic matter, - | 3.000 | - | not determined |

Proportions of (A,)

| | |
|---|---|
| Water, - - - | 56.138 |
| Dry matter, - - | - 43.862 |
| Ash, - - - | 3.260 |
| Do. calculated dry, - - | - 7.514 |

For the organic analyis of the fruit, see (S——)

645. Quince *(Pyrus Cydonia,) (a,)* native of the South of Europe; *(b,)* varieties few, cannot be eaten uncooked, seeds medicinal; *(c,)* propagated by seed—cuttings—grafts—layers. *(d,)* cultivation simple; *(e,)* injured by the *Borer*, and a worm that girdles the twigs; *(f,)* manures,—barn-yard—salt—woolen rags.

646. The tree and fruit do not appear to have been analyzed. Souchay gives the following inorganic constituents of the seeds:

| | | | |
|---|---|---|---|
| Potash, - - | 27.09 | Oxide of iron, - - | 1 19 |
| Soda, - - - | - 3.01 | Phosphoric acid, - | 42.02 |
| Lime, - - | 7.69 | Sulphuric acid, - - | 2 67 |
| Magnesia, - | - 13.01 | Chloride of Sodium, | 2.57 |
| Silica, - - | 0.75 | | |

647. Peach *(Persica vulgaris,)* *(a,)* native of Persia; said to have been found cultivated abundantly by the Indians by Hendrick Hudson, on his first voyage, but never discovered wild on this continent; supposed to be a cultivated variety of the almond *(amygdalus communis,)*; *(b,)* in Great Britain requires artificial heat; *(c,)* varieties exceedingly numerous; *(d,)* propogated by seed—budding—(grafting, and in New Zealand by cuttings); *(e,)* cultivation simple, pruning chiefly confined to *shortning in*; *(f,)* dried; *(g,)* fattening for hogs—owing to the *Cyanogen* of the kernel? *(h,)* distilled into brandy; *(i,)* manures —leached ashes; *(j,)* injured by the *Borer*, the *Aphis*, the *Curculio;* and diseases—the *Yellows*, *Curl*, &c.—causes and remedies.

648. Inorganic analysis of the leaves of the Peach tree, (pulled July 22), (A,) and of the leaves of a tree affected by the Yellows, (B,) *(Emmons.)*

| | A | B |
|---|---|---|
| Carbonic acid, | 13.300 | 13.200 |
| Silicic acid, | 0.600 | 0.800 |
| Phosphates, | 9,600 | 11.600 |
| Lime, | 16.220 | 14.300 |
| Magnesia, | 5.900 | 5.300 |
| Potash, | 14.280 | 14.440 |
| Soda, | 21.220 | 22.280 |
| Chlorine, | 5.120 | 4.740 |
| Sulphuric acid, | 4.420 | 4.430 |
| Organic acids, | 7.900 | 4.300 |

These analyses are peculiarly interesting, as showing that the disease called the "yellows" does not arise from a deficiency of inorganic matter. Should further examinations sustain this view of the case we may be enabled to find a remedy for this scourge of the peach tree. We throw out the suggestion, that, owing to the constant generations of plants on the same soil, a change takes place similar to that observed when animals are bred in-and in; or in other words a scrofulous constitution becomes inherent, which causes the absorption of too great proportions of inorganic salts, and thence disease, and early mortality. We cannot in this place do more than hint at this subject, but many facts and analogies may be adduced in support of this theory, and we submit it to the consideration of those who live in a part of the country where this disease prevails. In some soils, if long continued wet weather occurs in the early part of the summer, the leaves of this tree, even when perfectly healthy, become diseased, curl up, and fall off; an affection which we are inclined to attribute to an inordinate absorption of salts, but are, as yet, unable satisfactorily to prove it.

649. Inorganic analysis of a small seedling Peach tree, aged 23 years; mean diameter 3½ inches; thickness of bark 1-7 inch; growth rather slow. *(Emmons.)*

| | Bark of Trunk. | Wood of Trunk. | Bark of Root. | Wood of Root. |
|---|---|---|---|---|
| Potash, | } 1 20 | 7.11 | 3.162 | 8.58 |
| Soda, | | 11.15 | 1 92 | 15 92 |
| Chloride of Sodium, | 0.04 | 0.16 | 0.33 | 5.60 |
| Chloride of Potassium | —— | —— | —— | —— |
| Sulphuric acid, | 4.19 | 1.51 | 3.44 | 0.58 |
| Carbonic acid, | —— | —— | —— | —— |
| Lime, | 42.17 | 23.26 | 38 48 | 0.11 |
| Magnesia, | 2.[illegible]6 | 6.40 | 2.91 | 0.01 |
| Phosphate of iron, | 0.45 | 0.32 | } 10.40 | 1.02 |
| Phosphate of lime, | 18.79 | 29.19 | | 18.10 |
| Phosphate of magnesia, | 0.01 | 1 34 | —— | 30 00 |
| Organic matter, | 3.30 | 5.20 | 3.60 | 2.55 |
| Insoluble silica, | 4.15 | 1.35 | 9.40 | 6.46 |
| Coal, | —— | —— | 1.40 | —— |
| | **Leaves.** | **Pits.** | **Bark of Limbs.** | **Wood of Limbs.** |
| Potash | 12.41 | 18.47 | 8.85 | 19.21 |
| Soda, | —— | 5.21 | —— | 8.11 |
| Chloride of Sodium, | —— | 2.70 | 0.28 | 0 24 |
| Chloride of Potassium, | 0.36 | —— | —— | —— |
| Sulphuric acid, | 12.12 | 15.12 | 6 18 | 8.07 |
| Carbonic acid, | —— | —— | —— | —— |
| Lime, | 14.77 | 16.80 | 31.98 | 24.64 |
| Magnesia, | 8.00 | 1 33 | 6.00 | 9.76 |
| Phosphate of Iron, | 2.47 | 1.33 | 1 60 | 0.60 |
| Phosphate of lime, | 10.44 | 17.98 | 8 50 | 13.20 |
| Phosphate of Magnesia, | 3.15 | 0.02 | 0.20 | 0.20 |
| Organic matter, | 0.86 | 6.61 | 5.00 | 8.40 |
| Insoluble Silica, | 6.42 | 10.00 | 4.30 | 1.00 |
| Coal, | 4.48 | —— | 1.00 | 1.20 |

For organic analysis see § ——

650. The kernels, blossoms, leaves, and bark, possess poisonous qualities, apparently independent of the *hydrocyanic (Prussic) acid*, contained especially in the first. *(Pereira.)*

651. THE NECTARINE *(Persica lævis,)* is distinguished from the Peach by its smooth fruit; but it is believed to be merely a variety of the latter. In the United States it is rarely cultivated in consequence of the great injury done to it by the Curculio.

652. CHERRY *(Cerasus vulgaris,) (a,)* native of Asia, *(b,)* varieties numerous as *Heart*, *Bigarreau*, *Duke*, *Morello*, each of which has many sub-varieties. Best in France; many good American varieties, especially those produced by hybridizing by Dr. Kirtland, of Cleveland, O.; *(c,)* propagated by seeds—(for stocks and new sorts)—by budding—(grafts;) dwarfed by budding on the Perfumed Cherry *(C. Mahaleb;) (d,)* cultivation; pruning simple,—branches should be trained near the ground, with a short stem. *(e,)* Manures,—bones, ashes, salt, plaster.

653. Analysis of the leaves of the Oxheart Cherry, (picked, May 23rd,) (A;) and of the leaves of the Large Yellow Spanish Cherry, (picked, September 30,) (B.) *(Emmons.)*

| | A. | B. |
|---|---|---|
| Carbonic acid, | 11.450 | |
| Silicic acid, | 1.850 | |
| Phosphates, | 26.650 | 37.175 |
| Lime, | 3.941 | 21.975 |
| Magnesia, | 3.465 | 3.195 |
| Potash, | 23.757 | 13 948 |
| Soda, | 12.367 | 1.657 |
| Sulphuric acid, | not determined. | 10.260 |
| Organic acids, | do | 7.650 |
| Silica, | do | 4.225 |
| Chloride of sodium, | do | 0 410 |

PROPORTIONS OF THE LAST, (B.)

| | |
|---|---|
| Water, | 58.628 |
| Dry matter, | 41.372 |
| Ash, | 3.434 |
| Ash, calculated dry, | 8.300 |

For organic analysis, see §

654. THE PLUM *(Prunus domestica,)* is a native of Europe, with four indigenous species in the Northern United States. Owing to the destruction of the fruit by the Curculio, the culture of this tree has become insignificant. The principle inorganic constituents are Potash, Soda, Lime, and Phosphoric acid. *(See Patent Office Report,* '49, p. 480.) Many modes of preventing the attacks of the Curculio have been proposed, but none have proved entirely effectual. Dusting the tree with slaked lime is, at present, looked upon with most favor.

655. GRAPES *( Vitis,) (a;)* European grapes originally from Persia. Quite distinct species from native American Grapes, of which there are many species and varieties. *(b,)* European grapes difficult to cultivate in America. Large vineyards on the Ohio River, and other States south of that. *(c,)* Propagated by layers,—cuttings,—eyes,—grafts. *(d,)* Cultivation and pruning demand much skill and knowledge. Subject to a mould on the fruit, curable by sulphur.

656. Inorganic analysis of the leaves of the Catawba Grape, picked, June 2d, nearly full grown (A,) and the same picked, September 30, fruit abundant (B.) *(Emmons.)*

| | A. | B. |
|---|---|---|
| Carbonic acid, | 3 050 | 8.900 |
| Silicic acid, | 29.650 | Silica 23.150 |
| Sulphuric acid, | 2 062 | 1.426 |
| Phosphates, | 32.950 | 28.750 |
| Lime, | 4.391 | 26 258 |
| Magnesia, | 1.740 | 5.330 |
| Potash, | 13.394 | 1.710 |
| Soda, | 9.698 | 2.983 |
| Chlorine, | 0.741 | |
| Organic acids, | 2.250 | 3.450 |
| Chloride of sodium, | | 0.305 |

From Grapes are made: 1. Grape Sugar. 2. Bitartrate of Potash, *(Crude tartar or Argol.)* 3. Raisins, and small black "currants" imported from the Mediterranean. 4. Wine. 5. Brandy.

657. GOOSEBERRY *(Ribes Grossularia,) (a,)* native of Great

Britain—many cultivated sub-varieties—4 wild species in the northern United States—prefers a damp climate and soil; *(b,)* colors vary, red, yellow, green, differs also much in size, and in the prickles on the fruit; *(c,)*, propogated by cuttings—layers, suckers, *(c,)* cultivation simple, best in the U. S. in a damp, shaded place, or well mulched especially with salt-grass—pruning, annual shortening in, keeping the centre open to admit air; *(d,)* manure, ashes, salt, well-rotted organic matter; *(e,)* a mould similar to that on grapes, often destroys the fruit.

658. Organic analysis of the unripe (A,) and the ripe Gooseberry (B.) *(Berard.)*

| | A | B |
|---|---|---|
| Chlorophyl and coloring matter - - | 0,03 | |
| Sugar, - - - | 0.52 | 6.24 |
| Dextrine, - - - | 1.36 | 0.78 |
| Fibre, - - - | 8.45 | 8.01 |
| Albumen, - - - | 1.07 | 0 87 |
| Malic acid, - - - | 1.80 | 2.41 |
| Citric acid. - - - | 0.12 | 0.31 |
| Lime, - - - | 0.24 | 0.29 |
| Water, - - - - | 86.41 | 81.10 |

The leaves of the CURRANT are rich in Soda and the Phosphates; the blossom, in Potash. *(Emmons.)*

659. RHUBARB; *(Rheum rhaponticum,) (a,)* many species cultivated, from Asia, China, Turkey, and Tartary; many sub-varieties produced by cultivation; *(b,)* the petioles, or leaf-stalks, used for pies, preserves, making wine; the root as medicine—the best from Russian Tartary, on the confines of China—the root grown in Europe and America very inferior as a drug; *(c,)* cultivation requires deep rich soil, highly manured, and the plants covered during the winter with rough barn-yard manure—is sometimes *blanched*, by which the flavor is improved; *(d,)* the leaf, flower, stalks &c., poisonous, chiefly in consequence of the *Oxalate of lime* contained in them, which is decomposed in digestion; *(e,)* specific manures, bones—plaster—salt—ashes —organic substances.

660. Percentage of Water, Dry matter, and Ash, in various parts of the Giant Rhubarb, cut June 1, Plant in flower. (*Salisbury.*)

| | Root, | Stalk, | Petioles, | Leaf-blades, | Flowers & Pedicles. |
|---|---|---|---|---|---|
| Percentage of water, | 82.000 | 89 50 | 93.46 | 88.00 | 86.90 |
| —— Dry matter, | 18.000 | 10.50 | 6.53 | 12.00 | 13.10 |
| " Ash, | 0.925 | 1.13 | 0.94 | 1.53 | 1 32 |
| " ash calc. on dry mat. | 5.194 | 10.76 | 14.384 | 12.75 | 10.07 |

661. Inorganic analysis of various parts of the same plant—viz—Root (A,) Leaf stalk (B,) Leaf blades (C,) Stalk (D.)

| | A. | B. | C. | D. |
|---|---|---|---|---|
| Silicic acid, - - | 3.95 | 1.40 | 7.60 | 0.450 |
| Phosphates, - | 30.05 | 22 20 | 19.40 | 17.20 |
| Lime, - - | 4.78 | 2.47 | 5.74 | 3.57 |
| Magnesia, - | 2.92 | 0.20 | 1.16 | 0.20 |
| Potash, - - | 7.21 | 5.28 | 7.87 | 8.09 |
| Soda, - - | 24.73 | 33.26 | 27.36 | 33.26 |
| Sodium, - - | 0.14 | 1.65 | 2.11 | 0 97 |
| Chlorine, - | 0.22 | 2.50 | 3 21 | 1.48 |
| Sulphuric acid, - - | 5.15 | 5.27 | 4.27 | 10.72 |
| Organic matter, - | 7.35 | 15.60 | 6.40 | 12.15 |
| Carbonic acid, - - | 12.05 | 9.43 | 14.90 | 9.40 |

662. Proximate organic analysis of the Leaf stalks (gathered September 1st) of a very large and succulent Rhubarb.

| | |
|---|---|
| Percentage of water, - - - | 87.77 |
| " of dry matter, - - | 12.23 |
| " ash - - - | 2.27 |
| " ash calc. on dry matter, - | 18.56 |

| | With the Water. | Without the Water. |
|---|---|---|
| Fibre with a little starch and chlorophyl, | 1.26 | 9.89 |
| Malic acid and extract, with a little tartaric and oxalic acids, | 5.70 | 44 62 |
| Dextrine, - - | 0.55 | 4.30 |
| Fibre, - - - | 3.23 | 25.30 |
| Matter separated from fibre, albuminous, | 1.60 | 12.55 |
| Albumen, - - - | 0.27 | 2.11 |
| Casein, - - | 0.15 | 1.17 |
| Water, - - - | 87.77 | —— |

(*See Trans. N. Y. Agricul. Society, vol. ix, p.* 744.)

663. Comparative analyses of the large red Tomato, (*Sola-*

*num lycospersicum,)* (A,) and of Egg Plant, *(Solanum melongena,)* (B.) *(Salisbury.)*

I. Percentage of water, dry matter and ash:

| | A | B |
|---|---|---|
| Water, | 94.75 | 91.35 |
| Dry matter, | 5.24 | 8.64 |
| Ash. | 0.33 | 0.60 |
| Ash, calculated on dry matter, | 6.37 | 6.98 |

II. Composition of the ash of the above:

| | A. | B. |
|---|---|---|
| Carbonic acid, | 11.05 | 4.72 |
| Silicic acid, | 1.77 | 1.70 |
| Sulphuric acid, | 1.79 | 4.74 |
| Phosphoric acid and peroxide of iron, | 24.07 | 28.77 |
| Lime, | 0.07 | 0.07 |
| Magnesia, | 1.61 | 1.37 |
| Potash, | 20.80 | 20.51 |
| Soda, | 25.53 | 31.97 |
| Sodium, | 2.79 | 1.13 |
| Chlorine, | 4.24 | 1.73 |
| Organic acids, | 4.55 | 2.20 |

III. Proximate organic composition of the Tomato:

| | |
|---|---|
| Sugar and extract, with tartaric, citric and malic acids, | 3.32 |
| Albumen, | 0.21 |
| Casein, | 0.20 |
| Dextrine or gum, | 0.54 |
| Fibre with coloring matter, | 1.01 |
| Matter separated from the fibre | 0.32 |
| Water, | 94.75 |

With a small quantity of volatile oil.

Proximate organic composition of the Egg Plant:—

| | |
|---|---|
| Sweet water and extract, with a peculiar bitter principle, | 3.04 |
| Starch, | 0.36 |
| Albumen, | 0,25 |
| Casein, | 0.20 |
| Dextrine or gum, | 0.37 |
| Fibre, | 0.76 |
| Matter separated from the fibre, | 0.97 |
| Water, | 91.35 |

With a small quantity of volatile oil and wax.

*(See Trans. N. Y. Agricul Socy. Vol. viii, p. 370.)*

664. ASPARAGUS *(A officinalis,)* owes its flavor and properties to a peculiar, easily crystallizable neutral substance ($C_8$ $N_4$ $H_{16}$ $O_6$ which occurs in several plants, as the Marsh-mallow, Cumfrey, Potato &c, called *Asparagine.*

665. LETTUCE *(Lactuca sativa,)* owes its value to a narcotic principle called *Lactucin.* It acts upon the brain after the manner of Opium, and induces sleep; eaten during the day, it calms, soothes, and allays the tendency to nervous irritability. It is probable that it might be fed with a good effect to fattening animals; in a favorable soil, it is cultivated with great facility. *(See Blackwood's Magazine, Dec.* 1853, *p.* 679.*)*

666. Analysis of the Muskmelon *(Cucumis melo.)* (A;) Watermelon *(Cucurbita citrullus,)* (B;) and Cucumber *(Cucumis sativus,)* (C.) *(Salisbury.)*

Percentage of water, dry matter, and ash:—

| | A. | B. | C. |
|---|---|---|---|
| Percentage of water, | 90.987 | 94.898 | 96.364 |
| " of dry matter, | 9.013 | 5.102 | 3.636 |
| " of Ash, | 2.771 | 0.248 | 0.362 |
| " of Ash in dry matter, | 3.007 | 4.861 | 9.955 |

| Ultimate analysis of the above:— | A. | B. | C. |
|---|---|---|---|
| Nitrogen, | 2.231 | 1.739 | 1.236 |
| Oxygen, | 43.905 | 43.187 | 41.806 |
| Carbon, | 44.820 | 43.764 | 40.984 |
| Hydrogen, | 6.832 | 6.872 | 6.879 |
| Inorganic matter, | 3.007 | 4.861 | 9.955 |

| Inorganic analysis of the above:— | A. | B. | C. |
|---|---|---|---|
| Carbonic acid, | 11.55 | 11.42 | 13.25 |
| Silicic acid, | 2.20 | 1.21 | 0.70 |
| Phosphoric acid, | 25.40 | 14.93 | 18.90 |
| Sulphuric acid, | 3.90 | 1.63 | 0.90 |
| Phosphate of iron, | 2.30 | 4.52 | 3.10 |
| Lime, | 5.85 | 7.32 | 4.30 |
| Magnesia, | 0.60 | 1.31 | 0.20 |
| Potash, | 8.35 | 23.95 | 23.20 |
| Soda, | 34.35 | 30.63 | 33.75 |
| Chlorine, | 5.20 | 1.81 | 1.10 |
| Organic matter, | trace, | trace, | trace. |

Proximate organic analysis of the above *(fresh,)*:—

| | A. | B. | C. |
|---|---|---|---|
| Albumen, - - | 0.918 | 0.572 | 0.356 |
| Casein, - - - | 0.442 | 0.004 | 0.040 |
| Dextrine, - - | 1.142 | 0.318 | 0.354 |
| Starch, - - - | trace, | none, | 0.002 |
| Sugar and extract, - | 5.250 | 3.020 | 2.826 |
| Chlorophyl, - - - | 0.004 | 0.006 | 0.006 |
| Fat, wax, and resin, - | 0.038 | 0.022 | 0.031 |
| Citric acid, - - - | trace, | 0.007 | |
| Malic acid, - - | 0.007 | 0.009 | |
| Tartaric acid, - - | 0.0('5 | trace. | |
| Fibre, - - | 1.123 | 1.058 | 9.61 |
| Water, - - - | 90.987 | 94.898 | 95.354 |

The varieties above examined were the *Nutmeg Muskmelon;* the *Long Red Watermelon;* and the *Early Long Prickly Cucumber.* (See further, *Trans. of the N. Y. Agricul. Socy.*, vol. xii., (1852,) pp. 335—337.)

667. Analysis of the Vegetable Oyster-root—*Tragopogon porrifolius,)* (A;) of the Endive or Succory-leaf—*Cichorium Endivia,)* (B;) and of Celery, *(Apium Graveolens,)* (C.)—*(Salisbury in Trans. of N. Y. Agricul. Socy.*, vol. xii.)

Percentage of water, dry matter, and ash:—

| | A. | B. | C. |
|---|---|---|---|
| Percentage of water, - - | 81.22 | 91.925 | 88.225 |
| " of dry matter. - | 18.78 | 8.075 | 11.775 |
| " of ash, - - | 1.465 | 1.010 | 1.375 |
| " of ash in dry matter, - | 8·333 | 12.507 | 11.931 |

Ultimate analysis of the above:

| | A | B | C |
|---|---|---|---|
| Nitrogen, - - | 0.995 | 2.170 | 2.121 |
| Carbon, - - | 42.044 | 41.171 | 40.626 |
| Oxygen, - - | 44.017 | 40.257 | 40.352 |
| Hydrogen, - - | 5.058 | 5.617 | 5.371 |
| Inorganic matter, - - | 8.860 | 12.507 | 11.931 |

Inorganic analysis of the above:—

| | A | B | C |
|---|---|---|---|
| Carbonic acid, - - | 24.60 | 13.80 | 20.80 |
| Silicia acid, - - | 0.60 | 20.80 | 5.60 |

| | A | B | C |
|---|---|---|---|
| Phosphoric acid, - - | 15.60 | 9.90 | 5.40 |
| Phosphate of iron, - - | 1.85 | 2.95 | 4.95 |
| Lime, - - | 4.95 | 8.05 | 13.55 |
| Magnesia, - - | 0.75 | 3.65 | 0.90 |
| Potash, - - | 5.80 | 8.90 | 7.25 |
| Soda, - - | 39.20 | 27.80 | 28.80 |
| Chlorine, - - | 2.45 | 1.40 | 1.40 |
| Sulphuric acid, - - | 3.90 | 2.10 | 10.30 |
| Organic matter, - - | trace. | —— | —— |

Proximate organic analysis of the above:—

| | A | B | C |
|---|---|---|---|
| Water, - - | 80.610 | 91.925 | 88.225 |
| Fibre, - - - | 2.764 | 1.348 | 3.168 |
| Sugar and extract, - - | 3.665 | 4.300 | 5.685 |
| Dextrine, - - | 1.435 | 0.735 | 0.905 |
| Casein, - - - | 0.172 | 0.100 | 0.115 |
| Albumen, - - | 1.066 | 1.320 | 1.532 |
| Starch, - - - | 0.035 | none. | none. |
| Resin, - - - | 0.180 | 0 260 | 0.185 |
| Gluten, - - - | 0.014 | 0.055 | 0.095 |
| Chlorophyl, - - | —— | 0.052 | 0.055 |
| Wax, - - - | —— | 0.055 and oil | 0.120 |

# CHAPTER XXII.

## MANURES.

668. In order to understand the principles of manuring we must consider:—

(*a*,) A plant consists of two parts, an organic and a mineral part. The mineral part is drawn from the soil alone, by the roots; while of the organic part one portion comes from the soil through the roots, and another portion from the air through the leaves.

(*b*,) The organic part of plants consists of four simple bodies, or gases; carbon, hydrogen, oxygen, and nitrogen. In all the parts of plants these four are associated also, with minute quantities of sulphur and phosphorus.

(*c*,) Of these four substances nitrogen appears to be drawn by the plant almost exclusively from the soil; the hydrogen and oxygen are drawn partly from the soil and partly from the air—chiefly in the form of water. The carbon is derived only in small proportion from the soil, being for the most part sucked in from the air by the leaves, in the form of carbonic acid gas. Sulphur and phosphorus come from the soil only.

(*d*,) The mineral part of the plant, which forms from half of one per cent. to 15 to 20 per cent. of the whole weight of the dried plant, consists of about 12 different substances. (*See* § 93, *p.* 27.) Of these silica exists chiefly in the stems of grasses, grains, &c., and in smaller proportion only in the softer parts and juices of plants. Potash, soda, chlorine and sulphuric acid are, for the most part, found in the sap; lime, magnesia, and oxide of iron in the solid parts of plants. Phosphoric acid is necessary to, and is found in every part of a plant, but it collects in larger proportion in the grain or seeds as the season of ripening approaches. (*See Johnston's Experimental Agriculture, p.* 7.)

(*e*,) No plant therefore can flourish and come to maturity unless it is able to procure in a proper form, and absorb the above substances.

669. We must consider also:—

(*a*,) That a fertile soil consists of three portions, 1. Of one which is dormant, as the sand and clay which form by far the larger mass of it; 2. Of the above minerals and organic matter in a state in which they are *insoluble* in water, and therefore cannot become part of a plant; and 3. Of the same in a *soluble* form capable of dissolving in water, and of entering into the pores of the roots. (*See* § 113, *p*. 34.)

(*b*,) That every crop which is taken off the ground carries away a notable portion of the soluble materials; and, supposing that there existed no means of adding to them, all soil would rapidly become exhausted by cultivation.

(*c*,) But nature is continually rendering soluble that which she finds insoluble in the soil, by the action of the air, of carbonic acid gas, by heat, electricity, moisture, and complex chemical changes which are always in progress. Again, a porous soil into which air and water can find their way, is constantly receiving additions from the atmosphere, and from spring water laden with soluble salts, raised by evaporation and capillary attraction. (*See* § 29, *p*. 9, § 55, *p*. 17.)

(*d*,) If, therefore, we were content to commence cultivating a virgin soil, abounding in all that is requisite to form a plant; to take off one grain crop; and then leave the field uncultivated for a certain number of years, we might in this manner retain the fertility of the soil, and at each period reap an equally large crop, for any length of time.

(*e*,) But this mode of cultivating the soil is *unprofitable;* and, therefore, the ingenuity of man has discovered various modes of hastening or dispensing with the action of nature. These modes are 1. A *bare fallow*, where two grain crops were taken in succession, and then the land was left unfruitful for a year, but frequently plowed and stirred so as to expose every part of it to the dissolving action of the elements. 2. *Rotations*, so arranged that each succeeding crop abstracted only such materials as were not required by the other crops; so that when grain was again sown it found an accumulation of those peculiar elements which were requisite for its prosperity. 3. *Draining*, whereby the soil was rendered porous to a considerable depth, and enabled to receive and retain such elements as the air and water were capable of supplying; and 4. *Manuring*, which is procuring from some other source, and applying directly to the soil the elements necessary for the crop; or, in other words placing in the ground the raw material which nature is to work up into grain; as the paper-maker collects old rags, out of which white paper is to be made. (*See Farmer's Companion and Horticultural Gazette*, Vol. ii, p. 89.)

(*f*,) Manuring, therefore, may be defined to be the directly supplying to the soil those constituents which are necessary for the formation of the plant we wish to grow, and which, in a soluble shape, are either naturally deficient in the soil, or have become so by our carrying them off in the form of grain, meat, &c., we not being able to wait until nature performs this work for us,*

670. Manuring is probably the most costly mode of restoring the fertility of the soil that can be practiced.

671. But while many persons are content merely to retain, by manuring, their land at its natural point of fertility, others render it much more fertile than it ever was; on the principle that if a certain quantity of applied manure can be worked up into a grain crop, a still greater quantity will supply a larger proportion of grain.

672. From this it must be apparent that in order that a farmer may economically and skilfully manure his land, he must understand the composition of plants, the relative materials which constitute his soil, the constituents of the manures applied, and their chemical action. For were he to put on his field a salt in a soluble form which would immediately become insoluble in consequence of chemical changes, the manure would be lost to him.

In the following pages we shall chiefly confine ourselves to an account of the manures which are generally available in the Northern States, and the principles on which they act. For further information on this extended and intricate subject we must refer the reader to works especially bearing upon it.

673. The following diagram from *Dumas & Boussingault's Chemical and Physiological Balance of Organic Nature*, may be useful in this connection.

---

*A species of manurnig may be practiced, the principle of which differs from the above; as where a salt is applied, *not* for the purpose of directly entering into the plant, but to act, chemically, as a solvent, upon the insoluble constituents of the soil; o as a fixer of gases, or other to^ readily soluble materials, as charcoal and probably plaster.

| AN ANIMAL<br>is<br>AN APPARATUS OF COMBUSTION ; | A VEGETABLE<br>is<br>AN APPARATUS OF REDUCTION ; |
|---|---|
| Possesses the faculty of Locomotion ; | Is fixed ; |
| Burns Carbon,<br>Hydrogen,<br>Ammonium, | Reduces Carbon,<br>Hydrogen,<br>Ammonium, |
| Exhales Carbonic acid,<br>Water,<br>Oxide of Ammonium,<br>Nitrogen ; | Fixes Carbonic acid,<br>Water,<br>Oxide of Ammonium,<br>Nitrogen ; |
| Consumes Oxygen,<br>Neutral nitrogenized matters,<br>Fatty matters,<br>Amylaceous matters,<br>sugars, gums ; | Produces Oygen,<br>Neutral nitrogenized matters,<br>Fatty matters,<br>Amylaceous matters,<br>sugars, gums ; |
| Produces Heat,<br>Electricity ; | Absorbs Heat,<br>Abstracts Electricity ; |
| Restores its elements to the air,<br>or to the earth ; | Derives its elements from the air,<br>or from the earth ; |
| Transforms organized matters<br>into mineral matters. | Transforms mineral matters into<br>organized matters. |

673. Manures are generally classed under three heads :—(*a*,) vegetable ; (*b*,) animal ; (*c*,) mineral. Those that are of vegetable origin being formed of decaying vegetable matter, consist, like the plant, of an organic and mineral part ; of which the former is usually much the larger in quantity. But a new branch of study is connected with the decay or decomposition of this vegetable matter, and especially of its organic part, in the farm-yard, in the compost heap, or in the soil. This decay gives rise to new chemical combinations, which have much influence on the efficacy of the decomposed matter as a manure. The nature and products of this new series of chemical changes ought to be familiar to the farmer.

674. Those manures which are of animal origin resemble, in composition, the parts of the animal body from which they are derived—the blood, flesh, bone, &c. Or, if they consist of urine and dung of animals, they have a certain relation, especially the solid excrements, to the food on which the animals have lived. Here, however, a new kind of information is demanded. These animal substances, like the vegetable, putrify before they become directly useful to plants. In the bodies

of animals, also, changes take place, by which the food consumed is decomposed, and new compounds of much importance are, in consequence, introduced into the urine and dung. All these changes are, in some degree, connected with the richness and fertilizing quality of animal manures, or with the special action of the variety which may be used. To know on what the general efficacy or peculiar effect of such manures depends, their changes and the substances produced by them, should be understood. How different samples of the same kind of manures differ in virtue; how this virtue is modified, lost, preserved, or augmented—these questions are of much consequence in ordinary farming, if the best, or most profitable results are to be obtained by the practical man.

675. Mineral, or saline manures are combinations, or mixtures of different combinations of one or more of those mineral substances which exist and are found in living plants. These saline substances are fixed and definite in their composition. But to use them right—to apply them in the proper place, at the proper time, and in the proper quantity—to understand their action, how they ought to be mixed, and why their effects vary in different circumstances and localities—all this requires that they should be thoroughly known, and their mode of action, as single substances and as mixtures understood. (*See Johnston's Experim. Agricul., p.* 246)

676. In order to show the very complex action of plants and manures on the soil, we extract the following curious and instructive account of an experiment by a practical English farmer, from the *Journal of the Royal Agricul. Socy. of England, vol. xiii. p.* 417.—1852. It is worthy of careful study, and shows more clearly than any other document we are acquainted with, the difficulties which beset the farmer in the management of his crops and manures:

"In the autumn of 1846, a field of three acres was manured at the rate of 20 tons of farm-yard manure per acre, and sown with rye for soiling in the following spring. It produced a very heavy crop, but on account of the stalks becoming too hard for the horses, half the rye was allowed to remain for seed. The part of the field which had been cut for soiling was immediately plowed and sown with globe turnips, with a dressing of three cwt. of Peruvian guano per acre. The turnips were very fine. After the seed rye was harvested and the turnips cleared, the whole three acres were plowed and set with beans the following February; and now comes the curious part of the affair. The beans came up well all over the field; but a difference was soon perceived between those on the seed-rye and turnip ground, the former looking much more luxuriant than the latter, but we were not prepared for what afterwards took place. The beans that followed the turnips actually stopped all growth when six inches high, and, of course, did not seed, whereas, after the seed-rye they grew so luxuriantly as to injure the produce, and this difference extended to the line where we had discontinued cutting the green-rye—the more conspicuous as we had stopped in the middle of a land.

The result certainly astonished me, for it was in direct antagonism to all preconceived notions of farmers; as it is usually thought by them that crops do not impoverish the ground, nearly to the same extent when cut green, as when allowed to ripen their seed. Turnips, too, are generally supposed to extract the greater portion of their nourishment from the atmosphere. But here we find that beans actually refused to grow after the green-rye and turnips, notwithstanding the application of three cwt of guano, and the land being in much better tilth where the rye was allowed to ripen its seed, and no extra manure applied they grew luxuriantly.

I determined to inquire whether the researches of chemists would throw any light upon the question; and the difficulty I had in compiling the following small tables, fully accounts to my mind for the fact that chemistry has hitherto received so little assistance from practical farmers.

Probable Amount of Ingredients abstracted from or restored to One acre of Land by the several Crops and Manures of Rotation I, (Seeded Rye and Beans.)*

| For one acre of land in lbs. | Carbon | Hydrogen, | Oxygen | Nitrog'n | Potash | Soda | Lime | Phosphoric acid. |
|---|---|---|---|---|---|---|---|---|
| Amount added to soil by barn-yard manure, | 3320 | 400 | 2380 | 180 | 140 | 40 | 280 | 140 |
| Ditto by seed Rye, | 56 | 6 | 53 | 2 | 0.7 | .. | .. | 1 |
| Total added for rye crop, | 3376 | 406 | 2433 | 182 | 141 | 40 | 280 | 141 |
| Amount abstracted byditto | 2169 | 245 | 1868 | 34 | 25 | 0.1 | 10 | 14 |
| Balance after rye crop, | 1207 | 161 | 565 | 148 | 115 | 40 | 270 | 127 |
| Am't added by seed beans | 101 | 15 | 86 | 13 | 3 | .. | 1 | 2 |
| Balance left for Bean crop, | 1303 | 176 | 651 | 161 | 119 | 40 | 271 | 129 |
| Amount required by ditto | ? | ? | 164? | ? | 55 | 8 | 37 | 29 |
| Balance, | ? | ? | ? | —3 | +64 | +32 | +234 | +100 |

Rotation 2, (Green Rye, Turnips, and Beans.)

| For one acre in lbs. | Carbon | Hydrogen. | Oxygen. | Nitrog'n | Potash | Soda | Lime | Phosphoric acid. |
|---|---|---|---|---|---|---|---|---|
| Amount added to soil by barn-yard manure, | 3320 | 400 | 2380 | 180 | 140 | 40 | 280 | 140 |
| Ditto by seed rye, | 56 | 6 | 53 | 2 | 0.7 | .. | .. | 1 |
| Tot'l add for green rye crop | 3376 | 406 | 2433 | 182 | 141 | 40 | 280 | 141 |
| Amount abstracted by ditto | 1499 | 168 | 1233 | 12 | 17 | .. | 9 | 4 |
| Balance after ditto | 1877 | 238 | 1200 | 170 | 124 | 40 | 271 | 137 |
| Am't added by 3 cwts guano | ? | ? | ? | 48 | 10 | 4 | 38 | 49 |
| Balance left for turnip crop, | ? | ? | ? | 218 | 134 | 44 | 309 | 186 |
| Am't abstracted by ditto | ? | ? | ? | 159 | 166 | 5 | 102 | 33 |
| Balance left after the 2 crops | ? | ? | ? | 59 | —32† | 39 | 207 | 153 |
| Am't added by seed leaves, | 101 | 15 | 86 | 13 | 3 | .. | 1 | 2 |
| Balance left for bean crop, | ? | ? | ? | 72 | —29 | 39 | 208 | 155 |
| Am't required by ditto | ? | ? | ? | 164? | 55 | 8 | 37 | 29 |
| Balance | ? | ? | ? | —92 | —84 | +31 | +171 | +126 |

*Mr. Hemming calculated in the same manner *every* constituent of the plant, but the size of our page obliges us to give those only which are most essential to growth.

(†The mark (—) means *minus*, or that the turnips abstracted 32 lbs. more Potash, than had been supplied to the soil by the manure and other sources. In the last line,

When we come to compare the balance left in the soil after these two rotations, supposing the bean crop to have succeeded in both, we find that with the green rye and turnips there is a large deficiency both of nitrogen and potash, that of the latter amounting to 84 lbs. per acre, or in other words the soil would have had to supply 84 lbs. of potash, in addition to that supplied by the manure in order to grow a crop of beans, whereas in the rotation where the rye was allowed to stand for seed, there was a large excess of potash, and a sufficiency of nitrogen."

The above also elucidates a principle which the practical farmer should never lose sight of; viz, that a field may prove barren for a given crop, such as wheat, from the deficiency of only *one* or *two* constituents; and that, in order to supply this deficiency, our cheapest course generally is to give to the soil that peculiar material. Suppose I have a field which refused to grow wheat, in consequence of impoverishment. Am I to supply barn-yard manure, which contains *every thing* the wheat crop can require, but which is costly owing to the quantity which I must haul from a distance and spread? or shall I apply 3 cwt of guano, and 100 pounds of super-phosphate of lime, on the supposition that nitrogen and phosphoric acid alone are wanting? In the Michigan Oak openings we have reason to believe that it is a deficiency of these two materials only which renders the soil less fertile than it used to be; but a chemical analysis can alone positively decide the matter. In *practice* the question would be one of cost, supposing the barn-yard manure to be good: but the amount of *common* dung requisite to supply the nitrogen, phosphates and potash of the above named guano and bones, would have to be very much larger than we are in the habit of using to the acre. The above also teaches, that while a field may refuse to grow one crop profitably, it may be quite capable of growing another and different class of plants.

677. Before manures can produce their full and profitable effect upon the soil, the land must be laid dry by drainage or other means. It must also be cleaned and kept clean from weeds.

678. The value of the various constituents of manure may be thus classified; and the money cost, in the Western States, of any given manure can easily be estimated by the quantity of the following ingredients which it contains, in a *soluble* form.

1. Nitrogen.
2. Ammonia.
3. Phosphoric Acid.
4. Sulphuric Acid.
5. Soda.
6. Chlorine.
7. Potash.
8. Magnesia.
9. Iron and Manganese.
10. Lime.
11. Carbon.
12. Soluble Silica.

679. It is impossible to ascertain by theory alone and without actual experiment, the exact effect which a given manure will produce upon a given soil or crop. The mechanical con-

it shows that there were 92 lbs. less nitrogen and 84 lbs. less potash than the bean crop required, and it appears to be taken for granted that the soil contained none of these constituents except where they had been artificially supplied.)

struction of the soil, the climate, the season, the mode of cultivation, the salts already contained in the earth, but especially the period, mode, and form in which a manure is applied, all combine in influencing the final result. *Theoretically*, the value of a manure depends upon the amount of nitrogen which it contains, but, *practically*, this does not *always* prove to be the case; and in some instances, a salt, such as gypsum, wholly devoid of nitrogen, may return a larger crop than any nitrogenous manure we can apply. The rule, however, is general in its application, the exceptions comparatively few. The form of a manure, and the way in which we apply it are, in practice, of chief importance. Thus, in most instances, barn-yard manure well prepared and well rotted, is very superior in action to "long dung," unfermented, and with the vegetable matter undecayed. Yet there are soils and crops for which the latter is preferable. Again, bones owe much of their efficacy to the manner in which they are prepared. Whole bones, boiled bones, crushed or ground bones, bones dissolved in sulphuric acid, and applied in a powder, or in a solution with water, all differ in their effects and profitable results. Thus, in an English experiment, it was found that—

16 bushels of crushed bones gave 10 tons 3 cwt. turnips per acre.
2 " bones dissolved in acid and applied dry gave 11 tons 15 cwt.
4 " " " " " 14 " 11 "
8 " " " " " 16 " 1 "

But when applied in a *liquid form* at the time of sowing, the effect was still more remarkable, thus:—

| | Tons per acre. |
|---|---|
| 16 bushels of bone dust (dry) produced | 11 of turnips. |
| 8 " dissolved in 83 lbs of acid dried up and sown with the hand produced | 11 " |
| While 2 bushels, with 83 lbs. of acid, and 400 gallons water produced | 12½ " |
| And, again, in a third locality in Scotland, 76 lbs. of bones, 46 lbs. of acid, and 400 gallons of water produced | 17½ " |
| While 440 lbs. of bones, with 28 lbs. of acid applied dry, produced only | 17 " |

The same rule appears to hold good as regards barn-yard manures. In Flanders and Switzerland they have long been dissolved in water previous to application, and, of late years, in Great Britain, the steam engine has been employed for this purpose, and the liquid carried over the farm in iron pipes, similar to those used for Hydraulic works in our cities; the extra power of the manure being supposed to cover the greatly increased cost of preparation and application. *(See Prof. J. W. F. Johnston's Essay on Manures, written for the Farmer's Companion and Horticultural Gazette, vol.* 1, *p.* 98.) So in the same manner, Plaster has been found to act more efficiently when plowed in, instead of being scattered over the surface, and newly and finely ground gypsum is understood to act more efficiently than that which is coarse, and long kept, even in tight barrels. And again, common salt has been applied with beneficial results, in large quantities, to fruit trees in one locality, while a smaller application has killed trees in another.

There is no one subject in agriculture which demands, at the present day, more careful, continued, and widely extended experiments than the practice of manuring. Of the positive and relative constituents of common manures, the best quantities to apply, the condition in which, and the time when they should be used, the average effect which they produce, and the money profit derived from their application, we regret to believe that the great proportion of practical farmers are quite ignorant; and there can be no doubt but that this ignorance causes great individual and national losses.

680. I.—Animal Manures.

Flesh, is a rich manure in itself, and the rapidity with which it decays, enables it to bring other organic substances into a state of active fermentation. It is a very compound substance, in the shape in which we generally meet with it—that of dead animals—consisting of the lean muscle, or *Fibrin;* of fat or oil; and of blood, which again consists of Fibrin, Albumen, *(white of egg,)* coloring matter, several salts and water; while connected with the flesh are hair, horns, hoof, tendons, bones, again differing from the first in their relative composition. The only flesh, usually, at the farmer's disposal is that of animals accidentally dying, or, near cities, the refuse of the slaughter houses. A dead animal, if large, should be cut to pieces, and mixed with six or eight times its weight of peat, muck, earth, or even barn-yard manure; with plaster and salt; being sheltered from the rain; the whole of which will be converted into a very rich compost. A horse will supply sufficient ammonia to grow an acre of wheat.

681. An ox, on the average, yields of

| | | | | |
|---|---|---|---|---|
| Saleable meat | 58 per cent | Tallow, | 8 per cent |
| | Skin, | 5½ per cent. | |

The marketable meat contains,

| | | | |
|---|---|---|---|
| Dry bone, | 10 per cent | Muscle, with blood, lymph &c | 16 p. ct. |
| Cellular tissue & fat | 5 " | Water, | 71 " |

The chemical composition of flesh and blood is almost identical, so that blood may be called liquid flesh, and *vice versa;* the solid or liquid state being more dependent upon structure than upon the amount of water—blood only containing 3 per cent more water than flesh.

682. Ultimate analysis of Dry Beef (A,) and Dry Ox Blood, (B.) *(Playfair and Beekman.)*

| | A | B |
|---|---|---|
| Carbon, | 51.83 | 51.96 |
| Hydrogen, | 7.57 | 7.25 |
| Nitrogen, | 15.01 | 15.07 |
| Oxygen, | 21.37 | 21.30 |
| Ashes | 4.22 | 4.42 |

683. Inorganic analysis of the Blood of the Ox (A,) Calf (B,) and Sheep (C.) *(Enderlin.)*

| | A | B | C |
|---|---|---|---|
| Phosphate of Soda | 16.77 | 30.13 | 13.30 |
| Chloride of Sodium, | 59.34 | 52.65 | 66.57 |
| Chloride of Potassium, | 6.12 | | |
| Sulphate of Soda, | 3.85 | 2.94 | 5.38 |
| Phosphates of lime and magnesia, | 4.19 | 3.49 | 13.92 |
| Oxide and phosphate of iron, | 8.28 | 9.28 | |
| Gypsum and loss, | 1.45 | 1.46 | 0.83 |

The reader will notice the large quantity of common Salt *(Chloride of sodium,)* found in the blood of our domestic animals, and as our common forage plants contain but a small quantity of it, he will see the necessity of regularly supplying it with the food. In countries near the Sea, as in Great Britain, sufficient salt is deposited on the grass by the winds and spray, and there, salt is not given to cattle; but in the West, it becomes an essential necessary of life, and were it not for the "Salt Licks", the Deer and other wild, ruminating animals would perish.

(For the effect of blood as a manure upon wheat, in its yield and composition see *ante* § 177 p 68; upon rye § 211, p 87; upon barley § 237, p 94; and upon oats § 262, 103.

684. Hair, Horn, and Wool, are distinguished from the muscular parts of the animal body, by the large proportion—about 5 per cent—of sulphur which they contain. They consist of a substance, which, in other respects, closely resembles gluten and gelatine in its chemical composition. When burned they leave from one to 2 per cent of ash. The inorganic matter, therefore, is generally the same as is found in the muscular fibre and the bone.

685. Bones are, in reality, that portion of animals, to which, as a manure, the farmer is the most indebted. It has been observed that all useful plants contain *phosphorus*, which is one of the rarest minerals in the soil; which, when in a soluble form, is most rapidly withdrawn; and yet, without which, plants become useless, for the sustenance of animal bodies. It has occurred, that the old pasture lands of Cheshire, England, became impoverished of this element; and although grass continued to grow, it was inferior in quality, and animals fed upon it became diseased, especially as to their bony structure. Till lately bones and brains have been the only available source whence Phosphorus could be procured. The following is the composition of the Ileum of a sheep (A,) of an ox (B,) and the vertebræ of a haddock (C.) *(Thompson.)*

| | A | B | C |
|---|---|---|---|
| Organic matter, | 43.3 | 48.5 | 39.5 |
| Phosphate of lime, | 50.6 | 45.2 | 56.1 |

| | A | B | C |
|---|---|---|---|
| Carbonate of lime | 4.5 | 6.1 | 3.6 |
| Magnesia, | 0.9 | 0.2 | 0.8 |
| Soda, | 0.3 | 0.2 | 0.8 |
| Potash, | 0.2 | 0.1 | — |

The proportion of water in the bones of quadrupeds varies from 7 to 20 per cent according to the age of the animal, and the fat, or oily matter from 13 to 25 per cent. Those of the ox contain 64.5 per cent of earthy matter, and 35.5 per cent of cartilage; each family differing in this regard.

686. Bones do not benefit plants under all circumstances, and, as has been stated, the form and mode in which they are applied, is of much importance. In Great Britain where they are in especial demand for the turnip crop, it has been the fashion, till of late, merely to grind them in mills built for the purpose; the bones being of different lengths, from fragments 1 inch long to dust; and sometimes boiled, sometimes unboiled bones were preferred. It is now becoming general there, and in the United States, to employ them as *Superphosphate* or *Biphosphate of lime*, that is, dissolved in Sulphuric acid. This may be done by the Farmer himself procuring the ground bones, and in leaden vessels, boiling in Sulphuric acid diluted with water; but according to Johnston, the following is the *true* superphosphate. "When burned bones are reduced to powder, and digested in Sulphuric acid, diluted with once or twice its weight of water, the acid combines with a portion of the lime, and forms sulphate of lime (plaster) while the remainder of the lime and the whole of the phosphoric acid are dissolved. The solution, therefore, contains an *acid* phosphate of lime, or one in which the phosphoric acid exists in much larger quantity than in the earth of bones. The true bi-phosphate when free from water consists of 71½ phosphoric acid, and 28½ of lime." In a manufactured state, however, it is probably never found thus pure; and great complaints have, at times, been made that the manufacturers mix

plaster, earth, salt, and other cheap ingredients with it. When purchasing, the farmer should procure an analysis of the samples and afterwards compare them with the bulk. In Great Britain the manufacture of fictitious and worthless manures is said to have become an extensive trade, the farmers thus losing largely from their ignorance of chemistry. On a small scale, bones may be rendered partially soluble by breaking or grinding, and mixing with fresh wood ashes, to be kept moist for a month or two.

687. In the United States, *Mineral Phosphate of lime* or *Apatite* has been found and dug in considerable quantities at Crown Point, N. Y., and in New Jersey; some of which has been exported to England. So far, the purity appears to differ much, and the expense of mining and dissolving, has discouraged the progress of the works. The following are Dr. Jackson's analyses of pure specimens of the minerals, compared with Prof. Johnston's analysis of bones.

| | New York. | New Jersey. | Bones. |
|---|---|---|---|
| Lime, | 47.230 | | |
| Phosphoric Acid, | 45.710 | 92.405 | 55.50 |
| Carbonic Acid, | 1.218 | | |
| Lime, | 1.554 | —— | 4.00 |
| Chlorine, | 0.130 | | |
| Calcium, | 0.204 | 0.540 | —— |
| Fluoriae, | 0.590 | | |
| Calcium, | 0.855 | 7.012 | 3.00 |
| Protoxide of Iron, | 2.000 | 0.040 | |
| Water, | 0.500 | —— | 20.00 |
| Oxide of Manganese, | | 0.003 | |
| Phosphate of Magnesia, | | | 2.00 |
| Soda and common Salt, | | | 2.50 |
| Gelatine (animal matter,) | | | 33 00 |

(*See Jour. of Boston Socy. of Nat. Hist.*)

Many *Marls*, especially those formed of recent shell, and some lime rocks, contain notable proportions of the phosphates.

688. Fish are also a valuable manure, where they can be had in quantities. On parts of the New York and New England coasts they are annually caught in vast shoals for this purpose, and the time will come when the streams and lakes of the West

will supply their portion to the soil. The bones and flesh of fish very nearly resemble those of quadrupeds in their phosphates and nitrogen; fish, however, generally affording more free oil. They should always be composted with muck, peat, &c.

689. Shell fish are rarely found sufficiently numerous to be used as a manure, except in a mineral state. In New England, muscles and oyster shells are collected. In Alabama there are vast deposits of this kind; and according to Dr. Houghton (*M. S.,*) much of the marl of Michigan is formed of recent shells. They chiefly consist of lime, a little phosphoric acid, animal matter, and in salt water, iodine, and soda.

690. BARN YARD MANURES are composed of the dung and urine of animals, with hay, straw, &c., more or less decayed, and they necessarily differ much according to (*a,*) the species; (*b,*) the age of the animal; (*c,*) the food it eats; (*d,*) the mode in which the dung is preserved, whether exposed to rain, sun, &c.; (*e,*) the quantity of urine contained; (*f,*) the decomposition which has taken place; (*g,*) whether alkalies or lime are in connection with it during decay, and how long.

691. Table exhibiting the amount in pounds of carbon, &c., in the food and dung of two cows during fourteen days. (*Thompson.*)

| | BROWN COW. | | | WHITE COW. | | |
|---|---|---|---|---|---|---|
| | Grass. | Dung. | Consumption. | Grass. | Dung. | Consumption. |
| | lbs. | lbs. | lbs. | lbs. | lbs. | lbs. |
| Carbon, - | 161¾ | 67 | 94¾ | 161¾ | 64 | 97¾ |
| Hydrogen, - | 21 | 8 | 13 | 21 | 7¾ | 13¼ |
| Nitrogen, - | 6½ | 2 7-10 | 3 8-10 | 6½ | 2½ | 4 |
| Oxygen, - | 148 | 54½ | 93½ | 148 | 52 | 96 |
| Ash, - | 13¾ | 14⅓ | 4 4-10 | 18¾ | 13¾ | 5 |
| Water, - | 1070¾ | 902½ | 167½ | 1070¾ | 860 | 210¾ |
| | 1426¾ | 1049 | 377 | 1426¾ | 1000 | 426¾ |

(See also, *Liebig's Animal Chemistry*. Note 4.)

Or according to another estimate, a cow consuming 26.41 lbs. of grass daily, emits in shape of dung 11.13 lbs.; and consumes, in the support of its body, 15.28 lbs. 100 parts of fresh fallen cow-dung will afford 0.614 or five-eighths of a pound of pure ammonia, or about 2 lbs. 2 oz. of carbonate of ammonia *(sal volatile)* of the shops. *(S. L. Dana.)*

Analysis of 100 parts of cow-dung. *(Penot.)*

| | |
|---|---|
| Water, | 69.58 |
| Bitter matter, | 0.74 |
| Sweet substance, | 0.93 |
| Chlorophyl, | 0.28 |
| Albumen, | 0.63 |
| Muriate of soda, | 0.08 |
| Sulphate of potash, | 0.05 |
| Sulphate of lime, | 0.25 |
| Carbonate of lime, | 0.24 |
| Phosphate of lime, | 0.46 |
| Carbonate of iron, | 0.09 |
| Woody fibre, | 26.39 |
| Silica, | 0.14 |
| Loss, | 0.14 |

The amount of water, however, mentioned above, is too small. Boussingault gives the following comparative analysis:

| | Fresh dung. | | Dry dung. | |
|---|---|---|---|---|
| | Cow. | Horse. | Cow. | Horse. |
| Water, | 90.60 | 75.31 | | |
| Nitrogen, | 0.22 | 0.54 | 2.3 | 2.2 |
| Saline matter, | 1.13 | 4.02 | 12.0 | 16.3 |

So that in every 100 lbs, of fresh cow-dung, we have ¼ of a pound of nitrogen, and a little over one pound of salts.

692. Table exhibiting the food and water of a horse, consumed; and dung and urine, voided in 24 hours. *(Boussingault.)* *(See Liebig's Animal Chemistry.* Note 4.)

| | Food. | Dung. | Consumed. |
|---|---|---|---|
| Carbon, | 3938.0 | 1472 9 | 2465.1 |
| Hydrogen, | 446.5 | 191.3 | 255 2 |
| Oxygen, | 3209.2 | 1363.0 | 1846.2 |
| Nitrogen, | 139.4 | 115.4 | 24. |
| Salts and earthy matters, | 672.2 | 684.5 | +12.3 |

Analysis of horse-dung, in Rhode Island, *(Jackson.)* 500 grains, dried at a heat a little above that of boiling water, lost 357 grains of water. The dry mass weighing 143 grains was burned, and left 8.5 grains of ashes, of which 4.80 grains were soluble in dilute nitric acid, and 3.20 insoluble.

| | |
|---|---|
| Water, | 357 |
| Vegetable fibre and animal matter, | 135 |
| Silica, | 3.2 |
| Phosphate of lime, | 0.4 |
| Carbonate of lime, | 1.5 |
| Phosphate of magnesia and soda, | 2.9 |
| | 500.0 |

Horse-dung, in consequence of the smaller proportion of water, and more ammonia, ferments, or "heats," more rapidly than the solid excrement of the cow; the ammonia being evolved and lost; and in this mode it may be rapidly deteriorated.

693. The dung of sheep and of *fattening* hogs is richer in nitrogen than either of the above, and consequently ferments and acts more rapidly.

Boussingault found the following proportions:

| | *Sheep.* | | *Hogs.* | |
|---|---|---|---|---|
| | Recent | Dry | Recent | Dry |
| Water, | 63.0 | — | 81 | — |
| Nitrogen, | 1.11 | 2.99 | 0.63 | 3 37 |
| Ash | 12.7 | | — | — |

694. Dung of birds (Fowls, Pigeons, &c,) being mixed with urine, is still richer. In Belgium the dung yearly produced by 100 pigeons is valued at $5.00. Its immediate effect depends upon the quantity of soluble matter it contains, and this varies much according to its age, the mode in which it is preserved, &c. Thus Davy and Sprengel obtained respectively, of

| | Recent, | Six months old. | After fermentation. |
|---|---|---|---|
| Soluble matter in Pigeons dung, | 23 per cent | 16 per cent | 3 per cent. |

The soluble matter consists of uric acid, urate, sulphate and carbonate of ammonia, common salt and sulphate of potash; —the insoluble part of phosphate of lime, with a little phosphate of magnesia, &c. By fermentation it loses a portion of its ammonia. Every farmer should carefully clean his fowl-houses, at least once a week, and pack the dung in barrels with plaster, dry peat, earth, and a little salt &c; and in the spring sow it on his wheat at the rate of 300 cwt to the acre. If properly kept it differs but little from guano, for which $50 per ton is now paid at our shipping ports. In Michigan, 10 bushels more of wheat to the acre, might in many instances be thus obtained.

695. We give the following analyses of Guano, chiefly to show the composition of what has proved to be the most valuable manure in existence; and the nearer we can cause other manures to approach to it, the more perfect will our art become. It is merely the dung of salt-water birds preserved in the dry regions of the globe, chiefly on the coast of Peru. It has lately been stated, from actual measurement, that unless other deposites are discovered, and if the demand continues at the present height, the whole will be exhausted within 9 years. A patent has lately been granted in Great Britain for the preparation of an equivalent compound, at a lower price, from fish, fish offal, &c., and salts.

Analysis of 2 specimens of Peruvian Guano. *(Way.)*

| | | |
|---|---|---|
| Water, | 12.57 | 13.67 |
| Organic matter and Salts of ammonia, | 33.67 | 52.97 |
| Sand and Silica, | 1.72 | 1.42 |
| Phosphoric acid, | 20.21 | 14,56 |
| Sulphuric acid, | 4.00 | 2.52 |
| Lime, | 16.49 | 10.38 |
| Magnesia, | 0.80 | 0.31 |
| Oxide of iron, | 0.22 | 0.73 |
| Potash, | 3.60 | 1.42 |
| Soda, | 4.15 | none |
| Chloride of Potassium, | none | 2.02 |

| | | |
|---|---|---|
| Chloride of Sodium, - - | 2.57 | none |
| Or the average of | | per cent |
| Ammonia at - - - | | 17.41 |
| Phosphate of lime at - - | | 24.12 |
| Potash at - - - - | | 3.50 |

These three being the elements chiefly demanded by plants, and in which the soil is apt to be deficient: in Guano, they are in the proper state of solubility and combination.

696. Night Soil, or human excrements, are extensively used in Belgium, Germany, China, and other countries; but the English and Americans appear to have an insuperable objection to manuring with these substances. A few years ago they were prepared in Great Britain and in the Ciy of New York, in a dry form devoid of smell, and called *Poudrette and Urate*; but they seem to have gone greatly out of use, probably on account of the means taken to render them less obnoxious dispelling the gases, so as to reduce the value of the manure below the cost of production. The excrement of men living on animal food is richer in nitrogen and phosphates than of those living on vegetables. *(See Liebig's Aanimal Chemistry, Note* 1.)

697. Urine. It is to the urine, that barn yard manure chiefly owes its value, both as regards nitrogen and salts; and yet in our Western States how few take any pains to save the liquids; or prevent their being afterwards washed out of the dung. Liebig denies that there is any available nitrogen in horse *dung*, and *practically*, it probably is so; so that with from 3600 to 4000 lbs. of fresh horse dung, corresponding to 100 lbs of dry dung, we place on the land from 2484 to 3000 lbs of water, of 730 to 900 lbs of vegetable matter and altered gall, and also from 100 to 270 of salt, and other inorganic substances, a portion of which only are soluble; while in urine, rotted with water, we apply a large quantity of nitrogen, as well as of the most valuable salts, and these in a dissolved state ready at once to feed the plant, and therefore requiring a very small quantity, as we have already shown respecting bones. The urine of all animals bears a very

strong chemical resemblance. We give the following table from *Sprengel* showing the composition of Cow's urine when fresh (A,); putrified alone (B,); and when putrified with water (C.)

| | A | B | C |
|---|---|---|---|
| Urea, | 4000 | 1000 | 600 |
| Albumen, | 10 | — | — |
| Mucus, | 190 | 40 | 30 |
| Benzoin acid, | 90 | 250 | 120 |
| Lactic acid, | 516 | 500 | 500 |
| Carbonic acid, | 5256 | 16 | 1533 |
| Ammonia, | 205 | 487 | 1622 |
| Potash, | 664 | 664 | 664 |
| Soda, | 554 | 554 | 554 |
| Silica, | 36 | 5 | 8 |
| Alumina, | 2 | — | — |
| Oxide of iron, | 4 | 1 | — |
| Oxide of manganese, | 1 | — | — |
| Lime, | 65 | 2 | 8 |
| Magnesia, | 36 | 22 | 30 |
| Chlorine, | 272 | 272 | 272 |
| Sulphuric acid, | 405 | 388 | 332 |
| Phosphoric acid, | 70 | 26 | 46 |
| Acetic acid, (vinegar) | — | 1 | 20 |
| Sulphuretted hydrogen, | — | 1 | 30 |
| Insoluble earthy Phosphates and carbonates, | — | 180 | 150 |
| Water, | 92,624 | 95,442 | 93,481 |
| | 100,000 | 100,000 | 10.0000 |

It will thus be understood how *fresh* urine may destroy vegetation, and yet prove beneficial when decomposed.

| Urine of | Water in 1000 parts | Solid matter in 1000 parts, | | | Average quantity voided in 24 hours |
|---|---|---|---|---|---|
| | | Organic. | Inorganic. | Total. | |
| Man, | 930 to 970 | 22 to 52 | 8 to 18 | 30 to 70 | 3 lbs. |
| Horse, | 886 to 940 | 27 to 79 | 33 to 45 | 60 to 124 | 3 ? |
| Cow, | 880 to 930 | 50 to 70 | 20 to 47 | 70 to 120 | 40 |
| Sheep, | 930 to 960 | 28 to 50 | 12 to 20 | 40 to 70 | ? |
| Pig, | 926 to 983 | 9 to 56 | 9 to 18 | 18 to 74 | ? |

It is to the UREA which exists in urine in very much larger

quantity than in any other substance, that its beneficial effects are chiefly due.

*Urea* is a white salt-like substance, very soluble in water, consisting of—

| | Per cent. |
|---|---|
| Carbon, | 20.0 |
| Hydrogen, | 6.6 |
| Nitrogen, | 46.7 |
| Oxygen, | 26.7 |

Besides which, when the urine begins to ferment, this substance changes entirely into carbonate of ammonia. As this rapidly escapes into the air, the urine must be kept in covered vessels, and plaster, peat, sulphuric acid, &c., may be mixed with it; but burnt lime must not be brought into contact with it.

There are various modes of preserving the liquid manures of the barn yard, such as tanks, sawdust, &c.; but probably, in all respects, the best is the simple plan invented by Mr. Mechi, of England. This consists of a shallow, water-tight cellar under the stable, with a floor made of scantlings laid an inch and a half apart from each other, so that the dung adn urine fall below, and are preserved till carried to the field. It is of the utmost importance to the farmer to preserve this liquid; and if *one* must be lost, it ought to be the solid.

699. GOOD BARN YARD MANURE, then, is a mixture of dung, urine, and straw, kept from the rain and sun, decomposed to a certain extent; and its value, per ton, must depend equally on the various proportions of these matters which it contains; the food of the animals; and the state of the decomposition, &c.

Analysis of barn yard manure, just previous to being applied, at New Castle-upon-Tyne, England. (*Richardson*:)

| | Fresh. |
|---|---|
| Water, | 64.96 |
| Organic matter, | 24.71 |
| Inorganic salts, | 10.32 |

| | Dried at 212°. |
|---|---|
| Carbon, | 37.40 |
| Hydrogen, | 5.27 |
| Oxygen, | 25.52 |
| Nitrogen, | 1.76 |
| Ash, | 30.05 |

21

Inorganic matter, 1. Portion soluble in water.

| | | | |
|---|---|---|---|
| Potash, | 3.22 | Sulphuric Acid, | 3.27 |
| Soda, | 2.73 | Chlorine, | 3.15 |
| Lime, | 0.34 | Silica, | 0.04 |
| Magnesia, | 0.26 | | |

2. Portions soluble in muriatic acid only.

| | | | |
|---|---|---|---|
| Silica, | 27.01 | Carbonate of Magnesia, | 1.63 |
| Phosphate of Lime, | 7.11 | Sand, | 30.99 |
| Phosphate of Magnesia, | 2.26 | Carbon, | 0.83 |
| Phosphate of Iron, | 4.68 | Alkali and loss, | 3.14 |
| Carbonate of Lime, | 9.34 | | |

Thus, of 100 lbs. of barn yard manure, well made, well taken care of, and hauled on the field, 65 lbs. are pure water; of the remaining 35 lbs., 25 are inert carbonaceous matter, only serviceable as a source of carbonic acid, leaving only 10 per cent. of inorganic substances, and 0.6 of nitrogen, as true fertilizing matters. Of this 10 per cent. only 3 are of much value either as regards their commercial price or relative value. But the above manure is of extraordinary richness when compared with what we are in the habit of applying in the Western States. Ours is generally thrown out of the stables, every shower penetrating through it, and carrying into the next ditch whatever there may be soluble in water; then, through spring and summer, the heat of the sun and fermentation drives off all gases as formed; and when, at much toil and expense, we apply it, we find nothing which can feed a plant or assist it to grow. The "black water" found round manure heaps, where there happens to be a hole in the ground, is sufficient proof of this. The peat and marl of our marshes are much more valuable than *such* dung.

As this a point of great practical and economical importance, the teacher ought to impress it especially on the minds of his pupils, and may exhibit the effect of water and heat on fresh manure before them.

**We strongly recommend all farmers who take the trouble to haul their manure on to their soil, to save it either on Mr. Mechi's plan, or to have a cheap shed near the door of the stable into which it can be pitched, taking care to use sufficient straw, sawdust, peat, &c., to absorb all the liquids. One load of such dung is proved to be**

equal to at least eight that have been exposed. The best mode of saving sheep manure is to keep the sheep under sheds, giving sufficient straw to keep them clean. Not only is much manure thus saved, but less food is consumed, and the sheep are much more profitable. (*See Farmer's Companion and Horticultural Gazette*, VOL. 1, P. 6, 64.)

700. In America, the European mode of making *composts* of barn yard manures and other substances is not much employed. It is not only a greater expense of manual labor, and lower value of produce which forbid it, but there are serious reasons for believing that with our very hot summer climate, and comparative want of showers, composts will not act as effectively with us as they do in the Eastern Hemisphere. The subject, however, does not appear to have been yet tested by experiment, and we can only speak theoretically.

There are many other sources of animal manures enjoyed in various parts of the world, but which at present are of no practical interest to Western farmers.

701. MINERAL MANURES.

By this term we mean all substances of an inorganic nature, all of which are derived, either directly or indirectly, from the soil, such as wood and coal ashes, plaster, &c.

WOOD ASHES. These are the remains of trees, after the organic or vegetable matter has been consumed (driven off in the shape of gas,) by fire; and consequently, while they all bear a general resemblance, they differ much in the relative proportion of the constituents, according to the trees and soils from which they are derived. As manures they have a two fold action; *(a,)* they supply to the plant the inorganic constituents which it requires; *(b,)* they act chemically as solvents upon other insoluble salts already in the soil; or they neutralize acids, &c.

702. When we have burnt a tree and collected the ashes we find that they consist of two portions, those that are soluble in water and those that are insoluble. The average quantity of ashes from 100 parts of dry oak, beech, birch, &c., is 2.37. 100 parts of such ashes afford 13.57 parts soluble; 86.43 parts insoluble, the latter being left behind at our ash works, while the soluble have been boiled down and exported as potash. Pine

wood (dry,) affords only 0.83 in 100 parts of ashes; of which 50 are soluble, 50 insoluble. Wheat straw yields 4.40 in 100 parts, 19 per cent. being soluble, 81 insoluble.

Composition of the ashes of hard wood, (oak, beech, birch, &c., *(A)*; of Pine, *(Pinus abies,) (B)*; and of wheat straw, *(C)*. *(Dana.)*

| 100 parts of soluble contain | A, | B. | C. |
|---|---|---|---|
| Carbonic Acid, | 22.70 | 13.50 | —— |
| Sulphuric Acid, | 6.43 | 6.90 | 0.2 |
| Muriatic Acid, | 1.82 | —— | 13.0 |
| Silex, | 95 | 2.00 | 35.6 |
| Potash and Soda, | 67.96 | 69.70 | 50.0 |
| Water, | | 7.90 | |

| 100 parts of the insoluble contain, | A. | B. | C. |
|---|---|---|---|
| Carbonic Acid, | 35.80 | 21.50 | |
| Phosphoric Acid, | 3.40 | 1.80 | 1.20 |
| Silex, | 4.25 | 13.00 | 75 00 |
| Oxide of Iron, | 0.52 | 22.30 | 2.50 |
| Oxide of Manganese, | 2 15 | 5.50 | |
| Magnesia, | 3.55 | 8.70 | |
| Lime, | 35.80 | 27 20 | 5.80 |
| Charcoal, | | | 15.50 |

The following gives a comparative view of the entire ashes of the oak *(A,)*; elm *(B,)*; Beech *(C,)*; and fir tree *(pinus sylvestris,)*; *(D,)*; analysed in Europe. *(Johnston.)*

| | A. | B. | C. | D. |
|---|---|---|---|---|
| Potash, | 8.43 | 21.92 | 15.83 | —— |
| Soda, | 5.65 | 13.72 | 2.88 | 9 97 |
| Lime, | 75.45 | 47.80 | 63 33 | 46.15 |
| Magnesia, | 4.49 | 7.71 | 11.29 | 13.46 |
| Oxide of Iron, | 0.57 | 0.38 | 0.79 | 3·26 |
| Phosphoric Acid, | 3.46 | 3.62 | 3.07 | 4.49 |
| Sulphuric Acid, | 1.16 | 1.28 | 1.35 | 3.03 |
| Chlorine, | 0.01 | —— | 0.14 | 0.71 |
| Silica, | 0.78 | 307 | 1.32 | 8.38 |
| Percentage of ash in the dry hard wood, | | | | 0.143 |

It is thus obvious that, by leaching, little else is removed than potash, soda, and sulphuric acid, (the carbonic acid being a product of combustion, and of no intrinsic value); and when ashes are thus separated on a large scale, a notable quantity of the alkalies remains behind. Though the refuse is not *immediately* soluble, it will become available to plants in the soil by chemical action, and the power which roots appear to possess of decomposing mineral matter; while such alkalies as remain will act on the silica, and form soluble silicates for grass and the stalks of grain.

In leaching, more or less lime is always added for the purpose of depriving the potash of its carbon, and rendering it caustic, so that the common leached ashes are richer in lime than before the process commences. According to Dana, a bushel of good ashes contains about 5½ pounds of real potash. In leaching ashes, generally about one peck of lime is added to each bushel of ashes, and as it loses no bulk during the operation, a *cord* of leached ashes contains about the following proportions —allowing an average of 4¼ lbs. per bushel to be leached out:—

| | lbs. |
|---|---|
| Phosphoric acid, | 117 |
| Silex, | 146 |
| Oxide of iron, | 17 |
| Oxide of manganese, | 51 |
| Magnesia, | 119 |
| Carbonate of lime, including that added in leaching, | 3072 |
| Potash combined with silica, | 50 |

Spent ashes therefore belong to the class of carbonates; and to the farmer are worth very nearly as much as the unleached.

In nearly the whole range of soils, ashes are beneficial to cultivated plants; but much more so on sandy and gravelly lands than on clay, which being chiefly formed of granite rocks naturally contain potash. We have also seen, in the analyses of plants, that certain genera, such as turnips, carrots, potatoes, beets, &c., contain a very large amount of the alkalies; to such therefore ashes are found to be an essential manure. But the *immediate* benefit of such an application is most perceptible upon leguminous plants, such as clover, peas, beans, &c. Applied to grass land, as a top dressing, it roots out the moss, and promotes the growth of white clover, where it is indigenous to the soil. On Red clover, it will act more certainly in connection with plaster. If applied in *large* doses to poor thin soils it is believed to act injuriously by causing a rapid disappearance of the organic matter, but this may be prevented by the use of peat, barn-yard manures, &c., at the same time.

In connection with all wood-ashes is a large quantity of charcoal, and imperfectly burned carbonaceous matter, which also add to the value of the manure.

Unleached ashes act at once, most rapidly and powerfully; leached ashes act more slowly, but continue to act for many years after being applied. In the large heaps of such ashes, as everywhere accumulate in the west around the asheries, we neglect a most useful source of fertility; and where they have thus lain for a length of time, they are probably, to a considerable extent, again rendered soluble. Their effect on the *mechanical* condition of the soil is also worthy of notice. They render sands more compact and retentive of water, while they separate and render friable, heavy clays.

In practice, they should always be placed *in* the soil, where the roots can come in contact with them.

It is a general custom to apply ashes to corn, on the *surface* of the ground, but in this way the plant can receive no benefit except from the little that is soluble and is carried down by rain; but placed in the ground previous to planting, the roots and chemical action will afford many elements not available in the other way. The only advantage of placing ashes on the surface is the protecting of the plant against grubs. The seed, however, should not come in immediate contact with the ashes.

Prof. Way has lately ascertained that all clay soils contain a double silicate of alumina and one of the alkalies or alkaline earths, as :—

| Soda, | Lime, |
|---|---|
| Potash, | Magnesia, |
| Ammonia. | |

which is slowly soluble, but sufficiently so to supply what plants require; and that these silicates, without exception, are capable of absorbing and retaining ammonia; and, what is still more important, some of them have the faculty of abstracting ammonia from the air. "Whenever a salt of ammonia or potash reaches the soil, and gets distributed through it, a change occurs—a double silicate of alumina and ammonia is formed, and the salt which was added no longer exists there. The ammonia or potash henceforth exists in the soil only in the form of silicate, and is presented to the roots of a plant only in that form, or in the form of carbonate derived from it by the action of carbonic acid in the soil. And inasmuch as all average soils possess this property of conversion in more than the degree necessary for the quantity of manure which reaches them, the inference is obvious and incontestable, that nature has given to the soil this power for the specific purpose of preparing the food of plants, and we then have the soil occupying a place intermediate between that of mere dead matter, and the living organism of plants." We can only thus slightly mention this most important and beautiful discovery; and refer the reader to Prof. Way's own writings in the *Jour. of Royal Agricul. Socy. of England*, vol. xiii, &c.

703. LIME is everywhere an essential of a fertile soil, and in Great Britain is more extensively used than any other mineral substance. It is applied in a variety of forms, as *(a,)* carbonate of lime—lime rock—(44 lbs. of carbonic acid and 51 lbs. of lime;) *(b,)* the same lime rock burned, and the carbonic acid driven off, when it becomes caustic, but again absorbs carbonic acid and moisture rapidly from the air when it again returns to a carbonate, or is "slaked;" *(c,)* Gypsum, Plaster, *Sulphate of lime*. *(d,)* Phosphate of lime, as in bones, &c., of which we have already spoken. *(e,)* Silicate of lime, existing in many rocks and earths; *(f,)* Marls; *(g,)* Chalk, which is another form of carbonate of lime, chiefly found in England; *(h,)* Magnesian limestone, the base of which is lime, with a

varying proportion of magnesia. Of these, only common lime, plaster and marl, are of present interest to us in this part of the country.

Lime rocks are rarely pure, and they vary much in their exact composition. It is believed that those of Michigan have not yet been analyzed. The following are specimens from Seneca county, N. Y., examined by Mr. Delafield.

| | NO. 1. | NO. 2. | NO. 3. | NO. 4. |
|---|---|---|---|---|
| Insoluble sand and clay, - - | 6.7 | 15 0 | 4.0 | 78.0 |
| Alumina and peroxide of iron, - | 1.4 | 23.0 | 26.0 | 9.0 |
| Carbonate of lime, - - | 90.0 | 53.5 | 60.0 | 11.0 |
| Magnesia, - - | 1.5 | 2 8 | 5.5 | 2.0 |
| Oxide of manganese, - - | none, | none, | 1.0 | |
| Soluble saline matter, - | 1 4 | 1.2 | 2 4 | |
| Phosphoric acid, - - - | trace, | trace, | 0.1 | |

(*Trans. of N. Y. Agricul. Socy.*, vol. x, p. 611.)

The following are analyses of English lime rocks made by Prof. Johnston, in their unburned and burned states:—

| UNBURNED. | NO. 1. | NO. 2. |
|---|---|---|
| Carbonate of lime, - - | 94.86 | 95.89 |
| Sulphate of lime, - - | 0.23 | 0.32 |
| Carbonate of magnesia, - - | 1.26 | 0.54 |
| Alumina and oxide of iron, - - | 0.73 | 1.20 |
| Phosphate of lime, - - | ? | ? |
| Silica, - - - | 2.92 | 2.05 |

| BURNED. | NO. 1. | NO. 2. |
|---|---|---|
| Lime, - - - | 89.93 | 88.85 |
| Magnesia, - - - | 1.02 | 0.43 |
| Sulphuric acid, - - - | 0.22 | 0.30 |
| Phosphoric acid, - - - | ? | ? |
| Alumina and oxide of iron, - - | 1.23 | 1.98 |
| Silicate in the state of silicate, - - | 4.92 | 3.39 |
| Carbonic acid and moisture, - - | 2.68 | 5.05 |

(*Johnston on the use of lime in Agriculture*, p. 243.)

We shall shortly mention the effect of burned and slaked lime upon the land.

1. Mechanical; it opens and renders free, stiff clays, and con-

solidates sands. 2. Chemical. *(a,)* increases the fertility of all soils in which it does not already abound; and especially of tenacious, moist soils and those containing much inert vegetable matter; *(b,)* it improves the *quality* of the crop; *(c,)* it increases the effects of manure, calls into action that which is dormant, and less manures needs afterwards be applied; *(d,)* alters the natural produce of the land by killing some plants and favoring the growth of others—it kills moss and sour grasses and brings up sweet and tender herbage with clovers—wheat has a thinner skin, and yields more flour—runs less to straw—peas and beans are of better quality, and so with most plants; *(e,)* it hastens the maturity of the crop; *(f,)* it renders the whole country more healthy, and plants less subject to diseases.

Lime, indeed, can scarcely be applied judiciously to any soil without benefit; but it requires care and experience acting as it does with a varying effect under different circumstances.

The quantity of lime which ought to be added to a soil is of course a question of experiment and practice. Theoretically 3 per cent of lime *(finely disintegrated)* at least, ought to be present in a soil which contains an ordinary proportion of vegetable matter and of the other food of plants. In order to add 1 per cent of lime to the land, the quantity to be laid on will depend upon the depth. The following table shows the number of tons of burned lime as it comes from the kiln, which will give one per cent of lime to soils, respectively 3, 6, 9, and 12 inches in depth.

| If the depth of the soil be | 12 ins. | 9 ins. | 6 ins. | 3 ins. |
|---|---|---|---|---|
| Tons of burned lime, | *per cent* | *per cent* | *per cent* | *per cent* |
| 16 tons give | 1 | 1½ | 2 | 4 |
| 12 " | ¾ | 1 | 1½ | 3 |
| 8 " | ½ | ¾ | 1 | 2 |
| 4 " | ¼ | ⅜ | ½ | 1 |

Quantity of quicklime applied per Imperial acre in different localities:

| | Bush. | | Years. | | Bush. a year. | When applied. |
|---|---|---|---|---|---|---|
| Roxburgh, | 200 | every | 19 | or | 10½ | to the fallow |
| Ayr, | 40 | " | 5 | or | 8 | do., or lea |
| Carse of Stirling | 54 | " | 6 | or | 9 | do |
| South Durham, | 90 | " | 12 | or | 8½ | do |
| Worcester, | 70 | " | 6 or 8 | or | 10 | before grasses & tares. |
| Flanders, | {50<br>{12 | "<br>" | 12}<br>3} | or | 4 | |

Or at the average of 8 or 10 bushels a year per acre.

Lime is found, in some of its shapes, over a large portion of the United States; but so far, its application as burnt lime has been much neglected. For further information we refer the reader to *Prof. Johnston's Essay on the use of lime in agriculture, 12 mo, pp.* 259, *Edinburgh,* 1849.

704. GYPSUM OR PLASTER is a *Sulphate of lime.* 100 lbs of common gypsum consist of 46 lbs of sulphuric acid, 33 lbs of lime, and 21 lbs of water. When it is heated to redness this water is driven off, and the gypsum is very easily reduced to an exceedingly fine powder. In this form it is used by masons. It dissolves in 500 times its weight of pure water, or 50 gallons will dissolve one pound. Thus it is often found in spring water, and in streams which pass through a soil in which gypsum exists. In solution with water it is decomposed when mixed with fermenting animal or vegetable matter.

Gypsum acts very differently on different soils and in different localities; at times producing no visible effect whatever; and at others, becoming almost a necessary of profitable cultivation.

The theory of its beneficial action has long been a subject of dispute. The most probable solution is, that to a small extent it supplies lime and sulphuric acid to the plant, but is chiefly useful by the power it possesses of solidifying and retaining the ammonical gases of air and earth.

Benjamin Franklin first introduced it from France into the United States. It was afterwards imported from Nova Scotia; and as New York, and the other Western States were settled, it was discovered in abundance. Ohio and Michigan possess large beds of it in various localities. It is quarried, and ground in mills; but is supposed to differ in quality, some mines having a higher reputation than others, probably in consequence of greater purity. That used by masons is said to be ground from selected specimens.

It were interesting to try quick lime along side of plaster, so as to ascertain the relative effect and profit of each. At present, plaster in Michigan is expensive, costing $7.00 loose or $9.00 in barrels per ton at the mill; and most that is used is carried by land either from Detroit or Grand Rapids; while there are few farms in the interior of the State which cannot procure excellent marl at little more expense than digging. The late Dr. Houghton expressed the opinion that upon our sandy lands, the shell marls, even without burning, would prove quite as effective. Of the quantity consumed in this State we have no correct statistics. We find that during the year ending June 1853, the Central Railroad carried 2,613 tons; and allowing as much more for the Southern Railroad, and for private conveyance, we have a total of 5226 tons averaging $10 per ton delivered on the farm, which makes a total of $52,260 per annum for this one manure. It is very important that our marls and peats should be more fully investigated and their effects carefully tried.

Prof. Johnston states that when mixed with common salt, the action of gypsum upon clovers, beans, peas, &c., appears to be greatly increased.

W. Alexander, of Ballochmyle, Scotland, dressed an apparently worthlest crop of young beans with a mixture of 2 cwt. of gypsum, and one of common salt per acre. The effect was almost marvelous, and instead of a bad crop, his beans were the admiration of the country. He found a sensible effect produced by this mixture even after the beans were in flower.

Plaster acts as a stimulant, and its tendency is to impoverish the soil unless organic and other manures are liberally added.

705. Marl properly means an earthy mixture containing not less than 20 per cent of carbonate of lime. If the proportion of lime be less than this, the mixture is rather a marly clay, containing potash or silica in place of lime, as in the Green-sand marls of New Jersey, and Silicious marls of Massachusetts. (*See*

§ 117, 118, 119, 120, *p.* 37.) Of the true marls, there are many varieties, differing both in composition and external character; and consequently in value.

The following are analyses of marls in Seneca Co., N. Y.

| | No. 1, | No. 2, | No. 3. |
|---|---|---|---|
| Moisture, | 4.50 | 1.0 | 3.48 |
| Organic matter, | 8.50 | 4.20 | 1.65 |
| Insoluble sand, | 6.60 | 6.0 | 5.0 |
| Carbonate of lime, | 77.10 | 83.33 | 83.35 |
| Magnesia, | 2.10 | 2.16 | 4.0 |
| Phosphoric acid. } Alumina, } | 1.20 | 2.8 | 0.86<br>2.00 |
| Common Salt, | — | — | 0.20 |
| Sulphate of lime, | — | 50 | — |
| Sulphuric acid, | — | — | 0.46 |

The lime marls appear to be formed in two modes; *(a,)* by the deposite of lime brought to the surface by springs; *(b,)* by the accumulation of shells, and minute forms of animal life, or *Infusoria*, often microscopic, with calcareous coverings. "Some of these are so minute, that a cubic inch of stone has been calculated to contain the remains of 41 thousand millions of them —and yet deposites composed almost entirely of such remains have been met with of 20 and 30 feet in thickness. How very striking is it to find the united labors of these invisible creatures capable of producing such extraordinary effects! How very little we really know of what is going on around us!" *(Johnston.)*

The marls of Michigan are believed to consist of both these kinds, but especially of the latter. We believe they have never yet been analyzed, but will probably be found rich in phosphoric acid and ammonia. Mr. Delafield states of the New York marls above mentioned, that the *poorest* will afford 25 lbs of phosphoric acid to every ton of dry and weathered marl. This is equal to 45 lbs of phosphate of lime, a quantity found in 80 lbs of bone dust, and equal also to what a grazing cow annually takes from the land. The best Michigan marls will probably be found much richer than the above—and here is the very substance in which our oldest wheat lands are beginning to be deficient, *(See Genesee Farmer, August*, 1853,*)* and yet it is allowed to lie neglected and despised in almost every marsh and lake. Marls may be applied in two modes, *(a,)* burned as lime, in which respect they do not much differ in effect from the best agricultural lime rocks; *(b,)* in the natural state, but dried so as to powder. Like lime they produce a mechanical and chemical effect; the first differing with the soils and the character of the marl. The chemical effect consists in actually rendering the soil productive of larger crops. The exact mode of acting does not appear to be well understood. The *observed* effects of marl and shell sand, in so far as they are chemical, are chiefly the following:—They alter the nature and quality of the grasses when applied to pasture; they cover even the undrained bog, with a short rich grass—they extirpate coarse grasses and moss, and the weeds which infest unlimed wheat fields; they increase the quality and enable the land to grow a better quantity of wheat; they manifest a continued action for many years after they have been applied; like the purer limes, they act more energetically if aided by the occasional addition of other manure; and like them they finally exhaust a soil from which successive crops are reaped, without the requisite return of decaying animal or vegetable matter. *(Johnston.)*

In practice it is probably best to dig the marl, and leave it to dry and disintegrate for some months before applying. One ton and upwards may be applied to the acre, and plowed in *shallow* at the last plowing, or worked in with the cultivator. To act effectually, lime must be kept near the surface, and its constant effort is to sink below the reach of roots.

706. SALT is chemically composed of the metal *sodium*, and the gas *chlorine*, *chloride of sodium*, or called by the older chemists *muriate of soda*. It is procured by evaporating the

water of the sea or salt springs, and is rarely found in commerce perfectly pure; salts of lime and magnesia being mixed with it.

Salt is found in nearly all soils; in the ashes of all plants; and is necessary for animal life. It has been used in all ages and countries as a manure, and acts not only as a feeder of plants, but chemically as a solvent, and in this latter regard appears to be most efficient. In some soils it strengthens the straw, but it acts variously in different localities. *Theoretically*, it ought to prove very efficient in our Western States. Mixed with plaster it is said greatly to improve the latter. It must be used with care, and not applied *directly* to the plants. In dry climates, where seasonable rains seldom fall, salt will rarely do anything but injury. Root crops, and of those, beets, appear to be the most benefitted by salt. From one to ten bushels may be applied to the acre, sown broadcast and harrowed in, a few days before the seed is sown. In New York, three bushels to the acre have been found effective in destroying grubs, cutworms, &c.

707. Mud, Muck. This substance is found in great abundance in many ponds, marshes, &c., and in some localities it has been applied with great success as a manure. It necessarily varies much in its composition. Mr. Dana analyzed two specimens in Massachusetts, and he found them to consist of:—

| | | No. 1. | No. 2. |
|---|---|---|---|
| Soluble Geine, | Organic. | 5.10 | 8.10 |
| Insoluble Geine, | | 8.90 | 6.50 |
| Salts and Silicates, | | 86. 0 | 84.40 |

A cord of No. 1 weighed when dug 6117 lbs., and contained solid matter, 3495 lbs.; composed of geine, 495 lbs.; of silicates and salts, 3005 lbs. The salts of lime were 2½ per cent.; from which we judge that it would prove a vaulable manure.

Prof. Johnston examined a black mud from Leith Docks,

which was carted away by the farmers. He found a considerable quantity of animal matter, with much finely divided silica, which were found under the microscope to be infusoria.

Many mucks will probably be found to contain phosphoric acid, ammonia, vegetable matter, sulphur, and salts of lime and potash, and if so they are important to the farmer; but in our present state of ignorance regarding them, we can only recommend careful trials. We believe that, in practice, they are usually left exposed to the air, after digging, till dry and disintegrated; and if dug in the fall, so as to be frozen, they are found to be inproved.

708. III. Vegetable Manures.

These are practically of two classes; *(a.)* such as are grown for the purpose of being plowed in; *(b,)* and those which are collected from other sources, and applied as are ordinary manures, *e. g.* peat, leaves, &c. In the West, the first are employed in the shape of buckwheat, clover, and sometimes rye; and in other countries several plants are used for the same purpose; being turned under immediately before flowering. Such plants as collect their food chiefly from the air by the leaves, and contain much carbon, or those whose roots pierce deep into the subsoil, are preferred. Their value is owing to the elements which they supply directly to the next crop; and they are estimated according to the amount of nitrogen, carbon, and inorganic matter which they contain. In soils deficient in organic matter, such manuring is often very profitable when properly applied. The mechanical tendency of such applications is, also, to render stiff soils more friable.

In the second division a great variety of substances have been used, as straw, chaff, bran, rape cake, sawdust, malt-dust, &c.; but, in this country, Peat promises to prove the most important. Peat is a partially decayed moss or *sphagnum*, and is a real coal in an imperfect state. It is found in marshes and wet places, and is sufficiently abundant throughout Michigan and the other Western States. Like all other similar substances, it is subject to many variations in its composition. Some specimens contain a large proportion of ammonia, and they all appear to be rich in salts and carbon.

Analysis of peat from Paisley Moss, Scotland, viz: an upper peat, (A;) an under peat of the same bed, (B;) and of the Dutch ashes, formed of peat, (B.) *(Johnston.)*

| | A. | B. | C. |
|---|---|---|---|
| Organic matter, (charred peat,) | 54.12 | 3.02 | 25.77 |
| Sulphates and carbonates of potash, soda, and magnesia, soluble in water, | 6.57 | 5.1 | 2.78 |
| Alumina, soluble in acids, | 2.99 | 2.48 } | 11.19 |
| Oxide of iron, | 4.61 | 18 66 } | |
| Gypsum, | 10.49 | 21.23 | 16.35 |
| Phosphate of lime, | 0.90 | 0.40 | 1.24 |
| Carbonate of lime, | 8.54 | 3.50 | 1.21 |
| Carbonate of magnesia, | | | 3.39 |
| Insoluble siliceous matter, | 10.88 | 43.91 | 37.24 |
| | 99.10 | 98.36 | 99.17 |

Analysis of 10 varieties of Peat from Massachusetts. *(Dana.)*

| Locality. | Saluble Geine. | Insoluble Geine. | Total Geine. | Salts & Silicates. |
|---|---|---|---|---|
| 1. Dracut, | 14.0 | 72.0 | 86.0 | 14.00 |
| 2. Sunderland, | 26.0 | 56 60 | 85 60 | 14 40 |
| 3. Westborough, | 48.80 | 43 60 | 92.40 | 7.60 |
| 4. Hadley, | 34.0 | 60.0 | 94.0 | 6.0 |
| 5. Northampton, | 38.30 | 44.15 | 82 45 | 17 55 |
| 6. " | 32.0 | 54.90 | 86.90 | 13.10 |
| 7. " | 12.0 | 60.85 | 72.85 | 27.15 |
| 8. " | 10.0 | 49.45 | 59.45 | 40.55 |
| 9. " | 33.0 | 59.0 | 92.0 | 8.00 |
| 10. " | 46.0 | 46.80 | 92.80 | 7.20 |
| Average, | 29.41 | 55.03 | 84.44 | 15.55 |

By the word "Geine" this writer means the *vegetable matter of soils*, also called *Humus*, *Ulmin*, &c., and represented by the symbol C 40,

H 16, O 14, with, occasionally, an addition of ammonia. The term is now rarely used in agriculture.

All Peat shrinks by drying, and when perfectly dried at 240 ° F. loses from 73 to 97 per cent of water. When allowed to dry in the air, it still contains about two-thirds of its weight of water, and rapidly re-absorbs moisture. It shrinks from two-thirds to three-fourths of its bulk. Taking these data, 100 parts of fresh dug peat, of average quality, contain:—*(Dana.)*

| | |
|---|---|
| Water, | 85.0 |
| Salts of lime, | 0.50 |
| Silicates, | 0.50 |
| Geine, | 14.0 |

Owing to the difficulty of rendering Peat soluble, it has not been used in agriculture to the extent it deserves, in its natural state. It is frequently burned (or rather *charred*,) and the ashes are applied with good effect at the rate of from 50 bushels to two tons per acre.

Prof. Norton, says : "They usually contain from 5 to 6 per cent of potash and soda, considerable quantities of lime, magnesia, iron, &c., being therefore worth about as much as the poorer kinds of wood-ashes. In wet land, where varieties of peat abound, which are only decomposed with great difficulty, it is sometimes advisable to burn them on a large scale for the purpose of obtaining the ash as manure. Heaps are made at convenient distances directly upon the surface of the bog, and the fire started by means of a little dry peat in the centre of each heap; as it burns through to the outside, fresh peat is dug up and thrown on, and so the process may be kept up as long as desirable. It is to be observed as to all varieties of ashes, that their value is greatly impaired by exposure to the weather." But the best mode of using peat is to lay it in cattle stables, and to mix it with decomposing animal manures; when it will, if sufficiently dried, not only absorb the liquids, but itself undergo fermentation. According to Mr. Phinney, of Lexington, Mass., a cord of fresh dung converts twice its bulk of peat into a manure of equal value to itself—that is, a cord of clear stable dung, composted with two of peat, forms a manure of equal value to three cords of green dung.

Mr. S. L. Dana, of Lowell, Mass., wrote a book, a few years since, for the purpose of showing that peat mixed with an alkali, in all respects resembles, and, as a manure, is equivalent in effect to cow dung. The cost per cord, at that time, he estimates as :—

| | | | |
|---|---|---|---|
| 1 Cord peat and digging, - | | - - | $1.50 |
| 92 lbs. potash at 6 cents, | $5.52 | average of alkalies, | 3.65 |
| Or 61 lbs. soda ash at 4 cents, | 2.44 | | |
| Or 24 bush common wood-ashes at 12½ cents, - - - | 3.00 | | |
| | 3)10.96 | | |
| | $3.65 | Per cord.... | $5.15 |

Were they really good hard-wood-ashes, about 16 bushels would be sufficient, but an excess is allowed to compensate for variation. At that period, clear cow dung was purchased by the Print works at an average cost of 17 4-5 cents per bushel, or $17.45 cents per cord, at times even higher.

We must he e complete our very imperfect remarks on manures, as the subject is sufficiently extensive to fill a much larger volume than this. The teacher will find all that he can require in the *American Muck Book*, by D. J. Browne, 12 mo. pp. 429, published by C. M. Saxton, New York, 1852.

For the sake of convenience, however, we add a list of the articles used in various countries as manures, designating with an asterisk (*) such as can probably be of service in the United States.

I. Animal Manures.

Blood.*
Flesh.*
(Dried flesh, from South America.)
Bones.*
Skin.
Wool.
Hair.*
Feathers.
Woollen rags,* (England.)
——— Mill refuse,* (England.)
Fish, (New England, &c.)
Blubber, and other fish refuse.*
Refuse of Lard-Boilers,* (Cincinnati, &c.) The whole hog is boiled by a heavy pressure of steam, and all, but the oil. left as a dry power.)
Other refuse of Pork Packers.*
Bone Black, or animal charcoal, from Sugar Refineries.*
Refuse of Bone and Ivory Turners, &c.
Dung of Horses.*
" Cows.*
" Sheep.*

Dung of Hogs.*
" Men.*
(Pudrette.)*
Droppings of Birds.*
Guano.*
Urine of all kinds.*
(Urate.)*
Shells, (marine and fresh.*)
Infusoria in muck.*
Coral sand*?
Scutch, (Glue maker's refuse.)*
Refuse from Tanneries.*

II. Mineral.

Carbonate of Ammonia.
Nitrate of Ammonia.
Muriate of Ammonia.
Sulphate of Ammonia.
Water from Gas works.*
Lime from Gas works.*
Coal Tar.
Wood ashes, (unleached.)*
do (leached.)*
Coal ashes, (Anthracite.)*
do (Bituminous.)*
Ashes of Sea-weed, (Kelp, or Barilla.)
Soap maker's waste, (Soda.)*
Bitterns, (Refuse of Salt works.)*
Burnt clay.*
Rubbish of old buildings.*
Coprolites, (a mineral phosphate.)
Apatite, (a mineral phosphate.)*
Lime, (carbonate of.)*
Burnt lime.*
Sulphate of lime, (plaster.)*
Phosphate of lime.
Silicate of lime.
Nitrate of lime.
Marls, (Calcareous.)*
Potash.
Nitrate of Potash, (Saltpetre.)
Potash Marls, (Greensand.)*
Soda.
Chloride of sodium, (common salt)*
Nitrate of soda, (Peruvian Saltpetre.)
Sulphate of soda, (Glauber salts.)
Magnesia.
Sulphate of magnesia, (Epsom salts.)
Silica, (Sand.)*
Sulphuric acid.
Clay, or sand, of Granite, Greenstone, Serpentine, and Basalt Rocks.*

III. Vegetable Manures.

Straw.*
Chaff.*
Leaves of plants and trees.*
Spoiled hay.*
Saw-dust,*
Charcoal*
Vegetable matter, charred.*
Spent Tan, (appears to act specifically on strawberries.)*
Apple Pomace.*
Weeds.*
Cotton Refuse.*
do Seeds.*
Stems of Flax.*
Refuse of water of flax mills.*
Bran.
Rape Cake.
Rape Dust.
Cake of Linseed.
do Poppy seed.
do Cocoa nut.
Refuse of other oil-seeds.
Peat.*
Sea-weed,*
Tops & leaves of cultivated plants,*
Soot.*

To plow in—Green Manures.

Red Clover.*
Buckwheat.*
Rye.*
Corn, (Maize.)*
Turnips.
White Lupines.
Vetch or Tares.
Rape.
White Mustard.
Vine twigs, (for Vineyards.)*
Malt-dust.
Refuse of Starch manufactories.*

There are a few other expensive salts occasionally used in very high farming, but they are scarcely worth mentioning. (See *Johnston's Experimental Agriculture*, 1849.)

# CHAPTER XXIII.

## PLOWING.

709. Plowing is merely a means resorted to for stirring up the soil, and rendering it friable in order that it may receive the seed. Digging was probably the original mode of performing this operation, but as this is very laborious, although very effective, some sort of plow appears to have been invented as soon as oxen or horses were employed in agriculture. The history of the plow is the history of the art; for so intimately are good crops dependent upon good plowing. that just in proportion as this implement has been improved so has the product of the earth increased in quantity. But it is only of late years that this all important implement has been formed on *true* mechanical principles; and, with the exception of Great Britain and America, nearly all the world still cling to the use of antiquated and inefficient forms; nor can it yet be said that either the plow or the mode of using it are fully understood. The English and Americans form and use the plow on different principles, the first endeavoring to lay an unbroken furrow, the latter trying to break or pulverize the soil in the operation; while the proper depth of plowing in different classes of soils is very little understood by practical men. Notwithstanding the great skill with which the best American plows are made, there is still a wide field of improvement open in both these respects. Within a very few years, many efforts have been made to plow by steam, or by horse power, indirectly applied; and a Canadian is at this moment perfecting a machine in England; while there is one

in successful operation in that country which may be worked either by steam or horse power. This is not strictly *plowing*, in the usual sense of the word, but turning up the soil by rotary cutters. Should such machines become generally available they will probably revolutionize agriculture, as the introduction of the Spinning Jenny &c. revolutionized the manufacture of Cotton and Woolen cloths; since it will be impossible for small farmers, working on the old plan, to compete with large capitalists, with extensive farms, doing all their work by steam and other machinery. As however, the improvements introduced into manufactories have not only benefitted the world in general, but supplied work for a very much larger number of laborers, so may we expect this revolution in art to produce the same effect in agriculture.

710. Till within a century, all plows were made of wood with wrought iron plates &c, nailed on, for the land-side, mould-board, and point. In Great Britain, they were generally prepared with one or two wheels at the end of the plow-beam, as they still are in France and Germany, and were drawn by 4 to 8 horses; or by a pair of horses with the addition of four, and sometimes of six oxen, with one man to hold, and two to drive. About 1763, James Small, of the county of Berwick, Scotland, a manufacturer of Agricultural implements, turned his attention to the improvement of plows. In experimenting, he made the mould-board of *soft-wood*, by means of which it soon appeared where the pressure was the most severe, and where there was the greatest friction. He likewise applied true mechanical principles to the subject; introduced cast iron in place of wood; and so lightened the draft that two horses were quite as efficient as the heavy teams previously employed. This appears to have been the first invention of the light and elegant cast-iron *swing* plows which are now every where in use in this country. (Sir John Sinclair, in his *Account of the systems of husbandry adopted in Scotland*, 1812, gives the full history of this invention.) This introduc-

tion of an improved plow has not only had a most favorable bearing upon agriculture in every respect, by reducing the cost of working the soil, and doing the work in a much better manner, but it is very doubtful, whether a very large portion of America could yet have been settled, if so many animals and men had been requisite to perform the operation. Plows are made so as to be adapted to every sort of soil and work, and are arranged upon well known and accurately ascertained principles. These principles every farmer should understand; but as this knowledge presupposes an acquaintance with mathematics and mechanics we cannot enter upon it here.

711. The object of the plowman is so to turn over the soil as to render it the best adapted for the growth of plants with the least expenditure of labor and time. If the soil is so turned as merely to be reversed, lying, as it were, in long *ribbons*, friability is not attained, but must be produced by subsequent operations, with the harrow, cultivator, &c. If the soil is so broken, that part is reversed, and part is not, weeds are tempted to grow and the crop will be uneven. If there are inequalities, and deep holes, some seeds will be buried too deeply, others will be too shallow. The best plowmen, therefore, endeavor, while they separate the soil, entirely to reverse it, to lay the furrows perfectly even on the surface, and to plow as deeply, and as great a width at the same time as possible. In narrow furrows, the soil will be rendered friable most effectually, but time will be lost.

Depth is of great importance in successful agriculture, under nearly all circumstances. There may be subsoils of such a character that it would be injudicious at once to turn up much of them; but by annually plowing an inch or so deeper, by degrees great depth is attained without injury. Deep plowing acts in the same manner as thorough draining, but to a less extent. It gives the roots of plants a larger field from which to gather their food; it allows surface water to escape; atmospheric manures to be collected instead of running off; and it affords a more equal and probably a higher temperature and greater command of moisture. A field plowed three or four inches deep is easily exhausted; while such manures as are applied, soon escape beneath the reach of the roots; and, in many soils, in process of time, the plow passing at one equal and shallow depth forms an artificial and impervious *hard-pan.* According to Mr. Delafield in 1850, in Seneca county New York, "The evidence of every successive year, has clearly manifested the economy and profit of deep tillage; the mechanical operations on the soil require less force and labor; less seed is necessary; and all manures produce their full effect. Many of the best informed farmers are firm in the opinion that deep plowing and subsoil plowing are more effective on wheat soils when a judicious system of drainage has been adopted; for though deep tillage by the plow allows the roots of plants to seek their food at a greater depth from the surface, yet they will extend themselves (in some soils,) to the cold influences of retained waters, where drains do not exist, and be deprived of that full measure of health and vigor which the principle of deep tillage is intended to afford."

The *Jointer Plow,* invented in Michigan, is forcing its way into very general use. It is a miniature or small plow, which can be attached and detached from the beam of any other plow at pleasure, and is placed a short distance in advance of the main plow. It turns over 2 to 4 inches of the soil which is buried deeply and neatly under the furrow formed by the succeeding plow; and with four oxen or horses, 10 to 12 inches can easily be reached. (*See Transactions of Michigan State Agricultural Society, Vol, iv, p* 147.)

712. Horses cannot draw a plow for any very great distance without stopping. A length of 250 yards is believed to be the best for the size of a field, allowing the horses to rest at the turning. The following table shows the quantities of land plowed at different speeds, at given breadths of the furrow-slices. (*Stephens.*)

| Speed; rate per hour. | Distance walked in 8⅓ hours. | | Breadth of furrow plowed | Quantity of land plowed in 8⅓ hours at that speed. | | |
|---|---|---|---|---|---|---|
| Miles | Miles, | Yards, | Inches, | A | R | P |
| 1 | 8 | 1248 | 9 | 0 | 3 | 1 |
| | 8 | 440 | 10 | 0 | 3 | 14 |
| 1⅓ | 12 | 642 | 9 | 1 | 0 | 21 |
| | 12 | 220 | 10 | 1 | 0 | 34 |
| 2 | 17 | 808 | 9 | 1 | 2 | 2 |
| | 16 | 880 | 10 | 1 | 2 | 28 |
| 3 | 26 | 332 | 9 | 2 | 1 | 3 |
| | 24 | 1320 | 10 | 2 | 1 | 42 |

Table showing the comparative amount of time lost in turnings while plowing long and short ridges. (*Stephens.*)

| Length of ridge. | Breadth of furrow slice. | Time lost in turning. | | Time devoted to plowing. | | Hours of work. |
|---|---|---|---|---|---|---|
| Yards | Inches | H | M | H | M | H |
| 78 | 10 | 5 | 11 | 4 | 49 | 10 |
| 149 | " | 2 | 44 | 7 | 16 | " |
| 200 | " | 2 | 1 | 7 | 59 | " |
| 212 | " | 1 | 56½ | 8 | 3½ | " |
| 274 | " | 1 | 22 | 8 | 32 | " |

713. There are a variety of modes of plowing to suit the nature of the soil and season of the year; though this diversity is more practised in Europe than in America. (For illustrations see *Stephen's Farmer's Guide*, vol. 1 p. 171–186.)

FINIS.

# GENERAL INDEX.

*[The figures at the end of each line refer to the Sections.]*

## W

## ERRATA.

PAGE 62—Reverse the headings of the Table—"Water in the Flour per cent," and "Flour in the Grain per cent."

" 161, line 10 from top, for "Guined" read *Guinea.*

" 166, " 5 from bottom after "Randal Grass" ("***Festuca Pratensis and Elatior,***")

" 181 " 4 from top for "tree" read ***tres.***

" 187 " 2 from bottom for "them" read ***their.***

" 206 " 13 from top for "soil" read *oil,*

" 250. While the last sheet was going through the Press, the third number of Prof. Johnston's *Chemistry of Common Life* was received, in which it is stated "that the onion is remarkably nutritious. According to my Analyses, the dried onion root contains from 25 to 30 per cent. of gluten. It ranks in this respect with the nutritious pea, and the ***Gram*** (or Chick Pea) of the East."—*See* § 353, p. 148.

www.ingramcontent.com/pod-product-compliance
Lightning Source LLC
LaVergne TN
LVHW010143110826
845151LV00002B/414

* 9 7 8 1 4 2 5 5 3 7 9 3 7 *